JUSTICE FOR HEDGEHOGS

JUSTICE FOR HEDGEHOGS

Ronald Dworkin

THE BELKNAP PRESS
OF
HARVARD UNIVERSITY PRESS
Cambridge, Massachusetts
London, England
2011

Library of Congress Cataloging-in-Publication Data

Dworkin, Ronald.
Justice for hedgehogs / Ronald Dworkin.
p.   cm.
Includes bibliographical references and index.
ISBN 978-0-674-04671-9 (alk. paper)
1. Values.   2. Ethics.   I. Title.
BD435.D85   2011
170'44—dc22   2010033807

For Reni

Contents

Preface   *ix*

1 Baedeker   *1*

PART ONE

Independence

2 Truth in Morals   *23*

3 External Skepticism   *40*

4 Morals and Causes   *69*

5 Internal Skepticism   *88*

PART TWO

Interpretation

6 Moral Responsibility   *99*

7 Interpretation in General   *123*

8 Conceptual Interpretation   *157*

PART THREE

Ethics

9 Dignity   *191*

10 Free Will and Responsibility   *219*

PART FOUR

Morality

11 From Dignity to Morality 255

12 Aid 271

13 Harm 285

14 Obligations 300

PART FIVE

Politics

15 Political Rights and Concepts 327

16 Equality 351

17 Liberty 364

18 Democracy 379

19 Law 400

Epilogue: Dignity Indivisible 417

Notes 425

Index 489

Preface

This is not a book about what other people think: it is meant as a stand-alone argument. It would have been longer and less readable if packed with responses, distinctions, and anticipated objections. But, as an anonymous reader for the Harvard University Press pointed out, it would weaken the argument not to notice the great variety of prominent theories in the several fields the book touches. I compromised by discussing the work of contemporary philosophers in several extended endnotes spread throughout the book. I hope this strategy makes it easier for readers to decide which parts of my argument they wish to locate in the contemporary professional literature. Nevertheless, it proved necessary to anticipate objections more fully in some parts of the text—particularly in Chapter 3, which examines rival positions in greater detail. Readers who are already persuaded that moral skepticism is itself a substantive moral position will not need to linger over those arguments. Chapter 1 provides a road map of the entire argument and, at the risk of repetition, I have included several interim summaries in the text.

I have been fortunate in attracting critics in the past, and I hope this book will be criticized as powerfully as past books have been. I propose to capitalize on technology by establishing a Web page for my responses and corrections, www.justiceforhedgehogs.net. I cannot promise to post or to respond to all comments, but I will do my best to make additions and corrections that seem called for.

Acknowledging all the help I have had in writing this book is close to the hardest part of writing it. Three anonymous readers for the Press made a host of valuable suggestions. The Boston University Law School sponsored a conference of some thirty papers, organized by James Fleming, to discuss an earlier version of the manuscript. I am unboundedly grateful for that conference; I learned a great deal from the papers that I believe has much improved the book. (I acknowledge, in endnotes, several passages that I changed in response to criticism offered there.) The conference papers are published, together with my response to many of them, in *Symposium: Justice for Hedgehogs: A Conference on Ronald Dworkin's Forthcoming Book* (special issue), *Boston University Law Review* 90, no. 2 (April 2010). Sarah Kitchell, that review's Editor-in-Chief, did an excellent job of editing the collection and making it available to me as quickly as possible. I have not been able to include the bulk of my responses in this book, however, so readers might find it helpful to consult that issue.

Colleagues have been unusually generous. Kit Fine read the discussion of truth in Chapter 8, Terence Irwin the discussion of Plato and Aristotle in Chapter 9, Barbara Hermann the material on Kant in Chapter 11, Thomas Scanlon the section on promising in Chapter 14, Samuel Freeman the discussions of his own work and that of John Rawls in various parts of the book, and Thomas Nagel the many discussions of his views throughout the book. Simon Blackburn and David Wiggins commented helpfully on drafts of my endnote discussions of their opinions. Sharon Street generously discussed her arguments against moral objectivity discussed in the endnotes to Chapter 4. Stephen Guest read the entire manuscript and offered a great many valuable suggestions and corrections. Charles Fried taught a seminar based on the manuscript at the Harvard Law School and shared his and his students' very helpful reactions to it. Michael Smith corresponded with me in further discussion of the issues raised in his *Boston University Law Review* piece. Kevin Davis and Liam Murphy argued with me about promising. I benefited greatly from discussion of several chapters in the New York University Colloquium on Legal, Political and Social Philosophy, and in a similar Colloquium, organized by Mark Greenberg and Seana Shiffrin, at the UCLA Law School. Drucilla Cornell and Nick Friedman reviewed the manuscript extensively in their forthcoming article "The Significance of Dworkin's Non-Positivist Jurisprudence for Law in the Post-Colony."

I am grateful to the NYU Filomen D'Agostino Foundation for grants enabling me to work on the book during summers. I am grateful to the NYU Law School, also, for its research support program that allowed me to hire a string of excellent research assistants. Those who worked on substantial portions of the book include Mihailis Diamantis, Melis Erdur, Alex Guerrero, Hyunseop Kim, Karl Schafer, Jeff Sebo, and Jonathan Simon. Jeff Sebo reviewed substantially the entire manuscript and offered very valuable critical comments. These assistants, collectively, provided almost all the endnote citations, a contribution for which I am particularly grateful. Irene Brendel made many perceptive contributions to the discussion of interpretation. Lavinia Barbu, the most exceptional assistant I know, has been invaluable in a thousand ways. One more, rather different, acknowledgment. It has been my unmatched good fortune to have as my closest friends three of the greatest philosophers of our time: Thomas Nagel, Thomas Scanlon, and the late Bernard Williams. Their impact on this book is most quickly demonstrated by its index, but I hope it is evident in every page as well.

JUSTICE FOR HEDGEHOGS

I

Baedeker

Foxes and Hedgehogs

This book defends a large and old philosophical thesis: the unity of value. It is not a plea for animal rights or for punishing greedy fund managers. Its title refers to a line by an ancient Greek poet, Archilochus, that Isaiah Berlin made famous for us. The fox knows many things, but the hedgehog knows one big thing.[1] Value is one big thing. The truth about living well and being good and what is wonderful is not only coherent but mutually supporting: what we think about any one of these must stand up, eventually, to any argument we find compelling about the rest. I try to illustrate the unity of at least ethical and moral values: I describe a theory of what living well is like and what, if we want to live well, we must do for, and not do to, other people.

That idea—that ethical and moral values depend on one another—is a creed; it proposes a way to live. But it is also a large and complex philosophical theory. Intellectual responsibility about value is itself an important value, and we must therefore take up a broad variety of philosophical issues that are not normally treated in the same book. We discuss in different chapters the metaphysics of value, the character of truth, the nature of interpretation, the conditions of genuine agreement and disagreement, the phenomenon of moral responsibility, and the so-called problem of free will as well as more traditional issues of ethical, moral, and legal theory. My overall thesis is unpopular now—the fox has ruled the roost in academic and literary philosophy for many decades, particularly in the Anglo-American tradition.[2] Hedgehogs seem naïve or charlatans, perhaps even dangerous. I shall try to identify the roots of that popular attitude, the assumptions that account for these suspicions. In this introductory chapter I offer a road map of the argument to come that shows what I take those roots to be.

My advance summary could start in any chapter, fanning out from there, tracing the implications of that chapter for the rest. But I think it best to start at the end of the book, with political morality and justice, so that readers particularly interested in politics will have an advance understanding of why I think that the more abstract philosophical discussions of the book are required steps to what concerns them most. I hope that starting the summary there will also encourage other readers whose greater interest lies in more mainstream issues of philosophy—meta-ethics, metaphysics, and meaning— to find practical importance in what they might believe to be abstruse philosophical issues.

Justice

Equality. No government is legitimate unless it subscribes to two reigning principles. First, it must show equal concern for the fate of every person over whom it claims dominion. Second, it must respect fully the responsibility and right of each person to decide for himself how to make something valuable of his life. These guiding principles place boundaries around acceptable theories of distributive justice—theories that stipulate the resources and opportunities a government should make available to people it governs. I put the matter that way, in terms of what governments should do, because any distribution is the consequence of official law and policy: there is no politically neutral distribution. Given any combination of personal qualities of talent, personality, and luck, what a person will have by way of resource and opportunity will depend on the laws in place where he is governed. So every distribution must be justified by showing how what government has done respects these two fundamental principles of equal concern for fate and full respect for responsibility.

A laissez-faire political economy leaves unchanged the consequences of a free market in which people buy and sell their product and labor as they wish and can. That does not show equal concern for everyone. Anyone impover-

ished through that system is entitled to ask: "There are other, more regula-
tory and redistributive, sets of laws that would put me in a better position.
How can government claim that this system shows equal concern for me?" It
is no answer that people must take responsibility for their own fate. People
are not responsible for much of what determines their place in such an economy. They are not responsible for their genetic endowment and innate talent.
They are not responsible for the good and bad luck they have throughout
their lives. There is nothing in the second principle, about personal responsibility, that would entitle government to adopt such a posture.

Suppose government makes the extreme opposite choice, however: to
make wealth equal no matter what choices people made for themselves. Every few years, as would be possible in a Monopoly game, government calls in
everyone's wealth and redistributes it in equal shares. That would fail to respect people's responsibility to make something of their own lives, because
what people chose to do—their choices about work or recreation and about
saving or investment—would then have no personal consequences. People
are not responsible unless they make choices with an eye to the costs to others
of the choices that they make. If I spend my life at leisure, or work at a job
that does not produce as much as I could of what other people need or want,
then I should take responsibility for the cost this choice imposes: I should
have less in consequence.

The question of distributive justice therefore calls for a solution to simultaneous equations. We must try to find a solution that respects both the
reigning principles of equal concern and personal responsibility, and we must
try to do this in a way that compromises neither principle but rather finds
attractive conceptions of each that fully satisfy both. That is the goal of the
final part of this book. Here is a fanciful illustration of a solution. Imagine an
initial auction of all available resources in which everyone starts with the
same number of bidding chips. The auction lasts a very long time, and will be
repeated as long as anyone wishes. It must end in a situation in which nobody
envies anybody else's bundle of resources; for that reason the distribution
of resources that results treats everyone with equal concern. Then imagine a
further auction in which these people design and choose comprehensive insurance policies, paying the premium the market establishes for the coverage
each chooses. That auction does not eliminate the consequences of good or
bad luck, but it makes people responsible for their own risk management.

We can use that fanciful model to defend real-life distributive structures.
We can design tax systems to model these imaginary markets: we can set tax

rates, for instance, to mimic the premiums it seems reasonable to assume people would pay in the hypothetical insurance market. The rates of tax designed in that way would be fairly steeply progressive; more so than our tax rates at present. We can design a health care system mimicking the coverage it seems reasonable to assume people would seek: this would require universal health care. But it would not justify spending, as Medicare now does, enormous sums keeping people alive in the last few months of their lives, because it would make no sense for people to give up funds useful for the rest of their lives to pay the very high premiums required by that sort of coverage.

Liberty. Justice requires a theory of liberty as well as a theory of resource equality, and we must be aware, in constructing that theory, of the danger that liberty and equality will conflict. It was Isaiah Berlin's claim that such conflict is inevitable. I argue, in Chapter 17, for a theory of liberty that eliminates that danger. I distinguish your freedom, which is simply your ability to do anything you might want to do without government constraint, from your liberty, which is that part of your freedom that government would do wrong to constrain. I do not endorse any general right to freedom. I argue, instead, for rights to liberty that rest on different bases. People have a right to ethical independence that follows from the principle of personal responsibility. They have rights, including rights to free speech, that are required by their more general right to govern themselves, which right also flows from personal responsibility. They have rights, including rights to due process of law and freedom of property, that follow from their right to equal concern.

This scheme for liberty rules out genuine conflict with the conception of equality just described because the two conceptions are thoroughly integrated: each depends on the same solution to the simultaneous equation problem. You cannot determine what liberty requires without also deciding what distribution of property and opportunity shows equal concern for all. The popular view that taxation invades liberty is false on this account provided that what government takes from you can be justified on moral grounds so that it does not take from you what you are entitled to retain. A theory of liberty is in that way embedded in a much more general political morality and draws from the other parts of that theory. The alleged conflict between liberty and equality disappears.

Democracy. But there is another supposed conflict among our political values. This is the conflict between equality and liberty, on the one hand, and the right to participate as an equal in one's own governance, on the other. Political theorists sometimes call the latter a right to positive liberty and suppose that that right may conflict with negative liberty—the rights to freedom from government I just described—and also with the right to a just distribution of resources. The conflict is realized, on this view, when a majority votes for an unjust tax scheme or a denial of important liberties. I respond to that claim of conflict by distinguishing various conceptions of democracy. I distinguish a majoritarian or statistical conception from what I call the partnership conception. The latter holds that in a genuinely democratic community each citizen participates as an equal partner, which means more than just that he has an equal vote. It means that he has an equal voice and an equal stake in the result. On that conception, which I defend, democracy itself requires the protection of just those individual rights to justice and liberty that democracy is sometimes said to threaten.

Law. Political philosophers insist on yet another conflict among political values: the conflict between justice and law. Nothing guarantees that our laws will be just; when they are unjust, officials and citizens may be required, by the rule of law, to compromise what justice requires. In Chapter 19 I speak to that conflict: I describe a conception of law that takes it to be not a rival system of rules that might conflict with morality but as itself a branch of morality. It is necessary, to make that suggestion plausible, to emphasize what might be called procedural justice, the morality of fair governance as well as just outcome. It is also necessary to understand morality in general as having a tree structure: law is a branch of political morality, which is itself a branch of a more general personal morality, which is in turn a branch of a yet more general theory of what it is to live well.

You will by now have formed a suspicion. Poseidon had a son, Procrustes, who had a bed; he suited his guests to his bed by stretching or lopping them until they fit. You might well think me Procrustes, stretching and lopping conceptions of the great political virtues so that they neatly fit one another. I would then be achieving unity on the cheap: a meaningless victory. But I mean to submit each of the political conceptions I describe to the test of conviction. I will not rely on any assumption that a theory is sound just because it fits with other theories we also find agreeable. I hope to develop integrated conceptions that all seem right in themselves, at least after reflection. I do make an independent and very powerful claim, however. I argue throughout the book that in political morality integration is a necessary condition of truth. We do not secure finally persuasive conceptions of our several political values unless our conceptions *do* mesh. It is the fox who wins too easily: it is his apparent victory, now widely celebrated, that is hollow.

Interpretation

The first step toward that important conclusion, about integration and truth, requires facing up to an immediate challenge. I sketched a series of claims about the true meaning of a variety of political concepts. How can I show that one conception of equality or liberty or democracy is right and rival conceptions wrong? We must pause to consider what political concepts are and how we might be said to agree or disagree about their application. If you and I mean something entirely different by "democracy," then our discussion about whether democracy requires that citizens have an equal stake is pointless: we are simply talking past one another. My claims about the best understanding of the political virtues would then count only as statements about how I propose to use certain words. I could not claim that I am right and others wrong.

We must ask: When do people share a concept so that their agreements and disagreements are genuine? We share some concepts because we agree, except in cases we all regard as borderline, about what criteria to use in identifying examples. We mainly agree about how many books there are on a table, for example, because we use the same tests in answering that question. We don't always agree because our criteria are sometimes slightly different: we might disagree because you count a large pamphlet as a book and I don't. In that special borderline case our disagreement is illusory: we don't really disagree. Justice and the other political concepts are different, however. We think that our disagreements about whether progressive taxation is just are genuine even though we disagree, in some cases very sharply, about the right criteria for deciding whether an institution is just.

We must therefore recognize that we share some of our concepts, including the political concepts, in a different way: they function for us as *interpretive* concepts. We share them because we share social practices and experiences in which these concepts figure. We take the concepts to describe values, but we disagree, sometimes to a marked degree, about what these values are and how they should be expressed. We disagree because we interpret the practices we share rather differently: we hold somewhat different theories about which values best justify what we accept as central or paradigm features of that practice. That structure makes our conceptual disagreements about liberty, equality, and the rest genuine. It also makes them *value* disagreements rather than disagreements of fact or disagreements about dictionary or standard meanings. That means that a defense of some particular conception of a political value like equality or liberty must draw on values beyond itself: it would be flaccidly circular to appeal to liberty to defend a conception of liberty. So political concepts *must* be integrated with one another. We cannot defend a conception of any of them without showing how our conception fits with and into appealing conceptions of the others. That fact provides an important part of the case for the unity of value.

I describe interpretive concepts much more fully in Chapter 8. Chapter 7 takes up a more basic set of questions about interpretation. We interpret in many genres beyond politics: in conversation, law, poetry, religion, history, sociology, and psychodynamics. Can we provide a general theory of interpretation that holds for all these genres? We will better understand the standards that should govern our interpretation of the distinctly political concepts if we can. I describe a popular general theory of interpretation: that it always aims to retrieve the intention or other psychological state of some author or creator. That theory is apt in some circumstances in some genres and inapt in others; we need a more general theory of interpretation that explains when and why the intention-retrieval goal is plausible. I suggest a value-based general theory. Interpreters have critical responsibilities, and the best interpretation of a law or a poem or an epoch is the interpretation that best realizes those responsibilities on that occasion. The best interpretation of Yeats's poem "Sailing to Byzantium" is the interpretation that deploys or assumes the best account of the value of interpreting poetry, and reads the poem so as to show its value in that light. But because interpreters disagree about their responsibilities, because they disagree about the value of interpreting poetry, they disagree about how to read that poem or any other object of interpretation.

Truth and Value

I argue, then, that political morality depends on interpretation and that interpretation depends on value. It has become obvious by now, I suppose, that I believe that there are objective truths about value. I believe that some institutions really are unjust and some acts really are wrong no matter how many people believe that they are not. The contrary view is now common, however. It seems absurd to a great many philosophers—and to a great many other people as well—to suppose that there are values "out there" in the universe awaiting discovery by human beings who have some mysterious faculty of value apprehension. We must understand value judgments, they say, in some wholly different way. We must accept that there is no objective truth about value that is independent of the beliefs or attitudes of people who judge value: we must understand their claims about what is just or unjust, right or wrong, saintly or wicked, as simply expressions of their attitudes or emotions, or recommendations for others to follow, or personal commitments they undertake, or proposed constructions of guides for their own lives.

Most of the philosophers who take this view do not think themselves pessimists or nihilists. On the contrary. They suppose that we can live perfectly good lives—and intellectually more responsible lives—if we give up the myth of objective independent values and concede that our value judgments only express our attitudes and commitments. Their arguments and examples show that they have our private lives rather than our politics in mind, however. I think them wrong about private lives: I argue in Chapter 9 that our dignity requires us to recognize that whether we live well is not just a matter of whether we think we do. But they are even more plainly wrong about politics: it is our politics, more than any other aspect of our lives, that denies us the luxury of skepticism about value.

Politics is coercive: we cannot stand up to our responsibility as governors or citizens unless we suppose that the moral and other principles on which we act or vote are objectively true. It is not good enough for an official or voter to declare that the theory of justice on which he acts pleases him. Or that it accurately expresses his emotions or attitudes or aptly states how he plans to live. Or that his political principles are drawn from his nation's traditions and so need not claim larger truth.[3] Any nation's history and contemporary politics are a kaleidoscope of conflicting principle and shifting prejudice: any formulation of the nation's "traditions" must therefore be an interpretation that, as Chapter 7 argues, must be rooted in independent assumptions about what is really true. Of course, people will disagree about which conception of justice is really true. But those in power must believe that what they say is so. So the old philosophers' question—Can moral judgments really be true?—is a foundational, inescapable, question in political morality. We cannot defend a theory of justice without also defending, as part of the same enterprise, a theory of moral objectivity. It is irresponsible to try to do without such a theory.

I must now summarize what might seem philosophically the most radical view I defend: the metaphysical independence of value.[4] It is a familiar, perfectly ordinary idea that some acts—torturing babies for fun—are wrong in themselves, not just because people think them wrong. They would still be wrong even if, incredibly, no one thought so. You might not believe that; some form of moral subjectivism might seem more plausible to you. But whether it is true is a matter of moral judgment and argument. Most moral philosophers think, on the contrary, that the idea of what they call "mind-independent" moral truth takes us outside morality into metaphysics, that it urges us to consider whether there are chimerical properties or entities "in the world" that are half moral—how else could they make mind-independent moral claims true?—but also half nonmoral—how else could they "ground" moral claims or make them objectively true? They urge a colonial philosophy: setting up embassies and garrisons of science within value discourse to govern it properly.

Ordinary people sometimes express the idea that some acts are wrong in themselves by referring to moral "facts": "It is a moral fact that torture is always wrong." Trouble arrives, however, when philosophers make a meal of these innocent references by supposing them to make a further claim that adds something to the initial moral claim: something metaphysical about moral particles or properties—we might call these "morons." They therefore announce what I believe to be entirely bogus philosophical projects. They say that moral philosophy must aim to "reconcile" the moral and the natural worlds. Or to align the "practical" perspective we take when living our lives with the "theoretical" perspective from which we study ourselves as part of nature. Or to show how we can be "in touch" with the chimeras or, if we cannot, what reason we could have to think our moral opinions sound rather than mere accidents. These bogus questions and projects threaten puzzlement on all sides. Self-described "realists" try to make good on the projects, sometimes by claiming mysterious interaction between morons and ourselves. I discuss these attempts in Chapter 4. Self-described "anti-realists," discovering that there are no morons in "the world," or that in any case we have no way to be "in touch" with them, declare we must make up values for ourselves, an entirely bizarre assignment. How can they be values if we can just make them up? I describe these efforts in Chapter 3.

Each of these different "realist" and "anti-realist" projects evaporates when we take the independence of value seriously. Then there is no more need to "reconcile" a practical and a theoretical point of view than there is to reconcile physical facts about a book or psychological facts about its author with an interpretation of its poetry that ignores both. The only intelligible case for the "mind-independence" of some moral judgment is a moral argument showing that it would still be true even if no one thought it was; the only intelligible case against it is a moral argument for the opposite claim. In Chapter 6 I describe a theory of moral knowledge, responsibility, and conflict, and in Chapter 8 a theory of moral truth. These theories are drawn from within morality—they are themselves moral judgments. That is what independence means in moral philosophy. It is a natural and entirely familiar view: it is how we think. There is no noncircular argument against it. There is no argument that does not presuppose rather than establish a demand for philosophical colonialism.

Philosophers who deny independence insist on a distinction between two branches of moral philosophy. They distinguish between questions *of* morality—Does justice require universal health care?—and questions *about* morality—Can the claim that justice requires health care be true, or does it merely express an attitude? They call the former questions "substantive" or "first-order" questions and the latter "meta-ethical" or "second-order" questions. They assume that addressing meta-ethical issues requires philosophical argument rather than moral judgment. They then divide into the two camps I mentioned. Realists argue that the best nonmoral philosophical arguments show that moral judgment can indeed be objectively true, or are factual, or describe reality, or something of the sort. "Anti-realists" argue that the best arguments show exactly the contrary, whatever the contrary is. (Recently other philosophers have speculated whether these two views really are different and, if so, how to tell the difference.[5])

The independence of value plays an important role in the more general thesis of this book: that the various concepts and departments of value are interconnected and mutually supporting. The daunting philosophers' questions I mentioned seem to encourage a foxy response. Where do values come from? Are they really "out there" in the universe, part of what finally just is? If we understand these as metaphysical questions about the fundamental character of reality rather than questions calling for moral or value judgments, then we are well on the way to some important degree of pluralism about values. Suppose we think that values really are "out there" waiting to be perceived; that they are, in their own way, as brute as gasses and rocks. There would be no reason to think that these brute values are always nicely knit together in the mutually accommodating way that hedgehogs imagine.

On the contrary, it would seem more plausible that values conflict—as they certainly seem to do, for instance, when it would be an act of kindness to tell someone a lie or when the police can save some people from a terrible death only by torturing other people.

The contrary metaphysical opinion yields much the same result. We say: "It's crazy to think that values are 'out there' waiting to be discovered. So there is nothing that can make a moral judgment true. We don't find our values; we invent them. Values are just tastes and distastes gilded with honorifics." Then it would seem even sillier to insist on some grand unity of our values. We can, and do, want a large variety of things, and we cannot have all of them at the same time, or indeed ever. If our values are only our desires glorified, why shouldn't they reflect our undisciplined and contradictory greed?

On the other hand, if I am right that there are no nonevaluative, second-order, meta-ethical truths about value, then we cannot believe either that value judgments are true when they match special moral entities or that they cannot be true because there are no special entities for them to match. Value judgments are true, when they are true, not in virtue of any matching but in view of the substantive case that can be made for them. The moral realm is the realm of argument, not brute, raw fact. Then it is not implausible—on the contrary—to suppose that there are no conflicts but only mutual support in that realm. Or, what comes to the same thing, that any conflicts we find intractable show not disunity but a more fundamental unity of value that produces these conflicts as substantive results. Those are the conclusions I defend in Chapters 5 and 6.

How shall we classify the independence thesis? In what philosophical pigeonhole does it rest? Is it a kind of moral realism? Or constructivism? Or even anti-realism? Is it itself a nonmoral metaphysical theory? Or a quietist or minimalist theory that just ignores rather than really escapes troublesome metaphysics? None of these labels fits exactly—or exactly doesn't fit—because each is stained with the mistaken assumption that there are important philosophical questions about value that are not to be answered with value judgments. Please forget the pigeonholes as you read this book.

Responsibility

If, as I claim, a successful theory of justice is moral all the way down, then any sharp disagreement about justice is likely to survive all the way down as well. There is no neutral scientific or metaphysical plane on which we can stand finally to adjudicate which of different views about equal concern or liberty or democracy or any other opinion about right or wrong or good or bad is the best or true one. That means that we must pay considerable attention to another important moral virtue: moral responsibility. Though we cannot expect agreement from our fellow citizens, we can nevertheless demand responsibility from them. We must, therefore, develop a theory of responsibility that has sufficient force so that we can say to people, "I disagree with you, but I recognize the integrity of your argument. I recognize your moral responsibility." Or, "I agree with you, but you have not been responsible in forming your opinion. You've thrown a coin or believed what you've heard on a biased television network. It's only an accident that you've arrived at the truth."

We might call a theory of moral responsibility by a grander name: we might call it a moral epistemology. We cannot be, in any causal way, "in touch" with moral truth. But we can nevertheless think well or badly about moral issues. What is good and bad thinking is itself a moral question, of course: a moral epistemology is part of substantive moral theory. We use part of our overall theory of value to check our reasoning in other parts. So we must be careful to keep that part of our theory sufficiently distinct from other parts to allow it to function as a check on the rest. I have already anticipated my main claim about moral reasoning in this advance summary: I argue, in Chapter 6, that moral reasoning must be interpretive.

Our moral judgments are interpretations of basic moral concepts, and we test those interpretations by placing them in a larger framework of value to see whether they fit with and are supported by what we take to be the best conceptions of other concepts. We generalize, that is, the interpretive approach I described. We must take that approach to all our moral and political concepts. Morality as a whole, and not just political morality, is an interpretive enterprise. At the end of Chapter 8 I offer, as a classical and paradigm illustration of the interpretive approach, the moral, political, and ethical philosophies of Plato and of Aristotle.

In Chapter 10 I turn to an ancient threat that offers to make everything in my account of responsibility pointless: the apparently catastrophic idea that we can have no responsibility at all because we lack free will. I argue for what philosophers call a "compatibilist" view: that responsibility is compatible with any assumption we can sensibly entertain about what causes our various decisions and what the neural consequences are of those decisions. I argue that the character and extent of our responsibility for our actions turns rather on an *ethical* question: What is the character of a life well lived? I emphasize here and throughout the book the distinction between ethics, which is the study of how to live well, and morality, which is the study of how we must treat other people.

Ethics

How, then, should we live? In Part Three I argue that we each have a sovereign ethical responsibility to make something of value of our own lives, as a painter makes something valuable of his canvas. I rely on the authority of Part One, about truth in value, to argue that ethical responsibility is objective. We want to live well because we recognize that we should live well, rather than the other way around. In Part Four I argue that our various responsibilities and obligations to others flow from that personal responsibility for our own lives. But only in some special roles and circumstances—principally in politics—do these responsibilities to others include any requirement of impartiality between them and ourselves.

We must treat the making of our lives as a challenge, one we can perform well or badly. We must recognize, as cardinal among our private interests, an ambition to make our lives good lives: authentic and worthy rather than mean or degrading. In particular we must cherish our dignity. The concept of dignity has become debased by flabby overuse in political rhetoric: every politician pays lip service to the idea, and almost every covenant of human rights gives it pride of place. But we need the idea, and the cognate idea of self-respect, if we are to make much sense of our situation and our ambitions. Each of us bursts with love of life and fear of death: we are alone among animals conscious of that apparently absurd situation. The only value we can find in living in the foothills of death, as we do, is adverbial value. We must find the value of living—the meaning of life—in living well, just as we find value in loving or painting or writing or singing or diving well. There is no other enduring value or meaning in our lives, but that is value and meaning enough. In fact it's wonderful.

Dignity and self-respect—whatever these turn out to mean—are indispensable conditions of living well. We find evidence for that claim in how most people want to live: to hold their heads high as they struggle for all the other things they want. We find more evidence in the otherwise mysterious phenomenology of shame and insult. We must explore dignity's dimensions. At the outset of this summary I described two fundamental principles of politics: a requirement that government treat those it governs with equal concern, and a further requirement that it respect, as we may now put it, its subjects' ethical responsibilities. In Chapter 9 I construct the ethical analogues of these two political principles. People must take their own lives seriously: they must accept that it is objectively important how they live. People must take their ethical responsibility seriously as well: they must insist on the right—and exercise that right—to make ethical decisions finally for themselves. Each of these principles needs much elaboration. I offer part of what is needed in Chapter 9, but the application of the two principles in later chapters, as well as the discussion of determinism and free will I mentioned, furnish much more detail.

Morality

Philosophers ask: Why be moral? Some take this question as strategic. How can we tempt wholly amoral people to mend their ways? The question is more profitably understood in a very different way: as asking how we can account for the appeal of morality that we already feel. That is a profitable question because answering it not only improves self-understanding but helps to refine the content of morality. It helps us to see more clearly what, if we are to be moral, we must do.

If we can connect morality to the ethics of dignity in the way I propose, we will have an effective answer to the philosophers' question understood that way. We can then reply that we are drawn to morality in the way we are drawn to other dimensions of self-respect. I use many of the ideas already mentioned in this summary to make a case for that reply: particularly the character of interpretation and of interpretive truth and the independence of both ethical and moral truth from science and metaphysics. But I rely mainly on Immanuel Kant's thesis that we cannot adequately respect our own humanity unless we respect humanity in others. Chapter 11 sets out the abstract basis for that interpretive integration of ethics and morality, and considers objections to the feasibility of that project. Chapters 12, 13, and 14 take up a series of central moral issues. When must someone who properly values his own dignity aid others? Why must he not harm them? How and why does he incur special responsibilities to some of them through deliberate acts like promising and also through relationships with them that are often involuntary? We encounter old philosophical questions pursuing these various topics. How should numbers count in our decisions about whom we should aid? What responsibility do we have for unintended harm? When may we cause harm to some people in order to aid others? Why do promises create obligations? Do we have obligations just in virtue of our membership in political, ethnic, linguistic, and other communities?

Politics

Part Four ends with that transition to Part Five, and the book ends where I began this summary: in a theory of justice. My argument draws that theory from what has gone before. I hope, by presenting my argument backward in this introductory chapter, to emphasize the interdependence of the book's several themes. Chapter 15 argues that much political philosophy suffers from a failure to treat the main political concepts as interpretive, and the remaining chapters try to correct that mistake. I defend the conceptions of these concepts I summarized earlier and claim for them the kind of truth only a successful integration can claim. The last chapter is epilogue: it repeats the claim, now through the lens of dignity, that value has truth and that value is indivisible.

A Just So Story

I do not ask you to take the following conjectures seriously as intellectual history; they are not subtle or detailed or—I'm sure—correct enough for that. But whatever defects my account may have as history, it might help you to understand better the argument I just summarized by seeing how I conceive its place in a large historical story. At the end, in the Epilogue, I tell the same story more briefly and differently—and add a challenge.

The ancient moral philosophers were philosophers of self-affirmation. Plato and Aristotle saw the human situation in the terms I identified: we have lives to live and we should want to live those lives well. Ethics, they said, commands us to seek "happiness"; they meant not episodic glows of pleasure but the fulfillment of a successful life conceived as a whole. Morality also has its commands: these are captured in a set of virtues that include the virtue of justice. Both the nature of happiness and the content of these virtues are initially indistinct: if we mean to obey the commands of both ethics and morality, we must discover what happiness really is and what the virtues really demand. This requires an interpretive project. We must identify conceptions of happiness and of the familiar virtues that fit well together, so that the best understanding of morality flows from and helps define the best understanding of ethics.

The god-intoxicated philosophers of the early Christian period and of the Middle Ages had the same goal, but they had been given—or so they thought—an obvious formula for achieving it. Living well means living in God's grace, which in turn means following the moral law God laid down as the law of nature. That formula has the happy consequence of fusing two conceptually distinct issues: how people have come to hold their ethical and moral beliefs, and why those ethical and moral beliefs are correct. God's power explains the genesis of conviction: we believe what we do because God has revealed it to us directly or through the powers of reason he created in us. God's goodness also justifies the content of conviction: if God is the author of our moral sense, then of course our moral sense is accurate. The fact of our belief is in itself proof of our belief: what the Bible and God's priests say must therefore be true. The formula did not make for entirely smooth sailing. The Christian philosophers were troubled, above all, by what they called the problem of evil. If God is all-powerful and the very measure of goodness, why is there so much suffering and injustice in the world? But they found no reason to doubt that such puzzles were to be solved within the template provided by their theology. The morality of self-affirmation was firmly in control.

The philosophical explosions of the late Enlightenment ended that morality's long reign. The most influential philosophers insisted on a firm epistemological code. We can endorse our beliefs as true, they insisted, only if the best explanation of why we hold those beliefs vouches for their truth, and it can do that only if it shows those beliefs to be either the product of irresistible reason, like mathematics, or the effect of the impact of the natural world on our brains like the empirical discoveries of the nascent but already stunning natural sciences. That new epistemological regime posed an immediate problem for convictions about value, a problem that has challenged philosophy since. We are not entitled to think our moral convictions true unless we find these convictions either required by pure reason or produced by something "out there" in the world. Thus was born the Gibraltar of all mental blocks: that something other than value must underwrite value if we are to take value seriously.

The Christian and other religious philosophers could respect part of the new epistemological code because they did find something "out there" that underwrote conviction. But they could do so only by violating the naturalistic condition. Philosophers who accepted that further condition found the code more challenging. If the best explanation of why we think theft or murder wrong is to be found not in God's beneficent will but in some natural disposition of human beings to sympathize with one another's suffering, for instance, or in the convenience to us of the conventional arrangements of property and security that we have contrived, then the best explanation of these beliefs contributes nothing to their justification. On the contrary: the disconnection between the cause of our ethical and moral beliefs and any justification of those beliefs is in itself grounds for suspicion that these beliefs are not actually true, or at least that we have no reason to think them true.

The great Scottish philosopher David Hume is widely understood to have declared that no amount of empirical discovery about the state of the world—no revelations about the course of history or the ultimate nature of matter or the truth about human nature—can establish any conclusions about what ought to be without a further premise or assumption about what ought to be.[6] Hume's principle (as I shall call that general claim) is often taken to have a stark skeptical consequence, because it suggests that we cannot discover, through the only modes of knowledge available to us, whether any of our ethical or moral convictions is true. In fact, I argue in Part One, his principle has the opposite consequence. It undermines philosophical skepticism, because the proposition that it is not true that genocide is wrong is itself a moral proposition, and, if Hume's principle is sound, that proposition cannot be established by any discoveries of logic or facts about the basic structure of the universe. Hume's principle, properly understood, supports not skepticism about moral truth but rather the independence of morality as a separate department of knowledge with its own standards of inquiry and justification. It requires us to reject the Enlightenment's epistemological code for the moral domain.

The ancient and medieval conception of self-interest, which takes self-interest to be an ethical ideal, was another casualty of the new supposed sophistication. Disenchantment and then psychology produced a progressively bleaker picture of self-interest: from Hobbes's materialism to Bentham's pleasure and pain to Freud's unreason to the economists' *homo economicus*, a being whose interests are exhausted by his preference curves. Self-interest on this view can only mean the satisfaction of a mass of contingent desires that people happen to have. This new, supposedly more realistic, picture of what it is to live well produced two Western philosophical traditions. The first, which came to dominate substantive moral philosophy in Britain and America in the nineteenth century, accepted the new, meaner view of self-interest and therefore declared that morality and self-interest are rivals. Morality, this tradition insisted, means a subordination of self-interest; it requires taking up a distinct objective perspective that counts the agent's own interests as in no way more important than anyone else's. That is the morality of self-abnegation, a morality that spawned the moral philosophy of impersonal consequentialism, of which the theories of Jeremy Bentham, John Stuart Mill, and Henry Sidgwick are famous examples.

The second tradition, much more popular on the continent of Europe, rebelled against the bleak modern picture of self-interest, which it regarded as base. It emphasized the underlying freedom of human beings to struggle against custom and biology in search of a more ennobling picture of what a human life could be, the freedom that we grasp once we understand, as Jean-Paul Sartre put it, the distinction between objects in the world of nature, including ourselves so conceived, and the self-conscious creatures that we also are. Our existence precedes our essence because we are responsible for the latter: we are responsible for making our nature and then for living authentically up to what we have made. Friedrich Nietzsche, who has become the most influential figure in this tradition, accepted that the morality recognized by the conventions of Western community requires the subordination of the self. But he insisted that morality therefore stands exposed as a fake with no claims on us. The only real imperative of life is *living*—the creation and affirmation of a human life as a singular and wonderful creative act. Morality is a subversive idea invented by those who lack the imagination or the will to live creatively.

The first of these two modern traditions, the morality of self-abnegation, lost interest in self-interest, which it treated as the satisfaction of the desires people happened to have. The second, the ethics of self-assertion, sometimes lost interest in morality, which it treated as mere convention with no objective value or importance. The Greek idea of an interpretive unity between the two departments of value—a morality of self-affirmation—has survived only in a very degraded form. In the seventeenth century, Thomas Hobbes argued that conventional morality promotes everyone's self-interest, understood in the new, non-normative, desire-satisfaction way, and his contemporary followers have used the techniques of game theory to refine and defend the same claim. His suggestion unites morality with ethics, but to the discredit of both. It takes the desire view of ethics as fundamental, and it takes morality's function as only to serve desire. The Greek ideal was very different: it assumed that living well is more than having your desires satisfied and that being moral means taking a genuine, not just an instrumental, concern in the lives of others. Modern moral philosophy seems to have abandoned that ideal of ethical and moral integrity.

I have so far left Kant out of my Just So story, but his part is complex and crucial. His moral philosophy seems the paradigm of self-abnegation. The truly moral person, in his view, is moved only by the moral law, only by laws or maxims he could rationally will to apply to everyone equally. No act is morally good that is motivated only by the agent's interests or inclinations, even his altruistic inclinations of sympathy or desire to help others. There seems no space in this account for the idea that an agent's moral impulse can flow from his ambition to make something distinguished of his own life, to do a good job of living. Yet we can understand Kant to make exactly that claim: it is, on the best understanding, the foundation of his entire moral theory.

He claimed, in one stage of his evolving theory, that freedom is an essential condition of dignity—indeed, that freedom is dignity—and that only through legislating a moral law and acting out of obedience to that law can an agent find genuine freedom. So what seems a morality of self-abnegation becomes, at a deeper level, a morality of self-affirmation. Kant's unification of ethics and morality is obscure because it takes place in the dark: in what he called the noumenal world, whose content is inaccessible to us but which is the only realm where ontological freedom can be achieved. We can rescue Kant's crucial insight from his metaphysics: we can state it as what I shall call Kant's principle. A person can achieve the dignity and self-respect that are indispensable to a successful life only if he shows respect for humanity itself in all its forms. That is a template for a unification of ethics and morality. Just as Hume's principle is the anthem of Part One of this book, which describes the independence of morality from science and metaphysics, Kant's principle is the anthem of Parts Three and Four, which chart the interdependence of morality and ethics. In between lies Part Two, about interpretation, and after lies Part Five, about politics and justice.

PART ONE

Independence

2

Truth in Morals

The Challenge

"If we want to talk about values—about how to live and how to treat other people—we must start with bigger philosophical issues. Before we can sensibly think about whether honesty and equality are genuine values we must first consider, as a distinct threshold matter, whether there are any such things as values. It would not be sensible to debate how many angels can sit on a pin without first asking whether there are any angels at all; it would be equally silly to puzzle about whether self-sacrifice is good without first asking whether there is any such thing as goodness and, if so, what kind of thing it is.

"Can beliefs about value—that it is wrong to steal, for instance—actually be *true?* Or, for that matter, false? If so, what in the world can make such a belief true or false? Where do such values *come from?* God? But what if there is no god? Can values be just *out there,* part of what there really, finally, is? If so, how can we human beings be *in touch* with them? If some value judgments are true and others false, how can we human beings discover which are which? Even friends disagree about what is right and wrong; and of course we disagree even more strikingly with people of other cultures and ages. How can we think, without appalling arrogance, that we are right and others are just wrong? From what neutral perspective could the truth finally be tested and settled?

"Obviously we can't solve these puzzles just by repeating our value judgments. It would be unhelpful to insist that wrongness must exist in the universe because torturing babies for the fun of it is wrong. Or that I am in touch with moral truth because I know that torturing babies is wrong. That would just beg the question: torturing babies is not wrong if there is no such thing as wrongness in the universe, and I can't know that torturing babies is wrong unless I can be in touch with the truth about wrongness. No, these deep philosophical questions about the nature of the universe or the status of value judgments are not themselves questions about what is good or bad, right or wrong, wonderful or ugly. They belong not to ordinary ethical or moral or aesthetic rumination but to other, more technical departments of philosophy: to metaphysics or epistemology or the philosophy of language. That is why it is so important to distinguish two very different parts of moral philosophy: ordinary, first-order, substantive questions about what is good or bad, right or wrong, that call for value judgment, and philosophical, second-order, 'meta-ethical,' questions *about* those value judgments that call not for further value judgments but for philosophical theories of a quite different sort."

I apologize. I have been teasing for three paragraphs; I don't believe a single word of what I just wrote in quotes. I wanted to set out a philosophical opinion that is dear to a fox's heart and that has in my view hindered a proper understanding of all the topics we explore in this book. I stated my own contrary opinion in Chapter 1: morality and other departments of value are philosophically independent. Answers to large questions about moral truth and knowledge must be sought within those departments, not outside them. A substantive theory of value must include, not wait for, a theory of truth in value.

That there are truths about value is an obvious, inescapable fact. When people have decisions to make, the question of what decision they should make is inescapable, and it can be answered only by noticing reasons for acting one way or another; it can be answered only in that way because that is what the question, just as a matter of what it means, inescapably calls for. No doubt the best answer on some occasion is that *nothing* is any better to do than anything else. Some unfortunate people find a more dramatic answer unavoidable: they think nothing is *ever* the best or right thing to do. But these are as much substantive, first-order, value judgments about what to do as are more positive answers. They draw on the same kinds of arguments, and they claim truth in just the same way.

You will have gathered from Chapter 1 how I use the important words "ethics" and "morality." An ethical judgment makes a claim about what people should do to live well: what they should aim to be and achieve in their own lives. A moral judgment makes a claim about how people must treat other people.[1] Moral and ethical questions are inescapable dimensions of the inescapable question of what to do. They are inescapably pertinent even though, of course, they are not invariably noticed. Much of what I do makes my own life a better or worse one. In many circumstances much of what I do will affect others. What should I therefore do? The answers you give might be negative. You may suppose that it makes no difference how you live your life and that any concern for the lives of other people would be a mistake. But if you have any reasons for those distressing opinions, these must be ethical or moral reasons.

Grand metaphysical theories about what kinds of entities there are in the universe can have nothing to do with the case. You can be witheringly skeptical about morality, but only in virtue of not being skeptical about the nature of value further down. You may think that morality is bunk because there is no god. But you can think that only if you hold some moral theory that assigns exclusive moral authority to a supernatural being. These are the main conclusions of the first part of the book. I do not reject moral or ethical skepticism here: those are the subject of later parts. But I do reject Archimedean skepticism: skepticism that denies any basis for itself in morality or ethics. I reject the idea of an external, meta-ethical inspection of moral truth. I insist that any sensible moral skepticism must be internal to morality.

That is not a popular view among philosophers. They think what I quoted earlier: that the most fundamental questions about morality are not themselves moral, but rather metaphysical, questions. They think it would be a defeat for our ordinary ethical and moral convictions if we discovered that these were grounded in nothing but other ethical or moral convictions: they call the idea that it makes no sense to ask for anything else "quietism," which suggests a dirty secret kept dark. I believe—and will argue—that this opinion radically misunderstands what value judgments are. But its modern popularity means that something of a struggle is needed to free ourselves from its influence and to accept what should be obvious: that some answer to the question what to do must be the right one, even if this is that nothing is any better than anything else. The live question is not whether moral or ethical judgments can be true, but which are true.

Moral philosophers often reply that we must (in a phrase they particularly like) *earn* the right to suppose that ethical or moral judgments can be true. They mean that we must construct some plausible argument of the kind my teasing paragraphs imagined: some nonmoral metaphysical argument showing that there is some kind of entity or property in the world—perhaps morally charged particles or morons—whose existence and configuration can make a moral judgment true. But in fact there is only one way we can "earn" the right to think that some moral judgment is true, and this has nothing to do with physics or metaphysics. If I want to earn the right to call the proposition that abortion is always wrong true, then I have to provide moral arguments for that very strong opinion. There just is no other way.

However, I fear that this statement is just what the critics mean by "helping myself" to the possibility of truth. Part One defends this supposed larceny. Moral theory has become very complex in recent decades—it has produced a larger bestiary of "isms," I believe, than any other part of philosophy.[2] So Part One has several currents to navigate. This chapter describes what I take to be the ordinary person's view—or in any case the view that I shall describe that way. It holds that moral judgments can be true or false and that moral argument is needed to establish which are which. I elaborate, later in the chapter, the distinction I have already drawn between two different kinds of skepticism about the ordinary view—external skepticism, which claims to argue from entirely nonmoral assumptions, and skepticism that is internal to morality because it does not. Chapter 3 confronts external skepticism; Chapter 4 takes up crucial questions about the relation between the truth of moral convictions and the best explanation of why we hold the convictions we do; and Chapter 5 introduces what, in its global form, is by far the most threatening kind of skepticism—internal skepticism.

The Ordinary View

Someone who sticks pins into babies for the fun of hearing them scream is morally depraved. Don't you agree? You probably hold other, more controversial opinions about right and wrong as well. Perhaps you think that torturing suspected terrorists is morally wrong, for instance. Or, on the contrary, that it is morally justified or even required. You think that your opinions on these matters report the truth and that those who disagree with you are making a mistake, though you might perhaps find it more natural to say that your convictions are right or correct rather than true. You also think, I imagine, that sticking pins into babies or torturing terrorists would be wrong even if no one actually objected to it or was repulsed by the idea. Even you. You probably think, that is, that the truth of your moral convictions does not depend on what anyone thinks or feels. You might say, to make plain that that is what you think, that torturing babies for fun is "really" or "objectively" wicked. This attitude toward moral truth—that at least some moral opinions are objectively true in this way—is very common. I shall call it the "ordinary" view.

There is more to the ordinary view, some of it negative. You don't think that the wrongness of torturing babies or terrorists is just a matter of scientific discovery. You don't suppose that you could prove your opinion sound, or even provide evidence for it, just by some kind of experiment or observation. You could of course show, by experiment or observation, the consequences of torturing babies—the physical and psychological harm it inflicts, for example. But you couldn't show in that way that it is wrong to produce those consequences. You need a moral argument of some kind to do that, and moral argument is not a matter of scientific or empirical demonstration. Of course you don't conduct moral arguments with yourself—or anyone else—before forming your moral opinions. You just see or know that certain acts are wrong: these are your immediate reactions when you are presented with or imagine those acts. But you don't think that this kind of "seeing" provides evidence the way ordinary seeing does. If you see a burglar climbing through a window, you can cite your observation as a reason why the police should attend. But you wouldn't cite your seeing that the Iraq invasion was wrong as a reason why others who don't immediately agree should think it was. The difference is plain enough. The burglar's smashing the window caused you to see him smashing the window, so your observation is indeed evidence that he did smash it. But it would be absurd to think that the wrongness of the Iraq invasion caused you to think it wrong. You drew on the store of your convictions, education, and experience in judging the invasion as you did. If for some reason you wanted to defend your judgment, or consider it more carefully, you couldn't just cite what you saw. You would have to compose something by way of a moral argument.

You would be puzzled if someone told you that when you express a moral opinion you are not really saying anything. That you are only venting your spleen, or projecting some attitude, or declaring how you propose to live, so that it would be a mistake to think that what you had said is even a candidate for being true. You would agree, in response to that suggestion, that when you announce your opinion that torture is wrong you are doing some or all of these other things as well. Unless you are insincere, you are exhibiting your disapproval of torture and indicating at least something about your more general moral attitudes. But indicating or expressing these emotions or commitments is something you do through saying that torture is wrong, not instead of it. Even if you are insincere and only feigning your convictions and emotions, you are still, nevertheless, declaring that torture is wrong, and what you say is nevertheless true even if you don't believe it.

This ordinary view is committed to taking moral judgment at face value. If the Iraq war was wrong, then it is a fact—something that is the case—that it was wrong. On the ordinary view, that is, the war was *really* wrong. If your taste runs to drama, and you thought that war seeking regime change is always immoral, you might say that the wrongness of such war is a fixed, eternal feature of the universe. On the ordinary view, moreover, people who think that cheating is wrong recognize, in that opinion, a strong reason not to cheat, and to disapprove of other people who cheat. But thinking an act wrong is not the same thing as not wanting to do it: a thought is a judgment, not a motive. On the ordinary view, general questions about the basis of morality—about what makes a particular moral judgment true—are themselves moral questions. Is God the author of all morality? Can something be wrong even if everyone thinks it right? Is morality relative to place and time? Can something be right in one country or circumstance but wrong in another? These are abstract and theoretical questions, but they are still moral questions. They must be answered out of moral conscience and conviction, just like more ordinary questions about right and wrong.

Worries

That is the set of opinions and assumptions that I call the ordinary view. I assume that most people more or less unthinkingly hold that view. If you are philosophically disposed, however, then you may hold this ordinary view with some diffidence and concern because you may have some difficulty answering the philosophical challenges set out in the paragraphs I put in quotes earlier. First, you may be concerned about the kinds of entities or properties that we can sensibly suppose the universe to contain. Statements about the physical world are made true by the actual state of the physical world—its continents, quarks, and dispositions. We can have evidence—very often through observation of scientific instruments—about what the actual state of the physical world is. That evidence, we might say, provides an argument for our opinions about the physical world. But it is the physical world itself, the way the quarks actually spin, not the evidence we can assemble, that determines whether our opinions are actually true or false. Our evidence might be ever so powerful, but our conclusions nevertheless wrong, because, as a matter of brute fact, the world is not the way we think we have proved it is.

If we try to apply these familiar distinctions to our moral convictions, however, trouble appears. What do moral facts consist in? The ordinary view insists that moral judgments are not made true by historical events or people's opinions or emotions or anything else in the physical or mental world. But then what *can* make a moral conviction true? If you think the Iraq war immoral, then you can cite various historical facts—that the war was bound to cause huge suffering and was launched on the basis of evidently inadequate intelligence, for example—that you believe justify your opinion. But it is hard to imagine any distinct state of the world—any configuration of morons, for instance—that can make your moral opinion true the way physical particles can make a physical opinion true. It is hard to imagine any distinct state of the world for which your case can be said to be *evidence*.

Second, there is an apparently separate puzzle about how human beings might be thought to know moral truths, or even to form justified beliefs about them. The ordinary view holds that people do not become aware of moral facts the way they become aware of physical facts. Physical facts impinge on human minds: we perceive them, or we perceive evidence for them. Cosmologists take the observations of their huge radio telescopes to have been caused by ancient emissions from the edges of the universe; cardiologists take the shape of electrocardiogram printouts to be caused by a beating heart. But the ordinary view insists that moral facts cannot create any impression of themselves in human minds: moral judgment is not a matter of perception the way color judgment is. How then can we be "in touch with" moral truth? What could justify your assumption that the various events that make up your case about the Iraq war really do argue adequately for its morality or immorality?

These two puzzles—and others that we shall uncover later—have for centuries encouraged learned scholars and great philosophers to reject different aspects of the ordinary view. I shall call those who do that "skeptics," but I use that word in a special sense to include anyone who denies that moral judgments can be objectively true—true, that is, not in virtue of the attitudes or beliefs anyone has but true without regard to any such attitudes or beliefs. An unsophisticated form of such skepticism, which is often called "postmodernism," has been much in vogue in the unconfident departments of Western universities: in faculties of art history, comparative literature, and anthropology, for example, and for a time in law schools as well.[3] Devotees declare that even our most confident convictions about what is right or wicked are just emblems of ideology, just badges of power, just the rules of the local language games we happen to play. But as we shall see, many philosophers have been more subtle and inventive in their skepticism. In the balance of this chapter I distinguish different versions of philosophical skepticism about morality; in the rest of Part One we concentrate on arguments for each of those versions.

Two Important Distinctions

Internal and External Skepticism

Two distinctions are essential to my continuing argument; I set them out in more detail now. The first distinguishes internal from external skepticism about morality. I assume that people's moral convictions form at least a loose set or system of interconnected propositions with a distinct subject matter: people have convictions at different levels of abstraction about what is right and wrong, good and bad, worthy and unworthy. When we puzzle about a moral issue, we can bring a variety of these convictions to bear: we can appeal to more abstract or general convictions to test more concrete judgments about what to do or think. Someone asking herself whether it would be wrong to leave an unhappy marriage might reflect on more general issues about what people owe other people they have asked to trust them, for instance, or about the moral responsibilities children bring. She might then weigh her sense of those responsibilities against what might seem to her a competing responsibility to make something of her own life or perhaps competing responsibilities she believes she has assumed to someone else. Such reflection, we can say, is internal to morality because it claims to reach moral conclusions from more general assumptions that are themselves moral in character and subject matter. Moral reflection of that kind takes account of ordinary nonmoral facts as well, of course: facts about the impact of divorce on children's welfare, for instance. However, it appeals to such nonmoral facts only by way of drawing concrete implications from more general moral claims.

But someone can step back from the entire set of his moral ideas and reflect about these ideas as a whole. He can ask external questions *about* his or other people's moral values rather than internal questions *of* moral value. These include social-scientific questions: whether, for example, our economic or other circumstances explain why we are drawn to moral convictions that other cultures with different circumstances reject. This distinction between internal and external questions can be made about any body of ideas. We distinguish mathematical claims, which are internal to the domain of mathematics, from questions about mathematical practice. The question whether Fermat's theorem has at last been proved is an internal question of mathematics; the question whether a higher percentage of students study calculus now than formerly is an external question about mathematics. Philosophers use a different vocabulary to make the same distinction: they distinguish between "first-order" or "substantive" questions within a system of ideas and "second-order" or "meta" questions about that system of ideas. The claim that torturing babies is immoral is a first-order, substantive claim; the hypothesis that this opinion is almost universally held is a second-order or meta-claim.

Internal skepticism about morality is a first-order, substantive moral judgment. It appeals to more abstract judgments about morality in order to deny that certain more concrete or applied judgments are true. External skepticism, on the contrary, purports to rely entirely on second-order, external statements about morality. Some external skeptics rely on social facts of the kind I described earlier: they say that the historical and geographical diversity of moral opinions shows that no such opinion can be objectively true, for example. But the most sophisticated external skeptics rely, as I said earlier, on metaphysical theses about the kind of entities the universe contains. They assume that these metaphysical theses are external statements about morality rather than internal judgments of morality. So, as the metaphor suggests, internal skepticism stands within first-order, substantive morality while external skepticism is supposedly Archimedean: it stands above morality and judges it from outside. Internal skeptics cannot be skeptical about morality all the way down, because they must assume the truth of some very general moral claim in order to establish their skepticism about other moral claims. They rely on morality to denigrate morality. External skeptics do claim to be skeptical about morality all the way down. They are able to denigrate moral truth, they say, without relying on it.

Error and Status Skepticism

We need a further distinction within external skepticism: between error and status skepticism. Error skeptics hold that all moral judgments are false. An error skeptic might read the ordinary view as assuming that moral entities exist: that the universe contains not only quarks, mesons, and other very small physical particles but also what I called morons, special particles whose configuration might make it true that people should not torture babies and that optional military invasions seeking regime change are immoral. He might then declare that because there are no moral particles, it is a mistake to say that torturing babies is wrong or that invading Iraq was immoral. This is not internal skepticism, because it does not purport to rely on even counterfactual moral judgments for its authority. It is external skepticism because it purports to rely only on value-neutral metaphysics: it relies only on the metaphysical claim that there are no moral particles.

Status skeptics disagree: they are skeptical of the ordinary view in a different way. The ordinary view treats moral judgments as descriptions of how things actually are: they are claims of moral fact. Status skeptics deny moral judgment that status: they believe it is a mistake to treat them as descriptions of anything. They distinguish between description and other activities like coughing, expressing emotion, issuing a command, or embracing a commitment, and they hold that expressing a moral opinion is not describing but something that belongs in the latter group of activities. Status skeptics therefore do not say, as error skeptics do, that morality is a misconceived enterprise. They say it is a misunderstood enterprise.

Status skepticism evolved rapidly during the twentieth century. Initial forms were crude: A. J. Ayer, for example, in his famous little book *Language, Truth, and Logic,* insisted that moral judgments are no different from other vehicles for venting emotions. Someone who declares that tax cheating is wrong is only, in effect, shouting "Boo tax cheating."[4] Later versions of status skepticism became more sophisticated. Richard Hare, for instance, whose work was very influential, treated moral judgments as disguised and generalized commands.[5] "Cheating is wrong" should be understood as "Don't cheat." For Hare, however, the preference expressed by a moral judgment is very special: it is universal in its content so that it embraces everyone who is situated in the way it assumes, including the speaker. Hare's analysis is still status-skeptical, however, because, like Ayer's puffs of emotion, his preference expressions are not candidates for truth or falsity.

These early versions wore their skepticism on the sleeve. Hare said that a Nazi who would apply his strictures to himself, should he turn out to be a Jew, has not made a moral mistake. Later in the century external skepticism became more ambiguous. Allan Gibbard and Simon Blackburn, for examples, have called themselves, variously, "noncognitivists," "expressivists," "projectivists," and "quasi-realists," which suggests sharp disagreement with the ordinary view. Gibbard says that moral judgments should be understood as expressing acceptance of a plan for living: not "as beliefs with such and such content" but rather as "sentiments or attitudes, perhaps, or as universal preferences, states of norm acceptance—or states of planning."[6] But Blackburn and Gibbard both labor to show how, on their view, an expressivist who takes this view of moral judgment can nevertheless sensibly speak of moral judgments as true or false, and that he can also mimic in other, more complex, ways how people who hold the ordinary view speak about moral issues. But they treat these claims of truth as part of an activity that is nevertheless, they insist, different from describing how things are.

Internal Skepticism

Because internal skeptics rely on the truth of substantive moral claims, they can only be partial error skeptics. There is no internal status skepticism. Internal skeptics differ from one another in the scope of their skepticism. Some internal skepticism is quite circumscribed and topical. Many people think, for instance, that the choices that adult partners make about the mechanics of sex raise no moral issues: they think that all judgments that condemn certain sexual choices are false. They ground this limited skepticism in positive opinions about what makes acts right or wrong; they do not believe that the details of adult consensual sex, whether heterosexual or homosexual, have any right- or wrong-making features. Other people are internal error skeptics about the place of morality in foreign policy. They say that it makes no sense to suppose that a nation's trade policy can be either morally right or wrong. They reject positive moral judgments that many other people hold—that American policy in Latin America has often been unjust, for example—by appealing to the more general moral judgment that a nation's officials should always act with only the interests of their own citizens in mind.

Other versions of internal error skepticism are much broader, and some are near global because they reject all moral judgments except counterfactual ones. The popular opinion I mentioned—that because there is no god, nothing is right or wrong—is a piece of global internal skepticism; it is based on the moral conviction that a supernatural will is the only possible basis for positive morality. The more modern opinion that morality is empty because all human behavior is causally determined by prior events beyond anyone's control is also internally skeptical; it is based on the moral conviction that it is unfair to blame people or hold them responsible for behavior that they could not have avoided. (We consider that popular moral conviction in Chapter 10.) Another now popular opinion holds that no universal moral claim is sound because morality is relative to culture; this view, too, is internally skeptical because it relies on the conviction that morality rises only out of the practices of particular communities. Yet another form of global internal skepticism notices that human beings are incredibly small and evaporating parts of an inconceivably vast and durable universe and concludes that nothing we do can matter—morally or otherwise—anyway.[7] True, the moral convictions on which these examples of global internal skepticism rely are counterfactual convictions: they assume that the positive moral claims they reject would be valid if certain conditions were satisfied—if a god did exist or moral conventions were uniform across cultures or the universe was much smaller. Still, even these counterfactual convictions are substantive moral judgments.

I have no quarrel with any form of internal skepticism in this part of the book. Internal skepticism does not deny what I wish to establish: that philosophical challenges to the truth of moral judgments are themselves substantive moral theories. It does not deny—on the contrary it assumes—that moral judgments are capable of truth. We shall be much concerned with internal skepticism later in the book, because my positive claims about personal and political morality presume that no global form of internal skepticism is correct. However, we should at least notice now an important distinction often overlooked. We must distinguish internal skepticism from uncertainty. I may be uncertain whether abortion is wrong: I may think the arguments on both sides reasonable and not know which, if either, is stronger. But uncertainty is not the same as skepticism. Uncertainty is a default position: if I have no firm conviction either way, then I am uncertain. But skepticism is not a default position: I need as strong an argument for the skeptical thesis that morality has nothing to do with abortion as for any positive view on the matter. We return to the important distinction between skepticism and uncertainty in Chapter 5.

The Appeal of Status Skepticism

Both forms of external skepticism—error and status skepticism—are different from the biological and social-scientific theories I mentioned earlier. Neo-Darwinian theories about the development of moral beliefs and institutions, for instance, are external but in no way skeptical. There is no inconsistency in holding the following set of opinions: (1) that a wired-in condemnation of murder had survival value in the ancestral savannahs, (2) that this fact figures in the best explanation why moral condemnation of murder is so widespread across history and cultures, and (3) that it is objectively true that murder is morally wrong. The first two of these claims are anthropological and the third is moral; there can be no conflict in combining the moral with the anthropological in this way.[8] So external skeptics cannot rely only on anthropology or any other biological or social science. They rely on a very different kind of putatively external theory: they rely on philosophical theories about what there is in the universe or about the conditions under which people can be thought to acquire responsible belief.

In one way internal and external skepticism are in sharp contrast. Internal skepticism would be self-defeating if it denied that moral judgments are candidates for truth; it cannot rely on any coruscating metaphysics that has that consequence. External skepticism, on the other hand, cannot leave any moral judgments standing as candidates for truth: it must show them all to be error or all to have some status that rules out their being true. External skepticism would be immediately self-defeating if it exempted any substantive moral judgment from its skeptical scope.

In another way, however, internal skepticism and external error skepticism are alike. Internal skepticism plays for keeps. It has direct implications for action: if someone is internally skeptical about sexual morality, he cannot consistently censure people for their sexual choices or lobby for outlawing homosexuality on moral grounds. If he believes that morality is dead because there is no god, then he must not ostracize others because they have behaved badly. External error skepticism also plays for keeps: an error skeptic may dislike the war in Iraq, but he cannot claim that the American invasion was immoral. External status skeptics, on the contrary, insist that their form of skepticism is neutral about moral claims and controversies and permits them to engage in moral condemnation with as much fervor as anyone else. Suppose we conclude, with the status skeptic, that moral claims are only projections of emotion onto a morally barren world. We will have changed our minds about the status of our moral convictions, but not about the content of those convictions. We can continue to insist that terrorism is always wrong, or that it is sometimes justified, or to offer or deny any other moral opinion we may entertain. The later status skeptics (assuming they are skeptics) even allow us to insist that our convictions are objectively true. We only say to ourselves (silently in order not to blunt the impact of what we say out loud) that in so insisting we are only projecting more complex attitudes.

This apparent neutrality gives status skepticism a seductive appeal. I said earlier that some of us are troubled by the philosophical challenges I described. We cannot believe in morons. And we have other reasons for shrinking from bold assertion that our moral beliefs are true: it seems arrogant, in the face of great cultural diversity, to claim that everyone who disagrees with us is in error. But any form of error skepticism seems out of the question. We can't really believe that there is nothing morally objectionable about suicide bombers or genocide or racial discrimination or forced clitoridectomy. External status skepticism offers people torn in that way exactly what they want. It is agreeably ecumenical. It allows its partisans to be as metaphysically and culturally modest as anyone might wish, to abandon all claims as to their own morality's ultimate truth or even superiority to other moralities. But it allows them to do this while still embracing their convictions as enthusiastically as ever, denouncing genocide or abortion or slavery or gender discrimination or welfare cheats with all their former vigor. They need only say that they have revised their view, not about the substance, but about the status, of their convictions. They no longer claim that their convictions mirror an external reality. But they still hold these convictions with the same intensity. They can be as willing to fight or even die for their beliefs as they ever were, but now with a difference. They can have their moral convictions and lose them too. Richard Rorty called this state of mind "irony."[9]

External status skepticism is therefore much more popular among academic philosophers now than global internal skepticism or external error skepticism has ever been, and it is status skepticism that has infected contemporary intellectual life. I shall therefore concentrate on that form of skepticism, but I mean my arguments in the next few chapters to embrace all forms of external skepticism and, indeed, all forms of what might seem the opposite view: that we can have external, nonmoral reasons for believing that our moral opinions can be true. (Because the latter claim is often called philosophical "realism," I will sometimes refer to those who hold it as "realists.") Philosophy can neither impeach nor validate any value judgment while standing wholly outside that judgment's domain. Internal skepticism is the only skeptical game in town. Perhaps it is neither true nor false that abortion is wicked or that the American Constitution condemns all racial preference or that Beethoven was a greater creative artist than Picasso. But if so, this is not because there can be no right answer to such questions for reasons prior or external to value, but because that *is* the right answer internally, as a matter of sound moral or legal or aesthetic judgment. (I explore that possibility in Chapter 5.) We can't be skeptical about any domain of value all the way down.

Disappointment?

I have tried to answer the two questions that I said give people pause about the ordinary view: What makes a moral judgment true? When are we justified in thinking a moral judgment true? My answer to the first is that moral judgments are made true, when they are true, by an adequate moral argument for their truth. Of course that invites the further question: What makes a moral argument adequate? The answer must be: a further moral argument for its adequacy. And so forth. That is not to say that a moral judgment is made true by the arguments that are in fact made for it: these arguments may not be adequate. Nor that it is made true by its consistency with other moral judgments. I argue in Chapter 6 that coherence is a necessary but not a sufficient condition of truth. We can say nothing more helpful than what I just said: a moral judgment is made true by an adequate case for its truth.

When are we justified in supposing a moral judgment true? My answer: when we are justified in thinking that our arguments for holding it true are adequate arguments. That is, we have exactly the reasons for thinking we are right in our convictions that we have for thinking our convictions right. This may seem unhelpful, because it supplies no independent verification. You might be reminded of Wittgenstein's newspaper reader who doubted what he read and so bought another copy to check. However, he did not act responsibly, and we can. We can ask whether we have thought about the moral issues in the right way. What way is that? I offer an answer in Chapter 6. But I emphasize there, again, that a theory of moral responsibility is itself a moral theory: it is part of the same overall moral theory as the opinions whose responsibility it is meant to check. Is it reasoning in a circle to answer the question of reasons in that way? Yes, but no more circular than the reliance we place on part of our science to compose a theory of scientific method to check our science.

These answers to the two ancient questions will strike many readers as disappointing. I believe there are two reasons for this attitude, one a mistake and the other an encouragement. First the mistake: my answers disappoint because the ancient questions seem to expect a different kind of answer. They expect answers that step outside morality to find a nonmoral account of moral truth and moral responsibility. But that expectation is confused: it rests on a failure to grasp the independence of morality and other dimensions of value. Any theory about what makes a moral conviction true or what are good reasons for accepting it must be itself a moral theory and therefore must include a moral premise or presupposition. Philosophers have long demanded a moral theory that is not a moral theory. But if we want a genuine moral ontology or epistemology, we must construct it from within morality. Do you want something more? I hope to show you that you do not even know what more you could want. I hope you will come to find these initial answers not disappointing but illuminating.

The second, more encouraging, explanation for your dissatisfaction is that my answers are too abstract and compressed: they point to but do not provide the further moral theory we need. The suggestion that a scientific proposition is true if it matches reality is actually as circular and opaque as my two answers. It seems more helpful because we offer it against the background of a huge and impressive science that gives the idea of matching reality substantial content: we think we know how to decide whether a piece of chemistry does that trick. We need the same structure and complexity for a moral ontology or a moral epistemology: we need much more than the bare claim that morality is made true by adequate argument. We need a further theory about the structure of adequate arguments. We need not just the idea of moral responsibility but some account of what that is.

These are projects for Part Two. I argue there that we should treat moral reasoning as a form of interpretive reasoning and that we can achieve moral responsibility only by aiming at the most comprehensive account we can achieve of a larger system of value in which our moral opinions figure. That interpretive goal provides the structure of adequate argument. It defines moral responsibility. It does not guarantee that the arguments we construct in that way are adequate; it does not guarantee moral truth. But when we find our arguments adequate, after that kind of comprehensive reflection, we have earned the right to live by them. What stops us, then, from claiming that we are certain they are true? Only our sense, confirmed by wide experience, that better interpretive arguments may be found. We must take care to respect the distance between responsibility and truth. But we cannot explain that distance except by appealing once again to the idea of good and better argument. We cannot escape from morality's independence, no matter how strenuously we struggle. Every effort we make to find a trap door out of morality confirms that we do not yet understand what morality is.

3

External Skepticism

An Important Claim

In Chapter 1 I said that moral skepticism is itself a moral position. That is an important claim that has been and will be severely challenged. If it is true, then external skepticism defeats itself. An external error skeptic holds that all moral judgments are objectively false, and an external status skeptic that moral judgments do not even purport to be true. Each contradicts himself if his own skeptical judgment is itself a moral judgment; surely he must claim truth for his own philosophical position. So the philosophical leverage of my claim is very great, both in general and for the further arguments of this part of the book. Even most philosophers who insist that moral judgments can be true or false will disagree with that claim.[1] I must therefore take some care in explaining and defending it.

You might think it Pickwickean to insist that a philosophical statement that denies the existence of moral properties itself makes a moral claim. You might offer these analogies: the observation that astrology is bunk is not itself an astrological claim, and atheism is not a religious stance. That depends, however, on how we choose to define these categories. If we define an astrological judgment as one that asserts or presupposes some planetary influence on human lives, then the proposition that astrology is bunk, which denies any such influence, is not an astrological judgment. However, if we define an astrological judgment as one that describes the character and extent of planetary influ-ence, then the statement that there is no such influence is indeed an astrologi-cal judgment. If we define a religious position as one that presupposes the existence of one or more divine beings, then atheism is not a religious position. But if we define it as one that offers an opinion about the existence or proper-ties of divine beings, then atheism certainly is a religious position.

Cosmology is a domain of thought: it is a part of science more broadly understood. We can ask: What is true and false in that domain? What is true or false, that is, cosmologically speaking? Skepticism about astrology and God stake out answers to that question: they speak to the issue of what there is among the forces of our universe. We could hardly say, "Since we are athe-ists, we insist that nothing is true, cosmologically speaking." We have offered, in our atheism, an opinion about what is true in that domain. Morality is also a domain. Its topics, we might say, include these questions: Do people have any categorical responsibilities to other people—responsibilities, that is, that do not depend on what they want or think? If so, what categorical responsi-bilities do they have? Someone takes a position on these issues when he declares that the rich have a duty to help the poor. Someone else takes a contrary posi-tion when he denies that the rich have any such obligation because, he says, the poor have brought their poverty on themselves. A third person takes a broader form of that second position if he declares that no one ever has a moral obligation because moral obligations could be created only by a god and there is no god. A fourth person argues that no one ever has a moral obligation be-cause there are no queer entities that could constitute a moral obligation. The latter two skeptics offer different kinds of reasons, but the state of affairs each claims to hold is the same. The *content* of the two claims—what the different skeptics claim to be the case, morally speaking—is the same. Both of them, not just the third, make a moral claim and so cannot consistently declare that no moral claim is true. Compare: we may say that no claim anyone makes about the shape or color of unicorns is true because there are no unicorns. But we can't then declare that no proposition of unicorn zoology can be true.

As I said in Chapter 1, moral philosophers have characteristically insisted on a fundamental distinction between moral judgments and philosophical judgments about moral judgments. Russ Shafer-Landau claims that the dis-tinction is evident in other fields. "We are not doing mathematics when we ask about the ontology of numbers. We can stand apart from theological disputes and still query the basic assumptions of religious doctrine."[2] But many philosophers of mathematics do think we are doing mathematics when we declare that numbers exist.[3] And we certainly do not stand apart from religious dispute when we insist that there is no god. On the contrary, we stand at the center of that dispute. The distinction that philosophers like Shafer-Landau have in mind is at best semantic. Consider: "Victims of automobile accidents cannot recover compensation unless someone has been negligent" and "Tort law enforces the no-liability-without-fault doctrine." The second statement is in a sense about statements like the first, but it is nevertheless itself a legal judgment. We can treat skeptical moral theories as theories about more detailed moral judgments in the same way, but they are nevertheless moral judgments as well. Shafer-Landau adds, "We can leave our grammar books aside and still ask about whether grammatical facility is innate." Yes, because the latter question is biological, not grammatical. No view of biology disagrees with any opinion about correct grammar. But there is nothing else for moral skepticism to be but moral.

Some philosophers have found what they take to be a mistake in my argument: I suffer from a mental block, they believe, about the possibilities of negation.[4] An external skeptic, on their view, declares that acts are neither morally required nor forbidden *nor* permitted. Surely that does not stake out a moral position but instead refuses to make any moral claim at all. So I am wrong, they say, to suppose that external skepticism is itself a moral position.

Consider this conversation:

A: Abortion is morally wicked: we always in all circumstances have a categorical reason—a reason that does not depend on what anyone wants or thinks—to prevent and condemn it.

B: On the contrary. In some circumstances abortion is morally required. Single teenage mothers with no resources have a categorical reason to abort.

C: You are both wrong. Abortion is never either morally required or morally forbidden. No one has a categorical reason either way. It is always permissible and never mandatory, like cutting your fingernails.

D: You are all three wrong. Abortion is never either morally forbidden or morally required *or* morally permissible.

A, B, and C make moral claims. Does D? Because it is unclear what he could mean by his mysterious claim, we ask him to elaborate.

He might say, first, "Any proposition that assumes the existence of something that does not exist is false. Or (as I sometimes think) neither true nor false. A, B, and C are all assuming that moral duties exist. But no such thing exists, so none of them is making a true statement." D has fallen victim to morons—or rather the lack of them. If there are morons, and morons make moral claims true or false, then we might imagine that morons, like quarks, have colors. An act is forbidden only if there are red morons in the neighborhood, required only if there are green ones, and permissible only if there are yellow ones. So D declares that, because there are no morons at all, abortion is neither forbidden, nor required, nor permissible. His assumption that there are no morons, he insists, is not itself a moral claim. It is a claim of physics or metaphysics. But he has seriously misunderstood the conversational situation. A, B, and C have each made a claim about what reasons of a certain kind—categorical reasons—people do or do not have. D's claim that no duties exist means that no one ever has a reason of that kind. So perforce he expresses a moral position; he agrees with C and cannot say, without contradiction, that what C says is false (or neither true nor false).

D might say: "A, B, and C are each relying on the existence of morons to sustain their claim." But they are doing no such thing. Even if A thinks there are morons, he would not cite their existence and color as arguments in his favor. He has very different kinds of arguments: that abortion insults the dignity of human life, for instance. But once again, to be generous to D, let us assume that A, B, and C are unusual and would cite morons as arguments. That doesn't help D's case. What matters is not the arguments that the trio make but what they take to be the conclusion of those arguments. To repeat: each makes a claim about the categorical reasons people do or do not have with respect to abortion. The upshot of D's various arguments, whatever they are, is a claim of the same kind. He thinks there are no such reasons and therefore disagrees with A and B and agrees with C. He makes a much more general claim than C does, but his claim includes C's. He has taken a position on a moral issue: he has taken a substantive, first-order, moral stance.

Now D corrects himself. "I should not have said that the claims of A, B, and C are false, or that they are neither true nor false. I should have said that they make no sense at all: I cannot understand what they could mean by claiming or denying categorical reasons. It's all gibberish to me." People often say that some proposition makes no sense when they mean only that it is silly or obviously wrong. If that is what D now means, he has not changed his approach; he has just added emphasis. What else might he mean? He might mean that he believes the others contradict themselves, claiming something impossible, as if they claimed to see a square circle on a park bench. That changes his argument but not his conclusion. If he thinks that categorical reasons are impossible, then once again he thinks that no one has a categorical reason for anything. He still takes a moral stand. One more try. Perhaps he means that he finds what the others say literally incomprehensible. He concedes that they seem to have a concept he lacks; he can't translate what they say into a language he understands. Of course that is preposterous: he knows very well what A, B, and C mean to say about people's moral responsibilities. But if he insists that he doesn't understand, he ceases to be a skeptic of any kind. I can't be a skeptic in a language I can't understand.

The message of all this seems clear. When you make a statement about what moral responsibilities people have, you are declaring how things stand—morally speaking. There is no way out of or around the independence of value. Now, however, suppose that D replies in a very different way. "I mean that the arguments on both sides of the abortion issue are so evenly balanced that there is no right answer to the question whether abortion is forbidden or required or permissible. Any such claim assumes that the arguments for its position are stronger than those for the other, and that is false." In Chapter 5 I emphasize the difference between being uncertain about the right answer to some question and believing that there is no right answer—that the issue is indeterminate. D, in this new elaboration, has indeterminacy in mind: that is why he says that all the other positions are false, not just unpersuasive. His position is now obviously a substantive moral claim. He does disagree, finally, with C as well as A and B, but he disagrees with them all because he holds a fourth moral opinion. He assesses the strength of the three moral opinions and finds none of them stronger than either of the others. That is a form of skepticism, but it is internal skepticism.

Hume's Principle

If, as I argue, any moral skepticism is itself a substantive moral claim, then external moral skepticism contradicts itself in the way I said. It also violates the principle of moral epistemology I called Hume's principle. This holds that no series of propositions about how the world is, as a matter of scientific or metaphysical fact, can provide a successful case on its own—without some value judgment hidden in the interstices—for any conclusion about what ought to be the case. Hume's principle seems to me obviously true. Consider this attempt to violate it. "Jack is in great pain and you could easily help him. Therefore, just for that reason, you have a moral duty to help him." If this is a good argument, just as it stands, then some principle about what makes an argument a good one must be at work. What is that principle? It cannot be any form of induction or generalization, because these would assume that you have had a moral duty in the past, which is a moral assumption. It cannot be a principle of deduction or semantic entailment. It needs something more, and that must be something—a hidden premise or an assumption about the nature of good moral reasoning—that is infused with moral force.

Yes, the fact that someone standing before you is evidently in great pain does seem by itself a reason why you ought to help him if you can. Nothing more needs to be said. But I assume you think this because you unselfconsciously accept, as something that goes without saying, a general responsibility to help people in grave need when you easily can. Suppose you make it explicit that you are not relying on any such background moral assumption. You declare that you have no view one way or the other about any general responsibility to help people in pain in circumstances just like these. You simply insist that in this particular case the pain before you, on its own, without any further assumption of that kind, imposes a moral responsibility on you. Your point then becomes not obvious but opaque.

Some philosophers have offered a different objection.[5] Hume's principle, they agree, does show that a set of nonmoral facts cannot, on their own, establish a moral claim. But it doesn't follow that nonmoral facts cannot, on their own, undermine a moral claim. So external skepticism, which seeks only to undermine, may succeed in spite of Hume's principle. But this rescue fails if, as I claim, skepticism is itself a moral position. Undermining the moral claim that people have a duty not to cheat is the same as establishing the moral claim that it isn't true that they have that duty. Hume's principle has been challenged in other ways; I find these challenges all unsuccessful.[6]

Of course, Hume's principle does not outlaw the many disciplines—sociology, psychology, primatology, genetics, political science, and common sense—that study morality as a social and psychological phenomenon. Nor does it outlaw what I take to be at least part of Hume's own project: the natural history of moral sentiment and conviction. We can learn a great deal about morality and ourselves by attending to facts about what is and has been. We can speculate about why certain moral convictions are popular in some cultures and communities though not in others, about the varied forms of influence and pressure that have proved effective in perpetuating these convictions as social norms, about when and how children become sensitive to moral claim and censure, about why certain moral opinions are near universal among human beings, and about how the economic circumstances of a community, among other factors, correlate with the content of moral convictions current there.

These are all important and fascinating questions, and they have of course been set out much more precisely than I have just done. I distinguish them all, however, from the question before us now, the question that is usually of much greater interest to most of us: Which moral opinions are true? Hume's principle applies only to this latter question. This crucial distinction between moral judgments and descriptive studies about morality is sometimes obscured by an ambiguity in the idea of explanation. People ask: How can we explain morality? That might be understood as calling for the kind of factual explanation I just described. It might invite, for example, a neo-Darwinian account of the rise of certain practices among higher primates and early human beings. On the other hand it might call for a justification of moral practices and institutions. Justification is what someone has in mind who demands, in an angry tone, "Explain yourself!"

Error Skepticism

If external skepticism is itself a moral position, then it contradicts itself. External error skepticism seems most immediately vulnerable because it holds that all moral claims are false. Error skeptics might revise their view, however, to hold only that all positive moral judgments are false. Positive moral judgments, they might say, are those that offer guidance for action or approval: these include judgments that some action is morally required or forbidden, that some situation or person is morally good or bad, that someone has a moral virtue or vice, and so forth. They might call the alternatives to such claims— that some situation is neither good nor bad but morally neutral, or that some person is to be neither praised nor criticized for some trait of his character— negative moral judgments. But, as I said earlier, these are still moral judgments. They are as much moral judgments as the proposition that the law neither requires nor forbids drinking wine is a legal judgment. Error skepticism so revised would therefore be an example of global internal skepticism. It would have the same content, for instance, as the theory that God is the only possible author of moral duty and that he does not exist. An error skeptic might hope to rely on some argument parallel to that one: that only queer entities can impose moral duties and that there are no queer entities. I consider that odd claim in the next chapter. Or he might rely on two other familiar arguments that I consider now. We must inspect these, however, as arguments for an internal, not an external, skepticism.

Diversity

John Mackie, the most prominent recent error skeptic, argued that positive moral claims must be false because people disagree about which of them are true.[7] His sociological assumptions are largely correct. Moral diversity is sometimes exaggerated: the degree of convergence over basic moral matters throughout history is both striking and predictable. But people do disagree about important matters, like affirmative action, abortion, and social justice, even within particular cultures. Does that show that we actually have no moral duties or responsibilities at all?

Of course it should give us pause that others disagree with what we find so plain. How can I be sure that I am right when others, who seem just as intelligent and sensitive, deny that I am? But we cannot take the fact of disagreement itself to count as an argument that our moral convictions are mistaken. We would not count the popularity of any of our other convictions as evidence for their truth. The fact that almost everyone thinks that lying is sometimes permissible doesn't provide any reason at all for thinking that it is. Why then should we count disagreement about some opinion as evidence against its truth? Mackie and other skeptics have only one response to that sensible question. They take diversity to prove that moral conviction is not caused by moral truth. If it were, we would expect less disagreement. Suppose millions of people claimed to have seen unicorns but disagreed wildly about their color, size, and shape. We would discount their evidence. If there were unicorns, and people had seen them, the actual properties of the beast would have caused more uniform reports.

I argue, in the next chapter, that error skeptics are right to deny that moral truth causes moral conviction. People's personal histories, rather than any encounters with moral truth, cause their convictions. If so, some combination of convergence and diversity is exactly what we should expect. People's personal histories have a very great deal in common, starting with the human genome. Their situation, everywhere and always, is such that they are very likely to think that murder for private gain is wrong, for instance. But these histories also have a great deal not in common: the habitats, economies, and religions of people differ in ways that also make it predictable that they will disagree about morality too. In any case, because diversity is just a matter of anthropological fact, it cannot on its own show that all positive moral judgments are false. People, in their diversity, must still decide what is true, and this is a matter of the justification of conviction, not the best explanation of either convergence or divergence.

Morals and Motives

Mackie also said that positive moral judgments presuppose, as part of what they mean, an extraordinary claim: that when people come to hold a true positive moral opinion, they are just for that reason motivated to act in whatever way it commands. So if it is true that you ought not to cheat on your income tax, your coming to accept that truth must have the consequence that you feel drawn as by a magnet to report your income and deductions accurately. But that is, as Mackie put it, a "queer" consequence. In other domains, just accepting a fact doesn't automatically carry any motivating force: even if I accept that there is poison in a glass in front of me, I might, in certain circumstances, feel no reluctance to drink it. If moral propositions are different in this striking way—if belief about a moral fact carries an automatic motivational charge—then this must be because moral entities have a special and unique kind of magnetic force. The idea of an "objective good," Mackie said, is queer because it supposes that "objective good would be sought by anyone who was acquainted with it, not because of any contingent fact that this person, or every person, is so constituted that he desires this end, but just because the end has to-be-pursuedness somehow built into it. Similarly, if there were objective principles of right and wrong, any wrong (possible) course of action would have not-to-be-doneness somehow built into it."[8]

It is unclear how we should understand these supposedly lethal metaphors. We should certainly agree that there are no morons with automatic coercive moral force. But why should we think it follows that torture is not morally wrong? We might be driven to that conclusion if we held the theory of moral responsibility I just mentioned: that no positive moral opinion is justified unless that opinion has been produced by direct contact with some moral—and motivating—truth. We consider that theory, as I said, in the next chapter. In any case, however, it seems that Mackie misunderstood the connection that people think holds between morality and motivation. He thought that people suppose that *true* positive moral judgments move them to act as the judgment directs. If they did think that, then they would indeed be presupposing a strange kind of moral force. In fact, however, people who find some automatic connection between moral conviction and motivation think this connection holds for false as well as true convictions. They think that anyone who really believes that he is morally required not to walk under ladders will feel constrained not to walk under them. It is conviction, not truth, that supposedly carries the motivational surge. So it cannot be a matter of queer entities.

Morals and Reasons

There is another, now more fashionable, argument for external error skepticism. It begins by noticing a crucial assumption of the ordinary view: that the wrongness of an act gives people a categorical reason—a reason that does not depend on their own desires and preferences—to avoid it. I relied on that connection between morals and reasons just now in explaining why D, in the last invented discussion, really does disagree with A. A believes that people have a categorical reason not to countenance or assist abortion. D believes there are no categorical reasons, and therefore that what A says is false.

Some philosophers believe that D's position follows just from what it is to have a reason.[9] There is an essential internal connection, they insist, between having a reason and having a desire. You can't have a reason to do something unless you have a genuine desire (I mean a desire that you would have or retain even if you thought consistently and were well informed) that doing it would help to satisfy. So the idea of a categorical reason—a reason you have even if it matches no genuine desire—makes no sense at all. Because moral judgments assert or presuppose categorical reasons, they are all false.

On that view of what having a reason means, Stalin had no reason not to murder his colleagues. But should we accept that view? Bernard Williams argued for it by proposing this test: If someone has a reason to do something, that reason must be at least potentially capable of explaining how he behaves.[10] If I know that you want to help the starving poor, I can explain why you contributed to UNICEF by citing that desire. But if you don't want to help the poor and so don't contribute, I can't say that you had a reason to help them, because attributing that reason to you couldn't explain how you acted. Because Stalin had no desire to spare his former colleagues, we couldn't explain any of his actions by attributing to him any reason to spare them. So, on Williams's view, we must concede that he had no reason not to murder them.

But nothing requires us to adopt Williams's test, so nothing requires us to accept that people only have the reasons that serve their desires. We might adopt an alternative view: we might say that someone has a reason to murder his colleagues if (but only if) doing that would be good for him. Then it would not automatically follow that someone has a reason to murder whenever murder would suit his aims, because it might be that a career of murder would not in fact be good for him. This alternative view would not automatically support Williams's test. But it would not automatically contradict that test either. The alternative view would make everything turn on a further, ethical issue. What, in general, is good for a person? Even if we accepted the alternative view, we might nevertheless insist that the only thing that is good for a person is to have his genuine desires satisfied. We would then accept something like Williams's view of what it is to have a reason. But we might, on the contrary, think that it is good for a person to live with decency and self-respect, and that, whatever Stalin thought, his brutality was bad for him. The alternative view, that is, ties questions of rationality to questions of ethical theory.

How shall we decide which view of what it is to have a reason is correct—Williams's view, which automatically ties reasons to desires, or the alternative view that does not? Should we treat this as only a question of linguistic usage, to be decided, that is, by identifying the correct or standard use of that phrase? But there is no correct or standard use. We do sometimes use the phrase in an instrumental sense that might seem to support Williams's account. We say that because Stalin wanted to consolidate his power, he had a reason to murder potential rivals. But we also use it in the contrary way: it is hardly a linguistic mistake to say that people always have a reason to do the right thing. Shall we say, then, that the philosophical disagreement is only illusory? That because we can sensibly use the phrase "has a reason" in different senses, philosophers do not really disagree? That the choice can therefore have nothing to do with an important philosophical issue like error skepticism? But then why haven't philosophers spotted their mistake long ago? Why does the debate still seem real and important to them?

If the debate is not illusory, and if it is not about standard usage, then what is it about? In Chapter 8 I describe a class of concepts—I call these "interpretive concepts"—that we share in spite of disagreeing about which understanding of the concept is best. We argue for one conception over others by constructing a theory to show why our favored conception best captures the value locked in the concept. Conceptual theories are of course controversial; this explains why different conceptions compete in both ordinary and philosophical usage. The concept of having a reason is an interpretive concept.[11] We cannot usefully answer questions that turn on which conception is best, like the question whether Stalin had a reason not to purge his colleagues, by just declaring a definition one way or another and then drawing our answer from that definition. We must construct a larger structure of different kinds of value into which a conception of rationality fits—a structure that justifies a particular conception or understanding of what it is to have a reason.

That larger structure must answer the question, among others, why a person should care about what he has reason to do. But that is a normative question, not a psychological or motivational one; it asks not whether a person does care but whether he should care. A conception of rationality would be a poor one—it could serve no justifying purpose—if it declared that someone has a reason to get what he wants even if getting it would be bad for him. So an ethical theory—a theory about what is good or bad for people—must be part of a successful theory of reasons and rationality: the alternative conception I described, which ties rationality to ethics, is therefore a better conception. Later in this book, in Parts Three and Four, I argue for a particular ethics and then for an interpretive connection between ethics and morality. If I am right, then someone who lives as Stalin did has a bad life: his life is bad for him even if he does not recognize that it is. Williams had a different ethical theory. He thought that what is good or bad for people depends only on what they genuinely want. He was skeptical about any more-objective ethical or moral truth, and he therefore denied the possibility of categorical reasons. I believe, and will argue, that there are objective ethical truths and therefore that there are indeed categorical reasons. In any case, a philosopher cannot properly argue for external error skepticism by assuming that there are no categorical reasons. He must argue in the opposite direction: he can deny categorical reasons only if he has already and independently embraced an error skepticism about ethics.

Status Skepticism

Two Versions

Status skepticism is popular, I said, because it does not ask us to pretend we are abandoning convictions that we cannot actually abandon. It encourages us to keep our convictions and give up only bad metaphysics. The long arguments between status skeptics and their opponents, and among status skeptics about which form of their view is most persuasive, now dominate what is called "meta-ethics" in academic philosophy. I will not try to describe or assess this literature here. I want to focus on a different question: Is status skepticism a distinct and available position at all?

It is available, even as a position to contest, only if we can establish a distinction between what the two following judgments mean or come to: first, that torture is always wrong, and second, that the wrongness of torture is a matter of objective truth that does not depend on anyone's attitudes. If the second, supposedly philosophical, judgment is only a wordy restatement of the first concededly moral one, then no one can coherently embrace the first without the second and status skepticism is a bust from the start. It is hardly obvious that the necessary difference can be found between the two claims. It would certainly seem odd for someone first to insist that torture is wrong and then to declare that what he had just said is not true. It doesn't help to insist, as many status skeptics do, that the first-order judgment that torture is wrong is only the projection of an attitude and not really a judgment at all. If it is, then why isn't status skepticism just the projection of the opposite attitude and not a philosophical position at all?

That is the challenge status skeptics face. I believe the challenge fatal to all forms of that view. But status skeptics have tried to meet the challenge in at least two—contrary—ways. (1) Some take the challenge at face value. They insist that there is indeed a sufficient difference established in linguistic practice between the two speech acts—embracing a moral conviction and describing that conviction as true—so that there is no contradiction, logical or emotional, in performing the first of these speech acts while condemning the second. The first act is an engaged, first-order projection of emotion. The second is a mistaken, second-order philosophical judgment. (2) Other status skeptics concede that there is no such difference between the two speech acts as these occur in ordinary discourse; they agree that in ordinary speech someone would contradict himself if he declared that torture is always wrong but then added that what he had just said is not really true. But they insist on a difference between two enterprises or language games: ordinary speech and philosophical speech. The status skeptic, according to this second defense, occupies himself in the language game of philosophical speech, and within that game he is privileged to say that the moral judgments people rightly call true in ordinary speech are not true in philosophical speech. So in ordinary life a status skeptic may declare with undiminished enthusiasm that torture is wrong *and* that its wrongness is a matter of objective moral truth. Then in philosophical speech he may consistently declare that both those opinions are only projections of emotion on a morally inert universe. The speech-act version of external skepticism was long popular: it dominated moral philosophy for decades. It grew steadily harder to defend, however, and the two-language-games version is in fashion now. We should consider the two strategies in turn.

Speech-Act Skeptics: The Challenge

I am speaking at length about abortion. I begin: "Abortion is morally wrong." Then, drawing breath, I add a variety of other claims set out in the rest of this paragraph. "What I just said about abortion was not just venting my emotions or describing or expressing or projecting my own or anyone else's attitudes or my own or anyone else's commitment to rules or plans. My claims about the immorality of abortion are really, objectively, true. They describe what morality, quite apart from anyone's impulses and emotions, really demands. They would still be true, that is, even if no one but me thought them true—indeed, even if I didn't think them true. They are universal and they are absolute. They are part of the fabric of the universe, resting, as they do, on timeless, universal truths about what is fundamentally and intrinsically right or wrong. They are reports, that is, of how things really are out there in an independent moral reality. They describe, in short, real moral facts."

Call all the statements I made after drawing breath my "further claims." These further claims declare mind-independent moral truth in what seems an increasingly emphatic way. So there must be some red flag buried within them to draw a speech-act skeptic's attention; there must be something in them he wants to deny. But my further claims also appear themselves to be moral claims. If so, and he denies them, he makes a moral claim as well. If he says that my claims are just projections of my emotions, he has tarred his own brush: his own philosophical claims become only emotional outbursts as well.

He must find some way to understand my further claims as stating or presupposing some factual or metaphysical thesis so he can deny that thesis without self-destruction. But that seems difficult, because the most natural way to understand my further claims is precisely as moral claims—albeit particularly heated ones. Someone who thinks that abortion is always and deeply wrong might well say, in an enthusiastic moment, "It is a fundamental moral truth that abortion is always wrong." That would be only an emphatic restatement of his substantive position. Some of the other further claims do seem to add something to the original claim, but only by substituting more precise first-order moral judgments for it. People who use the adverbs "objectively" and "really" in a moral context usually mean to clarify their opinions in a particular way—to distinguish the opinions so qualified from other opinions that they regard as "subjective" or just a matter of taste, like a distaste for soccer or mustard. The claim that abortion is objectively wrong seems equivalent in ordinary discourse to another of my further claims: that abortion would still be wrong even if no one thought it was. That further claim, read most naturally, is just another way of emphasizing the content of the original moral claim, of emphasizing, once again, that I mean that abortion is just plain wrong, not wrong only if or because people think it is.

Another of my further claims, that abortion is universally wrong, can also be understood as only a clarification of my original moral claim. It clarifies its scope by making plain that in my view abortion is wrong for everyone, no matter in what circumstance or culture or of what disposition or from what ethical or religious background. That is different from saying simply that abortion is wrong or simply that it is objectively wrong. I might conceivably think that the wrongness of abortion is objective, since it depends on features of abortion and not the reactions of people to it, and yet that the wrongness of abortion is not universal because it is not wrong in certain kinds of communities: those whose religious life supports an entirely different conception of the sacredness of human life, perhaps. When someone says that the wrongness of abortion is universal as well as objective, it is natural to understand him as ruling out qualifications of that sort.

What about my further claim that the wrongness of abortion is absolute? It is most naturally translated to mean not just that abortion is always wrong in principle but that its wrongness is never overridden by competing considerations—that it is never true, for example, that abortion is the lesser of two evils when a mother's life is threatened. What about the baroque claims I added toward the end, about moral truths being "out there" in an independent "realm" or forming part of the "fabric" of the universe? These are not things people actually say; they are invented by skeptics in order to have something to ridicule. But we can make sufficient sense of them, as things people *might* say, by understanding them as inflated, metaphorical ways of repeating what some of the earlier further claims say more directly: that the wrongness of abortion does not depend on anyone's thinking it wrong. What about my very last phrase? I spoke of moral facts, but I am most naturally understood not as insisting that moral particles exist but yet again as emphasizing that I do not mean my comments to express only a subjective taste.[12]

None of these paraphrases helps the would-be external skeptic, because he contradicts his skepticism if he denies any of them. He can remain both external and a skeptic only if he can find something else in my further claims, something that is not itself a moral claim and yet whose denial has skeptical implications. I shall call these the twin conditions of semantic independence and skeptical pertinence. He would fail the latter condition, for instance, if he said that I am assuming, in my further claims, that people all agree about the immorality of abortion. I am certainly not assuming that; but even if I were, pointing out my mistake would have no skeptical implications. That people disagree about abortion is not, in itself, an argument against my thesis that abortion is in itself and always wrong. You may have begun to suspect that the two requirements I described, of independence and pertinence, cannot both be satisfied. Any skeptical thesis that is pertinent cannot be external.

I should, however, consider various possibilities. The philosophical literature makes one of these particularly important. A skeptic might purport to find, in my further claims, a psychological assumption—that I formed my views about abortion by apprehending their truth, that the best explanation of how I came to think abortion wrong is that I was "in touch" with the truth of the matter. The skeptic can then deny this—he can insist that so-called moral truth can make no impact on a human brain—and his denial is evidently not itself a moral claim. It meets the condition of independence. But it fails the pertinence condition: it carries no skeptical force. The issues it raises are complex, however, and I devote an entire chapter—the next one—to considering them.

What else might a speech-act skeptic find either explicit or buried in my further claims that he can deny so as to satisfy both conditions? I consider only three other possibilities because I believe these sufficient to reinforce my claim that he can find nothing. I try to ignore the details of particular schools and the arguments and refinements of particular writers, though I include notes about some of them.

Semantic Expressivism

First we must set aside semantic claims. Some status skeptics insist that when ordinary people declare that torture is morally wrong, they themselves intend only to express their own attitudes: they actually mean nothing more than to turn their thumbs down on the practice. That semantic story seems obviously wrong. What ordinary people mean when they say that torture is wrong is that torture is wrong. No restatement of what they mean can be as accurate. But these skeptical philosophers do not really doubt that: the semantics they invent are only the second act of their dramas. They first try to show that moral judgments make no sense if we take them at face value, that there is nothing for them to describe. Then they offer their new semantic theory to reinstate moral judgment as a sensible activity. If we reject the first act of the drama, we have no need of that next, reforming step. In any case, however, as I have already said, the arguments of this chapter cannot turn on these semantic issues. If a philosopher's supposedly second-order philosophical judgment is actually a first-order moral judgment, and if we take first-order judgments to be only spleen-venting occasions, then we must take the same view of the philosopher's own activities. We need to concentrate only on the drama's first act.

Morals and Motives Again

Some speech-act skeptics insist that the close connection between moral judgments and motives I mentioned earlier shows that moral judgments cannot be beliefs, and so cannot be true or false, because beliefs cannot provide motives by themselves. I may believe that aspirin will relieve my pain, but it doesn't follow that I am in any way inclined to take aspirin. I will feel that urge only if I have an independent desire that my pain cease. So if moral judgments do provide motives by themselves, they cannot be beliefs. We need a second act in which we declare them just emotional outbursts or declarations of some desire or plan; it is the emotion or desire or plan that supplies the near-automatic motivation we find.

This simple-sounding argument hides a great variety of complexities, re-finements, and definitions.[13] Its first step declares that moral beliefs necessarily motivate. It is quite unclear, at least to me, whether this claim is meant to be empirical, semantic, or conceptual. Much of the debate turns, for instance, on whether there are any "amoralists"—people in full mental health who claim to hold a moral conviction but who have no inclination to act in the way it directs. Is this a question of whether people with a certain personality in fact exist, and in what numbers? Or whether it would be a mistake to say of such a person that he really believes the conviction he endorses but ignores? If the latter, would that be a conceptual mistake, because being motivated is part of what it means to have a moral belief? Or semantic because our best linguistic rules for attributing moral beliefs to people rule this out? If you are tempted to ponder these issues, bear in mind Richard of Gloucester, who, descanting on his own deformity, declared, "I am determined to prove a villain" and counted his own plans "subtle, false and treacherous."[14] He wasn't vowing just to do what others think villainous but to do what was, in his own view, villainous.

The argument's crucial second step assumes another postulate also named after Hume, the eponymous father of so much doctrine. If moral convictions do automatically carry at least some weak motivational charge, then these convictions cannot express beliefs but can only testify to desires. This seems only dogma captured in an antique psychology. We often take behavior into account in deciding what beliefs people hold. Someone professes a fervent belief in an all-powerful and good god but does not reflect that conviction, even in the most marginal ways, in how he lives. Or declares all superstition rot but takes great trouble not to walk under a ladder or in a path crossed by a black cat. We are likely to say in either case that he does not believe what he says he does. But not that supposed beliefs about a god or magic are not really beliefs, that no one really believes in a god or rejects superstition.

Here is another popular argument supposed to show that moral judgments cannot express belief.[15] Beliefs and desires, it is said, differ in their direction of fit with the world: beliefs aim to fit the world, and desires aim that the world fit them. Moral judgments aim at the latter direction of fit, so they cannot express beliefs. This seems simply to beg the question: if moral judgments express beliefs, and do not aim to fit the world, then not all beliefs aim to fit the world. In any case, moral judgments do aim to fit the facts—the facts about morality. If a skeptic adjusts the distinction to say that beliefs aim to fit how things are physically or mentally, then the circularity of his argument is even more evident. So the debate about morality and motivation has gone, yet again, in the wrong direction. A skeptic can provide an argument that moral judgments do not express beliefs only by first demonstrating that there is nothing for them to be beliefs about.

Whatever natural connection we find between people's convictions about their moral duties and their behavior is much better explained by exploring a psychological question: Why do people take an interest in moral issues? If, as I believe, people want to live well and sense that living well includes respecting their moral responsibilities, then it is wholly natural that they mainly feel at least some impulse to do what they think they ought to do. That is not true of everyone. Some perverse people—Richard and Milton's Satan, for instance—want to know what is wrong because they take special or additional pleasure in doing what is wrong—doing, as Satan put it, what he should "abhor."[16] But it is hard to see why anyone would take any interest in moral issues at all unless he thought that his opinions should in some way and to some degree affect what he does next. The true amoralist, if he exists, would not have any moral convictions at all.

Notice now, moreover, that the two-step argument I first described, which aims to show that moral judgments are not beliefs, cannot in any case help a status skeptic out of his difficulty. If my initial claim about abortion is not the expression of a belief, because it normally supplies a motive, then none of my further claims express beliefs either because they normally supply motives as well. It would be bizarre for someone to claim that abortion is absolutely, objectively, furniture-of-the-universe wrong and then cheerfully to counsel it to his friends. And if none of my further claims describes a belief, then how can any of them be false? And if none of them can, then what philosophical mistake does the speech-act skeptic offer to correct? What can he be skeptical about?

Primary and Secondary Qualities

He might now claim to find a different philosophical assumption in my further claims. Philosophers distinguish between primary qualities, which things have in themselves and would still have if there were no sentient or intelligent creatures, such as the chemical properties of metals, and secondary properties, which things have in virtue of their capacity to provoke particular sensations or reactions in sentient or intelligent creatures. The disgustingness of rotten eggs, for example, is a secondary property: it consists only in the eggs' capacity to provoke a sensation of disgust in most or normal people. A status skeptic might take my further claims to declare that moral properties are primary properties. That reading would indeed provide a thesis for him to reject that is independent of my initial claim. Just as someone can deny that disgustingness is a primary property of rotten eggs and still believe that rotten eggs are disgusting, so a skeptic might deny that moral wrongness is a primary property of abortion and still believe that abortion is evil. But this strategy achieves independence from my initial claim not by endorsing an external, non-moral thesis but by embracing a *different* first-order moral claim. It fails the independence condition in that different way.

The thesis that moral wrongness is a secondary property is a first-order substantive moral judgment. Suppose social scientists discovered that, contrary to what you and I think, contemplating torture does not in fact outrage even most normal people. You would still think that torture is wicked, I assume, but someone who believed that moral properties are secondary properties, so that the wrongness of torture could only consist in its disposition to outrage most normal people, would then disagree with you about that substantive moral issue. Even if all normal people do think that torture is wicked, the dispositional account of its wickedness is not neutral about morality, because it claims not just that most or normal people do react to torture in a particular way but that the wickedness of torture just consists in that reaction, and that further claim yields conditional or counterfactual statements that are both substantive and controversial. Which conditional or counterfactual claims follow from the dispositional thesis depends on the precise form the thesis takes; it depends, in particular, on how far and in which way the extension of moral properties is supposed to be fixed by our own natural history.[17] That does not mean that moral properties are primary. But it does mean that the argument over whether they are is a substantive moral dispute.

Different Language Games?

Richard Rorty

Here is the state of play. I said that a status skeptic must find a way to reject the thesis he opposes, which is that moral judgments are candidates for objective truth, without also rejecting the first-order, substantive moral declarations he wishes to leave standing. I described two strategies he might use. He might claim, first, that what he rejects—one or all of my further claims—are second-order, philosophical claims that differ in meaning, because they are different kinds of speech act, from the first-order substantive judgments he does not mean to reject. That is the strategy we have so far been reviewing.

We turn to the second strategy. A status skeptic might embrace rather than reject my further claims. He might count them all as only repetitions or variations of my initial claim about abortion and raise no objection to any of them. His skepticism, he might say, is confined to a different universe of discourse; confined, in the phrase Wittgenstein made famous, to a different language game altogether. He might explain the structure of his argument by pressing an analogy to the way we sometimes talk about fictional characters. I declare, playing the world-of-fiction game, that Lady Macbeth was married at least once before she married Macbeth.[18] I do not contradict myself when I take up the different real-world game and say that there never was a Lady Macbeth, that Shakespeare just made her up. There is no contradiction between my two claims because I offer them in two different modes or universes of discourse. So a status skeptic might propose that we play a morality game in which we properly declare that torture is always and objectively wrong and also a different, reality game in which we can say that there is no such thing as wrongness.

Richard Rorty pioneered this response as a defense of status skepticism not just about moral and other value judgments but about propositions more generally. Here is a characteristic statement of his view:

> Given that it pays to talk about mountains, as it certainly does, one of the obvious truths about mountains is that they were here before we talked about them. If you do not believe that, you probably do not know how to play the usual language-games which employ the word "mountain." But the utility of those language games has nothing to do with the question of whether Reality as It Is In Itself, apart from the way it is handy for human beings to describe it, has mountains in it.[19]

Rorty imagined two language games, each with its own rules. The first is the geology game in which you and I mostly engage. In that game mountains exist, existed before there were people, will exist after there are people, and would have existed even if there had never been people. If you don't agree, you don't know how to play the geology game. In addition, however, there is a second, Archimedean, philosophical game in which a different question can be raised: not whether mountains exist, but whether Reality as It Is In Itself contains mountains. In that second game, according to Rorty, a dispute has broken out between misguided metaphysicians who say that It Does and pragmatists like him who say that It Doesn't, that mountains exist only in the ordinary geology game that people mostly play.

Rorty's strategy fails unless there is an actual difference in what people mean when they say, in the ordinary way, that mountains really exist and then say, with a philosophical air, that they don't. We have no difficulty in understanding that we are playing a special kind of game when we talk about fictional characters, because we can collapse the two discourses into one by rephrasing any statement about Lady Macbeth to make plain what we really mean. I can say, for instance: "If we were to think (or pretend) that Shakespeare was describing real historical events, then we should think (or pretend) that Lady Macbeth had children by another man before she married Macbeth." I could then add, now with no even surface contradiction, that of course Shakespeare invented those events and speeches.

Rorty's two-games metaphor can be redeemed only if we can dissolve the apparent contradiction about mountains in a parallel way: by offering a way to understand one or the other of the apparently contradictory claims that dissolves the conflict. But we cannot do that. Rorty's distinction between the proposition about mountains that belongs to the geology game and the one that belongs to the Reality game fails to identify any difference in meaning between the two propositions. He hoped to display a difference through capitalization: the second proposition sports capital letters that the first lacks. But that device is not helpful. If we give the sentence "Mountains are part of Reality as It Is In Itself" the meaning it would have if anyone actually said this, then it means nothing different from "Mountains exist, and would exist even if there were no people," and the contrast Rorty needs disappears. If, on the other hand, we assign some novel or special sense to that sentence—if we say, for example, that it means that mountains are a logically necessary feature of the universe—then his argument loses any critical force or philosophical bite because no one would or could think that mountains are logically necessary. That is in fact the same dilemma we explored in our discussion of speech-act skepticism. If the language-game skeptic satisfies the independence condition I described there, by showing that my further claims are not just repetitions of my initial claim, he fails the pertinence condition because his argument no longer has any force against the ordinary view.

Expressivists and Quasi-Realists

Rorty tried to distinguish ordinary judgments from the supposedly different philosophical claims he rejected, like my further claims, by placing them in different language games. We can construct another version of the two-language-games strategy for defending status skepticism, however, that places both ordinary moral judgments and my further claims in the same language game by identifying them *all* as first-order substantive moral opinion and then finding another kind of world—a distinct philosophical world—for a status skeptic to bustle in.

This version of the two-games strategy has an evident advantage: it allows an avowed status skeptic nevertheless to embrace at least the more natural, or perhaps all, of my further claims. He can agree that cruelty really is wrong, that it would still be wrong even if no one thought it was, and that these propositions are evidently true. He can say all this because he locates all these statements, and perhaps even my more extravagant further claims, as just more moves in the ordinary, day-to-day business of offering moral opinions. However, on a second look, and just for that reason, the strategy is self-defeating because it leaves no room for a status skeptic's skepticism to spread itself.

Suppose a self-described "projectivist," playing a philosophy game, declares that in reality moral convictions must be understood as emotional projections onto a morally inert world. But later, playing the morality game, he declares that the wrongness of torture has nothing to do with projecting attitudes of disapproval; torture, he says, would be wrong no matter what attitudes or emotions anyone had about it. Later still, now back in his philosophical game, he declares his last statement itself to be only the projection of an attitude. He treats all of my further claims in the same way. When in the morality game, he says that moral truths are timeless and stitched into the fabric of reality, and then, back in the philosophy game again, he reports his last statement to be a particularly florid projection.

Now the projectivist is in the difficulty I described for Rorty. He must show how his statements made in the morality game are consistent with those he makes in the philosophy game. He can do this, as we do in the world-of-fiction game, only by replacing his statement in either game with a translation that dissolves the apparent contradiction. But he cannot do that. He can't replace what he says in the morality game with any statement, while still in that game, that implies or allows that wrongness is only a matter of projection. He can't replace his statement in the philosophy game by declaring or implying there that wrongness does not depend on projection. His strategy swallows itself like the Cheshire cat leaving only a smile behind. (Michael Smith holds a contrary view.[20])

Have any actual philosophers employed this self-defeating version of the two-game strategy? I said, in Chapter 2, that the skepticism of the prominent philosophers Allan Gibbard and Simon Blackburn, who call themselves "expressivists" and "quasi-realists," is open to doubt. I do regard both as skeptical of the ordinary view. But both have denied this and suggested that their own views are much more like my own than I allow.[21] So I should put my claim more cautiously: if they can properly be regarded as skeptical, it is this second, two-games strategy they use to defend that skepticism. [22] The exegetical issue is not of direct importance, however; my aims in this book do not include defending particular interpretations of the work of other contemporary philosophers.

Constructivism

We have not yet considered a very popular, supposedly meta-ethical theory that has often been counted as skeptical. This is called "constructivism." It was made much more popular in recent decades by John Rawls, who described his famous book, *A Theory of Justice,* as an exercise in "Kantian" constructivism. On this view, moral judgments are constructed, not discovered: they issue from an intellectual device adopted to confront practical, not theoretical, problems. Rawls gave the example of Kant's Categorical Imperative: Kant said that we must construct our moral judgments by asking what moral principles we could will as maxims to be followed not just by us but by everyone.

However, the most famous example among moral and political philosophers now is Rawls's own original-position device. Rawls suggested that we fix principles of justice for the basic structure of our political community by imagining people who come together to establish such a community and who are well aware of general economic, technological, psychological, and sociological facts but ignorant of their own ages, genders, talents, social and economic positions, interests, desires, and ethical beliefs about how to live well. Rawls argued that people in that odd situation would agree on two principles of justice: one that assigns priority to certain liberties, and another that requires an economic structure in which the situation of the economically worst-off group is as good as a basic structure can make it. He said that you and I, here and now, therefore have reason to treat these two principles as defining justice for our own political community.

But why? Two strikingly different answers are possible. We might say, first, that the original position is an expository device for testing the implications of certain basic moral and political principles we take to be true. The original position, we might say, models those basic truths in its structure. I once proposed this understanding and suggested that the basic principles the device models are egalitarian. We believe that a coercive political community must treat everyone subject to its dominion with equal concern and respect; we can test what that requires, more concretely, by imagining a constitutional convention in which members have no ground for treating each other in any other way.[23] Rawls firmly rejected my suggestion. "I think of justice as fairness," he said, "as working up into idealized conceptions certain fundamental intuitive ideas such as those of the person as free and equal, of a well-ordered society, and of the public role of a conception of political justice, and as connecting these fundamental intuitive ideas with the even more fundamental and comprehensive intuitive idea of society as a fair system of cooperation over time from one generation to the next."[24] Rawls's triple emphasis on intuition in this sentence suggests that though he disagreed with my suggested basic principles of justice, he agreed that the original position rested on assumed moral truths, albeit a different and more complex set than I had suggested. Elsewhere he isolated and stressed one idea in the set. "Put another way, first principles of justice must issue from a conception of the person through a suitable representation of that conception as illustrated by the procedures of construction in justice as fairness."[25] We might suppose that a particular conception of the person would fill this role because it is correct.

But these statements are also consistent with (or perhaps a step toward) a very different understanding that Rawls seemed to express on other occasions. I shall state this briskly, in a way that emphasizes the contrast I have in mind, ignoring nuance. People of good will in political community who disagree in their ethical and moral convictions face an immense practical problem. How are they to live together with self-respect in a coercive state? They cannot each insist that the state enforce his own private convictions: the state would then disintegrate, as Kant put it, into a political tower of Babel. Their solution: to collect together what is sufficiently common among them, by way of strictly political principle, and construct a political constitution that appeals only to such principles. Everyone in the community—or at least everyone who is reasonable—can accept that constitution as falling within an "overlapping consensus;" each can see these principles as supported by, or at least not condemned by, what he takes to be the truth about the broader ethical, religious, and personal moral convictions that divide them. Everyone can accept the basic structure of a society ordered by those common principles and so can form a political community that is "well-ordered" in the sense that each member accepts and serves the same principles of justice. The original position models the common convictions into a suitable device of representation that allows us to construct principles of justice like the two principles I described. You and I, here and now, must accept those principles provided we accept the ambition to live together in a peace and dignity.

It is this second way of understanding the original-position device that is offered as an example of a constructivist approach. Constructivism, understood through this example, is not necessarily skeptical. Indeed, it is consistent even with the most extravagant versions of moral "realism." For it does not deny that one comprehensive view is true and all others false. However, it does not depend on that assumption. The principles modeled in the original position on this account are chosen not because they are true but because they are common. The method is therefore also consistent, on this understanding, with any form of skepticism about moral truth. Rawls seemed himself, at least on some occasions, to have accepted a fully skeptical view. "But in addition, the idea of approximating to moral truth has no place in a constructivist doctrine: the parties in the original position do not recognize any principles of justice as true or correct and so as antecedently given; their aim is simply to select the conception most rational for them, given their circumstances. This conception is not regarded as a workable approximation to the moral facts: there are no such moral facts to which the principles adopted could approximate."[26] So we might understand constructivism, at least as Rawls understood it, not as itself providing a skeptical argument but rather as showing that moral truth need play no part in defending an attractive and detailed theory of political justice. Constructivism challenges the ordinary view not directly but by trying to shove it aside.

Can this marginalization work? We must ask: How are these common principles, like a particular conception of the self, to be identified? As his ideas developed, Rawls placed greater emphasis on the history and political traditions of particular states. He aimed at finding shared principles within a particular historical community—the liberal, post-Enlightenment tradition in North America and Europe, for example—rather than to justify a more cosmopolitan constitution.[27] He could not hope to do even this, however, through what we might call a sociological method. He could not hope to find a useful consensus even in what all Americans actually now believe or would accept on reflection. Religion would on its own defeat that project: a great many Americans believe that it is more important to establish a state reflecting and nourishing their personal religious convictions than to create one that people with a different religion, or none at all, could comfortably embrace. The difficulty becomes even more evident if we try to work in the other direction. What set of views about the character of free and equal persons could generate either of the two principles of justice and yet be adopted at a Tea Party convention?

Rawls plainly had in mind, however, not a sociological but an interpretive search for overlapping consensus. He hoped to identify conceptions and ideals that provide the best account and justification of the liberal traditions of law and political practice. That is an important and, in my view, feasible project.[28] But it cannot be a morally neutral project, because any interpretation of a political tradition must choose among very different conceptions of what that tradition embodies—what qualities or properties it takes "free and equal" citizens to have, for instance—that all fit the raw data of history and practice. It must choose among these by taking some to be superior and hence to provide a more satisfactory justification than others.[29] If you ask the present justices of the United States Supreme Court to describe the principles embedded in American constitutional history, you will receive nine different answers. The point is not that any interpretive account must be idealized. Of course it must. It is rather that without a background moral theory we take to be true we can have no idea which idealization to choose. A constructivist strategy can indeed be used to argue for a kind of skepticism—the thesis that any acceptable theory of justice must be drawn from a plausible interpretation of the traditions of the community for which it is designed, for instance. That would rule out any claim to a transcendental theory like utilitarianism that is supposed to hold everywhere and for all time. But this thesis would itself rest on controversial moral theories and so would be an example of internal, not external, skepticism. Rawls's constructivist project, at least as he sometimes conceived it, is impossible.

Yes, Meta-Ethics Rests on a Mistake

In Chapter 2 I described the distinction most moral philosophers draw between ordinary ethical or moral questions, which they call first-order substantive questions, and the second-order questions they call "meta-ethical." Moral realism and external skepticism are all, on this view, meta-ethical positions. If I am right, however, the distinction is a mistake, at least as meta-ethics is traditionally conceived. Of course there are interesting questions of anthropology and of personal and social psychology that are second-order in the sense that they are about moral judgment but do not themselves call for moral judgment. But there are no distinctly philosophical questions of that kind; in particular the question whether moral judgments can be true or false is a substantive moral issue, not a distinct meta-ethical one. There is no meta-ethics unless (on the analogy I drew with astrology) we count the question whether there is meta-ethics as itself a meta-ethical question.

Some philosophers have identified what they call "quietism" as a meta-ethical position holding "that there is, in some sense, no way of getting outside of normative thought to explain it, and that therefore no answers to these questions [e.g., whether moral judgments can be true or false] are possible."[30] That would be the wrong conclusion to draw from this part of this book, and the wrong way to describe what it argues. It is true that we cannot justify a moral judgment (as distinct from explaining why someone believes that judgment) without relying on further moral convictions or assumptions. But that fact follows simply from the content of a moral judgment—what it claims—and the suggestion that we are therefore in some way trapped within the realms of value, as if it would be wonderful though impossible to escape, is as foolish as saying that we cannot escape from the realm of the descriptive when we describe the chemistry of combustion. That latter proposition might also have felt constraining—an unfortunate limitation—to an earlier age that reveled in the Great Chain of Being and found teleological explanations of natural phenomena particularly satisfactory. But it does not feel constraining to us. Nor is it right that no answer to the question whether moral judgments can be true or false is possible. On the contrary, our argument shows exactly the opposite: that answers are readily available to the question whether some particular moral judgments are true or false. The use of the term "quietism" is just more evidence that philosophers do not recognize the full independence of value.

External skepticism should disappear from the philosophical landscape. We should not regret its disappearance. We have enough to worry about without it. We want to live well and to behave decently; we want our communities to be fair and good and our laws to be wise and just. These are very difficult goals, in part because the issues at stake are complex and puzzling and in part because selfishness so often stands in the way. When we are told that whatever convictions we do struggle to reach cannot in any case be true or false, or objective, or part of what we know, or that they are just moves in a game of language, or just steam from the turbines of our emotions, or just experimental projects we should try on for size, to see how we get on, or just invitations to thoughts that we might find diverting or amusing or less boring than the ways we used to think, we should reply that these observations are all pointless distractions from the real challenges at hand. I do not mean that we can ignore moral skepticism. On the contrary. Genuine skepticism—internal skepticism—is much more worrying than these philosophical confusions. We will worry about it later.

4

Morals and Causes

Two Crucial Issues

What causes you to have the opinions you do about right and wrong? Where do these opinions come from? What produced in your brain the thought that the Iraq war was immoral? Or that it was not? Do the best answers to these questions validate your opinions? Or impeach them? Suppose I asked parallel questions about your scientific opinions. You might sensibly answer: the way the world is caused me to hold the opinions I do about the way it is. Our scientists form opinions about the chemistry of metals through a causal process in which the chemistry of metals itself plays an important part. It is because gold has the properties it does that experiments involving gold have the results they do. Because those experiments have those results, accredited scientists all believe that gold has those properties. You believe it has those properties because the accredited scientists do, and because they have in different ways told you so. The upshot of this causal chain is striking: the best explanation of why you hold most of your opinions is also a sufficient justification of those opinions. The explanatory story and the justifying stories are united: the best explanations of belief validate belief.

Is the same union of explanation and justification available for morality? Has the truth about the morality of gay marriage in some way caused you to think what you do about gay marriage? I suggested my own answer earlier when I ridiculed the idea of moral forces with causal powers as "morons." But perhaps I am wrong; many distinguished philosophers do think that moral facts can cause people to hold true moral opinions, though they disagree about how and why. We must examine their view more carefully. Suppose, however, that I am right: there is no causal interaction between moral truth and moral opinion. Wouldn't that make your opinions about gay marriage just an accident? Wouldn't you have to admit that even if there are moral truths "out there" in the universe, you have no possible way to be "in touch with" those truths?

I have just mooted two hypotheses. The first is the causal impact hypothesis (CI). This holds that moral facts can cause people to form moral convictions that match those moral facts. Moral realists accept CI and external skeptics reject it. I argue that in this matter realists are wrong and external skeptics right. The second is the causal dependence hypothesis (CD). This supposes that unless the causal impact hypothesis is true, people can have no sound reason to think that any of their moral judgments is a correct report of moral truth. External skeptics embrace this second hypothesis. So, apparently, do many realists, because they would otherwise not be so anxious to defend the causal impact hypothesis. I argue that in this matter both realists and external skeptics are wrong. There is an obvious and important difference between the two hypotheses. CI includes a claim of scientific fact: a matter of particle physics, biology, and psychology. CD is a moral claim: about what counts as an adequate reason for holding a moral conviction.

The Causal Impact Hypothesis

The Stakes

Affirmative action programs give preference in university admissions or employment to black and other minority applicants. Suppose you think that such programs are unfair.[1] Why do you think this? That question is ambiguous. It might mean: What reasons could you offer in defense of your position? So understood, the question asks for a moral argument. Or it might mean: What is the best causal explanation of why you have come to hold that view, given that so many others in your political culture have come to the opposite conclusion? We should concentrate now on this second question. A psychologist or social scientist or biologist might respond to that question in a professional way. He might point to features of your subculture or upbringing or self-interest, or, if he is madly ambitious, he might try to identify a gene that predisposes you to that opinion. He assumes that some explanation of this sort is a complete answer to the question of why you hold the opinion you do.

You might be tempted to offer a different and competitive answer to the same question. You might say, "I have come to think affirmative action unfair because I, unlike those others, have seen or perceived or intuited that it is unfair." Some philosophical realists believe that your answer is indeed competitive with any that the scientists might offer, that it makes sense, and, indeed, that it is often correct. They think that at least some people have a sensitivity to moral truth that allows them to perceive what is right or wrong, worthy or unworthy. They insist that when people have perceived moral truth, no explanation of the birth of their conviction is complete unless it includes that fact.[2]

If that causal impact thesis makes sense, and is persuasive, then any global moral skepticism must be false. As I just said, people's beliefs about the physical world are often caused directly or indirectly by the truth of what they believe, and when they are, that fact confirms the truth of their belief. The best explanation of why I believe that it rained earlier today includes the fact that it did rain. If realists can construct a successful explanation of why you believe that affirmative action is unfair along the same lines—if they can show that you believe this because affirmative action *is* wrong—then they would in that way justify your conviction as well as explain its existence. That would also show that, after all, Hume's principle is false. It is a matter of biological fact whether something has caused your brain to be in any particular state. If it follows from some biological fact of that kind that affirmative action is wrong, then Hume's principle must be scrapped.[3]

However the causal impact hypothesis (CI) is a high-risk strategy for defending the ordinary view from skepticism. For it risks encouraging the further thought that if, on the contrary, moral facts cannot cause moral convictions, then we have no reason to think that there are any moral facts and therefore no ground on which to reject skepticism. Suppose that though you believe that it rained in France today, no rain in France could possibly figure in any explanation of why you believe that. Perhaps you were hypnotized into that belief by a hypnotist who had no knowledge of Gallic rain. You would then have no reason at all to think it had rained there. External skeptics argue that CI is false and that moral facts, even if there were any, could never play any role in explaining people's moral convictions. They conclude that we have no more reason to believe in the truth of our moral convictions than you would have reason, in my latest story, to believe in the rain. That conclusion depends on rejecting the causal impact hypothesis. But it also depends on accepting the causal dependence hypothesis.

The Myth

We often realize that an act is wrong immediately we spot it. When I see someone beating a child, I "see" the wrongness of his act at once. However, that is not an instance of moral facts causing a moral conviction: I would not have "seen" the wrongness of beating the child had I not already formed the conviction that causing gratuitous pain is wrong. The latter conviction is the one whose existence CI hopes to explain.[4] We must distinguish CI from divine inspiration. Many people believe that a god has shared his infallible moral knowledge with them, but CI does not suppose divine intervention. It claims a more direct causal impact of moral truth on our minds. CI, in the stark form I present, was once more popular among professional philosophers than it is now.[5] It remains influential among many nonphilosophers, however, some of whom take more seriously than they should the familiar rhetoric of moral "insight." Moreover, many of the best philosophers are unwilling to entirely abandon the hypothesis; they hope to retain at least some remnant or faint echo of the idea that moral truth can cause moral belief, in order to avoid the frightening conclusion that moral beliefs are accidents.[6]

However, we do not have even the shadow of a hint how any such causal interaction could operate. Our scientists have begun, at least, to understand the optics, neural chemistry, and brain geography that figure in a competent explanation of how the rain in France produces thoughts about itself. But nothing in that story could be expanded to explain how the unfairness of affirmative action, if any, could produce thoughts about itself. We are ignorant, I assume, of most of what there is to know about what the universe contains or how our brains work. But it is difficult for us even to imagine how CI could be true. Compare mental telepathy. Relatively few people believe, I think, that one person, by concentrating mightily, can cause another person thousands of miles away to have stipulated thoughts. But we might well imagine at least the rough shape of discoveries that could change our minds about this possibility. We might construct controlled experiments that would make the phenomenon difficult to deny: masses of repeated instances of events that could be explained in no other way. We might then discover or at least speculate about external electrical fields that are created by the internal electrical transfers in brains that neurologists now report and measure. True, mental telepathy goes well beyond what science can so far test or explain. But CI goes much further. After all, we already believe in the causal power of mental events: we believe that emotions can cause physiological changes and that one thought can lead to another. CI cannot claim even to extrapolate from those phenomena. It supposes that a moral truth that has neither mental nor physical dimension can nevertheless have causal power.

We cannot imagine how any experimental evidence could suggest the truth of CI even in the absence of an explanation of how it works, as evidence might suggest the truth of telepathy even if we lacked any theory of its mechanics. For we cannot test CI in the way we most naturally test causal claims: by asking a counterfactual question. We can test the claim that someone in Australia sneezed because you willed this by asking whether he would have sneezed even if you had not so willed. But we cannot test CI in that way—if we think that affirmative action is unfair, we cannot produce or even imagine a different world in which everything else is the same except that affirmative action is fair. That is what philosophers mean who say that moral attributes "supervene" on ordinary facts: they mean that we cannot vary moral attributes except by varying the ordinary facts that make up the case for claiming those attributes. We can certainly ask whether you would still think affirmative action unfair even if you discovered that it made no one unhappy. But a negative answer would only confirm that you hold some moral opinion that connects wrongness and suffering. We can't sensibly ask whether you would still think affirmative action unfair even if it wasn't unfair, and it is that latter question we would need to ask to test CI's claim that the unfairness of affirmative action has made you think it unfair.

Because we can make no sense of that crucial counterfactual question, we have no way to test whether the offered explanation of your belief—that it was caused by a perception of moral truth—is accurate. The competing explanations a scientist might offer can be tested by asking whether, if your personal history had been sufficiently different, your beliefs would have been different. There might well be good reason to think they would have been. You can't offer a parallel counterfactual hypothesis to support your competing "perception" explanation: you can't show or even imagine that your belief would

be different if the moral truth were different. Your claim that you have perceived the truth is only an emphatic restatement of your belief, not an explanation of how it arose.

CI is a myth. It is, moreover, a pointless myth, because even if we assumed
that moral truth does have mysterious causal potency, that assumption could
be of no help whatsoever in justifying our moral beliefs. We would have to
know, independently, whether those beliefs were true before we could intelligibly cite truth as their parent. That requirement is particularly clear when
you offer to explain someone else's moral opinions. You think that affirmative action is unfair but your friend thinks it perfectly fair. You cannot think
that his belief is caused by the truth; if you want to explain his belief you
must compose a personal-history explanation. You find one that you think
complete and persuasive: you cite his education in a knee-jerk liberal family.
But now you change your own mind: you are suddenly convinced by his arguments that affirmative action is fair. You now think that what your friend
believes is true, but you have discovered nothing that could impeach your
earlier explanation of why he believes it. If the personal-history explanation
was adequate before, it remains adequate now. You may be tempted now to
say that, after all, the truth did play a role in the causal story of how he came
to think what he does. But that shows only that CI is never more than a fifth,
spinning wheel in any explanation.

It is this fact—that CI is otiose—that provides the final argument against
it. Perhaps there are as yet unimagined receptors in the human brain and as
yet unimagined forces in the universe such that those forces do cause people
to form moral beliefs. Perhaps the best explanation of this process is teleological: perhaps we will one day discover that the universe is evolving toward
a predestined goal and that the existence and convictions of self-conscious
creatures are parts of the plan. Imagine that scientists have discovered and
can measure these influences and can discern the trajectory of the universe's
great strategy. They find that whenever the pertinent instruments report a
peculiar force of a certain strength in a field, everyone in the neighborhood
declares that a morally wrong act is occurring. None of these people can explain why the act is wrong; they can say only that they "see" or "intuit" that
it is wrong. We form the hypothesis that the peculiar force causes moral conviction, and we test that hypothesis by developing protective clothing that
shields people from that force. We find that many people so protected form

and express moral beliefs different from those of nonprotected people, but that when the protective clothing is removed they change their mind and join the general opinion. We conclude that the peculiar force does cause people to form moral beliefs.

Nothing in this story even begins to suggest, however, that the force causes people to form true moral beliefs. Nothing suggests that the force is in some way equivalent to or evidence of moral truth. So nothing so far supports CI. How could we show that the beliefs the force causes people to have are true beliefs? Only by thinking about the moral issues ourselves, wearing the protective clothing. Only if we come to think, immune from the force, that these beliefs really are true.[7] But we are then back in our original situation. So this scientific way of trying to establish CI would actually undermine it. We could not think that the force caused our own belief in the truth of the beliefs it causes in others; if we did we would be begging our question. We would have to suppose that we could be "in touch with" moral truth in some other way that did not involve CI in order to know which of the beliefs any peculiar force causes are true. CI is pointless. I hope it is now clear that we need not be Luddite about unknown forces or teleological processes to reject the causal impact hypothesis. CI is not a mistake about what there is. It is a confusion about what can count as an argument for the truth of a moral conviction. Only moral argument can. CI is a mistake because it violates Hume's principle.

Some moral philosophers have fallen into the fashion of speaking of their "intuitions" in moral matters. There are two ways to understand that usage. We might take them to mean that they have in some way or to some degree perceived the truth of what they claim as an intuition. If so, then they mean to offer their intuition as an argument for the truth of what they say they have intuited, as an eyewitness does, for instance, when he says he saw the accused at the scene of the crime. They claim some version of CI. Or they might mean simply to report what they believe, which of course supplies nothing by way of argument. Several times in this book I report what I believe about ethical and moral issues, and I seek to elicit your agreement and to remind you of what, I hope, you also believe. In Chapter 6 I speak about the importance of such beliefs: they determine, in part, what counts as ethical and moral responsibility. But they are not independent arguments for what you or I believe.

The Causal Dependence Hypothesis

Too Quick?

CI is driven by fear of external skepticism, and that fear is in turn driven by CD, the causal dependence hypothesis, which holds that if moral truth does not cause moral opinion, then people can have no reliable or responsible grounds for those opinions.[8] A quick proof is available that CD is false: it refutes itself. I assume that CD cannot be restricted to the domain of morality. It can make sense, if at all, only as a general claim about knowledge. It must insist that we cannot form a reliable belief about anything (except, perhaps, purely logical truths) unless our belief has been caused by what it reports. So the hypothesis is victim to a paradox: if it is true, then we can have no reason for thinking it true. CD is not true by definition: it does not follow from the meaning of the concepts it employs. And whether or not we can make sense of moral causation, we can surely make none of philosophical causation. A great many philosophers, as I said, believe that CD is true. But almost none of them thinks, I assume, that the truth of CD has itself caused them to believe that CD is true, that the universe contains philons with causal power over human minds. If they did think that, they could not consistently deny the existence of morons. They would have to accept CI.

Many philosophers distrust that kind of argument. It seems too quick a refutation of what many very distinguished philosophers believe. I think, on the contrary, that the paradox is not only a decisive argument against CD but also a helpful one, because it suggests that if we are to discover why CD has had such great appeal for moral philosophers on both sides of the skepticism debate, we must look to something distinctive about morality—some fear that seems lively when we puzzle about substantive moral issues but not about issues in philosophy.

Another and slightly longer version of much the same argument is equally illuminating. CD is not directly a claim about the truth of moral judgments even though it does figure prominently in popular skeptical arguments. It is directly a claim only about the reasons people do or do not have to believe any judgment true. We count all sorts of reasons as good reasons for the judgments we make, and what we count as a good reason depends on the content of those judgments. Any theory about adequate physical evidence for some judgment—about the rain in France this morning, for instance—is itself a scientific theory. So any theory about adequate reasons for accepting a moral judgment must be itself a moral theory. CD, when applied in the moral domain, is itself a moral claim. You need a reason to accept it, and, given Hume's principle, this must be or include a moral reason. We can imagine some such reason. You might think it wrong to act on the basis of moral judgments that are best explained through your personal history rather than encounters with the truth. But this new judgment, you soon realize, also refutes itself. You did not reach that new judgment through any encounter with the truth. Once again, in this different way, CD undermines any possible reason for accepting CD.

Embarrassing Stories?

But if personal history best explains why we hold the opinions we do, and the truth of those opinions plays no explanatory role, then how can we have any confidence in those opinions? That personal history might have features that make confidence difficult. Suppose I discover that yesterday you had to decide whether to attend a lecture by an unusually charismatic opponent of affirmative action or watch a football game on television. You flipped a coin, it fell tails, you went to the lecture, and you were converted. Now you think affirmative action unfair. The coin flip is an indispensable part of any complete explanation of why you think what you do. That sounds embarrassing. But, still, you have reasons you can offer to anyone who challenges your opinion: the reasons, let us assume, that the lecturer provided. Whether you have good grounds for your new opinion must depend entirely on whether those reasons are, as moral reasons, good ones. That you came by those reasons through the toss of a coin is irrelevant.

In this example, you were persuaded to your new opinions by arguments. Does that matter? Imagine a more bizarre story. Until a year ago you thought affirmative action patently unfair. Then you had occasion to think about the matter again and were convinced, by arguments that suddenly seemed compelling, that it is not unfair. One Tuesday morning you read, in the Science section of your newspaper, of an astounding discovery. Everyone in the world who has had a scalotopic brain scan (don't ask) thinks that affirmative action is fair, whatever opinion he held before the scan. The evidence is vast and conclusive: there is no possibility of coincidence. You had a scalotopic scan shortly before you rethought and changed your views, and you are left in no doubt that you would not have changed them if you had not had the scan.

Of course you look again at the arguments that convinced you to change your opinion. Indeed, you subject them to much greater scrutiny than you had before. You test them the way a conscientious judge would test a principle he was about to lay down in an important case: you ask how your new view sorts with your more general opinions about the fairness or unfairness of various forms of discrimination or special advantage. You cast the net of your investigation wide: you ask yourself what you think about admissions discrimination in favor of athletes, people with interesting hobbies, and children of alumni, and what you think about positive discrimination in other areas: in choosing brain surgeons for your own operation, for instance. You probe your opinions backward into generality as well as sideways into related issues: you ask what is ever wrong with racial discrimination, and you then ask whether the best answers to that question must also condemn affirmative action. You engage in these complex reflections expecting to find conflict: the scan most probably targeted only your very concrete opinion about affirmative action in university admissions and therefore left you in a state of moral dissonance. But you find, on the contrary, that your new opinion survives all these examinations very well: it is your old opinion that would conflict with your other or more general convictions. The effect of the scan, you now assume, was more general and pervasive than you had thought: it affected widespread shifts throughout the full range of your moral convictions so that all your convictions are now thoroughly integrated with your new views about affirmative action. No matter how you test them, they all seem right to you.

What now? How should you react when you finish being bewildered? Surely your discovery should have *some* impact on either your opinions or your confidence in those opinions. If CD is correct, it must have a devastating impact. But in fact it can have no impact whatsoever. For a start, you cannot regret having had the scan, at least not for this reason. You have no reason whatever to think you were right before. Even if you embrace CI, and think that moral truth can cause moral conviction, you have no reason to think that your former views enjoyed that benefit. As I said, the only reason you could have to think that truth has caused your moral opinion is an independent belief that your conviction is true, and you now think your present opinions, not your past ones, true. Before the scan you would have had a very strong reason not to have the scan if its results could have been predicted. But now you have the same reason for not regretting the scan; indeed, for thinking yourself fortunate to have had it.

Do you have less reason to suppose your new views correct than you had to think your old ones correct before the scan? No; on the contrary, you now think you have more reason than you had then because you now think your earlier reasons were unsound. Should you now doubt your ability to form any responsible judgment at all on the question of affirmative action? No, because you cannot reject the hypothesis that the brain scan improved your ability to reason about morality. On the contrary, you have some evidence that it did so: you were in error about many moral matters before the scan but are now reasoning better, or so you cannot help but think.

Do you have any reason to think yourself irresponsible if you act on your new convictions? As it happens, a referendum proposing a ban on affirmative action is scheduled to be held in your state soon. Should you abstain in that election? Abstention means one less vote against what you think would be either serious injustice or stupid policy, and that one vote might be decisive. Nothing you believe licenses abstention; it would be irresponsible, not responsible. You might think that you should now treat your convictions about affirmative action as untrustworthy, no matter how right they seem to you, and not vote for that reason. But then you need a theory about the right way to form convictions, and no plausible theory paints your convictions as untrustworthy. You listened to arguments on both sides, composed a principled account of when racial criteria are and are not permissible, and tested your principles against your other convictions and hypothetical cases you took care to imagine. Very few of your fellow citizens have reflected as carefully. On what ground could you think your opinions less trustworthy than theirs? Their opinions, like your new opinions, reflect their personal history; their opinions are no more than yours downstream of any validating causal process. The difference is that your personal history seems more bizarre and that difference must be irrelevant.

Even in this absurd invented case, that is, when your opinions are laughably accidental, you cannot find any respect in which that matters. So we should have no fear in conceding that everyone's moral opinions are accidental in the following sense: if their lives had been different enough, their beliefs would have been different as well. Any sting in that concession will be drawn if we have taken the main lesson of this part of the book—the independence of morality—to heart. Morality stands or falls on its own credentials. Moral principle can be neither vindicated nor impeached except through its own connivance. I have been laboring the crucial distinction between the explanation and the justification of a moral conviction. The former is a matter of fact, and the latter of morality. Moral responsibility is also a moral matter: we need a theory of what questions we must have asked ourselves before we are entitled to hold and act on a moral opinion. That is the subject of Chapter 6. But no theory of moral responsibility can plausibly denounce someone as irresponsible just because some embarrassing feature of his personal history best explains why he came to think his moral arguments good ones, provided that those arguments are reasonable and adequately deep.

We must judge CD, which is a theory of moral responsibility, as a moral thesis: about moral epistemology. We can accept it only if we can make a compelling moral case in its favor. But we cannot. Facts about how someone tested his moral opinions are indeed pertinent, as we shall later see, in judging whether he has acted responsibly in holding, expressing, and following them. But nothing turns on the best causal explanation of how he came to the opinions he tests or, indeed, of how he decided what tests to use.

Conviction and Accident

But isn't it worrying that your most profound moral convictions are only accidents and therefore can be only accidentally true? If affirmative action is fair and you think it is, then haven't you been as lucky as the man who believes, correctly, that the time is 3:15 because his watch stopped at that time yesterday? You have been lucky because nothing in the best explanation of how you came to form your view—perhaps you did flip a coin to decide whether to hear a lecture—bears any relation to the truth of that view. That seems appalling: if it really is only an accident when your convictions are true, then—given the number of possible moral convictions—it is very unlikely that your convictions are true.[9]

But we must separate the two questions I just mangled together. Is it only an accident that you hold the convictions you do? Is it only an accident if what you believe is true? The first is a question of explanation and the second of justification, so we need different definitions of accident for the two. The first asks whether your history might well have been different in such a way that your opinions would now be different. If we set aside determinism, which holds that your history could not have been different, the answer is certainly yes. If you had not gone to the affirmative action lecture, you would not have heard the arguments that convinced you. More generally: if you had been raised in a very different moral culture, a great many of your convictions would probably have been different. You might well think that gun control laws are tyranny. You might, indeed, think that you have a moral duty to kill unbelievers.

But all our even mildly theoretical beliefs, not just our moral convictions, are accidental in the same way. I believe that the earth is about four and a half billion years old. If my parents had died young, however, and I had been adopted by a fundamentalist family, I might well have the different belief that a god created the universe only very recently. None of my beliefs about the physical world is immune from that kind of contingency. The great popularity, around here, of most of those beliefs doesn't make the fact that I hold those beliefs any less contingent. That is also true of my philosophical beliefs. Many of the philosophers who accept the causal dependence hypothesis might well have rejected it had their education led them to graduate studies in a different philosophy department from the one they chose. (We should not, however, exaggerate either the contingency of beliefs or the importance of that contingency.[10])

The second question invokes a different sense of accident. It is only an accident that someone believes what is true if his reasons for thinking it true are bad ones. That is why the true belief of the man with the stopped watch is only an accident. If you flipped a coin and then declared affirmative action fair just because it came up tails, your belief, though true, would be accidental in the same way. On this view of accident, whether our moral convictions can be true other than accidently is itself a large moral question. Are there ways of thinking about moral issues that are reasonably well calculated to identify moral truth and, if so, what are those ways? Any answer is, of course, itself part of an overall moral theory. If, as I claim in Chapter 6, there are such ways of thought, and if you have followed them, then it is no accident if the convictions you tested in those ways are true.

It will now be objected that I am cheating: that we must estimate the chances that our moral convictions are true not by assuming the truth of some of them, such as our convictions about good moral reasoning, but by imagining that we had no opinions at all and drew them all, one by one, randomly from a jar that held some true but mainly false ones. We should ask: What would the odds be that all or any of the convictions we drew from that jar turned out to be true? But this is a catastrophically misleading suggestion: we cannot imagine reasoning as a lottery. Even if we could separate all our convictions as distinct marbles drawn from a jar, we could not judge the odds of having drawn out a true one if we had put our mathematical opinions into the jar as well.

We must assume the truth of some convictions to make any judgment, even a probability judgment, about the truth of any other conviction, and once we have done that the truth of other convictions must be a matter of judgment or inference, not chance. Any thought of a lottery disappears. The key methodological question is always one of degree: What and how much should we assume is true in order to judge all or part of the rest? It would be pointless to ask what the chances are of any moral conviction being true without some assumptions about what makes a moral conviction true. The supposition that all moral opinions are equally likely to be true is itself a moral opinion—and a crazy one. But when you allow yourself even indispensable opinions about good moral reasoning, then any thought that your other moral convictions could be only accidentally true evaporates. The fear of accident, though epidemic, is only another symptom of not fully grasping the independence of value, of thinking that somehow, somewhere, there must be some tether to the causal order if morality is not to float away into airy nothing.

Integrated Epistemology

The causal dependence hypothesis is a piece of Archimedean epistemology, and Archimedean epistemology is misconceived. There is no such thing as an entirely abstract condition on knowledge.[11] Every thought is a thought about something and depends, for its sense and plausibility, on what it is a thought about. Responsibility in science means, at least for the most part, responding to evidence, and something is genuine evidence of some fact only if it exists because that fact exists. That explains why CD is plausible in science. It also explains why CD is senseless in those domains, like morality, that are matters of argument, not evidence. Archimedean epistemology fails because a theory of knowledge must take its place in and with the rest of our opinions. Abstract epistemology and concrete belief must fit and support each other, and neither must be given a veto over the other.

We need integrated epistemology: we must make assumptions about what is true in order to test theories about how to decide what is true. Our scientific method, for instance, assumes the truth of what we believe about optics and biology, even though we use scientific method to confirm our optics and our biology. The whole intellectual structure fits and stands together. So it is a mistake to give some epistemological axiom priority over the rest of our convictions. It is an equally grave mistake, of course, to give any concrete conviction priority over the general epistemology that we develop in this mutually sustaining way. We must not ask our epistemology to make way for whatever it would be nice to believe. Astrology makes causal claims—about the influence of planetary orbits on the arrival times of handsome strangers—that cannot be made to fit the requirements on causal explanation that we have developed in constructing the science in which we have overall such faith. We cannot arrive at an integrated set of theories and opinions that includes both science and astrology, and for a thousand reasons it is the latter that we must set aside.

The popularity of religious conviction is a more difficult challenge to integrated epistemology. Thoughtful people carve out, in the name of their religion, what seem to be stark exceptions to their general opinions about the conditions of respectable belief. These exceptions rely on "miracles"; these include the foundational miracle of an eternal mind existing without brain and with absolutely unlimited power to will anything else into existence. Religious philosophers have tried with great ingenuity to weld these miracles into a general epistemology. Some try to show that scientific method, as we have otherwise developed and conceived this, does indeed explain the miracles that religion claims. Some argue in the other direction: that general epistemology must be revised and expanded to include religious experience and acceptance of miracles. Both efforts respect the need for an integrated epistemology.

A recently popular argument for God's existence—the argument from intelligent design—illustrates the first of these strategies.[12] This insists that certain primitive forms of life are irreducibly complex: if anything in their structure were different, they could not survive; they therefore could not have evolved from simpler forms. We must conclude, according to this argument, that they were created by a supernatural being with the attributes traditionally credited to the Abrahamic God. I believe that this argument is scientifically weak.[13] But it is nevertheless an argument that hopes to explain the miracle of creation in a recognizably scientific way: by showing that the best causal explanation of certain phenomena requires us to accept what are in effect religious hypotheses. The advocates of intelligent design include many people who formerly held the opinion I described earlier: that a god made the earth and life on it only fairly recently and in seven days. No doubt their conversion to intelligent design was accelerated by legal decisions holding that "creationism," which is what they called their young-earth theory, could not be taught in public schools because it is based on biblical authority, not scientific evidence.[14] But the conversion may also have been hastened by a strong impulse to unite their religion with their more general opinions about proper reasoning.

The second strategy for reconciling religion with integrated epistemology is used by philosophers who argue that our theories about what and how we know must be sensitive to the full range of what we find we cannot help but believe. Some people—many hundreds of millions of people—believe that their lives include a vast variety of religious experiences. They believe they have transcendent perceptions of a god in the world: their sense of awe, they think, properly grounds their religious conviction unless the conviction is defeated by known arguments. They cannot make an independent case—independent of the bare authority of those perceptions—that the perceptions are correct and not illusions. But in the opinion of these philosophers we do better to take these perceptions at face value than to reject them, because we could reject them only by begging the question—by insisting on an Archimedean epistemology that rules them out.[15]

This argument seems to me also to fail, and for a reason that is pertinent to this chapter. If the validity of religious convictions is said to turn on the existence of a cognitive faculty analogous to perception, then a host of famously difficult questions arise. We can fit the more familiar forms of perception—those delivered by the five senses—into an integrated epistemology because our biology, physics, and chemistry explain how those senses function in a way that shows why they can be trusted. True, as I said, there is a certain circularity in this account: we rely on sense perception to confirm the tenets of biology, physics, and chemistry that we use to validate sense perception. But that is the kind of circularity that integrates conviction and epistemology across an entire domain of thought; that is what integrated epistemology means. If we declare our faith in some special religious form of perception, however, we have no way of integrating our belief in the faculty that delivers that perception with any more general account of how that faculty functions. We must just declare an ad hoc faculty of perception and then grant that others may sensibly claim a special faculty of detecting ghosts or communicating with the dead.

Moreover, if religious conviction rests on perception, then how can we explain the diversity of religious opinion among people? What explains why so many people—nonbelievers and believers in a very different faith—are mistaken? Some people hold an internal explanation of diversity and error: that their god grants his grace only to those he has chosen to receive it.[16] But that is too tightly circular to count as an answer when the claim of perception is challenged; once again it does nothing to integrate general epistemology and religious conviction. We need a less question-begging explanation, and none seems available except the unhelpful claim that some people lack a faculty that others have. Is there any evidence of this defect, in those who have it, other than their inability to "see" what true believers claim they have "seen"?

These are exactly the questions that have traditionally been used to embarrass the causal impact hypothesis. We can find no place in an integrated epistemology for a special moral faculty that enables people to "intuit" the fairness or injustice of affirmative action or the wickedness or wisdom of abortion. But we can defend the responsibility of our moral convictions without relying on the causal impact hypothesis, because the causal dependence theory is also false. So perhaps we can defend the reasonableness of religious conviction without supposing any special faculty of religious perception. But religious convictions face a formidable burden in finding a place within an integrated epistemology that moral convictions do not face. Moral convictions, just in themselves, make no causal claims. Of course, causal hypotheses about the physical, social, and mental world figure in the justification of particular moral claims. No plausible case for or against affirmative action ignores its consequences, and of course the evidence we cite for any view of those consequences must respect the requirements of the pertinent science.

But justifying a moral judgment never requires appeal to extraordinary modes of causation. Morality needs no miracles. Conventional religious judgments, on the contrary, are shot through with extraordinary causal claims about the creation of matter and life and the workings of nature. These causal claims are indispensable to the historical and contemporary appeal of most religions. Whether a believer attempts to vindicate these claims through an appeal to perception, or through some other explanation of their source, he must in any case justify the causal claims that are part of their content, and it is difficult to see how miracles—exceptions to the causal mechanics that must figure in any integrated epistemology—can be avoided. Even if the intelligent design movement were able to show that neo-Darwinian theory could not explain the origin of species, it would face an independent and formidable challenge in explaining how the hypothesis of a supernatural designer could explain it.

So integrated epistemology must guard against two tyrannies: the tyranny of an Archimedean ambition that is insensitive to the content of particular intellectual domains, and the rival tyranny of dogmatic adherence to some discrete conviction—about gods or ghosts or what is good or what is wrong—that requires an ad hoc, made-for-the-occasion exception to the best account of how we form reliable belief in the broad domain of that conviction. I agree, however, that in the end raw, undefeated conviction must play a decisive role in any honest search for an integrated epistemology; there may be propositions that we find we cannot but believe, even after the most sustained reflection. Then we must not pretend not to believe them but must instead struggle to explain why we are justified, in spite of the difficulties, in believing what we do. We may not succeed, but the struggle is better than the pretense.

That seems to me the situation of many people of deep religious conviction who cannot but believe: their faith endures even when they accept that they lack a good account of how that faith can be woven into a general account of causation that sustains its causal claims. If you can't help believing something, steadily and wholeheartedly, you'd better believe it, not of course because the fact of your belief argues for its truth but because you cannot think any argument a decisive refutation of a belief it does not loosen. In the beginning and in the end is the conviction. The struggle for integrity lies in between.

Moral Progress?

If we abandon the causal impact and causal dependence hypotheses, do we lose any other convictions of independent importance? Crispin Wright suggests one ground of concern.[17] If we abandon all claims of causal impact, then we can no longer explain moral progress in what might seem an appealing way: as the gradual falling away of impediments to the impact of moral truth on human sensibility. Of course we would not then have to deny the reality of moral progress. Anyone who is convinced that slavery is wrong and knows that his view is now shared by a great many people will think that general moral opinion has improved at least in that respect since slavery was widely practiced and defended. Perhaps sufficient other examples can be found to allow us the much more ambitious claim that moral opinion has improved broadly on all fronts. How much progress we think we can claim, in that simple comparative sense, depends only on our own moral convictions and our sociological and historical beliefs about the distribution of parallel convictions now and in the past.

True, we might be able to explain why what we take to be progress occurred. We might find personal-history explanations that show why the mistaken beliefs are outdated: that people who defended slavery held false empirical beliefs, for instance, or that the economy that sustained slavery has been transformed. Some people might offer different kinds of explanation. Those who think that a god is the source of moral knowledge may believe that that god has gradually unfolded his moral plan to more and more of his children. Utilitarians may suppose that moral error gradually disappears because people who suffer have a greater incentive to press for egalitarian principles than other people have for resisting those principles.[18]

It is important to notice, however, that none of these causal historical explanations helps to confirm our initial claim of moral progress. That initial judgment rests entirely on our conviction that slavery is wrong, and we assume rather than support that conviction when we describe past influences as distorting or assume that slavery is offensive to a god or suppose that economics has produced a better state of affairs. So we are entitled to no more confidence in our judgment of progress when we can offer such explanations than when we can say only that earlier generations did not "see" some moral truth that we do. In either case we are relying finally on our conviction and on the moral case that we believe supports it. We would be in no better situation if the causal impact hypothesis were true. We would need some independent judgment that our contemporary views were improvements before we could claim that moral truth figured in the explanation of the progress we claim, and that independent judgment of improvement, on its own, is all we could mean by progress.

5

Internal Skepticism

Typology

Global internal skepticism has long been a potent influence on literature; the ancient philosophers thought it an important position either to defend or to attack. It is a despairing conviction, particularly when it is trained on ethics. Then it holds that life itself has no value or meaning, and, as I argue later in this book, no value of any other kind can survive that dismal conclusion. Once a corrosive, global internal skepticism takes hold of someone, declaring, as Macbeth put it, that life signifies nothing, it may leave him but he cannot refute it. I shall try to confront that despairing form of skepticism in the only way I can: by trying to show, in Chapter 9, the kind of value that it makes sense to suppose a human life can have. I call this adverbial value: it is the value of a good performance in response to an important challenge.

In this brief chapter I concentrate not on rebutting internal skepticism but clarifying it. I offered examples of internal skepticism in Chapter 2. Many of these are negative moral judgments: they do not offer guidance or demand. It is a negative moral judgment, for instance, that morality neither requires nor condemns particular sexual mechanics among consenting adults. Some judgments of internal skepticism take a different form, however. They declare, not that some particular act is neither forbidden nor required, but that there is no

correct answer to the question whether it is forbidden or whether it is required—
that the wrongness of abortion, for instance, is indeterminate in that way.

We must take care to distinguish such judgments, which are instances of
internal skepticism, from certain forms of purported external skepticism. The
view I considered at length in Chapter 3, that first-order substantive moral
judgments are only projections of emotion or attitude, not reports of a mind-
independent moral fact, claims that moral judgments are never either true or
false. The indeterminacy judgments I have in mind now are patently substantive moral claims: someone who thinks that there is no right answer to the
abortion question, because the arguments on either side are not better than
those on the other, may subscribe fully to the ordinary view of morality and
hold that a great many other moral judgments are straightforwardly true or
false.[1]

Indeterminacy judgments are more familiar—and in my view much more
often persuasive—in domains of value outside ethics and morality. Some
people with either exceptional palates or nerve stand ready to rank the quality
of any two bottles of wine: one is always better than the other, they insist,
and they are always ready to tell us which. It is certainly an available view,
however, that in the case of some wines neither bottle is better than another
and they are not exactly equal in quality either. We might say that they are
"on a par" with one another.[2] Or we might take an even more radically skeptical view of this matter: that goodness in wine is entirely a subjective matter
and that, in spite of the cult of oenophiles, there is no room for objective valuation at all. Then we might say that there is never a right answer to the question which of two wines is best, but only answers to the different question
whether some particular person likes one wine better.

Consider two more nonmoral examples of this "no-right-answer" judgment.
It is an English country-weekend game (or used to be, before DVDs escaped
to the home counties) to compose and debate "greatest" lists. Who was the
greater athlete: Donald Budge or David Beckham? The greater statesman:
Marcus Aurelius or Winston Churchill? The greater artist: Picasso or Beethoven? It is a tempting response to such questions to deny their sense. We
want to say: it is pointless to try to compare talents or achievements across such
different challenges, roles, and contexts. The only sensible judgment, we think,
is that these talents and achievements are incommensurate. Picasso was neither
a greater nor a lesser artist than Beethoven, nor, of course, were the two exactly
equal in greatness. They were on a par.

Before the Supreme Court's recent 5–4 decision in the matter, lawyers debated whether the Second Amendment to the United States Constitution guarantees private citizens the right to keep handguns at home.[3] There were, and remain, popular arguments on both sides. Many lawyers and law students were therefore tempted to say that it is a mistake to think that there is a single right answer to the question. There are only different answers that appeal to different political constituencies and different parties of constitutional theory.

Internal skepticism about morality therefore includes not only negative moral judgments, like the judgment that anything is permissible in sex between consenting adults, but also claims of indeterminacy in moral judgment and incommensurability in moral comparison. We should distinguish both of these from a third and distinct form of internal skepticism, which is moral conflict. Many people think that Antigone had moral duties both to bury and not to bury her brother, so that whatever she did was wrong. They think, not that it is neither true nor false that she had either duty, but true that she had both.[4] This is a claim not of indeterminacy but, we might say, of too much determinacy. I include judgments of conflict for the sake of completeness: they are internally skeptical because they deny that morality provides any guidance in the premises. But they raise special problems for my later argument, and I return to issues of conflict later.

Indeterminacy and Default

In this chapter I discuss mainly "no-right-answer" claims of indeterminacy and incommensurability. When are such judgments appropriate? One surprisingly popular answer is this: in the domains of value—morality, ethics, art, and law—indeterminacy is the default judgment. When, after careful study, no persuasive argument can be found for either side of some moral or aesthetic or ethical or legal question, it is sensible to suppose that there is no right answer to that question. Suppose I am bewildered whether abortion is wicked. Certain arguments or analogies make it seem so to me sometimes, when I am in some moods. But other arguments or analogies make it seem not so at other times. I confess that I lack any secure or stable sense of which of these sets of arguments and analogies is better. Then, according to the default thesis, I ought to conclude that there is no right answer to the question. This approach assumes that though positive arguments are necessary to establish positive claims about moral issues, one way or the other, failure to find such positive arguments is enough to support the indeterminacy claim. Positive claims need arguments of their own: the indeterminacy judgment just needs the failure of argument for anything else.

This thesis is a familiar form of instruction in law schools. Lecturers construct elaborate arguments first for and then against a particular legal claim, and they then announce, generally to the delight of their students, that there is no right answer to the question in dispute. But the default thesis is patently mistaken, because it confuses two different positions—uncertainty and indeterminacy—that it is essential to distinguish. Confessions of uncertainty are indeed theoretically less ambitious than positive claims; uncertainty is indeed a default position. If I see arguments on all sides of some issue and do not find, even after reflection, one set of arguments stronger than the others, then I am entitled without more ado to declare that I am uncertain, that I have no view of the matter. I do not need a further, more substantive, reason beyond my failure to be persuaded of any other view. But in all these respects indeterminacy differs from uncertainty. "I am uncertain whether the proposition in question is true or false" is plainly consistent with "It is one or the other," but "The proposition in question is neither true nor false" is not. Once uncertainty is taken into account, in some such way, then the default thesis of indeterminacy collapses, because if one of these alternatives—uncertainty—holds by default, then indeterminacy, which is very different, cannot.

The difference between uncertainty and indeterminacy is practically, as well as theoretically, indispensable. Though reticence is generally appropriate when one is uncertain, it is wholly out of place for anyone genuinely convinced that the issue is not uncertain but indeterminate. The Catholic Church has declared, for example, that even those who are uncertain whether a fetus is a person with a right to live should oppose abortion, because abortion would be so terrible if it turned out that a fetus is a person. No comparable argument could move someone who has convinced himself that it is indeterminate whether a fetus is a person: that no claim one way or the other is correct. He might of course have other reasons for taking a stance. He might say that because those who mistakenly think that a fetus is a person are very upset by abortion, it should be legally banned for that reason. Or that abortion should be legally permitted because it is unjust for the state to limit liberty without a positive case. But he lacks the reason for reticence or agony that someone who thinks the issue uncertain has.

Once we distinguish uncertainty from indeterminacy, we see that we need as strong a positive case for claims of indeterminacy as for more positive claims. How might I support my judgment that, of two famous wines, one is not better than another nor are they equal? Or that it is a mistake to claim that either Beethoven or Picasso was the greater artist or Budge or Beckham the greater athlete? I need a positive theory about greatness in wine or art or sports. I assume that you, like me, are willing and think yourself able to make at least some comparisons of artistic merit: we think Picasso a greater painter than Balthus and also, though the case is closer, a greater painter than Braque. We also think Beethoven a greater composer than Lloyd-Webber. So we believe that comparisons about the merits of particular artists are in principle sensible.

I think, as I just said, that though Braque was a very important artist, all things considered Picasso was a greater one. If you challenge me, I will try to sustain that opinion in various ways—by pointing to Picasso's greater originality, inventiveness, and range of qualities from playfulness to profundity, while nevertheless admitting certain advantages in Braque's work: a more lyrical approach to cubism, for example. Because artistic merit is a complex subject and my claim is an all-things-considered one, the issue can tolerate a complex discussion. The conversation would not soon turn silly, as I think it would if I were trying to defend a claim about the greater nobility of Petrus over Lafite. I might or might not convince you, after sustained discussion, that I am right about Picasso and Braque; you might or might not convince me that I am wrong. But if neither convinces the other, I will continue in my opinion, as no doubt you will in yours. I might be disappointed if I could not convince you, but of course I would not count that fact as refuting my view.

But if I were asked whether Picasso was a greater genius than Beethoven, my answer would be very different. I would deny both that one was greater than the other and that they were exactly equal in merit. Picasso and Beethoven were both very great artists, I would say, and no exact comparison can be made between the two. Of course I must defend the distinction I have now drawn. Why can I rank Picasso and Braque but not Picasso and Beethoven? The difference is not that people agree about standards for comparing artists in the same period or in the same genre. They do not, and it would not follow that the agreed-upon standards were the right ones even if they did. The difference cannot be based on any cultural or social fact of that sort, but must be based, if it makes sense at all, on more general, perhaps even quite theoretical, assumptions about the character of artistic achievement or evaluation. I would try to defend my judgment about Picasso and Beethoven in that way. I believe that artistic achievement is a matter of response to artistic challenge and tradition, and that comparisons can therefore be more finely drawn within a genre than across them and more finely drawn between artists within a particular period of development of the same genre than between those who worked in the same genre though at very different times. So though I do think that Shakespeare was a greater creative artist than Jasper Johns, and Picasso a greater one than Vivaldi, I believe no precise ranking makes sense among evident geniuses at the very highest levels of different genres. This is not an evidently stable view, and I might well change my mind. But it is the view I now hold. I am certain that your own view, if you were to make it articulate, would be rather, or perhaps very, different.[5]

Now consider indeterminacy claims in the more consequential domain of ethics. People are sometimes faced with important life-shaping decisions, and they then wonder about the value of different kinds of lives they might lead. A young woman must choose whether to pursue a promising career as a public-interest lawyer in Los Angeles or to emigrate to a kibbutz in Israel. (Of course, she will have many other options as well. But suppose these are the only two now in question.) She might be puzzled about a great deal. Which life would she find day-to-day more fun? More satisfying in retrospect? In which role would she be more successful? In which would she help others more? She might be uncertain about the right answers to any of these questions taken separately, and she will very likely be uncertain about the right answer to the further question how to weigh her answers against one another. It is a very popular view that she faces not uncertainty but indeterminacy, because, since these are both rewarding lives, there is no right answer to what life would be better or to which choice she should make.[6] She must just choose. That view might be correct. But it is not correct by default. It needs as much or as little positive argument as the contrary claim that the best life, all things considered, really lies in emigration. No such argument is supplied only by citing the obvious fact that there are many values and that they cannot all be realized in a single life. For the question remains—as a challenging abstract issue for philosophers and an agonizing practical one for people—which choice is nevertheless best?

There is no more question of a default here than in the exotic comparison of wines or athletes or artists. I have some sense of how the indeterminacy claim might be defended in those less important cases. My discussion, later in the book, of the ethical challenge we all face in leading our lives might suggest some possible arguments for indeterminacy in the ethical case. The adverbial value of a particular way of leading a life depends, among other things, on the way that life connects with other kinds of value, and someone might have positive reasons to believe that the kind of value created in a kibbutz life is incommensurate with the value created through work in American poverty law. If so, these reasons are indistinct.

In any case it would seem at best premature to suppose that positive arguments for indeterminacy are always available when people are deeply uncertain about what lives would be best for them to lead, and it is therefore puzzling that philosophers who declare broad ethical indeterminacy offer so few arguments for the transition from uncertainty to indeterminacy. Few people faced with important career or other life decisions have taken that comforting step themselves. We face life-changing decisions with a variety of emotions—uncertainty, of course, but also foreboding, weariness, and a fearsome sense that though we do not know how to decide, it nevertheless and greatly matters how we do decide. That set of thoughts is for many people a terrible burden. If they are making a mistake—if there really is no right answer to the question they ask—it would be enormously helpful if the philosophers of indeterminacy were to explain why.

Now consider the popular claim, at least among academic lawyers, that there is often no right answer to a difficult legal question.[7] This cannot be true by default in law any more than in ethics. The no-right-answer claim is a legal claim—it insists that no argument exists that makes the case for one side stronger—and it must therefore rest on some theory or conception of law. Some theories of law do claim to support that conclusion: the cruder versions of legal positivism do, because according to those theories only past decisions of officials provide legal reasons and there might well be no past official decision on either side of an issue. There are more complex and plausible legal theories that might also be thought to generate indeterminacy in certain cases. So law nicely illustrates the point that claims of indeterminacy, unlike confessions of uncertainty, require a positive theory. In my view it also illustrates the difficulty of producing such a theory: the crude legal positivism that sustains no-right-answer verdicts appeals to very few thoughtful practicing lawyers. In any case, however, many contemporary legal scholars who claim to find it self-evident that there is no right answer to controversial legal questions do not subscribe to legal positivism or to any other theory that offers positive legal arguments for indeterminacy.[8] They just fall into the fallacy of supposing that indeterminacy holds by default.

Finally we come to the moral case. We are not, remember, now discussing cases of alleged moral conflict. We are considering the claim that the case for prohibiting abortion is no stronger and no weaker than the case for permitting it, even though the two cases are not of equal strength. How can that strong claim be defended? Commentators often say that someone's view about abortion depends on whether he finds one analogy—that abortion is like murder—stronger than the competing analogy that compares abortion to appendectomy. That is an innocuous observation. But many of them add, as if this were self-evident, that neither of the two analogies is stronger than the other. How could that further claim be defended? What would it take to show, a priori, that no matter how thoroughly and imaginatively the dozens of complex issues at stake are canvassed, no case can be constructed that will show, even if only marginally and controversially, that one side or the other has the better of the overall argument? In the easier cases we considered, about the comparison of wines, artists, and athletes, it seemed plausible that the right theory of aesthetic or athletic excellence might well provide grounds for limiting the range of sensible judgment so as to show why, for instance, trying to rank Picasso and Beethoven is silly. But it hardly seems obvious that the right account of morality could do that. On the contrary, it seems antecedently unlikely that a plausible view of the point of morality could teach us that debates about the permissibility of abortion are silly.

Hardheaded people like to ridicule—as woolly or dogmatic—the claims of other people who believe that one position in some deep and apparently intractable controversy really has the better of the argument. Critics say that these partisans overlook the obvious truth that there is no "fact of the matter," no "single right answer" to the issue in play. The critics do not pause to consider whether they themselves have any substantive arguments for their equally substantive position, and, if they do, whether these might not also be ridiculed as vague or unpersuasive or as resting on instincts or even bare assertions in the same way. Absolute confidence or clarity is the privilege of fools and fanatics. The rest of us must do the best we can: we must choose among all the substantive views on offer by asking which strikes us, after reflection and due thought, as more plausible than the others. And if none does, we must then settle for the true default view, which is not indeterminacy but uncertainty. I repeat my earlier caution. I mean to challenge only one form of internal skepticism about ethics and morality. I have said nothing yet about the internal skepticism that finds us alone at night when we can almost touch our own death, the terrifying sense that nothing matters. Argument can't help then; we can only wait for dawn.

PART TWO

Interpretation

6

Moral Responsibility

Responsibility and Interpretation

Agenda

To recapitulate: Morality is an independent domain of thought. Hume's principle—itself a moral principle—is sound: any argument that either supports or undermines a moral claim must include or presuppose further moral claims or assumptions. The only sensible form of moral skepticism is therefore an internal skepticism that depends on rather than challenges the truth-seeking character of moral conviction. The only sensible argument for the "realist" view that some moral claims are objectively true is therefore a substantive moral argument that some particular moral claim—that tax cheating is wrong, say—is true and would still be true even if no one ever disapproved of cheating on taxes. If we think that our reasons for accepting any such moral claim are good ones, then we must also think that we are "in touch with" the truth of the matter, and that its truth is no accident.

Some readers may find in this declaration of independence only a deeper form of skepticism; skepticism so deep that it is skeptical even about skepticism. But there is no skepticism here, even about skepticism. The independence thesis leaves you free to conclude (if that is what seems right to you) that no one ever has any moral duties or responsibilities at all. What could be a deeper form of skepticism than that? Would you be better off—intellectually or in any other way—if you were able to reach that dramatically skeptical conclusion through an Archimedean piece of metaphysics or sociology rather than through a moral argument? Would you be better off if you could reach the opposite conclusion, that people do indeed have moral duties, through an Archimedean Platonism of morons? You might think: "Yes, because I could then be more confident of my convictions than I am now." But you could not, because you would have to decide—through ordinary moral argument alone—which of your convictions were true in order to know which were made true by morons.

These are important conclusions; we have established, I think, that the ordinary view makes sense and that external critics of that view do not. But nothing more. Our limited conclusion will come as no surprise to nonphilosophers. What worries them is not whether moral claims can be true but which moral claims are true; not whether we can, but whether we do, have good reason to think as we do. Many people and some philosophers who press that question hope to find a litmus stick: a test for good moral argument that does not beg the question it tries to answer by already presupposing some controversial moral theory. If the argument of this book so far is sound, that is not a reasonable hope. Our moral epistemology—our account of good reasoning about moral matters—must be an integrated rather than an Archimedean epistemology, and it must therefore be itself a substantive, first-order moral theory.

We are always guilty of a kind of circularity. There is no way I can test the accuracy of my moral convictions except by deploying further moral convictions. My reasons for thinking that tax cheating is wrong are good reasons if the arguments I rely on are good ones. That is too crude an account of the difficulty: we hope that the circle of our opinions has a wider radius than that. But if I am faced with someone who holds moral opinions radically different from my own, I cannot count on finding anything in my set of reasons and arguments that he would be irrational not to accept. I cannot *demonstrate* to him that my opinions are true and his false.

But I can hope to convince him—and myself—of something else that is often more important: that I have acted responsibly in reaching my opinions and acting on them. The distinction between accuracy and responsibility in moral conviction is a further dimension of what I called the ordinary view. I may be right about affirmative action when I flip a coin and wrong when I reflect carefully, but I am irresponsible in the first case and responsible in the second. The difference between accuracy and responsibility is readily apparent in the third person. I may judge that your convictions are seriously wrong but nevertheless accept that you acted with full responsibility in forming them. The difference is substantially eroded in the first person: I cannot think myself responsible in believing that abortion is wrong unless I do believe that abortion is wrong. But the two virtues are different even from that perspective: I might have greater confidence that abortion is wrong than that I have reached that conclusion on adequate reflection. Or the other way around: I may be satisfied that I have thought about the matter properly and yet remain tentative about the conclusion I have reached. Indeed, I may be satisfied that I have thought about the matter as well as I can and yet be wholly uncertain about what conclusion to draw.

We can best approach the crucial question of how to think about moral issues—the question of moral epistemology—by studying the ordinary concept of moral responsibility. In this chapter, and more broadly in this Part Two, I argue that the nerve of responsibility is integrity and that the epistemology of a morally responsible person is interpretive. It might be helpful to summarize my conclusions in advance. We all have unstudied moral convictions, almost from the beginning of our lives. These are mainly carried in concepts whose origin and development are issues for anthropologists and intellectual historians. We inherit these concepts from parents and culture and, possibly, to some degree through genetic species disposition. As young children we deploy mainly the idea of fairness, and then we acquire and deploy other, more sophisticated and pointed moral concepts: generosity, kindness, promise keeping, courage, rights, and duties.[1] Sometime later we add political concepts to our moral repertoire: we speak of law, liberty, and democratic ideals. We need much more detailed moral opinions when we actually confront a wide variety of moral challenges in family, social, commercial, and political life. We form these through interpretation of our abstract concepts that is mainly unreflective. We unreflectively interpret each in the light of the others. That is, interpretation knits values together. We are morally responsible to the degree that our various concrete interpretations achieve an overall integrity so that each supports the others in a network of value that we embrace authentically. To the extent that we fail in that interpretive project—and it seems impossible wholly to succeed—we are not acting fully out of conviction, and so we are not fully responsible.

That is the burden of this chapter. If its conclusions are sound, we need to ask new questions. What makes one interpretation of fairness or generosity or justice better than another? Does it make sense to suppose a best—or true—interpretation of a moral concept? In Chapter 7 I will approach these questions by setting them in a wider context. We study interpretation in general—not just in morality but also across a wide range of interpretive genres that includes literature, history, and law. I argue that the interpretive process—the process of seeking meaning in an event or achievement or institution—differs in important ways from scientific investigation. If so, and if my claim is right that moral reasoning is best understood as the interpretation of moral concepts, we do well to treat moral reasoning not as sui generis but as a special case of a much more general interpretive method.

In Chapter 8 we will return to morality but with a different focus. If moral reasoning is interpretive of moral concepts, we need better to understand not just the nature of interpretation but the nature of such concepts. I suggest that we treat certain concepts as special by designating them as interpretive concepts whose nature cannot be explicated except through normative argument. If so, then moral philosophy is itself an interpretive project. I end Part Two by offering the moral theories of Plato and Aristotle as classic examples of moral philosophy so understood.

Types of Responsibility

Responsibility is an indispensable concept across our intellectual life. It is a tricky concept because we use the words "responsibility" and "responsible" in so many different and easily confused ways. First, we must distinguish responsibility as a virtue from responsibility as a relation between people and events. We say, in the virtue sense, that someone behaved responsibly or irresponsibly in acting as he did on some occasion (he acted responsibly in refusing the offer), or that it is or is not characteristic of him to behave responsibly (he is, in general, a highly responsible, or irresponsible, person). We say, in the relational sense, that someone is or is not responsible for some event or consequence (he alone is responsible for the company's turn into profit). We make further distinctions among types of responsibility in the first, virtue, sense: we distinguish intellectual, practical, ethical, and moral responsibility. A scientist who does not check his calculations lacks intellectual responsibility; a writer who does not back up his files lacks practical responsibility; someone who lives aimlessly lacks ethical responsibility; a voter who votes for a vice presidential candidate because he finds her sexy lacks moral responsibility. A political leader who sends a nation to war on plainly inadequate intelligence is irresponsible in all four ways.

We make a variety of distinctions within relational responsibility as well. A person is causally responsible for an event, we say, if some act of his figures (or figures substantially) in the best causal explanation of that event. I would be causally responsible for an injury to a blind beggar if I shoved him to steal his money or collided with him absentmindedly or while drunk or deranged or even just accidentally. But not when someone else has pushed me into him, because then no act of mine has contributed to the injury. (My body is part of the causal chain, but I am not.) Someone has assignment responsibility for some matter if it is his duty to attend to or look after it. The last person to leave a room, we say, is responsible for turning off the lights, and the sergeant is responsible for his platoon. Someone has liability responsibility for an event when he is required to repair, compensate for, or absorb any damage flowing from the event. I have liability responsibility for the damage I cause by my careless driving; an employer may have liability responsibility for any damage his employees cause. Causal, assignment, and liability responsibility are all, finally, to be distinguished from judgmental responsibility. Someone has judgmental responsibility for some act if it is appropriate to rank his act on some scale of praise or criticism. I have judgmental responsibility for walking past the beggar, giving him nothing, but not for the harm when someone else pushes me into him. These different senses of relational responsibility are conceptually independent: an employer may have liability responsibility for damage caused by his employees' negligence even though he is neither causally nor judgmentally responsible for that damage.

In this chapter we consider moral responsibility as a virtue. We begin with one aspect of that virtue. Morally responsible people act in a principled rather than an unprincipled way; they act out of rather than in spite of their convictions.[2] What does that mean? I ignore, though only to postpone, a familiar problem. Any account of moral responsibility must at some point face what philosophers call the free will challenge. If every decision anyone makes is fully determined by prior events over which he has no control, if full knowledge of the state of the world before someone is born, together with full knowledge of the laws of nature, would enable a computer to predict every decision he makes throughout his life, then it might seem that moral responsibility is always only an illusion, that it makes no sense to distinguish acting out of conviction from acting for any other reason. Everyone thinks or does what he is fated to think or do, and that is the end of the matter. I face that challenge in Chapter 10. We can assess judgmental responsibility from two perspectives: from within the experiential lives people lead, taking at face value the fact, inescapable from that perspective, that people have fresh decisions to make, or from a more Archimedean scientific perspective that treats their experiential lives as only part of the data for which a causal explanation should be sought. I argue in that chapter that the first perspective is appropriate when judgmental responsibility is at issue, and I make that assumption for the balance of this chapter.

Morally Responsible Action

Ways Not to Be Responsible

Count the ways in which someone might fail to act out of the principles he professes. The most obvious is crude insincerity. The leader who takes his country to war pretending to follow principles that in fact have no grip on him, principles that he has no intention of following when it is inconvenient for him to do so, is crudely insincere. He pays only lip service to the principles he offers as justification. Rationalization is a more complex phenomenon: someone rationalizes who genuinely believes that his conduct is governed by principles that in fact play no effective role in explaining what he actually decides to do. He votes for politicians who promise to end welfare programs and justifies his vote by telling himself that people should take responsibility for their own fates. But that principle plays no role in guiding his behavior on other occasions: when he appeals to the politicians he helped elect for a bailout for his industry, for example. His behavior is in fact determined by self-interest, not any principle that recognizes the importance of other people's lives. His alleged commitment does not promise evenhandedness, because he will follow the principles he cites only when these serve his own interests.

There are many other ways in which moral responsibility can be compromised. Someone might hold faithfully to moral principles of great abstraction but yield to self-interest or to some other parallel influence in deciding how these abstract principles apply to concrete cases. He may think that preventative war is always immoral unless absolutely necessary, but he may not have reflected on what "necessary" means in this context: whether it means unless preventative war is essential to save a nation from annihilation, for example, or, perhaps at the other extreme, necessary to protect a nation from trade competition that would compromise its citizens' standard of living. His conviction, vague though it is, may play a role in his decision whether to support a particular foreign policy. But it cannot play as full or consequential a role as a tighter principle or a principle supplemented by other pertinent convictions would do. The porosity of his principle allows some other part of his personal history—perhaps something as simple as his party affiliation—to play a more effective role in explaining his behavior than the abstract principle does.

Moral schizophrenia compromises responsibility in a still different way: someone feels himself committed to two contradictory principles and succumbs to whichever of the two comes into his mind at the moment, even when this is against his interests and more stable inclinations. He thinks, for example, both that people who have become rich deserve to keep what they have earned and that comfortable members of a community have a duty to help care for the neediest of their fellow citizens. He supports tax reductions when his mind is on the deserving rich but opposes them when his mind is on the wretched poor. He is morally irresponsible: his behavior is not even-handed but arbitrary and whimsical.

Very few people are so evidently schizophrenic as that, but almost everyone contradicts himself in a more subtle way: through moral compartmentalization. We have convictions about Middle East politics, the proper justifications for war, permissible acts in war, self-defense on city streets, abortion, capital punishment, fair trials, how the local police should behave, the character and limits of personal responsibility for the consequences of one's acts, a fair distribution of a community's collective wealth, patriotism, loyalty to one's friends and the limits of that loyalty, the nature of personal courage, and the importance of wealth, knowledge, experience, family, and achievement in making a life a good, successful life rather than a bad, wasted one. We have convictions about all these things, and our convictions may be locally sincere and effective. We may act out of these convictions on the occasions when each is directly relevant: when we ask ourselves whether the invasion of Iraq was immoral, for example, or whether taxes should be raised or lowered, or whether we should take up skiing. But when we step back we may find that the coherence of our convictions is *only* local, that the principles or ideals that govern one compartment are at war with, or anyway disconnected from, those that govern another.

The degree of potential conflict depends on how narrow our compartments are. I may have powerful convictions about the Iraq war, but if these
do not match my convictions about other military incursions—in Kosovo or
Bosnia, for example—then my views about Iraq are more likely to be explained by my dislike of the Bush administration or my party affiliation. The
moral responsibility I show by voting out of my sincere conviction may be
only skin deep. More subtle—and debatable—contradictions appear when
we compare convictions across larger categories. We have instincts and convictions, I said, about the special loyalty we owe to family and friends and the
limits of that loyalty. We may and should, as individuals, show greater concern for the well-being of family and friends than we show for strangers. But
there are limits to that special concern: we may not subject strangers to risks of
grave injury that we would not accept for ourselves or those close to us. Those
are our moral convictions, but we may betray them in the political policies we
support. We may think it right to subject foreigners to injuries and risks of
injustice to which we would not expose our own citizens, as many Americans
did in approving our treatment of the prisoners in Guantánamo Bay.

These possibly contradictory convictions cut across the boundary between
personal and political convictions. Now consider convictions drawn from
categories that seem even further separated—convictions about political and
personal virtue, for instance. It is quite common just now to say that terrorist
atrocities show the need for a new balance between liberty and security: that
we must curtail the individual rights we normally respect in our criminal process in the interest of greater protection from the terrorist menace. But does
that opinion match our convictions about the character and value of personal
courage? Courage, we think, requires that we accept increased risks in order to
respect principle.

Now notice convictions drawn from compartments yet further separated:
political justice and personal standards. Suppose I embrace, self-consciously
or by instinct, a roughly utilitarian account of distributive justice that makes
justice depend on advancing some collective social goal like making the community richer or happier on balance. But I myself, in my personal ambitions
and accounting, do not rate wealth or even happiness high: I might think
that certain achievements are much more important than happiness in making a success of my life. Or suppose I insist on an egalitarian redistribution of
a community's wealth without regard to whether recipients are able and willing to work. I say that people's industry and dispositions for work are them-

selves created by social conditions and that it is therefore improper to deny someone a decent life just because he is lazy. But I adopt very different standards in criticizing myself: I struggle against sloth, and I blame myself when I fail to achieve what I set out to do.

Each of these various examples of apparent conflict or compartmentalization of principles is of course subject to reexamination. The conflict may be dissolved by further reflection or discussion. I may think, or decide after further thought, that the differences between the political situations in the Balkans and in Iraq justify my differing views about intervention in the two regions; that political officials have different and greater responsibilities to their citizens than we as individuals have to our own families; that courage is distinct from foolhardiness in a way that shows that our treatment of terrorist suspects is not cowardly; that a theory of justice may properly rest on assumptions about well-being and responsibility that those who embrace the theory would not accept in their private lives. If I do think so, or decide so after reflection, then my moral personality is more complex and has greater unity than at first appeared. But this is hardly inevitable: it might be that further reflection would instead reveal my inability to unify my apparently conflicting convictions through distinguishing principles that I could also claim wholeheartedly to accept. If so, then I have discovered a further shortfall in my moral responsibility. It is not deep conviction but something else— self-interest, perhaps, or conformity or just intellectual laziness—that best explains how I treat other people in at least some circumstances, and I therefore deny them the respect that moral responsibility is meant to provide. I do not, after all, treat others in a principled way.

Filters

We can summarize these various threats to responsibility in a metaphor. Imagine that your effective moral convictions—convictions that exert some control over what you do—bind together as a filter surrounding your decision-making will. Insincere convictions and rationalizations are not effective convictions and so have no place in that filter, but abstract, contradictory, and compartmentalized convictions are and do. Your personal history explains, let us assume, which effective convictions are part of that filter: they explain why you have developed those convictions rather than the different convictions that other people with different personal histories have developed.

Personal history also explains the great variety of other inclinations and attitudes you have—emotions, preferences, tastes, and prejudices—that might
also influence your decisions. Moral responsibility requires that these other
influences pass through the filter of effective convictions so that they are
censored and shaped by those convictions, as light passed through a filter is
censored and shaped.

Insincere convictions and rationalizations, as I just said, can play no part
in that filter. Porous effective convictions play some role, but because they are
porous their protection is incomplete. If I believe only that preventative war
is wrong unless it is necessary, and have no more detailed convictions about
what necessity means in this context, then my decision whether to support or
oppose a war may reflect unfiltered personal history like party affiliation or
political ambition. Flatly contradictory convictions, like the opinions that
the rich are entitled to keep what they have earned and that the community
is obliged to do what is necessary to help the poor, provide almost no filter
even when each is sincerely held, because the choice between them, on any
particular occasion, will be determined not by principle but by other, unfiltered influences. Convictions whose inconsistency is hidden in compartmentalization are also ineffective filters, even though they are not nakedly capri-
cious in that way, because compartmentalization allows unfiltered influences
decisively to define and distinguish departments. Inconsistency across departments of moral personality shows inattention, rather than genuine respect
and concern for others, and permits what further examination shows to be
arbitrary difference rather than principled distinctions.

Our moral responsibility requires us to try to make our reflective convictions into as dense and effective a filter as we can and in that way to claim as
much force as possible for conviction within the more general causal matrix
of our personal history as a whole. This requires that we seek a thorough coherence of value among our convictions. It also requires that we seek authenticity in the convictions that cohere: we must find convictions that grip us
strongly enough to play the role of filters when we are pressed by competing
motives that also flow from our personal histories. Our convictions are initially unformed, compartmentalized, abstract, and therefore porous. Responsibility requires us critically to interpret the convictions that seem initially
most appealing or natural—to seek understandings and specifications of these
initially appealing convictions with those two goals of integrity and authenticity in mind. We interpret each of these convictions, so far as we can, in the

light of the others and also in the light of what feels natural to us as a suitable way to live our lives. In that way we aim both to expand and thicken the effective filter. Much of the rest of this book is an illustration of how we might pursue that responsibility project.

Responsibility and Philosophy

I mean to describe how the mental life of a fully responsible person could be pictured, not the moral phenomenology of a responsible person. It must be plain by now, however, that the goal of responsibility would be impossible to achieve fully, even if we set out self-consciously to achieve it. We cannot hope to construct a dense, detailed, interwoven, wholly coherent filter of conviction wrapped around our will that is effective without exception and that brings us a constant glow of fittingness. That would be the achievement of Kant's man of perfectly good will, and no one is that intelligent, imaginative, and good. So we must treat moral responsibility as a work always in progress: someone is responsible who accepts moral integrity and authenticity as appropriate ideals and deploys a reasonable effort toward achieving them. In principle this must be an individual effort, not only because each person's initial convictions are somewhat different from everyone else's, but because only the person whose settled convictions they become can gauge their authenticity for him. But it would be absurd to expect everyone to engage in the kind of philosophical reflection that any full-blown attempt at moral responsibility would demand. So moral interpretation, like so much else of high importance, is a matter for social formation and also for division of labor.

As I emphasize in later chapters, a community's language and culture, and the occasions these present for conversational exploration and collective thought, play an inevitable and indispensable role in anyone's search for his own responsibility. Moral and political philosophers have their own role to play in that culture. It falls to them—though not only to them—to try to construct self-conscious articulate systems of value and principle out of widely shared but disparate moral inclinations, reactions, ambitions, and traditions. They must try to establish connections and to winnow out inconsistencies across familiar families and departments of morality and ethics, making theory at once more abstract and detailed, broader and more widely integrated. In that way a school or group of philosophers who share roughly similar general moral attitudes might hope together to provide a template of what responsibility requires for people with those general attitudes: a template of liberal responsibility, for example. Such templates are valuable to other people who are reflective and well disposed to moral responsibility, either because they already hold the same general values or because they find those values newly attractive when presented in that integrated way. Even those who reject a particular philosophical template can nevertheless discover in its structures what moral responsibility would require for them out of their different convictions.

In that way moral philosophy can influence people; it can make them more responsible as individuals. Village-idiot skeptics mock what they take to be philosophy's pretensions: they say that a moral philosopher never converts anyone who begins with a different moral instinct or education. That claim is as silly as the opposite claim that every philosopher invariably convinces anyone who listens to him. No doubt the truth lies somewhere in between, and it would take a pointlessly grand empirical program even to give us some idea where in between it lies. But the role we are now imagining for philosophy is anyway immune from the complaint, because that role makes no claims about radical conversion. Indeed, philosophy would have an important role to play on this account even if, as seems unbelievable, it actually never dramatically changed anyone's opinion or behavior. For a community or a culture has moral responsibilities of its own: its collective arrangements must show a disposition toward realizing that responsibility. Whatever the Athenians thought, history has made Socrates an ornament to Athens.

Indeed, it is easier to understand philosophy's ambitions, and test its achievements, on the space of responsibility than that of truth. Kant's moral philosophy, for example, is best understood in those terms. As John Rawls emphasized in his lectures on Kant, that philosopher did not suppose himself to have discovered fresh truths about moral duties.[3] His various formulations of the categorical imperative were in the spirit of the responsibility project I described. Being able to universalize the maxim of our conduct is hardly a test of truth; different agents will produce different schemes responding to that requirement. But it is a test of responsibility, or at least an important part of such a test, because it provides the coherence that responsibility asks. It also tests the authenticity that responsibility demands: Kant said we must be able to will as well as imagine the universality of a maxim. Politics is for most people among their most important moral theaters and challenges. So a community's political philosophy is a major part of its conscience and claim to collective moral responsibility.

These last few paragraphs might be open to a misunderstanding I have been helpfully warned to avoid.[4] I do not suggest what is patently false: that moral philosophers have a more accurate moral sense than ordinary people do. The philosopher's assignment is more explicit, but his concrete judgments are not necessarily more sensitive. Nor is ordinary moral judgment innocent of philosophy: people's opinions about good and bad, right and wrong, reflect a generally intuitive sense of how a host of more concrete moral concepts relate to one another. In Chapter 8 I try to explain why it is difficult to account for moral agreement or disagreement on any other assumption.

The Value of Responsibility

Responsibility so understood is impossible to achieve fully. But why does responsibility matter? Of course it matters to us individually. Anyone who cares about acting as he should must aim to act coherently out of principle. But why do we care that others act responsibly? We care about what they do: we want them to act properly. But why should we care, independently, whether they act out of conviction or for some other reason? Consider two imaginary leaders of democracies, both of whom bring their nations into war in the Middle East. Each says that he acts to free an oppressed people from a savage dictator. One is sincere: he believes that powerful nations have a duty to liberate oppressed people, and he would not have committed his nation to war had he not thought the population oppressed. The second is insincere: he goes to war because he thinks it important that his nation have greater control over the oil resources of the region. His appeal to a moral duty is only window dressing: if the nation he attacks had not been oppressed by a dictator, he would have invented some other excuse. (These descriptions are so crude that I need not add that I have no actual politicians in mind.) One, we say, has acted responsibly, even if wrongly; the other has not acted responsibly, and we despise him. Why is the difference so important?

It might be tempting to think that people who follow some principle rigorously, rather than acting on impulse or for their own narrow advantage, are more likely to do what is in fact the right thing. But that assumption is not justified: there are more mistaken convictions than sound ones. Indeed, people who act out of mistaken principle are sometimes more dangerous than those who only feign principle: the latter act wrongly only when this is to their advantage and hence can more easily be deterred by fear of political retribution or criminal prosecution. Why do we nevertheless praise sincerity as valuable for its own sake? We cannot say that when sincere people are in the right they are guided by moral truth, while insincere people can be right only by accident. We have rejected the causal impact hypothesis: even sincere people's convictions never stand causally downstream of moral truth.

The sincere leader's behavior, let us for now assume, is caused by his beliefs about the moral duty of powerful nations. No moral conviction figures in any causal explanation of the insincere leader's behavior. But even if we grant this, the causal role of conviction cannot be exhaustive or even particularly deep. We can explain why the sincere leader invaded by citing his conviction. But we must then ask why he came to have that conviction rather than the different convictions many other people have, and our answer to that question will end in the expanded personal history I described, or in some supposition about what we would find if we knew that history in more refined detail. If we go far enough back in the causal chain, that is, we find that culture, education, genes, and even perhaps self-interest play much the same role, finally, in explaining the behavior of sincere and insincere people. If the sincere leader had been educated in a different culture or family, or perhaps if his genes were differently arranged, he might well have thought that powerful nations have a duty not to intervene in the affairs of other people, even to save them from a savage dictatorship. So the behaviors of the sincere and the hypocritical leaders have a parallel deep causal origin. Why is it so important that in one case the causal route runs, toward the end, through a filter of conviction, while in the other it does not?

In Chapter 7 I will propose a connection between morality and ethics. In brief: we try to act out of moral conviction in our dealings with other people because that is what our own self-respect requires. It requires this because we cannot consistently treat our own lives as objectively important unless we accept that everyone's life has the same objective importance. We can—and do—expect others to accept that fundamental principle of humanity. It is, we think, the basis of civilization. But we know that many other people draw very different conclusions from ours about what further moral convictions the principle entails. In Parts Four and Five I defend a detailed view of its implications, but that view is and will remain controversial. Only a minority of Americans now accept, for instance, that the fundamental principle requires even a roughly equal distribution of a political community's wealth. Community and civility nevertheless require a high level of tolerance: we cannot treat everyone who disagrees with us as a moral outlaw. We must respect the contrary opinions of those who accept the equal importance of all human lives but who disagree with us, in good faith, about what that means in practice. We must respect them, however, only so far as they accept the burden of responsibility we have canvassed in this chapter, because only then do they *really* accept that equal importance. Only then do they try to act consistently with what they take, rightly or wrongly, to be its demands.

The most vulnerable members of any community are likely to benefit most by our treating responsibility as a distinct virtue and requirement, because they are most likely to suffer when people do not give everyone the advantage of principles they generally endorse. But everyone benefits in a more diffuse way by living in a community that, by insisting on responsibility, signals a basic shared respect even in the face of moral diversity. These benefits are particularly important in politics, because politics are coercive and the stakes are invariably high and often mortal. No one can sensibly expect that his officials will act always out of principles that he himself thinks right, but he can expect his officials to act out of the principles they themselves endorse. We feel cheated when we suspect corruption, political self-interest, bias, favoritism, or whimsy. We feel cheated of what those in power owe those subject to that power: responsibility that expresses equal concern for all. Nothing in these social and political values of responsibility is undermined by the further assumption I said might seem to threaten moral responsibility: that even sincere people's convictions are causally explained not by encounters with truth but by a varied and contingent personal history.

Responsibility and Truth

Evidence, Case, and Ground

Morally responsible people may not achieve truth, but they seek it. It might seem, however, that the interpretive account of responsibility compromises that search. Responsibility seeks coherence and integration. But the truth about morality, some philosophers think, is crowded with conflict and compromise: moral values are plural and incommensurate. So insisting on coherence, they say, blinds us to obdurate conflict that is really just there.[5]

Is responsibility therefore misconceived? I began this chapter by distinguishing responsibility from truth. Now we must consider how these two virtues are connected. In Chapter 4, in the course of an argument against the causal impact hypothesis, I used a philosopher's term: I said that moral properties "supervene" on ordinary properties. I must now say more about what that means and entails. Judgments about the physical and mental world can be *barely* true in the following sense. We can imagine another world that is now exactly like ours in every detail of its present composition save one: in place of the black pen on your desk in this world, on the otherwise identical desk of a person otherwise identical to you in that other world, the pen is blue. Nothing else need now be different in the two worlds in consequence of which those pens, otherwise exactly alike, are of different colors. Physical facts like that one can stand alone: that is what it means to say that they can be barely true.

That is not the case with moral and other value judgments, however. They cannot be barely true; if two worlds differ in some value they must differ in some other, nonevaluative, way as well. There cannot be another world just like this one except that in that world *The Marriage of Figaro* is trash or that in that world it is morally permissible to torture babies for fun. That would indeed be possible if value judgment were a matter of perceiving value particles. Then it would make perfect sense to suppose that moral judgments can be barely true: that they could be true in one world but false in another one otherwise exactly alike if morons were configured differently in the two worlds. But there are no moral particles or anything else whose bare existence can make a value judgment true. Values are not like rocks that we might stumble across in the dark. They are not just stubbornly there.

When a value judgment is true, there must be a *reason* why it is true. It can't be *just* true. That is not necessarily the case in science. Our scientists aim to find the most fundamental and embracing laws of physics, biology, and psychology that they can. But we must accept the possibility—or in any case the sense of the idea—that at some point in the scarcely imaginable future the possibility of further explanation will give out: that at some point it would be correct to say, "That's just the way things are." We may say this too early or with only error in hand. Scientists may one day find the comprehensive principles they seek: a principle of physics, perhaps, that explains everything physical and encapsulates biology and psychology as well. Or their search for unifying principles may turn out to be misconceived. The universe might be finally untidy: as Einstein put it, God might have missed an opportunity for elegance. There may be a way the world had to be. Or perhaps not; perhaps it might have been different. All that remains to be seen—or not, depending on the survival and improvement of intelligent creatures.

In any case it makes sense to think there is a way the world just is and therefore a theoretical end to explanation. In his lectures on quantum electrodynamics to a general audience, the physicist Richard Feynman said, "The next reason that you might think you do not understand what I am telling you is, while I am describing to you *how* Nature works, you won't understand *why* Nature works that way. But you see, nobody understands that. I can't explain why Nature behaves in this peculiar way . . . So I hope you can accept Nature as She is—absurd."[6]

Can you imagine a moral philosopher speaking that way? "I will tell you *how* morality works—progressive income taxes are wicked—but no one can understand *why* they are wicked. You must understand Morality as She is—absurd." It is always appropriate to ask why morality requires what we say it does, and never appropriate to say: it just does. Very often, of course, we cannot say much more than that. We might say: "Torture just is wrong, and that's all there is to it." But this is only impatience or lack of imagination: it expresses not responsibility but its opposite.

True, single-minded philosophers sometimes offer their moral opinions in the form of an axiomatic system: some utilitarians say, for instance, that all our obligations flow from a most basic obligation to do whatever will produce the greatest surplus of pleasure over pain in the long run. But when other philosophers make trouble by producing apparent counterexamples—by pointing out, for instance, that this supposed basic obligation might require inflicting intense torture on one or a few innocent people to avoid a tiny inconvenience to billions of others—those utilitarians try to find reasons why their principle would not have that consequence.[7] Or they try to modify it so that it would not, or they argue that adhering to their principle even when it has such unappealing consequences is nevertheless justified for some other reason: in order to respect the equal importance of all human lives, for example. They do not say: "It is too bad that our principle has such consequences but that is how the cookie crumbles. Our principle is just, as it happens, true." We would be appalled if they did: it makes sense to ask for support even for a very abstract moral principle, and in some circumstances it would be irresponsible not to try to provide one. Once again, philosophers' habit of claiming "intuitions" might mislead us. In its innocent use, the claim is only a statement of conviction. It might also suggest an inability to provide a further reason for that conviction. But it should not be meant or understood to deny the possibility of a further reason.

Here is the same point through a different distinction. In the formal and informal sciences we seek *evidence* for propositions, and in the domain of value we make a *case* for propositions. Evidence signals the likelihood—perhaps the extreme likelihood—of a further fact. But it does not help to constitute that further fact or make it true. The further fact it signals is entirely independent: it is genuinely another fact. If there is water on some planet in a distant galaxy, then the proposition that there is water there is true. What makes it true— what supplies, we might say, the ground of its truth—is the water there. We may well have evidence of its truth, in the form of spectrographic data, but it would be a silly mistake to think that that evidence *made* the proposition true.

We cannot, however, make the same distinction in the case of moral judgment. Suppose we think that America's invasion of Iraq was immoral and we offer, as part of our case, that the Bush administration was culpably negligent in relying on faulty intelligence. If we are right, the administration's negligence is not evidence of some further, independent fact of immorality that we might establish in some other way. It is part of what makes the war immoral. The distinction is easy to illustrate in law. When the prosecutor shows the jury fingerprints, he is introducing evidence that the accused was at the scene. When he cites a precedent to show that the law does not recognize a particular defense, he is making a case for that conclusion. The precedent is not evidence of a further and independent legal fact. If the prosecutor's case is sound, the precedent he cites helps to make his claim true.

The first distinction I drew explains the second. Because value judgments cannot be barely true, they can be true only in virtue of a case. The judgment that the law does not permit a particular defense, or that invading Iraq was immoral, can be true only if there is an adequate case in law or morals that supports it. Given Hume's principle, that case must contain further value judgments—about the right understanding of the doctrine of precedent or about the responsibilities of political officials. None of those further value judgments can be barely true either. They can be true only if a further case can be made supporting each of them, and that further case will ramify into a host of other judgments about law and blame that cannot themselves be barely true but need yet further cases to show them true if they are true. How can this process of justification come to an end? Any actual person's attempt to justify a moral judgment will of course come to an end soon, no matter how energetic and conscientious he is, in exhaustion or lack of time or imagination. He can then say no more than that he "sees" its truth. But when *must* a moral justification end because there is no more to say? It cannot end in the discovery of some master fundamental principle that is itself barely true, in some foundational statement about how things just are. There are no moral particles, and so there is no such principle.

The best we can say is: the argument ends when it meets itself, if it ever does. We can elaborate the metaphor I used earlier. If you organized all your moral convictions into an ideally effective filter encapsulating your will, they would form a large interconnected and interdependent system of principles and ideas. You could defend any part of that network only by citing some other part, until you had somehow managed to justify all parts in terms of the rest. Justifying your condemnation of the Iraq war might in that way include, at some point in an extraordinarily extended account, appealing to principles about negligence in personal matters, trustworthiness as a virtue, and caginess as a vice, and then to further principles purportedly justifying each of these convictions, and so on nearly forever. The truth of any true moral judgment consists in the truth of an indefinite number of other moral judgments. And its truth provides part of what constitutes the truth of any of those others. There is no hierarchy of moral principles built on axiomatic foundations; we rule that out when we dismiss morons from our ontology.

How vast a vast network of conviction should we imagine? Morality is only one department of value, only one dimension of conviction about what ought to be. We also have convictions about what is beautiful, for instance, and what it is to live well. Morality itself has departments: we distinguish personal from political morality and the morality of obligation, right and wrong from the morality of virtue and vice. Is there any limit to the range of convictions to which we might appeal in making a case that some action is morally right or morally wrong? Or that someone is virtuous or vicious, or that something is beautiful or ugly, or that some life is successful or unsuccessful? Could a case for the unfairness of affirmative action include an aesthetic judgment as well as a moral one? Could a case for the right way to live include claims about the natural evolution of the universe or about the biological heritage of animals in human beings?[8] I see no conceptual or a priori reason why not. What can count as an argument for a moral conviction is a substantive matter: we must wait to see what connections among different departments of value seem pertinent and appealing.

Conflicts in Value?

But might we not discover conflict as well as coherence in our constructions? Some distinctions are necessary. We must distinguish, first, values from desiderata. Values have judgmental force. We ought to be honest and not cruel, and we have behaved badly if we are cruel or dishonest. Desiderata, on the contrary, are what we want but do no wrong not to have. Or not to have as much of as we might. Desiderata almost always conflict: I like lemonade and lemon tart, but I have only one lemon. A community wants the highest level of security, the best educational system, the most efficient transport network, and the best available health care. But its budget is tight.

The serious and important question is whether values conflict with one another. Values often conflict with desiderata. Some steps we might take to improve safety from terrorists, which we certainly desire, would compromise liberty or honor. Some apparent conflicts of that sort may dissolve on further study. We may find that a better understanding of liberty shows that the measures that improve security do not compromise liberty after all. But sometimes further study reinforces the conflict: a nation's honor is indeed sacrificed when alleged terrorists are tortured. There is no moral conflict in such cases, however, because morality requires that we give up whatever security our dishonor would achieve.

Moral conflict—conflict between two values—is our worry now. Richard Fallon describes an awkward situation.[9] A colleague asks you to comment on a draft of his book, and you find it bad. You will be cruel if you are frank but dishonest if you are not. Two questions arise. First, does it follow that there is no right answer to the question what you should do? That the case for honesty is neither stronger nor weaker than the case for kindness in these circumstances? Second, even if there is a right answer to that question, must you necessarily have compromised some moral value whatever you do? Does doing the right thing in such circumstances, all things considered, mean nevertheless doing something bad? Do kindness and honesty really conflict?

The first question raises the issues of Chapter 5. I urged the importance of distinguishing uncertainty from indeterminacy, and that distinction is essential here. Of course you might be uncertain whether it is better—or perhaps less bad—to be cruel or dishonest in these circumstances. But I cannot imagine what ground you could have for the alternate conclusion that neither would be better. There are no bare moral facts: moral reasoning, as I said, means drawing on a nested series of convictions about value, each of which could in turn draw on still other such convictions. What ground could you have for thinking that you would never see a reason, no matter how long you wrestled with the issue, why one choice of conflicting values in one set of circumstances is morally preferable to the other choice? What ground could you have for the even more ambitious hypothesis that there is no such reason to discover?

Turn to the second question. Is there really a conflict here at all? Do honesty and kindness really conflict, even from time to time? If I am to sustain my main claims in this book, about the unity of value, I must deny the conflict. For my claim is not just that we can bring our discrete moral judgments into some kind of reflective equilibrium—we could do that even if we conceded that our values conflict, by adopting some priorities for values or some set of principles for adjudicating conflicts in particular cases. I want to defend the more ambitious claim that there are no genuine conflicts in value that need such adjudication. It is, I agree, natural to say in a case like Fallon's that we are torn between kindness and honesty. We might disagree, however, as to why it seems natural.

Here is one story. Moral responsibility is never complete: we are constantly reinterpreting our concepts as we use them. We must put them to work day by day even though we have not yet refined them fully to achieve the integration we seek. Our working understanding of the concepts of cruelty and dishonesty is good enough for most cases: it allows us comfortably to identify and, with a good will, avoid both vices. But sometimes, as in this case, that working understanding seems to pull us in opposite directions. We can do no better at this stage than to admit this by reporting an apparent conflict. It doesn't follow that the conflict is deep and genuine, however. Just now I distinguished two questions. What is the right thing to do? Is the apparent conflict real? These questions cannot be so independent as my distinction suggested. The first question requires us to think further, and the way we think further is to further refine our conceptions of the two values. We ask whether it is really cruel to tell an author the truth. Or whether it is really dishonest to tell him what it is in his interests to hear and no one's interests to suppress. However we describe the process of thought through which we decide what to do, these are the questions that, in substance, we face. We reinterpret our concepts to resolve our dilemma: the direction of our thought is toward unity, not fragmentation. However we decide, we have taken a step toward a more integrated understanding of our moral responsibilities.

On this story, apparent conflict is inevitable but, we can hope, only illusory and temporary. We confront it at retail, case by case, but we confront it through a conceptual rearrangement that works toward eliminating it. What other story might one tell? Consider this one: "Moral conflict is real, and any theory that denies this is false to moral reality. Once we understand the nature of kindness and of honesty, we see that, in cases like this one, they just *do* conflict. That conflict is not an illusion produced by incomplete moral interpretation; it is a matter of plain fact." But what in the world could that supposed plain fact consist in? Kindness and honesty cannot *just* have one content or another, because moral claims cannot be barely true. I repeat tediously: no moral particles fix what these virtues just are. Nor do the concepts have a precise and conflicting content just in virtue of linguistic practice. Moral concepts are (as I have already begun to call them) interpretive concepts: their correct use is a matter of interpretation, and people who use them disagree about what the best interpretation is. Many people do believe that it would be an act of kindness to tell your colleague the truth. Or that it would not be dishonest, in this circumstance, to trim. They are not making a linguistic mistake.

There is another possibility. It might be that for some reason the best interpretation of our values *requires* that they conflict: that they serve our underlying moral responsibilities best if we conceive them in such a way that from time to time we must compromise one to serve another. Values don't conflict just because they do, but because they work best for us when we conceptualize them so that they do. That is a conceivable view, and perhaps someone might make it seem plausible. That would not, however, show that conflict is just a stubborn fact we must recognize. It would provide an interpretation that reconciles values in a different way: by showing conflict as a deeper collaboration.

Do We Need Truth?

We have reached the foothills of full value holism—the hedgehog's faith that all true values form an interlocking network, that each of our convictions about what is good or right or beautiful plays some role in supporting each of our other convictions in each of those domains of value. We can seek truth about morality only by pursuing coherence endorsed by conviction. We cannot will ourselves to embrace some conviction simply because it fits and unifies the rest of our convictions. We must also believe it or find something else that fits that we do believe. Equally, we cannot rest satisfied with convictions we find we believe if they do not fit. We must find convictions that we believe and that do fit. That is an interpretive process, as I said, because it seeks to understand each part and strand of value in the light of other strands and parts. No one can manage this fully, and there is no guarantee that we will all be able, even together, to manage it very well.

I intend no kind of relativism. I do not suggest that a moral opinion is true only for those who think it true. I mean to describe method, not metaphysics: how you must proceed if truth is on your agenda. Two people who both reason responsibly and find conviction in what they believe will reach different conclusions about what is right and wrong. But they will share the belief that there is a getting it right and a getting it wrong about what is right and wrong. A third person may challenge that shared belief: he may think that the fact of their disagreement indicates that there is no truth to be had. But that is only a third position of the same kind, a third moral stance to assess. Perhaps the third contestant cannot convince the first two to abandon the belief they share. Then he is in the same position as they are: there is no philosophical safe harbor in the neighborhood. We must each believe what we responsibly believe. We are all out on some limb, even if it is not the same limb.

Why then talk about truth at all? Why not retire truth and speak only of responsibility? People seem more comfortable saying of some moral opinion not that it is true but that "it is true for me" or "it works for me." These are sometimes taken to be skeptical confessions, but they are better understood as claiming responsibility in lieu of truth. I said, earlier in this chapter, that the value of moral philosophy depends more on its contribution to responsibility than to truth. Why then not drop truth altogether? We could just make and criticize arguments. That would come to the same thing as seeking and claiming truth, but without raising hackles as the vocabulary of truth seems always to do.

We would purchase that peace at considerable cost, however. Explicitly declaring a lack of interest in truth would pass for skepticism, and that would encourage all the confusion we uncovered in Part One. Insisting on truth has more positive virtues as well. It keeps before us the deepest philosophical challenge of this domain: to make sense of the idea that there is unique success to be had in inquiry, even when that inquiry is interpretive rather than empirical or logical, even when that inquiry admits no demonstration and promises no convergence. External skepticism is no threat to that idea. Internal skepticism exploits it—as in the case of wine, for instance. We must not only make sense of unique success in interpretive inquiry but struggle to achieve it.

Perhaps the vocabulary of truth seems more appropriate in science because we can more sensibly expect convergence there. It is worth noticing, however, that if we are thorough realists about science, we are threatened with an especially deep kind of error that is no threat in morals or other genres of interpretation. In science, if the physical world is as it is no matter whether there is any reason to think it is that way, we may be in irretrievable error. Our beliefs may be wrong in spite of the fact that we could find no evidence that they are wrong. We might be in fundamental and uncorrectable error about events in some other universe, for example, or about events so far away that their light cannot reach us before our universe expires. But because the truth about morality just is what the best case shows, our moral convictions cannot be irretrievably mistaken. Our culture or education or other factors of personal history may prevent us from appreciating the best case. But people with different personal histories might well discover and appreciate it. Moral truth is always within human grasp in a way that scientific truth may not always be.

One final observation. Earlier I disparaged Archimedean second-order meta-ethics. I should therefore say that I understand these preliminary remarks about truth in morals as themselves part of first-order moral theory, albeit the most abstract part. My claims about truth are drawn from the substantive theory of moral responsibility offered in this chapter and also from Hume's principle, which is itself a thesis about moral responsibility. But my remarks are indeed only preliminary. We need to explore the idea of truth in morals further and more substantively; we do that at several points in the argument to come. First—immediately—as part of a wider inquiry into what interpretation is.

7

Interpretation in General

Interpretive Truth?

You are interpreting me as you read this text. Historians interpret events and epochs, psychoanalysts dreams, sociologists and anthropologists societies and cultures, lawyers documents, critics poems, plays, and pictures, priests and rabbis sacred texts, and philosophers contested concepts. Each of these genres of interpretation houses a large variety of apparently different activities. Lawyers interpret contracts, wills, statutes, chains of precedent, democracy, and the spirit of constitutions; they dispute how far the methods appropriate to each of these exercises hold good for the others. Critics in art and literature count, as interpretations, such very different claims as that the value of art lies in moral instruction, that Piero della Francesca's *The Risen Christ* is a pagan rather than a Christian painting, and that Shylock's Jessica betrayed her father because she hated being a Jew.

In this chapter we consider interpretation in general. I argue that all these genres and types of interpretation share important features that make it appropriate to treat interpretation as one of two great domains of intellectual activity, standing as a full partner beside science in an embracing dualism of understanding. I try to answer the following questions. Is there truth to be had in interpretation? Can we sensibly say that one lawyer's interpretation of the First Amendment, one critic's reading of Yeats's *Among School Children*, one historian's understanding of the meaning of the American Revolution, is true and all conflicting interpretations false? (Or, what comes to the same thing, that one is the soundest or most accurate and the others each to some degree less sound or accurate?)

Or must we say that there are no true or false or even most or least accurate interpretations of these objects but only different interpretations of them? If there is truth (or unique success) in interpretation, then in what does this truth (or unique success) consist? What makes one reading of Yeats's poem or the Constitution true or sound and others false or tinny? Is there some important difference between truth in interpretation and truth in science? Are these great domains of investigation sufficiently different in their structure to justify my large claim of an all-embracing dualism? Can the truth about interpretation take the form of internal skepticism? Can the unique truth be that there is no uniquely right interpretation but only a family of interpretations on a par with one another?

Of course, that we use a single word "interpretation" to describe all the apparently disparate genres I named is far from itself conclusive that they have some important feature in common. They may be related only by what Wittgenstein called "family resemblance": perhaps, that is, legal reasoning shares some feature with conversational interpretation that makes it appropriate to say that lawyers interpret statutes, and historical argument shares a different feature with conversational interpretation that makes it appropriate to say that historians interpret historical events, but legal reasoning and historical argument nevertheless share no feature in virtue of which they are both examples of interpretation.[1] Language is often misleading in that way: there may be nothing we can usefully call interpretation in general.[2]

Certainly there is no such thing as interpreting in general, that is, interpreting in the abstract rather than in some particular genre. Imagine that flashing dots of color suddenly appear on the wall in front of you as you read, and someone asks you to interpret those dots. You could not even make a beginning without some working assumptions about how the dots were created. You would have to decide whether to treat them as a coded message, perhaps from an extraterrestrial source, or as a light show designed by some artist, or as a template for a child's drawing lesson, or as created in some other way for some different purpose. Only then could you begin to construct an interpretation; you would need, that is, to take up a particular genre of interpretation before you could interpret at all. That might suggest that the different genres have little in common. However, there is one important contrary indication. We find it natural to report our conclusions, in each and every genre of interpretation, in the language of intention or purpose. We speak of the meaning or significance of a passage in a poem or a play, of the point of a clause in a particular statute, of the motives that produced a particular dream, of the ambitions or understandings that shaped an event or an age.

Ambivalence

In Part One we several times noticed people's characteristic ambivalence about their moral and other value judgments. We cannot resist thinking our moral convictions true, but many of us seem also unable to resist the contrary thought that that they can't *really* be true. We find the same phenomenon throughout interpretation. Interpreters seem characteristically to assume that an interpretation can be sound or unsound, correct or incorrect, true or false. We accuse some people of misinterpreting us or Yeats or the Renaissance or the Sale of Goods Act; we suppose that there is truth to be found or missed about the meaning of each of these objects of interpretation. We distinguish between an accurate interpretation and one that is admirable in some other way. A musician might find great pleasure in listening to a Glenn Gould performance of a Beethoven sonata, for example, but nevertheless think that as an interpretation of the sonata Gould's performance is a travesty. An American lawyer might wish that the equal protection clause could properly be interpreted as requiring states to spend as much educating students in poor neighborhoods as in rich ones, but agree that it cannot be so interpreted.[3]

True, in some contexts it would sound odd as well as unusual for an interpreter to claim a unique truth. A director or actor who offers a new interpretation of *Hamlet* need not (and better not) claim that his interpretation is the only correct one and that all other approaches to the play are wrong. (The idea that there is no one best way to perform *Hamlet* on the stage is an example, as I shall argue later in the chapter, of successful internal skepticism about productions of a classic.) But it would be equally odd for a critic who has devoted his life to understanding that play to add, in a coda to his great work, that his study is only one among many interesting approaches and that other approaches are equally valid. In some circumstances skepticism would seem not only odd but outrageous. Imagine a judge sending an accused criminal to jail, perhaps to death, or awarding a huge verdict against a civil defendant, and then conceding in the course of his opinion that other interpretations of the law that would have required contrary decisions are just as valid as his own. Or a friend who insists that you keep a burdensome promise though he concedes that a different interpretation of what you said, which contains no promise, would be an equally successful report of your meaning.

So at least in most cases the phenomenology of interpretation—how it feels to interpreters—includes a sense that interpretation aims at truth. An eminent critic of an earlier day, F. R. Leavis, emphasized the demand of sincerity in criticism and said that aiming at truth was of the essence: "A real critical judgment, of its very nature, always means to be more than merely personal . . . Essentially, a critical judgment has the form, 'This is so, isn't it?' "[4] Another, probably equally influential, critic, Cleanth Brooks, said, "I suppose that the practicing critic can never be too often reminded of the gap between his reading and the 'true' reading of the poem . . . The alternatives are desperate: either we say that one person's reading is as good as another . . . or else we take the lowest common denominator of the various readings that have been made."[5]

Nevertheless, just as some of us are uncomfortable flatly claiming truth for our moral convictions, many of us are uncomfortable making unqualified claims of truth for our interpretive judgments. Many lawyers, for example, who would be shocked to find the language I just imagined in a judge's opinion, are nevertheless also troubled when legal philosophers suggest that there is always one best interpretation of a legal provision or precedent and that all the other interpretations are wrong. They prefer locutions that avoid that flat claim. An academic lawyer might say, for example, that though a particular interpretation of the equal protection clause seems the best to him, he knows that others disagree, and he cannot say that there is only one correct interpretation or that those who disagree with him are simply mistaken.[6] That bizarre form of words makes no sense at all: if in his opinion one interpretation is best, then, also in his opinion, contrary interpretations are inferior and he contradicts himself when he asserts that some of them are not. But the popularity of such incoherent statements underscores the uncertainty many people feel about the truth-seeking status of interpretation.

External skepticism is, of course, a constant temptation: some critics delight in saying that there is never one correct reading of a poem or a play but only different ones that happen to appeal to different people. They think their skeptical posture is justified by the fact that eminent critics often disagree. But external skepticism is as confused in art as it is in law and morals. Once we take care to distinguish uncertainty from indeterminacy, we see that a skeptical interpretive claim—that there is no one right way to read the poem or the clause—is itself an interpretive claim. Global interpretive skepticism must be internal—a dramatically ambitious claim that could only be redeemed by a heroically ambitious theory. This striking parallel between ambivalence in interpretation and in moral conviction reinforces the claim I made in Chapter 6: that moral reasoning is interpretive. It also poses an immediate challenge for this chapter. I must try to show how the account of truth and responsibility I offered in Chapter 6 fits not only moral interpretation but interpretation in general and explains the ambivalence we find in both the larger and the narrower domains. I must also respond to the other questions and challenges I described.

Most interpreters assume, in some moods at least, that their interpretive judgments can be true or false. But in what can that truth or falsity consist? And how can it follow from the truth of one that another is false—rather than simply about something else? In many genres interpreters differ strikingly not only in the conclusions they reach but in the methods they use to reach those conclusions. In literary interpretation, for example, new tribes of critics emerge daily claiming an entirely different—and better—way to read Spencer or Kerouac: we are treated to psychodynamic readings, all-within-the-text readings, reader response readings, cultural myth readings, Marxist and feminist readings. Can we make any sense of the competition among these tribes? Competition not just for academic promotion or power but for accuracy? Or should we say that each tribe pursues a different project, so that there is no more competition between them than between a doctor and a financial advisor? Scholars can be in conflict, after all, only when they are trying to answer the same question, and though these scholars seem to take themselves to be disagreeing with one another, often heatedly, they also set out very different questions to answer.

The phenomenology of interpretation raises other puzzles as well. Often we are struck by a particular reading of a poem—it feels right—yet we have nothing to say in favor of our opinion to other people who have other opinions. Nothing to say, that is, beyond just pointing to some passage and waiting for the conversion to take place. In some genres interpretation is characteristically ineffable. We sense that some performance of a sonata or production of a play is right, that it brings out what is really in the work, but that sense far outruns our ability to explain why it is right. In the case of some genres, moreover, we feel that interpretation would be spoiled by any self-conscious attempt at justification. It might be deadening for a musician to try to explain in any detail just why an interpretation that seems right is right. Perhaps he really should—whatever this means—just let the music speak to and for him. We often fall back on troublesome metaphors and personifications like that one: we say that the right interpretation leaps from the page or that the sonata itself dictates how it must be played or—most common—that a skilled and sensitive interpreter just "sees" what a work of art means or says.

In spite of these hesitations and opaque metaphors, however, the distinctive truth-seeking and argumentative phenomenology of interpretation survives. Interpretation would be a radically different intellectual activity if interpreters did not characteristically claim truth and assume disagreement rather than only difference. The ineffability we sense is therefore troubling: it makes a poor match with truth. If our instincts are right, and one reading of Yeats or the equal protection clause really is better than another, then why can't we explain why it is? Interpretive judgments, like moral judgments, can't be barely true. It can't be just a brute fact with no further explanation that Shylock's Jessica betrays her father because she is ashamed of being a Jew. There must be some further explanation of why that is true, if it is true. What in the world could make it true?

Psychological States

One answer to that daunting but inescapable question has seemed, to some interpreters, compelling across the range of interpretive genres. This is the familiar psychological state theory of interpretation. It holds that interpretive claims are made true, when they are true, by actual or counterfactual facts about the mental states of one or more people. If Jessica did hate being a Jew, that is so only in virtue of Shakespeare's intention or assumption in writing her lines. If the equal protection clause forbids all racial quotas, that is so because the nineteenth-century authors of that clause, or the public for whom they acted, believed it would do that. If commerce rather than liberty was the moving ideal of the American Revolution, that is because a very large number of people who played central roles in that drama had commerce somehow in mind.

The mental states that make an interpretive claim true need not, on this view, be simple or even transparent to the people whose states they are. Shakespeare's intention might have been subconscious. The congressmen who adopted the Fourteenth Amendment might not have thought about affirmative-action racial quotas; it may only be true that they would have wanted their clause to forbid such quotas if they had thought about the matter. The thoughts that made commerce the point of a great revolution might have been made up by many hundreds of very different thoughts of many thousands of different people who were not aware of having any joint thought at all. But in the end it is psychological states of some kind that make an interpretive claim true, or nothing does.

It is easy to explain the popularity of this psychological state theory. It makes the truth of interpretive claims depend on an ordinary kind of fact; if it succeeds, therefore, it dissolves the mystery that seems to surround the idea of interpretive truth. There is nothing particularly mysterious about playwrights having intentions: after all, everyone does. The psychological state thesis also explains why we find it natural to speak of meanings and purposes in all genres of interpretation. The meanings and purposes in question are those, on this view, of the people whose mental states make interpretations true.

Nevertheless the psychological state thesis fairly obviously fails if we take it as a general theory of interpretation fit for all genres. It is normally correct about conversational interpretation. What makes you right in your understanding of what your friend said to you, if you are right, is essentially what he intended you to understand in speaking to you as he did. But in some genres the psychological state theory is plainly wrong, and in others it is both highly controversial and very implausible. It seems wholly implausible in historical interpretation: it is silly to think that whether the American Revolution should now be seen as dominated by commercial interests or political ideals turns on which thoughts were in the minds of either key actors or the relevant populations at large. It is now widely thought preposterous, among sophisticated lawyers, that the correct interpretation of a statute depends on the mental states of the legislators who enacted it.[7] Lawyers do speak of a "statutory intention" in explaining how they think a particular enactment should be read. But they cannot mean, by the intention of the statute, what the legislators had in mind as they voted. Many legislators do not understand the statutes they vote on, and those who do are as often moved by their own political motives—to please constituents, financial backers, or party leaders—as by any principles or policies that a lawyer might attribute to what they enact.

In the literary and artistic genres, what is called the "author's intention" theory of interpretation has been popular in some periods but unfashionable in others. It played little or no role in early accounts of the point or value of art: both Plato and Aristotle, for example, assumed that whatever value art has lies in imitation, so that understanding a work of art consists only in identifying what it can be seen as copying. (Two millennia later Hamlet said that art is nature's mirror.) The author's intention theory was popular in the nineteenth and early twentieth century, particularly among critics who styled themselves romantics. But it has been under sustained attack since and is now generally dismissed as based on what extremely influential critics deemed the "intentional" fallacy.[8] On the newer view, once an author has released his work to the public he has no more authority than anyone else over what that work should be understood to mean. The author becomes, in a nice phrase of Paul Ricoeur's, only "first reader."[9] A successful theory of interpretation must explain both the popularity and the shortcomings of the psychological state theory; it must explain why that account of interpretation seems so natural in some genres, familiar but controversial in others, and ineligible in still others. It must also explain why, even in genres in which the psychological state theory is ruled out, we still find it natural to report our interpretive conclusions as claims about what something means.

The Value Theory

A successful theory of interpretation must achieve a tenuous balance. It must account for the sense and possibility of truth in interpretation, but it must also account for the ineffability of that truth and the familiar, irresolvable clash of opinion about where it lies. Neither skepticism nor simplicity will serve. I shall now formulate, though still only in a rough and perhaps cryptic way, the theory of interpretation that I try to defend in this chapter. Interpretation is a social phenomenon. We can interpret as we do only because there are practices or traditions of interpretation we can join: these are the practices that divide interpretation into the genres I listed. We can talk about the meaning of a statute or a poem or an epoch only because others do that: they understand what we mean to claim when we say that the equal protection clause permits affirmative action or that Lady Macbeth was or was not married before.

These social practices are truth-seeking. In each case, when we offer an interpretation of something, we state and are understood to be stating what we take to be the truth of some matter. We do not treat these interpretive practices as pointless exercises: we assume that something of value is and ought to be served by forming, presenting, and defending opinions about the scope of the equal protection clause or Lady Macbeth's sexual history. We accept a responsibility, as interpreters, to promote that value. When we interpret any particular object or event, therefore, we are also interpreting the practice of interpretation in the genre that we take ourselves to have joined: we interpret that genre by attributing to it what we take to be its proper purpose—the value that it does and ought to provide.

Interpretation is therefore interpretive, just as morality is moral, all the way down. A particular interpretation succeeds—it achieves the truth about some object's meaning—when it best realizes, for that object, the purposes properly assigned to the interpretive practice properly identified as pertinent. Interpretation can therefore be understood, analytically, to involve three stages. We interpret social practices, first, when we individuate those practices: when we take ourselves to be engaged in legal rather than literary interpretation. We interpret, second, when we attribute some package of purposes to the genre or subgenre we identify as pertinent, and, third, when we try to identify the best realization of that package of purposes on some particular occasion. There is space, at each level but particularly at the latter two, for a skeptical opinion: that there is no right answer to the question what value a genre serves or what best serves that value on this occasion. I return to that possibility later in this chapter, but it is important to notice, now, that a skeptical opinion is only a different interpretation. It rests as much on assumptions about value as any of the positive interpretations it challenges.

The level of convergence or divergence a particular interpretive community exhibits in these various judgments determines whether interpretation flourishes within that community or whether it dissipates into mere difference. The convergence required is greatest at the first stage. If there is no substantial agreement about what counts as literary rather than some other form of interpretation, then no genuine disagreement in literary interpretation is possible. It is greater at the second stage than the third: if lawyers did not agree that the interpretation of a statute is a political exercise, there could be no recognizable statutory interpretation. How much agreement is necessary at each stage to sustain the practice is not fixed a priori. We discover how much and what kind of disagreement can be tolerated only ex post: only by judging whether some particular practice of agreement and disagreement remains fruitful or runs into argumentative sand.

I warned that this skeletal account of the value theory of interpretation might seem cryptic. But it will prove helpful, I believe, to have at least this skeleton in hand before elaborating the theory through examples. Two immediate clarifications are necessary. First, few interpreters have a self-conscious articulate theory of the boundaries or point of any interpretive genre, though some academic interpreters do have such theories. Most interpreters collect a set of inarticulate assumptions unreflectively in and through their experience of interpreting; these may simply reflect the parallel and unquestioned assumptions of an interpretive subculture to which they belong because of their distinctive education and training. That helps to explain the ineffability I described: why an interpretation can seem compelling to someone, just as a matter of what he "sees" in the object being interpreted, even though he could not give any extended account of why.

I do not assume that interpreters adopt a self-conscious value strategy or that they are aware that they are interpreting a larger practice as they interpret a statute or a poem. I offer the value strategy as a reconstruction not as a psychological report of how they think. That account exposes, we might say, the submerged assumptions that we can sensibly attribute to interpreters to explain how they support or oppose interpretive claims—assumptions that redeem their intuitive sense that there is truth to be had in such claims.

Second, no sensible reconstruction of any interpreter's judgment could reduce the sense he has formed, through training and experience, of the point of interpretation in his genre to a single crisp maxim. That is why I described an interpreter's assumptions as an inarticulate package. If an interpreter in any genre actually tried to make an articulate and reasonably full case for any particular interpretive claim, he would draw on a complex web of background convictions that he could not have set out in advance but rather develops as he explains. We might be able to set out a single background assumption that all interpreters in a genre would endorse. We might say, for example, that a musical performance serves the purpose of recreating a work of art to make it come alive. But that anodyne level of description obliterates the complexity of what it tries to capture. The judgment that a particular interpretation of a particular object or event best realizes a practice's value is always, therefore, a very complex claim, which of course adds to its inherently controversial character.

This is still very abstract. I can offer a quick example from legal practice because the structure of interpretation in that genre is relatively transparent.[10] Statutory interpretation aims to make the governance of the pertinent community fairer, wiser, and more just. That description fits what lawyers and judges do when they interpret statutes; it justifies that practice, in a general way, and it suggests, also in a very general way, what standards are appropriate for deciding which interpretation of a particular statute is most successful. But it is too abstract to be helpful in practice. Lawyers must rely on more refined and complex statements of the value of their practice actually to decide between competing interpretations.

They must decide, for example, what division of political authority among different branches of government and civil society is best, all things considered. That question in turn forces upon American lawyers, at least, further and more general questions of democratic theory; they must assume or decide, for instance, drawing on theory or instinct, how far unelected judges should assume an authority to decide for themselves which of the semantically available interpretations of a controversial statute would produce the best law. Each of these further questions, in its turn, implicates still further questions that would require, if they were pursued, deeper expeditions into political and moral theory that take lawyers even further from the particular statute that is their initial challenge. Disagreements among lawyers about the best interpretation of particular statutes are therefore symptoms of submerged and often unrecognized disagreements about these extensions and refinements. Lawyers who disagree about the best conception of democracy are likely to disagree, for that reason, about the best interpretation of the equal protection clause or even the Uniform Commercial Code.

Here is another, quite different and more concrete, example to bear in mind. A 2009 issue of the *New York Review of Books* reviewed the changing history of critical interpretations of the eighteenth-century French painter Antoine Watteau.[11] The change in critics' understanding of Watteau's work over the centuries is striking. Initially he was celebrated (and later dismissed) as light, joyful, frivolous, even effeminate, an expression of the pleasure-seeking Parisians' rapturous emancipation from the cultural oppression of the dour Sun King, a bridge to the rococo. Then, in the more severe nineteenth century, a new orthodoxy took hold: Watteau was very far from frivolous; on the contrary his "robust and virile" paintings, in the words of a prominent twentieth-century critic, were drenched in isolation and melancholy. In the latest book, under review in the article, the critic "wants to steep the paintings in the world he currently inhabits, and vice versa; in the process, Watteau's own moment of novelty gets overlaid with the many versions of the modern that ensued . . . [his painting of the pierrot Gilles] taps us into the revival of mime theater in 1830s Paris and the resuscitation of that revival in Marcel Carné's great film of 1945, *Les Enfants du Paradis*—not to mention Cézanne's pictorial dalliances with pierrots in the 1880s, and Picasso's after the Great War. And these give us a larger sense of what Watteau was up to . . . *Gilles* suggests a characteristically modernist anxiety."[12]

This kaleidoscope of contradictory interpretation does not reflect revolutionary discoveries about Watteau's artistic intentions. Nor is it helpful simply to say that later critics saw in the pictures what earlier ones had missed; on the contrary, the fact that different critics saw different things is part of what needs explaining. If we are to make sense of what seems undeniable—that each of the long succession of critics took himself to be right and others seriously wrong about "what Watteau was up to"—we must study not the critics' research into the painter's thoughts and ambitions but their sense of where value lies in art and of their own role in creating that value.

Important Distinctions

Collaborative, Explanatory, and Conceptual Interpretation

The legal example crisply illustrates the skeleton description I offered of the value account. We reconstruct an interpretation by distinguishing three elements explicit or buried within it: first, a background identification of a practice or tradition to which the interpretation belongs (statutory or constitutional interpretation); second, a set of assumptions about the purpose of that practice (a theory of democracy that divides authority between parliaments and adjudicators); and third, a claim that the proffered interpretation realizes those purposive assumptions better than any alternative understanding. This still skeletal account is artificial in a variety of ways: it neglects, for instance, the interaction among the different steps. My sense of what the equal protection clause means and requires is not just drawn from but in turn colors my sense of the role of constitutional constraints in a democracy. Interpretation is holistic: just as a moral philosopher aims at holding together concrete moral opinions and abstract justifying principles, reinterpreting each of these as necessary to achieve that integration, so an interpreter seeks, though usually unawares, an integration of background values and concrete interpretive insights. Some surprising reading of a play may strike an interpreter as so suddenly illuminating—that the murder of King Hamlet was a desperate act of self-defense by discovered illicit lovers, for example[13]—that he comes to reject any abstract account of literary interpretation that would rule out that reading.

The skeleton is nevertheless important because it allows us to focus on the crucial connection between value in and standards of interpretation. The value account blurs the line between two questions we might have thought very different. What does some object—a law or a poem or a painting— mean? What kind of value does that object have, in itself or for us? The value account makes answers to the first of these questions sensitive to answers to the second. It supposes that as an interpreter's understanding of a diverse mix of values shifts, so will his concrete interpretive opinions in any number of genres. The several authors of a recent and comprehensive anthology of literary theory and criticism, summarizing its over 2,500 pages of readings, report this connection between theories of the character and value of literature and theories about how to read that literature.

> Theories of literature and theories of reading have affinities with one another. Here are four instances. First, the formalist idea of literature as a well-made artistic object corresponds to the notion of reading as careful explication and evaluation of dense poetic style. Second, when viewed as the spiritual expression of a gifted seer, poetry elicits a biographical approach to criticism focused on the poet's inner development. Third, dense historical symbolic works presuppose a theory of reading as exegesis or decipherment. Fourth, literature conceived as social text or discourse calls for cultural critique. While we can separate theories of literature from theories of interpretation, they often work hand in hand.[14]

The value account of interpretation extends this thesis across the different genres of interpretation. It encourages further and crucial distinctions among the different types of value that a genre or an occasion of interpretation might be thought to exhibit. It allows us to distinguish, for example, collaborative, explanatory, and conceptual occasions of interpretation. Collaborative interpretation assumes that the object of interpretation has an author or a creator and that the author has begun a project that the interpreter tries to advance.

Conversational interpretation is almost always collaborative, and much literary and artistic interpretation is collaborative as well. Listeners or readers typically take themselves to be partners in a project initiated by a speaker or writer: they aim at a successful communication of what the latter intends to communicate. Sartre said that "creation can find its fulfillment only in reading, since the artist must entrust to another the job of carrying out what he has begun."[15] Law is also collaborative: a judge takes himself to aim at the same goal—justice—as the statesmen who made the laws he interprets. Even when he sees his role as entirely subordinate to theirs, the subordination is, in his view, itself justified by the overall goal of justice he shares with them.

Explanatory interpretation presupposes something different: not that interpreters are in partnership with those who created some object or event, but that an event has some particular significance for the audience the interpreter addresses. Historical, sociological, and psychodynamic interpretation are usually cases of explanatory interpretation. A historian who constructs a theory about the meaning of the French Revolution or the Holocaust is not in partnership with Jacobins or Nazis. Instead he tries to find the significance of these epochs and events for those he addresses. Conceptual interpretation is structured by yet a different assumption: that the interpreter seeks the meaning of a concept, like justice or truth, that has been created and recreated not by single authors but by the community whose concept it is, a community that includes the interpreter as a creator as well. In conceptual interpretation, that is, the distinction between creator and interpreter that marks collaborative and explanatory interpretation disappears, not because an interpreter is free to use these concepts as he wishes but because his use of the concept, in response to what he believes the right interpretation, will at least imperceptibly change the interpretive problem future interpreters face. I noticed conceptual interpretation earlier in this book: in explaining the concept of an agent's having a reason. We take up conceptual interpretation in much more detail in Chapter 8.

In collaborative interpretation there is a direct connection between the value an interpreter assigns to the class of objects he interprets and the value he assigns to interpreting such objects. He treats himself as having joined an author in an attempt to realize, in a conversation, a law, a poem, or a picture, the value he believes it can and should have; how he interprets hinges on the latter judgment. A negative critic takes that process a further step. He argues that he cannot make a success of the collaboration. The author has not produced anything that can be interpreted as realizing the kind of value at which he should aim: the speaker has hidden his meaning in garbled syntax, the parliamentary draftsman's text plainly commands injustice, the poem cannot be rescued from banality. These judgments assume that the interpreter has made the object he interprets the best it can be and that, on his lights, that is not good enough.

The most influential literary critics focus their skills, understandably, on success rather than failure—on universally acclaimed masterpieces—and they are explicit in relying on particular standards of literary excellence to justify that title. Consider the similarities and differences between the two critics I mentioned who insisted so forcefully on truth in interpretation. Leavis and Brooks were equally direct in rejecting the psychological state explanation of where that truth lies; they insisted that the meaning and value of a poem must be found in its text with no assistance from biography or from the author's own account of what he was trying to achieve. They were therefore both, in that sense, formalists, but while Brooks dismissed any distinction between content and form, and denigrated the idea that literature should yield to "paraphrase," Leavis emphasized the necessity of what he called moral seriousness in art. That emphasis is evident both in his ranking of the achievement of novelists (he counted Austen, Eliot, James, Conrad, and Lawrence as alone "great" English novelists because they best represented what he called the special "moral tradition" of that language) and in his interpretive reading of those novels: in his broad characterization of *Portrait of a Lady* as a "moral fable," for example, and his confidence in such minute observations as that Lord Warburton would not have offered an English girl, with her different "ethics," what he offered Isabel Archer: to "light your candle."[16]

The difference between Brooks's and Leavis's visions of greatness in literature is alive in their different readings of Yeats. Leavis found few of Yeats's poems great because he found them morally inaccurate; Brooks thought Yeats a master poet because he found Nietzsche in him. Compare Leavis's account of *Among School Children,* which he counted among the few great Yeats poems because it "has the force of convinced and irresistible truth,"[17] with Brooks's treatment of the poem.[18] Then compare both their readings with that of Yeats's biographer, Roy Foster, who begins his study by reporting the impact that Yeats's visit to St. Otteran's School in Waterford had on his theories of education. Yeats mentioned the visit "more than once" in his Senate speeches on the subject and wrote *Among School Children* a few weeks after the visit. Foster has no doubt that the "Ledaean body" evoked for Yeats by a school child was that of his early lover, Maud Gonne, who had had an unhappy childhood and was now, like himself, "hollow of cheek," and Foster describes the poem as "carrying a political charge" and as occupied with "the inadequate approaches to a philosophic understanding of the world epitomized by classical theories of education."[19]

Brooks, writing decades earlier, anticipated and warned against both these ideas. He declared it as hardly worth saying that the poem is not some "abstract proposition" about education, and he regarded the identification of the Ledaean body with Gonne as a corrupting mistake—a mistake he attributed to "the perils of biographical bias."[20] Now consider a very different kind of critic, Northrup Fry, who utterly denied the anthem of "new critics" like Brooks that the value and meaning of a work of art is self-contained. Fry insisted that the greatness of literature required tapping effectively into archetypical cultural myths. (He made the grave-digger scene in Hamlet a memory of the myth of *Liebestod,* the operatic linking of love and death.[21]) Leavis read Yeats's *Sailing to Byzantium* poem as a meditation coupling optimism and pessimism about death; Foster, as preoccupied "not so much with a heavenly city on earth" as with "artistic absorption in the act of creation"; Fry, as a superb example of the "comic" vision.[22]

When we turn from collaborative to explanatory interpretation, we see ascriptions of value operating at several levels. A historian may explain an event by ascribing purposes to particular historical actors: to the Austrian diplomats reacting to the archduke's murder at Sarajevo, for example. Or, what is very different, by ascribing a collective intention to a great mass of people that could not be replaced by any description of the discrete intentions of individual people: that Americans were moved to independence by economic rather than political ambitions, for instance. But a historian's general approach to history—which ascriptions of purpose he takes to be important or relevant, if indeed he takes any to be—depends on his own sense of the point and value of historical interpretation. Historians seek to make the past intelligible to the present, but they differ in their understandings of what dimensions of information or report best serve that purpose.[23]

Herbert Butterfield's polemic against what he called the Whig interpretation of history beautifully illustrates that disagreement.[24] "The Whig historian," Butterfield declared, "can say that events take on their due proportions when observed through the lapse of time. He can say that events must be judged by their ultimate issues, which, since we can trace them no farther, we must at least follow down to the present. He can say that it is only in relation to the 20th century that one happening or another in the past has relevance or significance for us."[25] Butterfield contrasts his own opinion: "It is easy to see the fight between Christianity and Paganism as a play of forces and to discuss it so to speak in the abstract; but much more illuminating to watch it as the interplay of personalities and people . . . much more interesting if we can take the general statement with which we began . . . and pursue it in its concrete incidence till we discover into what manifold detail it differentiates itself. It is along this road that the historian carries us, away from the world of general ideas."[26]

The differences in what two historians regard as "illuminating" or "interesting"—between Thomas Macaulay's fascination with big ideas as moral lectures and Butterfield's with minute details he found interesting just in themselves—shapes what each finds in history; what he takes to be the "meaning" of epochs and events. Butterfield says that the Whig historians were ignorant of the suffering that the religious wars caused. That is almost certainly untrue—how could they be?—but they may well have thought that the suffering, however deplorable, could contribute nothing of instruction to what makes the history of those wars valuable to us now. Marxist historians are different still; they write what the British Marxists called "history from below"—from the point of view of the poor and oppressed. That perspective cannot be explained, certainly not fully, by any assumption of historical materialism. It is better explained on the assumption that focusing attention on the history of oppression will help in the battle for a better society. If a historian thinks that history can be a weapon in the hands of the masses, that thought will teach him what to find important in history.

Independence, Complementarity, and Competition

We need yet another set of distinctions, however, before we can do even limited justice to the practices and attitudes of interpretation. We must distinguish between occasions on which two different interpretations of the same object or event are independent of one another, because each can either accept or deny the other, or be complementary to one another, because each takes itself to be adding insight to the other without challenging its accuracy or importance, or competitive with one another because each makes claims that assume that the other is in some way defective. A causal account of the genesis of some work of art—that the artist was commissioned to paint a donor's portrait as worshipper and to use a good deal of expensive cobalt blue in the composition—would in itself be independent of any interpretive reading of the work: that the work is religious or ironic in character, for instance.

Carl Jung thought psychological explanations of why an artist writes or paints as he does independent of interpretation in the same way: "Though the material he works with and its individual treatment can easily be traced back to the poet's personal relations with his parents, this does not enable us to understand his poetry."[27] Laurence Olivier's *Hamlet,* however, reflected a psychodynamic interpretation in every gesture and intonation: the famous actor, like so many others of his time, used Freud not simply to speculate why Shakespeare wrote the closet scene as he did but to fix what the closet scene means, and though Olivier's interpretation might be regarded as complementary rather than conflicting (I discuss that possibility later), it was certainly meant to teach audiences something about the play, not simply about its author.

How shall we tell whether two different interpretations of a particular work are independent, complementary, or conflicting? Whether Foster's reading of *Among School Children* is meant simply to add information to nonbiographical readings like those of Brooks or Leavis, or rather to supply a better reading than either of theirs? That is itself a question of interpretation—not of Yeats, of course, but of these various critics. Consider this different example. The popular Shakespearean critic J. Dover Wilson argued that it is incontestable "that Shakespeare and his audience regarded Bolingbroke as a usurper."[28] He argued that *Richard II* must therefore be read as a defense of the legitimate order and that this reading is "evident from the whole tone and emphasis" of the play. Stephen Greenblatt, speaking for a movement he described as the "new historicism," criticized Dover Wilson's reading, not because he doubted the latter's understanding of Tudor political opinion (though he noted that Elizabeth I appeared to take a different view), but because Dover Smith, though no New Critic, was assuming that the correct interpretation of a classic remains fixed over time—what the artist produced at a particular moment rather than a social artifact that changes as circumstances do. Greenblatt disagrees. Interpretations, he thinks, "are not intrinsic to the texts; rather than are made up and constantly redrawn by artists, audiences, and readers . . . In this light, the study of genre is an exploration of the poetics of culture."[29] He thus cites the importance of the fact that Dover Wilson's lecture on the play was given in Weimar in 1939, when a defense of a legitimate though weak government might have seemed still very much in point.

We may be tempted to think that Greenblatt is not really disagreeing with Dover Wilson about the best interpretation of *Richard II;* that he is rather taking up a different project so that his work is independent, or perhaps complementary, but not conflicting. E. D. Hirsh, another prominent critic who favors the psychological state school of literary interpretation, distinguishes what he calls the significance of a work of art for its audience, which of course changes over time and place, from the meaning, which Hirsh believes is fixed.[30] We might say that Dover Wilson lectured about the meaning of *Richard II* and Greenblatt about its significance, including its significance for Dover Wilson and his Weimar audience, so that the two critics did not really disagree. But this won't work. We can't read Greenblatt in that perhaps tempting way: he plainly thinks that the methods of interpretation once in vogue, now to be replaced by the new historicism he champions, are in some way not just limited *to* interpretation as distinct from social history but wrong *as* interpretation because they are insufficiently steeped in social history. It is the same with postmodernism, deconstructionism, critical feminist interpretation, and all the rest of the new small talk. They pick fights when they could settle for comfortable compatibility.

What are these fights about? What does Greenblatt think his new tribe of critics can do that is not just different from but better than what was done before? That is a difficult and neglected question: we need the value theory of interpretation to answer it. The projects Brooks or Leavis or Foster or Hirsh or Dover Wilson or Greenblatt announce are too different from one another to allow us to say that they follow the same interpretive methods but reach different conclusions. We can generate no more conflict just by comparing the methods these critics use than Jung saw between his psychology and any critic's interpretation. We need to focus on what I called the second stage of a reconstructed interpretation—on the values the critics assign to a practice they take themselves to share—to find space for disagreement.

An interpretive school is a shared interpretation of the point of the larger practice a group of interpreters take themselves to have joined. For there is tradition in criticism as much as in creation: what T. S. Eliot said about poets—that they cannot write poetry except as part of a tradition that they interpret and through interpretation retrospectively shape—is true of critics as well.[31] Literary critics see their craft as a tradition instinct with value and hence responsibility. They disagree about what that value is and therefore what responsibility they have. The New Critics did not simply choose a new occupation to take up, like a doctor switching specialties. They saw a defining responsibility in the traditions of literary criticism—a responsibility to make something grander of literature and particularly poetry than other techniques could. They thought their methods better suited to a better understanding of what the long practice of criticism demands of its practitioners. Marxist critics see a very different responsibility in the same tradition. Frederic Jameson said that in Marxist interpretation, "The individual text retains its formal structure as a symbolic act: yet the value and character of such symbolic action are now significantly modified and enlarged. On this rewriting, the individual utterance or text is grasped as a symbolic move in an essentially polemic and strategic ideological confrontation between the classes."[32]

This is the deep dynamic that explains large and small shifts among schools and vogues of interpretation: the shared assumption of responsibility to a practice together with different assumptions about what that responsibility now demands. Judges, historians, and literary critics all take themselves to have responsibilities, roles to play given by the traditions of some genre. Their theories of those responsibilities are as much creative, and are even more evidently in conflict, than the discrete interpretations they propose in the light of those theories. Contrast the claim of Terry Eagleton, a Marxist critic, that "modern criticism was born of a struggle against the absolutist state" with the histories of critical tradition offered by representatives of almost any other interpretive style.[33] We can find room for disagreement rather than just difference among interpretive schools only when we push that far back in an interpretive reconstruction of their arguments. It is only when we take seriously what the critics themselves say, noticing the other critics they take themselves to be disagreeing with, that we ourselves, interpreting them, can decide what independence and conflict there is in their different projects and styles. Only then can we see the independence of a Jungian explanation from a Freudian interpretation of *Hamlet* and the genuine conflict between Whig and Marxist understandings of religious wars and traditional and revisionary interpretations of *Richard II*.

Compare the deep conflicts among schools of interpretation in law. We see the parallels most clearly when we focus on judges, not because judges are the only interpreters of law—they are certainly not—but because both the responsibility and the tradition are clearer in their case than in that of advocate, professor, or citizen. The history of western adjudication, from Justinian to the International Criminal Court, shows a considerable variety in judges' interpretations of their own responsibilities. What we now call "mechanical" or "conceptual" jurisprudence is part of that story, as are the more modern interpretive schools of judicial deference, legal realism, social policy, economic efficiency, interpretive analysis, and whatever comes next. It is easier to see these schools of adjudication as in competition than to see competition in other interpretive genres, because the institutional demands and consequences of adjudication remain constant as the schools of legal interpretation shift. But the shifts in conceptions of other interpretive roles even in our own time—of historians from Hugh Trevor Roper to Eric Hobsbawm, of journalists from Walter Lippman to Edward R. Murrow to Hunter Thompson, of art critics from Bernard Berenson to Svetlana Alpers and Michael Freed—shows a parallel interpretation and reinterpretation of responsibility.

I must not exaggerate the importance of these various distinctions among types of interpretation and relationships among them. It rarely matters in which box or boxes we place a critic's work. We can profit from what seems illuminating without pursuing distracting issues of categorization or deciding how far different critics really disagree with one another. But sometimes the distinctions are essential, either to avoid confusion or to locate genuine and important disagreement we might have missed. In recent years, in universities and particularly in law schools, a variety of self-styled "critical" schools of interpretation have flourished and waned. Critical feminist interpretations of the oeuvre of Walt Disney point to the stereotyping of Minnie Mouse and her unquestioned subordination to Mickey.[34] These seem, at first glance, exercises in explanatory, not collaborative, interpretation. The feminist critics certainly do not regard themselves as Disney's partners in some aesthetic adventure. They seek to expose what they take to be one significant and malign aspect of popular culture: its sexist roots and hidden influences. Yet we cannot ignore the anger these writers feel at more conventional criticism that finds charm in the naiveté of anthropomorphized animals. In these critics' opinion, ignoring the sexism is a failure in an important and traditional critical responsibility and helps to perpetuate what it ignores.

The rise and fall of what was called "critical legal studies" in American law schools provides an even better example of the same phenomenon. The "Crits," as they called themselves, were anxious to debunk the widespread assumption that law is the product of legal officials trying to work out a coherent set of principles of personal and political morality for the regulation of social and commercial interaction. Crits aimed to expose the contradictions in legal doctrine produced by powerful groups pursuing their own interests rather than the impact of moral and political principle. That is explanatory interpretation: it claims contemporary significance in a particular account of how the law developed. There is no reason why critical legal studies, so understood, should think itself competitive with conventional collaborative interpretation that aims to improve the law by imposing some greater degree of integrity and principle on doctrine whose causal roots may well have been what the Crits claim they were. On the contrary, the two enterprises might well be thought complementary: aiming to improve law both by demystifying the origins of doctrine and then bending doctrine through enlightened interpretation to better ends. There is no conflict in finding the causes of legislation in greed and interpreting that legislation so as to thwart greed; it takes rose-colored glasses to deny the first but not to insist on the second.

But critical legal studies did take itself, and noisily, to be competitive with what its acolytes called "liberal legalism." This combat may have reflected a crude confusion between interpretation and explanation, as I once perhaps uncharitably suggested.[35] However, the posture of antagonism these scholars took up may have reflected a more profound judgment about the proper responsibilities of legal scholarship. If the proper goal of a demystifying explanatory interpretation is radically to change opinion and practice, then it might best achieve this by wearing collaborative clothing. It might try to interpret the practice it hopes to change in the worst light it can, which of course requires it to insist that this is the best light possible, and so to oppose any attempt to picture it better. That reading does make critical legal studies the enemy of liberal legalism.

Interpretive Skepticism

These are examples of actual competition hidden by apparent independence or complementarity. It is often more soothing to suppose, in the opposite direction, that apparently contradictory interpretations are actually complementary or independent. In that way we might diffuse the tension between our inescapable sense that there is unique truth to be had in interpretation and our unease in actually claiming that truth in controversial cases. We tell ourselves that the unique truth is that there is no unique truth, that a work of art is greater when it can sustain wildly different readings, and we invoke the tired metaphor of a multifaceted diamond. But the occasions on which this strategy succeeds are relatively few.

One attempt to avoid direct competition is relativism—the thesis that correct standards of interpretation are relative to different schools or communities of interpreters. If so then different interpretations that appear to contradict one another really do not because they must be judged against different standards. Consider the various formulations of this view by the critic and columnist Stanley Fish. He argued, once, that certain crucial aspects of a poem can be appreciated only temporally, by a reader who has a series of reactions, some of which are cancelled or modified as he progresses. "Thus, in the case of three sonnets by Milton, what is really happening depends upon a moment of hesitation or syntactic slide . . . In a formalist analysis that moment will disappear, either because it has been flattened out and made into an (insoluble) crux or because it has been eliminated in the course of a procedure that is incapable of finding value in temporal phenomena."[36] There is nothing skeptical in this argument: on the contrary, it insists that any analysis that denies force in "temporal phenomena" like a "syntactic slide" inevitably misses something of objective value.

But later in the same essay (as published) Fish, in what he called a "self-consuming" act, took all this back. "I must give up the claims implicitly made in the first part of the essay. There I argue that a bad (because spatial) model had suppressed what was really happening, but by my own principles the notion 'really happening' is just one more interpretation." Of course it is just one more interpretation. But it is not yet clear why it is not a better interpretation. Or a worse one. It doesn't help to say, as Fish does, that a poem is created by a reading and that there is therefore no text independent of a particular reading and no reading independent of a particular reader. If we are drawn to that way of putting the point—there are others—our question then becomes: Why does one reading not create a better poem and therefore show the reader to be a better reader?

Still later Fish seemed to offer a flatly skeptical answer. He called his way of reading a "fiction" and declared, "My fiction is liberating. It relieves me of the obligation to be right (a standard that simply drops out) and demands only that I be interesting (a standard that can be met without any reference at all to an illusory objectivity)." But still later he called that last statement "the most unfortunate sentence I ever wrote," and repudiated it because it implies "relativism."[37] But immediately thereafter he declared that standards of right and wrong in interpretation are indeed relative—to "community goals and assumptions." That statement of relativism, too, is just one more interpretation, and we need to ask why *it* is true. Why are the goals and assumptions of one community not better than those of another? Why are they not the best they can be? If they are the best, then they are not just correct relative to that community. They are just correct, and the goals and assumptions of other communities are mistaken. Fish denies this possibility; he insists on relativism. But he needs a positive argument for this piece of internal skepticism, and I cannot find one. We cannot find one just in the familiar fact of the diversity of interpretive schools. Or in the lack of any Archimedean platform from which interpretations can be judged without any interpretive assumptions. That would only send us back to the failed arguments for external skepticism we canvassed in Part One.

I do not deny, however, that there are good positive arguments for internal skepticism in literary interpretation. A critic might think he shows a poem to be greater, and therefore better acquits his critical responsibility, when he insists that there is no single right way to read it. Earlier I mentioned Leavis's reading of *Sailing to Byzantium,* which contains this: "Intensely the soul interrogates itself and its images of fulfillment and finds no answer that doesn't turn into an irony . . . the ambiguity is essential and undeniable: Which is it—nostalgia for the country which is not for old men, or nostalgia for the eternal posited as the antithesis? The poet couldn't, I think, have said, and in any case the question isn't his but ours."[38] In this case, reading this poem, Leavis thinks moral seriousness best served by an understanding that depends on, rather than resolves, ambiguity. Two films of Michael Haneke, *Hidden* and *The White Ribbon* (English titles), provide further, though very different, examples. In both there is crime, but the criminals remain unidentified; what might (but needn't) be the best interpretation of these films is that there is in fact no answer to who the criminals are, that in *this* case the world of fiction is incomplete in a way that, for a realist about history, the actual world cannot be.

I have already mentioned a yet different example. The public performance of a classic performed many times before is itself a subgenre of interpretation, and it is plainly part of the point of that subgenre that each performance offer some fresh claim about the work. Of course this understanding does not license a markedly inferior reading of an honored play or piece of music. But as I said, the director of a new production of *Hamlet* need not think that his interpretation is competitive with and superior to all different interpretations. It is enough if his interpretation displays something of character or poetry or connection with other literature or pictorial art or contemporary political or social significance that others have not, and that the text can reasonably sustain that interpretation. That is a daunting enough challenge, and many fewer directors than try actually succeed. But in any case complementarity is the presumption of this subgenre: the requirement of reasonable originality, as a distinct virtue of the genre, justifies our sense that it would be a mistake for any director to claim unique truth for his reading.

These are just samples: there are many other examples of successful skepticism in literary and other forms of the interpretation of art. But these are all cases of internal, not external, skepticism, and none of them justifies any wholesale or default skepticism. When interpretations of a work of art diverge, seeing conflict is more often a better and more instructive diagnosis than seeing facets of a brilliant diamond—more instructive because it requires us to trace out the roots of the conflict in deeper divergent understandings of the critical responsibilities in play.

Radical Translation

I should mention one more example of alleged interpretive skepticism—one much more studied by philosophers than the others we have considered.[39] It is drawn not from art or law but from a genre of interpretation rare in practice but topical in philosophy: translation from a language of which we have initially no even partial understanding. If we find speakers of that language, we can attempt translation through extensive study of their behavior. We attribute sense to the words they use by attributing different packages of beliefs and desires to them and trying to make sense of what they say against that background. But the same behavior will almost always be explicable through a large variety of very different packages: if we change our opinion about what these people think is true, or about what they desire to happen, then we would attribute very different meanings to what they say. Each of a great many different packages, taken as a whole, might fit their behavior equally as well. Willard Quine, whose study of the problem has greatly influenced philosophy of language, put the matter this way: "Manuals for translating one language into another can be set up in divergent ways, all compatible with the totality of speech disposition, yet incompatible with one another. In countless places they will diverge in giving, as their respective translations of a sentence of one language, sentences of the other language which stand to each other in no plausible sort of equivalence however loose."[40]

We might therefore be tempted by a skeptical conclusion: there is no right answer to questions of radical translation but only different answers. Philosophers have said essentially that in different ways: that there are no such things as meanings, for example, or that translation is essentially indeterminate. These skeptical claims assume, however, that we must judge what makes best sense of behavior by asking only what package of attributes fits the raw facts of behavior; it claims indeterminacy because many packages fit those raw facts just as well. But radical translation is best understood as a kind of collaborative interpretation—we imagine ourselves in conversation with speakers of the language for the great variety of purposes that normally provoke conversation. It is therefore sensible to adopt assumptions about the language and its speakers that seem necessary to achieving any such purpose: assumptions such that, if they do not hold, any project of useful communication or transaction is anyway doomed.

We can understand Donald Davidson's suggested principles of charity and coherence in that light.[41] We assume that the speakers we aim to understand employ the same logic as we do and that their beliefs are in general true, though not necessarily true in each case. Because the purposes of translation would have no point except on those assumptions, we proceed on that basis. Suppose that even then, accepting these constraints, we produce two markedly different radical translations of the same language: two packages of belief, desire, and meaning, each of which fits all the evidence. These are competitive; if we label one "correct," then we must suppose the other not correct. Is one better, all things considered?

We must take care, as always when such a question is posed, to distinguish uncertainty from indeterminacy. We would be entitled to the latter very strong positive conclusion only if we had uncovered some positive reason for supposing that there is nothing to choose between divergent translations, given the broad range of purposes an interpretation must serve. In fact different translators have achieved a great deal of uniformity in meeting actual challenges in radical translation; this might suggest that indeterminacy, as distinct from uncertainty, is rare.[42] We would think otherwise, of course, if we supposed that success in this kind of interpretation means only fitting the raw behavioral facts.

Perhaps Davidson made that last assumption when he said: "The totality of evidence available to the interpreter determines no unique theory of truth for a given speaker . . . because all possible evidence cannot limit acceptable theories to one." But, as he insisted, there is more to interpretation than fit. Though he allowed that "we may say, if we please, that interpretation or translation is indeterminate," he also compared that indeterminacy to the fact that a bath's temperature can be measured in either Fahrenheit or centigrade.[43] He must have thought that though a huge number of different packages of attribution would fit the behavioral data, the interpretive strategies that served our actual purposes would normally narrow those packages to a few whose differences were only terminological. If that is true, then there may be little indeterminacy in the sense Quine had in mind. Perhaps we are not often faced with equally good interpretations that "stand to each other in no plausible sort of equivalence."

The Value Account: A Summary

Does the value account of interpretation satisfy the conditions I laid down earlier in this chapter for a successful theory of interpretation? It is adequately general: it claims application over all the genres of interpretation I listed. It also explains why there is nothing that might be called interpreting in general, apart from a particular genre. If the success of any particular interpretive claim depends on a successful account of the value of interpreting in some genre, then of course interpretation cannot begin until that genre is specified or assumed in what I called the first stage of interpretation. Interpreting light flashes as a message has a dramatically different point from interpreting them as artistic expression.

The value account also explains, as I said any general theory of interpretation must, why the role of some creator's psychological state is so often controversial. Authors' states of mind are pertinent when, and in the way that, they are made pertinent by the best account of the value served by interpreting in the genre in question. Conversational interpretation is dominated by speakers' intentions because the point of interpreting in conversation is almost always the communication of such intentions. Legal interpretation is not dominated by the actual mental states of legislators and other officials because the best understanding of the purpose of interpreting statutes and other legal data makes irrelevant most of what those officials actually think or intend. The role of an author's intention is controversial in the interpretation of literature, and the importance that critics attach to that intention fluctuates, because it is controversial among critics how far the value of a work of art depends on an author's inspiration and its realization in the work.

In the early nineteenth century, when the author's-intention tradition was particularly strong, its supporters argued that an author's intentions should control interpretation because only in that way could the real value of literature be realized. Here is Coleridge:

> What is poetry? is so nearly the same question with, what is a poet? that the answer to the one is involved in the solution of the other. For it is a distinction resulting from the poetic genius itself, which sustains and modifies the images, thoughts, and emotions of the poet's own mind . . . He diffuses a tone, and spirit of unity, that blends, and (as it were) *fuses,* each into each, by that synthetic and magical power, to which we have exclusively appropriated the name of imagination.[44]

How could anyone who embraced that romantic, dancer-and-dance view of poet and poem not assume that the point of criticism is to bring that genius of imagination into proper view? Contrast Tom Stoppard's very different view of the critic's role: he said a critic is like a customs inspector who finds much in a work that the author must admit is there though he claims, truthfully, that he did not pack it.[45] Still other views about the role and importance of "the first reader" reflect yet different assumptions about the value of the critical enterprise. Many of them subordinate any alleged authorial genius to something quite different: to the work of art judged on its own, as orphan or *objet trouvé,* to the opportunities for surprise offered to a contemporary reader, to the moral instruction or social or political consciousness of a new age. The author's authority rises and falls, dies and is reborn, as opinion shifts about what interpretation is for.

The value account answers other questions I posed. As I said, it explains the ambivalence we everywhere find about truth in interpretation. Disagreement is patent, but its source almost always is obscure, buried in a large variety of unarticulated assumptions about law or art or literature or history that rarely surface and that can be explained only as the upshot of some combination of inherent taste, training, acculturation, allegiance, and habit. No wonder we speak so naturally of just "seeing" a poem or a picture one way or another: that is often and inescapably how the judgment feels. Of course, it seems arrogant to thoughtful people to insist that there is then one exclusive truth about the interpretive issue in hand, that those who do not see the statute or painting as they do are simply in error. It seems more realistic and modest to say that there is no one right interpretation but only different acceptable or responsible ones.

And yet that is exactly what we must not say if we are honest, because it is not what we believe or can believe. To repeat: a scholar who labors for years over a new reading of *Hamlet* cannot believe that his various interpretive conclusions are no more valid than the contradictory conclusions of other scholars; a judge who sends someone to jail on an interpretation of the law he believes no better than, but only different from, rival interpretations should be jailed himself. The value account redeems our conviction of truth in the face of all the complexity, controversy, and ineffability. If interpreters accept that some complex web of value defines success in their enterprise, then they can sensibly believe that these values can be identified and better served by one particular interpretation, on any interpretive occasion, than by others. Conversely, if they have come to think that one interpretation of something is best, they can also sensibly think that that interpretation meets the test of what defines success in the enterprise, even if they cannot articulate that test in much or any detail. So they can think there is objective truth in interpretation. But only, of course, if they think there is objective truth in value. The argument of Part One of this book is a necessary foundation for the argument of this part.

We have already noticed one maneuver that helps people think they are not arrogant in insisting on their favored interpretations. They say that while scientific claims are true or false, interpretive judgments are something different. They are sound or unsound, or more or less reasonable, or something of that sort. These distinctions are empty. Of course we can stipulate that "true" is to be used as the endorsing operator for scientific judgments and "most reasonable" as the endorsing operator for interpretive judgments. But that stipulation would be pointless because we can claim no utility for it.[46] We cannot map the distinction onto any more familiar distinction by explaining, for instance, that "true" indicates objectivity while "most reasonable" indicates only subjectivity, or that "true" marks a cognitive judgment while "most reasonable" marks some form of noncognitive expression. On the contrary, any alternate endorsing term for interpretive judgments would have to signify, if it is to fit what we think, exactly what "true" signifies: unique success. The important differences between scientific and interpretive judgments reflect differences in the content of the two kinds of judgment rather than the eligibility of one, though not the other, for truth.

Science and Interpretation

What are those differences? I asked, among the questions I posed at the start of this chapter, how interpretation differs from science. Philosophers, historians, and social scientists have proposed a grand distinction between two kinds of investigation: what some philosophers have called explanation and understanding.[47] Those who believe the distinction fundamental hold that the natural sciences seek explanations that do not suppose purposes whereas history and sociology, among other humane disciplines, seek comprehension through purpose. This chapter has offered a somewhat different version of the same distinction. I take understanding to mean interpreting. Interpretation differs from science because interpretation is purposive, not just in the vocabulary of its claims but in the standards of its success.

We start by distinguishing between the intrinsic and justifying goals of any inquiry. Whenever we investigate anything—black holes or the causes of the First World War or the demography of the Cayman Islands or the ambiguities in Yeats's poetry—our intrinsic goal is to find the truth about something. If we did not have that goal, we would not be inquiring. But we can also identify justifying goals of inquiry: these are the goals or purposes that we believe justify trying to find that truth. We believe that medical research is justified, for example, because it prevents and cures disease. Many of what we take to be justifying goals of science are practical in that way: research in agricultural biology is justified because it promises to feed more people; research in consumer electronics because it will provide desired entertainment and prosperity.

The justifying goals of science are not always that immediately practical, however. We study cosmology out of fascination with its mysteries, excited by the sheer drama of our universe's history. That is not a practical goal, but it is nevertheless a justifying one, because it includes an ambition not only for truth but for truth about something we deem of fundamental importance for us to know. We do not try to discover how many rocks weighing two pounds or more there are in Africa. If we did, then the intrinsic goal of the study would be to determine the truth of that matter, but we do not because the study would not serve any justifying goal, practical or theoretical.

Justifying goals play an evidently important role in science. They explain not only which questions scientists try to answer and which studies governments or foundations finance, but also when we think it right to rest content with some claim of truth that falls far short, as many significant scientific claims do, of certainty. Nevertheless, in spite of these important effects, we must never conflate the justifying goals with the intrinsic goals of science; in particular we must not suppose that justifying goals enter into any test of success in finding truth.[48] We may study cosmology because we are enchanted with the vastness of space, but the truth of the big bang theory does not turn on whether it enchants us. That we want to cross rivers is no part of the case for the truth of the principles that predict when bridges stay up or fall down. To think otherwise would collapse the indispensable distinction between scientific truth and our reasons for wanting the truth. It is part of the organizing structure of our science—part of what it is essential to understand if we are to achieve our justifying goals—that justifying goals have nothing to do with truth. It may be, as some great philosophers have insisted, that this crucial separation between truth and purpose in science reflects and serves human purposes at some higher level of abstraction. (I touch on that possibility in the next chapter.) But that speculation confirms rather than challenges the importance of the distinction.

Interpretation is dramatically different. In that realm justifying purpose is at the heart of success. If the value account is right, our standards for success in an interpretive genre do depend, in the way I tried to describe, on what we take to be the best understanding of the point of interpreting in that genre. In interpretation, we might say, justifying and intrinsic goals merge. Interpreters make or just have assumptions about these purposes and the values that support them, and these assumptions, though often inarticulate and unrecognized, are determinative of which interpretive claims they accept and which they reject.

That great difference between the two great worlds of inquiry, science and interpretation, matches and explains several of the differences we noticed in earlier chapters between science and morality. Unlike scientific claims, interpretive propositions cannot be barely true: they can be true only in virtue of an interpretive justification that draws on a complex of values, none of which can be barely true either. It cannot be that the best interpretation of the equal protection clause makes it unconstitutional for states to refuse driving licenses to infants, just as a matter of how things actually are, though no lawyer has any reason to think so, or that *Sailing to Byzantium* is really an attack on British imperialism even though there can be no deeper explanation of why that is so. An interpretation is not evidence of some further fact. A true interpretive claim is true because the reasons for accepting it are better than the reasons for accepting any rival interpretive claim. That is why, when we reconstruct the reasoning of a great critic, we must speak of a web rather than a chain of value.

Interpretation is pervasively holistic. An interpretation weaves together hosts of values and assumptions of very different kinds, drawn from very different kinds of judgment or experience, and the network of values that figure in an interpretive case accepts no hierarchy of dominance and subordination. The network faces the challenge of conviction as a whole; if any one strand is changed, the result may be locally seismic. Someone's second-best interpretation of a poem or a picture may be radically different from his first best; a third interpretation that is only slightly different from the first may seem much worse. True, some persuasive philosophers argue that science is holistic too: that our science, as Quine put it, also confronts the bar of experience as a whole.[49] They say that there is no belief about the physical world, however established and indubitable it now seems, that we could not give up if we also surrendered all the other beliefs we now hold and began again to describe and account for the physical world in an entirely different vocabulary.

But holism in science, if we accept it at all, is almost entirely academic and passive: it can play no part in almost anyone's practical life. In ordinary practice we think about physics and plant ecology and how far personality depends on genes in a straightforwardly linear way. We reason to new beliefs from the same incalculably great mass of what we all take for granted, and we reason on evidence whose force and limits we mainly all recognize. Our acquisitions and shifts in belief are almost all incremental: we test hypotheses on the assumption that they, and nothing else, are at risk in the test. That is not invariably true. It is not true in the more speculative regions of theoretical physics or, perhaps, in basic biology. New evidence can call into question a good deal of what seemed settled. Let Stephen Hawking say that black holes do not, after all, destroy information, and suddenly formerly intriguing theories about alternative universes evaporate.[50] But the difference between what one responsible scientist thinks about the world we actually encounter and what others think, because he accepts some controversial opinion that they reject, is generally small compared to what they all think in common. Matters stand very differently in interpretation: literary critics or constitutional lawyers whose values are strikingly different in some pertinent respect are likely to disagree across a very broad area of interpretive convictions. We saw ample evidence of that kind of leverage in this chapter. In interpretation, holism is not passive; it is very active.

Recognizing these differences between science and interpretation offers yet more help in explaining our unease about claiming truth for our interpretations. What interpretation lacks is exactly what gives science a sense of solidity. The permissibility of bare truth gives us an enormous boost in metaphysical confidence. Not, of course, confidence that we have the truth about the world—indeed, we noticed that the idea of bare truth makes possible a very deep, irremediable kind of mistake—but confidence that there is truth to be had. When no truth can be bare, that comfort disappears. Any doubts we may have about the soundness of our interpretive case remind us of the possibility, which we cannot automatically exclude, of deep internal skepticism: that there is no best case and therefore no right answer. The fact that the justifying goals of science are irrelevant to truth is another source of solidity in science. Knowing that people's differences in what they take to be the justifying goals of science can play no role in fixing what they take to be scientific truth makes it profitable for us to expect convergence of opinion in that domain.

In interpretation, on the contrary, differences in justifying purpose and ambition are automatically differences in method; argument is not shielded from these differences but is rather shaped by them. Convergence therefore seems problematic and, so far as it does occur, accidental. The linearity of science is another source of comfort: controversy about novel claims or hypotheses is not threatening because, even in speculative regions, castles of sand are built on what seems undeniably firm ground. The active holism of interpretation means, on the contrary, that there is no firm ground at all, that even when our interpretive conclusions seem inescapable, when we think there really is nothing else to think, we are still stalked by the ineffability of that conviction.

We cannot escape a sense of the airiness and contingency of our interpretive convictions because we know that other people do think what we cannot think and that there is no lever of argument that we can press to convince them. Or they us. There is no experiment that must reconcile our disparate certainties. Still, for all that, we are left only with uncertainty, not nihilism. If you want more—if you want the quietus of an interpretive skepticism— you must argue for it, and your arguments will be just as airy, just as controversial, just as unconvincing to others as the positive arguments that dissatisfy you now. So—yet again—everything depends in the end on what you actually and responsibly think. Not because your thinking makes it right, but because, in thinking it right, you think it *right*.

8

Conceptual Interpretation

How Is Disagreement Possible?

Moral reasoning is interpretation, but it is not collaborative or explanatory interpretation. It belongs to the third type I distinguished in the last chapter: conceptual interpretation. People have together developed a great variety of moral concepts—the concepts of reasonableness, for instance, honesty, trustworthiness, tactfulness, decency, responsibility, cruelty, shabbiness, insensitivity, deceit, and brutality, as well as the special political concepts of legitimacy, justice, liberty, equality, democracy, and law. We develop our moral personalities through interpretations of what it is to be honest or reasonable or cruel, or what actions of government are legitimate, or when the rule of law has been violated. In conceptual interpretation the distinction between author and interpreter vanishes: we have together created what we each and together interpret. Much of the long history of philosophy is a history of conceptual interpretation. Philosophers interpret the concepts they study in a much more self-conscious and professional way, but they also help in creating what they interpret.

The title for this section must sound odd. Of course we agree and disagree about morality and politics. We join campaigns because we agree and fight wars because we disagree. But pause to consider what makes this possible. Many words sound alike but have different meanings, and this linguistic fact can produce comically spurious agreement. If you and I agree to meet at the bank tomorrow and you mean the river's edge but I mean the money storehouse, our agreement is illusory, as we will soon discover. We also seem to attach different meanings to the words we use to express moral concepts. When we think we disagree about whether a progressive income tax is unjust, for instance, it may turn out—it probably will turn out—that our tests for injustice are very different. I may think a law unjust if it disturbs the upshot of a free economic market and you if it increases overall suffering. Why is our apparent disagreement not then illusory like our supposed agreement in the bank case?

Types of Concepts

In this chapter I argue that we can account for genuine agreement and dis-agreement about moral issues only by distinguishing among types of the concepts that we use, separating them by identifying the different ways in which people share them. The moral and political concepts I just listed are all examples of a type I shall call "interpretive." We share an interpretive concept when our collective behavior in using that concept is best explained by tak-ing its correct use to depend on the best justification of the role it plays for us. I can best elaborate that complex idea by first trying to explain how we share concepts that are not interpretive: the concept of a bank, for instance, a book, an equilateral triangle, or a lion.

Some of our concepts are *criterial* in this sense: we share the concept when, but only so far as, we use the same criteria in identifying instances. People share the concept of an equilateral triangle, for example, when they all use a particular test—figures with three equal sides are equilateral triangles—to identify specimens. People who share a concept in this way may nevertheless fall into illusory disagreement about its proper use in some circumstances. The criteria we share for an equilateral triangle are precise, but those we share for applying other criterial concepts are not. If we seem to disagree about whether our mutual friend who is losing his hair is now bald, even though we agree about how much hair he actually has, our apparent disagreement is spurious—or, as we sometimes say, only verbal. Our apparent disagreement about how many books there are on a table is illusory if you count large pam-phlets as books but I do not. The concepts of baldness and of a book, we may say, are vague criterial concepts because although people mainly agree about the correct criteria for their application, they differ over a range of application that each regards as marginal. It makes sense to say either that we share the concept in such cases because we use the same criteria in standard cases or that the concepts we use are only so slightly different that we should treat them as the same concept. The point is the same: it is the identity of our criteria that makes disagreement genuine when it is genuine.

However, we cannot account for the way all our concepts make agreement and disagreement possible by treating them all as criterial concepts. You and I disagree, say, about whether an animal we encounter in Piccadilly is a lion, and it turns out that I identify lions by their size and shape and you only by what you believe to be their distinctive behavior. I say the animal we have met is a lion because it looks like a lion, and you deny this because instead of roaring it speaks an accented English. We are using very different criteria and yet we really are disagreeing. We are not, as in the "bank" case, talking about entirely different things. Nor is our disagreement fake because the concept of a lion is vague. In the baldness case, once we understand that our criteria differ over some range and accept that this range counts for both of us as borderline, we agree that we are not really disagreeing.[1] But in the lion case, even after we understand that we use very different identifying criteria, we insist that our disagreement is genuine. We still disagree about whether that beast standing near the Ritz really is, as it looks to be, a lion.

Some concepts are not criterial concepts, we must say, but rather (as many philosophers now call them) "natural-kind" concepts.[2] We need not pause over the exact character of these concepts, about which philosophers disagree, but can say (very roughly though adequately for us now) that natural kinds are things that have a fixed identity in nature, such as a chemical compound or an animal species, and that people share a natural-kind concept when they use that concept to refer to the same natural kind. People can refer to the same natural kind even when they use, and know they do, different criteria to identify instances. You and I assume that "lion" names a distinct biological kind and that the beast we met is a lion if it has a lion's biological essence, whatever that is, whether or not it meets the criteria either of us normally uses to identify lions. If you understand DNA, and if tests showed that the creature we saw had the DNA of a lion, you would likely change your opinion to recognize talking lions. Criterial concepts do not work that way: nothing you discovered about the molecular structure of my copy of *Moby Dick* could convince you that it was not a book.

We cannot take either criterial or natural-kind concepts to be only a special case of the other. There is no essential nature of baldness that finally determines who is bald in spite of appearances. We must accept what Wittgenstein pointed out: that concepts are tools and that we have different kinds of tools in our conceptual toolbox. However, criterial and natural-kind concepts do have something important in common. People do not share a concept of either kind unless they would accept a decisive test—a kind of decision procedure—for finally deciding when to apply the concept (except in cases they agree are marginal). Genuine disagreement about application is ruled out once all pertinent facts are agreed upon. We would not share the concept of a lion if we disagreed about the lionhood of an animal even when we agreed that it did or did not belong to the biological species historically designated as lions.

Does this condition for sharing a concept—that we share an idealized decision procedure for applying it—hold for all the concepts we share? The assumption that it does has dominated—and in my view spoiled—much recent philosophy of law.[3] In fact we must recognize at least one more family of concepts—a family that we share in spite of not agreeing about a decisive test. These are our interpretive concepts.[4] We share these concepts, as I said, not because we agree in their application once all other pertinent facts are agreed upon, but rather by manifesting an understanding that their correct application is fixed by the best interpretation of the practices in which they figure. I must explain this further.

Interpretive Concepts

Paradigms

People participate in social practices in which they treat certain concepts as identifying a value or disvalue but disagree about how that value should be characterized or identified. The concept of justice and other moral concepts work in that way for us. We agree—mainly—that these are values, but we do not agree about the precise character of these values. We do not agree about what makes an act just or unjust, right or wrong, an invasion of liberty or an act of tactlessness. Nor do we agree about what response, if any, would be required or justified by a correct attribution of the concept. But we agree sufficiently about what we take to be paradigm instances of the concept, and paradigm cases of appropriate reactions to those instances, to permit us to argue, in a way intelligible to others who share the concept with us, that a particular characterization of the value or disvalue best justifies these shared paradigms.[5]

We agree, for instance, in spite of great disagreements in other areas, that it would be unjust for government to tax wealth produced by the industrious poor for the sole benefit of the lazy rich or to convict and punish someone known to be innocent of any crime. We agree sufficiently about such paradigms to permit each of us to propose a theory or conception of justice that justifies the judgments we make in those paradigms, one that others can recognize as a theory or conception of that concept. Because these theories are different, and may be strikingly different, the attributions they license beyond the paradigms are different. Sharing an interpretive concept does depend, as sharing criterial and natural-kind concepts depends, on agreement. But the kind of agreement that is required in the case of an interpretive concept is very different: it is not agreement on a decision procedure as a decisive test for instances. On the contrary, sharing an interpretive concept is consistent with very great and entirely intractable differences of opinion about instances. It is also consistent with some people who share the concept denying that it expresses any value at all. Someone who declares that there is no value in what is expressed by a certain concept—chastity, perhaps, or etiquette or patriotism—must suppose ample agreement on paradigms of that concept among those who do count it as valuable. Otherwise his debunking argument could not take hold.

It would be a mistake to try to make this general account of interpretive concepts more precise: we cannot say just how much or what detail of agreement about paradigms is required in a particular community to justify treating a concept as interpretive for that community. It is in each case itself an interpretive question whether we make more sense of how the concept functions there on that assumption than we do on any competing assumption that declares agreement or disagreement spurious. (It is at least an open interpretive question, for example, whether the concept of democracy alive in the rhetoric of liberal societies is the same concept as the one deployed in so-called people's democracies.) The question always remains, in spite of even very radical disagreement, whether the pattern of that disagreement is better explained by the hypothesis that those who disagree share a single interpretive concept and disagree about its character, or by the alternative hypothesis that the disagreement is illusory like our agreement to meet at the bank. We noticed in Chapter 7 that the first stage in collaborative or explanatory interpretation is the identification of a genre to which an interpretive question belongs. There is a parallel basic stage in conceptual interpretation: treating a concept as interpretive supposes that this way of understanding a practice better interprets that practice than a rival interpretation that makes apparent agreement or disagreement spurious. Here too interpretation is interpretive all the way down.

There seems no doubt which of the alternative assumptions—shared interpretive concept or spurious disagreement—is more persuasive in the case of justice. We fight campaigns, even wars, about justice, and it is obviously false that if we only reflected on what we mean by the term, we would see that we really had nothing to disagree about. Because we share the interpretive concept of justice, we can recognize the theories of a great variety of political philosophers as competing conceptions of that concept. Utilitarian and other consequentialist philosophers interpret the practices in which claims of justice figure by supposing those practices to aim at the general happiness or some other desirable goal. Political philosophers in the Kantian tradition offer very different interpretations. Few of the politicians who argue about universal health care are sophisticated political philosophers, nor are their arguments self-consciously interpretive. But we can reconstruct their arguments by identifying theories of justice that each, on inspection, can be seen to exhibit and treating these theories as interpretations of the shared practices of calling institutions, people, and actions just and unjust. If we could not do this, we would have to accept what seems ludicrous: that the most fervent and passionate of our political arguments are just silly misunderstandings.

But can interpretive arguments about justice escape a narrow circularity? It was relatively easy to illustrate the value account of interpretation in Chapter 7 because the objects of interpretation we considered there—a poem or statute or an epoch—are not themselves values. There is no circularity in interpreting a statute by supposing it to serve the value of equality. But moral concepts themselves designate values. How can someone identify the value latent in the practices of justice without appealing, unhelpfully, to the concept of justice itself? I anticipated an answer in the discussion of moral responsibility in Chapter 6. We defend a conception of justice by placing the practices and paradigms of that concept in a larger network of *other* values that sustains our conception. We can in principle continue this expansion of our argument, exploring other values until, as I said, the argument meets itself. The circularity, if any, is global across the whole domain of value. That is the method of formal moral and political philosophy: the method of the social contract or the ideal observer, for example. At the end of this chapter I offer a more extended example in the moral and political theories of Plato and Aristotle. But what I hope will prove the most convincing illustration lies further on, in the later parts of the book—in particular in the analysis of moral concepts that begins in Chapter 11 and of political concepts beginning in Chapter 15. The idea of interpretive concepts plays an important and obvious role, that is, in the overall theme of this book: the unity of value.

Concepts and Usage

Though the distinctions we draw among criterial, natural-kind, and interpretive concepts are justified by usage—by the way people use and respond to concepts—these distinctions are interpretations of usage, not themselves part of usage. Few people who use the concept of democracy would agree that what a democracy is depends on which political theory provides the best justification of paradigms of the concept. Most would insist that they rely on a criterial or commonsense account of the matter, or none at all. But we nevertheless need the idea of an interpretive concept to explain their behavior: why they support or oppose theories of democracy in the way they do, and why their agreements and disagreements about whether particular governments are democracies are genuine, as they certainly suppose them to be. People are not always or even often aware of the buried theoretical structure needed to justify the rest of what they think.

Nor do I suppose that people who talk about books, lions, and justice understand that they are using different kinds of concepts. They need not— and most of them do not—have the concept of a concept at all, let alone the concept of a type of concept, let alone the concept of a criterial, natural-kind, or interpretive concept. These are philosophers' ideas: they are not recognized in practice but justified by their role in making sense of practice. Our account of the concepts that structure an intellectual domain is itself an interpretation of that domain, a device for making sense of the inquiry, reflection, arguments, and strategies that mark the domain. So in one sense all concepts are interpretive: because we must interpret the practice of "baldness" to decide that that concept is both criterial and vague, we might say that it is an interpretive fact that it is both.[6] The concepts I call interpretive concepts are interpretive not just in that sense, however, but in the further sense that people who use them are best understood as interpreting the practices in which they figure. There is enough leeway in this description, as I said, to allow for hard cases when it might be thought uncertain or even indeterminate whether a group agrees sufficiently about the paradigms to allow us to say that its members share a particular interpretive concept.

If most people do not understand what an interpretive concept is, why is it important nevertheless to insist that the concepts they use are interpretive? Part of the answer is explicit in what I have so far many times said: we want to understand as well as describe how and why people disagree and argue. We want to see whether their disagreements are genuine. But we also need to recognize interpretive concepts to guide our own arguments. Most of the rest of this book explores interpretive concepts. Understanding what kind of concepts these are, and what kinds of argument we therefore need, will help us construct and test conceptions of judgmental responsibility, a good life, moral obligation, human rights, liberty, equality, democracy, and law. It will also help us explain why the best conception of each of these concepts must both draw on and contribute to conceptions of the rest of them.

When Concepts Migrate

Because the assignment of any particular concept to one of the types we have distinguished is an interpretive conclusion, it need not hold for all uses of what seems the same concept. In most circumstances it would be bizarre to treat the concept of a book as other than a criterial concept. We would treat almost any disagreement about whether to count a flat-backed pamphlet as a book, however heated, as a silly, verbal disagreement rather than as a deep disagreement about the best interpretation of the practices in which the concept of a book figures. In some circumstances, however, a novel interpretation of a normally criterial concept would be appropriate, and indeed necessary, because in these circumstances the concept does function not as criterial but as interpretive. Imagine a statute declaring that bald men are entitled to a special income tax exemption. This silly statute would convert the question of baldness into a genuine interpretive issue: officials, lawyers, and judges would have to contrive some highly artificial definition of baldness (not necessarily a hair-counting definition) by asking which such definition would make most political sense of the exemption. Less silly examples are more plausible: a statute exempting books from sales or value-added tax but leaving "book" undefined, for instance. Concepts that are normally criterial often become interpretive when embedded in law in that way.[7]

In some circumstances, moreover, we must treat concepts that normally function as natural-kind concepts, not as interpretive because they do not house values, but rather as up for grabs in a different way. It seems settled now—no other assumption makes sense of our practices—that animal and mineral species are fixed by the most basic biological or chemical properties of these natural kinds: the animal's DNA and the metal's molecular structure. If I insist that some animal before us is a small lion rather than a very large pussy cat, even after I had grasped genetics and learned that the beast had the DNA of a cat, this would show either that I had misunderstood what a lion is or that you and I appeal to different concepts when we speak of a "lion." But the assumptions that DNA and molecular composition are decisive of an animal or metallic kind is a scientific achievement and, in the case of DNA, a relatively recent one. Experts treat these properties as settling issues of application because DNA or molecular structure provides the most comprehensive available explanation of a natural kind's other features, including its appearance.[8] In that way they explain why the differing criteria that people use to identify instances do pick out the same animals or metals.

But we can imagine further scientific discoveries that might disturb that assumption. Imagine that a newly invented form of radiation changes an animal's cells, not just randomly but into those produced by the DNA of a different animal. Zoologists would then have to choose between two ways of reporting this phenomenon: they might assume that an animal's species is fixed by the DNA it inherits from its parents, so that this form of radiation changes a lion's DNA, or that an animal's species is fixed by its DNA from time to time, so that the radiation turns lions into cats. Scientists might divide, at least for a time, in their choices and therefore in their opinions about which beasts are lions. If their arguments then took the form of a debate about the most useful way of continuing the established classificatory practices of zoology, we might well say that the concept of a lion had become for a time something like an interpretive rather than a natural-kind concept.

Criterial concepts can be up for grabs too. Consider the recent reformulation of the concept of a planet in a world congress of astronomers.[9] That concept is ordinarily criterial—planets are not natural kinds. So whether to call Pluto a planet might be treated as a borderline issue to be decided by arbitrary fiat and perhaps decided differently by different astronomers. But the settled practice of calling it a planet collided with the discovery that consistency would then require calling many insignificant solar system residents planets as well. The astronomers therefore adopted a legislative attitude—which conception of planethood would best fit the uses astronomers make of the distinction between planets and other bodies?—and spent a week debating that issue under the world's gaze with headlines daily declaring shifts in position and no doubt bookmakers setting odds on Pluto's fate. Finally Pluto was demoted, with various results including my consequent demotion as an astronomer in the eyes of my grandson. The concept of a planet is now, with a shiny new set of criteria, a criterial concept again. But it passed through, as we might put it, a brief different phase.

Moral Concepts

Moral concepts are interpretive concepts. That claim has great significance for moral and political philosophy. It offers to explain, for example, why the popular idea is mistaken that philosophers can provide an "analysis" of justice or liberty or morality or courage or law that is neutral about the substantive value or importance of these ideals. It supports the opinion I offered that "meta-ethics" is a misconceived project. It would therefore be wise to consider at some length how this strong claim might be resisted.

Politicians and philosophers disagree about instances of injustice. They do not think that questions like whether a progressive income tax is unjust are peripheral or borderline like the question whether some balding man is yet bald. One side takes the progressive income tax to be a firm requirement of justice, while the other calls it plainly unjust. They have no temptation to accept, once they see how different their criteria are, that their disagreement is not genuine. So it seems plausible, as an interpretive conclusion, to suppose that justice and other moral concepts are interpretive.

It might be objected, however, that in spite of these surface facts justice is nevertheless a criterial concept because people do agree at some high level of abstraction about the right criteria. But at how high a level? In his treatise John Rawls says that people who disagree about justice nevertheless "agree that institutions are just when no arbitrary distinctions are made between persons in the assigning of basic rights and duties and when the rules determine a proper balance between competing claims to the advantages of social life."[10] It is far from plain, however, that people do agree on criteria even at that very abstract level. It is a popular view in some parts of the world, for instance, that political institutions are unjust when they fail to respect God by providing authority and preference to his priests. That opinion objects not when arbitrary distinctions are made but when necessary ones are not made, and the complaint contains no claim about the proper distribution of advantages created by social life.

It is unclear that we can find any form of words, however abstract, that describes a consensus among those we take to share the concept of justice. But even if we could, that consensus would not describe a decision procedure for identifying justice or injustice. On the contrary, it would simply point to further apparent disagreements, whose nature as genuine disagreements would then have to be explained. If we accepted Rawls's suggestion, for instance, we would have to identify criteria that people who disagree about justice all accept for determining which distinctions are "arbitrary" and what is a "proper" balance of advantages. There are no such criteria.

We might try a different tack. We might say that people who disagree about justice actually do share criteria of application, because they agree about the connections between justice and more basic moral judgment. Disagreements about what is just and unjust, we might say, are really disagreements about what kinds of political institutions are good or bad, or about how officials or other people ought or ought not to behave. On this view, we could actually do without the concept of justice and argue directly about which institutions ought or ought not to be established or, if they exist, ought or ought not to be dismantled. One difficulty with this solution is evident: people have reasons for thinking that institutions ought or ought not to exist that are not reasons of justice. So we cannot treat every argument about whether officials ought to abolish the progressive income tax as an argument about the justice of that institution, and it is far from plain that we can explain what is distinctive about the particular arguments we have in mind without reintroducing the concept of justice. On the contrary, it seems impossible to do that. But there is an even more fundamental and pertinent difficulty: the strategy begs the central question, because it assumes that the very abstract moral concepts of goodness, badness, duty, and what ought or ought not be done are themselves criterial concepts.

So let us set complex moral concepts like justice aside for the moment and ask whether *any* of our moral concepts, including the most general and abstract among them, can be understood as criterial. On first appearances none can. People who disagree about what is good or about what ought to happen plainly do not share decisive criteria for settling those disagreements.[11] Can we say that these concepts are nevertheless criterial because people do agree that something ought to be done whenever there is an authoritative or categorical reason for doing it? No, this only pushes the problem back further—and not much further at that. People disagree about the right criteria for deciding when something is a categorical or authoritative reason for action. Nor would it help to try to specify shared criteria through consequences: to say, for instance, that people share the concept of goodness because they agree that something that is good is to be promoted or protected. Or that if some action is wrong then anyone who acts that way should be criticized or punished. People do not even agree on those propositions—any apparent agreement disappears when we ask what kind of promotion or protection or criticism or punishment is called for—and of course people do not share criteria for deciding what ought to be protected or promoted or punished. Moreover, there are many reasons for promoting something other than its goodness and for criticizing someone other than for his badness; as in the case of justice, there is no way to specify what is distinctive to moral reasons for promotion or criticism without using a moral vocabulary.

It seems hopeless, then, to try to account for agreement or disagreement about what is right or good by treating these concepts as criterial. However, we have noticed another possibility: perhaps we can treat these abstract concepts as natural-kind rather than criterial concepts. Let me explain. Some moral philosophers believe that there is a distinct property of goodness—a property that figures in what they call the actual inventory of the universe—and that moral argument is therefore about where this distinct property is to be found. Some of them suppose this to be a "non-natural" property—a matter of morons—that at least some human beings can perceive through a faculty of intuition. Others that it is a "natural" property that we perceive in the ordinary way. I gave my reasons for rejecting both these views, and the causal impact hypothesis on which they rest, in Chapter 4, but it might be helpful to return to the issues they raise.

Both versions treat moral concepts as in effect natural-kind concepts. On that view, goodness is like lionhood. We say that a particular animal is (or is not) a lion because it has (or does not have) the property (whatever it is) that provides the essential nature of a lion. Most people who say this have no idea what that property is and therefore may disagree about whether some animal is a lion. So, on this new story, people may sensibly say that capitalism is (or is not) good because it has (or does not have) the property (whatever it is) that provides the essence of the natural or non-natural property of goodness. People who say this will disagree about what that essence is. They disagree about whether it is a natural or non-natural property and, if the former, what natural property it is. But that does not mean, according to this new strategy, that their disagreement about the goodness of capitalism is not genuine.

The new strategy fails, however, because people can share a natural-kind concept only when they largely agree about which objects fall under that concept. Suppose you and I agreed that there is some essential property that defines which animal is a lion but disagreed not only about what that essential property is but also and consistently about which of the animals in our zoos and picture books are lions. That would suggest that we use "lion" to refer to entirely different animals and that our disagreement about the beast in Piccadilly is spurious after all. Our disagreement about a particular case is real only if we otherwise agree, by and large, when we are called on to identify lions. Philosophers of language explain this phenomenon historically: history has attached the name "lion" to a particular zoological kind, so that when people suppose that "it" has an essential nature, they refer to the animal kind people have called by that name.[12] This explanation presupposes convergence, not in criteria but in instances: though people may use different criteria in deciding what is a lion, they mainly all agree, at least after the other pertinent facts are known, about which animals are lions. But we don't mainly and consistently agree on which objects or people are good or which acts are wrong. Far from it. There is sufficient agreement about paradigms to allow us to say that these moral concepts are shared. But that minimal agreement leaves legions of crucial cases in which disagreement persists even after all other pertinent fact are agreed upon.

We must accept, then, that moral concepts are interpretive. But here is one final attempt to avoid that conclusion. "We should understand the very abstract vocabulary of morals—the concepts of goodness and of what we ought to do—as primitive concepts, concepts that cannot be defined in terms of something else. We all know very well what it means to say that something is good or right or that someone ought to do something, even though we cannot define these concepts by setting out tests on which we all agree. Just as we all know what we mean by yellow, and can therefore disagree about which fruits are yellow, so we all know what we mean when we say that something is good, and can therefore disagree about whether the triumph of capitalism is good." That final argument also fails. Of course we all know what we mean when we say that something is good or ought to be done. Our question is: what makes it true that we all mean the same thing? It is not enough to say that we all think we do. We must explain how we can be right. We suppose we mean the same thing by "yellow" because the objects we identify as yellow are the same objects, and when we disagree we think we can explain why by calling attention to light or perceptual apparatus. But that is not true in the case of moral concepts. I should add that because moral concepts are interpretive it is a mistake to say that they cannot be defined. Moral and political philosophy, as we shall see, is in large part an effort to define them. We should rather say that because any definition of a moral concept is a piece of moral interpretation, any helpful definition will inevitably be controversial.

Relativism?

Do these arguments threaten a new relativism? The practices that employ the concepts of justice, honesty, and the other concepts I called interpretive vary from place to place. We count racial or gender discrimination as a paradigm example of injustice; other cultures think that justice permits or indeed even requires such discrimination. Does it not follow that the best interpretation of these practices would vary correspondingly, so that the best conception of what justice requires in Toledo might not be the best conception in Tehran? We might worry that if justice is interpretive, someone in a culture that practices systematic discrimination against women makes no mistake when he says that such discrimination is not unjust. His interpretation, we might think, is correct for the practices of his community. Parallels with legal practice might seem to suggest this. Legal practice is different in different political communities, and so, of course, are people's legal rights and duties. If justice is an interpretive concept, why should this not also be true about justice?

We have an antecedent problem even in understanding this threat. Why should we assume that the various practices that differ so much around the world are all practices built around the same concept—the concept of justice? In most of these places the English word "justice" is not used; we suppose that the practices of people there are practices of justice because we suppose that some word they use invokes the value we use that word to invoke. (Even if they do use a word that sounds like "justice," we make the same assumption, of course.) But if those practices are really so different, what justifies that piece of translation? Why should we not say, rather, that they do not have the concept of justice at all?

So the threat presupposes enough structural similarity to justify the assumption that their concept is our concept. They must call many acts we judge unjust by the word we translate as "unjust," and they must suppose that their designation has sufficiently similar consequences to those we recognize when we call something unjust. Otherwise our translation would be mistaken. (Compare the discussion of radical translation in Chapter 7.) Those structural similarities, which we need to notice even to pose the threat, also dissolve it. We can count a great proportion of the substantive claims other cultures make about justice as mistakes; we do this when we suppose that the best available justification of the paradigms of attribution and response we share justifies rejecting those claims. We must judge for ourselves what justification of these shared paradigms and structures is adequate, and no justification that approved gender discrimination would be. They share the concept of justice with us, but—at least so we can sensibly suppose—they misunderstand that concept profoundly. There is no relativism in this story, only error on their part.

What if our translation exercise fails? We find no word in some linguistic community that we can sensibly translate as "justice," and we conclude that that community does not have the concept. It remains true that their behavior may be deeply unjust: acting unjustly does not require having the concept of justice. There is no relativism in this different story either.

Why is law different? Why do we not say that nations that have adopted zoning regulations different from ours have misunderstood the concept of law, so that, contrary to what they think, it is actually illegal to tear down Georgian buildings there as well as here? Because any plausible conceptions of law and of justice must suppose that local decisions have a force in fixing what law requires that they do not have in fixing what is just or unjust. Different legal theories understand the force of local decisions differently; but any competent theory assigns such decisions much greater force in law than in morality. Even when we understand that law is a branch of morality—that is what I argue in Chapter 19—we must accept this indispensable distinction between that branch and the rest of the domain.

Truth

Disagreement about Truth

I suggested that many of the concepts that occupy philosophers—not just moral and political concepts, but concepts that challenge philosophers in other ways—are best treated as interpretive concepts. Disputes about the concept of truth seem perennial among philosophers. Is that concept, as it figures in their theories and controversies, an interpretive concept? We certainly disagree about what truth is and about what is true. Some of these disagreements are philosophical: I disagree with some external skeptics about whether moral judgments can be true. And of course people disagree about truth in thousands of more mundane ways all the time: about whether it is true that Cleopatra slept with Caesar or that our universe started with a big bang or that Glendower was a fool or that the Iraq invasion was immoral. If these various philosophical and more mundane disagreements are genuine, as they certainly seem to be, then people, including philosophers, must share a concept of truth. But do they? How?

It is high time I raised these questions. In Part One I argued that moral claims can be objectively true. In this part I have argued, more generally, that interpretive judgments can be true. I tried to state the truth conditions of interpretive judgments and how these differ from the truth conditions of scientific claims. Truth has been my subject all along. But if external skeptics and I do not share a concept of truth, then these long discussions have been silly, as illusory as the pseudo-agreement we had about the bank. In Chapter 7 I said that those who balk at calling interpretive judgments "true" could substitute some other word—perhaps "most reasonable" or "most acceptable." But am I entitled to say that they would be using the same concept?

It is now a popular view that truth is a primitive idea that cannot be defined.[13] But (as we saw in the case of goodness) that is not a helpful response to these questions. We need to ask whether philosophers and other people share the same primitive concept. They do not share criteria for applying the concept: for deciding whether "true" is properly used of propositions in some particular domain like morality or mathematics. They might agree on what Crispin Wright has called "platitudes" about truth: that the proposition that snow is white is true only if snow is white, for instance, or that a proposition is true if it accurately reports the facts of the matter.[14] But these platitudes do not yield decision procedures for answering the questions they ask. Philosophers do not agree about what kinds of facts there are.

I distinguished, a moment ago, mundane from philosophical uses of the concept of truth. If we look only at the former, we might be tempted by what has been called the "deflationary" theory of truth.[15] This holds, roughly, that to claim that a proposition is true is just to repeat the proposition. Calling it true that Sam is bald or that water flows downhill or that gratuitous torture is bad is just saying that Sam is bald, that water flows downhill, or that gratuitous torture is bad. So we might say that in such contexts truth functions as a criterial concept, because we all agree on a decision procedure: that if things are as a statement asserts them to be, then it is correct to call that statement true. The concepts we use in stating how things are may themselves be criterial or natural-kind or interpretive concepts: all three occur in those examples. But truth itself, we might think, remains criterial.

We cannot, however, take this view of the concept of truth as it appears in philosophical controversies about truth—for example, in the controversy about whether moral claims can be true (or, indeed, whether the deflationary theory of truth is correct). In the mundane use, any worry about the nature of truth disappears once we understand its redundancy. We needn't worry about what truth is: we are concerned only with Sam's scalp, water's behavior, and whether gratuitous torture is bad. But in philosophical contexts truth remains the focus of attention: we cannot transfer our concern about its nature to concern about something else. It is correct, but wholly unhelpful, to say that the sentence "Moral judgments can be true" is true if and only if moral judgments can be true. The fact remains that philosophers disagree about whether moral judgments can be true because they disagree about what truth is.

We can rescue philosophical arguments about the nature of truth if we can understand truth as an interpretive concept. We should reformulate the different theories of truth that philosophers have proposed, so far as we can, by treating them as interpretive claims. We share a vast variety of practices in which the pursuit and achievement of truth are treated as values. We do not invariably count it good to speak or even to know the truth, but it is our standard assumption that both are good. The value of truth is interwoven in these practices with a variety of other values that Bernard Williams called, comprehensively, the values of truthfulness.[16] These include accuracy, responsibility, sincerity, and authenticity. Truth is also interwoven with a variety of other kinds of concepts: conspicuously the concept of reality, but also the concepts of belief, investigation, inquiry, assertion, argument, cognition, proposition, assertion, statement, and sentence. We must interpret all these concepts—the entire family of truth concepts—together, trying to find a conception of each that makes sense given its relations with the others and given standard assumptions about the values of truth and truthfulness.

The familiar philosophical theories of truth should therefore be judged by asking how well they interpret this great network of concepts and practices taken together. The once-popular correspondence theory, for example, should be seen as an attempt to construct interwoven conceptions of correspondence and reality such that it makes substantial interpretive—not just platitudinous—sense to treat truth as correspondence with reality. If successful, that interpretation of these concepts would provide a successful interpretation of the other truthfulness concepts as well: it would sustain Williams's accounts of the value of sincerity, for instance. If suitably elaborated it would also make good sense of the familiar and intuitive connection between truth and causation in the domains to which it applied: that the proposition that Jupiter is the largest planet is true not just if, but because, Jupiter is the largest planet.

However, the project of connecting truth with correspondence has proved difficult. Ingenuity is required, for example, to show that there is something in reality to which a negative proposition (that Caesar did not dine with Casca on his last night) or a complex proposition (if Caesar had dined with Casca, he would have discovered the conspiracy) might be thought to correspond. It has also proved difficult, moreover, to specify any substantial and appropriate sense of correspondence. How can propositions be thought to *correspond* with anything?

But for now assume (just as an illustration, and not because we believe it) that these problems have been or can be solved.[17] Assume that philosophers can produce conceptions of correspondence and reality that generate something in reality to which propositions, including negative and complex propositions, can be said to correspond. We then face the following important interpretive question. Should we take the best correspondence theory (whatever it turns out to be) to exhaust the concept of truth? Or should we take the best such theory to be the upshot of applying to science (or some other particular domain of inquiry) a yet more abstract interpretation of the truth concepts and practices? A yet more abstract interpretation whose application to other domains, like mathematics or morality, might yield not a correspondence theory but a very different theory for that domain?

We faced a parallel question in Chapter 7 when we discussed the popular psychological state theory of interpretation. I distinguished two views. The first holds that this popular theory exhausts interpretation, so that truth in interpretation is always just a matter of correspondence with some psychological state, like the intention of a poet or lawmaker. It would follow that no claim could be said to be true when, as often occurs in interpretive genres like law and history, there is no psychological state that can make it true. The second, rival, view argues that the psychological state theory holds only for certain particular genres of collaborative interpretation, like conversational interpretation; it holds for those genres in virtue of the application to them of a more abstract account—I called this the value account—that fits a broader range of genres as well. I argued for the second view. The psychological state account is illuminating for some genres but misplaced in others, and the more abstract value account explains which and why.

I mean now to press the same distinction about theories of truth. We might, first, take the correspondence theory of truth (or some rival like a coherence theory) to exhaust the concept of truth—to state conditions that any kind of judgment in any domain must meet if it is to count as true. We would then demote as not "truth-apt" any domain of apparent intellectual activity in which the chosen exclusive conception of truth has no application; this might be, for instance, mathematics or morality. Or we might, second, try to formulate some very abstract concept of truth, and of the associated ideas of reality, objectivity, responsibility, sincerity, and the rest, that would allow us to construct different less abstract theories as candidates for explaining truth in, the different domains in which claims of truth play a role.

If we took up the second strategy, we would treat the various theories of truth that philosophers have proposed, including the redundancy, correspondence, coherence, and pragmatist theories, as attempts to apply some more abstract account of truth to some particular domain or domains, just as we treat the author's intention theory as a candidate for a theory of interpretive truth in some genres rather than across all genres of interpretation. A truth theorist might then claim that his favored theory supplies the best application of that more abstract theory to one particular domain, such as science, without thereby claiming that the same theory is also successful as an application of that abstract idea of truth to other domains.

The first, monolithic strategy has been popular. Philosophers have offered theories of truth that seem to fit science well and then declared morality, for instance, not to be truth-apt because it is not truth-apt on that theory. In Part One we discovered a fatal difficulty in that strategy. We cannot understand the thesis that it is not true that torture is wrong as other than a denial that torture is wrong, which itself claims not just truth-aptness but truth for a moral judgment. Nor can we understand the more contorted and mysterious thesis that it is neither true nor false that torture is wrong other than as claiming truth for the moral judgment that those who believe that torture is wrong are wrong. We considered and dismissed various ways of avoiding that paradox. We noticed apparently more sophisticated versions of skepticism, including what I called the two-language-games strategy. But these founder because they leave themselves no space in which to deny that any discourse is really (or fundamentally, or at the explanatory or philosophical level) not suitable for truth. So the first of the two strategies for truth theories ends in failure.

We must take up the second strategy. This has obvious initial advantages. It fits a much broader range of the practices in which the concepts of truth and truthfulness now play an important role. The brigade of virtues collected in the idea of truthfulness—sincerity, authenticity, intellectual responsibility, and the rest—is not limited to the domains of physical science and psychology. These virtues are equally important in morality, law, and other genres of interpretation. The first strategy is therefore committed to what seems bad interpretive strategy: seeking an interpretation that ignores from the start vast parts of the interpretive data. The second strategy begins, on the contrary, by noticing all the data.

We would make a more convincing case for the second strategy, however, if we could set out a very abstract, highest-level account of truth that we might think holds for all the genres—of science, mathematics, philosophy, and value—in which claims of truth are standard. Perhaps that would not be absolutely necessary. We might perhaps study truth as a wide-ranging interpretive concept just by attending to its various paradigms in different domains without any overall abstract formulation. I defended that possibility in the case of justice earlier in this chapter. Still, it would be helpful to find some very abstract statement of the concept of truth, some formulation that is independent of any intellectual domain and explains why the different standards for pursuing truth in different domains are nevertheless all standards for pursuing truth.

That statement would have to be even more abstract than the value theory of interpretation discussed in Chapter 7, because the latter theory, which is a theory of truth in interpretation, would then have to be seen as itself an application of an even more abstract theory of truth to the entire domain of interpretation. That supremely abstract theory of truth could not be wholly formal or platitudinous, however. If we can formulate such a theory at all, it would have work to do: it would have to fit and justify our truth-seeking practices and the allied practices of truthfulness across all domains. That is a tall order, and I do not know how to satisfy it.

Here is one tentative and incomplete suggestion. We might build a suitable supremely abstract theory by taking inquiry and truth to be paired and interwoven concepts, so that we can usefully characterize truth, as I did in the last chapter, as the intrinsic goal of inquiry. We could offer, as our most abstract characterization, that truth is what counts as the uniquely successful solution to a challenge of inquiry. We could then construct more concrete specifications of truth for different domains by finding more concrete accounts of success tailored to each domain.[18] These different accounts would be nested. The value theory would be a candidate account for success across the whole domain of interpretation, and the theory of moral responsibility I described in Chapter 6 would be a candidate application of the value theory to the more specific interpretive domain of morality. A different account of success, and hence truth, would be offered for science. The distinction Chapter 7 offered—that investigative success must be defined by purpose in interpretation but must be divorced from purpose in science—would distinguish conceptions of truth at a very abstract level, but these would both be conceptions of truth viewed from the most abstract level.

These sketchy remarks are reminiscent, at least, of much of what Charles Saunders Peirce said about truth.[19] But we must not say, as Peirce once said, that truth is always or just what enables us to satisfy some desire we have.[20] That is correct in some cases—when the question we take up is the question of what will satisfy us—but not generally. His statement was ill-advised because it misidentifies the level of his pragmatism. It treats his pragmatism as a theory of truth competitive with a correspondence, coherence, interpretive, or some other kind of theory; his pragmatism seems better understood as a more abstract directive about how to decide which other more particular such theory is right for some particular domain. That reading draws the sting of an old joke: that the trouble with pragmatism is that it doesn't work. In

Peirce's hands, at least, it was meant to "work" not by itself, but only by rec-ommending to us some other, distinctly not pragmatic, less abstract theory. In any case, the practices that make the truth concepts valuable in science rule out, decisively, any suggestion that what is true in science is what is useful—or delightful or intriguing or ironic. It is an important human achievement to have recognized this.

Skepticism Again

If we are to pursue some such suggestion, we must be able to treat the various forms of internal skepticism, including the indeterminacies I described in Chapter 5, as also uniquely successful solutions to challenges of inquiry. I said there that (in my tentative opinion) claims about the relative superiority of great artists working in very different genres at very different times are misjudged; according to the best account of artistic value, I said, no such claim, including the claim that these great artists were of equal worth, can be sustained. That is internal skepticism because it relies on a positive theory of artistic value. We might take something of the same view about the concept of humor. We might find it ludicrous that something could be really funny though it never produced even a tinge of amusement. We might conclude that it would be a mistake to claim objective truth for ascriptions of humor.[21]

We must now consider how such internal skepticism sorts with the su-premely abstract theory of truth I just sketched. We take at face value claims of truth in all the domains in which such claims are familiar; we then ask, as an initial question, whether a particular domain can be understood as orga-nized around inquiry. If so, we then consider whether the best theory of suc-cess in that inquiry supports the assumption, either in general or over some part or aspect of the practice, that no uniquely successful culmination of that inquiry exists. We treat that question as substantive within the area of in-quiry, and the skepticism at stake is therefore only internal skepticism. I offered this example in the last chapter. A director contemplates a new production of *Hamlet*. He might ask: Which interpretation of the play as a whole and of each speech should guide any production of the play anytime, anywhere? Or he might ask: Given my own reactions to the play, the cast and funding I have available, the time and place in which I work, and recent productions of the play around here, which interpretation should guide me now? In my own view, for reasons I offered in that chapter, the best theory about the proper goals of a fresh production of a classic shows that there is no uniquely right answer to the first of these questions. But that same theory might hold that there is indeed a uniquely right answer to the second question, even though our director is entirely uncertain what that right answer is. Of course, I might be wrong in my view about the proper goals of a new production of a classic, in which case my views about right answers would be wrong as well. Everything is substantive here, and everything is therefore in play.

Truth and Method

Our approach is different in another crucial respect. More conventional accounts draw a sharp line between theories of truth, which are meant to hold across all domains, and theories of proper investigative methodology, which must of course differ according to subject matter. Our approach recognizes, on the contrary, only differences of degree in abstraction between the two kinds of theory. We begin with a near-formal and supremely abstract account of the concept of truth—unique success in inquiry, for instance. When we apply that near-formal account of truth to specific domains, we produce more concrete theories, and these merge through further specification into discrete methodological manuals for each domain and subdomain. If, for instance, we take some form of correspondence theory to be the more concrete upshot of applying that very abstract formulation to the physical sciences, that more concrete theory would already supply the rudiments of a theory of scientific method: limiting evidence for propositions about the physical world to what can plausibly be thought to be caused directly or indirectly by facts that would make those propositions true, for instance. Each more detailed account or specification of scientific method—a special theory for particle physics or for the biological sciences, for example—would also be a more detailed specification of a theory of truth.

That progression from truth to method holds equally for the domains of interpretation. There is no sharp break, but only a difference in degree of abstraction, between a theory of truth for some interpretive genre and a more detailed theory defending some claim about sound method in that genre. A psychological state theory of truth in literary interpretation is a more abstract version of some particular critic's view about how to read *Among School Children*. In Chapter 6 I emphasized the distinction between moral truth and moral responsibility. But I also said that the interpretive reasoning required for moral responsibility is our best hope for achieving moral truth. I can now put the connection rather differently. Our theory of moral responsibility must be an appropriately concrete specification of our theory of moral truth, and any skepticism about the possibility of truth for some class of moral judgment must be secured through the exercise of moral responsibility. That is just another way of rehearsing what is by now a familiar song in these pages. Any genuine moral skepticism must be an internal skepticism. But now we reach that conclusion in a different way: through a study of the best conception, for morality, of what truth is.

Nothing in this argument even hints that truth is ever up to us. That is already ruled out by the most abstract formulation of truth as success in inquiry. There is nothing optional or pale or minimal or quietist in the kind of truth we claim for either domain. Nor are we talking past one another in our philosophical arguments over truth. We really do disagree.

At least since Plato identified the problem in the *Meno,* philosophers have worried about what they call the paradox of analysis. They set out to analyze familiar concepts—truth, causation, justice, and the rest—by telling us what each means. But if they succeed, then, because these are our concepts, they tell only what we already know. It follows that if an analysis is correct, it is uninformative. The idea of interpretive concepts dissolves the paradox. A successful conception of an interpretive concept is indeed something new.[22]

Thin and Thick Concepts

We return to the main argument. I said that moral concepts such as those of justice, honesty, treachery, and friendship are interpretive: we account for agreement and disagreement about cases not by finding shared criteria of application but by supposing shared practices in which these concepts figure. We develop conceptions of these concepts through interpretation. We suppose that even the most abstract moral concepts—the concept of what is good and of what we ought to do—are interpretive: we have no other way of explaining how disputes about what is good or right are genuine.

But the idea of interpretation might not seem easily to fit these very abstract moral concepts. It makes evident sense to treat our disagreements about friendship—whether someone should be criticized for giving the police incriminating evidence about a friend—as reflecting different interpretations of friendship. It seems odd to think of goodness and duty that way, however: odd to think that an argument about whether we have an obligation to help people in poverty is an argument about the best interpretation of what obligation is. The difference reflects the fact that when we disagree about the application of very abstract moral concepts—about what someone ought to do in certain circumstances, for instance—we interpret an open-ended and large set of practices rather than a smaller and more focused practice.

Bernard Williams gave the names "thick" and "thin" to two families of moral concepts, and he took the difference between them to be fundamental. He called the ideas of moral rightness and wrongness, of what ought and ought not be done, thin concepts, because they are very abstract vehicles of commendation or disparagement that can be attached to an almost unlimited range of actions or states of affairs. We can intelligibly say, of almost any human action, that it is morally required or wrong. Thick moral concepts, on the other hand, mix the praise or disparagement they offer with more concrete factual descriptions. "Brave," "generous," "cruel," and "trustworthy" are thick concepts: each of these praises or condemns a particular kind of behavior that it also describes. So each of the thick concepts can sensibly be applied only to a certain kind of act, an act, we might say, that is a candidate for that particular kind of commendation or condemnation. It is at least intelligible, though preposterous, to say that acts of charity are morally wrong. It is not even intelligible (except, perhaps, in a very special context) to say that charitable acts are cowardly.

The distinction between thin and thick moral concepts has been misunderstood by some philosophers: its importance has been underestimated by some and exaggerated by others. Some philosophers have insisted on analyzing the distinction away. They say that a thick concept like the concept of cowardice should be understood as a hybrid: it combines a straightforward criterial concept, shared only by those who follow the same criteria for identifying acts of cowardice, with an emotional charge: that such conduct is wrong.[23] This is a serious mistake. The thick concepts cannot be dissected to reveal a criterial base concept.

It is not true that we all agree about what conduct is factually described by "cowardice" and disagree only about whether and how much we disapprove of such conduct. Nor can such concepts be dissected by supposing that "cowardly" is a compound of some other descriptive concept (what could this be?) and a negative emotional charge. Whether someone is properly called brave—or tactless or cruel or generous—depends not simply on how he has acted but also on a judgment about the moral valence of his act. Deciding what bravery or tact or cruelty or generosity means—what acts are properly described in these terms—requires interpretation: what one person deems bravery or tact another calls foolhardiness or dishonesty.[24]

Other philosophers take the distinction to mark important divisions within moral theory. Williams, for instance, argued that moral knowledge is possible only of thick concepts, because only these concepts are sufficiently embedded in and given meaning by the practices of particular communities to allow members of those communities to claim knowledge of them.[25] Many contemporary philosophers call themselves "virtue theorists" because they emphasize the importance of certain thick concepts. They hope in that way to distinguish their general approach from that of the more numerous moral philosophers who offer general theories of thin concepts: Kantians, for example, who defend a formal account of moral duty, and consequentialists absorbed with defining the good that morality requires us always to pursue. In fact, however, the two kinds of concepts are so interrelated and interdependent in their functions that neither can be said to be more fundamental or central or more a matter of knowledge than the other. We could hardly have either without the other. We use thin concepts as conclusions, to report overall moral judgments, but without offering much, if anything, by way of a case to ground those judgments. Thicker concepts often provide the case that the thin concepts presuppose but do not supply.

The distinction is not polar but one of degree: moral concepts have different degrees of thickness, and each has different degrees in different contexts. In many circumstances, reminding someone of a promise he has made would supply much more by way of a substantive case than accusing him of treachery, but in other circumstances it would supply less. The virtue concepts are among the thickest of moral concepts, but they differ in thickness as well. Saying that someone is generous or tactful is certainly more informative than saying that he is a good or virtuous person, but it is less informative than saying that he is punctilious. The concepts of duty and obligation are commonly treated as thin, but they are thicker than the concept of the good or the impermissible; declaring that someone has a duty or an obligation signals at least a general kind of case for the demand it embodies: it suggests a promise or undertaking or some special responsibility of role or status. The familiar concepts of political morality vary in thickness as well. Describing a tax system as unjust says more than simply declaring it morally objectionable but less than calling it oppressive.

Neither thick nor thin concepts are more central or important to morality than the other kind: they are all part of a single system that would be unrecognizable without both. On some occasions idiom or practice or context makes it more natural to say that an act is just plain wrong than that it is treacherous, inconsiderate, cruel, dishonest, indecent, niggardly, unreasonable, cheap, unworthy, unfair, or contemptuous, or that a person has a good character rather than that he is generous, courageous, noble, or selfless. On other occasions the more concrete charges or claims would seem more natural. In either case, more concrete or more abstract judgments are waiting in the wings, though they may never appear. It is usually pointless to call an act unreasonable or tactless without suggesting that it is for that reason, at least to some degree and in some way, wrong as well. It is usually fraudulent to call something wrong or someone bad without supposing that there is some more informative description that begins at least to say why it is wrong or he is bad. Concrete and abstract concepts all have roles to play, and to exchange, in morality's repertory.

The flexibility provided by moral concepts of different thickness is useful in a variety of ways. Concepts that differ in thickness allow us to distinguish *pro tanto* considerations from overall judgments, for example. We might say that though someone did act cruelly on some occasion, it was the right thing for him to do at the time. Or that though what he did was selfish, he had a right to do it, and so no one has a right to complain. (I discussed in Chapter 6 whether the conflict in value these claims might suggest is genuine.) The thinner concepts are particularly appropriate when we want to state moral conclusions about difficult or very evenly balanced cases. We might want to say, for example, that though someone who does not report a friend's serious crime does the right thing, he would not have been treacherous if he had reported it. Thin concepts are also useful when we want to contrast moral with other kinds of reasons that we might entertain on some occasion. It is not necessary, on those occasions, to specify our moral reasons in any greater detail: "I know this is wrong, but I can't resist!"[26] In all these and many other ways, our moral experience is reflected in and facilitated by the distinctions we draw between more and less conclusory and more or less informative moral concepts.

So it is no obstacle to an interpretive understanding of morality and moral reasoning that some of the thinner concepts on which modern moral philosophers have most steadily fixed their attention—the concepts of rightness or goodness—are not so apparently interpretive as thicker concepts are. They do function as interpretive—otherwise we could not disagree using their vocabulary as we plainly do—but the interpretation they require must be focused, at least in the first instance, on other concepts, because the thinner concepts draw conclusions but do not themselves suggest much by way of argument. When argument is needed, we interpret the thicker concepts, including the relatively thinner of those thicker concepts, like the ideas of what is reasonable and what is just, to find grounds for redeeming the less clothed conclusions we offer in the very thin concepts we first use.

Plato and Aristotle

Because moral concepts are interpretive, both quotidian moral reasoning and high moral philosophy are interpretive exercises. Does that hypothesis help us to better understand the influential moral philosophers of the past? I shall try to answer that question by discussing the arguments of particular philosophers at different stages later in the book. I begin here with what I believe to be classic, obvious, and particularly instructive examples of interpretive moral philosophy.

Plato and Aristotle constructed their moral and political theories around interpretations of virtues and vices, ranging from those we regard as distinctly personal, like wisdom, to the great political virtue of justice. Their arguments were actively holistic. Each offered an elaborate interpretive argument that developed in two significantly different stages. First, they analyzed each of the virtues and vices they took up by constructing conceptions of each that draw upon and reinforce the conceptions they favored of the others. They showed these virtues, that is, as forming a mutually supportive network of moral values. Then, as a second stage, they found interconnections between that network of moral concepts and ethics.[27] They argued that their conceptions of the moral values were correct because a life that exhibits those values understood through those conceptions is best calculated to provide a state of being, "eudemonia," that modern translators into English characteristically call "happiness" but that we might better call "a good life"—the life that people, in their own best interests, should try to live.

Terence Irwin has argued that the arguments of Socrates in Plato's earlier dialogues were not interpretive.[28] The earlier Socratic method supposed that a successful definition of individual virtues would be reductive: that is, that it would characterize a virtue only descriptively. One of the straight men in an early dialog offers a reductive definition of bravery, for instance: bravery, he says, is holding steadfast in the face of danger.[29] The earlier Socrates shows that all the attempts at reductive definitions he is offered are inadequate, but he does not offer a reductive definition of his own. On the contrary, he says repeatedly that he is unable to construct one. The Socrates of the *Republic,* on the other hand, is quite willing to offer conceptions of each of the virtues, but he has abandoned the reductive constraint and adopted the interpretive style.

He offers conceptions of bravery, temperance, wisdom, and justice that show each of these to be distinct from the others—he rejects the earlier Socratic idea that all the virtues are one because knowledge comprises all the virtues—but to be interdependent nevertheless, so that the definition of each virtue incorporates an appeal to the value of other virtues. Bravery, for example, is not the same as temperance, but bravery cannot be defined independently of temperance. However, the great challenge of the *Republic,* put in different ways first by Thrasymachus and then by Glaucon and Adeimantus, takes Socrates to the second stage of interpretation I distinguished. He is asked to find connections between justice and happiness—between the moral virtues collected in the former and the ethical ambition of the latter—such that any just person must be happier than any unjust person.

Plato did not form his ideas of justice and of the good life independently and then discover their interdependence. He did not argue that justice, as this was then commonly understood, provides happiness. On the contrary, he denied that what Thrasymachus counted as happiness is genuine happiness. Plato's conception of justice is strikingly counterintuitive: he analyzes that concept to include a psychic condition of the agent. He seeks an account not of just actions but of a just person, and he identifies a just person, in the first instance, not as someone who cares about others but as someone who cares about the goodness of his own being. True, Plato does labor, as any philosopher using an interpretive approach must, to show that his conception of justice is not too counterintuitive to count as a conception of that virtue. He tries to explain how the enlightened promotion of self gives one an interest in the well-being of others. As we shall see, many other philosophers, including Kant, have followed much the same strategy. Plato's argument may be unpersuasive—Irwin discusses potent objections to it—but it is plainly directed by an interpretive strategy.

Plato's interpretive argument is multidimensional; it embraces an account of bravery and temperance as well as justice and happiness. It aims, moreover, at conceptions of the virtues that are not hierarchal but mutually supportive. He does not begin with an account of happiness and mold his discussion of the virtues to fit it. On the contrary, his account of happiness is also initially counterintuitive and can finally be justified only through its interpretive accommodation with the virtues. It is hardly obvious that happiness is the ordering of the soul: that seems to leave out pleasure and the other familiar components of happiness. So Plato must take up the further challenge of showing that his account of happiness is, after all, a good interpretation of what people commonly seek under that name. He must therefore expand the interpretive network still more broadly, to include the account of pleasure that he offers in book 9 of the *Republic* and then in the *Philebus*.[30] This shows pleasure to be not simply a desired experience but an indispensable part, though only part, of a good life. The entire remarkable construction, successful or not, is a paradigm of morality as interpretation.

Aristotle's *Nicomachean Ethics* is also a superb illustration of the interpretive method. He sets out his account of the virtues by situating each as the mean between two vices: we are to understand what bravery requires by contrasting what is brave both with what is cowardly and what is foolhardy; what temperance means by contrasting temperance with both intemperance, which is too great a concern with nonrational impulses for food, drink, and sex, and insensibility, which is too little concern with them; and so forth. The doctrine of the mean is an interpretive device. Conceptual interpretation often seeks to defend a particular conception of a virtue, as Aristotle also does, by showing how recognizing that virtue, so conceived, helps to promote some other value. The doctrine of the mean works differently: it defends a particular conception of a virtue by constructing a parallel account of that virtue and two recognized vices that might be seen, initially, as bracketing it.

The representation of the virtue as a mean between the two vices is not an interpretive conclusion but rather a strategy for guiding interpretation: the interpretive challenge is to find an account of the virtue that explains its apparent intermediate position between two vices. We cannot do this by identifying some Goldilocks commodity such that intemperance has too much of it, boorishness too little, and temperance just the right amount. Temperance is a virtue and intemperance a vice, not because the intemperate person takes more pleasure in life than the temperate one, but because he takes pleasure in the wrong things. We can sustain the bracketing strategy, therefore, only by identifying the right things in which to take unlimited pleasure and then the wrong things to take any pleasure (or much pleasure) in having.

Aristotle puts a great many other, neighboring concepts to work in identifying these right and wrong things: the concept of fineness, for example, which some commentators take to be an aesthetic concept, and the ethical concept of bestiality. This bracketing device is only one of his interpretive tools: he triangulates each virtue not only by drawing on some familiar sense of a related vice but also by appealing to other virtues that intersect the virtue under study. So though the brave man does not fear what the coward fears, he properly fears dishonor and disgrace. Even apparently unrelated virtues like civic pride and responsibility figure in the account of bravery: the brave man stands firm, not necessarily in the face of natural threats like the threat of death at sea, but in even hopeless battle when he fights as a citizen for his community. For a citizen, fear of dishonor "is caused by a virtue; for its cause is shame and desire for something fine—for honor—and aversion from reproach, which is disgraceful."[31]

Aristotle's discussion of individual virtues corresponds to the first stage of conceptual moral interpretation: it concentrates on moral concepts. His discussion is set against a prior and more general discussion that supplies the second, ethical stage. He starts on a discussion of the virtues only after he has first argued that "eudemonia" consists in activity in accordance with the most complete virtue, in a complete life. Living virtuously is necessary to a good life, he says, even though it is not sufficient, because a virtuous life might be marred by great misfortunes, such as Priam suffered in Troy, or by poverty. No one would call a life cursed by poverty or terrible misfortune a good life, even it was virtuous. But someone might be rich, fortunate, and maximally content with his life—he might, in the common view, be perfectly happy—and yet not have happiness in Aristotle's conception, because he does not lead a life of virtuous activity.

The connection Aristotle draws between virtues and happiness is interpretive, just as Plato's is. It is multidimensional and mutually supporting rather than hierarchal. How we understand happiness—a good life—depends on how we understand each of the virtues, which in turn depends on how we understand each of the others. But how we understand the virtues also depends on our independent sense of what happiness is. Aristotle constantly checks his account of the virtues by asking whether common opinion—particularly the opinion of "the wise"—would endorse a life lived in accordance with virtue so understood as a happy or successful life. (See, for example, his account of the role of pleasure in happiness.[32]) This last requirement is yet another turn of the interpretive screw, if we assume that the wise are particularly good judges of virtue because they are themselves virtuous. It would be a serious misunderstanding to condemn Aristotle's argument as circular, not because it is not in its broad sweep circular, but because that is its achievement, not its failure.[33]

We should notice, finally, a further dimension of interpretation that Aristotle treats as particularly important. He declares that the project of better understanding happiness, and therefore virtue, is not an abstract, theoretical enquiry but one aimed at action, and principally political action. The *Nicomachean Ethics,* he says, is an exercise in political science. We need to understand happiness so that we can construct a good state, which is a state in which people are enabled and encouraged to lead good lives. Once again this is not a one-way connection. We understand good government better by better understanding happiness and the virtues, which good government fosters. But we also better understand the virtues, and therefore happiness, by thinking in the other direction as well: by asking which personal qualities make for good citizenship in the kind of state we assume to be good. Politics adds a third stage to Aristotle's interpretive analysis. It will, eventually, for us as well.

PART THREE

Ethics

9

Dignity

Is Morality Closed?

Plato and Aristotle treated morality as a genre of interpretation. They tried to show the true character of each of the main moral and political virtues by relating each to the others, and then to the broad ethical ideals their translators summarize as happiness. As I said in Chapter 1, but remind you now, I use the terms "ethical" and "moral" in what might seem a special way. Moral standards prescribe how we ought to treat others; ethical standards, how we ought to live ourselves. We can—many people do—use either "ethical" and "moral" or both in a broader sense that erases this distinction, so that morality includes what I call ethics, and vice versa. But we would then have to recognize the distinction I draw in some other vocabulary in order to ask whether our desire to lead good lives for ourselves provides a justifying reason for our concern with what we owe to others. Any of these vocabularies would allow us to pursue the interesting idea that moral principles should be interpreted so that being moral makes us happy in the sense Plato and Aristotle meant.

In this chapter we begin that interpretive project. We aim to find some ethical standard—some conception of what it is to live well—that will guide us in our interpretation of moral concepts. But there is an apparent obstacle. This strategy seems to suppose that we should understand our moral responsibilities in whatever way is best for us, but that goal seems contrary to the spirit of morality, because morality should not depend on any benefit being moral might bring. We might try to meet this objection through a familiar philosophical distinction: we might distinguish between the content of moral principles, which must be categorical, and the justification of those principles, which might consistently appeal to the long-term interests of agents bound by those principles.

We might argue, for example, that it is in everyone's long-term interests to accept a principle that forbids lying even in circumstances when lying would be in the liar's immediate interests. Everyone benefits when people accept a self-denying rule of that kind rather than each lying when that is in his immediate interest. However, this maneuver seems unsatisfactory, because we do not believe that our reasons for being moral depend on even our long-term interests. We are drawn to the more austere view that the justification and definition of moral principle should both be independent of our interests, even in the long term. Virtue should be its own reward; we need assume no other benefit in doing our duty.

But that austere view would set a severe limit to how far we could press an interpretive account of morality: it would permit the first stage I distinguished in Plato's and Aristotle's arguments, but not the second. We could seek integration within our distinctly moral convictions. We could list the concrete moral duties, responsibilities, and virtues we recognize and then try to bring these convictions into interpretive order—into a mutually reinforcing network of ideas. Perhaps we could find very general moral principles, like the utilitarian principle, that justify and are in turn justified by these concrete requirements and ideals. Or we could proceed in the other direction: setting out very general moral principles that we find appealing, and then seeing whether we can match these with the concrete convictions we find we can approve. But we could not set the entire interpretive construction into any larger web of value; we could not justify or test our moral convictions by asking how well these serve other, different purposes or ambitions people might or should have.

That would be disappointing, because we need to find authenticity as well as integrity in our morality, and authenticity requires that we break out of distinctly moral considerations to ask what form of moral integrity fits best with how we want to conceive our personality and our life. The austere view blocks that question. Of course it is unlikely, as we recognized in Chapter 6, that we will ever achieve a full integration of our moral, political, and ethical values that feels authentic and right. That is why responsibility is a continuing project and never a completed task. But the wider the network we can explore, the further we can push that project.

The austere view is disappointing in another way. Philosophers ask why people should be moral. If we accept the austere view, then we can only answer: because morality requires this. That is not an obviously illegitimate answer. The web of justification is always finally, at its limits, circular, and it is not viciously circular to say that morality provides its own only justification, that we must be moral simply because that is what morality demands. But it is nevertheless sad to be forced to say this. Philosophers have pressed the question why be moral because it seems odd to think that morality, which is often burdensome, has the force it does in our lives just because it is *there,* like an arduous and unpleasant mountain we must constantly cross but that we might hope wasn't there or would somehow crumble. We want to think that morality connects with human purposes and ambitions in some less negative way, that it is not all constraint and no value.

I therefore propose a different understanding of the irresistible thought that morality is categorical. We cannot justify a moral principle just by showing that following that principle would promote someone's or everyone's desires in either the short or the long term. The *fact* of desire—even enlightened desire, even a universal desire supposedly embedded in human nature— cannot justify a moral duty. So understood, our sense that morality need not serve our interests is only another application of Hume's principle. It does not rule out tying ethics and morality together in the way Plato and Aristotle did, and in the way our own project proposes, because that project takes ethics to be, not a matter of psychological fact about what people happen to or even inevitably want or take to be in their own interest, but itself a matter of ideal.

We need a statement of what we *should* take our personal goals to be that fits with and justifies our sense of what obligations, duties, and responsibilities we have to others. This characterization seems to fit Kant's moral program, or so I will suggest later. His conception of metaphysical freedom is most illuminating when it is understood as an ethical ideal that plays a dominant justifying role in his moral theory. Our own interpretive project is less foundational because more evidently holistic. We look for a conception of living well that can guide our interpretation of moral concepts. But we want, as part of the same project, a conception of morality that can guide our interpretation of living well.

True, people confronted with other people's suffering do not normally ask whether helping those people will create a more ideal life for themselves. They may be moved by the suffering itself or by some sense of duty. Philosophers debate whether this makes a difference.[1] Should people help a child because the child needs help or because it is their duty to help? In fact both motives might well be in play, along with hosts of others that a sophisticated psychological analysis might reveal, and it might be difficult or impossible to say which dominates on any particular occasion. Nothing important, I believe, turns on the answer: doing what you take to be your duty because it is your duty is hardly disreputable. Nor is it culpably self-regarding to worry about the impact of behaving badly on the character of one's life; it is not narcissistic to think, as people often say, "I couldn't live with myself if I did that." In any case, however, these questions of psychology and character are not relevant now. Our question is the different one whether, when we try to fix, criticize, and ground our moral responsibilities, we can sensibly assume that our ideas about what morality requires and about the best human ambitions should reinforce one another.

Hobbes and Hume can each be read as claiming not just a psychological but an ethical basis for familiar moral principles. Hobbes's putative ethics is unsatisfactory. At least for most of us, survival is not a sufficient condition of living well. Hume's sensibilities, translated into an ethics, are much more agreeable, but experience teaches us that even people who are sensitive to the needs of others cannot resolve moral—or ethical—issues simply by asking themselves what they are naturally inclined to feel or do. Nor does it help much to expand Hume's ethics into a general utilitarian principle. The idea that each of us should treat his own interests as no more important than those of anyone else has seemed an attractive basis for morality to many philosophers.[2] But, as I shall shortly argue, it can hardly serve as a strategy for living well oneself.

Religion can provide a justifying ethics for people who are religious in the right way; we have ample illustration of this in the familiar moralizing interpretations of sacred texts. Such people understand living well to mean respecting or pleasing a god, and they can interpret their moral responsibilities by asking which view of those responsibilities would best respect or most please that god. But that structure of thought could be helpful, as a guide to integrating ethics and morality, only for people who treat some sacred text as an explicit and detailed moral rule book. People who think only that their god has commanded love for and charity to others, as I believe many religious people do, cannot find, just in that command, any answers to what morality requires. In any case, I shall not rely on the idea of any divine book of detailed moral instruction here.

The Good Life and Living Well

If we reject Hobbesean and Humean views of ethics and are not tempted by religious ones, yet still propose to unite morality and ethics, we must find some other account of what living well means. As I said, it cannot mean simply having whatever one in fact wants: having a good life is a matter of our critical interests, the interests we should have.[3] It is therefore a matter of judgment and controversy what a good life is.[4] But is it plausible to suppose that being moral is the best way to make one's own life a good one? It is wildly implausible if we hold to popular conceptions of what morality requires and what makes a life good. Morality may require someone to pass up a job in cigarette advertising that would rescue him from great poverty. He would lead a better life in most people's view if he took the job and prospered.

Of course an interpretive account would not be limited by these conventional understandings. We might be able to construct a conception of a good life such that an immoral or base act would always, or almost always, makes the agent's life finally a worse life to lead. But I now suspect that any such attempt would fail.[5] Any attractive conception of our moral responsibilities would sometimes demand great sacrifices—it might require us to risk, or perhaps even to sacrifice, our lives. It is hard to believe that someone who has suffered terrible misfortunes has had a better life than he would have had if he had acted immorally and then prospered in every way, creatively, emotionally, and materially, in a long and peaceful life.

We can, however, pursue a somewhat different, and I believe more promising, idea. This requires a distinction within ethics that is familiar in morals: a distinction between duty and consequence, between the right and the good. We should distinguish between living well and having a good life. These two different achievements are connected and distinguished in this way: living well means striving to create a good life, but only subject to certain constraints essential to human dignity. These two concepts, of living well and of having a good life, are interpretive concepts. Our ethical responsibility includes trying to find appropriate conceptions of both of them.

196

ETHICS

Each of these fundamental ethical ideals needs the other. We cannot explain the importance of a good life except by noticing how creating a good life contributes to living well. We are self-conscious animals who have drives, instincts, tastes, and preferences. There is no mystery why we should want to satisfy those drives and serve those tastes. But it can seem mysterious why we should want a life that is good in a more critical sense: a life we can take pride in having lived when the drives are slaked or even if they are not. We can explain this ambition only when we recognize that we have a responsibility to live well and believe that living well means creating a life that is not simply pleasurable but good in that critical way.

You might ask: responsibility to whom? It is misleading to answer: responsibility to ourselves. People to whom responsibilities are owed can normally release those who are responsible, but we cannot release ourselves from our responsibility to live well. We must instead acknowledge an idea that I believe we almost all accept in the way we live but that is rarely explicitly formulated or acknowledged. We are charged to live well by the bare fact of our existence as self-conscious creatures with lives to lead. We are charged in the way we are charged by the value of anything entrusted to our care. It is *important* that we live well; not important just to us or to anyone else, but just important. (I return to the idea of objective importance later in this chapter.)

We have a responsibility to live well, and the importance of living well accounts for the value of having a critically good life. These are no doubt controversial ethical judgments. I also make controversial ethical judgments in any view I take about which lives are good or well-lived. In my own view, someone who leads a boring, conventional life without close friendships or challenges or achievements, marking time to his grave, has not had a good life, even if he thinks he has and even if he has thoroughly enjoyed the life he has had. If you agree, we cannot explain why he should regret this simply by calling attention to pleasures missed: there may have been no pleasures missed, and in any case there is nothing to miss now. We must suppose that he has *failed* at something: failed in his responsibilities for living.

What kind of value can living well have? The analogy between art and life has often been drawn and as often ridiculed. We should live our lives, the Romantics said, as a work of art. We distrust the analogy now because it sounds too Wilde, as if the qualities we value in a painting—fine sensibility or a complex formal organization or a subtle interpretation of art's own history—were the values we should seek in life: the values of the aesthete. These may be poor values to seek in the way we live. But to condemn the analogy for that reason misses its point, which lies in the relation between the value of what is created and the value of the acts of creating it. We value great art most fundamentally not because the art as product enhances our lives but because it embodies a performance, a rising to artistic challenge. We value human lives well lived not for the completed narrative, as if fiction would do as well, but because they too embody a performance: a rising to the challenge of having a life to lead. The final value of our lives is adverbial, not adjectival. It the value of the performance, not anything that is left when the performance is subtracted. It is the value of a brilliant dance or dive when the memories have faded and the ripples died away.

We need another distinction. Something's product value is the value it has just as an object, independently of the process through which it was created or of any other feature of its history. A painting may have product value, and this may be subjective or objective. Its formal arrangement may be beautiful, which gives it objective value, and it may give pleasure to viewers and be prized by collectors, which properties give it subjective value. A perfect mechanical replica of that painting has the same beauty. Whether it has the same subjective value depends largely on whether it is known to be a replica: it has as great subjective value as the original for those who think that it is the original. The original has a kind of objective value that the replica cannot have, however: it has the value of having been manufactured through a creative act that has performance value. It was created by an artist intending to create art. The object—the work of art—is wonderful because it is the upshot of a wonderful performance; it would not be wonderful if it were a mechanical replica or if it had been created by some freakish accident.

It was once popular to laugh at abstract art by supposing that it could have been painted by a chimpanzee, and people once speculated whether one of billions of apes typing randomly might produce *King Lear*. If a chimpanzee by accident painted *Blue Poles* or typed the words of *King Lear* in the right order, these products would no doubt have very great subjective value. Many people would be desperate to own or anxious to see them. But they would have no performance value at all. Performance value may exist independently of any object with which that performance value has been fused. There is no product value left when a great painting has been destroyed, but the fact of its creation remains and retains its full performance value. Ucello's achievements are no less valuable because his paintings were gravely damaged in the

Florence flood; Leonardo's *Last Supper* might have perished, but the wonder of its creation would not have been diminished. A musical performance or a ballet may have enormous objective value, but if it has not been recorded or filmed, its product value immediately evaporates. Some performances—improvisational theater and jazz concerts—find value in their ephemeral singularity: they will never be repeated.

We may count a life's positive impact—the way the world itself is better because that life was lived—as its product value. Aristotle thought that a good life is one spent in contemplation, exercising reason, and acquiring knowledge; Plato that it is a harmonious life achieved through order and balance. Neither of these ancient ideas requires that a wonderful life have any impact at all. Most people's opinions, so far as these are self-conscious and articulate, ignore impact in the same way. Many of them think that a life devoted to the love of a god or gods is the finest life to lead, and a great many, including many who do not share that opinion, think the same of a life lived in inherited traditions and steeped in the satisfactions of conviviality, friendship, and family. All these lives have, for most people who want them, subjective value: they bring satisfaction. But so far as we think them objectively good—so far as it would make sense to *want* to find satisfaction in such lives—it is the performance rather than the product value of living that way that counts.[6]

Philosophers used to speculate about what they called the meaning of life. (That is now the job of mystics and comedians.) It is difficult to find enough product value in most people's lives to suppose that they have meaning through their impact. Yes, but for some lives, penicillin would not have been discovered so soon and *King Lear* would never have been written. But if we measure a life's value by its consequence, all but a few lives would have no value, and the great value of some other lives—of a carpenter who pounded nails into a playhouse on the Thames—would be only accidental. On any plausible view of what is truly wonderful in almost any human life, impact hardly comes into the story at all.

If we want to make sense of a life having meaning, we must take up the Romantic's analogy. We find it natural to say that an artist gives meaning to his raw materials and that a pianist gives fresh meaning to what he plays. We can think of living well as giving meaning—ethical meaning, if we want a name—to a life. That is the only kind of meaning in life that can stand up to the fact and fear of death. Does all that strike you as silly? Just sentimental? When you do something smaller well—play a tune or a part or a hand, throw a curve or a compliment, make a chair or a sonnet or love—your satisfaction is complete in itself. Those are achievements within life. Why can't a life also be an achievement complete in itself, with its own value in the art in living it displays?

One qualification. I said that living well includes striving for a good life, but that is not necessarily a matter of minimizing the chances of a bad one. In fact many traits of character we value are not best calculated to produce what we independently judge to be the best available life. We value spontaneity, style, authenticity, and daring: setting oneself difficult or even impossible projects. We might be tempted to collapse the two ideas by saying that developing and exercising these traits and virtues are part of what makes a life good. But that seems too reductive. If we know that someone now in poverty courted that poverty by choosing an ambitious but risky career, we may well think that he was right to run that risk. He may have done a better job of living by striving for an unlikely but magnificent success. An artist who could be comfortably admired and prosperous—Seurat, if a name helps—strikes out in an entirely new direction that will isolate and impoverish him, require immersion in his work to the cost of his marriage and friendships, and may well not succeed even artistically. If it does succeed, moreover, the success is unlikely to be recognized, as in Seurat's case, until after his death. We may want to say: if he pulls it off, he will have had a better life, even taking account of the terrible costs, than if he had not tried, because even an unrecognized great achievement makes a life a good one.

But suppose it doesn't come off; what he produces, though novel, is of less merit than the more conventional work he would otherwise have painted. We might think, if we value daring very highly as a virtue, that even in retrospect he made the right choice. It didn't work out, and his life was worse than if he had never tried. But he was right, all things ethically considered, to try. This is, I agree, an outré example: starving geniuses make good philosophical copy, but they are not thick on the ground. We can replicate the example in a hundred more commonplace ways, however—entrepreneurs pursuing risky but dramatic inventions, for instance, or skiers pressing the envelope of danger. But whether we are ourselves drawn to think that living well sometimes means choosing what is likely to be a worse life, we must recognize the possibility that it does. Living well is not the same as maximizing the chance of producing the best possible life. The complexity of ethics matches the complexity of morality.

Being Bad and Moral Luck

Our ethical responsibilities are as categorical as our moral responsibilities. That is why we not only regret not having lived well but blame ourselves. The despair of Sydney Carton or Ivan Illyitch was not self-pity for bad luck but self-excoriation for weakness and indolence, in Carton's case, and fatal ethical misjudgment in Illyitch's. We are not simply passive vessels in which a good life may or may not occur.

But having a bad life does not always mean not having lived well: that discrimination is one of the most important consequences of distinguishing the two ideals. Someone may have a bad life in spite of living well, as we have already noticed, because he dared greatly and failed. More generally, he may live well and have a bad life because the goodness of his life does not depend entirely on his own decisions and efforts: it depends critically on his circumstances and luck as well. If he has been born in great poverty or to a despised race, or is severely crippled, or dies very young, his life has been disadvantaged in ways he could not have changed. And the distinction may cut the other way: someone may have a very good life and not live well at all. We read of a Medici prince who lived what strikes us as a particularly wonderful life of achievement, refinement, cultivation, and pleasure. Then we learn more: he made this life possible by a career of killing and betrayal on a very grand scale. If we were to insist that living well is just having a good life, we would then have to say either that he lived well after all, which seems monstrous, or that, on a second look, his life was not a good one because his immorality made it much worse than it would otherwise have been.

That latter choice would revive the implausible view we rejected a moment ago, that immorality always and necessarily makes a life overall worse. In fact, on any plausible standard of what makes a life good, our prince had a better life than he would have had if he had scrupulously respected his moral responsibilities. But it does not follow that he lived well. He failed his ethical responsibilities; he should not have committed the crimes he did, and he should have settled for the less spectacular life he would then have had. So even though we may think that he made his life a better one by his immoral acts, we should still say that he did a worse job of living.

The distinction between the two ideals helps to explain a further phenomenon that has intrigued philosophers.[7] We inevitably carry a sharp burden of regret for serious harm we did that was in no way our fault. Oedipus blinded himself because he killed his own father, unaware of his patricide. A school bus driver who crashed his bus, killing a dozen children, carries a special sorrow for the rest of his life, even if his driving was faultless and the accident no one's fault. His is not just an impersonal sorrow for the event—the sorrow anyone reading a newspaper might feel—but special sorrow because it was he who was driving the bus. Some philosophers have called this not merely bad luck but bad *moral* luck: the driver not only is likely to feel a special deep regret but would be defective in moral sensibility if he did not.

This is puzzling for those who believe that guilt should track only fault, that nothing is morally bad, to paraphrase Kant, except a bad will. We can resolve the puzzle and yet recognize the force of "moral luck" through our distinction. Whether I have lived well is not affected by harm I did without fault, but it nevertheless makes perfect sense—it is in fact irresistible—to suppose that how good my life has been is very much affected. Just as I can regret that my life was spoiled by the injustice of others for which I was blameless, so I can equally regret that my life was spoiled by the fact that but for my blameless acts a tragedy would not have happened. Guilt tracks fault when we ask whether we have lived well or badly, but regret tracks luck when we ask how good our life has been.

The distinction between a good life and living well is also helpful in confronting another ancient question. Can what happens after your death affect the quality of your life? It was bad for Priam when Achilles dragged Hector's body three times around the walls of Troy. But was it bad for Hector? Is it good for you if your children are happy after your death? Bad for you if your books are all destroyed? We cannot understand people's intense concern with their posthumous fate without recognizing that it does matter to them what happens then.[8] Yet that can seem silly: why should they care? Our distinction helps. Whether people have lived well is not affected by what happens after they have ceased to live; nothing can affect that, any more than whether a painter has painted well depends on how his painting fares in the market. But whether someone has had a good life can be influenced after his death by anything that adds to or takes away from its achievements or hopes. How good a life you have had waxes and wanes after you are no more.

I said earlier that the two ideas—living well and having a good life—need each other. But our Medici prince teaches us that the ideals may whisper opposite advice. Which is then the more fundamental ethical responsibility? Living well. It is ethically irresponsible for you to live less well in order to make your life a better one, and inappropriate for you to take pleasure or pride in your life's goodness when you achieved this at the cost of living badly. We might say (using a term developed by economists that John Rawls made popular among philosophers) that the value of living well is lexically prior to the value of a good life.[9] But the goodness of a life nevertheless has independent value. You should feel glad when your life is good, but not if you cheated to achieve it. You should regret a life that is less good because your luck has been bad or because others have cheated you.

Two Ethical Principles

The distinction between living well and having a good life, remember, is in service of a hypothesis. We cannot integrate ethics and morality in an overall interpretive web by supposing that being moral is essential to a good life. But we can entertain the hypothesis, at least, that morality is essential to living well. It will not help much, however, to establish that proposition in only one direction: that people do not live well unless they respect their moral duties. That is an appealing proposition, but it cannot help us decide what those duties are. It makes ethical responsibility depend on moral responsibility, but not the other way around; only a bilateral interpretive connection can do that. If the connection is to serve any useful purpose in our interpretive project, it must be a matter of integration, not simply incorporation.

I must explain the difference. There are two views we might take about the substantive connection between being good and living well. We might think that living well requires being moral, so that our prince did not live as well as he might have done, but that the content of morality is nevertheless fixed by reflecting only on morality itself and is in no way determined by any other aspects or dimensions of living well. We might think, that is, that living well simply incorporates morality without that connection in any way affecting what morality requires. Or we might treat the content of morality as fixed at least in part by the independent character of ethical responsibility: we might suppose that just as our ethical responsibilities are partly fixed by our moral responsibilities to others, so the latter are fixed in part by what our ethical responsibilities are. On this second view, morality and ethics are integrated in the interpretive way we have been exploring over the last few chapters.

Most religions take the first view of the central values of their faith. They insist that living well requires devotion to one or more gods, but they deny that the nature of these gods, or their standing as gods, in any way derives from the fact that living well includes respecting them, or that we can advance our understanding of their nature by asking how, more precisely, they would have to be in order to make respecting them part of living well. The gods, they insist, are who or what they are, and it falls to us, in our responsibility for our own lives, to try to discover this so far as we can and to act in the light of what we discover. That is also the view we take of scientific fact. In science, I said, we draw a sharp distinction between the intrinsic goal of seeking the truth and our justifying reasons for seeking that truth.[10] We think that trying to understand the structure of the universe is part of living well, but we do not think—unless we are crude pragmatists or mad—that we identify that structure by asking what view of it would help us to live well.

Many people take the same view about the value of art. We are responsible for discovering what is wonderful in art and respecting its wonder, they say, but we must take care not to commit the fallacy of supposing that something is beautiful because it makes our life better to appreciate it, or that we can identify and analyze its beauty by considering what it would do us good to admire in that way. On that view, living well incorporates art but is not integrated with it. That is a controversial view. I described my own, not wholly different, view in Chapter 7: that the meaning and value of a work of art do depend on the proper reasons for evaluating and interpreting it. I believe that art, like morality, connects with the ethical hub.

If moral values are best understood as integrated with, rather than simply incorporated in, ethical responsibility, we might hope to capitalize on the connection in a more powerful exploration of moral conviction. We can achieve that integration, however, only if we can find some compelling aspect or dimension of living well that is not itself, at least at first glance, a matter of our duties to others but yet both affects and is affected by those duties. I believe that we can find that interpretive lever in the twin, connected ideas of self-respect and authenticity.

I now introduce two principles that I believe state fundamental requirements of living well. In other work I have discussed related though different principles as political principles; I stated these political principles in Chapter 1 and I will employ them in later chapters.[11] I describe these now, however, only as ethical principles. The first is a principle of self-respect. Each person must take his own life seriously: he must accept that it is a matter of importance that his life be a successful performance rather than a wasted opportunity.

The second is a principle of authenticity. Each person has a special, personal responsibility for identifying what counts as success in his own life; he has a personal responsibility to create that life through a coherent narrative or style that he himself endorses.

Together the two principles offer a conception of human dignity: dignity requires self-respect and authenticity. The distinction between the two principles may seem artificial; each could easily be called by the other's name. You cannot think it important that you choose values around which to live your life unless you think it important that your life have value. Otherwise why should it be through values that you seek to identify yourself? And you cannot think you have created something of value in living your life unless you find what you have created valuable. You may think that subscribing obediently to the traditions of some culture or faith is, at least for you, the right path to success in living. But that must be what *you* think, not because others require you to live that way. Nevertheless I shall discuss the two principles separately because they raise different philosophical issues.

One preliminary word about the overall title I offer for the two principles together. The idea of dignity has been stained by overuse and misuse. It appears regularly in human rights conventions and political constitutions and, with even less discrimination, in political manifestos. It is used almost thoughtlessly either to provide a pseudo-argument or just to provide an emotional charge: campaigners against prenatal genetic surgery declare it an insult to human dignity for doctors to repair disease or deficiency in a fetus.[12] Still, it would be a shame to surrender an important idea or even a familiar name to this corruption. We should rather take up the job of identifying a reasonably clear and attractive conception of dignity; I try to do this through the two principles just described. Others will disagree: dignity, like so many of the concepts that figure in my long argument, is an interpretive concept.

Later chapters of this book use the idea of dignity to help identify the content of morality: acts are wrong if they insult the dignity of others. Other philosophers—notably Thomas Scanlon—believe we should argue in the other direction: an act is an insult to dignity when and because it is morally wrong in some other way.[13] I am unsure how great this difference turns out to be once some conception of dignity is specified. Scanlon, for instance, believes that an act is wrong if condemned by a principle no one could reasonably reject. If it is always and automatically a reason for someone to reject a principle that it does not treat his life as intrinsically important, or that it denies his freedom to choose values for himself, then the two approaches come together. I use dignity as an organizing idea because it facilitates our interpretive project to collect widely shared ethical principles under one port-manteau description.

Self-Respect

The two principles I described might seem obvious stated so abstractly. But it is far from clear what actual force they have as ethical imperatives, that is, as concrete conditions of living well. I begin with self-respect. That principle insists that I must recognize the objective importance of my living well. I must accept, that is, that it would be a mistake for me not to care how I lived. I do not mean simply to repeat the orthodox claim that each person's life has intrinsic and equal worth. It is not clear what that orthodox claim means. If we understand it as a claim about the product value of human beings, we must reject it. The world does not go better when there are more people in it, as we might well think it does go better when there are more great paintings painted. If we understand the orthodox claim to insist that each life has the same per-formance value, then it is false as well. Many lives have little performance value, and the performance value of all lives is certainly not equal.

In practice, the equal-worth principle is usually understood not as an ethi-cal principle but as a moral principle about how people must be treated. It insists that all human lives are inviolable and that no one should be treated as if his life were less important than anyone else's. Some philosophers cite the equal value of human lives to support more positive claims: that the people of rich nations should make sacrifices in order to help the miserable poor of other nations, for example. Our project hopes to connect the principles of dignity we are now exploring with those and other moral principles, but that is a matter for later chapters. Our principle of self-respect is different: it is not in itself a moral claim. It describes an attitude that people should have toward their own lives: they should think it important that they live well. The prin-ciple of self-respect requires each of us to treat his own life as having that kind of importance.

Stephen Darwall has made a useful distinction between recognition respect and appraisal respect.[14] The latter is the respect we show someone in virtue of his character or achievements; the former includes the respect we must show people just out of recognition of their status as people. The self-respect that dignity demands is recognition, not appraisal, respect. Only a few people are fully satisfied with their own character and record, and they are fools. We may—some sad people do—completely lose appraisal respect for ourselves. But that does not mean or entail that we have lost recognition self-respect. It is, in fact, only in virtue of our recognition respect for ourselves—our sense that our character and achievements matter—that our misery at what we are or have done makes any sense at all.

Not everyone acts as if he had self-respect. Sydney Carton, until his redemption, drank his life away beside the winding sheet in his candle. But most of us do act as if we respected ourselves. We have ideas about how best to live, and, at least in fits and starts, we try to live up to those ideas. True, none of us lives self-consciously thinking day by day that he is giving performance value to his life or that he is facing up to the importance of his living well. Most people would hardly recognize these ideas, and it would not improve their lives to spend much time over them. Still we can best interpret our lives—make sense of how we live and what we feel—by supposing that we have at least an inarticulate but powerful sense of the importance of our lives, inarticulate but powerful beliefs about what achievements would give them performance value.

I assume you have that sense: that you suppose that it is important how your life goes. You want your life to be successful because you think its success is important, not the other way around. Is my assumption correct? Can you plausibly interpret the way you live as reflecting the rival assumption that it is only subjectively important how you live—important that you live well only if and because you want to live well? Please take some care over that important question.

You might think, "I don't in fact care about living well. I care only about enjoying myself so far as I can; all my decisions and plans aim in that direction. As it happens, caring for others and achieving some personal success are among the things I enjoy. If I didn't enjoy them, I wouldn't bother. But living well, whatever that means, has no independent grip on me." There is a well-known difficulty in that reply. Enjoyment in most cases is not a freestanding state of mind like hunger. It is normally an epiphenomenon of the conviction that we are living as we should.[15] Of course, there are pleasures that are just pleasures: pleasures of the body, as we call them, that other animals share with us in some way, including some pleasures of sex and food. But pleasure in most of its modes—including most of the pleasure of food and sex—is not a frisson of pure feeling independent of belief about what gives rise to that feeling.[16] We don't just *take* pleasure. We take pleasure *in* something, and the pleasure we take is mostly contingent on thinking that it is good—living as one should—to take pleasure in it. True, some pleasures are "naughty"; we enjoy them for the opposite reason: because we know we shouldn't. The phenomenology of enjoyment is almost always suffused, one way or another, with ethical flavor.

There are dramatic—and often comical—illustrations of that fact: people struggling to come to like sophisticated and expensive foods, for instance, because they want to be the kind of people who do. But even when they are drawn immediately to an activity they find intensely pleasurable, much of the pleasure is parasitic on a more complicated aesthetic evaluation. Listen to a skier describing the thrill of his sport: he reports not the flow of endorphins but the physical and visual sensations of the activity itself. Philosophers are fond of pointing out that no one wants the pleasure apart from the event: no skier would sacrifice an hour on the slopes for two hours connected to a laboratory pleasure machine.[17] Yes, some people are proud to count themselves hedonists: they think that success in finding pleasure, and refining the pleasures they find, is a measure of how well they are living and have lived. Some of them think that their lives have gone worse because they have not found enough pleasure. But this meaning-of-life hedonism, as we might call it, is not an alternative to thinking it important to live well. It is only a sadly popular answer to the question of what living well means. Otherwise there could be no regret for pleasures missed: this makes sense only as regret for failure.

You might entertain a curter reply to my question: that you just want what you do and for no further reason. You do not think that your life has any importance or that there is a right and wrong way for you to live. You just happen to want to live in a particular way. You also happen to love cashew nuts; you can't resist them when they are offered. Your overall plans and projects are just more and bigger cashew nuts. This down-market, crudely subjective interpretation of your behavior is indeed a genuine alternative to the grander one I proposed. But can you really accept it? Don't you have an overall self-image: a sense of who you are that guides you in choices and styles, even, perhaps, in whether you like martinis or beer? Yes, you might say, you do have a self-image. You not only want to have certain things, like nuts, but also to be a certain way. That is just part of what you find you want. But that reply misunderstands the character of a person's conception of himself. Self-images—choices of personal identity—play the critical role they do because they are constructed not of what we just find we like but of what we find we admire and think appropriate. These are themselves critical judgments: we aim to meet a standard, not just pick at random from a menu. Don't you have other critical attitudes that also play a part in your life? Don't you sometimes feel pride, shame, and regret, for instance? These critical attitudes make sense only to and for someone who thinks that it is important what he makes of his life and that he has a personal responsibility to create value in it. They make no sense for someone who just happens to want one kind of life. He has no platform on which to build any regret at all.

If these critical attitudes do play a prominent role in your emotional life, then their prominence confirms the more ambitious interpretation and rules out the down-market one. In fact, the critical attitudes are pervasive in almost everyone's life, and I shall now assume that they are important in yours. They can surface anytime. But as I suggested, they are most dramatically in play from the perspective of a deathbed or near it. People are then often reminded, with pride, of the children they have raised, their war service, their reputation. I read once that when Beethoven was dying he said, "At least we made some music." (Perhaps he didn't say that, but he might have.) Other people are full of regret: at chances not taken, at opportunities, pleasures, and experiences missed. Sometimes the regret is intense and self-flagellating.

I mentioned two examples earlier. Ivan Illyitch, who thought he had all he wanted, suddenly thought that he had wanted the wrong things and realized, in panic, that it was too late to correct his mistake. For Sydney Carton it was not too late, because an extraordinary coincidence made it possible for him to do a far, far better thing than he had ever done, and to achieve his life's redemption in doing it. Nothing like that could make any sense for someone whose concern for his life is only a matter of liking nuts. The critical attitudes make sense only if we accept that it is objectively, and not just subjectively, important what we do with our lives. We worry when we suspect that we have misunderstood and betrayed our responsibility; we take pride and comfort—we say our lives have meaning—when we believe we have met it.

Of course it is possible still to survey all these claims with a skeptical eye: to say that the objective importance I describe is a myth and that the pride, regret, shame, anxiety, and redemption most people feel are only part of the myth. But if that kind of hardheadedness tempts you, please remember the lesson of Part One. Your ethical skepticism cannot be an Archimedean, external skepticism. It can only be an internal skepticism, which means that you need just as strong a set of value judgments to support your nihilism as others need to support their very different intuitive sense. You cannot undermine their conviction of ethical responsibility with metaphysical arguments about the kinds of entities there are in the universe or sociological arguments about the diversity of opinions about what living well means. That would be to repeat the mistakes of external skepticism. You need an internally skeptical argument in two parts: positive claims about what would have to be true for our lives to have meaning, and then a negative case explaining why these conditions are not or cannot be met. Nihilism so earned has its own dignity. Macbeth found internal skepticism—indifference to the rest of his life—once he realized he was in the hands of supernatural tricksters. You are not, I expect, of his mind.

Authenticity

Now we turn to the second principle of dignity. I called it the principle of authenticity, though that virtue has a mixed reputation now. In a famous essay Lionel Trilling contrasted authenticity with sincerity, to the discredit of the former.[18] He had in mind, however, a sentimental and distinctly inauthentic popular use of the ideal. People say, without much thought, that they need to discover themselves and to be in touch with their deepest feelings. Our blue-eyed troubadour said, by way of anthem, that he did it his way. But a more genuine form of the ideal has had an important and entirely unsentimental life in our literature and in much of our most influential philosophy. Authenticity is central in the work of many of the most prominent modern philosophers—Kierkegaard and Nietzsche, for example, and also Sartre and other philosophers who called themselves Existentialists. Even Shakespeare's villains and clowns—Gloucester and Iago, Parolles and Pistol—find moments of dignity in soliloquies of sudden and scorching authenticity in which they recognize and endorse who they really are.

Authenticity is the other side of self-respect. Because you take yourself seriously, you judge that living well means expressing yourself in your life, seeking a way to live that grips you as right for you and your circumstance. This need not be commitment to a single overriding ambition or to a set hierarchy of values. It may instead amount to what we call character, or what Nietzsche called a "style": a way of being that you find suited to your situation, not one drawn mindlessly from convention or the expectations or demands of others.[19] That does not necessarily mean eccentricity or even novelty. What is crucial is not that you live differently from others, but that you live in response to, rather than against the grain of, your situation and the values you find appropriate. These may be expressed in commitment to a revered tradition; they may be beautifully expressed in loving, providing for, and educating children. They may be expressed even in a life so severely constrained that only very limited choices are available. Or in a life that, seen from the outside, seems wholly conventional or even tedious. Nor does authenticity require studied planning or a road map drawn in youth. We can discover a character or style as we live, interpreting what we do as we do it, in search of rather than following a thread. Sartre called that "existential psychoanalysis."[20]

It would be a mistake to find this account of authenticity elitist. On the contrary, it is elitist to suppose that only people of high education or imagination or sensibility or favored by wealth can lead authentic lives. Nor does endorsement require the absurdity of a constantly examined life. It does not require anyone explicitly to recognize that his life can have adverbial value and that he has a responsibility to seek that value. Few people wonder, tired in front of a television screen, whether they could add more value to their lives doing something else. Authenticity does make important demands, however. It requires a personal sense of character and commitment to standards and ideals out of which we act. It requires that we recognize some acts as self-betrayal.

Responsibility

In Chapter 6 I distinguished responsibility as a virtue from responsibility as a relation, and I also distinguished different forms of responsibility in both senses. The second principle of dignity demands both that I be responsible in the virtue sense and that I accept relational responsibility when appropriate. I do not treat an act as my own, as issuing from my personality and character, unless I regard myself as judgmentally responsible for it. People who blame their parents or other people or society at large for their own mistakes, or who cite some form of genetic determinism to absolve themselves of any responsibility for how they have acted, lack dignity, because dignity requires owning up to what one has done. "The buck stops here" is an important piece of ethical wisdom.

It is a more complex question how far authenticity requires that I accept liability responsibility for my acts. When may I properly demand that others bear all or part of a financial burden that I have assumed or that has fallen upon me? I may need money because I have suffered an accident that makes me unable to work or that requires expensive medical treatment, or because I have chosen to comb beaches instead of working, or because I have vowed to build a monument to my god.[21] Does the right view of my own ethical responsibilities entail that it would be wrong to demand help in some of these circumstances but not in others? If it is part of living well not only to make choices but to live with the consequences of those choices, do I have reason to distinguish what I need because I have cancer from what I need because I chose not to work? Does it matter whether my needs are basic—I will starve without help—or spiritual? Does it matter whether I can support myself comfortably, but only at a boring job I loathe? These questions have direct analogues, as we shall see, both in moral questions about what we owe others and in important political questions about distributive justice. But they are also, distinctly, ethical questions.

Ethical Independence

Authenticity has another dimension: it stipulates what dignity demands we try to establish in our relations with other people. We must strive for independence. That does not mean trying to escape influence or persuasion. People cannot invent wholly new styles of living; we all live in an ethical culture that provides, at any time, the palette of recognizable ethical values from which possibilities can be drawn. We can rearrange conventional priorities among those values—we can become people of brute honesty instead of tact—and we can cleave to personal values that others disdain, like sexual abstinence. But it is not possible to live a life of medieval chivalry in Brooklyn now: that life required a social and even political background of which no sufficient vestiges remain. The opinions and models about how to live that are alive in our folklore, literature, and advertising are pervasive in our lives—we are born into and raise our children in the environment these create. This has been, in my own time, a rapidly shifting environment. Styles of living were possible and admired in the late 1960s and early 1970s that were not admired and were barely possible before; they remain, barely, possible now, but again they are not much admired.

We cannot escape influence, but we must resist domination. The distinction is of great ethical importance. Authenticity is in this aspect a narrowly relational concept. A person's authenticity is not compromised by limitations of nature or circumstance: not because he lacks athletic ability, or because taxation makes it impossible for him to live as he would most like, or because he lives in a technologically backward community. He does not then have many colors on his palette, but the life he designs with the colors he has may be just as fully authentic, just as firmly the life that he rather than anyone else has designed. On the other hand he does not live authentically, no matter how great the range of options he is offered, if others forbid him some options otherwise available because they deem those options unworthy. The indignity lies in usurpation, not limitation. Authenticity demands that, so far as decisions are to be made about the best use to which a person's life should be put, these must be made by the person whose life it is.

So authenticity is not autonomy, at least as some philosophers understand that protean concept. They suppose that autonomy requires only that some range of choices be left open by the sum of circumstance, whether these be natural or political. A person's autonomy is not threatened, on this view, when government manipulates its community's culture so as to remove or make less eligible certain disapproved ways of living, if an adequate number of choices remain so that he can still exercise the power of choice. Authenticity, on the other hand, as this is defined by the second principle of dignity, is very much concerned with the character as well as the fact of obstacles to choice. Living well means not just designing a life, as if any design would do, but designing it in response to a judgment of ethical value. Authenticity is damaged when a person is made to accept someone else's judgment in place of his own about the values or goals his life should display.

This principle of ethical independence has evident political implications, and I shall identify and explore these later, in Chapter 17. Now, however, I emphasize the principle's distinctly ethical importance: the role it plays in protecting the individual dignity that living well demands. Coercion is plain when it is achieved or threatened by the criminal law or by other forms of state action. In other circumstances more subtle discrimination is needed to distinguish influence from subordination. Someone who prizes his dignity must refuse to shape his ethical values out of fear of social as well as political sanction; he might decide that he lives well when he conforms to the expectations of others, but he must make that decision out of conviction, not laziness or that kind of fear.

Some orthodox religions establish priests or texts as supposedly infallible reporters of a god's will; they declare the overriding importance of religious conviction to living well. Theocratic communities that impose an ethical regime by coercion compromise their subjects' authenticity. In liberal political communities, in contrast, those who subject themselves to the ethical authority of their church do so voluntarily. They are nevertheless inauthentic if their adherence is so mechanical and unthinking that it does not flow into and shape the rest of their lives, if their religion is dutiful or social or self-congratulatory rather than a source of narrative energy. Fundamentalist Christians who denounce unbelievers and vote as they are told by televangelists, but who seem otherwise untouched by Christian charity, lead inauthentic lives even though their religion is not coerced.

Authenticity and Objectivity

The modern philosophers who preach authenticity most energetically deny the possibility of objective values: they insist that value can be created only by imposing a human will on an ethically inert universe. But that assumption makes it difficult to see why we should value authenticity at all. It might be said that some people just have a taste for authenticity. They just want to impose a narrative structure on their lives. But this seems unsatisfactorily lame. Our ethical responsibilities seem as categorical as our moral responsibilities: we think that authenticity is not a taste but a necessary virtue, that there is something *wrong* with an inauthentic life. We think that authenticity has objective importance; it is not just a taste some people happen to have.

Indeed, our common convictions assume something more, that we must seek the right values for our lives, the right narrative, not just any narrative. Otherwise we would be ethically free to choose any life so long as that life's principle was coherent: a life of relentless, unmitigated indolence, for instance. The analogy to artistic value is useful here again. We do count a work of art's integrity as indispensable to its value, but we do not count integrity as a stand-alone value. Otherwise we could not distinguish banal monotony from the brilliant coherence of complexity. That is equally true in ethics. We seek coherence in imposing a narrative on a life, but coherence endorsed by judgment, not just a coin flip. Nietzsche is sometimes taken to be a nihilist in value. But he had no doubt that some lives really are better than others. In fact he said he was aware of only three people whose lives were truly great. One of them was himself.[22]

It must therefore seem mysterious why the champions of authenticity have been so anxious to reject the very intelligibility of objective value; why they present authenticity as a replacement for the objective values they insist are only myths. I suggested an explanation in the Just So story of Chapter 1. Enlightenment and post-Enlightenment philosophers inherited part of the metaphysics of the age of religion: they continued to think that values can be objective only if the best explanation of how people come to hold those values also certifies the values as correct. Religion offers to show values objective in that way, but the secular philosophers turned their backs on religion. Nietzsche said that God was dead, and others that they must do without God's help. They insisted that only naturalistic explanations are competent to explain why people hold the convictions they do, and they recognized that no such explanation could also vindicate those convictions. So they rejected all objective value.

But they could not deny the inescapable phenomenology of value in people's lives. So they declared that it is we—human beings who long for value—who create that value for ourselves, by acts of will and fiat. This strategy fails because it does not redeem the phenomenology that inspires it. We do create our lives, but we do it aiming at value, not trying to invent it. Otherwise the struggle for authenticity these philosophers salute would be barren and pointless. We cannot escape, in how we think, an assumption that value exists independent of our will or fiat. So though we follow these philosophers in celebrating authenticity, we cannot accept their special form of external skepticism. Nor need we: once we break the supposed connection between the explanation and justification of our convictions, we have no need for their failed strategy.

The Religious Temperament

For most people, living well requires a *situated* life: living appropriately to their circumstances—their own history, attachments, locality, region, values, and environment. E. M. Forster's famous instruction—only connect—has its greatest resonance in ethics. People want their lives to have the kind of point we give some event or act by finding its place in a larger story or work of art, as a scene is given point by the whole play and an arc or diagonal by the whole painting. We cherish complexity of reference in poetry, painting, and music not just or even for instruction but out of a sense of the beauty of what is embedded rather than what is detached. We cherish it also in life. We might try to capture the importance of connection in the idea of ethical parameters: features of our situation, such as our political and national identification, ethnic and cultural background, linguistic community, locality and region, religion, education, and associations that we can, if we wish, shape our life generally to embody and reflect. People sometimes describe the importance of such connection by saying that their nationality or ethnicity or some other parameter has a *claim* on them.

People similarly situated will give these parameters different orders of priority and will form different ideas about how to live accordingly. However, the larger and denser the canvas which these parameters occupy, the more each is interwoven with others, the more point a life reflecting these parameters can be seen to have. The most inclusive parameter of all, for many people, is their conception of the universe. They believe, as they often put it, that the universe houses some force "bigger than we are" and they want to live in some way in the light of that force. Thomas Nagel calls the desire for such a permeating connection the "religious temperament."[23]

People who are religious in the orthodox way locate that force in their god. Some of them believe in Heaven and Hell and also in the power of their god as benefactor and disciplinarian even in this life. But many people who count religion as important in their lives have less instrumental connections in mind. Few of the Oxford chaplains and students who pray for the success of their college's boat in the university races or the Siennese who take their contrada's horse to church before their Palio actually believe in divine intervention, at least at this level of triviality. They take these occasions as opportunities to exhibit their religious convictions in the way they live.

Nagel describes a secular version of the same impulse. Even nonbelievers think, as he puts it, that the universe has a "claim" on us. Atheists too, he says, face this dramatic question: "How can one bring into one's individual life a full recognition of one's relation to the universe as a whole?" He considers three responses. The first is dismissive: it insists that nothing is missing from a life in which no such attempt is made. The second is humanist: it treats each individual life as an episode in the career of our species or, in a yet grander version, in the story of life evolving from its primitive beginnings. The third response is grander still: it places life, particularly human life, as itself part of the vastly larger story of the natural evolution of the universe. The unmatched exhilaration of that grandest answer tempts even some atheists to suppose some secular trajectory of purpose in the universe, a trajectory in which life and therefore their lives provide a pivotal event: the birth of consciousness.

Two large questions arise. First, why should people find value in this speculative aggrandizement of their individual lives? How do they benefit by seeing their lives as either a celebration of a transcendent but indifferent god or an event in an unconscious cosmic drama? Second, how can people shape their lives to record that aggrandizement? How can one bring it "into one's individual life?" I just suggested an answer to the first question. We want to live in a way that is not arbitrary but is salient, suited to our circumstances. If our circumstances include the background of a cosmic drama, then we respond most appropriately by recognizing that noble background. Of course, we cannot think that the drama adds to the product values of our own lives. Our consciousness may be to the credit of the universe, perhaps its greatest achievement so far. But it is not our achievement. No, the value we think we find in our connection with the universe must be adverbial, performance value. Recognizing our tiny role is part of living well.

That makes the second question—Nagel's question—crucial. How can recognizing a secular cosmic trajectory change how we live? Less grand parameters can easily make a difference. Some Jews who are atheists nevertheless celebrate religious holidays and even observe rituals of diet and weekly ceremony. They say that in that way they can belong, even without religion, to a cultural tradition they cherish. The second response Nagel identifies, humanism, can also change how we live. It might give us a heightened interest in conservation and in fighting climate change. Nietzsche, in Nagel's reading, insisted on a still more dramatic consequence: he urged us to replace conventional values with others, like power, that better reflect our animal heritage and therefore better identify our place in evolution. Moral philosophers who speculate about human nature exhibit the same thirst for connection. No fact about how we are—about the natural phenomenon of human sympathy, for instance—can on its own yield any conclusion about how we should live. But the ethics of salience can provide a link. If there is such a thing as human nature, then living so as deliberately to express that nature is another avenue of connection to our situation, another way not to fall into an arbitrary life.

But what about the universe? We may be happy to learn that the appearance of conscious beings, at our stage of the long cosmic story, was not a chance accident but rather part of an unfolding plan. But how can this discovery change how we live? The universe has no temple at which we can worship. The discovery can, perhaps, affect our lives in a way parallel to worship: it can increase the interest we take in science, particularly cosmology. People who believe that the universe has evolved according to principles, and that they are an achievement of that evolution, will presumably try hard to secure at least an outsider's sense of what the best scientists now think, the way a great many people take an intense interest, now often commercially exploited, in their own family history. I believe, however, that the main ethical importance of the secular "force larger than we are" conviction, for most people, is not to provide a distinct way of living but rather to provide a defense against the frightening thought that *any* way we live is arbitrary. If the universe just *happens* to be some way or other, if there is no purpose or plan at the most fundamental level of explanation, then it might seem absurd that we can give value to our lives by responding appropriately to more concrete parameters of our situation. How can we create any kind of value, even adverbial value, by responding to a personal or even species history that is itself only the most arbitrary of accidents? Nagel ends his discussion in pessimism. If there is no final order, he says, "since the cosmic question won't go away and humanism is too limited an answer, a sense of the absurd may be what we are left with."

But why? Suppose we think—as we have no reason not to think—that there is no point or purpose in the universe. Finally, at the distant end of the relentless discovery of unifying laws of nature, there are only facts—bare facts—about what there just was and is. We need not then ignore or dismiss Nagel's cosmic question: we can answer it in that way. Of course it then would be absurd to try to live pretending to some great universal law. But what is absurd about living with no such pretense? If the value of living up to the universe is adverbial—if it is connection that counts—then why is it not as valuable to live up to the pointlessness of eternity, if the universe is pointless, as to live up to its purpose if it has one? For it is not true that nothing makes sense or creates value unless there is universal sense and value. Even if there is no eternal planner, *we* are planners—mortal planners with a vivid sense of our own dignity and of good and bad lives that we can create or endure. Why can we not find value in what we create, in response to what there just happens to be, as we find value in what an artist or musician makes? Why must value depend on physics? From this perspective, it is the assumption that ethical value does depend on eternity, that it can be undermined by cosmology, that seems absurd. It is just another in the endless string of temptations to violate Hume's principle. But we have now touched issues among the deepest of moral and ethical philosophy. How vulnerable is value to science? What are the sources and character of absurdity? Turn to Chapter 10.

10

Free Will and Responsibility

Two Threats to Responsibility

I have been writing about responsibility in its various modes and forms, so far ignoring a view popular among philosophers that there is no such thing. People are responsible for their acts only when they are in control of what they do—only, in the standard philosophical jargon, when they have and act out of a free will. You are not responsible for the injury when someone else pushes you into a blind beggar or when a hypnotist makes you steal from the beggar's cup. Many philosophers—millions of other people as well—believe that this apparently innocent observation is wholly destructive of at least large and central parts of ethics and morality. They press what we might call the "no free will" challenge in the following form.

"People are never actually in control of their own behavior, even when it seems to them that they are. Their will is never free because their behavior is always caused by some combination of forces and events entirely beyond their control acting on their brains. It is never true that they could have done anything else but what they did. Indeed, people's decisions are not only caused by prior events, but do not even cause the actions for which they think themselves responsible. Responsibility is therefore an illusion, and it is always inappropriate to hold people blameworthy or to punish them for what they do."

It will be useful to name the different phenomena I just mentioned. I use "decision" to describe the familiar conscious event we sense as deciding; I mean to include not just reflective, thoughtful decisions we take after deliberation, but also the unreflective decisions we make minute-by-minute to continue what we are doing rather than do something else.[1] You took a reflective decision when you decided to read this book, I assume, but I hope only unreflective ones to continue reading. I understand "determinism" to hold that every one of these decisions, reflective as well as unreflective, is fully determined by processes and events that precede it and lie outside the control of the decider. "Epiphenomenalism" denies more: it denies that decisions even figure in the causal chain that ends in movements of nerve and muscle.[2] It supposes that the internal sense of having decided to do something is only a side effect of the physical and biological events that have actually produced the behavior decided upon. Epiphenomenalists think, for instance, that the series of physical events that culminated in my typing the last word in this sentence began before I actually decided which word to type assiduously. It began while I was still, or so I thought, hesitating over my choice of words. If every conscious decision is only a side effect, then whatever part of me forms that decision, whether we call it my "will" or by some other name, can hardly be in charge of what happens. It is only the fraud of Oz, pulling levers and pluming steam to no effect whatsoever.

Determinism and epiphenomenalism may both be true: I am not competent to judge either of them as scientific theories. Neither has been demonstrated to be true. Everything is possible. Every Tuesday brings fresh surprises about brain geography, physics, and chemistry, about potent alleles on neglected chromosomes, and about the interrelations among all these and our mental life. Every dinner party brings fresh speculation about the sexual reasoning of baboons, the religious lives of chimpanzees, the reptilian brain beneath your cerebrum, and the neo-Darwinian explanation of the trolley problem I discuss in Chapter 13. Our grandchildren had better be ready for anything.

The Issues

The free will challenge is probably the single most popular philosophical issue to have escaped the textbooks and entered popular literature and imagination: it is the theme of earnest speculation everywhere. The philosophical literature is in itself vast and dauntingly complex.[3] (Two particularly influential and contrasting positions are those of Thomas Nagel and Peter Strawson.[4])

This literature weaves together three groups of issues that we should take care to separate. We find, first, discussions of the causes and consequences of thought and action. Is all human behavior fully determined by prior events over which people themselves have no control? If not, is some behavior caused by random, chance physical or biological events over which, equally, people have no control? Or can some faculty of the human mind—the "will"—exercise a kind of purposeful agency that is not itself caused by anything but its own occurrence? I shall call these "scientific" issues, but many philosophers would regard this name as inappropriate. They think that at least one of the questions I listed—whether a human will can act spontaneously as an uncaused cause—is a metaphysical question rather than one of biology or physics. Thomas Nagel finds the last hypothesis—that a complete explanation of action can begin in an act of will with no prior physical or biological explanation—unintelligible. But he also finds it irresistible.[5]

The literature also contains discussions of what is styled "freedom." Under what circumstances is someone free to act as he wishes? Is his freedom compromised only when he is subject to some external constraint—only when he is tied up or locked up, for example? Or when he is mentally ill? Or when he cannot govern himself or control his appetites as he would wish? Or when he does not behave as right reason and true morality require? Or is his freedom illusory whenever his choices and behavior are inevitable, given prior events or forces beyond his control? Is he free, that is, only if and when his own will acts as the uncaused cause of his behavior?

Finally we find discussions of our own topic: judgmental responsibility. When is it appropriate for someone to judge his own behavior critically and for others to judge him that way? When is it appropriate for him to feel pride or guilt, for example, or for others to praise or blame him? Whenever he acts rather than is acted upon? Whenever he makes decisions for himself rather than being, for instance, hypnotized? Or only when his will is the uncaused cause of his actions? These questions about responsibility hang like swords over Chapter 9. I argued that people have a foundational ethical responsibility to live well, to make something of their lives, and that living well is a matter of making appropriate decisions over one's life. But if no one is ever responsible for his decisions, the idea of living well or badly makes little sense. No decision can ever make a life better or worse lived.

It is crucial now to notice the large logical space between the first set of issues—the scientific or metaphysical questions that can be answered, if at all, only through empirical investigation or philosophical speculation—and the last set, about responsibility, which are independent ethical and moral issues. Because Hume's principle applies just as firmly in the ethical context as it does in the moral context of Part One, no conclusion about responsibility can follow directly from any answers we give to questions in the first set. Any inference from the first to the third set of issues requires a further evaluative premise. The literature of the free will problem has not, in my view, paid sufficient attention to this requirement—perhaps because philosophers assume that it is obvious which ethical and moral principles are available to bridge the gap. I believe that this is very far from obvious.

The second set of issues—about freedom—are not, however, independent of the other two groups. There is no pertinent question about whether people are free that is not either the scientific or the ethical question in disguise. Some people use "freedom" simply to mean nondeterminism: people are not really free, they assume, unless determinism is false. Others use the word simply to mean responsibility: they say that people are or are not free when they mean that they are or are not judgmentally responsible for their actions. Neither of these ways of speaking is mistaken: it is not a linguistic mistake to say either that people are not really free because determinism is true or that people are really free, even if determinism is true, when they are subject to no external constraint. But talk of freedom in this context is unhelpful and often sponsors confusion. I propose not to discuss freedom much in this chapter, even though my subject is the free will controversy.

Classical discussions of free will and responsibility almost always begin in a moral rather than an ethical issue. Is it right to criticize someone else for what he did when he was hallucinating or suffering from some other mental disorder? Or if he had an unfortunate upbringing or acted under duress? Would it be fair to jail someone who committed a crime while acting under one or another of these disabilities? These questions and the anticipated answers prepare the way for the supposed impact of determinism. If everyone's actions are determined by forces beyond his control, in the way we think mentally ill people's actions often are, then it is just as unfair ever to blame anyone as it is to blame the mentally ill. I propose to begin differently: by asking how and why people normally hold *themselves* responsible for what they have done, and why, in some circumstances, they do not and should not do so. I begin, that is, in ethics rather than morality. That different tack brings this chapter into line with the general strategy of the book; it allows us to concentrate on something important that the more classical approach tempts us to ignore. When we begin in the first rather than the third person, we pay more attention to how it feels to be confronted with a decision.

The Stakes

Chapter 6 distinguished modes and varieties of responsibility. We concentrated in that chapter on the virtue of responsibility; now we are concerned with one form of relational responsibility. Someone has judgmental responsibility for an act if it is appropriate to appraise his act against critical standards of performance: of blame or praise. Further terminology will now be helpful. The literature of the free will problem divides philosophers into two camps. Compatibilists believe that full judgmental responsibility is consistent with determinism, and incompatibilists that it is not. Some incompatibilists are optimists: they believe that judgmental responsibility is genuine because they believe, as a matter of either science or metaphysics or both, that behavior is not always determined by past events beyond the agent's control. Other incompatibilists are pessimists: they believe that all behavior is determined by past events and that it is therefore never appropriate to attribute judgmental responsibility to anyone. Can pessimistic incompatibilism be right?

It is important to notice, right from the start, that we cannot actually believe it. I do not mean only that we would find it hard to believe the way someone might find it hard to believe that a lover has betrayed him or that slavery was overall good for the slaves. You cannot be convinced, even intellectually, that you are not responsible for your actions, because you cannot make any reflective decision without judging which decision it would be better to make. You may be convinced, after you pass the beggar by, that you were forever destined to ignore him. Nevertheless, as you approach him you cannot repeal either the thought or the fact that you have a decision to make. You cannot lift yourself above yourself just to watch how you choose. You must choose. You might pause, frozen in your tracks, to see what will happen. But then nothing will happen, and even then you have chosen to stop, and eventually you will choose to do something else.

I repeat: you cannot choose, except in particularly banal matters, without supposing that there is a better and a worse choice for you to make; you cannot choose, that is, without supposing that your choice is a matter appropriate for self-criticism. You cannot wrestle apart the thought "What shall I do?" from the thought "Which decision would it be better for me to make?" This need not be a matter of moral or even ethical criticism: it rarely is. You may criticize yourself on what you take to be purely instrumental grounds—Can you afford to give to every beggar you confront? But you will still be holding your choice to a normative standard, still considering what reasons you have to act one way or another, not treating your action as a tic or a cough.

After you choose, you might be able to treat your decision that way: you might insist, even to yourself, that because you were destined to ignore the beggar, you are not to blame and have nothing to regret in having done so. But the threatened conclusion, that you never have judgmental responsibility, claims more than that. It claims that your decision, like a cough you cannot stop, is immune from critical judgment from the start, and that is what you cannot believe as you act. In the first person, deciding includes assuming judgmental responsibility; the connection is internal and independent of any premise about the causes of decision. Pessimistic noncompatibilism is not an intellectually stable position. It asks us to believe what we cannot believe. You may say: I can believe in pessimistic incompatibilism even though I do not act as if I believe it; I'm only pretending. That misses the point: there is no way to behave as if you *did* believe it, so no ground for attributing the belief to yourself.

What about third-person judgments? Could we continue to judge other people in the way we do if we accepted pessimistic incompatibilism? Philosophers normally focus, as I said, on third-person judgments: incompatibilists argue that if determinism is true, then it is wrong to blame or punish anyone for what he does; unfair, in Galen Strawson's hyperbole, for God to send anyone to hell.[6] They insist that this would not rule out any number of other ethical or moral judgments. It would still be possible, they say, to declare that a criminal has done something morally wrong even though he is not blameworthy for having done it. Or that he has a bad character. It would still be possible to think, they say, that someone has acted prudently or imprudently or that some states of affairs are better than others. I believe all this is wrong.[7] Morality is an integrated web of standards. It is not a collection of detachable modules, each of which can be eliminated, leaving the rest even more or less intact. Judgmental responsibility is the weft of all moral fabric.

If I cannot believe that I myself lack judgmental responsibility, even when I accept that my own actions are determined, I have no ground for supposing that anyone else lacks judgmental responsibility just because his actions are determined. Some lawyers and criminologists insist that we must abandon traditional criminal law, with its apparatus of guilt and punishment, and substitute only therapeutic treatment because people are never responsible for what they do.[8] They contradict themselves. If no one ever has judgmental responsibility, then officials who treat accused criminals as responsible for their actions are not responsible for their own actions, and it is therefore wrong to accuse them of acting unfairly. Of course, it would then also be wrong of me to accuse the criminologists of acting wrongly in accusing the officials of acting wrongly, because the criminologists are not responsible either. And wrong of me to accuse myself of accusing them wrongly, because I am not responsible either. And so on. This recursive nonsense shows, even if nothing else did, that we cannot believe the proposition on which it hinges, which is that we all lack judgmental responsibility for anything.

There is yet a further difficulty. If determinism extinguishes our judgmental responsibility, then it must extinguish our intellectual responsibility as well. So we would act no more responsibly in declaring determinism true when we have read the literature, done the experiments, and reflected for a decade than if we had simply thrown dice and come up boxcars. If pessimistic determinism is true, no one could responsibly think that he had made a wise decision in believing it. He had no choice but to believe it.

Six Billion Characters in Search of a Life

The Responsibility System

The fact that no one can actually believe pessimistic incompatibilism is not in itself much of an argument against it. We can't believe Zeno's "proof" that an arrow never reaches its destination, but we need to explain why that proof is wrong.[9] Perhaps we can find no decent reason *not* to believe what we cannot believe; perhaps we are condemned to that kind of incoherence. As I said, there may be no consistent and interpretively satisfying theory of judgmental responsibility. But whether that is so depends on the ethical and moral issues we now begin to explore. No doubt the causes of our decisions do in some way affect our judgmental responsibility for those decisions. The question is, how? To repeat: we seek an *ethical* principle that defines the connection.

We should begin with our ordinary ideas about when judgmental responsibility is extinguished or abated. Remind yourself of the ordinary economy of judgmental responsibility: the way you and others use the idea, day to day.

Deliberate behavior has an internal life: there is a way it feels deliberately to act. We intend to do something, and we do it. There is a moment of final decision, the moment when a die is cast, the moment when the decision to act merges with the action decided on. That internal sense of deliberate action marks the distinction, essential to our ethical and moral experience, between acting and being acted upon: between pushing and being pushed. We think that we are judgmentally responsible for what we do, but not for what happens to us: for driving too fast but not for being hit by lightning. Our more complex ideas about responsibility depend on refinements of these crude ideas.

We distinguish the normal occasions in which people decide to act not just from those in which they are acted upon but also from those when they act under the control of someone else, as in hypnosis or higher-tech forms of mind control, or when they are victims of certain forms of mental deficiency or illness. We say, in the mind-control case, that the decision reflects not their own judgment or intention but rather that of the mind-controllers. We say, in the mental deficiency case, that though they acted on their own judgment or intention, they nevertheless ought not to be held responsible, because they lacked some capacity essential to responsibility.

We distinguish two such capacities. First, to be responsible, people must have some minimal ability to form true beliefs about the world, about the mental states of other people, and about the likely consequences of what they do. Someone who is unable to grasp the fact that guns can harm people is not responsible when he kills. Second, people must have, to a normal degree, the ability to make decisions that fit what we might call their normative personality: their desires, preferences, convictions, attachments, loyalties, and self-image. Genuine decisions, we think, are purposive, and someone who cannot match his final decisions to any of his desires, plans, convictions, or attachments is incapable of responsible action.

The responsibility system we have now briefly summarized plays a crucial role in the ethical project described in Chapter 9. Living well is a matter of making the right decisions; how well we have lived is a matter of how far we did that. But not every decision counts: we do not count what we did before we gained the capacities the responsibility system makes prominent—the capacity to form true beliefs and to match our decisions to our values—or (if we are later in a position to identify these) decisions we made while we had lost those capacities. The latter decisions, at least, figure in the judgment of how good our lives have been. Any period of insanity or deep compulsive obsession endangers the goodness of a life. But when we make the different judgment whether someone has lived well or badly, we filter out these infirm decisions. A person who is mentally incapacitated for substantially all his life has not, in the ethical sense, lived at all. Others pity him for the horribly damaged life he has endured, but they do not blame him or suppose that if he recovered in time he should blame himself.

When the responsibility system is described that abstractly, it seems uncontroversial; it is at least very widely accepted. Much of the system becomes controversial, however, when specified in greater detail. People disagree, for instance, about whether someone is judgmentally responsible who is unable to resist impulses stemming from blind rage, or who is forced to act against his convictions by threats of grievous harm, or whose sense of right and wrong has been warped by watching violence on television. A plausible theory of responsibility must explain the wide appeal of the abstract responsibility system and also explain when and why its details become controversial.

Two Conceptions of Control

The responsibility system embeds, hidden from view, ethical principles of the kind we seek—principles that connect the causes of our decisions with our responsibility for those decisions. Which principles are these? That is an interpretive question of the kind by now familiar in this book. We need to ask: Which ethical and moral principles provide the best overall justification of the system? It might be thought—I believe it is commonly thought—that the strongest argument for incompatibilism can be identified in that way. We cannot justify our ordinary convictions about judgmental responsibility, on this story, except by making responsibility depend on the ultimate causes of an action.

We must test that claim. Join me in a speculative experiment. We have discovered that determinism makes sense and is true: every one of our thoughts and acts has been made necessary by prior events or forces or states of affairs over which we had no control. In what way, if any, does that discovery undermine the point and sense of our responsibility system? We realize that our discovery cannot change the way we actually live. After the original shock, we find we must live pretty much as before. We are then like characters in a play who know they are scripted but lack the script—a variation of the situation of Pirandello's *Six Characters in Search of an Author*. We know we cannot live but as our author, nature, has decided. But we must nevertheless live: we, like Pirandello's characters, must still decide minute by minute what to do. We must still decide what the best reasons are and require.

Should we think ourselves absurd for carrying on in that way, even if we can't help it? Are we then like cigarette addicts or alcoholics, unable to kick the responsibility habit? We might be tempted to that view of our situation—many philosophers have been tempted—by the following line of thought. The responsibility system shows that we have responsibility only when we are in control of our behavior. Only when we are in charge can we give or deny ethical value to our lives. That explains why our responsibility system exempts acts under hypnosis or while we are insane. But if determinism is true, then we are never in control. So we can never create that kind of value, no matter how we act: we are only marionettes pretending that we are pulling the strings ourselves.

But this is too quick. This argument depends not just on the assumption that control is necessary to responsibility, but on a particular understanding of what control means. It supposes that someone is not in control when his decision is determined by external forces in the way determinism holds that all behavior is. I shall call this the "causal" sense of control, because it makes judgmental responsibility turn on the ultimate, originating historical causes of decision. We are in control when the causal chain that explains how we act travels back only to an impulse of our own will, not when it travels further back to past states and events that, together with natural laws, explain that act of will.

There is an alternate understanding of what it means to be in control. On this different view, an agent is in control when he is conscious of facing and making a decision, when no one else is making that decision through and for him, and when he has the capacities to form true beliefs about the world and to match his decisions to his normative personality—his settled desires, ambitions, and convictions. This is the "capacity" sense of control.

The two senses of control provide two different principles as candidate ethical foundations for the responsibility system: the causal control principle and the capacity control principle. The first insists that causal control is essential to responsibility; the second that capacity control is essential. Many philosophers—and many nonphilosophers—assume that the causal principle is obviously sound and the capacity principle just an evasion.[10] But the difference between the two principles is more profound. They take very different views of the nature, point, and, as we might put it, the location of judgmental responsibility.

The causal principle views the question of responsibility from outside an agent's own ordinary sense of his situation. It asks us to step back from our day-to-day life to try to see our situation as an all-knowing god might view it. It places our mental life in the context of the natural world; it asks us to try to explain our processes of decision the way we explain the workings of our internal organs. It ties the ethical judgment of responsibility to the scientific judgment of causation. The capacity principle, on the contrary, locates responsibility within the brackets of an ordinary life lived from a personal perspective. It makes an assumption of ethical independence: that our conscious decisions are, in principle, crucially and independently important in their own right and that their importance is in no way contingent on any remote causal explanation. Even if we are Pirandello characters, our decisions are genuine facts and whether we live well depends on how good those decisions are.

The two principles are contradictory: we cannot assume that one is true without denying the other. We cannot defeat the capacity principle by appealing to the control principle. It would beg the question to say that the former cannot be right because people cannot be responsible for what they were determined to do. Nor can we defeat the causal principle by appealing to the capacity principle. It would equally beg the question to argue that the control principle fails because the ethical importance of a decision depends on its circumstances, not its causal pedigree. We need denser arguments and these can only be interpretive.

I will offer an interpretive case for the capacity principle. In my view, it makes much better sense of the rest of our ethical and philosophical opinion. The causal principle, on the other hand, is an interpretive orphan: we can find or construct no good reason why it should be part of our ethics. But argument may in the end be unavailing. Interpretation depends finally on conviction, and anyone's choice between the two principles will probably reflect deeper attitudes and dispositions that lie beyond argument. In Chapter 9 we encountered a very closely related issue: Is life absurd if the universe is accidental? That issue and the question of judgmental responsibility that we are now exploring seem to be mirror images of each other. They both turn on the independence of ethics from science.

Whether a philosopher joins the compatibilist or incompatibilist camp turns on which of the two principles of control he adopts and therefore on how far he thinks ethics is independent. The Greek dramatists assumed a form of the capacity principle; their heroes were responsible even when the gods caused them to act as they did.[11] Aristotle, Hobbes, Hume, and, among prominent contemporary philosophers, Thomas Scanlon, also accepted the capacity principle.[12] Hume said that whether someone is in control depends on whether he could have acted otherwise if he had wanted to.[13] Hume's view is sometimes criticized by pointing out that if determinism is true, someone could not have wanted to do anything but what he did want to do.[14] That misses his point: he was endorsing an ethically independent attitude. Scanlon has suggested what he called a "psychological" test of responsibility; he challenges "the incompatibilist" to explain why that test is not satisfactory.[15] However, many contemporary philosophers assume that the causal principle is correct.[16] They think no one has judgmental responsibility when there is available in principle a full external causal explanation of what he wanted and did.

This deep contrast in opinion has, I believe, a further dimension. The idea of ethical responsibility I described in Chapter 9 rests on a fundamental assumption: that a human life can have value in the way it is lived. That assumption seems to suppose that self-conscious creatures are special in the universe: that they are not just more of the homogenized physical stuff that surrounds them. But why are they special? Billions of people find confirmation of their special importance in religion. They think a god gave us free will as a miraculous act of grace. Or, if not, that at least our predestination is decreed not by a soulless mechanics but by a supreme intelligence who made us, alone, in his image. Enlightenment deism or atheism blocked that escape for most philosophers, however, even as Enlightenment physics magnified the threat.

We might nevertheless hope for a different kind of independence from the natural order. There are two possibilities. We might hope that our decisions and acts actually are free of the causal transactions of the physical and biological world: that somewhere, perhaps only in a noumenal world, we have a free will, whatever that means. That hope encourages us to take up the external perspective of the causal principle because it can be redeemed only there. But once we do, our hope becomes vulnerable to scientific discovery or metaphysical skepticism. Or, on the other hand, we might think that the fact of our consciousness itself, together with the phenomenal challenge of lives to lead, itself gives us all the dignity we need or should crave. The universe may know what we will decide, but we do not. So we must struggle to choose, and on this view we do create value—the adverbial value of living well—just through our choices. We might reinterpret the long existentialist tradition in philosophy, or at least extract what is most persuasive in it, through that second view of our dignity. It gives a different and more plausible meaning to Jean-Paul Sartre's declaration that our existence precedes our essence.[17] Each of these two possibilities has its own emotional appeal. Which makes better sense of the rest of what we think?

Causal Control?

I emphasize yet again that the two contrasting principles—the causal and the capacity principles—are ethical, not physical or biological or metaphysical, principles. It is hardly obvious which better fits and justifies our familiar responsibility system: each of them has been embraced by many distinguished philosophers. We must pursue our interpretive question at some length.

We begin with causal control. I am an adult, suppose, of normal intelligence. I do not suffer from mental disease, and my decisions mainly correlate in the normal way with my preferences and convictions. I see a beggar on the street, and I wonder whether to give him something. I quickly rehearse reasons for and against. He looks hungry; I won't miss a dollar or two. He'll spend it on drugs; I gave at the office. I decide against giving; I walk past. I assume that I am judgmentally responsible for my action, that it makes sense for me or others to blame me for stinginess or praise me for good judgment.

If the causal principle is correct, however, my assumption of responsibility is hostage to science or mystery. If my decision was causally determined by forces or events in place before I was born, then my sense of responsibility, however unshakeable, is only an illusion. If, on the other hand, my decision to walk past the beggar was uncaused by anything in the past, if it represented a spontaneous intervention in the causal order that flowed from my brain to my legs, then my sense of responsibility is genuine: I am responsible. The causal principle might seem, at first blush, to capture the essence of responsibility. If external forces made me do something, how can I be myself responsible for doing it? But in another respect the principle seems arbitrary, even at first blush. How can the presence or absence of some physical or biological or metaphysical process of which I cannot possibly be aware as I act, and that cannot possibly be revealed in any account, either introspective or observational, of the intentions, motives, convictions, and emotions with which I act, make any moral or ethical difference at all?

Epiphenomenalism

The causal principle has two components: it denies responsibility if either determinism or epiphenomenalism is true. I begin with the second component: we are responsible only if our decisions are causally potent. Assume that everything you do is initiated in your nervous and muscular system before you make a decision to do it. All your decisions, from the simplest to the most complex and far-reaching, are only part of an after-the-fact documentary film playing on the screen of your mind: what you do causes your sense of having decided to do it, rather than the other way around. The hypothesis is of course amazing. But what can it have to do with judgmental responsibility?

Responsibility is an ethical or moral matter: it attaches to final decisions whether or not these are causally effective. We might say that someone who decides to injure someone else, but whose decision is only epiphenomenal, is guilty merely of an attempt. He is trying with all his heart to do something bad. But he fails because his decision is not the cause of what happens. He wants to kill his rival, he decides to do so, the gun he is holding fires, the rival dies. But it wasn't he who killed him; it was (we might say) only his programmed reptilian brain. So what? At least in this kind of case an attempted murder is morally as bad as a successful murder.

Lawyers like to invent cases like this one: A puts arsenic in B's coffee intending to kill him, but just as B is about to drink, C shoots him dead. A is not guilty of murder but only of attempted murder. Nevertheless A is morally as much at fault as if he were a murderer; that is the assumption that makes the lawyers' question—why should A be punished less severely than C?—difficult to answer. Lawyers discover or invent policy or procedural reasons to explain why attempted murder should be punished less severely than murder. We want to encourage people to change their minds at the last moment; we can't be sure that A wouldn't have warned B just before he sipped the coffee. But these reasons of policy have no application here. So why shouldn't we say that the person who tries to kill his rival but fails, because his decision is not the cause but only an epiphenomenal consequence of his behavior, is nevertheless morally culpable? He is judgmentally responsible for having tried, for having done his best.[18]

I agree that this comparison between the action of a single person and those of two distinct people is strange. It is strange to treat a person and his reptilian brain as separate actors, the way we treat A and C in the lawyers' imagined case. But that artificial bifurcation of a person is exactly what the causal control principle itself relies on. We normally treat people as whole people: the same person who has a mind also has a brain, nerves, and muscles, and his acting involves all of these. The causal control principle separates mind from body, personifies part of mind as an agent called the will, and then asks whether that agent actually causes the body it inhabits to act in a certain way or is only a fraud pulling levers disconnected from anything. It is an odd picture, and you may think the causal principle odd for that reason alone. If we accept the picture, however, we must hold the person-within-the-person responsible for what he has tried to do, unless we have some other reason for exempting him.

Determinism and Chance

I said earlier that we could not integrate the causal control principle with our other beliefs if we thought determinism true, because the principle would then contradict convictions of judgmental responsibility that we cannot disbelieve. In fact the principle finds no basis in the rest of our convictions even if we assume that determinism is *false* or not generally true. Consider this fantasy. Imagine that determinism is false as a universal claim. People often make decisions caused only by an original act of will. There are, however, exceptions. Sometimes people's decisions are indeed only the result of past events and forces wholly beyond their control. But we know this only as a possibility sometimes realized. We have no statistics about how often it is realized. No one can tell the difference on any particular occasion: no one can know which of his decisions is original and which was determined. They *all* seem, from the internal phenomenal perspective, free choices. It seems bizarre to suppose that you are responsible for some of your decisions but not others though no one can ever tell which. If you nevertheless accept the causal principle, how are you supposed to criticize yourself, even after you act? You can't even think that you are probably responsible for the damage you caused. Or probably not.

One day a breakthrough produces an instrument that can identify which decisions were determined and which not, though only through evidence not detectable until two weeks after the act in question. Two men are arrested for plotting and then executing a murder in cold blood; after lengthy police tests, the instrument declares that one of their wills, by a inscrutable mental spasm of some kind, initiated the causal chain that produced his crime, while the other's act was determined from the beginning of time. That difference produced no difference in the way the two villains thought, plotted, or acted, and nothing but the new instrument could have detected it. Should the second villain be freed and the first jailed for life or executed? That seems absurd: the hidden causal distinction seems too disconnected from anything we think should matter in a decision of that kind. The responsibility system does make distinctions in blameworthiness. But the qualities that lead us to excuse young children and mentally ill people are also qualities that affect their behavior and their lives, and our relations with them, in hundreds of other ways. People who lack the capacity to reason or properly to organize their desires lead very different lives from those who have those capacities. People who are hypnotized or whose brains are manipulated by mad scientists have become subordinated to alien wills. For all such people, their lack of responsibility is a general status, not a haphazard piece of quantum whimsy.

If I am right that it would be crazy to make responsibility turn on what the instrument displays in my fantasy, then the causal principle must be wrong. It makes no difference how we change the fantasy. I might have supposed, not that everyone's behavior is sometimes determined and sometimes not, but that some people's behavior is always determined and other people's behavior never is. It would make no ethical or moral sense to treat the two classes differently once an instrument had identified their category. Because the causal control principle would seem arbitrary in these various different circumstances, we cannot accept it as a sound ethical or moral principle. If the bare, brute fact of determinism does not undermine judgments of responsibility when that fact is randomly distributed, it cannot undermine them when it is pervasive.

Determinism and Rationality

The causal principle seems bizarre in a further way. People make decisions on the basis of their beliefs and values. These are the ingredients of a rational decision. But we do not have the kind of control over our beliefs and values that the causal principle demands for the decision itself. You can't choose your beliefs about the world by an act of free will. On the contrary, you hope that your beliefs are determined by how the world is. Nor can you just choose your values: your tastes, preferences, convictions, allegiances, and the rest of

FREE WILL AND RESPONSIBILITY   235

your normative personality. I argued in Chapter 4 that our moral convictions are not caused by moral truth: the causal impact hypothesis is false. If it were true, however, then our convictions would of course be caused by something outside us—moral fact—not an originating will inside. If it is false, as I believe, then any competent causal explanation of convictions must lie in the kind of personal history I described in that chapter, which means that a complete explanation would include not only facts about a person's genes, family, culture, and environment but also the causes of these: it would include the laws of physics and chemistry and the history of the universe. This is even more evidently true of our tastes, desires, and preferences. We cannot create these from nothing by some act of will.

Yes, to some degree people are able to influence their preferences and convictions. We struggle to like caviar or sky diving or to become better people by enrolling in churches or extension philosophy courses. But we do this only because we have other convictions or preferences or tastes we did not choose. People try to train themselves to like caviar or skiing because for a variety of reasons they desire to be the kind of people who do like them, and they did not choose to have that desire. They join churches or self-help groups to acquire or strengthen convictions they already want to have. The responsibility project I described in Chapter 6 requires people to try to work their various convictions into a coherent and integrated whole. But these efforts at integrity respond to still deeper aspirations that we do not originate by any act of will either, and they are, sadly, often frustrated by what we find we just cannot believe.

The fact that we cannot just choose what to believe or want makes the causal control principle ethically and morally otiose. If I am rational, I choose as my beliefs and desires directly; in that sense my decision is caused by factors beyond my control, even if I have free will. Why should I then be thought more responsible if I had the power to act irresponsibly—that is, contrary to my beliefs, convictions, and preferences? The causal principle is offered, remember, as an interpretation of the more abstract principle that people are liable to praise or blame only when they are in control of their own behavior. Someone who acts irrationally is not in control, and it therefore seems perverse to insist that a person is not in control unless he has the power to lose control. We might as well say that a society isn't free if it doesn't allow people to sell themselves into slavery.

Galen Strawson is right: causal control over actual decisions cannot provide judgmental responsibility on its own. "To be truly morally responsible for what you do," he declares, "you must be truly responsible for the way you are—at least in crucial mental respects."[19] Because we cannot be responsible for the way we are in these respects, he concludes, responsibility is an illusion, whether or not determinism is true. Strawson's premise is inescapable and important. If the key to judgmental responsibility is causal control, then we are not responsible unless we can freely choose the beliefs and preferences that are the ingredients of our decisions, as well as the decisions themselves. But he draws the wrong conclusion. We should rather conclude that the causal control principle is false. We are responsible (if we are) because what we believe is at least in large part fixed by how things are. We could not be responsible if what we believed was just up to us, if we could whimsically decide for ourselves which beliefs would take root in our minds.

Nor would we be responsible if we could freely choose which convictions to adopt or preferences to embrace. We would then have no ground for any choice we made. If we supplied a reason for our choice, that would simply raise a further question of justification—why did we choose that particular desire or that particular conviction?—and so backward into infinity. We must just *have* ultimate convictions and tastes that we cannot abandon by fiat, to be capable of rational action. Once again the causal control principle ends not by defining, but by undermining, the conditions of responsibility.

Psychological and Metaphysical Impossibility

Suppose determinism is false. People's decisions are for the most part causally downstream of original acts of their will. The causal control principle holds that they are therefore responsible for what they do. But the familiar phenomenon of psychological impossibility remains. Martin Luther speaks psychological truth when he declares that he can do no other than declare his new faith before the world; Mother Teresa is incapable of a selfish thought or action; Stalin is incapable of a generous or noble one. Commentators sometimes say that people have put themselves in that situation by prior deliberate decisions. Mother Teresa may have squashed any selfish thought she had until she no longer had any. But that is not necessarily (or, I think, even usually) so. Someone who was born into and grew up in a rigid military environment may never have been capable of shirking disagreeable or dangerous duty; someone born into a fundamentalist religious family or into a resentful and mistreated minority may never have been capable of acts that seem natural to others. We say that these people's character makes it psychologically impossible for them to act, in certain instances, other than as they do.

If we are tempted by the causal principle, we must decide whether this kind of psychological impossibility negates judgmental responsibility so that though we may blame ordinary political leaders for their infrequent acts of cruelty or tyranny, it would be wrong to blame anyone so double-dyed in evil as Stalin, and though it would be right to praise generally selfish people for their occasional acts of generosity, it would be wrong ever to praise someone so instinctively good as Mother Teresa. This seems implausible.[20] But if we therefore decide that psychological impossibility does not count, so that we can praise or condemn Stalin and Mother Teresa as we do everyone else, then the causal principle seems arbitrary in a different way. We must be distinguishing between psychological and some other kind of inevitability—call it metaphysical. We must think that someone's will can be the uncaused cause of his actions in spite of the fact that his character, formed by events wholly beyond his control, makes it impossible for him to act other than as he does. But that only offers another puzzle. If inevitability is what defeats the ethically important kind of control, then the source of the inevitability shouldn't matter. If inevitability does not in itself defeat the ethically and morally important kind of control, then why would metaphysical inevitability defeat it?

The Responsibility System

The causal control principle has what might appear to be roots within the popular responsibility system I described. We are not responsible when someone pushes us or manipulates our mind through hypnosis or chemical or electrical intervention. That is understandable; these are not our acts. But we are also not responsible when we are small children or seriously mentally ill. It might seem an important strength of the causal principle that it identifies and justifies all these exceptions. Indeed, the familiar pessimistic argument that I described at the outset begins with that claim. Pessimistic incompatibilists argue that if we accept that mentally ill criminals should be excused because they are not responsible, we must for that reason accept that no one is ever responsible, because everyone is actually in the same position. People who are mentally ill are not in control of their behavior, but neither are people whose actions are caused entirely by events and laws beyond their control.

The structure of that familiar argument is important. It is addressed to people who think that they and other people are normally judgmentally responsible for what they do, but who also assume that children and the mentally ill, among others, are not. It aims to show such people that they already accept the causal control principle. "You assume," it tells them, "that there are crucial differences between your normal situation and that of children and the mentally ill. The causal control principle captures what you must take the crucial difference to be. You must think that in these exceptional cases people's decisions are caused by events they could not control, while in the normal cases people's acts of will initiate the causal chain that ends in action. We now show you, by demonstrating the truth of determinism, that your own decisions are never original in that way but are always the product of events wholly beyond your control." The strategy assumes that the distinction ordinary people see between normal and exceptional cases is best explained as a difference in causal paths: they think that decisions in the exceptional cases, but not in normal cases, are causally determined by past events over which the agent had no control.

But that cannot be what ordinary people think. They do assume that they are responsible for their decisions and that young children and the mentally ill are not. But the causal control principle cannot be, for them, what justifies that distinction. Consider first young children. Senior citizens make decisions that give effect to their beliefs, desires, and preferences. We have no reason to think that young children, who certainly make decisions, make them in any other way. We therefore have no basis for ascribing a different internal agency or cause of decision to them. Whatever view we take about the freedom of an adult will must therefore hold for a young child as well. But of course there is a difference: it is the difference that the rival interpretation of the responsibility system, the capacity control principle, picks out. Young children have a defective capacity, judged by normal adult standards, to form correct beliefs about what the world is like and about the consequence, prudence, and morality of their doing and having what they want. They are often ignorant of "the nature and quality" of their acts. It is these incapacities, not any assumption about the causal pedigree of their decisions, that strikes people as requiring that children be relieved of some or all judgmental responsibility.

Now consider someone suffering from a serious mental disease: he thinks himself Napoleon or God, and he also thinks that this identity entitles or even requires him to kill or steal. He lacks the normal capacity to form beliefs that are guided by facts and logic. He is crazy, and the familiar responsibility system holds him exempt from judgmental responsibility for that reason. But there is no reason to suppose that his decisions have either less or more initiating power than they would have had if he were not crazy. Like normal people, he acts in a way that is fully predictable, given a full knowledge of his beliefs and normative personality. True, we find it natural to say that his disease has made him kill, which might suggest something special about the pedigree of his decisions. But that is only a figure of speech. Taken literally it is absurd. We speak more accurately when we say that the disease has distorted its victim's judgment. But then, once again, we are invoking the capacity, not the causal, principle to justify the exception.

Now consider a different form of mental disease: someone who though he has normal powers to form true beliefs, and though he is committed to unexceptional moral, ethical, and prudential convictions, nevertheless constantly makes fateful decisions that contradict all those convictions. Instances range from psychopaths—the killer who begs society to catch him before he kills again—to the physiological or psychological addict, the smoker or shooter or alcoholic or compulsive hand-washer who is desperate to stop but cannot. I distinguish these unfortunates from people who have been hypnotized into behavior they would reject or whose minds are manipulated by a villain with a thought-control ray gun. I do not know what it feels like to be hypnotized, and no one knows what it feels like to have his impulses zapped into being. I shall assume, however, that people in those latter cases do not make what I called final decisions: real, felt decisions that merge into the actions the decisions contemplate. Their behavior is like a cough or other production of their autonomic nervous system. They do not act, and so their behavior raises no question of judgmental responsibility. (If I am wrong, then their cases raise the same problem as those of the ill people I discuss.) I do suppose, however, that psychopaths and addicts make final decisions: to kill or to light or shoot up. Would it make sense for ordinary people, who take themselves to be responsible for their acts, to excuse psychopaths or addicts because of some perceived difference in the causal genesis of their own and their decisions?

We ordinary people, who believe that we are responsible for what we do but that psychopaths and addicts are not, concede that we ourselves are sometimes unable to overcome temptations of various sorts: we sometimes decide to do what our reflective values condemn as imprudent or wrong. We might or might not deliberate much; we might or might not struggle. But temptation wins. We say, "Just this once" or "The hell with it," and we light up or order steak and fries. We do not think that on these occasions we have been hypnotized or zapped; we do not think our wills have been robbed of their ordinary originating power. We think, on the contrary, that the state of our wills is to blame: we say we have been weak-willed, and we resolve not to sin again. We count the occasion as showing, not a conquest of our minds by some alien force, but a failure of our mind's ordinary capacity to organize and direct our reflective convictions.

We can find no reason, in this account of our own lapses, to think that an addict's situation is an entirely different matter rather than only different in degree. We have no reason to suppose that some alien force has usurped the role of the addict's will, either. We may say that because he yields even though he knows that the result will be disastrous, he is very much weaker than we are. He is in fact incapable of controlling his immediate impulses; perhaps, in the moment of acting, he is even incapable of understanding his peril. But then we are not assuming that the causal path of mental events distinguishes his case from ours. We count the difference between us and him as one of capability and therefore of degree. That latter explanation does not invoke the causal control principle; it makes no assumption, either way, about determinism or epiphenomenalism.

Summary: Causal Control?

I must first make clear what my argument is not. I started this discussion by noticing that pessimistic incompatibilism would require us to abandon practically the entire body of our ethical and moral convictions and practice; so much that we could not, I said, actually believe it. It might therefore be tempting to say that no matter how strong the arguments are for the causal control principle, we must reject it just for that reason.[21] That has not been my argument. I have rather tried to show that there are no arguments *for* the causal principle: nothing that we need to sweep under a carpet and try to forget.

The causal control principle is an ethical or moral principle, so any argument for it must be interpretive. It does not just follow from any scientific or metaphysical discovery: that is the lesson of Part One. It can find support only in other moral and ethical principles. But it is supported by none of them. It is contradicted by the principle that people are responsible when they attempt harm, even when the attempt is unsuccessful. We can find no moral or ethical explanation why, if some acts are caused by external circumstances and others are not, an agent should be responsible for the latter but not the former. Nor why it matters whether a final decision is uncaused by external forces when all the factors that make any decision rational—the beliefs and value on which it is based—are clearly caused by external forces. The principle is also contradicted by the practices that allow us to praise or blame people who are psychologically unable to act otherwise. Nor does the ordinary responsibility system we identified presuppose, as many philosophers suppose it does, the causal principle. On the contrary, that principle cannot explain the cardinal features of that system. So we do not reject causal control because, though the best arguments support it, we can't believe it. We reject it because no argument supports it. As I said, a great many philosophers, including some very distinguished ones, nevertheless do accept it. They report a "robust intuition" that we cannot be responsible for an action unless we are the first cause of that action. But that claim presupposes rather than argues for the control principle; it offers nothing else by way of a link between ethics and science. Intuitions are not arguments.

It does not follow that the second principle I distinguished, the capacity control principle, is automatically preferable as an interpretation; perhaps we can make no good sense of that principle either. But the failure of the causal principle prepares us for a more sympathetic inspection of that alternative. Our original conviction that responsibility depends on control now seems itself at stake. Perhaps the capacity principle can make it more intelligible.

Capacity Control

The Inescapable Importance of Decision

Can we do a better or worse job of making decisions even if, unknown to us, the decisions we make are inevitable? I believe we can. Another fantasy. The painter begins on a giant canvas. He dreams and imagines. He sketches, draws, paints, rubs out, paints over, despairs, smokes, drinks, returns, paints violently, stands back, sighs, lights up. He is done. His canvas is exhibited; we adore it and we celebrate him. Then a guru in the Arctic Circle calls a press conference. He unveils an exact replica of the great painting; newly sophisticated dating techniques prove that it was created a second before our artist began his own work. The guru explains that he has an instant painting machine directed by a powerful computer at whose disposal he has placed an exact description of every event since the beginning of time, including, of course, information about the artist's various abilities, his convictions about greatness in art, and his beliefs about the tastes of rich collectors. We are amazed.

But do we value the artist's efforts or achievement less? Before the press conference we valued what he did because we admired the way he made the many thousands of large and small decisions that ended in the wonderful picture. He made those decisions splendidly. None of that has changed; our amazing discovery cannot have cheapened the worth of a single brush stroke. They remain his decisions; he made them self-consciously with no guidance from any of the guru's information. We praise the *artist* for those decisions. We are not praising some internal homunculus person—his "will"—who made him do it.

Of course, if we discovered that he had in some way cheated—employed some other artist and taken the credit—we would not have praised him. The decisions we praise would not then have been his.[22] But predictability itself cannot cheapen achievement.[23] That explains why Mother Teresa and Stalin were responsible for what they did. A sharp-eyed critic discovers a few square inches in the artist's canvas that the replica did not replicate exactly. The guru interrogates his machines and checks his base of information. No mistake was made. The artist has free will after all! We do not suddenly value his achievement more, however. Perhaps he would have painted better if he had done exactly what the machines predicted.

We find, in this fantasy, the same account of the performance value of a work of art as we identified in Chapter 9. This lies in an artist's own creative decisions and not in any more remote causal account of those decisions. Now we apply the same account, as we did there, to a more embracing creative career: your living your life and trying to live it well. The value you achieve in that larger career also depends on the character of your decisions, not their remote ancestry. It does not matter whether your decisions were fixed by the world's history or initiated in some spontaneous festering of neural molecules. The remote natural etiology of your decisions is irrelevant to the performance value or disvalue these decisions create.

The struggle I described in Chapter 6, to create integrity among our convictions, is part of the unfolding drama of self-conscious life. If all our decisions are determined, then so are these. That does not make integrity less crucial to our ethical success. Is it an objection to this entire line of thought that it makes us judgmentally responsible for our character even though we did not choose our character? Strictly speaking, it makes us responsible for our decisions, not our character. But of course decisions flow from character. So, yes, we are responsible for our character. If this were not so—if we treated character as the good or bad luck someone has had—there would be no person left whose luck that could be. I cannot excuse my indolence, or you your impatience, because neither of us chose to have these qualities. But can we be responsible for what we have not chosen? Yes. The causal control principle denies that we can, but it is mistaken. Handicaps and accidents are different precisely because they do not reflect character. As we shall see in Chapter 16, that difference matters to distributive justice.

An Ethical Justification for Exemption

These are the assumptions—about character, decision, and performance value in living—that we need in order to explain why we have judgmental responsibility for our decisions generally. Now we confront a different question. Why do we not have responsibility for all our decisions? What justifies the exceptions our responsibility system recognizes? I argued that, contrary to first impressions, the causal control principle cannot justify these exceptions. We must now ask whether the alternative understanding of control, the capacity principle, provides a better justification.

I cannot deny, as I write a paragraph or end a love affair, that I must count my act in any overall self-assessment. But we do exempt certain decisions from counting, when we think we have good reason to do this. We can do this for other people as they act and for ourselves in retrospect. Which decisions, if any, should we exclude? What screening filters would be justified? We cannot screen out decisions just because we regret them; that would altogether erase the possibility of living well. But we do have reason to adopt a much less forgiving filter. Often in various contexts we distinguish between doing a job badly and not being able to do it at all. A blind person does not read badly. We must see the responsibility system in that light. The capacity principle describes capabilities we believe someone must have if he is sensibly to be judged successful or unsuccessful in his effort to live well.

Bernard Williams pointed out that a screening filter can be constructed in various ways; the combination reflected in Greek literature was, he believed, very like our own, but in certain important ways different.[24] We treat even temporary insanity as negating responsibility, but Sophocles' Ajax thought himself responsible for his stupid slaughtering of cattle, even though Athena made him do it by making him mad.[25] The capacity principle holds, instead, that someone lacks control in the pertinent sense when he has insufficient capacity to form true and pertinent beliefs about the world in which he acts, or to match his decisions to his normative personality. That principle therefore provides a different screening filter. We must judge whether it is a better one by asking whether it reflects a better conception of adverbial ethical value.

People have these two capacities to very different degrees. Almost any scientist is better at forming true beliefs about the physical world than I am, and someone who is less impulsive is better at conforming his decisions to what he actually thinks good for him to have or do. The capacity principle supposes a threshold level of these capacities, and much of the argument among lawyers and laymen about when it is proper to hold someone responsible for his behavior is actually argument about where that threshold should be set. It is a virtue of the capacity principle that it shows these disputes to be ethical rather than psychological in character. They turn on micro value judgments that people who accept the capacity principle in the abstract will make differently.

In some cases, however, failure in one of the other of the capacities is egregious and undeniable, and we should concentrate first on those cases. An idiot cannot form a large enough stock of stable true beliefs about the world to make his life safe, let alone profitable; he lacks the minimum level of the first capacity.[26] Someone with serious frontal lobe brain injury may be wholly unable to avoid aggressive and violent behavior, even though nothing he thinks or wants or approves recommends that behavior. The capacity principle holds that the idiot and the victim of serious brain damage are not judgmentally responsible for the decisions that manifest these incapacities. The principle does not deny that an agent's other incapacities, properties, or situation may also be grounds of exemption. (I consider some candidate examples toward the end of this chapter.) But we concentrate now on those incapacities that the capacity principle recognizes.

How can we justify these incapacity exceptions? They assume a more basic ethical conviction: that living well means creating not just a chronology but a narrative that weaves together values of character—loyalties, ambitions, desires, tastes, and ideals. No one creates a narrative of perfect integrity: we all act, as we say, out of character sometimes. Many people's lives, judged as narratives, are picaresque or even a shambles—Hubbard's "one damned thing after another" or Millay's "one damn thing again and again."[27] But just for that reason those lives are not lived well, no matter how full of worldly success they turn out to be, unless they are redeemed by a new, late-in-life integrating interpretation or by conversion to a new integrity. Our responsibility system reflects that—at least to me—attractive ethical judgment.

In this light, the first capacity seems indispensable. Creating a life requires reacting to the environment in which that life is lived; a person cannot sensibly be treated, or in retrospect treat himself, as creating a life unless he can form beliefs about the world that are largely responsive to how the world is. People whose senses are impaired in some way, or who have had an unsatisfactory education, may be able to compensate enough to form mainly correct beliefs about their immediate environment. But an idiot or someone who thinks he is Napoleon or that pigs can fly lacks that minimal ability. Philosophers sometimes ask you to imagine that you are only a disembodied brain in a nutrient vat, comprehensively deceived by a master intelligence into thinking that you are an embodied bipedal organism living on a planet Earth. If that were true, then you would not be leading a life. Assuming that we are not brains in a vat, almost all of us have the epistemic capacity we need for most of our lives. But from time to time some of us lack or lose that normal ability in one way or another, and then our judgmental responsibility for what we do is called into question.

The second capacity is regulative; it seems essential as well. If I am to respond to the challenge of living well, I must have the capacity to match my decisions to a sense of what living well would mean. My personality has been molded by forces gathered in my personal history; these have shaped my personality, but they do not limit my ability to match my decisions to the personality they have shaped. It destroys that capacity, however, when others take over my decision-making capacity to serve their own ends: when I am hypnotized or governed through electrodes implanted in my brain. That usurpation disconnects my decision from my personality, so that it is at best an accident when these match. It is therefore sensible that when I ask how well I have lived, I distinguish between what I did when I had the capacity to reflect my own desires and convictions in my decisions and what I did when I lacked that capacity. I take responsibility only for the former. Some people are in that position temporarily or even over extended periods of their lives, not because others have stolen their capacity to shape their behavior to their own personality, but because they lack the capacity in themselves. A beginning infant does not make decisions at all, I suppose. A very young child does, but he does not have the cognitive or critical ability needed to match his decisions to any self-consciously recognized ambitions or desires. The victims of severe mental disease I described earlier—the killers who beg to be caught—are in the same case. Indeed, mental illness may savage either or both of these judgmental capacities; serious loss of either might be a defining condition of mental disease.[28] The history of the insanity-defense debate that I describe briefly later in this chapter shows a pendulum swing between a strict doctrine that requires loss of epistemic capacity and a more generous doctrine that also makes regulative capacity critical.

The Moral Application

We have now constructed an ethical justification of the capacity principle. The principle functions as a moral as well as an ethical principle, however. In that different role it plays no direct part in anyone's judgment of how well he or anyone else has led his life; instead it serves, among other purposes, as a threshold condition for blame and sanction. We must therefore ask what justification we have for exporting the principle from the ethical to the moral arena in that way. It is a central demand of self-respect, I argued in Chapter 9, that we must not only take personal responsibility for making something of our own lives but also treat the principle that requires this as an objective principle of value. In the next chapter I argue that this means recognizing and respecting the same responsibility in others. That requirement cannot be met—we cannot be treating the principle of personal responsibility as having objective standing—unless we understand personal responsibility to have the same character and dimension for everyone. So we must give that principle the same character and force in morality that it has in ethics.

I rely on the capacity principle in criticizing myself; in deciding whether it is appropriate to feel shame or guilt or only deep regret for some decision I wish I had not taken. I hold myself responsible unless I am satisfied that I lacked some capacity essential to responsibility when I took that decision. What justification can I have for using a different—stricter or more lenient—standard for judging the guilt of someone else? Using a different standard would mean judging him as I refuse to judge myself. It would be an act of disrespect to him.

We have already met a dramatic form of that failure. Some criminologists say that because science has shown that no one has free will, it is wrong to punish anyone for anything. We should treat those we now style criminals medically rather than as criminals, hoping to reprogram rather than punish them. This declaration supposes that "we" have responsibility that other people lack, that we can judge ourselves to act wrongly while we can only judge everyone else to act dangerously or inconveniently. Most people have a strong negative reaction to the proposal that outlaws should be treated medically rather than punished criminally. They think that this would dehumanize outlaws. They sense, I believe, that this proposal fails the cardinal requirement that we treat responsibility in others as we treat it in ourselves.

Illusion?

I have neglected epiphenomenalism for several pages. Of course, in judging the merits or demerits of our final decisions, we and others pay great attention to the consequences that we foresee, or ought to foresee, of acting as we decide to act. But, strictly speaking, that attention presupposes no causal efficacy. It presupposes only what logicians call material implication. If I decide to pull the trigger, someone will die without the intervention of any other agent; if I do not, he will not. I can know the truth of such conditionals from my experience, without making any assumption about the causal force of my decision on the muscles that pull my trigger finger back. The conditionals are consistent with epiphenomenalism as well as determinism. They are also consistent, of course, with denying both.

The capacity principle makes exceptions for what it treats as pathological cases: it conditions judgmental responsibility on the capacities of the agent. But these are not causal conditions. The principle makes capacities crucial to responsibility, not because normal people have wills that are in charge while a child or an idiot or a madman does not, but because it sets conditions on responsibility with an eye to the overall ethical responsibility to live well. It declares that assignment in play only when a person is capable of pursuing the assignment. A toddler or idiot or madman makes decisions, and makes them, perhaps, with some sense of responsibility for them. But he should reject judgmental responsibility for those decisions later, when he grows or if he recovers, and the rest of us should reject them now. We think—and the toddler, at least, will later come to think—that it would be right not to count those decisions in deciding how well he has lived. If we accept the capacity principle as the ethical basis for our responsibility system, we can await the latest discoveries about the electrodynamics of our brains with boundless curiosity but no terror.

There is no delusion in this story. Nothing in my description of the role the capacity principle plays in fixing or denying responsibility makes any ultimate causal assumptions at all. No doubt many people who accept the responsibility system do believe that determinism and epiphenomenalism are both wrong: in fact, absurd. They believe that it has not already been decided what they will think best to do; that this is a matter of their spontaneous manufacture here and now. But whether that further thought is coherent or not, it plays no part in our story. We are not like the brains floating in a vat. They live in complete ignorance of their situation; they have no way to discover it. They wholly lack the capacity to form beliefs based on evidence. Most of us have that capacity in ample degree; indeed, we are now supposing that we have the capacity even to discover that all our decisions are determined by ancient events. We are not in either complete or terminal ignorance.

One more challenge. It might be said that if determinism or epiphenomenalism is true, people never have the capacities the capacity control principle assumes they normally do have, because these capacities require some kind of ultimate causal originality or power. But they require no such thing. The first is the capacity to form true beliefs about the physical world and the mental states of other people. It does not impeach that capacity that our beliefs about the world are caused by events beyond our control; on the contrary, as I said, it is exactly that fact that endows us with that capacity. Nor can it damage that capacity that our final decisions do not enter into causal relations with our nerves and muscles; that fact, if it is a fact, is completely irrelevant to the existence of the first capacity. The second, regulative capacity the principle assumes is that people can normally make final decisions that can be understood as serving their desires and convictions in the light of their beliefs. That is an assumption about the character—not the etiology or causal consequence—of final decisions. People have that capacity whether or not they were fated to have it. A fast car, whose behavior is certainly determined by events beyond its control, nevertheless has the capacity to exceed the speed limit.

Responsibility in Practice

The Insanity Defense

The choice between the causal and the capacity control principles is important for reasons that go beyond the free-will controversy. The choice is decisive for both explaining and debating the much more practical controversies I mentioned among people who accept the general structure of the responsibility system but disagree about its application to particular cases. If we think that people are responsible only when their actions flow from a spontaneous, un-caused act of will, then we will think that these practical controversies turn on an all-or-nothing psychobiological fact. When someone claims that he com-mitted his criminal act in a blind rage or when overcome by an irresistible im-pulse or under duress or because he grew up in a ghetto or because he had watched too much violence on television, we would ask: were these forces or influences strong enough in the circumstances so that they displaced his will's normal causal role, like a drunken sailor pushing the helmsman aside and tak-ing the wheel? So that it was not his will but rather an overwhelming surge of sexual jealousy or some such force that provided the efficient cause of his mus-cles contracting around the trigger? I doubt that many of the citizens, lawyers, and judges who would have to answer those questions, if they accepted the causal principle, would understand them. Perhaps the popularity of the causal principle among philosophers has contributed to the confusion that marks this area of the criminal law.

If we reject the causal in favor of the capacity control principle, however, we pose a different question. Did the accused lack one or the other of the pertinent capacities to such a degree that it is inappropriate to ascribe respon-sibility to him? That question calls for two distinct judgments: an interpre-tive judgment about his behavior and an ethical and moral judgment that reasonable people make differently. It is therefore often a difficult question but not, I think, a mysterious one. People who must try to answer it—jurors after hearing volumes of testimony, perhaps—will have different opinions about the interpretive issue. They will disagree, for instance, about whether the defendant's general behavior revealed an admiration for violence as part of his self-image, so that his violent act confirmed rather than contradicted his general capacity to suit his decision to his tastes. They will also disagree about the more evidently normative issue—about what level of incapacity is sufficient to let someone off the responsibility hook. We admire people who at least begin to answer that question introspectively. Would I think myself responsible, in retrospect, if I was in the defendant's shoes? That is the spirit of the attractive thought, "There but for the grace of God go I."

The history of the insanity defense suggests that many people do not ap-proach the issue in that introspective way, however. Outrage is a more frequent spur. When the public has been particularly anxious for vengeance after some crime, judges and legislators have responded by cutting back the scope of the insanity defense. The M'Naghten Rule, named after the woodcutter who killed Peel's secretary while trying to kill the prime minister himself, shrunk the defense to allow only the first, cognitive, capacity to count, and stipulated that only a particularly low level of even that capacity could excuse. Over many decades most American states moved from that strict rule to a more forgiving one that permitted the accused to argue that he was confronted with an irresistible impulse. But asking juries to judge the appropriate level of the second, regulative capacity proved unwieldy, and the results often seemed too permissive to many scholars as well as to the general public. The argument, made to a Florida court, that the defendant lacked the necessary regulative capacity because he had watched too much television, seemed a *reductio ad absurdam* that called the standard itself into question.[29] It was, however, the attempted assassination of President Reagan that provoked the greatest complaints about the leniency of the insanity defense.

In any case, for whatever reason, many American states have now adopted a different approach based on a recommendation of the American Law Institute: the defense is available to a defendant only "if at the time of such conduct as a result of mental disease or defect he lacks substantial capacity either to appreciate the criminality of his conduct or to conform his conduct to the requirements of the law."[30] That rule by no means eliminates the need for judgment, and different lawyers, judges, and jurors make the judgment differently. But the rule does change the focus from discrete event to general capacity. This has evidentiary advantages: it is easier to judge whether a defendant has shown a general incapacity, manifested in other ways, rather than just a single-shot temporary incapacity exhausted in the crime it is alleged to excuse. Requiring a showing of mental disease or defect also reduces the vagueness of the defense: the label "disease," even if not a medical term of art, is itself a classification. We do not regard someone as suffering from mental disease if his cognitive and regulative capacities fall only somewhat short of what we take to be normal. They must be very poor.

Duress, Injustice, and Responsibility

When we recognize the crucial connection between our ethical responsibility to live well and our judgmental responsibility for discrete decisions, we can more adequately understand and argue about other controversial features of the responsibility system. It is controversial, for example, whether and when duress diminishes responsibility. Usually when someone obeys an order to kill because he is threatened with death himself, he does not lack either of the pertinent capacities. He obeys because he understands his situation accurately and because he is able to conform his decision to his reflective judgment of what is best for him. His responsibility is not diminished, though his situation may nevertheless provide an excuse. Torture, at least in extreme forms, is different. Someone who threatens torture hopes to change his victim's options just as someone does who threatens death. Someone facing torture retains both the capacities necessary for responsibility in his choice whether to obey to avoid it. But when the torture begins, the torturer's aim is different: he hopes to reduce his victim to a screaming animal who is no longer able to reason in that way. He aims to extinguish, not to invoke, his victim's responsibility. But if duress short of torture diminishes responsibility, this must normally be for some other reason.[31]

It is also controversial whether someone born into a ghetto of poverty is less responsible for any antisocial behavior than people from more privileged backgrounds. He does not suffer from any pertinent incapacity. Someone with a mental disease may lack the capacity to conform his behavior to the law, but that is not true of someone condemned to an impoverished inner-city life who decides to push drugs. He knows that what he does is illegal and has every opportunity to consider whether it is immoral as well; he is no less capable than others of forming accurate views about the world or of matching his decisions to his desires or convictions. Again, if we think him less responsible than others, as a great many people do think, we must find some other ground.

We cannot find that different ground so long as we take the causal principle to govern responsibility. However we understand the idea of a free will, we can make no sense of the hypothesis that either threats or poverty can displace its normal causal operation. But the picture of judgmental responsibility we have now drawn opens the way to a very different suggestion: we are tempted to find diminished responsibility in these circumstances because—but only when—duress or poverty is the product of injustice. Our foundational responsibility to live well provides a ground for claiming moral and political rights. (I discuss some of these rights in Chapters 17.) We might—or might not—think that these rights should be protected by a further, distinct, responsibility filter in addition to the capacity filters we have been discussing. The authors of injustice cheat their victims of opportunities or resources that would very likely have led to different decisions.[32] Perhaps we should therefore not count these corrupted decisions in assessing how blameworthy we or others are. Or at least we should not count them fully: we should discount their responsibility in view of the injustice. This distinct, further filter is conceptually available because the root questions for the responsibility system are not metaphysical but ethical and moral; this further filter is controversial for exactly that reason.

It is important that this last argument for diminished responsibility is grounded in justice, not capacity. People who live in ghettos of poverty in a nation of affluence have been cheated of opportunities and resources they are entitled to have. But people who live in an age or space of relative privation that is no one's fault cannot claim diminished responsibility for that reason; otherwise no one would be judgmentally responsible for anything until some millennium of wealth and cultural sophistication had been reached. The poverty that even arguably mitigates judgmental responsibility is only unjust poverty. That is why those who deny the injustice deny the mitigation as well.

PART FOUR

Morality

11

From Dignity to Morality

Self-Respect and Respect for Others

Universal or Special?

We hope, remember, to integrate ethics with morality, not simply by incorporating morality into ethics but by achieving a mutually supportive integration of the two in which our thoughts about living well help us to see what our moral responsibilities are: an integration that responds to the traditional philosopher's challenge about what reason we have to be good. We start by considering the implications for morality of the first of our two principles of dignity—that you must treat the success of your own life as a matter of objective importance. In Chapter 1 I described Kant's principle. This holds that a proper form of self-respect—the self-respect demanded by that first principle of dignity—entails a parallel respect for the lives of all human beings. If you are to respect yourself, you must treat their lives, too, as having an objective importance. Many readers will find that principle immediately appealing, but it is important to pause over its sources and its limits.

If you believe that it is objectively important how your life goes, then you should consider this important question. Do you value your life as objectively important in virtue of something special about your life, so that it would be perfectly consistent for you not to treat other human lives as having the same kind of importance? Or do you value your life in that way because you think all human life is objectively important?

The relationship between you and your life is indeed special: the second principle, of authenticity, assigns you responsibility for it. But that is a different matter. I am asking about the first principle. Do you have a reason to care whether every person's life succeeds or fails, or just whether yours does? True, few people care as much about your situation as you do: your own fate may capture your attention as almost no one else's does. But that can be explained by the special responsibility I just mentioned. So you should focus further on the question whether the objective importance of your life reflects a universal importance—your life has that value only because it is a human life—or a special importance because you have some property that some other people do not have.

Subjective value is in its nature special. Coffee has value only for those who like coffee, and though this might conceivably be all the people alive at a given moment, that could be true only by accident. But objective importance is independent of taste or belief or desire, and it is therefore independent of any distinct emotional relationship, including one based on identity. Because there are no metaphysical value particles, objective value cannot be a bare fact: there must be some case to be made for it. What case could someone make that his importance is special?

Many people hold the opposite, universal view. Many religions teach that a god made human beings in his own image and has equal concern for them all. Secular humanitarians believe that human life is sacred and that the failure of any life is a waste of a cosmically valuable opportunity.[1] Most people react emotionally to the actual and even fictional tragedies of complete strangers on either a small or very grand scale. We weep for Adonis and we weep for the anonymous foreign victims of earthquakes and tsunamis. The universal view hangs together admirably with this set of familiar opinions and reactions.

What case could someone make for the opposite, special view: that only the lives of people like him have objective importance? He cannot rely on any form of global skepticism, because he accepts that his own life has objective and not merely subjective importance. He needs a positive case. It would not be enough, as I said, to point to his special responsibility for his life. Curators have distinct responsibilities for protecting particular paintings, but they accept that paintings in other museums have objective value as well.

One other claim has been all too popular in history, however, and remains sadly popular over much of the world still now. He might think that some property he has makes his life specially important from an objective perspective. He is an American or a Jew or a Sunni or a talented musician or brilliant collector of matchbook covers, and he might think that whichever of these properties he has gives objective importance to the life of any person who has it. I doubt that many readers of this book hold any such view—no religion with any genuine traction in the Western democracies would countenance it—but its more general popularity makes it important to notice it.

Of course there is much that does distinguish you from other people: your talents, nation, religion, and race. Some of these properties, at least, might be important to you in considering how you should live: you might take them to be parameters of success for you.[2] You might think that you do not live well unless your life reflects the fact that you are an American or a Catholic or talented at music or matchbook collecting. But we are considering a different claim: not whether personal properties should affect how you live, but whether they account for the objective importance of your living well.

Someone who thought his special properties made his life particularly important would find it difficult to integrate that view with other responsible opinions. Consider Richard Hare's Nazi who thinks it would be right for others to kill him if it was discovered, to his surprise, that he was actually a Jew.[3] It might be easy enough for him to integrate his opinion into a slightly larger scheme of value: he might insist, for instance, that Jews and other non-Aryan races are naturally inferior human beings. Or perhaps not human at all. But that further opinion would be unlikely to survive much further expansion toward overall integrity. It would be necessary to explain, for example, why Jews are inferior in spite of so many points of biological similarity, confirmed by DNA analysis, between them and Aryans, and any proposed explanation would be likely to make trouble somewhere else in his system of convictions. Are Jews inferior because their ancestors (on a bizarre but popular assumption) killed Christ? But that requires visiting sins of presumed but unidentifiable ancestors on very remote descendants, and Hare's Nazi might not think himself inferior because of the crimes of some Germanic tribe in the first century. Are Jews inhuman because of the role a few of them played in Weimar economics? Were there no troublemaking Aryan financiers? Is it a matter of a tendency to hook noses? Are these unknown in the Waffen SS? And how, exactly, could objective importance be thought to depend on nasal structure?

Now consider the potential role of religion in defending someone's claim to special objective importance. Much of the slaughter inspired by religion has presupposed, or at least not denied, the equal importance of the lives of

those slaughtered: their death has been thought necessary to save their im-
mortal souls or to spread the true faith and the true laws among their people
or simply to stop their real or imagined attempts at desecration. Much more
would be necessary to justify a faith's ethical claim to some special objective importance for its members' lives. It would be necessary, I imagine, to suppose the creative benediction of a biased god who cares nothing about the
conversion of infidels to his worship. Other stories are possible, no doubt, but
they are each likely to founder, at least for monotheistic religions, on further
embedded assumptions about the range and catholicity of that god's attention.
Monstrous ideas of that sort have been all too popular and all too powerful
in our history. But they are impossible to defend responsibly.

There is yet another hurdle for anyone to overcome who thinks his importance special. I said, in Chapter 9, that dignity requires recognition, not appraisal, respect. But there is an important relation between the two: they must
divide the territory of self-esteem between themselves, because thinking your
life important is a presupposition of thinking that it matters how you live.
Hare's Nazi fanatic would have to think that if he was discovered to be a Jew,
it would not then matter at all what he had done with or to his life. Few people
could honestly accept that counterfactual release of ethical responsibility.

Nietzsche?

Does the universal view of objective importance reflect only a parochial egalitarian, liberal, democratic political sensibility? It might be useful briefly to consider
whether the most famous philosophical critic of that sensibility rejected the
universal view. Nietzsche certainly thought that only a few people—he counted
himself among them—were capable of truly distinguished lives. But did he
think what is plainly different: that it is important only how those few creative
supermen live and unimportant what happens to the rest—the ordinary rabble
of the earth who are incapable of great lives anyway?

Interpretations of Nietzsche's ideas differ sharply. But according to several
critics Nietzsche accepted (at least in some parts of his not always consistent
work) the main themes of our argument so far. He seemed to insist on the
surpassing importance of people living well. It is a cosmic shame, he thought,
that the priests have imposed on the world the kind of morality that makes
living well impossible, the ascetic morality that fights rather than celebrates
human nature and tries to sublimate the will to power that is not only natural

but the spur and motive to great lives. We must recreate ourselves, he declared, because we have become, in part through this morality, people of slave mentality rather than heroic struggle.

He rejected the subjective view of the importance of living well.[4] We must recreate ourselves not only if we happen to want to be great but because we are not faithful to our human legacy unless we do strive to be great. He insisted that living well is very different from living a good life. Living well, he insisted, might include great suffering, as his life did, which hardly makes for a good life. He also insisted on the sovereign importance of integrity to living well. "The organizing 'idea' that is destined to rule . . . slowly . . . leads us *back* from side roads and wrong roads; it prepares *single* qualities and fitnesses that will one day prove to be indispensable as means toward a whole—one by one, it trains all *subservient* capacities before giving any hint of the dominant task, 'goal,' 'aim,' or 'meaning.' Considered in this way, my life is simply wonderful."[5]

But it is indeed a further question whether Nietzsche thought that these imperatives hold for all of us or only for those who are capable of greatness. His early spokesman, Zarathustra, speaks not only to the great but to everyone he finds, to all those who he hopes, however pessimistic he may be, will become the next man, not the last man.[6] The "gift" he brings is a gift for the species in general. "A tablet of the good," he declares, "hangs over every people."[7] Nietzsche expressed unmitigated disdain for equality, democracy, and the rest of what he called "servile" morality. But he rejected the morality he despised not because it assumes that it matters how everyone lives but because it offers what he thought a despicable account of how everyone should live.

He ridiculed the idea that living well means being happy. He had special contempt for the utilitarians, whose views make no sense except on the assumption that pleasure and happiness are alone important.[8] (He called that assumption "Anglo-angelic shopkeeperdom."[9]) To him pleasure and happiness were close to pointless. He also ridiculed Kantians, who recognize the intrinsic value of a human life but suppose that this value can be realized only through a life of moral duty.[10] So though he certainly thought morality as commonly understood a terrible mistake, I know of no reason to suppose that he thought it unimportant, rather than sad, how people in general live. He did think that the will to power makes everyone who has it, on appropriate occasions, angry, competitive, and anxious to show himself special in some way. These are, as he saw, human motives that most of us can subordinate or sublimate only with some difficulty and with, he thought, tragic costs.

But there is nothing in the will to power that holds that the same emotions are not just absent but illegitimate in the herd of people.

According to at least one commentator, Nietzsche embraced a form of aggregative consequentialism about good lives: he thought it important that the best lives be lived as greatly as possible, even if that meant less good lives for most people.[11] But that odd view does not presuppose the subjective view of a life's importance. It supposes, on the contrary, that there is an overall objective importance in great lives being lived that prescinds from any concern with which people live them. A connoisseur who wants the greatest painting painted, even if that means fewer paintings are, does not think it antecedently important which artist produces those great paintings. Another scholar reports that "in spite of the widespread opinion that Nietzsche opposes all universalization," "he does not object to seeing one's values as universally valuable, where one considers them essential to any human flourishing."[12] If so, Nietzsche's hatred of ordinary morality only underscores his assumption that it is important, even if impossible, that everyone live well.

Two Strategies: Balance and Integrity

The first principle of dignity, recast to make plain the objective value of any human life, becomes what I called Kant's principle. Your reason for thinking it objectively important how your life goes is also a reason you have for thinking it important how anyone's life goes: you see the objective importance of your life mirrored in the objective importance of everyone else's. Aristotle distinguished different kinds of love, including friendship, romantic love, and what he called *agape*, often translated as "altruistic" love, the love we show to everyone.[13] Agape is the most selfless form of love, but, we now see, it is also love that embraces oneself. Polonius was garrulous and silly, but his final advice to his son was profound and remains so when we invert it. Be not false to any man and you remain true to yourself.

Our question for the rest of the book is this. What are the implications of Kant's principle for how you must treat other people? It might strike you, initially, that fully accepting the equal objective importance of everyone's life means always acting so as to improve the situation of people everywhere, counting benefit to yourself and those close to you as each having only the same weight in your calculation as that of any stranger anywhere. This is certainly the conclusion that many philosophers, including but not limited to utilitarians, draw from that equal importance. If so, then it is close to impossible for human beings—as distinct from angels—actually to live as their self-respect requires. The second principle, of authenticity, assigns each of us a personal responsibility to act consistently with the character and projects he identifies for himself. It would seem psychologically impossible for almost anyone to satisfy that principle while nevertheless treating everyone's plans and projects with as much concern and attention as his own.[14] Most people in the world are very poor. Many of them lack even the essentials of life, so anyone of even modest wealth who accepted the first principle would, on this view of what it means, have to give everything away and become poor himself. Certainly he would have to abandon dedicating his life to any other projects, no matter how compelling he thought them.

A few philosophers have grasped this nettle: in principle we should try, as best we can, to live the saintly life demanded by the demanding interpretation.[15] Others have taken a different view that softens the impact (though not the demands) of the first principle out of concern for the second. Thomas Nagel distinguishes two perspectives from which a person might decide how to live.[16] The first is a personal perspective dominated by his own interests and projects. The second is the impersonal perspective from which his own interests, ambitions, attachments, and projects matter no more than those of anyone else. In Nagel's view, we find truth from both these perspectives and our difficulty arises because these truths are inconsistent. What seems to make most sense from the personal perspective will often contradict some requirement of the impersonal one. How should we then decide what is, all things considered, the right thing to do? How do we balance the two perspectives? Nagel suggests that a balance would be reasonable if it could be accepted as appropriate by everyone, no matter what his personal situation. He is doubtful that there is in fact a particular balance that satisfies that test. But he is clear that that is the test that must, as an ideal, be satisfied.[17]

However, once we call for a balance or compromise between two perspectives, each of which we take to speak truth, it becomes unclear how we could justify a particular settlement without circularity. Suppose we ask how much of his income it would be reasonable for a university professor to give away and how much it would be reasonable for him to retain for a summer holiday in Europe. It seems impossible to answer without first deciding which of Nagel's perspectives should govern: from the impersonal perspective, reasonableness looks very different than it does from the personal perspective of someone desperate for a holiday. There is no third perspective—no perspective of "reason" itself—from which the balance might be struck. We can't know what reason requires without first deciding from which perspective that question should be decided.

Nagel suggests, as I said, a procedural test. He seeks principles for balancing the impersonal and personal perspectives that everyone would find reasonable if he was motivated by the desire to settle on one standard. (Nagel cites and follows Thomas Scanlon's moral contractarianism.[18]) Nagel is rightly pessimistic that such principles can be found. Why should someone whose situation is worse than anyone else's not insist that, given the equal importance of human lives, the only reasonable principle is one that divides material wealth in equal shares? Why should someone else, whose situation is somewhat better, not reply that it is unreasonable to remove from the world all the pleasures and achievements that unequal wealth makes possible? No doubt it helps to assume, unrealistically, that everyone wants an agreement. But that is often true of labor negotiations that end in a prolonged strike ruinous for both sides.

Even if there were consensus on how people should act in some particular situation, however, it is unclear why that would be relevant. The consensus would, presumably, contradict the deliverance of either the personal or the impersonal perspective. More likely both. From which perspective should we then decide whether to do what everyone says is reasonable? Suppose everyone thinks it reasonable to do what the impersonal perspective condemns. How can that excuse doing what we think is, from that perspective, wrong? We would have to have already decided that the impersonal perspective is not sovereign about what to do. From what perspective could we have decided that? Nor does it help to say that the final decision must be a practical one. That declares that a decision must be made but is of no help in making it. "Practical" names no third, distinct, perspective. Nor can the right balance be found by asking what we do or should most care about, all things considered. That is just a way—or perhaps two ways—of restating our question.

Our two principles of dignity, on the other hand, do not describe different perspectives that a person might take up that he must then choose between. They describe a single perspective he must occupy if he is ethically responsible. We must not ask for a compromise between these two principles: they are too fundamental and important to compromise. They state conditions necessary to our self-respect and authenticity, and these are not negotiable. So our agenda must be different. We need to find attractive interpretations of the two principles that seem right in themselves—that seem to capture what self-respect and authenticity really do require—and that do not conflict with, but rather reinforce, each other. We need to treat our principles as simultaneous equations to be solved together.

Someone might object: it is fraudulent to set out, right from the beginning, to find interpretations of our principles that avoid conflict. We should rather seek the correct interpretations, and if these produce conflict, we must simply accept this as our fate. That objection ignores the argument of this book so far. Ethical judgments are not barely true. We do seek the correct understanding of our two principles, but that means, for us, an understanding of each that finds support in our understanding of the others and that feels right to us. We have to believe each part of a mutually supportive system of principles in order to suppose that together they are sound.

Our assignment is difficult and we are not promised success. It is easy enough to identify plain violations of one or the other principle. Treating someone else's suffering or failure with indifference denies the importance of his life; forcing him to practice the rituals of a religion he rejects outrages his ethical responsibility. The issues we confront in the next several chapters are more difficult and controversial, however. We shall have to consider when a failure to help a stranger does show indifference to his life, whether and how the numbers of those we affect count in determining what we should do, what pertinent differences fall between killing someone and letting him die, why we must keep our promises, and whether we owe more by way of aid to members of our own political communities than to those of other communities. So we must push our analysis further to generate more concrete interpretations of our principles, interpretations that we can test in other contexts.

We have no crisp decision procedure to follow. Each of us will finally judge differently from others the issues we consider. But we have a standard each can use to adjudicate. Do the interpretations of self-respect and authenticity we reach support one another and so require no compromise in either dimension of dignity? Can we accept these interpretations in good faith as each sound? Our challenge is in some ways like that posed by John Rawls's method of reflective equilibrium, but it is more ambitious and more hazardous. Rawls aimed at a kind of integrity among abstract and concrete convictions about justice, but one that allowed subordination, compromise, and balancing among different values. He insisted on a "lexical priority" of liberty to equality, for example. He did not aim to interpret each value in the light of others so that each supported rather than challenged the others. That difference reflects a deeper one. Our strategy is driven by a theory of moral and interpretive truth—the theory described in Chapters 7 and 8—a topic that Rawls did not pursue. Even if we interpret Rawls's methods to include an ethical component, as I suggest later in this chapter we should, the range of the values he meant to pose in equilibrium is much smaller than those in our field of concern. He thought it wise, particularly as his views developed, to bracket philosophical issues beyond those that can be seen as distinctly political. Our integration project has a centrifugal force that does not allow bracketing: we must attempt as wide a comprehensive theory as we are able to construct, not out of a taste for complexity but out of a philosophical necessity. We need to integrate theories of truth, language, and metaphysics with and into the more familiar realms of value. If you continue to join in that ambition, we are still both out on a limb. You may think we have fallen already; if not we must see whether we fall now.

More Moral Philosophers

Kant

I pause, before we begin on our list of topics, to pick up a different thread. It is an ancillary project of the book to see how far the interpretive approach to morality helps us understand the important classics of moral philosophy. In Chapter 8 I described the explicitly interpretive arguments of Plato and Aristotle; I said that each aimed at the integration of ethics and morality that is our goal as well. I end this chapter by considering how far the work of other philosophers, although less explicitly interpretive in the same way, might be recast with profit in that mode.

The most influential philosophical theories owe their influence—even among professional philosophers, but certainly any wider influence—not to the power or cogency of their arguments but to the imaginative impact of their conclusions and the metaphors in which these are presented. That is true, I believe, of Plato's cave and Rawls's original position, for example. It is most dramatically true of Kant. The very general principles he declared—that we must never act in ways we could not rationally wish that everyone act, for instance—have had enormous influence even among academic philosophers who reject many of his more concrete opinions. His powerful warning that we must treat other people as ends and never merely as means is daily repeated in legal and moral argument across a great part of the world.

But the arguments he supplied for these very influential principles are comparatively weak, in my own view, and the theories of freedom and reason he offered are opaque to almost all of those who are drawn to those principles.

However, Kant's writings on moral philosophy contain all the ingredients of what I believe to be a more accessible interpretive argument for those principles. It is not my aim (nor is it within my power) to add to the formidable volume of Kant exegesis. I want rather to suggest a way of reading Kant (whatever else it ignores in his writing) that tracks the methods I propose to follow here. That reading begins in ethics: with ethical demands that match the two principles of dignity we have now recognized. Kant's "principle of humanity" is in the first instance about the mode in which we must value ourselves and our own goals: we must see these as objectively, not just subjectively, important. We must think, as our first principle insists, that it is objectively important how our lives go.

We draw the appropriate conclusion in what I called Kant's principle: if the value you find in your life is to be truly objective, it must be the value of humanity itself. You must find the same objective value in the lives of all other persons. You must treat yourself as an end in yourself, and therefore, out of self-respect, you must treat all other people as ends in themselves as well. Self-respect also requires that you treat yourself as autonomous in one sense of that idea: you must yourself endorse the values that structure your life. That demand matches our second principle: you must judge the right way to live for yourself and resist any coercion designed to usurp that authority.

These two demands of dignity pose the interpretive challenge I have described. There could be no option, for Kant any more than for us, of resolving this stark conflict by balancing or compromising the two demands. Any compromise would necessarily be, for Kant as for us, a sacrifice of our dignity. His response was therefore to offer better interpretations of the two demands. He understood autonomy to mean not freedom to pursue whatever inclinations we might have but freedom that includes freedom *from* those inclinations. We are autonomous when we act out of respect for the moral law rather than to serve some particular goal: our own pleasure, for example, or what we take to be a good life, or some more transcendent value, or even to relieve the suffering of others.

That interpretation explains why autonomy has the commanding importance he assigned it. We would not respect our lives as having intrinsic and objective value if we dedicated our lives to achieving some one or another of these particular goods. We would be treating our lives as having value only as means to those ends. We must rather treat our freedom as an end in itself rather than a means to something else, and we do that by supposing that we are free when we act out of the moral law, not when we ignore it. That does not mean simply acting consistently with what the moral law demands. "For if any action is to be morally good, it is not enough that it should conform to the moral law—it must also be done for the sake of the moral law."[19]

That view of autonomy matches our account of moral responsibility in Chapter 6. When we take up the project described there, we aim that our moral convictions provide our actual motives, filtering out those influences of our personal history that press for contrary behavior. But Kant's reconciliation of autonomy with respect for others requires something more substantive: some statement of the content of what autonomy so understood requires. How do I treat others along with myself as ends in themselves? Kant does not answer that I must act impartially in all matters. He offers a different and much less demanding kind of universalism: we must act in such a way that we can will the principle of our action to be universally embraced and followed. A person respects his own intrinsic ethical value through such principles because, as Kant puts it, "it is precisely the fitness of his maxims to make universal law that marks him out as an end in himself."[20]

Kantian scholars puzzle and disagree about what that somewhat opaque formula, about willing a law to be universal, actually means, as they puzzle and disagree about much else in his theories.[21] But the general thrust is clear enough: treating people with the respect we accord ourselves requires, at a minimum, that we claim no right in ourselves that we do not grant others and suppose no duty for them we do not accept for ourselves. In the language of American constitutional lawyers, respect for all requires equal protection of the moral law. That constraint does not, in itself or by likely implication, require each of us always to act as if his own life was of no more concern to him than that of anyone else. Kant offers his theory as an interpretation of ordinary moral practice, and his various examples of what laws we cannot coherently will to be universal are designed to produce moral requirements that are familiar.[22]

This reconstruction of Kant's argument bends it toward the argument of this book—perhaps past the breaking point, though I hope not. I mean to show that Kant's claims are most persuasive when understood as an interpretive account linking ethics and morality. Each element in this structure of moral and ethical ideas contributes to the case for the other elements. Whether we start in the moral law or in the ethics of self-respect, we generate the same structure. Certainly Kant did not suppose that acting for the sake of the moral law necessarily or even usually produces a good life. But he did think it would mean living well, with full self-respect and autonomy. The Kantian system so understood is an impressive piece of active holism.

I concede that I have entirely ignored much argument that many Kantian scholars think most distinctive and important: his metaphysics and the theory of reason articulated in his critiques. He supposed himself to have shown, in the first two sections of his *Groundwork,* that autonomy is possible only if we are capable of acting out of the moral law whose form he described. In the third section he undertook to defend that possibility against the threat of determinism. In the phenomenal world we occupy, the world of science, autonomy seems impossible, because in that world our actions are determined by prior events beyond our control. But we inhabit another world as well—the world as it is in itself, not as it appears to us. We cannot in the nature of the case discover the nature of that noumenal world, but we can and must assume that in that world we do have the freedom that makes autonomy and morality possible. Kant held, that is, that responsibility and determinism are incompatible. I argued in the last chapter that his view is mistaken. If he had accepted a compatibilist position, he would have thought judgmental responsibility a phenomenon entirely explicable within what he called the phenomenal world.

Rawls

In Chapter 3, discussing the constructivist approach to moral theory, I said that Rawls's theory is not best understood as skeptical of objective moral truth in any but a limited internal sense. He meant to rely only on principles inherent in the political traditions of the community he addressed, but he needed substantive moral assumptions to decide what those traditions should be taken to be. Now we may consider his theory again, on that assumption. I quoted his important remark that "first principles of justice must issue from a conception of the person through a suitable representation of that conception as illustrated by the procedure of construction in justice as fairness."[23] That representation must suppose that people are "autonomous in two respects: first, in their deliberations they are not required to apply, or to be guided by, any prior and antecedent principles of right and justice . . . Second, they are said to be moved solely by the highest-order interests in their moral powers and by their concern to advance their determinate but unknown final ends."[24] He described these "moral powers" as, first, "the capacity for an effective sense of justice" and, second, "the capacity to form, revise and rationally to pursue a conception of the good."[25] This set of assumptions about people's attitudes and interests, Rawls thought, justifies the structural features of his original position strategy.

But it cannot do this unless we interpret this "conception of the person" in a very special way. If we read Rawls's account in what might seem the most natural way, nothing in it helps to justify the veil of ignorance. His people are assumed to have the capacity for a sense of justice. They are assumed to want to advance their "final ends" and to have the further capacity rationally to consider what those ends should be. They know that each of the others also has these capacities to a "minimum" degree. But nothing explains why they should not have exercised these two capacities before instructing their representatives at the convention. Each representative could then negotiate to secure what his principal believes a more just society, having due regard to his own view of the right final ends for him and, perhaps, everyone. This conception of the person seems, so far, to contribute nothing to the explanation of why the original position has the design Rawls gave it.

We might, however, interpret Rawls's account in a different way: we might read much more into the stipulation that his people are "autonomous." We might assume, for instance, that this means that they treat their lives as having objective importance, that they therefore think that every other human being has a life of the same objective importance, and that they therefore believe that they insult their own dignity when they urge political arrangements that neglect the importance of anyone's life. Suppose we assume, also, that autonomous people not only want to pursue what they take to be a good life for themselves but also, and more fundamentally, want to live well, and that they think, moreover, that living well means living in a way that does not insult their own dignity in that way. If we elaborate Rawls's conception of the person in that fashion, then the conception does figure as a supporting element for the original position device and its veil of ignorance. It can then be seen as serving the participants' shared interest in living well, on the ethical assumptions just described, because it allows them to concentrate on the crucial question of which institutions would respect their dignity—by defining, for instance, a share of community resources that respects the equal importance of everyone's life.

This interpretation puts Rawls's disclaimer, that the parties in the original position do not rely on any antecedent theory of justice, in a more nuanced way.[26] They accept, and bring to the original position, the political consequence of the theory of autonomy just described. They assume that the basic structure of government they choose must show equal concern and respect for all the political community's members. In that very abstract sense they do assume an egalitarian account of justice. But they do not assume any more concrete interpretation of that egalitarian standard: that is for their representatives to construct behind the veil of ignorance. We shall see, in Part Five, that there are many candidate interpretations of that abstract principle: these range from a utilitarian to a libertarian interpretation. So we understand Rawls's disclaimers as denying that his participants assume any particular interpretation, such as, for instance, what I call equality of resources in Chapter 16.

The suggested understanding of the original position makes use of our distinctions and, once again, it bends Rawls's theories toward our own. But again, I hope, not past the breaking point. However, interpreting Rawls's "conception of the person" in this way might change certain of the conclusions he reaches. It might not vindicate his "difference" principle that allows inequalities in wealth only so far as these benefit the worst-off group in the community; our two principles require the rather different conception of economic equality I describe in Chapter 16. I must also concede that this interpretation does not respect the distinction Rawls emphasized in his later work between a strictly political theory, drawn from what he called "public reason," and a more comprehensive ethical and moral theory. I have relied, throughout this book and in this reading of Rawls's argument, on comprehensive ethical and philosophical claims about the objective importance of human life and the nature and limits of various forms of ethical as well as moral responsibility. I have argued elsewhere that Rawls's "public reason" constraints are unwise and would bar his own most influential arguments from official political discourse.[27] If I am right, that fact offers another reason for interpreting his main argument in this more comprehensive way.

Scanlon

In his book *What We Owe to Each Other,* Thomas Scanlon argues that we should treat other people in ways required by principles that no one could reasonably reject.[28] He imposes no veil of ignorance on people who are called upon to judge which principles these are: they must decide themselves what aspects of their situation and which of their preferences and convictions are pertinent to that judgment. Nor does he suppose that people would all reach the same judgment. He indicates a range of judgment that reasonableness would require of people without supposing that everyone would make all the judgments within that range in the same way. His exercise is nevertheless sufficiently ex ante to show the reciprocal impact of ethical and moral ideas. He thinks that living well includes having or developing a certain attitude toward other people, and that one of the manifestations of that attitude is a desire to be able to justify one's conduct to them in the way he describes. He supposes that living well requires certain attitudes, which is not yet a moral claim, and that these attitudes essentially define which moral principles we should accept.

The idea of reasonableness plays a crucial role in Scanlon's overall argument. Some commentators have complained that because reasonableness is itself a moral ideal of just the kind his theory is meant to explain, the theory is circular for that reason.[29] But that objection is seriously misplaced, because it overlooks the interpretive complexity of Scanlon's argument. True, the concept of reasonableness is often used to make moral claims: "Under the circumstances," we might say, "it was reasonable of him to lie." But reasonableness is also an ethical standard: we think that someone who devotes a substantial part of his life to collecting matchbook covers is not just wrong but silly: his choice is not ethically reasonable. In fact the concept plays just the bridge role, between dignity and morality, that we are now exploring. It is unreasonable of you to favor your own interests in circumstances when the benefit to you is relatively trivial and the cost to others very large. That is unreasonable because it is inconsistent with recognizing the objective as well as subjective importance of your own life. It is not unreasonable to favor yourself, however, when that means only that you have weighed the impact of some decision on your own life more heavily than its impact on someone else's life: that does not imply any failure to accept that his life is objectively just as important as yours.

12

Aid

A Calculus of Concern

Dignity and Wrongdoing

What must we do for strangers—people with whom we have no particular connection, people who may live at the other end of the earth? We have no special relationship with them, but their lives are of equal objective importance to our own. Of course, special relationships are numberless and embracing. Politics, in particular, is a fertile source of them: we have distinct obligations of aid to those who are joined with us under a single collective government. But I ignore these special relationships in this chapter; they are the subject of Chapter 14. I discuss here, moreover, only what we must do for strangers, not what we must not do to them. In the next chapter I argue that we have much stricter responsibilities not to harm strangers than we have to help them.

I have already described the strategy of these chapters. We try to decide what we must do for—and not do to—other people by asking what behavior would fail to respect the equal importance of their lives. That might strike you as topsy-turvy: acts deny someone's equal importance only when they are wrongful, you might think, so we must first decide what acts are wrong, not the other way around. Under our interpretive strategy, however, as I said earlier, neither of these two directions of argument has final priority over the other. We need convictions about the two principles of dignity and about right and wrong behavior that all seem correct after reflection and that fit together so that the inferences hold in both directions. I stress one of these directions here, from dignity to morality, because our ambition is now to locate morality in ethics and that means beginning in the conception of dignity I sketched in Chapter 9.

Dignity and Welfare

Wealth and luck are very unevenly distributed among human beings, so we often find ourselves in a position to help strangers who are in worse case than us either generally or because they have suffered some accident or are in some special danger. Two kinds of conflict may arise on such occasions. First, we may face a conflict between our own interests and those of the people we might help. How far need we go out of our way to help them? Second, we may face a conflict about whom to help when we can only help some of them. If we can rescue only some victims of an accident and must leave others to die, how shall we decide whom to save? Together these puzzles pose the question of aid.

Kant's answer to that question—he said in different ways that we should treat strangers as we would wish them to treat us—is helpful because that formula fuses ethics and morality in the way we now seek: it takes an ex ante approach that integrates our hopes for our own lives with our sense of our responsibilities to others. We must find an allocation of the costs of bad luck that seems right from both an ethical and a moral point of view. If we think we have no moral duty to help others bear their bad luck, it must also seem right, as a matter of ethical responsibility, that we ourselves should bear the costs of our own bad luck in similar circumstances. But though Kant's formulations tie the underlying issues together in that helpful way, they do not help us decide them.

I restate the simultaneous-equation problem described in the last chapter. We must show full respect for the equal objective importance of every person's life, but also full respect for our own responsibility to make something valuable of our own life. We must interpret the first demand so as to leave room for the second, and the other way around. You would find that impossible, I said, if you were once persuaded of the ultra-demanding interpretation of the first principle I mentioned—that it requires you to act with the same concern for the well-being of any stranger, day by day, as you do for your own well-being. You would then be unlikely to find any plausible interpretation of the second principle that did not conflict with the first.

Fortunately the ultra-demanding interpretation is a poor reading of the first principle. We should notice, first, that this reading makes no sense as I just described it, because we have no metric of well-being that could sensibly supply the comparisons it requires. Someone's well-being is not a commodity that can be measured. It is a matter of having a good life, and we have no appropriate way to measure or compare the goodness or success of different lives. "Well-being" consequentialists, as they might be called, have tried to invent conceptions of well-being that do make it a commodity of some kind. Some say that a person's well-being at any moment is the surplus of the pleasure he enjoys over the pain he suffers, and that we can therefore calculate a person's overall well-being by measuring the total glows of his pleasure and then subtracting the total stabs of his pain. Others say that someone's well-being is a matter of how many of his ambitions are realized, so that we measure total well-being by counting up ticks of desire satisfaction and subtracting ticks of desire frustration. Still others claim that well-being can be defined in terms of people's capabilities for achieving what they do or might want to achieve. For reasons I have described elsewhere, none of these familiar philosophical conceptions of well-being can provide a plausible basis for a personal or political morality.[1]

The concepts of welfare, well-being, and a good life are interpretive concepts. People disagree about the right conception of what makes a life good—about how important it is to enjoy oneself or to satisfy desires or to develop capabilities, for instance. So a policy of making any of these particular commodities "equal" would shortchange many people and so destroy any initial appeal that an abstract statement of welfare consequentialism might enjoy. Of course, each of us can try to make it easier for other people to live well according to their own lights. We can work, for example, toward a more equal distribution of wealth and other resources. To some extent—particularly in the circumstances discussed in Part Five—we do have that responsibility. But that is not the same as trying to make their lives better lives to have lived. Well-being egalitarianism is not just impossibly demanding; it is a philosophical mistake.

Kant's principle changes the subject: it speaks not to well-being as a goal but to attitude as a guide. We must treat other people consistently with accepting that their lives are of equal objective importance to our own.[2] Failing to help someone else is not necessarily inconsistent with that attitude. That is true of other kinds of value as well. I might recognize the enormous objective value of a great collection of paintings and yet accept no personal responsibility for helping to protect that collection. I might have other priorities. So I may recognize the objective importance of the lives of strangers without supposing that I must subordinate my life and interests to some collective or aggregate interest of them all, or even to any single one of them whose needs are greater than my own. I can accept with perfect sincerity that your children's lives are no less important objectively than the lives of my own and yet dedicate my life to helping my children while I ignore yours. They are, after all, my children.

I do not deny the equal importance of human life just by refusing to make admirable sacrifices. Perhaps I can save many people from a catastrophe by embracing or risking the catastrophe myself. The soldiers who volunteered to be bitten by mosquitoes carrying yellow fever are rightly treated as heroes. But I would not imply that I regarded the lives of others as intrinsically less important than my own if I refused to volunteer. I have won an Aegean cruise in a lottery; I look forward to it but then learn from a mutual friend that a classical scholar whom I don't know has longed for such a cruise for years but is unable to afford it. It would be an act of generosity for me to let the scholar take the cruise. But I don't imply that his life is objectively less important than mine if I take the cruise myself.

However, there is a limit to how far I can consistently ignore something that I claim has objective value. I cannot be indifferent to its fate. If I am in a gallery that is bursting into flames and I can easily take an important painting with me as I leave, I cannot leave it to burn and expect people to take seriously my tributes to the painting's surpassing value. In some circumstances—philosophers call these "rescue" cases—failing to help a stranger would show the same indifference toward the importance of human lives. You are on a beach, and not far off shore an elderly lady, Hecuba, cries out that she is drowning. You are nothing to her and she nothing to you. But you can easily save her, and if you do not you cannot claim to respect human life as objectively important. How shall we draw the line? The test is interpretive. Which acts, in which circumstances, show a failure to respect the objective and equal importance of human life? This is not a matter of what someone, even sincerely, happens to believe. He shows disdain for human life by turning away from a drowning victim, even if he disagrees that he does. We need an objective test, even though an objective test cannot be mechanical because it must pose questions of interpretation that different interpreters will answer somewhat differently. Our test must aim to structure this interpretation by pointing to the factors that must count and in what way, but it cannot be sufficiently detailed to render verdicts in advance in difficult or marginal cases. Any plausible test will make room for three factors: the harm threatened to a victim, the cost a rescuer would incur, and the degree of confrontation between victim and potential rescuer. These factors interact—a very high or low score on any of them will lower or raise the threshold of impact of the others. But it will be easiest to discuss them separately.

Metric of Harm

It is obviously pertinent what kind and level of threat or need a stranger faces. How shall we measure this? We have already rejected a strict comparative measure: you have no duty to help someone just because his situation is in some way worse than your own. You can acknowledge the objective importance of a stranger's life without supposing that you must not have more money or opportunity than he does. The comparative standard is indeed of the essence of certain special obligations. I argue in Chapter 14 that it is at the heart of certain political obligations: in your political capacity as voter or official, you must do your part to ensure that your state shows equal concern for the fate of all under its dominion. That political obligation may in some way extend beyond national boundaries. But you do not, just acting as an individual, have any such obligation to all human beings just out of respect for their humanity.

So we need to measure the character of the threat or need the victim faces independently of whether his situation is overall worse than the potential rescuer's. But should we use a subjective test? Should we judge the degree of harm or loss as the victim judges it? Thomas Scanlon offers this case: a stranger asks our help in the enormously expensive project of building a temple to his god, a project he deems more important than life itself.[3] It seems clear, as Scanlon says, that we have no duty to help. We have no such duty even if he is right to treat his project as so important; indeed, even if his life will be ruined in his eyes if he cannot achieve it. That follows from the allocation of responsibility imposed by the two principles of dignity. It falls to each of us to design his life with an eye to the resources that he can expect will be at his disposal, at least if he is treated fairly. We cannot expect others to subsidize the expensive choices we make.[4]

Scanlon's reminder is necessary for those who believe that morality begins in a categorical requirement to treat everyone's interests as equally important in whatever we do. For it seems natural from that beginning to allow people themselves to judge when their position has been improved by what we do; we could reject the victim's judgment only by supposing that we know better than he where his overall interests lie. But once we reject that categorical requirement and base our morality instead on an interpretive judgment about what shows disrespect for human dignity, the calculations in play are very different. We must measure a victim's danger or need objectively by asking, not how bad he believes it to be, given his plans and ambitions, but how far it deprives him of the ordinary opportunities people have to pursue whatever ambitions they choose. That measure is more appropriate to identifying cases in which the threat or need is so great that a failure to respond displays an improper lack of concern for the importance of another human life.[5]

Metric of Cost

Whatever the character and magnitude of the harm threatening a stranger, my responsibility to prevent that harm is greater when I can do so with less risk to or interference with my own life. Again, the interpretive character of our test makes that point clear. When I can prevent a serious harm with relatively little risk or inconvenience to myself, failing to do so is less easily defended as consistent with an objective respect for human life. When the risk or inconvenience is greater, it is more plausible to plead the importance of my personal responsibility for my own life. When lawyers are asked to offer examples of the difference between law and morality, they are very likely to say, out of ancient law school tradition, that we have no legal duty to shove a child's face out of a puddle in which it is drowning as we stroll by. The example is powerful because the moral duty the law refuses to enforce is so uncontroversial. The threat to the child is at one extreme of harm, and the effort required of us at the other extreme of cost.

But now the hard question. Shall we measure the cost of rescue by taking a potential rescuer's own sincere assessment at face value, or should we strive for a more objective measure? Reverse Scanlon's story: suppose you can help save someone from starvation, but only by diverting funds from your life-long, arduous, and expensive attempt to build a temple to your god. Could you claim to respect human life if you refuse to help? That is a fanciful example, but it is easy to find real ones. Need you give any money to starving people in Africa when you need every cent for your own expensive research? Or to buy a more expensive lens for your camera in search of greater photographic fulfillment?

It may seem, at first, that it must be your own assessment of the cost that counts. The question is still interpretive—it asks when your refusal to help signals a lack of respect for the objective importance of human life—and that depends on what the cost of that help would mean to you, not what it might mean to someone with different ambitions. But there is another dimension to the question: does your total dedication to the temple or research or your hobby itself reflect the proper respect for the importance of other people's lives?[6] In Chapter 9 I conceded that someone might have a good life in spite of his callous indifference to the suffering of others: I imagined a murderous Renaissance prince whose life was nevertheless a good one. It is a different question whether someone who chooses such a life through those means has shown the self-respect his dignity demands.

I do not suggest what I earlier denied: that self-respect requires each person to view his own life as entirely at the service of others. Some saintly people have done that, and perhaps authenticity would have permitted nothing else for them. Lives lacking a normal attention to the needs of others may also be consistent with self-respect: the life of a dedicated artist or scientist, for instance. In those lives a sense of the objective importance of other people's fate may be visible even though it does not command rescue in all circumstances in which a less single-minded life would. But anyone who embraces projects that require him to ignore the suffering of others altogether is either irredeemably selfish or fanatical. In either case he lacks self-respect: his sense of an appropriate life is inconsistent with the right regard for the objective importance of the lives of others and therefore of his own. Yes, there is an asymmetry between how we judge the needs of a victim and the cost of rescue to the rescuer. We must take into account not what everyone would regard as an important cost to a rescuer but what is important to him given his sense of what his living well requires for him. But the asymmetry is limited by the condition dignity imposes on that ethical judgment.

Confrontation

The third scale is more difficult to state and justify, but it is real and we cannot make sense of much common moral opinion unless we find place for it.[7] This is the scale of confrontation. It has itself two dimensions. The first is particularization: the clearer it is who will be harmed without my intervention, the stronger the case that I have a duty to intervene. The second is proximity: the more directly I am confronted with some danger or need, the stronger the case that I have a duty to help. I am on the beach too far from the drowning Hecuba to help. There is a man with a boat on the shore who will row me out, but only for fifty dollars, which I can easily afford. Cursing, I promise it to him, as I plainly have a duty to do. He tells me, once the rescue is complete, that he is on the beach every day and will undertake to rescue the next swimmer in trouble by himself, if no other rescuer is there, if I will pay him another fifty dollars in advance. I believe I have no duty to do that or to make any other provision for rescue when I myself am not there. Why not?

From an impersonal moral perspective of the kind I described earlier, it would be hard to justify a duty to pay the boatman to rescue Hecuba but not a duty to pay him to rescue the next person in danger of drowning. I would owe no less to the anonymous person who will otherwise drown next week than I owe to Hecuba today. We might try to distinguish the two cases by appealing to the role of salience. It would be too demanding to expect any person to respond to even grave danger wherever and whenever it arises. A general understanding that only people in the immediate area of present danger have an actual duty both eliminates that risk and puts the duty on the person who is in most cases best able to help.[8] But that explanation, even if generally satisfactory, is not available here, because salience is guaranteed by the details of the selfish boatman's carefully limited offer. He has made the offer to no one else, and if he does make the offer to another visitor to the beach, well in advance of the rescue he promises, that visitor will be in no more salient position than I am now.

Once we reject any general moral duty to show the same concern for all strangers as for ourselves, however, and we ask instead the interpretive question whether refusing aid would deny the objective importance of human life, we can explain the distinction between the cases by citing the confrontation scale of assessment. If a tragic death of a particular, identifiable person is staring us in the face, or unfolding at our feet, we cannot walk away unless we actually are indifferent to life's importance. Ignoring the impending death of a particular person dying before us would require a callousness that mocks any pretended respect for humanity. My point is not that our duties are generated directly by visceral impact. It is rather that the morality of rescue hinges on an interpretive question, and that we must take natural human instincts and behavior into account in answering that question. We aim to make best sense of behavior, and we therefore cannot ignore the responses that a genuine respect for life normally provokes.[9]

The confrontation scale is also at work in a different kind of example, one that has puzzled economists. Any political community must judge, on some cost-accounting basis, how much to spend to prevent accidents of different kinds, whether through public or private spending. No community spends until no more spending would marginally improve safety: that would be deeply irrational. Yet when an accident does occur—a cave-in traps miners below ground, or an equipment failure traps astronauts in space—and particular identified people are at risk of death, we expect a community to spend much more than it would have cost to prevent accidents of that kind. Again, the dimension of confrontation explains the difference. We cannot ignore the threatened deaths of particular people in the way we can discount even highly probable deaths so long as the people who will die remain statistical and anonymous. Even in collective decisions of that kind, however, the confrontation metric does not always outweigh the other two dimensions—of harm and cost. It does not seem wrong for a community to devote so much of its total health care budget to disease prevention that it cannot afford expensive end-of-life care that prolongs life for only a short time.[10]

Great suffering may seem to make confrontation irrelevant. The starvation and disease of a massive number of peoples in Africa and elsewhere stands very high on the needs scale: even a moderate amount of foreign aid judicially used could save a great many of their lives. Their plea also stands very low on the cost scale: very large sums could be raised in aid if the peoples of rich nations each gave an amount small enough as to make no difference at all to the success of their lives.[11] Those who suffer are very far away, we have no idea who they are, and we have even less idea which of them will die, or why, if we do not contribute to general relief funds. But these facts seem in no way to diminish our obligation to help. If the case for a duty of aid scores high and low enough on the first two scales, of need and cost, that duty cannot be defeated by a low score on the third, confrontation, scale alone.

But even in such cases, I believe, confrontation plays various roles. Though we each have a duty to contribute to charities that try to rescue anonymous people immiserated far away, I do not believe we have a duty to contribute anywhere near as much, in either money or time, for each of them as we must spend, just out of respect for humanity, for a stranger who has fallen at our feet. The greater the publicity given to suffering far away, moreover, the greater is the duty to respond and the shame in not responding. The devastation of the 2004 tsunami in the Indian Ocean and the 2010 earthquake in Haiti was dramatically reported: the huge response of contributions from the first world shows what a difference the impact of immediacy produces. Should it? Lack of television publicity does not excuse us from trying to help relieve suffering we know is there. But the impulse is right that leads us to give more to help those whose suffering is thrust upon us. Consider two charities. One collects aid for distribution to starving people in very poor countries now. The other promises to accumulate its capital to help many more people a century from now. Suppose you do not doubt that the second charity's capital will grow as its managers promise. I believe you should nevertheless contribute to the first charity now.

Do Numbers Count?

We turn to the second situation I distinguished. Several people need aid, and it would plainly be wrong to ignore them all. But though you are in a position to help some of them, you then cannot help the others. How should you choose among them? There is a standard case—a variation on the drowning swimmer case. One person clings to a life preserver in a storm that has wrecked her boat; sharks circle her. Two other passengers cling to another life preserver a hundred yards away; sharks circle them as well. You have a boat on shore. You can reach one life preserver in time, but then not the other. Assuming all three are strangers, do you have a duty to save the two swimmers and let the lone swimmer die?

That is a staggeringly artificial hypothetical case, designed to focus attention on a philosophical issue without the distraction of reality. But we are surrounded by very real issues that pose the same puzzle. I just described one of them: there are continents of people living in poverty and disease. We can no longer ignore their misery without shame, but most of us can help only a small number of them. Suppose there are several charities we can give to; these operate in different African countries. Must we give to the charity that we judge will save the most people?

It is widely thought that in such situations, if we have a duty to aid at all, we have a duty to aid the most people possible, at least if the harm that threatens them all is comparable. So we have a duty to save two swimmers from the sharks rather than one and to contribute to the charity that we believe will save the most lives with the money we contribute. If we had accepted the impersonal perspective I rejected, which assumes a welfare consequentialist imperative, that would seem the right solution. Well-being is overall improved, we might well think, when two lives rather than one are saved.

But if we approach the decision in another way—by concentrating not on consequences but on rights—it is far from plain that we should automatically save the greater number. We might think that each victim has an equal antecedent right to be saved, and we might therefore be tempted by a lottery in which each shipwreck victim has at least a one-third chance to be saved.[12] (The sharks agree to circle while the lottery is conducted.)

Which approach is the right one? In which of these two ways should numbers count—as part of a consequential analysis or in giving effect to an assumed right to equal treatment? Philosophers have argued strenuously over this issue. But on the interpretive approach we are now exploring, neither of these approaches is the right one. We have rejected the consequentialist imperative and cannot revive it to justify our conviction, if we have it, that we do better to save a greater over a lesser number of people. We have also rejected any basis for supposing that everyone we can aid has an automatic right to that aid. He has a right only if, under the circumstances, ignoring his need would show disrespect for the objective importance of his life. If you reluctantly allow the lone swimmer to die because you can save two other human beings from death, you have not ignored the importance of anyone's life.

Suppose you make the opposite choice: to save the lone swimmer and let the others die. If you have a good reason for the choice—the lone swimmer is your wife—then you do not imply or assume that the lives of the two you abandon are objectively less important than hers.[13] On our interpretive test, that reason need be nothing beyond the fact of your love or your special responsibility. You will also need no further reason if the lone swimmer is not your wife but your friend. Or even if all the swimmers are perfect strangers, the lone swimmer is much younger than the two swimmers, and you think that saving the life of a young person is more important. Or if the swimmers are all strangers, but you know that the lone swimmer is a brilliant musician or philosopher or peacemaker and music or philosophy or peace is particularly important to you or you deem it particularly important to the world.

You do not deny the equal importance of all lives when you make such a choice: you know that some must die, and you make judgments of fairness or value to others to decide which. Remember, you would have no duty to rescue the two swimmers even if there were no third swimmer elsewhere but the risk of the rescue to you would be very great. You may put your own safety first without denying the equal objective importance of the two lives you might have saved. Why should you not then be permitted to put the safety of someone else first, whose life you deem to have particular instrumental value either to yourself or to others?

Now a different danger looms. Are there no limits to the proper grounds of a preference you might show among people whose lives are in danger? Suppose you know nothing about the three swimmers but that one of the two who are together is black and the other Jewish while the one who is alone is white and Christian. Would it be consistent with your accepting the equal objective importance of all human lives for you to save the white Christian swimmer and let the others die just because they are a black and a Jew? No, because there are certain grounds of preference that respect for humanity rules out: it rules out preferences that we have good reason to think are expressions or the residue of the contrary conviction that some lives are more important than others.

Once again we can justify our intuitive reaction as an interpretive assumption. In a world in which prejudice thrives, or in which social structures can best be explained by historical prejudice, attitudes and acts that track that prejudice are best understood as reflecting the prejudice absent some strong contrary indication. You can offer a reason why it is particularly important that a musician or a peacemaker survives without supposing that it is objectively more important that their lives flourish than anyone else's. You can supply a different kind of reason—a reason of fairness—why you should prefer saving the life of a young man rather than of two much older ones. They have already lived substantial lives and he has not. But you can point to nothing about the race or religion of perfect strangers that does not suggest a role in your decision of the conviction that people's lives are not, after all, really of equal importance.

Now consider the most abstract version of the three-swimmers-and-many-sharks case. Suppose you have no even thin personal reason to save the one who is alone rather than the two who are together, and you have not thrown dice to give each an equal chance to live. But you save one rather than two just because that is what you feel like doing. Perhaps you want to show your freedom from conventional bourgeois expectations. Is that behavior consistent with the conviction that all human life has great objective importance? I think not: it insults the gravity of the occasion. There are occasions for whimsy, but someone who thinks this is one cannot honestly claim to recognize that objective importance. The default decision—when nothing else, even a fair lottery, recommends one decision over another—must be to save two lives, not because this makes the world overall better but because the occasion demands taking life seriously and therefore having some reason beyond whimsy to justify how one acts. The principle that it is better to save more rather than fewer human lives, without regard to whose lives they are, is a plausible, even if not inevitable, understanding of what the right respect for life's importance requires. The competing principle, that it is better to save fewer than more lives, cannot. That supposed principle is only perverse.

Crazy Cases?

In this chapter I have relied on contrived and bizarre examples of the kind philosophers often use. Some people are suspicious of such examples because, they say, since we do not encounter the situations they describe in our ordinary life, we cannot trust the reactions we have—about whether we should save one drowning person or two, for instance—when we are presented with these examples in academic seminars and texts. That objection presupposes an account of the nature and point of moral philosophy that we have rejected, however. It supposes that moral reflection is in some way a matter of perception: that moral truth impinges on us through some distinct moral sensibility so that our moral "intuitions" are guides to truth in some way at least analogous to perceptions of the world of nature.

If that were right, then it would make good sense to be suspicious of moral perceptions that are provoked not by actual exposure to real events but by descriptions of barely possible events invented as supposedly useful fictions. (We would rightly be suspicious of our impressions of strange animals in an exotic jungle we had never seen.) The interpretive method we are pursuing, however, gives a very different force to bizarre examples. They are like the purely hypothetical cases lawyers imagine to test a principle they propose for an actual case. We confront imaginary cases, not to speculate about what we would perceive if we were actually exposed to them, but in order to see what integrity would require us to accept if we embraced the principles we test in that way. We need not reject proposed principles, however, when we are be-wildered or even doubtful whether we would accept them in unrealistic in-vented cases. It is only principles we are confident we would reject in such cases that we must therefore reject in an ordinary case before our eyes.[14] I return to this point at the end of the next chapter, in which examples grow even more exotic.

13

Harm

Competition and Injury

Here are two sad stories. (1) You are hiking in the Arizona desert with a stranger, you are both bitten by rattlesnakes, and you both see a vial of antidote lying in the scrabble. Both race for it, but you are nearer and grab it. He pleads for it, but you open and swallow it yourself. You live and he dies. (2) As before, but this time he is closer to the antidote, and he grabs it. You plead for it, but he refuses and is about to open and swallow it. You have a gun; you shoot him dead and take the antidote yourself. You live and he dies.

According to a pure version of impersonal consequentialism there is no intrinsic difference in the moral dimensions of these two stories because the result, in itself and judged from a raw impersonal perspective, is the same. If you are young and a popular and accomplished musician, and he is old and useless, you are justified both in taking the antidote yourself in the first story and in shooting him in the second. But if your qualities are the opposite— you are old and untalented and he is the young musician—you are not justified in either action. Your duty is to produce the best result with the resources you have, and the best result is fixed by the properties of the people who die and remain alive, not the mechanics used to produce that best result. Of course, if your act in either story has further consequences, these might make all the difference—for instance, if your act in the second case weakens a useful taboo against murder, that might make your act wrong even though taking the antidote yourself in the first story would not be wrong. But if we suppose that the two acts have exactly the same consequences, because the world learns of neither, then a pure consequentialist must treat them the same.

Stories like these rattlesnake stories are widely regarded as an embarrassment for consequentialism. But many consequentialists are happy in other contexts to rely on the supposed equivalence between killing and letting die. They say that because only consequences count, there is no overall moral difference between allowing someone to die when you can save him and killing him outright. They argue that indifference to starving Africans is morally tantamount to killing them. To most people, however, killing someone seems much worse than simply letting him die. Indeed, to generalize, it seems much worse to injure someone than to decline to help him when you can. According to this more popular view, you are justified in saving the antidote for yourself in the first story but not in killing the stranger to get the antidote in the second one, and even though it is wrong of you not to contribute more to African relief programs, that is not the moral equivalent of flying to Darfur to kill a few Africans yourself. If that is our view, however, we need to explain the difference, since the consequences seem so similar in the two pairs of situations.

Someone might say, as one attempt to justify what seems the natural position, that the consequences in the two stories are not really the same because those consequences include murder and theft in the second story but not the first, and murder and theft are bad. But this supposed explanation only treats itself to the conclusion we want to reach. Why is the murder of a stranger a worse consequence than simply allowing him to die when you could have saved him? It is worse only if killing someone is, just in its nature, worse than letting him die, and that is just what the explanation purports to demonstrate. Nor does it help to say, as some philosophers do, that it is a particular moral crime to aim at someone's death, that this is worse than just standing by while someone dies even when you could have prevented it. That is how most of us feel, to be sure, but we need to understand why it is worse, because the stranger is dead in both cases and our motive—to save ourselves life, or trouble, perhaps—might be the same in both cases. Some philosophers say that killing someone is worse than not helping him because killing involves a violation of the inviolability of persons. But the claim of inviolability merely restates the general conviction; it does not offer an argument for it.

The consequentialist I described, who thinks that killing and letting die are morally equivalent, follows a morality of self-abnegation. He sees himself as only one of the billions of people whose interests and fate he must weigh impersonally with no special attention to his own position. We are now exploring, in these chapters, a very different approach: a morality of self-affirmation, not anonymity, a morality drawn from and flowing back into our sovereign ambition to live well with dignity. Kant's principle is the spine of that morality. Dignity requires us to recognize and respect the objective importance of other people's lives. In that way ethics merges with morality and helps fix its content.

I appealed to Kant's principle in the last chapter to explain why in some circumstances people do have a duty to aid strangers in great need. I mainly relied, in that argument, on the first principle of dignity. That first principle will not be helpful in solving the puzzle of this chapter, however, because it is equally in play in both of the rattlesnake stories. You do not denigrate the objective value of human life in the first story when you swallow the antidote you grabbed rather than saving the stranger's life. You only exercise a perfectly consistent preference for your own life. You would not violate the first principle, of course, if you heroically sacrificed you own life so that the stranger might live. But you do not violate it in making the opposite choice either. If so, it cannot be the objective importance of human life that you offend when, in the second story, you shoot the stranger. The same preference for your own life is still at work. Now we must put the second principle of dignity to work in integrating our instinctive moral convictions with our developed sense of living well.

I offer this hypothesis. The second principle insists that you have a personal responsibility for your own life, a responsibility you must not delegate or ignore, and Kant's principle requires you to recognize a parallel responsibility in others. We need to reconcile these parallel responsibilities by distinguishing between two kinds of harm you might suffer because other people, like you, are leading their own lives with their own responsibility for their own fates. The first is bare competition harm, and the second is deliberate harm. No one could even begin to lead a life if bare competition harm were forbidden. We live our lives mostly like swimmers in separate demarcated lanes. One swimmer gets the blue ribbon or the job or the lover or the house on the hill that another wants. Sometimes, when one swimmer is drowning and another can save him without losing much ground in the race, the latter does have a duty to cross lanes to help. That is the duty we studied in the last chapter. But each person may concentrate on swimming his own race without concern for the fact that if he wins, another person must therefore lose. That inevitable kind of harm to others is, as the old Roman lawyers put it, *damnum sine injuria*. It is part of our personal responsibility—it is what makes our separate responsibilities personal—that we accept the inevitability and permissibility of competition harm.

Deliberate harm—crossing lanes not to help but to hurt—is a different matter. We need the right to compete to lead our own lives, but we do not need the right deliberately to injure others. On the contrary, if our responsibility for our own lives is to be effective, we each need a moral immunity from deliberate harm by others. In Chapter 6 I distinguished various strands in the overall idea of responsibility; assignment responsibility, I said, fixes who must perform specified tasks and who is therefore to be charged with failure if those tasks are not performed adequately. The second principle fixes on each of us an assignment responsibility for his own life. But assignment responsibility must include a power of control: some power to select which acts are performed in the exercise of the purported assignment. You would not have assignment responsibility for playing black at chess if someone else had the right and power to push the pieces with your hand.

The moral prohibition on deliberate bodily injury defines a core of control that we could not abandon without making a parallel nonsense of our assignment responsibility for our lives. Our responsibility requires at a minimum that we be in sole charge of what happens to or in our own bodies.[1] The prohibition on deliberate injury to property is less important but also central. We cannot lead a life without a high level of confidence in our right and power to direct the use of resources that have been put at our sole disposal by settled political arrangement. It is important not to confuse the right of control we must have to lead our own lives with the right to ethical independence we reviewed in Chapter 9 and will study again in Chapter 17. The latter is compromised when others attempt to make ethical decisions for us; the former when they interfere with our control over our bodies or property for any reason whatever.

The distinction between competition and deliberate harm is therefore crucial to our sense of dignity, even when the injury is trivial. Touching someone without his permission, however gently, violates a taboo. We do consent to others holding a temporary and revocable power over our bodies—lovers, dentists, and rivals in contact sports, for example. In some very limited circumstances paternalism justifies others in seizing temporary control over my body—to stop me harming myself in a moment or hour of madness, for example. But any general transfer of control over the integrity of my body, particularly to those who do not have my interests at heart, would leave my dignity in shreds. Only when we recognize that connection between dignity and bodily control can we understand why killing someone is intuitively horrifying when letting him die, even out of the same motive, is not.

Something makes us recoil from the killing in the second rattlesnake story, though not from self-preservation in the first one, and I believe it is the sense, which may be inarticulate, that granting people a personal responsibility for their own lives requires recognizing for each a zone of immunity from deliberate harm, though not an immunity from competition harm. The image I used, of swimmers keeping to separate lanes, may seem repugnant to the siblinghood of humankind. But it is not Darwin's picture of nature red in tooth and claw either, and the distinction is crucial. In the first rattlesnake case you are swimming in your own lane and ignoring a stranger drowning in his. In the second you have invaded his lane, usurping his responsibility to control his own life. The difference is invisible from the impersonal perspective; it emerges only when the idea of dignity, also invisible from that perspective, is brought into foreground light.

The connection between harm and personal responsibility explains not only why the distinction between act and omission is genuine and important, but also those special circumstances in which, on the contrary, it has no moral significance at all. It has no significance when the injured person has consented to the injury in the exercise of his own responsibility for his life. It is no violation of dignity for one football player to tackle another or for a doctor to kill a dying patient at the latter's urgent and reflective request. These are cases of permission, not usurpation. When the Supreme Court considered the constitutionality of laws forbidding doctor-assisted suicide for patients dying in great pain, those who challenged those laws pointed out that the Court had struck down laws forbidding doctors to remove life support from dying patients.[2] Some of the justices replied, rejecting the analogy, that it is morally much worse to kill a patient by administering poison than to let the patient die by removing lifesaving equipment.[3] In the rattlesnake cases that distinction is crucial; in the assisted suicide case it seems bizarre. Focusing on the importance of responsibility to dignity shows why.

Unintended Harm

The baseline picture I drew, of people forbidden to cross lanes deliberately to injure others, is in at least one respect too crude, because it ignores unintended harm. I may sell you a drug that has unanticipated side effects and makes you ill. Or I may drive carelessly and hit you. Or my lion may escape from my apartment to yours, in spite of my efforts to detain him, and maul your sofa. In these events you are injured because of what I have done. I did not harm you deliberately, but these are not stories of pure competition either. You suffer, but not just because I succeed in gaining something you wanted.

These stories take us to the question of liability responsibility that I first described in Chapter 6. Who should bear the cost of these accidents? In the first instance the loss I cause falls on you: you have become ill or have a broken leg or a ruined sofa. Is it appropriate that I compensate you? That is a moral question about compensatory and distributive justice, and also an ethical question about the appropriate connection between judgmental and liability responsibility. I need control over my body and my property to identify and pursue what I take to be a life well lived, and I must grant a like control to you. What scheme of liability responsibility for my choices, and hence for the choices of everyone else, should I therefore endorse? That question demands further interpretation of our second principle.

It requires us to seek a scheme of risk management that maximizes the control we can each exercise over our own fate, given that we must each recognize and respect the same control in others. We can rank schemes on a scale of risk-transfer magnitude. A scheme is lower in risk transfer the more it allows accidental losses to remain with the person on whom they initially fall, and higher in risk transfer the more it places liability responsibility for such loss on someone else. In one sense I gain more control from schemes that are higher in risk transfer, because they leave my plans less impaired when I am accidentally injured than if my loss remained on me. But in another sense I gain more control from schemes lower in risk transfer, because such schemes make me less liable to compensate others for accidents to which I contribute and therefore freer to pursue my plans unchecked by the threat of such liability.

We should therefore aim to identify a scheme of liability responsibility that achieves the greatest antecedent control, trading off gains and losses in control from both these directions. As a first approximation, we insist on a scheme that holds people responsible for losses that could have been prevented by them with greater care and attention. That stipulation allows me greater control over the liability responsibility I will bear for damage I cause to others—I can take greater care—and greater protection from the carelessness of others. The familiar principle that we must take care not to harm others carelessly, like the other principles canvassed in this chapter, is supported by ethics as well as by morality.

But how much care shall we say is due? It would destroy my life, not enhance it, if I were to take as much care as is possible not to harm others. I could not even cultivate my garden. So my goal of enlarging my control over my life needs a more sensitive metric of liability responsibility. In fits and starts, Anglo-American common law has moved toward a standard that was first formulated in quasi-mathematical form by the great judge Learned Hand. He said that the legal standard of due care should depend on what it is fair to expect people to do to avoid the risk of harming others, and that what is fair depends on how great a harm is risked and how probable or improbable it is.[4] His own formulation of that test was designed for commercial contexts and is too crudely monetary for other circumstances. But its structure reflects a general strategy that people anxious to maximize control over their own lives would do well to sponsor.

People each achieve the maximum control when everyone accepts, in principle, that he should bear liability responsibility for damage he has inadvertently caused to others when that damage could have been prevented had he taken precautions that would not have impaired his opportunities and resources as much as the damage he was likely to cause would likely impair the opportunities and resources of others.[5] Of course that is only the template of a standard: it requires appropriate metrics, techniques for discounting uncertainty, and so forth. But in many ordinary circumstances its upshot will be clear enough to common sense. The common law of torts is better explained by that set of interwoven ethical and moral principles than it is by any assumption that the law aims at some stipulated version of economic efficiency.[6]

Double Effect

Hard Cases

We have so far concentrated on our responsibility not to harm others in pursuit of our own interests. Moral philosophers have spent more time over a different puzzle: whether and when we may injure some people in order to protect or benefit others. Medical success has supplied these philosophers with outlandish examples. Suppose two patients are in a hospital, each of whom will die without an immediate liver transplant. A doctor has one liver available for transplant; it seems plausible that he is morally permitted to choose between the two potential recipients in a variety of ways. He may flip a coin. Or he may choose the patient whose chances of surviving the operation are better. Or he may choose to save the life of the younger patient rather than the somewhat older one, even though the latter's prospects for survival with the transplant are just as good. If the doctor chooses any of these decision procedures, he does not violate any rights of the patient who loses, even though the loser will quickly die as a result of his choice.

But now suppose there is only one dying patient, who will survive with a new liver but no liver is available. There is, however, an elderly cardiac patient in the hospital who cannot live more than a few weeks and whose liver could be harvested if he were to die immediately. The doctor may not kill the old man for his liver. Nor may the doctor shut down his respirator in hopes that he will die, or withhold the medication that is keeping him alive for those few more weeks, or not try his best to resuscitate him if he falls into cardiac arrest, assuming that he has not asked not to be resuscitated in that event. Each of these various conclusions seems inescapable, but taken together they may seem troubling. In the two-patient, one-liver case, giving the liver to the younger patient with likely more years to live might be said to show respect for the value of human life. But then why wouldn't killing the old cardiac patient, or letting him die in cardiac arrest, show the same respect? It would trade a few weeks of an old man's bedridden life for what would probably be decades of fully active life for the younger patient.

We answer: because the old man has a right not to be killed, even for a great benefit to others, even if he will die soon anyway. His doctor may secretly hope, when he applies the paddles to the old man's chest, that the shock treatment won't work. But he must nevertheless do his best to make it work. And it is not just a doctor, who has special professional duties, who has that responsibility. You happen to be in the hospital. You may not kill the old man either, and if you happen to walk past his room and see that his breathing has stopped, you have a duty of rescue. The conditions of that duty plainly hold in these circumstances: the old man would wish to be saved, you can save him at trivial cost to yourself, and he is dying in front of you. You must press the button that will summon the emergency team. But why? In this case turning your back would not indicate disdain for the importance of human life. On the contrary, you would be acting to save life. If two complete strangers are drowning in front of you on a beach, and you can and do save only one, you have violated no duty of rescue to the other one. What is different in this case?

There is an ancient and still fashionable answer; this is called the principle of double effect. It is permissible to let someone die when that is the necessary consequence of rescuing others. So it is permissible for the doctor to save one of two patients who each needs a liver, or for you to save one of two drowning swimmers, even though as a result the other patient or swimmer dies. But it is not permissible to kill someone or even to let him die when this is not just a consequence of your rescuing others but a means you adopt to that end.[7] So it is not permissible to kill the old heart patient who is anyway dying, because the point of killing him—or not saving him—would be that he dies so that his liver is available.

Other ingenious examples of the double-effect principle crowd journals of moral philosophy. You are invited to assume, for instance, that it would be permissible to turn a runaway trolley headed toward five people, who are for some reason strapped to the track ahead, onto another track even though the trolley would then strike one person who is for an equally unknown reason strapped to that other track.[8] But also to assume that if no alternate track was available, it would not be permissible to throw a large stranger who happens to be passing by onto the single track in order to stop the train with his bulk before it reached the others.

The principle of double effect can seem puzzling in just the way that the difference between the two rattlesnake stories can seem puzzling. Why does it matter whether you save five people by turning the trolley so that it kills only one, though you did not intend that death, or whether you throw one person onto the single track intending that he be struck? In both cases the outcome seems better if you act in that way than if you do not; in both cases one person dies and five lives are spared. In neither case is your intention bad or unworthy. Why then should the single difference in your state of mind—whether you treat the unfortunate death as a by-product or a means—make any moral difference at all?

We can inflate the difficulty by switching from the ex post mode in which these puzzles are mainly discussed to the ex ante mode. In the ex post mode we imagine a fat stranger ambling past a track who is killed when consequentialist enthusiasts throw him onto it. There is nothing in that decision for him. But if we consider the matter ex ante, that is no longer true. John Harris imagines a "spare parts lottery" in which people agree that each time at least five of them need an organ transplant and the needed organs can all be harvested from a single body, the healthy members of the group will draw lots to see which of them will be killed for that purpose.[9] Each member of the group would increase his life expectancy by agreeing to this arrangement, and as transplant technology improves the gain in life expectancy might well be considerable. What reason would anyone have not to join? True, the possibility of being swept up for fatal surgery when your number is announced is chilling, and so is the prospect of participating in the murder as one of the surgeons. But dying of cirrhosis or other diseases of organ failure is also a chilling prospect—being murdered is not obviously five times as bad—and American prisons have had no difficulty finding willing executioners for their death rows. True, it would be unsettling to know that at any moment one's number might be drawn. But is it five times as unsettling as knowing that any casual visit to the doctor might produce a death sentence?

It would seem to be in everyone's interest to join a spare-parts lottery. We could amend the terms to make this even more evident. We might stipulate that only the names of people past a certain age whose organs were still useful, and who were already in hospital when their organs were needed there, would be in the hat. Then it would be even more plainly in everyone's interests to subscribe, even though the chance of anyone's life being saved would be less. Why then is it wrong for us to treat people as if such a lottery had always been in place? Then old people in hospital when their organs were needed could be deemed to have lost a fair lottery they would, if rational, have joined long ago. Enforcing that hypothetical lottery would indeed mean that someone else would treat them, at that point, as only a means—would aim at their death for the sake of others. But if everyone would benefit by the arrangement, why does that matter?

Philosophers have offered various replies. Impersonal consequentialists, horrified that their theory might seem to license spare-parts murders, argue that allowing the practice would erode the taboo against taking life and cause much greater suffering in the long run than it would prevent. That is the kind of whistling-in-the-dark speculation that is often used to save consequentialism from embarrassing implications. As I said, there is no obvious reason why this practice would erode the taboo against killing any more than capital punishment has. On the contrary, capital punishment seems senseless, and this practice might seem humane. We must do better. Other philosophers say that it is always wrong to aim at someone's death, no matter what the gain. That explains our reactions to the transplant and trolley examples, they say, and also explains why a spare-parts lottery would be wrong: it would mean people one day aiming at someone's death. But that explanation simply restates the problem. If someone's motives are good—to save as many people as possible—why should it matter whether he actually aims at the death of a smaller number or simply knowingly produces their death?

The principle of double effect, as it is commonly understood, offers no answer by itself. It makes intention relevant without saying why. However, I believe that the second principle of dignity, which insists that decisions about the best use of someone's life must be left to him, shows how and why intentional assumptions are important in these contexts.[10] (Thomas Scanlon, on the contrary, argues against the relevance of intention in double-effect cases and offers an alternative explanation of those cases.[11]) Sometimes I suffer harm only because I am in the wrong place at the wrong time; I stand in the way of others achieving their aims. Competition harm is typically like that; I am harmed because my small grocery store is in the town chosen by a supermarket chain. But in other circumstances I would suffer because others have usurped a decision that dignity requires me to make for myself—the decision what use is to be made of my body or my life. I suffer that indignity when, fat, I am thrown onto a track to save the lives of others.

My dignity is at stake in the latter, though not the former, case. That explains not only the double-effect distinctions we make but a variety of other familiar convictions. Even those who think it would be immoral for a doctor to help someone commit suicide also think that it would be wrong for doctors forcibly to insert lifesaving equipment into his body against his will. Even Felix Frankfurter was "shocked" by police forcing a stomach pump down a suspect's throat to obtain evidence; the Supreme Court declared that unconstitutional.[12] People have a right, in all these cases, that nothing be done to them that supposes that they are not the final judges of how their bodies are best used.

The second principle does not forbid any act, like choosing a patient for a liver transplant, that saves one life and dooms another. Or any act, like diverting a trolley, that puts a life in peril that was formerly safe. It forbids such acts only when they are based on a usurping judgment that the best use of one person's body is to save another's life. The difference explains the morality and law of unintended harm that we discussed a moment ago. You are entitled to drive with normal care in my street, even though driving there even with normal care increases the risk to my children. But you are not entitled to kidnap my children even for an hour to induce me to give more to Oxfam. In some circumstances warring nations are entitled to bomb enemy munitions factories, knowing that innocent civilians will be blown apart. But they are not entitled to bomb some civilians to terrify others into pressing for surrender. Aiming at death is worse than just knowingly causing it, because aiming at death is a crime against dignity.

The double-effect examples elicit the convictions they do through that distinction. Just as I may act in a way that causes or risks harm to you, entirely for my own benefit, so I may act in a way that causes or risks harm to you for the benefit of others, again provided that my justification does not suppose my right to decide what it is desirable should happen to you. If two of us need a transplant but there is only one liver available, or if two of us are drowning and there is only one rescuer, then it is only a matter of chance—that someone else in the neighborhood happens to need help as well—that the loser will die. No one has determined that in all the circumstances it is more desirable that he should die than live, that in these circumstances that is what should be done with or to his body. It would suit the rescuer's purposes perfectly if the loser were not where he is, if he were in a position of greater safety.

But cases in which a dying person can be saved only by actually killing someone else are different: in those circumstances the rescuer who takes that step has formed and acts on a certain conviction. He has decided that the heart patient with only weeks to live should die at once in order that someone younger live. The heart patient may of course make that decision on his own: he may insist that he not be resuscitated the next time this is necessary—or even, if the law permits, that he be killed at once—so that his organs can be used to save another person. Then *he* would be deciding that the best use of his life would be to save someone else's. We might applaud his decision. Or we might not: we might think that a life ends badly if it ends sooner than it might, and that it would be better for the transplant patient to die young naturally than for the old man to take or surrender his own life in that way.[13] But however we think that decision should be made, the decision falls squarely within the patient's own responsibility, a responsibility no one else is permitted to steal, even to bring about an overall better result. That is the consequence, once again, of our convictions about the scope of human dignity.

Crazy Cases Again

I concede that a great artificiality still hangs over these examples. Can the distinction between competition harm and deliberate harm really have so much force, when people will die however we classify the case? Yes. Philosophers can invent examples that make any principle or distinction seem arbitrary. When such examples are properly used, they test principles the way hypothetical cases test proposed legal doctrine. As I said in Chapter 12, it is no objection to a principle that the result it requires in a bizarre invented case does not strike us as immediately or evidently right. Or because, even when it does, it can be made to seem arbitrary. It is enough, given our interpretive ambitions, that we are not confident, after reflection, that it is wrong. The principles of dignity—including the principle that people must have sovereign control over the use made of their bodies—are not compelling because they deliver what seems the intuitively right verdict in crazy trolley cases. It is the other way around: the verdict they deliver in those cases seems intuitively right, even though in some respects odd, because these principles are compelling in ordinary social and political life. They help to integrate ethics and morality there. We test them in silly invented cases, and they pass the test: they do not deliver verdicts we must believe wrong. Most philosophy students do, apparently, think it right, or in any case not wrong, to throw the switch, dooming a single victim to save five others, but not to throw the fat passerby onto the track.

True, philosophers who are expert in trolley problems have invented variations that do not attract a similar consensus.[14] Suppose, again, that five people are tied on the trolley track and that the trolley can be diverted to a second track on which a single person is tied. In this variation, the second track loops around to join the first in a circle, and the unlucky five are tied at that circle's exact midpoint. So in this case the death of the single person tied on the second track is a necessary means to saving the five people; if the single person were not there, stopping the trolley, it would kill the five people anyway and just as quickly, though from the other direction. So diverting the trolley might—or might not—be thought to assume a judgment about the best use of the single person's life. Students' reactions seem to depend on whether they see the proposed switch as one away from five people or toward a buffer person. Perhaps it makes a difference whether the simpler trolley case is presented first and then the even more bizarre loop case, or the other way around. In any case, however, neither reaction would be so evidently wrong as to disqualify the distinction because it fails in this hyperartificial case.

What about the ex ante argument for a spare-parts lottery? Of course, my earlier suggestion—that it is permissible to kill you to harvest your organs because it would have been in your interests to join a lottery scheme if one had been established—is mistaken. A hypothetical contract is not a contract. But what if there was a lottery and you did join it? You sold yourself into a kind of slavery. Imagine your number is called and surgeons advance on you. You might think then that as you could have benefited from the scheme, it is only fair that you now be killed in its name. You might think it your duty to submit. But you might not: you might then think the fate too horrible or the arrangement unjust after all, or simply that your wish not to die trumps everything else. No matter: the decision is no longer yours. You have consented to an arrangement under which you no longer have the minimum control over what use is made of your body that is essential to your dignity. That is why we must not sell ourselves into slavery, even for our own good—we might have longer lives, but we live in indignity. Volunteering for danger—volunteering for the army, for instance—is different. Volunteers have made their own decision that the best use of their lives includes a heightened risk of danger. But they have not granted anyone the authority, as distinct from the power, deliberately to take their lives.

Letting Nature Take Its Course

One difference between the two-drowning-swimmers case of the last chapter and the initial trolley case of this one might seem pertinent, but is not. In the drowning case both swimmers will die if the rescuer does nothing—if, as we might be tempted to put it, he lets nature take its course. But in the initial trolley case a sole person on the second track will not be harmed if the agent does nothing: in throwing the switch he places him in new danger. Should the agent let nature take its course in this bizarre case? Should we not say that an agent's decision to intervene *in itself* abrogates someone else's responsibility for his own life? That the agent should simply have walked away?

It is unclear what it means to let nature to take its course. If it is natural to try to rescue five people at the cost of one, then throwing the switch is letting nature take its course. But perhaps "nature" means nonintelligent nature, so that a potential rescuer lets nature take its course by pretending that he is not there. But why should he? Suppose you and I, shipwrecked, are equidistant from a bobbing life jacket. We do not let nature takes its course, which would mean both drowning. We race for the life jacket. If I lose, it is the presence of a rescuer trying to save another person—you trying to save yourself—that leads to my death. Why does it matter if your rescuer is not you but a third party who is a better swimmer—your wife?—tossing you the jacket instead of me? The harm I suffer then is only competition harm—only my bad luck. But if your wife shoots me so that you will get to the life jacket first, then this is not just bad luck. She has usurped my right to decide whether my life should end immediately.[15]

Criminal punishment usurps that right as well. Prison is a dramatic violation of dignity because, as I said, control over what happens to my body is a particularly important part of personal responsibility. Capital punishment is the most dramatic violation of all. We all think jail sentences sometimes necessary, and some of us think that capital punishment is as well. But we all insist that no one be punished who has not acted badly and so forfeited the rights his dignity would otherwise demand. We insist, moreover, that it is better that many guilty people go free than that one innocent person be punished, and in that judgment, too, we confirm the importance of the distinction between bad luck and the choice of others about how our lives should be used.

I4

Obligations

Convention and Obligation

We seek concrete interpretations of our two principles of dignity—that we must respect the equal importance of human lives, and that we have a special responsibility for our own lives—that allow us to live in the light of both without compromising either. In Chapters 12 and 13 we identified guides. We may swim mainly in our own lanes: we need not show strangers the concern we have for ourselves and those close to us. But we must not be indifferent to their fate. We owe them duties of aid when that aid is crucial, when we can give it with no great damage to our own ambitions, and, particularly, when we are directly confronted by suffering or danger. In these circumstances, to refuse our aid would show a contempt for other people's lives that would deny self-respect as well. Our responsibility not to harm strangers is different and much greater. We may not deliberately injure someone else, even as a means to our own prosperity or survival. We have explored these moral injunctions—to aid and not to harm—in rough dimension. What they require and forbid in real circumstances is a matter for more refined judgment, and too much turns on detail for any more concrete rules to be set out in advance. Everything turns, case by case, on further and very often ineffable interpretive judgments. Politics, which comes later, is different.

So much for strangers. In this chapter we consider the ethical and moral challenge when those we might aid, at cost to ourselves, are not strangers but rather people in one or another kind of special relationship with us. These relationships fall into two main categories: performative and associational. First, we make some people special through datable and voluntary acts like making a promise to them. Second, some people just are special in virtue of some associational bond: a bond of family, kinship, or partnership in a joint enterprise, for instance. One associational relationship is particularly important: this is political association, and I set it aside for separate discussion later in the chapter.

Both performative and associational relationships give rise to what we call "duties" or "obligations"; these terms connote particularly strong responsibilities of aid. So we say that parents have a duty to care for their children, and colleagues to help one another professionally, and also that people who make promises are obliged to keep them. Philosophers and lawyers have given much attention to what they call the "nature" or "logic" of obligations and duties.[1] What is the difference, if any, between the claims that someone ought to help a suffering human being and that it is his duty to do so? What is the connection between obligations and rights? If you have an obligation to help me in some way, does it follow, automatically, that I have a right to your help? Can duties or obligations always be waived by those to whom they are owed? Some of these questions are interesting, but I shall not take them up here because they do not touch our main question, which is how the duties and obligations that are attached to your special relationships are drawn from and affect what it is for you to live well.

Both performative and associational obligations are dramatically affected by social facts. What counts as a promise or an excuse for ignoring that promise varies from context to context, place to place, and time to time. The variations are sharp and evident when performative acts change legal relations—through the laws of contract, marriage, or employment, for instance—but they are impressive even when only moral obligation is in play. The role obligations of a parent or child or colleague or citizen are also defined by contingent conventions. In some communities the duties of kinship are thought to extend to more distant degrees of relationship than in others, for example, and what parents are thought entitled to expect from their children in old age is fixed by what is customary in their social milieu. What business or professional colleagues expect from one another, as of right, depends on custom that might be very different from trade to trade or from profession to profession. In some cases obligations are fixed even more contingently by some form of election or vote. People are widely thought to have a moral obligation to obey almost any law their parliament happens to enact, for instance.

The crucial role of convention and social practice in fixing obligation poses a philosophical difficulty. Conventions are only matters of fact. How can they create and shape genuine moral duties? How can I be obliged to treat my second cousin like a brother if we live in one place but entitled to ignore him if we live in another? Why isn't the difference just a matter of social anthropology that should cut no moral ice? How can the expression "I promise" gain moral force just because people take it to have moral force? Doesn't Hume's principle condemn the entire phenomenon of obligation as an enormous mistake? Yes, the moral responsibilities we discussed in the last two chapters do vary as facts vary. Whether you have a duty to try to rescue Hecuba depends on whether you can swim, have a lifeline, and so forth. But that is because a very general moral principle—the principle that governs duties of aid to strangers—makes them relevant. Social practices seem to create performative and associational obligations from scratch. They seem alchemy: making something moral out of nothing moral.

Philosophers have replied to this challenge by proposing other very general moral principles that might, like our general duty to help strangers in need, give contingent facts genuine moral force. They say that conventions give rise to expectations and that people have a moral right to have their expectations protected.[2] There is much in that claim, as we shall see, but it is incomplete. Not all expectations give rise to rights: we need to know why those generated by a particular vocabulary or role have special moral power. Other philosophers cite a general moral duty to respect useful and just social institutions.[3] But there are many useful and just institutions that I have no duty to respect— agricultural production arrangements among African tribes, for example— even though I could benefit them by respecting their production quotas and even if they expected me to respect them.

Still other philosophers say that general principles of fairness require me not to take advantage of social institutions without respecting the burdens of those institutions: not to be, as they put it, a free rider.[4] That principle could explain relatively few role obligations: parents may do nothing that gains them advantage from that role, and yet have moral as well as legal responsibilities associated with it. The free-riding principle might seem more apt in the case of promising, because people who make promises usually do seek to benefit from the institution. People often promise in order to extract benefits from those to whom the promise is given. But not always, and they still incur an obligation when they promise gratuitously.

Should we say that even a gratuitous promisor takes advantage of the institution of promising because that generally useful institution helps him on other occasions and, indeed, makes his gratuitous promise possible, whatever his purpose in making it? No, because there is no general moral principle that requires me to contribute to the cost of producing what benefits me: I may be selfish when I pass a street musician by without tossing him a bill, but I violate no obligation even if I have enjoyed his music—even if I have paused to hear more of it.[5] Of course promising is different: I do have an obligation when I promise because—well—I promised. But philosophers who appeal to a general principle of fairness to explain why promising creates obligations cannot count, as part of the reason why fairness requires keeping promises, that promises create obligations. We need a better account of the moral force of promises and role conventions. We can find it further back, in the two root principles of dignity whose implications we have been exploring for several chapters now.

Promises

Mystery

Promises create obligations. That is accurate enough for ordinary purposes, particularly when there would have been no obligation but for a promise. But there is a danger in putting the matter that simply, a danger realized in much philosophical literature. It makes promising look like magic. Hume put the problem with characteristic bite.

> I shall further observe, that, since every new promise imposes a new obligation of morality on the person who promises, and since this new obligation arises from his will; it is one of the most mysterious and incomprehensible operations that can possibly be imagined, and may even be compared to transubstantiation or holy orders, where a certain form of words, along with a certain intention, changes entirely the nature of an external object, and even of a human creature.[6]

Even when we put alchemy aside, we are likely to fear circularity. How can we explain why saying "I promise" creates a moral obligation without begging the question?[7] We are tempted to say: an obligation arises because the promisee—the person to whom the promise is made—will then rely on the promise and may be damaged if it is broken. But the promisee will not rely on the promise—it gives him no further reason to expect that the promise will be kept—unless he supposes that the promise creates an obligation. So we cannot appeal to the promisee's reliance without already assuming that promises create obligations, which is what we are trying to explain.

These problems arise, however, only because so many philosophers think of promising as an independent, distinct ground of moral responsibility. Some believe it to be finally the sole ground of all duty: they believe we have the moral and political responsibilities we do because, in some mythic mode or dimension, we have agreed, and therefore promised, to follow the community's moral conventions, which include the convention that we must keep our promises. That argument begs the question even more obviously and directly. We canvassed, just now, other arguments philosophers have offered to explain why we have at least a qualified duty to support standing moral conventions— a general duty to serve the greatest good, for instance, or to support just institutions, or not to ride free. These fail in general, for the reasons I offered, and they fail in particular to explain the moral force of promises.

We must kick the bad habit. Promising is not an independent source of a distinct kind of moral duty. Rather it plays an important but not exclusive role in fixing the scope of a more general responsibility: not to harm other people by first encouraging them to expect that we will act in a certain way and then not acting in that way. That general responsibility is itself a case of the even more general responsibility we are exploring throughout this Part Four: to respect the dignity of others and in that way to respect our own dignity. So we can study the detailed morality of promise-keeping as part of our interpretive project of deciding what our two principles of dignity require in practice. Once we see the question in that light, we can explain why promises create obligations without begging any question. We have a general responsibility not to harm other people, and this sometimes includes a responsibility to fulfill expectations that we have deliberately encouraged. This responsibility is particularly clear when we encourage the expectation through a promise, but only because promises clarify, through means fixed partly by convention, underlying responsibilities that would otherwise be muddy.

Encouragement and Responsibility

You cannot live without tempting or even encouraging others to make predictions about what you will do and to rely on those predictions in making their own plans. Governments, advertisers, rivals, family, lovers, friends, and opponents try to predict what you will do or want or buy or prefer. It would be impossible—a crippling compromise of your responsibility to live well—for you to avoid encouraging such expectations or to avoid defeating some of them. I may agree to attend some conference because I think you are coming, but you do me no wrong, even if you know this, by deciding not to attend after all. If we are friends, you should tell me, but that is all. But what if you have deliberately encouraged me to think you would attend the conference? You might have said: "I know this doesn't look to be a riveting conference. But wouldn't it be a good idea if we both went? We don't get a chance much to talk, and this would be an excellent opportunity." Then matters would be different. But how different?

If you were lying—you had no intention of attending—then you have harmed me just in that act. Dignity explains why: any lie (except in circumstances, like some games, in which lying is permissible) contradicts the second principle, because lying is an attempt to corrupt the base of information through which people exercise their responsibility for their own lives. You harm me when you lie to me even if your lie makes no further difference because I don't believe you, or because your lie makes no difference to what I do, or because I suffer no further harm in acting on it. Your lie harms me because it insults my dignity even to try to corrupt my responsibility in that way. It harms you, too, because the insult to my dignity compromises the respect you should have for yourself.

Suppose, however, that you were perfectly sincere. You did intend to attend the conference when you encouraged me to join you there. But after I accepted and agreed to give a paper, you saw a list of the other speakers and realized that the conference would be worse than you thought: in fact mainly a waste of time. You should tell me that you have changed your mind, of course. But do you have any obligation actually to attend the boring meeting just because I have already accepted and must go? Now the question is different and more difficult. Do you violate your responsibility not to harm me if you fail to do what you encouraged me to think you would? We might break this into two questions. Have you harmed me? Did you have a responsibility not to harm me in that way?

You would plainly have harmed me if I would not have gone but for your encouragement and the conference was useless to me—the discussion of my paper uncritical and the rest boring. But suppose, on the contrary, that I would have gone anyway and that the conference was so exciting that I didn't miss talking to you at all. Indeed, I wouldn't have had time for you even if you had come. Have you harmed me then? Obviously not as badly. But at all? Yes, in two ways.

First, you created a risk of harm, and creating a risk is itself a kind of harm. You harmed me in the same way that it harms me when you drive carelessly in my street even if you miss me. When you decided not to come to the conference, after having encouraged me to think you would, you did not know—certainly not for certain—whether I would have gone anyway or whether I would find the conference profitable. Had we been in touch before you decided not to come, I might have assured you that you would do me no harm by not coming. Then you would not have harmed me. But if you acted in even partial ignorance of the impact that disappointing me would have, then you harmed me just by risking harming me in other ways. Second, you harmed me in something like the way you harm me when you lie. You changed the information base on which I made decisions and then—though this time only retrospectively—falsified that base. You corrupted, in two steps, the information base on which I made my decisions: first by encouraging me and then by falsifying your encouragement. You did not intend to mislead me when you suggested the conference, but you later deliberately made what you had said misleading. As in the case of lying, that is in itself a harm quite apart from whether it generates any further harm.

So we must consider the second question. Did you have a moral responsibility not to harm me either in the obvious way—if I had hated the conference—or in those more subtle ways? This was not mere competition harm that you plainly had no moral responsibility to avoid. You had singled me out for encouragement—crossed into my lane—in order to change my expectations and intentions. This act, just in itself, must have *some* moral consequence. You needed a reason of some sort to justify not doing what you encouraged me to think you would. Indifference or whimsy would not be good enough. But, as I said, it would be much too serious an invasion of your control over your own life to accept that changing your mind would always be wrong no matter what justification you had. We need a more lenient interpretation of what you owe me out of respect for my dignity. It is, however, a very difficult matter to determine where that more lenient line should be drawn.

This turns, in particular cases, on a great host of factors. How strenuously did you encourage me? How difficult would it be for you not to defeat that expectation? Were these difficulties wholly unexpected when you encouraged me? Or could they have been predicted? How likely was it, when you decided not to attend, that I would suffer in any of the obvious ways? Did I in fact suffer? We might disagree about that latter issue, either at the time or in retrospect. We might disagree, for instance, about whether in fact I profited from attending the conference. Whose opinion on that issue is relevant to the question of moral responsibility? Yours or mine?

That only scratches the surface. Many further factors are also relevant when we ask whether someone does wrong when he disappoints those he encouraged. Thomas Scanlon's discussion of promising has greatly influenced contemporary discussions of the issue; my argument follows the same general strategy as his. (There are differences in our approaches.[8]) He endorses the following "Principle F."

> If (1) A voluntarily and intentionally leads B to expect that A will do X (unless B consents to A's not doing so); (2) A knows that B wants to be assured of this; (3) A acts with the aim of providing this assurance, and has good reason to believe that he or she has done so; (4) B knows that A has the beliefs and intentions just described; (5) A intends for B to know this, and knows that B does know it; and (6) B knows that A has this knowledge and intent; then, in the absence of special justification, A must do X unless B consents to X's not being done.[9]

There are several matters of degree in this formal statement. How much assurance must A intend to provide, for instance? But it is at least plausible that Principle F is satisfied by the conference case I describe. Other commentators apparently disagree: Charles Fried, whose work on promising has also been very influential, imagines that I want to sell you a house next to a vacant lot, and, to encourage you, I tell you that I plan to build a house for myself on that lot and live there for the rest of my life.[10] But a few years later I change my mind and sell the still vacant lot to a gas station chain. Fried believes, on balance, that I break no duty to you when I sell, although Scanlon's Principle F seems to argue otherwise.

Now consider a case in which the stakes are much higher than in the conference example. A young doctor starting in a small community is anxious to demonstrate his intention to remain there so as to acquire patients. He might, for instance, furnish and equip his surgery lavishly with that aim in view. After most local patients have shifted to the new doctor, and the only other doctor in the community has retired and moved away, the young doctor suddenly has a chance to join a teaching hospital with wonderful re-search facilities far away. What does he owe his new patients out of his re-sponsibility not to harm them? What does his ethical responsibility to make something valuable of his own life require? These are difficult questions, be-cause so many variables compete.

Many opinions seem reasonable. Scanlon's principle would suggest that because the doctor did what he could to persuade people to give up their old doctor, he must not leave them stranded now. But Fried and others might reasonably think that this asks too much. People should understand that circumstances change, and that they necessarily run some risk when they rely on even deliberately cultivated predictions. They should have appreciated the possibility that a young and ambitious doctor might be tempted to leave and cannot now complain when he does. Much may turn, for most people, on further questions I have not so far listed. Suppose the young doctor has him-self found someone to replace him. Would that extinguish any obligation he had to stay?

The Role of Promising

Such deep moral uncertainty would often be frustrating and crippling. Sup-pose I wanted you to help me plow my field tomorrow and I knew I could obtain your help only if you were convinced that I would then have an obliga-tion to help you the following day. You would be reluctant if you thought there would be any serious question about my continuing moral responsibility to do that if my circumstances changed overnight. So I might try to eliminate all the grounds you might think I could have for not doing what I said I in-tended to do. I might drive to your farm every few hours to assure you, loudly, that I intended to help no matter what happened in my life. I would then have encouraged you so strenuously that my responsibility would be close to unde-niable even if my circumstances did change. The level of excuse I would then need to escape responsibility would be much higher than if I had not encour-aged you so fervently—and you know this. You would be much more confi-dent, assuming you think me to be a morally responsible person, in your pre-diction that I would do as I tried to make you think I would.

Please notice that there is no circularity in this story.[11] You do not assume that I will do what I predict because you assume I have an obligation because you assume that I will do what I predict. Your confidence is grounded in the more fundamental assumption we have just been exploring: that I can incur responsibility to you just by crossing into your lane to try to make you act differently. We both understand that it can be controversial whether someone does incur that kind of responsibility in any particular set of circumstances, and if so how strong the responsibility is. We know that in many cases people can reasonably disagree. So I undertake to make the case for my responsibility as strong as I can make it, to reassure you that my responsibility will be undeniable. I do that in my own interests: in order that you will plow my field tomorrow.

The conventions of promising provide me with a much more efficient device for doing the same thing. They provide a vocabulary through which someone can immediately ratchet up his encouragement to the level—whatever it would otherwise take—so that other factors that might in different circumstances argue against responsibility become close to irrelevant. The same conventions also provide a means to all but eliminate uncertainty in the opposite direction. "But I don't promise" diminishes encouragement to such a low level that any justification of even minimum substance would be enough to avoid moral responsibility.

This is not magic. The conventions are parasitic on underlying and independent moral facts: that the degree of encouragement matters, that some very heightened levels of encouragement practically ensure responsibility, that some very diminished levels practically eliminate it. We might usefully compare the function of these promising conventions with that of the very different conventions of stylized insult. Convention has made certain words terms of grave abuse: these include what are known as racial or sexual slurs. The practices that attach special abuse to those phrases do not create new and distinct obligations. We normally do wrong to treat anyone with contempt; convention establishes these epithets as stylized and therefore efficient ways of showing that contempt. Promising is entirely different from stylized abuse, but it is similar in that both institutions clarify and refine nonconventional ways of harming people, and both therefore create new ways of breaching old duties.

No degree of encouragement can entirely eliminate the impact of other mitigating or damning factors, and so promising cannot do this either. There are circumstances in which no responsibility arises, in spite of a formal promise, because the promise was ill-judged or the promisor had a particularly urgent need to ignore it. And even "I don't promise" does not permit someone who has deliberately encouraged an expectation to disregard it for no reason at all. Promising and explicit not-promising signal, by convention, limiting cases of a kind of moral responsibility, cases that would exist even in the absence of convention. The convention cannot achieve what the rationale of the underlying moral facts would not sanction.

Promises and Interpretation

Promises—or alleged promises—raise moral questions as well as settling them. A promise does not preempt the moral neighborhood. A bare promise without any background of responsibility or connection may be inert. I pick your name at random from a telephone book and write you thus: "I hereby promise you that next July I will walk from Land's End to John O'Groats. Signed Yr. Obt. Servant Ronald." Even in saner cases we may be uncertain whether someone has really promised, what he has promised, and whether he really has to keep his promises. Because promising is not a self-contained practice that generates obligations automatically, but is instead parasitic on the much more general duty not to harm others, these questions do not call for inspection of some special promising rule book. They ask for an interpretation of the practices of promising that locates those practices within the wider network of ethical and moral conviction.

We begin with what seems the essential core of any successful interpretation. The point of promising is to set the bar very high for successful excuses for disappointing deliberately encouraged expectations. A promise makes a whole range of excuses ineligible that would be sufficient if reliance had been encouraged in some other and less heightened way. It follows, I believe, that we must also set the bar high for counting some act or gesture as a promise: the burden lies on someone who claims rather than denies a promise, and genuine ambiguity counts against the putative beneficiary of the promise. (Contract law is a more complex matter.) But once a promise is assumed, we must test the excuses someone offers for breaking that promise against a standard as demanding as that we use to test excuses for undoubted harms— assault or deliberate damage to someone's property, for instance.

In each of these cases, of course, as I said earlier, the level of excuse required is sensitive to the harm actually suffered as well as risked. Breaking a promise to dine is ordinarily not grave, but neither is a trivial assault or a token injury. But the fact that damage is negligible—or even that there is no damage at all—is not in itself an excuse. I am entitled that you keep a promise to dine even if one guest less doesn't really matter, because in these circumstances it falls to me, not to you, to assess what to count as harm. Your having received a better invitation won't do if I insist on your coming, even if you would be losing more than I gain. The manner of your intervention in my affairs raised the bar of excuse higher than that. But it could not have raised the bar so high that, for instance, your son's illness would not excuse you. None of these near platitudes offers an algorithm for testing promises and their breach. We can only say that we must assign a high level of seriousness to promises—but not too high—when we draw our judgments about promise-keeping from, and integrate them with, our other and more general convictions about not harming people.

Associative Obligations

Responsibility and Role

Why should the fact that everyone else in my community thinks that I have moral obligations to my children, parents, lovers, friends, colleagues, and fellow citizens mean that I do have those obligations? The answer lies, once again, in a creative interaction between our very general responsibility not to harm other people and the social practices that refine that responsibility. In some cases the mechanism of interaction is straightforward. Children need special care; if the community's practices assign the responsibility for that care to a child's parents, then no one else will supply it and his parents, just for that reason, have a duty to do so. In such cases, though conventions might have been different—in some kibbutzim they are—the fact that they have taken the shape they have accounts for the responsibilities they impose.[12]

But in other cases the alternative to assigning some people a special responsibility of care is not that others will be assigned that responsibility but that no one will. A community in which no one has special responsibilities to sexual partners or colleagues or in virtue of friendship, or in which children have no special responsibility to take care of parents, would seem impoverished to us, but no one else would be expected to pick up the special responsibilities we think these relationships bring. It is the internal character of these relationships, not the fact that some assignment of special responsibility is evidently needed, that drives the responsibilities that the community's conventions recognize and shape. So we must find a justification of the role those conventions play.

The best justification, I believe, describes a repeated feedback loop between a special responsibility we have to people in certain relationships with us, just in the nature of the case, and a set of social practices that progressively reduces the uncertainties inherent in that kind of responsibility. The second principle of dignity requires that we assume a special responsibility for our own lives: among other consequences, it forbids what I described in Chapter 9 as subordination. In certain relationships we defer to the interests, opinions, authority, or well-being of others in a way that would count as subordination if it was not in some way a reciprocal deference. The deference takes different forms in different relationships, and the necessary reciprocation need not be in kind. But unless the parties to such a relationship both accept some kind or degree of special responsibility to one another, the dignity of the party denied that special concern is compromised.

In our political life, for example, we defer to the authority of others—a sovereign, a parliament, or our fellow citizens—when we accept that we have an obligation to do what they command even when we disagree with its fairness or wisdom. That kind of obligation lies at one end of a spectrum of intimacy; I discuss it separately later in the chapter. Sexual intimacy defines the other end of that spectrum: people who accept that they are lovers place themselves, body and soul, in each other's hands. Political association, sexual intimacy, and other forms of association we discuss in this section are enormously valuable ethically. They contribute to both the goodness of our lives and our success in living our lives. But it is important to that benefit that they are risky relationships. They make each party not only open to a special kind of benefit but vulnerable to a special kind of harm. You do not deny or compromise your special responsibility for your own life if you have made the goodness of your own life vulnerable to what happens to a few others, or if you have granted them partial control over your own life, when these mergers of life and fate are matched by a like heightened concern for you. But, except in very special circumstances, a person's responsibility is compromised when that merger is unilateral; when the other party to what you take to be a special relationship treats you as he would any stranger. The benefit you sought, just in the fact of a relationship you value, is then replaced not just by disappointment but also by a kind of subservience.

The special importance of a parent's love for his children and their love for him, and the responsibilities that flow naturally from that love, redeems what would otherwise be slavery in both directions. Parents' freedom to direct their own lives is dramatically compromised by the responsibility of parenthood; children's subordination to their parents' will is, for a time, almost complete. Dickens caught the moral implications of these facts in his invention of Mrs. Jellyby. She neglected her own children, who lived in chaotic squalor, in order to pursue her "telescopic philanthropy." We do not count her as saintly for that choice; her show of greater concern for the poor of Africa made the total control she nevertheless exercised over her own family seem tyranny. She was ridiculous, not because she cared less for her children than for strangers, but because she did not care much more for them.

Other, less intense, relationships have their own internal logic. Partnership enterprises of various sorts, whether formal or informal, are deceitful if one partner lacks a commitment to the joint success of both. The special concern that partnership demands is of course much more limited than relationships to which love is central. I must show special concern for my fellow worker in his professional life but not for his life overall. Unless, of course, he is also my friend, because friendship is special in yet a different way. Seeking and finding pleasure in the continued company of another person need not imply love, but it would be meanly instrumental if it did not involve, as Aristotle put it, a concern for that person for his own sake that is greater than one's concern for strangers. Displays of friendship would be another kind of indignity if they were not matched by a special and reciprocal concern.

I anticipate two contrary objections. My account may strike you as too moralized. You might prefer to emphasize the evolutionary importance and continuing benefits of the relationships I have in mind and therefore the instrumental value of the obligations that protect them. You might think it entirely natural, for instance, that lovers and parents and children should feel responsibility for one another. As throughout, however, we seek a justification for these obligations, not an explanation of their origin or subsistence. The natural, ubiquitous, and powerful emotional force of these relationships does indeed have justifying importance: it is because the relationships almost invariably carry a natural and powerful emotional force that indignity is palpable when that force is absent or bogus. But it is the harm inflicted by that indignity, not the evolutionary value of those emotions, that grounds the obligation not to inflict that special kind of harm.

You might, on the other hand, think my account ethically deflated. Decent people do not see themselves as obliged to care for their children or lovers or parents or friends: they just do care for them and act wholly instinctively out of that concern. If they were to pause to reflect on exactly what they owe, or on when their failure would compromise someone's dignity, they would be guilty of the now-famous one thought too many. Once again, however, the objection misses the point. Perhaps decent people are never aware of their obligations to those close to them; perhaps they would resent the suggestion that a sense of obligation in any way explains their behavior. But they do have those obligations nevertheless, and from time to time they do sense their force: when they feel no desire, for instance, to endure a troublesome old parent. Their obligations do not disappear when they do ignore them, as the troublesome old parent may make plain when the occasion arises. So we must account for the obligations as well as the behavior of people who are never conscious, and never need to be reminded, of them.

Convention and Responsibility

We found a rough basis for role obligation in the general moral principles we identified in earlier chapters, principles that demand heightened concern in certain relationships, without relying yet on the moral force of convention. But the relationships that generate these obligations cannot appear except in society and therefore cannot be entirely innocent of the impact of convention. Even those relationships most dominated by biology carry cultural freight: identifying someone as a parent adds something to, and does not even assume, a biological fact, and what it adds differs to some degree from place to place, time to time. That fact does not make role obligation "only conventional." The obligations are genuine because convention does not create but only focuses and shapes the more general principles and responsibilities it assumes.

First, the more detailed the conventions, the less room for uncertainty they leave as to what would count as the forbidden harm. It would be at best unclear, absent any conventional instruction, who counts as a member of my family to whom I owe special concern. Or what friendship permits or requires by way of favoritism in employment. Social practice reduces these areas of uncertainty; it does this differently in different cultures and also over time. Second, convention sharply increases the risk to dignity when these responsibilities, so refined, are ignored; it increases the risk by attaching a social, and not merely personal, meaning to any failure to respect the relationship. Because role conventions stipulate which acts are required or forbidden by a special relationship, they establish a vocabulary of behavior that either confirms or denies the mutual concern that a particular form of association presupposes. These two features establish the progressive feedback loop I mentioned.

The analogy I offered to other forms of social meaning, including racial slurs, is in point here as well. Just as a word that has been brought into the lexicon of hate cannot be freed from that meaning without elaborate scaffolding of explanation, so it is not possible to free a denial of help demanded by a role convention from the disrespect it signals without an equally elaborate and hazardous explanation. So convention strengthens as well as shapes role obligations. The expectations they nourish cannot be dismissed as mere predictions with no moral force, because they are supported not just by the practices themselves but by the more basic responsibilities the practices refine and protect. The obligation drives the expectation rather than the other way around, and the obligation does not cease when the expectation perishes—when parents become resigned to their children's indifference, for instance.

Reciprocal interaction between background responsibility and social convention explains a further and crucial feature of these obligations. Role conventions do not impose genuine associative obligations automatically: the conventions must satisfy independent ethical and moral tests. Sexist or racist practices, or those that define honor among murderers, drug dealers, or thieves, impose no genuine obligation on those they purport to oblige, no matter how thoroughly adherents seem to accept those obligations. Mafia soldiers form expectations, they find the practices of their organization distinctly useful, they take advantage of those practices, and they regard any breach of loyalty by others as an indignity. They dangerously regard other soldiers as free riders when these shirk the burdens of the organization. But once we realize that role practices impose genuine obligations only because— and therefore only when—they allow their members more effectively to meet their standing ethical and moral responsibilities, then we also realize that these practices cannot impose obligations when they act as obstacles rather than means to that goal. Social practices create genuine obligations only when they respect the two principles of dignity: only when they are consistent with an equal appreciation of the importance of all human lives and only when they do not license the kind of harm to others that is forbidden by that assumption. They demand special treatment for certain people, but they cannot license hatred or murder.

Interpretation and Role

We have so far focused on how social practices and conventions impose actual obligations. The question which obligations they impose is of much greater practical importance. Role practices reduce the uncertainty people face in deciding what they owe people close to them, but they hardly eliminate that uncertainty. Even the most explicit of role conventions—those defining the duties of parents toward young children, for example—leave many questions unresolved. They do not settle, for instance, just as a matter of convention, the troubling question whether parents who can afford private education are permitted or required to use relatively poor state schooling instead. Many important role practices—the conventions of friendship, for instance—do little more than recognize a category calling for and justifying special treatment without any precise account of what that special treatment must or may entail. Who exactly is my friend? Where is the line to be drawn between friendship and acquaintance? Can I terminate an inconvenient friendship at will, just by so declaring? Or do friendships, once formed, have more staying power? If so, how and when do they end? What must I do for even a close friend? Help hide his crimes from the police?

These familiar questions roll on indefinitely, even about only one role practice. The traditional explanations of associative obligation I mentioned early in this chapter offer no help in answering them. We may accept a duty to bear the burdens as well as the benefits of a social practice, but that cannot help us decide what those burdens are. We may recognize a duty to support an existing institution that we believe useful, but that doesn't help in deciding what that existing institution actually does require. We may commit ourselves to respect the expectations that a social practice generates, but that commitment does not help us choose between people's expectations when these disagree. These purported justifications of role practices are unhelpful because they take the practices to be *only* matters of convention, and pure conventions are exhausted by the scope of consensus.

Once we recognize that role practices clarify genuine but indeterminate responsibilities that flow from the internal character of the relationships on which they build, we have a basis for interpreting them in the way we interpret anything else. The long discussion of interpretation in Chapters 7 and 8 is therefore pertinent here. In an earlier book I offered an example specifically tailored to the interpretation of conventional practices thought to impose obligations.[13] We sometimes disagree, even within a single community, about what courtesy requires, particularly when old conventions of respect are eroding. We each form our opinions through mostly unreflective but nevertheless controversial assumptions about the practice's underlying point.

When a friend asks you for financial help and you are reluctant, you do not ponder the underlying point of friendship to decide whether you must. But some reaction to his request will seem right to you because of your unstudied understanding of what friendship is and means, and your decision will solidify as well as give effect to that understanding and so govern your reaction to later and parallel questions about what you owe to friends. These are interpretive reactions. If we tried to reconstruct them in argumentative form, we would begin with some assumption about what form and degree of heightened concern friendship presumes and requires. You might well be unaware of having made any such assumption and, indeed, unaware that you were engaged in any process of reasoning at all. You might say that you just "saw" that this is what friendship does or does not require. But there was nothing for you to "see": we can make sense of your reactions only by assuming that your experience has embedded an interpretive understanding of the concept that has become unreflective and instantly available.[14] All that is simply to repeat the claims of our earlier discussions of interpretation and to apply them to the phenomenon of associative obligation.

Political Obligation

Paradox

Legal and political philosophers debate whether people have a moral obligation to obey the laws of their community just because they are its laws—whether, that is, people have what is often called "political" obligation. This is not the question whether people have any reason to submit themselves to political authority. It is a philosophers' parlor game to imagine that people might live in a "state of nature" under no scheme of governance and then to consider what reasons people in that situation would have to institute governments among themselves. The popularity of this exercise helps account for the popular but mistaken assumption that legitimacy depends on the unanimous consent of the governed and therefore on some fantastical history or fiction about that consent. In any case, that is not our question now. Familiar governments do exist, their boundaries and hence claims of dominion are the product of historical accident, and almost all of us are born or brought into one of them. Do we have an obligation to obey the laws of the state we happen to be born into?

Of course, we usually have an independent moral reason to do what the law requires and not to do what it proscribes. Laws condemn murder, and murder is wrong. But the question of political obligation arises when we have no other reason to do what the law requires. A law is adopted by officials I voted against, and I believe that law unwise in policy and wrong in principle. I probably have an important practical reason to obey this law; I may well be arrested or fined if I do not. But does the bare fact that this is the law give me a further, distinctly moral, reason to obey it? That is not to ask whether we are ever justified in disobeying a law. I can accept that I have a standing obligation, in principle, to obey the laws of my community and yet think that some particular law is so unjust or so brutally unwise that I am justified in disobeying it. That is the opinion of people who believe that civil disobedience—disobedience to protest unjust laws—is sometimes morally permitted and even required. For them, the moral permissibility of disobedience in these circumstances is an exception to a more general principle that requires obedience even to laws they disapprove but do not think wicked.

Some philosophers—they are called "anarchists," though few of them have bombs or beards—deny that the bare fact that a law has been passed, even in a community whose structures and laws are generally just, can provide any independent moral reason for obeying that law.[15] We have a duty to obey the law when some independent reason argues that we must: if the law improves social justice, for example, or if obeying it would make the community as a whole better off. But not, they insist, just because the law was adopted according to the constitutional procedures that the political practices and conventions of our community stipulate.

Anarchists often rely on a general philosophical thesis: they believe that no one has an obligation unless he has voluntarily accepted that obligation. They are right to think that political obligation is not voluntary, except in the relatively rare cases of naturalization. The once popular idea that people voluntarily accept an obligation to obey the laws of their community when they do not leave that community is too silly any longer to take seriously. Political philosophers have tested many other ways of defending the idea that political obligation depends on consent. But these have all failed, and they are anyway unnecessary because the popular assumption that obligations are genuine only if voluntary is itself untenable. The moral responsibilities we studied in the last two chapters are not voluntary: I have no choice whether I must rescue someone drowning in front of me when I can do so easily. Some of the associational obligations discussed earlier in this chapter are also involuntary—children have no choice in selecting parents—and most of the others are only partly voluntary: most friendships, for instance, arise casually, and we each have friends we had no conscious intention of making friends. Philosophers who assume that only voluntary obligations can be genuine contradict themselves, moreover, because they must assume that the obligation to keep a promise or respect an oath is genuine even though that obligation was itself never accepted. An involuntary obligation lies behind any voluntary one.

But that is not a positive argument for political obligation: it only denies that anarchists can win their case quickly by appeal to some general principle about obligation and consent. They are right to reject many positive arguments that have been suggested. You do not have a moral obligation to obey the law of your community just because others expect you to obey. Or because, since you have taken advantage of the benefits of political association, you have an obligation to accept the burdens. If people do have political obligations—if the anarchists are wrong—then this must be a special case of associational obligation. We must have political obligations because we are related to our fellow citizens in some special way that gives each of us special responsibilities to the others independently of any consent.

It might seem problematic that we could have that kind of special relations with all fellow citizens, however. We know our parents, children, lovers, and friends intimately, and we have at least a personal acquaintance with colleagues and even neighbors. But that is not true of fellow citizens of anything larger than a tiny community: many Americans have denser personal relations with foreigners than with all but a few fellow citizens. It may therefore seem mysterious what associational obligations could hold among people just because they salute—if they do salute—the same flag. We will not find the answer in any history of how political communities came to be formed or reformed. It is only a series of historical and geographical accidents—where rivers run and kings slept—that has made the political boundaries of the United States or France or any other place what they are. We must seek the moral force of fellow citizenship not in anything that preceded these accidental political groupings or explains them historically, but rather in the contemporary consequences of these accidents.

Political obligation flows from political association in the same way as the other associative obligations we just reviewed flow from other kinds of association. Coercive political organizations undermine the dignity of their members unless each accepts a reciprocal responsibility to the others to respect collective decisions, provided that these decisions meet appropriate conditions. We begin explaining why by noticing the paradox of civil society. Collective coercive government is essential to our dignity. We need the order and efficiencies that only coercive government can provide to make it possible for us to create good lives and to live well. Anarchy would mean the end of dignity altogether. But coercive government also threatens to make dignity impossible. Some members of the community must exercise vast power over the rest: they must threaten punishment for disobedience, and they must sometimes carry out the threat.

That state of affairs threatens both of our principles. How can I, given my special responsibility for my own life, accept the dominion of others? How can I, given my respect for the objective importance of other people's lives, join in forcing them to do as I wish? Everyone who is not a dictator faces the first of these challenges. A great many people—in a genuine democracy, almost all adults—face the second as well, and it is equally sharp. We may not deliberately harm even strangers for our own advantage. That applies to collective action as well as individual acts: if I combined with allies to imprison someone or steal his property, I would show the same contempt for our victim and therefore for myself as if I acted alone. Democratic politics raises the possibility that we all harm each other in that way every day.

The challenge the paradox poses is, once again, interpretive. We must develop our conception of what dignity requires further than we yet have, so that we can identify a politics that is consistent with it. We have already accepted that the second principle of dignity—that we must take responsibility for our own lives—permits us, under certain conditions, to share that responsibility with others. We considered examples earlier: relationships of intimacy, for instance, that are supported by mutual heightened concern. Political association is another example. We find ourselves in associations we need and cannot avoid but whose vulnerabilities are consistent with our self-respect only if they are reciprocal—only if they include the responsibility of each, at least in principle, to accept collective decisions as obligations. If we did not have that obligation, and supposed ourselves morally free to disregard those decisions whenever we wished and safely could, then we would have to concede a like moral freedom to everyone in the community. Our state would then be a tyranny that forced people to do what they had no obligation to do. We would abandon our dignity whenever we bowed to the community's threats and also whenever we joined in creating or enforcing those threats against others. It is an important part of our own ethical responsibility, and therefore part of our moral responsibility to others, that we accept for ourselves and require of them the particular associative obligation—political obligation—that we are now considering.

Political obligation is in one way more precisely defined than the other associative obligations we have been canvassing. What it requires is fixed by constitutional structure and history: by the processes of legislation and, in some cases, adjudication as well. But in another way its moral impact is often more contestable. It is debatable when civil disobedience is an appropriate response to a citizen's more general obligation to help improve his community's sense of what its members' dignity requires. In some terrible circumstances it is arguable that political obligation has lapsed entirely: when a government in power is no longer a legitimate government. No associative obligation holds when the purported association is itself a force for bad: the Mafia, as I said, creates no obligations among its members. Political obligation is a more complex matter, because laws are so different and have such different point and consequence from one another. But political obligation may also be extinguished altogether. Revolution rather than disobedience is then in the cards.

Legitimacy

Political obligation holds, I said, only under certain conditions. The government of a political community is legitimate, let us say, when it meets those conditions. Legitimacy therefore has two dimensions: it depends on both how a purported government has acquired its power and how it uses that power. I discuss the acquisition dimension in Chapter 18 and the exercise dimension first here and then throughout Part Five.

Legitimacy is a different matter from justice. Governments have a sovereign responsibility to treat each person in their power with equal concern and respect. They achieve justice to the extent they succeed. But it is controversial what success means: nations, political parties, and political philosophers disagree about justice. This book sets out, in Part Five, one among many controversial theories. Governments may be legitimate, however—their citizens may have, in principle, an obligation to obey their laws—even though they are not fully, or even largely, just. They can be legitimate if their laws and policies can nevertheless reasonably be interpreted as recognizing that the fate of each citizen is of equal importance and that each has a responsibility to create his own life. A government can be legitimate, that is, if it strives for its citizens' full dignity even if it follows a defective conception of what that requires.

Evaluating legitimacy therefore requires a distinct interpretive judgment that will often be difficult. Do we make better sense of some piece of injustice by taking it to express a flawed understanding of what equal concern and respect requires? Or rather as an outright rejection of that responsibility? Naked tyrannies—Nazi Germany and Stalin's Soviet Union—fall plainly into the second hole, but states less openly unjust present harder cases. The interpretive judgment must be sensitive to time and place: it must take into account prevailing ideas within the political community. When it was near-universally accepted that everyone's fate is better protected, and his dignity better expressed, when he is governed by royal or ecclesiastical appointees of a god and when a state religion is established as canonical, the interpretive case for the legitimacy of a genuine monarchy or theocracy was stronger than it now is. In any case, the interpretive judgment must take into account the full range of a government's laws and practices. Does the monarchy in fact work for the good of everyone it purports to govern, or only for some privileged group or to perpetuate and expand its own power? Does the theocracy try to convert dissenters only by persuasion? Or does it punish them for their opinions and coerce their conversion? It may be impossible to sustain some government's trumpeted claim to equal concern when the policies it hopes to defend are placed in a larger context.

Justice is, of course, a matter of degree. No state is fully just, but several satisfy reasonably well most of the conditions I defend in Part Five. Is legitimacy also a matter of degree? Yes, because though a state's laws and policies may in the main show a good-faith attempt to protect citizens' dignity, according to some good-faith understanding of what that means, it may be impossible to reconcile some discrete laws and policies with that understanding. A state may have an established democracy, provide for free speech and press, offer constitutional tests through judicial review, and provide adequate police service and an economic system that enables most of its citizens to choose their own lives and prosper reasonably. Yet it might pursue other policies that cannot be understood other than as a flat denial of the principles on which that attractive general structure is based. It may exclude some particular minority—of race or economic class—from benefits its policies assume to be requisite for others. Or it may adopt coercive laws that threaten liberty in misperceived emergencies or to enforce some cultural imperative: to improve the sexual ethics of the community, for example. These particular policies may stain the state's legitimacy without destroying it altogether. Its legitimacy then becomes a matter of degree: how deep or dark is that stain? If it is contained, and political processes of correction are available, then citizens can protect their dignity—avoid becoming tyrants themselves—by refusing so far as possible to be party to the injustice, working in politics to erase it, and contesting it through civil disobedience when this is appropriate. The state remains legitimate, and they retain political obligation, to a degree that may be substantial. If the stain is dark and very widespread, however, and if it is protected from cleansing through politics, then political obligation lapses entirely. The unfortunate citizens must contemplate, as I said, not just civil disobedience but revolution.[16]

Tribal Obligations?

We have been discussing obligation that arises from the special facts, powers, and vulnerabilities of human association. Many, perhaps most, people cherish other special relationships beyond those I discussed: these center largely on relationships that are in different ways cultural and historical rather than biological, social, or political. American Jews very often feel a special concern for other Jews: they give particularly to charities that benefit Jews, for instance, or work for causes they think, in the conventional phrase, good for their people. Blacks, ethnic Poles across the world, people who speak the same language whether across national political boundaries or within multilingual states, often feel a similar tug to favor other members of that group in some way. They sometimes, in some circumstances, speak of a right of such groups to something they call self-determination.

I recognized in Chapter 9 that many people treat these relationships as parameters in their decisions how to live. For some people they are crucial parameters: they think it essential to identify themselves with some group and to live in a manner that expresses that identification. They may be right. I am anxious now only to deny that these are matters of associational obligation. My argument for that kind of obligation fixed on standing ethical and moral features of our relationships with others: relationships that for different reasons threaten indignity if they are not structured by some special and shared concern. Political association is among these because coercive govern-ment destroys dignity without partnership. But the different popular forms of tribal association have no such features.

Many people do believe, as I do not, that their racial, ethnic, religious, and linguistic connections bestow associational rights and obligations. Per-haps some of these convictions have a genetic foundation; if so they will prove particularly hard to ignore and perhaps pointless to disparage. But the idea of these special rights and obligations has been and remains a powerful source of evil. Throw a dart at a spinning globe, and the odds are good that it will land where tribes of race, religion, or language are killing each other and destroying their communities in the name of some supposed group right or destiny. These hatreds may be as enduring as they are destructive, and we should have no illusions that they will disappear or even ebb from human affairs. But I insist that nothing in the argument of this chapter lends them any moral or ethical support.

PART FIVE

Politics

15

Political Rights and Concepts

Rights

Rights and Trumps

The final discussion of Chapter 14, about political obligation and legitimacy, turned an important corner. Parts One and Two of this book discussed the possibility and character of truth in morality, ethics, and other departments of value. Parts Three and Four discussed the central concepts of ethics, captured in the two principles of dignity, and then the central concepts of personal morality—our duties to aid others and not to harm them, and the special duties we have in virtue of performative acts like promising or relationships like friendship. Political obligation belongs to this last topic because it springs from a relationship that holds among fellow subjects of a political community. But it marks the transition from the personal to the political, because citizens acquit their political obligations in part through a separate, artificial collective entity. Political communities are only collections of individuals, but some of these individuals have special roles and powers that allow them to act, singly or together, on behalf of the community as a whole. So we must recognize a distinct department of value: political morality. Ethics studies how people best manage their responsibility to live well, and personal morality what each as an individual owes other people. Political morality, in contrast, studies what we all together owe others as individuals when we act in and on behalf of that artificial collective person.

The shift of topic from personal to political morality allows a shift in style as well. I have written little about personal morality before, and so the last several chapters were necessarily expository and somewhat detailed. In contrast, I have written a good deal about political morality, particularly in my books *Life's Dominion, Sovereign Virtue,* and *Is Democracy Possible Here?* so the remaining chapters can be more summary. I ask you to treat those books as incorporated into this one by reference, and I direct you to particular portions of those books that amplify arguments summarized here. I aim to redeem the suggestion of the first pages of Chapter 1 by showing how the other parts of this book converge on political morality, just as each of them, together with political morality, can be seen to converge on any of them singly. I try to weave political morality into the overall interpretive structure. There is a good deal of new wine in what follows. But there is old wine as well, and then the point, as I said much earlier, is its new bottles.

We studied ethics and personal morality through the concept of responsibility—what people must do for their own sake or for others—rather than the often corresponding idea of a right: what people are entitled to have. Responsibility is a particularly suitable focus for ethics, because it is more natural and accurate, when judging what it is to live well, to think of what we are responsible for doing than of what we have a right to demand. We might have studied morality through the idea of rights. We might have asked, for example, what aid we all have a right to have, even from strangers, or what help friends or lovers or citizens are entitled to expect from one another. When we come to political morality, however, rights plainly provide a better focus than duties or obligations, because their location is more precise: individuals have political rights, and some of those rights, at least, are matched only by collective duties of the community as a whole rather than of particular individuals.

We begin with the idea of a political right itself: its nature and force. What kind of rights do we each as individuals have against our state—against ourselves collectively? We must be careful because people use the word "right" in so many different senses. We speak of the "right" agricultural policy, for example, or the "right" approach to global warming. Politicians often say that people have a "right" to something—a more restrictive immigration policy, for instance—when they mean only that the public wants that policy or that, in the politicians' view, the public would be better off having it. Sometimes, however, people use the idea of a political right in a stronger and more discriminating way: to declare that some interests particular people have are so important that these interests must be protected even from policies that would indeed make people as a whole better off.[1]

We might say, capturing that idea, that political rights are trumps over otherwise adequate justifications for political action.[2] A policy is normally justified, for instance, if it would make the community safer by reducing violent crime: that is a good all-things-considered justification for increasing taxes to pay for more police. But increased safety is not an adequate justification for forbidding unpopular speeches on street corners or for locking up suspected terrorists indefinitely with no judicial review of the charges against them. Those latter policies violate political rights—the right to free speech and not to be punished without a fair trial. This trump sense of a right is the political equivalent of the most familiar sense in which the idea is used in personal morality. I might say, "I know you could do more good for more people if you broke your promise to me. But I have a right that you keep it nevertheless."

This chapter studies political rights understood as trumps. It therefore treats only part of political morality; it ignores the much broader question of what are in general good reasons for a political community's exercising its coercive power in one way rather than another. We say that the government should negotiate trade treaties because these are good for America's trade balance, or that government should subsidize farmers because that would improve the economy as a whole, or that government should abolish capital punishment because its use demeans our society. Many such claims are informal versions of a utilitarian trade-off argument. We concede that a new airport will make those who live nearby worse off but still insist that the airport is in the general interest because the number it will benefit directly and indirectly is much larger. But not every claim about the general interest appeals to a utilitarian argument. We might think, for example, that even if capital punishment decreases murder, and therefore contributes to a net gain in happiness, it is still unjustified because the moral blight that official killings imposes on the community outweighs the suffering caused by a small increase in murders.

I will not discuss any of these varied justifications for political action, but it is important to bear their range and diversity in mind when we ask our present question. What interests of individual people could be so important as to trump almost all these varied other justifications? For utilitarians and other consequentialists who think that justice is necessarily a matter of aggregation—of improving the overall welfare of the community as a whole—the correct answer is: nothing. We have rejected that aggregative thesis, however, so the question is open for us. Are any interests of particular individuals so important that they must be allowed to trump the general welfare or any other all-things-considered justification? If so, which interests are these—and why? In fact, we have already begun to answer these crucial questions. We began in the last chapter when we discussed political legitimacy and the deep connections between that pivotal idea and the two principles of human dignity we take to be fundamental for both ethics and morality.

I summarize the conclusion of that discussion. A political community has no moral power to create and enforce obligations against its members unless it treats them with equal concern and respect; unless, that is, its policies treat their fates as equally important and respect their individual responsibilities for their own lives. That principle of legitimacy is the most abstract source of political rights. Government has no moral authority to coerce anyone, even to improve the welfare or well-being or goodness of the community as a whole, unless it respects those two requirements person by person. The principles of dignity therefore state very abstract political rights: they trump government's collective policies. We form this hypothesis: All political rights are derivative from that fundamental one. We fix and defend particular rights by asking, in much more detail, what equal concern and respect require.

That hypothesis explains the capital importance in contemporary political theory of certain interpretive concepts, including the concepts of equality and liberty. In mature democracies people almost all recognize, as an abstract thesis, that government must treat those it governs with equal concern and must allow them the liberties they need to define a successful life for themselves. We disagree, however, about what more concrete rights follow from these abstract ones. We disagree, for instance, whether it follows that government must strive to make the wealth of its citizens less unequal and, if so, how far it must try to make wealth absolutely equal. We also disagree about how far and in what way government may limit its citizens' freedom of action consistently with recognizing their responsibility for their own lives; we disagree, for instance, about whether laws banning pornography or abortion or requiring seat belts in cars offend that requirement of human dignity. We develop a substantive theory of political rights as trumps through our answers to such questions. That is why political rights are so controversial across political cultures and even within them.

A substantive theory of political rights can be produced most economically by constructing and defending conceptions of these master interpretive concepts. That is what I attempt in the following chapters. We aim, remember, to interpret the two fundamental principles of dignity so that no compromise between the two is necessary; so that each complements and reinforces the other. So we must reject the opinion now popular among political philosophers that liberty and equality are conflicting values. We hope to define equality and liberty together: not only as compatible but as intertwined.

Political Rights and Legal Rights

Legal rights must be distinguished from other political rights, though the distinction is less easy to draw than many legal theorists suppose. I discuss legal rights and the distinction between political and legal rights in Chapter 19. For now we may take a standard example as a paradigm for legal rights: a right enacted by a legislative body of a legitimate government to be enforced on the demand of individual citizens through the decisions, if necessary, of an adjudicative institution like a court. A legal right may be designed to give effect to a preexisting political right: a general law forbidding public schools from excluding students of a minority race, for example. Some political communities give a special status to certain legal rights of that character: they make them constitutional rights that can be cancelled, not by the ordinary processes of legislation, but only, if at all, by a special process that requires extraordinary popular approval. The United States Constitution, for example, forbids government to create any law that denies freedom of religion. The constitutions of some states, including South Africa, impose a duty on government to provide a level of health care for all.

But no nation turns all political rights into constitutional rights or even ordinary legal rights. Americans have a political right to adequate health care or insurance, but for many long decades—until 2010—they had no proper legal right to either. Their government failed in its duty to them by not making their political right into legal rights. And every nation creates legal rights that are not designed to match preexisting political rights. A law awarding farmers a subsidy for not growing corn, for instance, creates a legal right that matches no prior political right. That legal right is nevertheless itself a political right with the power of a trump: a court must order the government to pay a subsidy stipulated by law even if for some reason withholding it from a particular farmer would be in the general interest.

Human Rights

What Are They?

Human rights have had a good press since the Second World War. Dozens of human rights conventions and treaties have been signed, among them the Universal Declaration of Human Rights enacted by the United Nations General Assembly in 1948, the European Convention on Human Rights, and the Cairo Declaration of Human Rights. Hundreds of books, monographs, and studies on the subject have been published. Some people and some institutions use the phrase casually and even hyperbolically. Campaigners declare a human right when they mean that some policy goal—some way of making the world better—is particularly important or urgent. They announce, for instance, a human right that no nuclear power plants be built or that no food be genetically modified or that workers have a stipulated vacation each year. I use the phrase in a stronger way that matches the strong sense of a political right: to designate a trump.

But how shall we then distinguish human rights from other political rights that also act as trumps? It seems widely agreed that not all political rights are human rights. People who all accept that government must show equal concern for all its members disagree about what economic system that requires. An unfettered free market? Socialism? Redistribution according to some standard or goal? Which standard or goal? Egalitarians, libertarians, and utilitarians each present their opinion as indispensable to genuine freedom and equality. But almost none of them would suggest that the many nations that disagree with his opinion are guilty of human rights violations: libertarians argue that taxation is theft, but few claim that it is a violation of a human right. Why not? Human rights are widely thought to be special and, according to most commentators and to political practice, more important and fundamental. In what way?

This is in the first instance only a classificatory question. It asks for a standard that a right must meet to count as a human right, though it need not supply or even point to a suitable test of what rights meet that standard. But, as

Charles Beitz has emphasized, our classification cannot be arbitrary.[3] It must be drawn from an interpretation of what he calls the "discursive" practice of human rights that now includes claims in treaties and other international documents and by political officials, international associations of states, judicial bodies, nongovernmental organizations, and academic discussants. Our classification must fit that practice sufficiently well to make our discussion pertinent to it, though it should not prejudge whether the particular rights widely recognized in the practice should in fact be accepted as human rights.

A number of writers have suggested the following classificatory strategy.[4] Human rights are those that trump not merely collective national goals but also national sovereignty understood in a particular way. (This is often called the Westphalian conception of sovereignty because it was prominent in the understanding of the system of nation-states that the Treaties of Westphalia achieved.) According to this conception, one nation or group of nations must not interfere in the internal affairs of another nation. Nations must not attempt, by actual force or threats of force or other sanction, to dictate another nation's policy or choose its rulers. These writers suggest that we should classify as human rights only those rights important enough to trump national sovereignty on that conception. If those who claim authority over any territory violate these human rights of people in their power, then other nations are permitted to attempt to stop them by means that would otherwise not be permitted—by economic sanctions or even military invasion.

If we accepted that classification and consequence, we would then have to decide, on other grounds, which political rights are sufficiently important to justify sanctions. Important provisos would also be necessary. Any proposed military incursion or severe economic sanction would have to meet two further tests. First, the organization or state proposing such sanction must be authorized to do so under international law. Many international lawyers believe that only a single international institution, the Security Council of the United Nations, can authorize such action; other international lawyers disagree. The second condition is equally important: any such sanction must reasonably be expected to do significantly more good than harm. Even if the invasion of Iraq in 2003, led by the United States, had been licensed under international law, it would nevertheless have failed that second stipulation.

Still, even when we take due account of these further conditions, the trumps-over-sovereignty idea seems to set too high a bar. Human rights conventions describe a variety of rights as human rights that would not justify even economic sanctions, let alone military force. The Universal Declaration of Human Rights lists, as human rights, a right to education, to adequate housing and health care, to marriage, to adequate compensation for work, to equal pay for equal work, and to a presumption of innocence in criminal trials. A protocol to the European Convention on Human Rights prohibits capital punishment. It would nevertheless be wrong for the community of nations, even if licensed by the Security Council and likely to be successful, to march into any nation to establish equal pay for women or more adequate primary schools or to invade Florida to shut down its gas chambers or establish gay marriage there. Economic or military sanctions that inevitably inflict great suffering—most often on the most vulnerable members of the target state—are justified only to stop truly barbaric acts: mass killing or jailing or torturing of political opponents or widespread and savage discrimination.

If you are drawn to the trump-over-sovereignty classification, you might respond to that objection by insisting that the human rights conventions have greatly inflated the category of human rights: that only rights whose violation would be truly barbaric should count in that category, that the rest should be downgraded to some different category. That would seem a shame, however, because it has proved valuable, for international political activists and organizations and, particularly, domestic and international courts developing international customary law, to treat the large variety of rights designated in such documents as having the kind of universal authority the idea of human rights suggests. If we shrunk the category, we would have to invent a new one for rights suitable for recognition and enforcement in those other contexts. It would be better, therefore, to use a more encompassing classification; this need not require us to recognize all the rights set out in the more extravagant conventions, but it should at least explain why nations and groups have been tempted to include such rights.

Other writers have tried a different way to mark off human rights from other political rights: focusing not on the force of human rights to license sanctions but on their substantive content. They seek formulas that show why human rights are in some way particularly important among political rights. These formulas have proved elusive, however, because it has proved difficult to frame a distinction in that way. All political rights are particularly important. If I think that a state denies equal concern, on the right conception of that requirement, because it does not sufficiently redistribute the economic result of free-market transactions to its poor, then I think it denies some people the lives they are entitled to have. It condemns some of them to unjust poverty. What could be more fundamental or important than that? How could we identify, in demarcating human rights, a more fundamental level of support than what people's dignity requires? As that question suggests, scholarly attempts to define some more fundamental and more sternly required level have proved arbitrary.[5]

I suggest a different strategy, one based on the distinction I introduced in our discussion of legitimacy in Chapter 14. We disagree, across nations and among ourselves, about what political rights people have. We disagree, as we just noticed, about what economic system the right conception of equal respect requires. We also disagree about what counts as the proper respect for people's individual ethical responsibility: some nations make a particular religion the official religion of the state, while others, including the United States, regard religious establishment as unconstitutional. We disagree about political rights in countless other ways as well. We must therefore insist that though people do have a political right to equal concern and respect on the right conception, they have a more fundamental, because more abstract, right. They have a right to be treated with the attitude that these debates presuppose and reflect—a right to be treated *as* a human being whose dignity fundamentally matters.

That more abstract right—the right to an attitude—is the basic human right. Government may respect that basic human right even when it fails to achieve a correct understanding of more concrete political rights—even when its tax structure is, as we think, unjust. We distinguish and deploy that basic human right through the interpretive question described in our discussion of legitimacy. We ask: Can the laws and policies of a particular political community sensibly be interpreted as an attempt, even if finally a failed attempt, to respect the dignity of those in its power? Or must at least some of its laws and policies be understood as a rejection of those responsibilities, toward either its subjects at large or some group within them? The latter laws or policies violate a human right.

That distinction between human rights and other political rights is of great practical importance and theoretical significance. It is the distinction between mistake and contempt. The test, I emphasize, is interpretive; it cannot be satisfied simply by a nation's pronouncement of good faith. It is satisfied only when a government's overall behavior is defensible under an intelligible, even if unconvincing, conception of what our two principles of dignity require. Nations and lawyers will of course disagree even about how and where that line should be drawn. But some judgments—those that match the world's consensus about the most basic human rights—will be obvious.[6] Nothing could be a plainer violation of the first principle of dignity than acts that exhibit blatant prejudice—assumptions of supposed superiority of one caste over another or of believers over infidels or Aryans over Semites or whites over blacks. These are the attitudes most horribly evident in genocide. Sometimes the contempt is more personal: people in power sometimes humiliate, rape, or torture their victims just as a demonstration of contempt or, what comes to the same thing, just for amusement. No nation that supposes that some people are of inferior stock or that condones humiliation and torture for amusement can claim that it embraces an intelligible conception of human dignity.

Now look quickly at the second principle: that individuals have a personal responsibility to define success in their own lives. That principle supports the traditional liberal rights of free speech and expression, conscience, political activity, and religion that most human rights documents include. Different nations and cultures take different views about how those liberal rights should be defined and protected in detail. Societies also differ about what we might call surface paternalism. Most of us think that compulsory education until late adolescence and mandatory seat belts are permissible forms of paternalism, because the first unqualifiedly enhances rather than diminishes a person's capacity to take charge of his own life and the second helps people achieve what they actually want in spite of moments of acknowledged weakness. Some societies indulge more serious paternalism, but they do not violate human rights unless that level of interference could not plausibly be understood in one of these ways. Different political cultures, we might say, take different views about how the personal responsibility of individuals is to be protected.

But once again some acts of government express not a good-faith effort to define and enforce that responsibility but rather a denial of personal responsibility altogether. Governments that forbid the exercise of any but a designated religion or that punish heresy or blasphemy or deny in principle the right of free speech or of the press violate human rights for that reason. So do governments that intimidate or kill or torture people because they hate or fear their political opinions. The right not to be tortured has long been thought the paradigm human right, first on everyone's list. Offering inducements like a reduced sentence to an accused criminal in exchange for information, however objectionable it might seem on other grounds, leaves a prisoner's ability intact to weigh costs and consequences. As I said in Chapter 10, torture is designed to extinguish that power, to reduce its victim to an animal for whom decision is no longer possible. That is the most profound insult to his dignity as conceived in our two principles. It is the most profound outrage to his human rights.

The case for other human rights on this test is equally compelling. Respect for the importance of any life forbids harming (as distinct from failing to aid) some people for the benefit of others. It is therefore a violation of human rights deliberately to punish people who have committed no crime, even when this is supposedly for the general good; it is also flatly inconsistent with human rights to punish except through procedures reasonably well calculated to protect the innocent. It is controversial which form of trial, subject to which procedures and safeguards, is necessary, but it is not controversial that some form of trial is required, and imprisonment without trial is therefore a violation of a human right. Some forms of paternalism are at least arguably consistent with personal responsibility, as I said. But in our age, laws that forbid property, profession, or political power to women cannot be reconciled with women's responsibility for their own destiny. These are the clear, indisputable cases. Some such acts may be sufficiently serious as to require formal economic and even, if barbaric, military intervention, provided the two crucial conditions I described earlier are met. In less grave and more controversial cases the proper forum of enforcement is not an economic or military battleground but the chambers of international courts and tribunals that rely on treaties, international law, or more informal international pressure to secure compliance.

This understanding of human rights helps explain the abstract character of the human rights treaties and documents I mentioned earlier. The preamble to the Universal Declaration begins with a reference to the "inherent dignity . . . of all members of the human family," and many of the rights it specifies seem simply to restate that perfectly abstract idea. Even the relatively concrete provisions—about education, work, and equal pay, for instance—require interpretation aimed at limiting their scope before they become applicable in practice. We should understand these provisions and comparable provisions in other treaties and documents not as attempts to define human rights in any detail but rather as directions pointing to sensitive areas in which a nation's practices might well reveal the unacceptable attitude that violates the basic human right. They invite interpretive questions. Does a nation's record of regulation of political speech or journalism, or its provision of health care or public education, or its broad economic policy, show a good-faith attempt to respect the dignity called for in the Declaration's preamble? Or does it rather show an indifference to or contempt for that dignity? In the latter case, the Declaration declares, that nation has violated a human right. On this understanding human rights treaties and conventions pose questions that await interpretive answers.

Our understanding is also helpful in answering a familiar question of human rights theory. Are human rights truly universal? Or is any list only parochial? Do human rights depend on features of local culture or history that universal declarations ignore? Or are some human rights, at least, independent of such circumstance? We answer each of these questions: yes and no. The interpretive judgment must in its nature be sensitive to different economic conditions and political and cultural profiles and histories. It must be sensitive to such differences because these plainly affect which of the available interpretations—an effort to realize equal concern and respect or indifference to these ideals—is more accurate, all things considered. A health or education policy that would show good-faith effort in a poor country would show contempt in a rich one. But the abstract standard itself—the basic understanding that dignity requires equal concern for the fate of all and full respect for personal responsibility—is not relative. It is genuinely universal.

I do not mean that that abstract standard has been or is universally endorsed. On the contrary, it plainly has not and is not. But if we believe in human rights at all—or in any other rights, for that matter—we must take a stand on the true basis of such rights. My understanding of human dignity might be defective. You must judge for yourself and, if necessary, correct my account. But unless you are tempted by a global skepticism about human and political rights, you must find a basis for such rights in some formulation of that kind, and you must embrace that formulation not because you find it embedded in some culture or shared by all or most nations but because you believe it to be true. You must make applications of your basic premise sensitive to a variety of circumstance that vary across regions and nations. But your judgments must be grounded finally in something that is not relative: your judgment about the conditions of human dignity and the threats that coercive power offers to that dignity.

You might worry that it is both arrogant and impolitic to claim absolute truth as the basis of a theory of human rights. One critic calls my account of dignity "theological or dogmatic" and argues that because different cultures embrace different values, it is wrong to ground a theory of human rights on any single one of these.[7] But we must do that—not to prefer one culture to another, but to prefer truth as we judge it. We have no option. If we proceed in any other way—by seeking some common denominator across cultures, for instance—we still need a justification for picking that strategy, and our justification for that choice must claim not popularity but truth. An ecumenicist strategy, all the way down, is deep logical confusion.

No doubt we must take pluralism into account in deciding what account of human rights could possibly be agreed upon in treaties and enforced in practice. Perhaps—though this is far from evident—it would be wise tactics not to stress the principled foundations of our views when we know others would reject those foundations. But we need to know what we ourselves believe about human rights before we begin to negotiate or persuade. Otherwise we can have no proper aim in view.

Human Rights and Religion

Our practical and diplomatic difficulties have been pointlessly magnified, however, because so many people in Europe and America insist on connecting human rights with some religious tradition. If we insist that human rights have finally a religious source and ground, then our appeal to those rights will inflame people whose religious traditions and convictions are very different from our own, particularly those who believe that their religion commands the very acts that we decry and try to punish. If we insist that human rights rest on religion, we also confront a paradox in our own values. We believe that religious tolerance is among the most basic of human rights, and we therefore think that it violates people's rights to force upon them religious doctrines and practices that they do not accept. But is not that exactly what we do when our invading armies march under a banner of religious rhetoric?

The idea that generates these difficulties—that human rights have a religious foundation—is a very old one. Human rights are widely thought to descend from natural rights; these in turn were supposed to be deliverances of natural law, which, at least in the central expository tradition of that idea, was understood to be divine law. Thomas Jefferson may well have been an atheist—there is a dispute among historians about that—but he was only reporting received ideas and common rhetoric when he declared it self-evident that a human being is "endowed by his Creator with inalienable rights to life, liberty and the pursuit of happiness." Former president George W. Bush often announced that "freedom is God's gift to everyone," as if our freedom were an act of divine charity. The religious origin of human rights is even more manifest in Islamic countries. Article 24 of the 1990 Cairo Declaration of Human Rights, for example, states, "All rights and freedoms mentioned in this statement are subject to the Islamic Shari'a," and Article 25 adds, "The Islamic Shari'a is the only source for the interpretation or explanation of each individual article of this statement."

In fact, however, no divine authority can provide a ground for basic human rights. On the contrary, the logic of argument runs the other way: we must assume the independent and logically prior existence of human rights in order to accept the idea of divine moral authority. I assume no particular view about the existence or character of a god or gods in making that perhaps radical claim. I do not base my rejection of ungrounded divine authority on atheism or any other form of skepticism. In fact I shall assume, for the purpose of this chapter, that a single anthropomorphic god as conceived in traditional monotheistic religions has existed and will exist forever; that that god has created the universe and all forms of life in it; that he has in particular created human beings in his own image; that he is, moreover, an all-powerful creator and destroyer; and that he is all-knowing and all-foreseeing. I know that many people who regard themselves as religious do not accept this traditional picture. They express their faith differently and in my view more mysteriously: in the declarations I mentioned in Chapter 9 that the universe contains a higher force or that it houses something bigger than we are or that we can glimpse the divine nature only through a glass darkly and hence must not suppose an anthropomorphic god of which we are an image. But it will be easier for me to put the argument I intend if I assume a more traditional supernatural cosmology.

I said nothing about goodness or morality in that crude account of a god. I supposed that a god is an all-powerful creator, but that is not to say—or to deny—that that god is good. Or that he has moral authority, by which I mean that his commands impose genuine moral obligations. Of course, the Abrahamic religions attribute moral virtue and authority as well as omnipotence and omniscience to their god, but I mean to separate those these two components of an overall religious view. Religions commonly have two parts: cosmological and evaluative. First, they answer the question of what there is and why. How did the world and its parts, including life and human life, come to exist? What or who determines how the world will go? Is there a soul? If so, what happens to the soul after death? Second, religions also—but separately—answer the question of what there should be and why. What is right and what wrong? What is important and not important? What must I do with my life? When must I sacrifice it, for example? How must I treat other people? When, if ever, may or should I kill?

Many theologians and some philosophers find this distinction between two parts of a religion illegitimate. They think that goodness is an inherent quality of a god, so that imagining his extraordinary power without also imagining his goodness is impossible. Indeed, some versions of the still-robust ontological argument for a god's existence include goodness as a necessary property. But the ancient Greek conception of the gods was very different; this shows at least the conceptual possibility of separating omnipotence from goodness, and that is all I am assuming. Moreover, to repeat, I do not deny that the god I am assuming, the all-powerful and omniscient creature who has created everything, really is good, and that his commands do have moral authority. I only ask what the source of that goodness and moral authority is.

Hume's principle holds that these moral properties cannot follow directly from a god's omnipotence and omniscience: we cannot derive an ought from an is. You can sensibly declare that a god is good and that his commands should be obeyed only if you accept some further background premise about value on which you rely. You may suppose that a god created the universe and created you as well. You may suppose that he has issued commands like those of the Ten Commandments. But you cannot infer just from those facts that you have any moral reason to obey those commands or that the commands will conduce to a morally good state of affairs or, indeed, a state of affairs desirable in any other way. You need an additional premise to draw God's moral authority from his power and knowledge. Consider the analogy to governments. Terrestrial rulers are legitimate only if they satisfy certain procedural and substantive principles of legitimacy. That philosophical requirement holds for divine as well as mundane rule.

I am taking sides in an ancient theological controversy.[8] Is a god good because he obeys moral laws, or are certain laws moral laws only because a god had commanded them? This is sometimes presented as a dilemma. If a god is bound by moral laws, he is not all-powerful because he cannot change what is finally right or wrong, good or bad. If, on the other hand, his commands create morality, then he is good only in a trivial, tautological sense.

The dilemma is a false one: the proposition that someone's power is less than it might be because he cannot turn bad into good is just another way of violating Hume's principle. No exercise of creative power, however great, can shift fundamental moral truth. So the familiar idea that a god is the ultimate source of morality is confused: the old churchmen who said that his goodness reflects some independent moral law or truth had the better of the argument.

It does not follow, of course, that a god cannot have moral authority: that he cannot create genuine moral duties through his commands. Parliaments have no moral authority unless they act in accordance with fundamental principles of political morality, but they nevertheless can create new moral obligations when they do. I have a moral duty to pay taxes at a certain rate only because a parliament has declared that I must. So the fact that a god has no automatic moral authority does not refute the claim that he is responsible for human rights. These rights may be morally imperative only because a god has commanded us to respect them. If that is so, however, then it is because some more basic principle has endowed god with the moral authority to create new moral rights. What could that more basic principle be?

The god I am imagining, who has unlimited creative and destructive capacities, enjoys stick-and-carrot power over all human beings. He can send an AIDS epidemic to Greenwich Village to punish homosexuals or provide a battalion of virgins in heaven for murderous suicides. Many people credit their god's moral authority to these powers of punishment and reward. But threats and bribes do not supply legitimacy. Others credit their god's moral authority to the fact that he created them.[9] There is a widespread opinion that someone who created something—a sculptor who mixes his labor with a marble block—owns what he has created and therefore has moral authority, though no doubt limited, over what happens to it. But blocks of marble have no moral duty to obey their creator, and people are in any case not blocks of marble. Children do owe duties to their parents, and these include, though only for a limited time, some limited obligation to do what their parents direct. But so far as this authority includes the power to create moral obligation—an obligation to participate in some joint family project, for instance—it depends on a host of social practices and understandings of the kind we reviewed in the last chapter. Parental authority does not in any case stem from mere creation: adoptive parents have the same moral authority as biological ones. If God has the authority to create fresh moral obligations, this must be in consequence of some principle different from John Locke's theory of property.

It may now be objected, by people whose religion is instinctive, that we do not need to find any principle that gives a god moral authority over us. It is enough to say that his authority is just a moral fact we perceive or intuit as an act of faith. That would not be to lapse back into the tautology that whatever a god does is by definition good. We might concede that his goodness is substantive but still insist that we can perceive or intuit his moral authority directly, as a brute moral fact, just as many people insist that they perceive or intuit his existence and power as brute facts. This claim neglects, however, the crucial difference between the domains of fact and value that we have now several times noticed.

A god's existence and achievements, if any god does exist, are matters of fact, albeit rather special and exotic facts. Any god's moral authority, if this exists, is a matter of value. Claims of fact can be barely true: the kind of god I am imagining might exist, not in virtue of any law of nature but just as an independent brute fact. The world of value is different: nothing is barely true there. Something can be right or wrong only in virtue of a principle that ramifies across a whole terrain of morality. It cannot be a bare moral fact, one we can just intuit, that genocide is wrong or that poor people in an affluent society have a right to basic medical care. We cannot be right or wrong about those claims without also and in consequence being right or wrong about a great deal else. We may be ignorant of the principles in virtue of which an omnipotent and omniscient being has moral authority over us. But if we believe that he does have that moral authority, we must also accept that some principled account of that authority can, in principle, be constructed. This is just to repeat, in this rarefied context, the lessons of Part One and of Chapter 7.

The arguments for a god's moral authority we have been reviewing to this point all begin in some fact that makes a god unique: his power to impose punishments or grant favors, his role as creator of the universe, or the special epistemic power of religious faith. We need a very different argument: one that focuses not on the uniqueness of some supernatural creature but on the general conditions of moral authority, conditions that hold even in less exalted contexts of power. We are then immediately back in familiar terrain. Political rulers claim moral authority: they claim the power to impose fresh moral obligations on those subject to their dominion through legislation and decree. But we do not recognize that moral authority unless the rulers' governance is legitimate, and we do not accept government as legitimate unless it treats those over whom it claims moral authority with the right attitude. It must show equal concern for the importance of their lives, and it must allow each of them responsibility for his own life. If we claim that a god has moral authority over all peoples, then we must suppose an equal divine concern and respect for all peoples. The idea popular in some religions, that their god cares only or mainly for subscribers to their religion or for the particular ethnic stock of its faithful, subverts the claim of that religion to their god's moral authority.

We must, I said, stand on our own convictions, here as everywhere in the domain of value. We must insist, with due courtesy and after full reflection, that we are right. But we must not appeal to our religion or our god as proof of that claim. We may, if so persuaded, treat our god as a moral legislator on less fundamental issues: on elements of our ethics or personal or even political morality. We may come to think that a god's declaration makes some ethical ideal, some theory about how to live, true. But we cannot, without disabling circularity, treat any god as the source of the most fundamental part of our political morality: our convictions about legitimacy or about human rights.

My argument does not denigrate religion, which has been a remarkable force for good as well as evil over human history. Though the evil may be more prominent in our minds right now, fixed by terror and bigotry, history is too complex to allow that as the final word. My aim has rather been to place the case for human rights on a different plane. We need not rely on our own religion, leaving those of other faiths behind, when we argue for the innate rights of all human beings. We can argue not from what divides us but from what unites us. We all—Muslim, Jew, or Christian, atheist or zealot—face the same inescapable challenge of a life to lead, death to face, and dignity to redeem.

Concepts

Criterial Error

We have found our two principles of dignity at the end of many brick roads—personal ethics, personal morality, political legitimacy, political rights, and human rights. Now we unwind these principles further to explore equality and liberty, the two interpretive concepts that dominate politics and political philosophy. I understand liberty to include both negative and positive liberty, and I therefore count the concept of democracy as part of this study. We disagree about what those concepts really mean: about what genuine democracy, political equality, and negative liberty really are. Those are topics for the following three chapters. I use a short advance summary here—which looks back to Chapter 8 and anticipates later arguments of this Part Five—to show why it is so important to understand that these are interpretive concepts. Much energy has been wasted by the defeating assumption that liberty, equality, and democracy are criterial concepts that can be explicated through some neutral analysis that makes no assumption about their value or importance. These efforts have each ended in paradox.

Liberty

Consider, for example, John Stuart Mill's classic account of liberty: this is the freedom, he said, to do what one wants. If that is what liberty is, then of course any government must constantly abridge liberty; it does so when it prohibits rape or arson. But we are then confronted with a dilemma. It is necessary to make arson and rape criminal, but do we nevertheless commit a special kind of wrong, a compromise of an important value, when we do so? If we think not then, because we have defined liberty so that these laws infringe liberty, we do not really value liberty for its own sake or take liberty as such to be essential to dignity. We only value something else often associated with liberty. But what is that something else? It does not help to say that we value only fundamental liberty. We must explain what makes one liberty more fundamental than another, and we cannot explain that by supposing that some commodity we name liberty is more at stake when a fundamental liberty is in question.

Suppose, on the other hand, we insist that it is in itself a special kind of wrong to stop people from doing what they want to do—in itself bad to stop some people from raping others—even when this wrong is overall justified. We then need to say why. If we are utilitarians, as Mill was, we might think that any constraint that causes unhappiness or frustration is harmful, and therefore an occasion for regret, even when necessary. But that strategy does not show that stopping someone from doing what he wants is a special kind of harm; it simply counts any unhappiness it causes in the cost column of a felicific calculus, along with other, very different, sources of unhappiness, like government's failure to provide air conditioning in public buildings. It makes liberty into nothing special.

We cannot say that preventing rape is a special kind of harm because any constraint on freedom is an insult to dignity. If the argument of Chapter 14 about political obligation is right, a legitimate government does not compromise dignity when it acts to protect some citizens from the violence of others. If we did think that every prohibition of crime automatically compromises dignity, then we would have to treat much of what government now does as gravely wrong. My town council could not fairly stop me from painting my Georgian house purple. It could hardly claim that this constraint is necessary to protect the safety or freedom of others, so it would be sacrificing my dignity to mere aesthetics.

Equality

Treating equality as a criterial concept has been at least equally unfortunate. It encourages the dismissive view that equality means *flat* equality—everyone having the same wealth throughout their lives—because no other definition is plausible if we take equality to be criterial.[10] It is now respectable even among liberals to say that equality is a false value because what is important is not that people have equal wealth but that those at the bottom not have less than is necessary for a decent life, or to avoid great inequality, or something of the sort. That view has been encouraged by a dispute sparked by John Rawls's account of distributive justice. His "difference principle" requires that any deviation from flat equality of "primary goods" be such as to improve the position of the worst-off group.[11] In some circumstances that principle would justify offering people with wealth-producing talents high incomes as an incentive to exercise those talents, because that would make everyone, including the poor, better off. Some critics object that the difference principle is insufficiently egalitarian. For a variety of social and personal reasons, they declare, it is better that everyone has the same wealth, and so share a common fate, than that some be rich and others poor, even if everyone then has less material wealth.[12]

But other, more numerous, critics declare the difference principle too egalitarian because it restricts its focus to the worst-off group: it would be better, they say, to settle for what many of them term a less rigid "priority" for the poor.[13] In general, they say, policy should favor those at the bottom. But suppose a community must choose between an economic strategy that would bring much greater wealth to the large middle and lower-middle classes and a different strategy that would instead make a small poorest group marginally less poor. It would be silly, these critics insist, to choose the latter strategy. Or, at least, silly unless the difference the latter policy made to the condition of the poor transformed their lives rather than making only a notional improvement. Still other critics reject even this apparently moderate position. They declare equality a demeaning goal and argue that a political community must put its faith in liberty. Some of them announce a further, though by now discredited, faith: that incentives for the talented will produce enough wealth so that some "trickles down" to the poor.[14] Others simply say, or at least believe, that the poor should look after themselves.

The argument among these various opinions is spoilt by the assumption that when we debate how important equality is, or when it should yield to other values like prosperity for the middle classes, we are debating how important it is that everyone have the same thing. We then face difficulties like those created by the supposedly neutral sense of liberty. Is equality, so understood, a value in itself? Is it intrinsically good that different people have the same wealth, so that any deviation from flat equality is regrettable even if it is justified by some overriding consideration like economic rationality? That seems implausible. Why is it desirable that people should have the same wealth, when some spend while others save, or when some work and others play?

We may decide, for these reasons, that flat equality is not in itself of any moral significance. Then why should we debate how far we should strive to approach that goal? Why should we then suppose, for example, as Rawls does, that deviations from flat equality need special justification? But if, on the other hand, we decide that flat equality of wealth is indeed good in itself, then why should that value be compromised at all? If at all, when? What competitive value requires that compromise and measures the desired extent? How should we decide whether it is better overall to have less of the intrinsic value of equality so that the middle class can be more prosperous, for instance? From what neutral perspective or metric can we make and defend that judgment? Again, nothing seems available except a sterile clash of "intuitions."

Democracy

The debate about democracy—equality in the political sphere—has suffered in the same way. Philosophers and political scientists have gravitated to a supposedly neutral account of democracy: democracy is government according to the will of the majority expressed in reasonably frequent elections with nearly full suffrage after political debate with free speech and a free press. With some such definition in hand, lawyers and politicians argue about whether the American practice of judicial review (now emulated to a greater or lesser extent in many other nations) can be justified. Under that practice, a court—finally, in America, the Supreme Court—can rule that a law adopted by a parliament that represents majority will is nevertheless so offensive to fundamental constitutional rights that it has no legal effect. Some lawyers and philosophers condemn the practice as offensive to democracy. Others defend it on the ground that while democracy is important, it is not the only value and must sometimes be compromised to serve other values like human rights.

Once again this approach produces only dilemma: we encounter the same, now familiar, problem. Is democracy, understood as majority rule, something valuable in itself? That seems at least doubtful. Why should the fact that numerically more people favor one course of action over another signal that the more favored policy is either fairer or better? We might say: when people locked in a joint enterprise disagree about what should be done, the only fair solution is to count heads. But that must be rejected as a universal default principle of fair play: it is not automatically true. Another hoary philosophical example: When a lifeboat is overcrowded and one passenger must go overboard to save the rest, majority vote would seem close to the worst method of choosing the victim. Personal attachments and antagonisms would play a role they should not play, and so a lottery would be much superior. Those attachments and antagonisms spoil politics as well, but on a much larger scale, and this makes the idea that majority vote is intrinsically or automatically fair in that context seem at least dubious.

But if democracy means majority rule, and majority rule is not something desirable in itself, then why should we care so much to protect our democracy? Or to expand democracy in other countries through any means we can adopt? Why do we argue so much about whether judicial review is democratic or whether replacing our first-past-the-post election machinery with proportional representation would make us more democratic? In these and a hundred other ways we do treat democracy as a value, and accepting that it is not—that there is nothing intrinsically good about it—would make much of our political life silly.

A Better Program

There is nothing to be said for the standard definitions of equality, liberty, and democracy proposed by Mill, Rawls, and most political scientists. They do not track the criteria everyone uses when he identifies egalitarian policies, liberal societies, or democratic institutions. There are no such shared criteria; if there were, we would not argue in the way we do. Some philosophers who assume that all concepts are criterial conclude that the failure of agreement makes the concepts useless and that we should manage without them. We should ask not what is democratic but what system of government is better on the whole; not whether equality or liberty is good but what distribution of resources or opportunities is best. This reductive approach is deceptive, however. It is appropriate only for those who already hold some theory, like the more fantastic versions of utilitarianism, that offer a single factual metric of political value against which all policies and institutions can be tested. Without such a fantasy we are left with no rudder in the current. How do we even begin to decide what form of government or distribution of resource is better, if we have no background ideals to guide us?

We do better when we accept that the familiar concepts of political virtue are interpretive concepts. Then we understand why they are so prominent in the politics of nations whose political cultures were dramatically reformed in the Enlightenment. We understand why the defining revolutions of those nations were explicitly dedicated to liberty, equality, and democracy and yet settled very little about what these actually mean. We also understand how we should proceed to develop our own conceptions of these values: our own convictions about the concrete political rights they name. The proper distribution of wealth into private and collective property is the distribution required by the community's obligation to treat the lives of every member with equal concern. For a community that accepts the first principle of dignity, a theory of economic equality just is a theory of distributive justice: the two concepts are identical. For a community that accepts the second principle, a conception of liberty must show the proper respect for the responsibility of each person to identify and pursue success in his own life. A conception of liberty includes a conception of that responsibility. In such a community, the distribution of political power must reflect both these principles: the structure and decisions of government must acknowledge both people's equal importance and their personal responsibility. A conception of democracy is a conception of how that challenge is best met through political structures and practices. Because we aim to interpret our two principles as mutually supporting, not conflicting, we must try to develop conceptions of equality, liberty, and democracy that support one another as well.

This strategy for studying political rights is strikingly different from what is often called the historical approach. Many philosophers—Isaiah Berlin and Bernard Williams were prominent recent examples—have argued that we cannot appreciate the character or force of a political concept like liberty until we have gained a sense through history of what it meant to our political predecessors.[15] In one sense the project I recommend is historical: it is right to treat liberty, equality, and democracy as interpretive concepts only if those concepts function as interpretive, and the question whether they do has a historical dimension. In that way interpretation engages history, but history does not fix interpretation.

I do not mean that a concept is interpretive only if those who use it understand that it is interpretive. As I said earlier, very few people have the concept of a concept, let alone the concept of an interpretive concept. I mean that we must be able to make best sense of the concept's use over history—best sense of the ways in which people take themselves to be agreeing and disagreeing— by supposing that it is interpretive. If the great political concepts are indeed interpretive, however, then history is no privileged guide to their best interpretation. The fact that throughout modern history many people have supposed that taxes infringe liberty or that democracy means absolute majority rule does not mean that an interpretation that denies this is false. They may have been—I think they were—mistaken. Perhaps those philosophers who believe that a study of these concepts must be densely historical have simply assumed that the concepts are criterial. If so, it is their approach, not the one I recommend, that is unhistorical.

16

Equality

Philosophy and Shame

Poverty makes an odd subject for reflective philosophy; it seems fit only for outrage and struggle. In most of the rich countries the distance between the comfortable and the poor is unconscionably great; in some, including the United States, the distance increases relentlessly. In these circumstances academic political philosophy must seem artificial and self-indulgent. Theories of distributive justice almost inevitably urge radical reform in the advanced capitalist communities in which they are most avidly studied. But the practical possibility of anything like the reform they recommend is remote. Left-of-center politicians struggle, with at most moderate success, to achieve incremental gains for those at the bottom, and the best politics is politics that does not ask more than the comfortable majority is willing to give. The gap between theory and politics is particularly great and depressing in racially or ethnically diverse communities; majorities continue to be reluctant to help poor people who are markedly different from them.[1] It is nevertheless important to continue to trouble the comfortable with argument, especially when, as I believe is now the case, their selfishness impairs the legitimacy of the politics that makes them comfortable. At a minimum they must not be allowed to think that they have justification as well as selfishness on their side.

Theories of distributive justice are highly artificial in a further and different way. They rely heavily on the furniture of fantasy: fictitious ancient contracts, negotiations among amnesiacs, insurance policies that will never be written or sold. John Rawls imagines people negotiating terms of an original political constitution behind an opaque curtain that hides from each what he really is, thinks, and wants. I imagine desert-island auctions that might take months to complete. This second kind of artificiality is inevitable, however. If we are to reject politics as the final arbiter of justice, we must supply something else to define what justice requires, some other way of showing what equal concern and respect really do demand. Given our complex and deeply unfair economic structure, with its own dense history, it is difficult to do this without heroically counterfactual exercises.

It would be worse than pointless, however, for political philosophers to describe angelic societies that actual human beings could not even approach. Or to suppose that our own communities could be improved only by an actual completely fresh start: by a voluntary return to a state of nature or an isolated island with convenient veils or bidding chips at hand. A useful theory of distributive justice must show which of the minimal steps we can actually take now are steps in the right direction.[2] If philosophers build ivory towers, they must set some Rapunzel at the top so that we can, slowly, climb higher. The economist Amartya Sen has criticized what he calls the "transcendentalist" theories of justice offered by Rawls and others, including me, for their exclusive concern with "one-shot" achievements of perfection and their corresponding neglect of comparative judgments of actual political systems. His criticism is unfounded, but it would be damning if accurate.[3]

False Conceptions

Laissez-faire

Coercive government is legitimate only when it attempts to show equal concern for the fates of all those it governs and full respect for their personal responsibility for their own lives. (Edwin Baker had reservations about this claim even at that abstract level.[4]) Because we know that moral truth cannot be bare truth, we must seek an interpretation of those two demands that produces not conflict but mutual reinforcement. One interpretation of the first requirement is popular among political conservatives and would indeed avoid conflict. This denies that the distribution of material resources is a proper function of government at all. On this view, government treats people with equal concern simply by allowing them all the freedom they need to work, buy and sell, save or spend, as they themselves can and think best. Their wealth would then be very unequal, because some people are much more talented in production and management than others, wiser in investment and more frugal in spending, and some inevitably have better luck than others. But that is not the doing of government and therefore cannot be taken to signal any lack of equal concern for those who fail, any more than the fact that most runners lose a race signals a lack of concern for the losers by the race organizers.

This popular argument is silly because it assumes that government can be neutral about the results of the economic race. In fact, everything the government of a large political community does—or does not do—affects the resources that each of its citizens has and the success he achieves. Of course, his resources and success are also a function of many other variables, including his physical and mental abilities, his past choices, his luck, the attitudes of others toward him, and his power or desire to produce what others want. We might call these his personal economic variables. But the impact of these personal variables on his actual resources and opportunities must in every case also depend on the political variables: on the laws and policies of the communities in which he lives or works.

A community's laws and policies constitute its political settlement. Tax laws are of course central to a political settlement, but every other part of the law belongs to that settlement as well: fiscal and monetary policy, labor law, environmental law and policy, urban planning, foreign policy, health care policy, transportation policy, drug and food regulation, and everything else. Changing any of these policies or laws changes the distribution of personal wealth and opportunity in the community, given the same choices, luck, capacities, and other personal variables of each person. So we cannot avoid the challenge of equal concern by arguing that the resources an individual has depend on his choices, not government's choices. They depend on both. The political settlement, which is under the community's control, fixes the opportunities and consequences of choice for each individual for each of the sets of choices about education, training, employment, investment, production, and leisure he might make, and for each of the events of good or bad luck he might encounter. It is a clumsy evasion to say that a laissez-faire policy, which simply means one set of laws rather than another, is not the act of government.

The footrace analogy reveals the weakness of the claim that government can be neutral about distribution. Properly designed races are not neutral: they are rigged so that people with particular skills are more likely to win. That kind of rigging is not bias; it treats people as equals because they are assumed to share that sense of the purpose of the enterprise. But the point of living together in legitimate political communities subject to the principles of dignity is not to identify and reward any particular set of skills, qualities, or luck, so laws that will predictably have that result may well be biased.

Utility

That observation might suggest a different strategy for defending laissez-faire government, however. On this view, the point of government is to identify and reward productive skill, not as an end in itself but in order to make the community more prosperous overall. We can put that claim more formally in the vocabulary of utilitarianism: we treat each person as an equal by valuing his pleasure (or happiness or welfare or success) equally in choosing policies that will increase the aggregate of pleasure (or one of those other commodities) in the community as a whole. Utilitarianism has been and remains an influential position in political theory. But it offers an unpersuasive interpretation of equal concern. Parents would not show equal concern for all their children if they spent their entire available budget educating only those who were likely to earn heavily in the market. That would not treat the success of each child's life as equally important. Concern for a large group of persons is not the same thing as concern for its members one by one. Yes, an aggregation strategy values happiness or welfare or some other interpretation of utility, no matter in which person it resides. But that is concern for a commodity, not for a person.

Welfare

These two responses to the challenge of equal concern—that the distribution of resources is not the business of government, and that government's goal should be to maximize some aggregate good—have at least this virtue: they recommend policies that respect people's individual responsibility for their own lives. But neither offers a reasonable conception of what it is to treat people with equal concern. Now we should notice a group of theories that fail in the opposite way. These aim to make people equal in welfare or well-being or capability according to some conception of what counts as well-being or what opportunities or capabilities are important.

They aim, for example, at making people equally happy or giving priority to the least happy, all as tested by some happiness Geiger counter. Or they aim to make people equally successful in their own lights. Or equal in their opportunities for achieving happiness or well-being.[5] Or equal in their over-all capabilities.[6] But people disagree about what happiness is, and they value happiness differently; some are ready, even anxious, to sacrifice happiness for other goals. They also disagree in their views about what makes their lives successful: some have much more ambitious—and expensive—plans than others. So they also differ, for both these reasons, in their view about what they need by way of opportunities to be happy or what capabilities are more important than others. If a community set out to make people equal in any of these welfare commodities, then it would necessarily be imposing on everyone its collective judgment of what lives are good and how to live well. It would annihilate personal responsibility even more fundamentally in another way, moreover: it would aim to insure that people were equal in the designated welfare commodity, no matter what choices they had made or risks they had run. Personal responsibility would count for almost nothing.

We must try to avoid both these errors: we need a theory of distributive justice that satisfies both our two principles. The welfare-based theories of the last paragraph show that we can do that only if we choose, as our basic metric, not people's happiness or opportunities or capabilities for achieving happiness but some test for equality that is as shorn of assumptions about welfare or well-being as possible. We must concentrate on resources, not welfare, and we must distinguish between personal and impersonal resources. Someone's personal resources are his physical and mental capacities; his impersonal resources consist in his wealth, measured as abstractly as possible. Only impersonal resources can be measured without welfare assumptions, and only these can be distributed through economic transactions and redistributed through taxation or other government programs. We must aim, as a first approximation, to make members of our political community equal in those material resources. That goal might seem perverse, because it aims to make people equal in what they value only as a means.[7] Reasonable people want resources not for their own sake but to make their lives better or better lived.

But that is the point. A community that respects personal ethical responsibility must concentrate on a fair distribution of means when it fixes its political settlement. It must leave the choice of ends to its citizens one by one.[8]

Equality of Resources

The Envy Test

What political settlement, seeking what distribution of resources, fits our two principles taken together? I have proposed a fantasy answer.[9] Imagine people shipwrecked on an empty island with diverse natural resources. They are each given an equal number of clamshells as bidding tokens, and they compete in an auction for individual ownership of the island's resources. When the auction finally ends, and everyone is satisfied that he has used his clamshells most efficiently, the following "envy" test will necessarily be satisfied. No one will want to trade his bundle of resources for anyone else's bundle, because he could have had that other bundle in place of his own if he had so wanted. Because the result is an envy-free distribution in that sense, the strategy treats everyone with equal concern. Each person understands that his situation reflects that equal concern: his wealth is a function of what others want as well as what he wants. The strategy also respects the personal responsibility of each bidder for his own values. He uses his clamshells to acquire the resources that he deems best suited to the life he deems best. He is limited, in designing that life, by what he discovers are the choices of others, and therefore of what he can have available for whatever life he designs. His choices are not limited by any collective judgments about what is important in life, but only by the true opportunity costs to others of what he chooses. (I discuss the nature of true opportunity costs and their role in establishing a theory of justice, together with Samuel Freeman's comments on that role, in a note.[10])

The fantasy distribution respects both our principles: it provides attractive conceptions of both equal concern and full respect. But you and I are not shipwrecked passengers on a newly discovered and abundantly stocked island. How far and in what way can we be guided by the fantasy in the very different situation of modern economies? The story has an immediate negative lesson. A command or socialist economy in which prices, wages, and production are set collectively by officials would be a very imperfect realization of our values. The decisions of a command economy are collective: they reflect a collective decision about what ambitions, and hence which resources, are best suited to a good life. A free market is not equality's enemy, as is often supposed, but indispensable to genuine equality. An egalitarian economy is a basically capitalist economy.

That bald claim must, however, quickly be qualified in two crucial ways. First, it is essential to the justice of the island auction that the price someone pays for what he acquires reflects the true opportunity cost to others of his acquiring it, but actual markets in capitalist economies are often corrupted in ways that defeat that condition. Regulation is therefore often needed to perfect the freedom or efficiency of a market: to protect it against distortions of monopoly or externality. These distortions include (as we have recently come to learn) exaggerated risk in search of exaggerated profit when the risk falls largely on those who took no part in the decision and would have little share in any gain. Climate impact is another important example of distortion: because the market cannot easily be structured to reflect the opportunity costs of energy consumption now to future generations, extra-market regulation seems necessary. These adjustments to a free market do not contradict the spirit of this understanding of equal concern; on the contrary, they enforce that understanding by better matching people's resources to the true opportunity cost of what they do or consume.

The second qualification is very different and must occupy us at some length. The fantasy auction scheme shows equal concern, I said, because the result satisfies the envy test I described. What each islander has is fixed by his own choices, given the choices others make from an equal base. When the auction is finally over, however, and the islanders begin their economic lives, the envy test soon fails. They plant, manufacture, and consume using the resources they acquired in the auction, and they enter into transactions with one another, each trading to improve his situation. Some of the differences this activity generates reflect their choices—to consume rather than save, to rest rather than work, or to produce poetry that others do not much want rather than corn, which is popular. The envy test is still met in spite of these differences if we apply that test over time: people's resources continue to be sensitive to their choices. But other differences do corrupt the envy test. Some islanders do not have much talent to produce what the markets value, or they fall sick, or they make responsible investments that nevertheless fail. They then have fewer resources with which to build a life, not as a consequence of, but in spite of, the choices they have made. Now the envy test fails because their resources do not depend, after all, only on their choices. The market is no longer egalitarian.

Ex Ante or Ex Post?

How should we respond? Runners in a fair race are equally placed, all at the starting line, before the race begins. They are ex ante equal. But they are not equally placed after the race has been run: ex post one has beaten the others. Which is the right temporal focus for justice? Does equal respect require trying to satisfy the envy test, so far as we can, ex ante, before the impact of transactions and luck? Or ex post, after those events have run their course? A government committed to ex post equality undertakes, so far as this is possible, to bring citizens who lack market skills to the same economic level as those with more skills and to restore those who have fallen ill or suffered handicaps to the position they would otherwise have occupied. A government that aims at ex ante equality, on the other hand, responds differently. It aims that its citizens face these contingencies in an equal position; in particular, that they have an opportunity to buy appropriate insurance against low productive talent or bad luck on equal terms.

At first blush ex post compensation might seem the more appropriate goal. People who are unemployed or who are badly injured or crippled and who receive only what an insurance policy might pay by way of compensation remain in a much worse position than others. Insurance payments typically do not compensate fully, and for some instances of bad luck—terrible physical disability—they fall sickeningly short of restoring people to their prior position. So long as the community can improve the situation of someone who has been a victim of bad luck, then equal concern might seem to require that it do that. In fact, however, the ex post approach, even so far as it is possible, is a very poor understanding of equal concern. The ex ante approach is better.

Investment luck, very broadly understood, is an important reason why people's income and wealth differ. You and I study financial charts with equal care and make equally intelligent though different choices. Your stocks thrive and mine wither; you are rich and I am poor and this is only because your luck has been better than mine. But if our political community undertook to erase this consequence of luck, it would undermine the responsibility each of us exercised; if it made our investment choices pointless in that way, we would cease to invest. Many of the most important decisions we make are also investment decisions whose consequences turn on luck: any educational or training decision might be undermined by unforeseeable technological shifts that make our particular training useless, for instance. If the community aimed to insure that our fate in no way depended on how any such investment gambles fare—if it guaranteed that we are equal in wealth, whether or not our choice of career turned out to be suited to our tastes or talents or market conditions—it would end by crippling our own responsibility for our choices. So any plausible version of an ex post approach would have to draw a distinction between investment and other forms of luck and rule out the former as a ground for redistribution.

That distinction would be difficult to draw. But ex post compensation would be not a reasonable goal, even if restricted to noninvestment luck. Any community that undertook to spend all it could to improve the position of its blind or crippled members, for example, until further expenditure would not even marginally benefit them, would have nothing left to spend on anything else, and the lives of all other citizens would be miserable in consequence.[11] That policy would reflect no one's actual priorities, including the antecedent priorities of the victims of terrible accidents. If the choice had been up to them before they were injured, they would not have spent everything they had to buy the best possible accident insurance policy, because they would not have thought, given the odds, that it made sense to compromise their lives in every other respect to secure the most expensive possible insurance. The ex post compensation approach to bad luck is irrational.

It remains wrong even if we apply it to erase the consequences, not of bad luck as ordinarily understood, but only of the bad genetic luck of not having talents prized in the contemporary market. If the community restores people to a condition of equal wealth, no matter what choices they make about work and consumption, then, as I said, it destroys rather than respects this dimension of responsibility. But there is no way fully to erase the consequences of differences in talent without adopting that foolish remedy. It is impossible in principle, not simply practically impossible, to distinguish the consequences of choice and capacity across the range of economic decision, because preference and capacity interact in both directions. Our preferences both shape the talents we are disposed to develop and are shaped by the talents we believe we have. So we cannot separate choice from genetic luck in what might seem the most direct way: by making sure, ex post, that people's wealth reflects only the former and no tinge of the latter.

Equal concern does indeed require that a community compensate in some way for bad luck. But we need an understanding of compensation that is compatible with the right respect for individual responsibility, and we must therefore seek an ex ante approach. This aims, as I said, to situate people equally as they face both economic decisions and the contingencies that hedge those decisions. An economic market for investment, wage, and consumption is a crucial step toward that equality, because it allows people's decisions to carry costs or gain rewards that are measured by the impact of those decisions on other people. But we need a further step: we need to place people in the position they would have occupied if they had been, at a point before the decisions and events that shaped their lives began, equally able to protect themselves against these different dimensions of bad luck through appropriate insurance. That step unfortunately requires the kind of fantasy speculation that I referred to earlier. For of course it is impossible that people could ever be equally able to insure in any real insurance market; certainly impossible before their genetic luck begins, because before that point they do not even exist.

Hypothetical Insurance

We must return to our island. Now we notice that insurance is among the resources auctioned. Some islanders undertake to insure others, in competition with other insurers, at market clamshell rates. When the auction ends, ex ante equality has been preserved and future transactions maintain it. How does this expanded story help us? It teaches us the importance of the following hypothetical question. What level of insurance against low income and bad luck would people in our own actual community buy if the community's actual wealth was equally divided among them, if no information was available that would lead anyone or any insurer to judge that he was more or less at risk than others, and if everyone otherwise had state-of-the-art information about the incidence of different kinds of bad luck and the availability, cost, and value of medical or other remedies for the consequences of that bad luck?

We can sensibly speculate about answers to that question from information readily available about what kinds of insurance insurers actually do offer and people actually do buy. Of course, there must be a large range of uncertainty in any answer we give. We cannot specify any particular coverage level that we can be confident any specific number of people would buy under the fanciful counterfactual conditions we imagine. But that need not be our aim. We can try to identify a top coverage level at which we can sensibly assume that most people in our community would have chosen to insure, given what we know about their needs and preferences, and given the premium structure that that coverage would require. We cannot answer even that question with any pretense to exactitude. But we can dismiss some answers as plainly too low. We can identify a coverage level such that it would be foolish for most people, given their preferences as we can ascertain them, not to buy coverage at that level.

We can then insist that our officials use at least that coverage level as a guide to redistributive programs of different kinds. We might aim to collect from the community, through taxes, an amount equal to the aggregate premium that would have been paid for universal coverage at that level and then distribute, to those who need it, services, goods, or funds that match what that coverage would have provided them in virtue of their bad luck. We would fund unemployment and low wage insurance, medical care insurance, and social security for people in retirement in that way. It is important to notice that by hypothesis any community can afford the programs that this insurance scheme describes: those programs would not be irrational in the way those mandated by a goal of ex post compensation would be. On the contrary, because the programs the scheme identifies reflect reasonable assumptions about the overall preferences of the community over risk and insurance, a government that did not provide them would fail in its economic responsibilities.

Paternalism?

Our overall ambition, remember, is to provide a scheme of distributive justice that satisfies both principles of dignity. It might now be objected that the hypothetical insurance scheme I just summarized offends the second principle because it is, in effect, mandatory. (Arthur Ripstein offers this objection and another concern.[12]) The scheme assumes that most citizens would have purchased insurance at least at the coverage levels and for the premiums it stipulates. But perhaps some would not, and taxing those citizens under the scheme (or indeed, awarding them benefits under it) is therefore, according to this objection, a paternalistic imposition of a supposedly reasonable choice upon them.

The point calls for further explanation, but the objection is not yet well framed. Paternalism means imposing a decision on someone supposedly for his own good but contrary to his own sense of what that is. The hypothetical insurance scheme makes assumptions, on the contrary, about what citizens' preferences would have been in circumstances very different from those anyone has actually encountered. It is no more paternalistic to assume, for any individual, that he would have chosen to buy the insurance at what we judge to be a level at which most people would have insured than it would be to suppose that he would not have bought that insurance and to treat him accordingly.

So the scheme is not paternalistic. But it is probabilistic. No one can sensibly think or argue that he would not have made the decision we assume most people would have made. The counterfactuals are too deep for any such individualized judgment: the scheme's claims can only be statistical. But he can rightly say that he might not have made it. That fact presents an issue not of paternalism but of fairness. We can treat individual citizens on either of two assumptions, and it seems fair to treat them, lacking any information to the contrary, as if each would have done what we judge most would have done.

This is our justification. We aim to charge people the true opportunity costs of their choices. Though we must rely on actual markets in production and wage, we must supplement and correct those markets in a variety of ways. In particular we must try to eliminate the effects of bad luck and other misfortunes by judging what a more comprehensive and fairer market would have revealed as the opportunity costs of provision against those misfortunes. We must make probabilistic counterfactual assumptions in that exercise, to be sure. But that seems fairer than the alternatives, which are either to leave the misfortunes uncorrected or to choose some level of redistributive transfer payments through politics guided only by raw reactions of fairness that have no ground in theory and are likely to be stingy in practice. We choose the hypothetical insurance device, even though it requires rough judgments of probability, as more faithful to the overall opportunity costs conception of fairness. That is the best we can do to show equal concern and the right respect for individual responsibility. Our overall interpretive project endorses a redistributive scheme modeled on hypothetical insurance assumptions for that reason. (Amartya Sen offers a number of further objections to the hypothetical insurance scheme.[13])

Laissez-faire Again

That completes my summary sketch of a design for a political settlement that merges equal concern by government and personal responsibility for citizens.

(I have elsewhere described in much more detail the tax structure that this exercise would generate and the social programs it would justify.[14]) But we must take care not to confuse our ex ante approach, which features ex ante compensation, with a different ex ante approach—misleadingly called equality of opportunity—that is popular among political conservatives. This holds that we show equal concern by letting the chips fall where they may: it allows no redistribution of market rewards and insists those who have bad luck must bear it themselves. This is just a form of the laissez-faire doctrine I mentioned at the outset of this discussion. Proponents say that laissez-faire rewards individual responsibility. But people with little market talent or bad luck can reply that it does not show equal concern, because a different economic arrangement is available that also satisfies the requirements of individual responsibility and that shows more appropriate concern for them.

Equality of resources, understood as I have described it, may reward qualities of productive intelligence, industry, dedication, shrewdness, or contribution to the wealth of others. But that is not its aim. It does not even suppose that these are virtues; it certainly does not suppose that a life earning more money is a better or more successful life. It presumes only that we treat people with equal concern when we allow each to design his own life, aware that his choices will have, among other consequences, an impact on his own wealth. However, it is crucial to this understanding that the character and degree of that impact reflect the effect his choices have on the fortunes of others: the cost to others, in lost opportunities for themselves, of the various decisions he has made.

17

Liberty

The Dimensions of Freedom

Two Kinds of Liberty?

Equality may be in decline, but liberty is in vogue. We fight wars in its name, and political parties denounce other parties for ignoring it. But, like equality, liberty is an interpretive concept: politicians all promise to respect it, but they disagree about what it is. Some say that taxation destroys the freedom we cherish; others that taxation makes that freedom possible. Some think that the proliferation of pollution controls has compromised liberty; others that it has made people more free. We might be tempted to say: given that people mean such different things when they talk about liberty, we should stop using that term and instead just argue about what kind of government is good government. But as I said earlier, that reductive suggestion comes to nothing. We believe that it is a condition of good government that it respect the second principle of dignity, and so we must ask what that means. Whatever language we use, we are then asking for the best understanding of liberty. So we must treat liberty as an interpretive concept and treat our disagreements about liberty as genuine.

However, we face the further question whether there are not one but two interpretive concepts of liberty. Two famous essays make that claim— Benjamin Constant's *The Liberty of the Ancients and the Liberty of the Moderns,* and Isaiah Berlin's *Two Concepts of Liberty.*[1] The argument they make in different ways seems plausible, and it has been very widely accepted among political philosophers and thoughtful lawyers.[2] In political theory the distinction comes to this. We must distinguish two very different questions. Both assume that government, at least of and by human beings, is inevitably coercive. The first asks: By whom—and with whom—should I be coerced? The second asks: How much should I be coerced?

A political theory calls for positive liberty if it insists, in response to the first question, that people must be permitted to play a role in their own coercive governance: that government must in some sense or another be *self-government*. A theory calls for negative liberty if it insists, in response to the second question, that people must be free of coercive government over some substantial range of their decisions and activities. Both these ideas—of positive and negative liberty—are initially puzzling. How can coercive government by a group larger than a single person be self-government for everyone? If coercive government is legitimate at all, then how can we carve out some area of decision and activity that government has no right to regulate?

The second principle of dignity explains why we should regard answers to these two questions, which seem so different, as both theories of liberty. People must be allowed responsibility for their own lives, and, as I said when we considered political obligation in Chapter 14, that responsibility is compatible with governance by others only when certain conditions are met. I described those conditions abstractly there. First, everyone must be permitted to participate in the right way in the collective decisions that make up his governance, and second, everyone must be left free from collective decision in matters that his personal responsibility demands he decide for himself. Because responsibility has those two dimensions, so does liberty. A theory of positive liberty stipulates what it means for people to participate in the right way. It offers, that is, a conception of self-government. A theory of negative liberty describes which choices must be exempt from collective decisions if personal responsibility is to be preserved. The latter is the question for this chapter; the former for the next one. Henceforth I use "liberty" to mean negative liberty unless the context requires a distinction from positive liberty.

Must They Conflict?

One preliminary remains. It is a popular idea, defended in those famous essays, that these two kinds of liberty may conflict with one another, so that a choice or compromise between them is necessary. Of course, conflict is certainly possible and perhaps likely if a community pursues a mistaken conception of either positive or negative liberty or both. Berlin pointed out that the goal of positive liberty has been used by totalitarians to call for a political regime that oppresses citizens in the name of their supposed true or higher interests, interests that they do not recognize for themselves. When the ideal of self-government is corrupted in some such way, it can be used to justify appalling violations of negative liberty. A totalitarian will muzzle people or shut them up in jails or kill them to save their better souls. But so corrupted, the idea has nothing to do with personal responsibility; on the contrary, it plainly violates rather than serves the second principle of dignity. It cannot serve as even an eligible conception of liberty. Berlin's history warns us that bad philosophy is dangerous, but it does not show that better philosophy must end in conflict.

Berlin thought that conflict was likely even on a correct understanding of both concepts. "Both [positive and negative liberty] are ends in themselves. These ends may clash irreconcilably . . . Should democracy in a given situation be promoted at the expense of individual freedom?"[3] He assumed, rightly, that positive liberty requires some form of democracy. But why should promoting democracy, which requires a range of personal freedoms, be thought to conflict with negative liberty? True, there are times and places in which democratic government is so weak and unstable that some constraint on freedom of political activity is thought necessary to prevent antidemocratic forces from destroying it. But such constraints are as much injuries to democracy itself as they are to negative liberty: these are circumstances in which— allegedly—both democracy and negative liberty must be compromised immediately to protect both from graver loss later, not cases in which one of these virtues is preferred to another.

Berlin thought conflict between the two forms of liberty inevitable for a different reason: because he held a problematic view not of positive but of negative liberty. I need a terminological stipulation to explain his view. Though the terms "liberty" and "freedom" are sometimes used interchangeably, I shall distinguish them in the following way. Someone's total freedom is his power to act in whatever way he might wish, unimpeded by constraints or threats imposed by others or by a political community. His negative liberty is the area of his freedom that a political community cannot take away without injuring him in a special way: compromising his dignity by denying him equal concern or an essential feature of responsibility for his own life.

Berlin treated total freedom and negative liberty as coextensive, so that any limit to the former is an invasion of the latter. (This was Mill's conception too, and that of many other philosophers: H. L. A. Hart, for instance, among others.[4]) This equation of liberty with freedom cannot be defended by supposing that liberty is a criterial concept and that our shared criteria for its application have that consequence. Liberty is not criterial: people who debate whether taxation limits our liberty patently use different criteria. We make sense of such disagreement only by assuming, as I now have, that liberty is an interpretive concept and that we understand its meaning best when we tie it to the deeper value of personal responsibility. In any case our question now is whether liberty and democracy conflict as values, not just as phenomena, and only by connecting liberty to dignity in that way can we treat liberty as a value.

So we should treat the equation of liberty with freedom as Berlin's conception of liberty as a value. If that conception is sound—it if realizes what is good about liberty—then of course democracy conflicts with liberty, because any form of government, including democracy, is impossible without criminal law and other forms of regulation. It must follow that good government is inevitably a matter of compromise: any government must compromise one good—liberty—in order to achieve others. But this interpretation is not sound: government does not compromise its citizens' dignity when it forbids them to kill one another. Certainly it is regrettable when people are punished for disobeying the law: it harms those who are punished, and it ought to dismay those who do the punishing. It is also regrettable when someone obeys the law only out of fear. It would no doubt be better if laws and citizens were both sufficiently just so that neither the threat nor the fact of coercion was ever necessary. But a collective decision to impose a duty not to kill and to threaten a serious sanction for any violation is not in itself an insult to the dignity of subjects.

On the contrary, your dignity as an equal citizen requires that government protect you in this way. It is not demeaning for you to accept that a majority of your fellow citizens has the right to fix traffic rules and enforce the rules they fix, provided that the rules they choose are not wicked or desperately foolish. Or that they have the right to define who owns what property and what rights and protections that ownership carries. However, it would certainly be demeaning for you to accept that even a large majority has the right to dictate your religious conviction or practice, or what opinions you should or should not express in political debates. You might be forced to obey those dictates as well, but you should not accept that they are legitimate or that you have a duty to accept them. Berlin's equation fails to capture the difference between the two kinds of constraint. We must attempt a more complex interpretation that does.

We might be tempted by an amendment to Berlin's equation: that liberty is not total freedom but substantial freedom. Laws invade liberty, on this view, when they seriously curtail freedom. But how can we measure the amount of freedom lost through any particular edict? A psychological test, like frustration, won't do. What people find frustrating varies, and in any case, a great many people are more frustrated by speed limits than they would be by political censorship. We need a more radical shift: we need a more explicitly normative conception of liberty.

An Integrated Conception

Dignity Again

We turn once again to our two principles of dignity. These principles are now richer in content than when we encountered them first in Chapter 9. We have steadily elaborated and refined them through our study of ethics, then personal morality, political obligation, and political legitimacy, and then, in our study of distributive equality, how government properly melds equal concern with full respect. We began with an inchoate sense of dignity and worried that it might be too flaccid for our purpose, as some commentators have suggested. Our conception of dignity has much more content now. Can it help us to define liberty? If so, we will have integrated that important political value with the others we have been exploring.

Ethical Independence

We return to a distinction we made in a discussion of ethical independence in Chapter 9: between what a government may not do to its citizens for any reason and what it may not do to them for certain reasons. Some coercive laws violate ethical independence because they deny people power to make their own decisions about matters of ethical foundation—about the basis and character of the objective importance of human life that the first principle of dignity declares. These include choices in religion and in personal commitments of intimacy and to ethical, moral, and political ideals. A plurality of American Supreme Court justices, refusing to allow American states to flatly prohibit early abortion, called these "matters involving the most intimate and personal choices a person may make in a lifetime, choices central to dignity and autonomy." People have a right to independence in such decisions, provided that they do not threaten the like independence of other people. So government may not constrain foundational independence for any reason except when this is necessary to protect the life, security, or liberty of others. Which other decisions are also foundational, if any, is open to dispute. But any more detailed account of liberty must take a stand on that issue.

Other laws violate ethical independence in virtue, not of the foundational character of the decisions they inhibit, but rather of government's motives in enacting those laws. Government must not restrict freedom when its justification assumes the superiority or popularity of any ethical values controversial in the community. Censorship of sexual literature or mandated flag salutes or other demonstrations of patriotism fall into that category, because they depend, directly or indirectly, on a choice about the personal virtues that a good life reflects. Some laws violate ethical independence in both ways. Prohibitions on same-sex intercourse or marriage constrain foundational choices, and they are almost always motivated by a desire to protect some conceptions of living well and blot out others. Political censorship may also violate independence in both ways. The freedom to speak or write honestly as your conscience or conviction or belief requires is foundational. In some circumstances, moreover, political censorship can be justified only by ethical assumptions.

But ethical independence is not jeopardized when a matter is not foundational and government's constraint assumes no ethical justification. Government relies on moral rather than ethical arguments when it pressures me to conserve scarce resources, forces me to pay taxes, and forbids me to drive carelessly. Certainly laws that do not offend ethical independence—in either of the two ways—may nevertheless have serious consequence for how people can live. Prohibiting physical violence and theft makes it less likely that I will judge the life of a Samurai or Robin Hood ideal for me and much more difficult for me to pursue that life if I do. Taxation makes it less likely that I will judge collecting Renaissance masterpieces the ideal life. None of these laws denies my responsibility to define ethical value for myself, however, because none aims to usurp my responsibility to identify a successful life. Properly motivated laws of my community are part of the background against which I make my ethical choices. My own ethical responsibility for making those choices is not diminished by that background.

Much of the philosophical literature about paternalism seems to me to underrate the importance of this distinction. Making people wear seat belts to prevent or mitigate injury is not ethical paternalism: medical paternalism may be offensive, but it is not an offense against authenticity. True, many people claim (perhaps a few of them sincerely) that a life that courts danger is attractive and that seat-belt legislation restricts people's opportunity to lead such a life. But seat-belt convictions are not foundational, and government need not assume that courting danger is a bad way to live in order to justify measures that reduce the costs of accidents to the community. It used to be easy to cite real cases of ethical paternalism: the Inquisition, for instance, was firmly in that line of work. Even during part of the last century the most popular arguments for censoring pornography appealed to ethical paternalism. The great Oxford bookseller, Basil Blackwell, testified that *Last Exit to Brooklyn* should be banned because it degraded those who read it; he then offered himself as an example of someone who had become depraved in that way.[5] But ethical paternalism has had a bad press in recent decades, and it is no longer a popular political cause.

Instead the most popular arguments for constraints once justified in that way now cite fairness, not ethical paternalism. They insist that people who form a political majority have a right to the ethical culture they deem best: they have a right to live and raise their children in a culture that permits and encourages a lifestyle they admire.[6] It is much easier for people to hew to their inherited religion with the almost blind conviction and fervor they long to achieve, and to transmit their own intense faith to their children, when that faith is officially endorsed and celebrated; it is harder when competing religions and triumphal atheism have equal voice. It is easier to feel comfortable in conservative attitudes to sex when striking sexual images are not freely available on magazine covers or dominant in advertising. Why, then, should the majority not be able to impose the religious or sexual culture it prefers on everyone? It has the right, within reasonable limits, to protect what it deems to have impersonal value by taxing for museums and forbidding despoliation of forests. It may forbid me to build a skyscraper on my land or put billboards or plastic flamingoes on my lawn. Why should it not be permitted to protect in the same way the religious and sexual culture it favors?

We need arguments like those of this book—the distinctions and interconnections among responsibility, authenticity, influence, and subordination that we have reviewed—properly to answer that question. The second principle of dignity makes ethics special: it limits the acceptable range of collective decision. We cannot escape the influence of our ethical environment: we are subject to the examples, exhortations, and celebrations of other people's ideas about how to live.[7] But we must insist that that environment be created under the aegis of ethical independence: that it be created organically by the decisions of millions of people with the freedom to make their own choices, not through political majorities imposing their decisions on everyone.

I proposed an image in Chapter 13: of people swimming in their own lanes who may cross into someone else's lane to help but not to harm him. Morality, broadly understood, defines the lanes that separate swimmers. It stipulates when one must cross lanes to help and what constitutes forbidden lane-crossing harm. Ethics governs how one must swim in one's own lane to have swum well. The image is helpful here again because it illustrates one way in which morality must be treated as prior to ethics in politics: it must be treated as prior in defining what opportunities and resources people are rightfully entitled to have, and in that way to establishing what rights they have to liberty. The interpretive conception of liberty we are now constructing explains why that philosophical fact entails no subordination of either morality or ethics to the other. They cooperate, not compete.

Other Liberty: Due Process, Free Speech

Certain rights are by tradition called "liberal." These include rights I have so far cited—freedom of religious practice and of political speech—but also such different rights as the right to leave the community and "due process" right not to be punished for an alleged crime without a trial conducted with proper procedural safeguards against convicting innocent people. Liberal rights are widely accepted in the abstract, at least in Western democracies, but they are controversial in detail. Lawyers and nations disagree to a considerable extent about whether, for example, the right to free speech includes a right to advertise cigarettes or a right to spend unlimited sums in political campaigns, and whether due process rights include a right to a jury trial or a privilege against self-incrimination. What arguments are available for these rights, either in the abstract or in some controversial specification?

The right to religious freedom is obviously grounded in ethical independence; I return to that right and its implications later in this chapter. Due process rights, on the other hand, seem to have little to do with ethical responsibility: we have those rights in virtue of government's obligation, flowing from the first principle of dignity, to treat each person's life as of distinct, objective, and equal importance. I have tried to explain elsewhere why punishing an innocent person inflicts a special and great harm on him—I called it a moral harm—and why that fact justifies the assumption that, in the popular slogan, it is better that a thousand guilty people go free than that one innocent one be punished.[8] It is a nice calculation, in which history and tradition have a part to play, how much expense a community must incur to avoid that terrible injury. But a community that is careless of proof or niggardly in protecting against error—and of course any community that countenances deliberate conviction of the innocent—violates the first principle of human dignity.

The right to free speech, which is equally central in the traditional account of liberal rights, requires more nuanced treatment.[9] It is now very widely accepted among American constitutional lawyers that the First Amendment, which forbids government to abridge "the freedom of speech," is justified by a variety of principles and purposes. One important set of these is grounded in positive liberty. Free speech must be part of any defensible conception of self-government for at least two distinct and equally important reasons: self-government requires free access to information, and government is not legitimate, and so has no moral title to coerce, unless all those coerced have had an opportunity to influence collective decisions. (We consider these two claims further in the next chapter.)

But free speech, as it has come to be understood in Western democracies, covers more than political speech even broadly construed: we must take more into account than positive liberty to explain all that it covers—and does not cover. Though a state may in different ways promote what it collectively deems intrinsically valuable in literature, art, and music, it may not forbid its members to read, look at, and listen to what they please when its only justification is that certain opinions about what is worthy of enjoyment are offensive in themselves and may be contagious. Sexually explicit material is protected by a right to free speech, not because it expresses a political position—that is far-fetched—but because the only available arguments for banning it are, as I said, offensive to ethical independence.

Censorship might not only undermine positive liberty but also, as I said, violate the right of ethical independence in both the ways we distinguished. Consider how a variety of factors interact when government tries to ban hate speech. Ohio courts convicted a Ku Klux Klan leader of a crime because he had advocated hatred of blacks and Jews.[10] The law so interpreted violated his right to positive liberty because it prohibited him from attempting to rally other citizens to his political opinions. It violated his right to ethical independence because the right to bear public witness to one's political convictions is foundational and any violence to others he advocated was not imminent. It violated his ethical independence in a different way if, as seems likely, the prosecution was motivated not by fear of violence but by wholly justified revulsion at his lower esteem for the importance of certain lives. The Supreme Court reversed the conviction, but I cite the example not to illustrate American constitutional law but to show the confluence of aspects of both positive and negative liberty at work, honorably, to protect the rights of the detestable.

We should distinguish these liberty-based arguments, which appeal to positive or negative liberty or both, from policy-based arguments for free speech. Mill, Oliver Wendell Holmes, and others stressed the value of unrestricted speech as a source of knowledge. Holmes, who loved evolutionary images, expressed it by saying that better ideas have a better chance of surviving in an intense Darwinian competition from which no thought, however unattractive or implausible, is initially excluded. This may well be true on the whole and over some very long run, though less plainly so in matters of political morality and aesthetic taste than in science. A second policy-based argument focuses on commercial speech: the public has an important economic interest in a free flow of information about the availability, price, and features of products offered for sale. The Supreme Court has developed an elaborate and unimpressive jurisprudence about the degree to which the First Amendment protects commercial speech from regulation. The upshot of its wandering decisions is that commercial speech has some constitutional protection but not as much as political speech.

It is commonplace that no political right is absolute and that even free speech has its limits. But the character and justification of these limits differs, depending on which of the justifications for the right I mentioned is in play. The policy-based arguments suggest their own limits. The public has at best a dubious economic interest in reading false or misleading advertisements, for example, or in advertisements that do not include reasonable warnings about the dangers of the products they advertise, or advertisements for illegal activities. Such advertisements are on balance not helpful but harmful to the public interest.

The liberty-based arguments of both kinds suggest their own limits in a different way: because the justification they offer is not engaged at all on certain occasions. I have argued (I summarize that argument in the next chapter) that reasonable limits on a candidate's expenditures in political campaigns do not cramp positive liberty. On the contrary, they enhance it because they help provide something at least closer to self-government for all citizens than politics can drenched in money and dominated by rich candidates and backers. The case for free speech drawn from ethical independence is self-limiting in the same way. When government forbids conspiring with confederates in crime, it does not constrain a foundational right. Nor does it act to vindicate some collective judgment of worthy behavior or to impose some uniform orthodoxy in ethics. It acts to improve safety; its motives, like its motives in taxation or economic regulation, are moral, not ethical.

This brisk review of free speech and its limits is not legal analysis: it does not confront the hard cases that a court charged with enforcing a constitutional right faces. Higher courts must draw reasonably rigid distinctions that can serve as a guide to lower courts and other departments of government. I mean here only to illustrate the different dimensions of argument that are required, on this conception of liberty, both to defend and limit this famous right.

Freedom of Property?

I have not yet mentioned a kind of freedom that is dear to conservative hearts and much celebrated in certain periods of American history: freedom to acquire property and use it as one wishes, except to harm other people. Is this freedom a liberty too? It is the freedom people have in mind when they claim that financial and industrial regulation strikes at liberty and that taxation is tyranny. These claims are no doubt exaggerated, but should we not recognize some liberty of this sort?

We already have. Some liberty to acquire and use property is assumed in the conception of distributive justice defined in Chapter 16: equality of resources. Some liberty of that sort is assumed, indeed, in any conception of distributive justice. For the resources people have cannot be defined or measured without taking into account people's freedom to acquire, trade, and use those resources as they wish. It would make no sense to urge an equal distribution of wealth, however equality is conceived, without assuming some kind or degree of such freedom, because bare ownership of some property means nothing unless we specify or assume a general background of freedom in its use. Ownership, lawyers say, is a bundle of rights, and we make assumptions about the contents of that bundle whenever we specify any distribution of resources as fair.

What the bundle of rights should contain is not, however, an independent question that belongs exclusively to a study of liberty. The right bundle obviously depends on the rest of political morality as well. The most we can say here is that your liberty includes the right to use property that is rightfully yours, except in ways your government can rightfully restrict. That proposition is not as anodyne as it sounds when it is integrated into the right general theory of justice. The opportunity-cost justification of equality of resources I defended assumes a very wide latitude of alienable ownership and control, and so does the second principle of dignity, which asks us to take responsibility for our own lives.[11]

Some resources must inevitably be held as public goods, and others should be under public control to protect against the externalities that corrupt the opportunity-costs metric. Some strict regulation is necessary for the same reason—pollution controls, for example—and some public programs, like a health care system, are necessary as the most efficient forms of redistribution in search of fairness. But the default required by equal concern and respect is a system of private property: we need a justification for any deviation from that default. The familiar right-wing complaint that taxation is an assault on liberty is mistaken. But the mistake is not conceptual: it is a mistake about justice. The structure and level of taxation in force may invade liberty if it is unjust—if it does not show equal concern and respect for all. Taxation in many countries now is unjust, but because it takes too little, not too much. It does not deprive people of what is rightfully theirs; on the contrary, it fails to provide the means of granting them what is rightfully theirs.

Religious Freedom and Ethical Independence

A right to religious freedom is plainly required by ethical independence. It has pride of place in the United States Constitution and in documents like the Universal Declaration of Human Rights and the European Convention on Human Rights. True, other justifications beyond dignity have been offered for that right. It is said, for example, that because religion is particularly divisive, religious tolerance is the only route to civil peace. But though that justification was cogent in Europe and America in the seventeenth and eighteenth centuries, it is much less cogent now. The main beneficiaries of tolerance in the West now are small minority religions and people with no religion at all, and they would not and could not provoke much civic disturbance if they were denied the freedoms they now enjoy. In certain other countries one religion is established as official and other religions are tolerated only barely, or not at all, without any apparent danger to stability. For us, now, dignity provides the only available justification for freedom of religious thought and practice.

But once we accept that proposition, we can no longer consistently think, as many people do, that religion is special and that other foundational ethical choices—about reproduction, marriage, and sexual orientation, for instance—may properly be subject to collective decision. We cannot declare a right to religious freedom and then reject rights to freedom of choice in these other foundational matters without striking self-contradiction. For if we insist that no particular religion be treated as special in politics, then we cannot treat religion itself as special in politics, as more central to dignity than sexual identification, for example. So we must not treat religious freedom as sui generis. It is only one consequence of the more general right to ethical independence in foundational matters. Government needs a compelling justification to regulate reproductive or sexual acts, and its justification may not rely on either the truth or the popularity of a collective ethical judgment. I have written at length elsewhere about some of these ethical issues and return to them here, though only briefly, to consider what fresh light the argument of this book throws on them.[12]

Abortion is the most complex as well as the most divisive of these issues. The first principle of dignity holds that human life is of intrinsic importance, and that principle necessarily includes the life of a human fetus, which is undeniably a human life. Earlier in the book we recognized dual consequences of that first principle. Each of us must live so as to acknowledge and respect the objective importance of his own life. We fail in dignity when we do not. And we must treat others consistently with recognizing the objective importance of their lives as well. It is a further question, however, what that latter requirement means more concretely. In earlier chapters we considered how far respect for human life requires that we aid other people and when it requires that we not harm them. Do these moral requirements shift when human life has only just begun? Do we owe an early fetus the same duty to aid and not to harm that we owe human beings who have reached a more complex state of development?

These are moral as well as ethical questions: the morality of abortion hinges on how we answer them. I have argued that we must answer the second: no. Because an early fetus has no interests of its own, any more than a flower does, a fetus cannot be supposed to have rights protecting its interests. In fact, very few people actually believe that we owe the same moral duty to a fetus that we owe to an infant: even most people who think that abortion should be prohibited in principle nevertheless believe it should be permitted when a pregnancy has begun in rape or when abortion is necessary to save a woman's life. But even if we accept that negative answer to the moral question, and hold that a woman has no moral duty not to abort the fetus she carries, critical ethical issues remain. For it remains a vivid possibility that abortion is nevertheless inconsistent with the respect for human life on which our dignity depends. Paintings and great trees have no interests of their own, and hence no moral rights to protect their interests, but it is still inconsistent with recognizing their intrinsic value to destroy them. That is why it is crucial, in discussing abortion and related issues, to take care to distinguish the moral from the ethical issues in play.

The moral question must be decided collectively within a political community. When the United States Supreme Court was asked, for the first time in 1973, whether an American state can constitutionally forbid all abortion, it had to answer that moral question one way or the other. It answered it negatively. Many critics of the decision insist that the Court should not have decided the question at all but should rather have allowed the states to decide it for themselves one by one. That objection is confused: states cannot be allowed to decide for themselves whether any particular class of their members may be murdered. It is a more sensible objection that, having decided that abortion is not murder and that states are therefore not required by the Constitution's equal protection clause to prohibit all abortion, the Court should have allowed them to decide for themselves whether abortion should be banned on ethical grounds—on the ground, that is, that abortion displays contempt for the intrinsic value of human life. That was the crucial issue that the Court actually faced in *Roe v. Wade,* and faced again, with a more accurate recognition and better response, in the later *Casey* case in which it reaffirmed its support for limited abortion rights.[13]

The right of ethical independence allows only one answer. That right is violated and liberty denied when government restricts freedom in order to enforce a collective ethical judgment—in this instance the ethical judgment that a woman who aborts an early pregnancy does not show the respect for human life that her dignity demands. I myself believe that in many circum-stances abortion is indeed an act of self-contempt.[14] A woman betrays her own dignity when she aborts for frivolous reasons: to avoid rescheduling a holiday, for instance. I would reach a different ethical judgment in other cases: when a teenage girl's prospects for a decent life would be ruined if she became a single mother, for example. But whether the judgment is right or wrong in any particular case, it remains an ethical, not a moral judgment. It must be left to women, as their dignity demands, each to take responsibility for her own ethical convictions.

18

Democracy

Positive Liberty

Slogans and Questions

The second principle of dignity protects personal ethical responsibility. In the last chapter we studied one aspect of that responsibility. Dignity requires independence from government in matters of ethical choice, and that requirement is at the foundation of any plausible theory of negative liberty. But dignity does not require independence from government in other matters: a political community must make collective decisions about justice and morality, and it must be able to enforce those decisions coercively. That sets the stage for the question of positive liberty. I cannot be free from coercive control in matters of justice and morality, but my dignity requires that I be allowed a role in the collective decisions that exercise that control. What role must that be?

We are soon knee-deep in slogans. Only democracy can provide dignity. Government must be of the people, by the people, and for the people. The people must govern themselves. Each citizen must be offered an equal and meaningful role. One person must have one vote and no one more than one vote. No man, Locke said, is born to rule or be ruled.[1] We must try to rescue positive liberty from these slogans because it is wholly unclear what they mean. The concept of democracy is an interpretive and much contested concept.

What can it mean that "the people" govern themselves when very few of them have any significant power over what the laws will be? The winner-takes-all style of electing parliamentary representatives in each electoral district, common in the United States and Britain, is very different from the proportional representation system common in other countries. Given the same distribution of interests, convictions, and preferences, rather different laws are likely to emerge, depending on which of these two systems is in place. Is one system more democratic than the other? Is the practice of judicial review, which allows judges appointed for life to declare legislative and executive acts unconstitutional, illegitimate because it is undemocratic? Or is that practice rather a necessary and desirable corrective to democracy? Or—a third possibility—is the practice actually essential to creating a genuine democracy? Each of these positions is widely defended, and we cannot choose among them without choosing among conceptions of democracy and defending our choice.

Who Are the People?

We face a further, threshold question before we can tackle those traditional questions. Who *are* the people? One day Japan grants equal voting rights to the citizens of Norway so that they can elect a small party of Norwegians to the Japanese Diet if they wish. Then the Diet by majority vote levies taxes on Norwegian oil and directs its transfer to Japanese refineries. This fantasy would hardly supply self-government to the Norwegians. If some form of majoritarian process is to provide genuine self-government, it must be government by a majority of the *right* people.

   Government by the right people has seemed more important to more people—to the peoples of Africa following the Second World War, for instance, or the white citizens of the antebellum American South—than their role as individuals in that government. People want to be governed by people relatively like themselves. It is often unclear what that means. It has been taken to justify many different forms of tribalism or nationalism: of race, religion, language, kinship, or even, as in the Old South, economic circumstance or interest. Historians, statesmen, and politicians cannot ignore the strength of these various centripetal forces: they continue to drive people into the most terrible violence. But they have no intrinsic normative force. There is no nonhistorical right answer to the question: on what principle should people be divided into political communities? We cannot find an answer in the ideal of democracy itself because that ideal presupposes a political community and cannot be used to define one. Nor in the emotionally powerful but terminally vague idea of national self-determination—the supposed right of ethnocultural groups to govern themselves. There is no concept of nonpolitical nationhood precise enough to make sense of that right, and even if there were, there is no satisfactory answer to the question why any individual member of any group so defined has a duty to associate himself politically with the rest of them.

There are indeed reasons—sometimes imperative reasons—for altering historical or established patterns of rule. Colonial systems in which the people of one political state governed other peoples far away could not have been reformed without severing that formal association and creating new states. Though the patriots who dumped tea into Boston Harbor shouted "No taxation without representation," Jefferson's Declaration of Independence did not suggest extending the Westminster franchise as a solution to King George's crimes, and no one thought, a century or two on, that franchise extension would end colonial empire in Africa or on the Indian subcontinent.

Even when there is no colonial domination to undo, the boundaries that geography, history, war, and politics have created may be untenable. When different tribes or races or religious groups prove incapable of living together without violence, separation into new political communities may be the only available alternative. Or if one minority group has become a perennial victim of injustice, a reformulation of boundaries may help, provided of course that this can be achieved without more injustice and without great suffering. When an illegitimate conquest—Saddam's incursion into Kuwait, for instance—can be undone, it must be undone. But a plausible statute of limitations provides a necessary limit even to that principle, so that even if it was wrong to establish Israel sixty years ago, the original boundaries of that state should now be respected.

These are examples of dramatic change in political boundaries. Less dramatic changes and regroupings are often wise and can normally be achieved with little or much less pain. Federalism and decentralization, creating subdivisions of established communities, often permit more rational political decisions and provide a greater sense of participation in self-government. Shifts in the other direction can be even more valuable: the now long-running and so far disappointing efforts to create a new constitutional structure for the European Union illustrate both the wisdom and the difficulty of a shift to larger and more diverse political communities from smaller and more homogeneous ones. Both the European nations and the world will gain, I believe, if the EU is able to form a common foreign policy and execute it with the economic power of its community giving strength to its united arm.

Still, the boundaries created by accidents of history remain the default. We are born into political communities and these are our legitimate governors, provided they also meet the conditions of legitimacy discussed earlier in this book and later in this chapter, which include imposing no legal barriers to emigration. Those who live a mile inside California's border with Nevada or France's border with Germany are governed rather differently from those who live a mile on the other side, and no abstract principle of political philosophy can justify that difference. Most attempts to draw supposedly more rational lines only create new uncomfortable minorities to replace newly comfortable old ones. If we rule out a one-world global democracy with one vote for everyone in every continent (which is impossible and would in any case raise all the old questions when the necessary subdivisions were created), we rarely find a persuasive argument for correcting what history has achieved.

Two Models of Self-Government

Assume, then, that some particular political community is the right community or at least not the wrong one. The right people govern. They govern by electing officials of various kinds and levels, and these officials exercise coercive power on their behalf. But the officials can be elected and the structures through which they govern constructed in a variety of ways: the systems we recognize as democratic across the world vary significantly. Some reserve major decisions for referenda in which people at large vote directly on matters of policy; others shun such referenda. Some elect officials more frequently than others, some use proportional representation and others winner-takes-all electoral schemes, some give considerable power to nonelected officials, including the judges of constitutional courts. By what principles should we judge these different constitutional arrangements? Are some more consistent with the dignity of the people than others? Do some provide more, and others less, by way of positive liberty or genuine self-government? Is there some deep standard we can use to test these various versions of democracy for democratic superiority or authenticity?

Democracy, to repeat yet again, is an interpretive concept: people disagree about what democracy is. We choose among competing conceptions by locating some distinct value or set of values that best explain, if any can, what is good about it. As always, some philosophers are tempted by a reductive solution: they suggest giving up the debate about what democracy is and arguing instead simply about what form of government is best. As always, that reductive strategy is self-defeating; it forces us to ignore important distinctions between different values at stake in that latter, overall, question. A good government is democratic, just, and efficient, but these are not the same qualities, and it is sometimes important to ask, for instance, whether some constitutional arrangement that is likely to make a community's economy more efficient must nevertheless be resisted because it is undemocratic. It is then crucial to consider, as an independent question, what we should understand the point and nerve of democracy to be. We can avoid the word if we wish: we can ask about the meaning of positive liberty or self-government instead. But we ask the same question.

It is instructive to contrast two answers to that question: two models of how people can be thought to govern themselves. I have elsewhere called these the majoritarian and partnership conceptions of democracy.[2] The majoritarian conception holds that people govern themselves when the largest number of them, rather than some smaller group within them, holds fundamental political power. It therefore insists that the structures of representative government should be designed to enhance the likelihood that the community's laws and policies will be those that the largest number of citizens, after due discussion and reflection, prefer. Elections should be frequent enough so that officials will be encouraged to do what most people want; federal units and parliamentary districts should be drawn, and constitutional power divided among types and levels of officials, with that aim in view. Further questions—referenda? proportional representation?—should be debated and decided in the same way. Which system is more likely to reliably enforce the reflective and settled will of a majority of citizens in the long run?

We must take care not to confuse this majoritarian conception of democracy with some aggregative theory of justice, like utilitarianism, that holds that laws are just when they produce the greatest possible sum or average of happiness (or some other conception of well-being) within a targeted community. (The phrase "majority will" is dangerously ambiguous because it is sometimes used to describe a majoritarian process and sometimes a utilitarian or other aggregative result.[3]) There is no reason to think that a majoritarian electoral process will even typically produce a result that would be deemed just on any particular aggregative standard. On the contrary, a majoritarian process might well produce—and often has produced—laws that injure total or average well-being on any conception of what that is. That is why proponents of the majoritarian conception believe it important to distinguish democracy from justice. An autocrat might decree a more just distribution of resources than a majority would approve.

The partnership conception of democracy is different: it holds that self-government means government not by the majority of people exercising authority over everyone but by the people as a whole acting as partners. This must inevitably be a partnership that divides over policy, of course, since unanimity is rare in political communities of any size. But it can be a partnership nevertheless if the members accept that in politics they must act with equal respect and concern for all the other partners. It can be a partnership, that is, if they each respect the conditions of legitimacy we discussed in Chapters 14 and 15—if each accepts a standing obligation not only to obey the community's law but to try to make that law consistent with his good-faith understanding of what every citizen's dignity requires.[4]

That brief description reveals the most important difference between the two conceptions of democracy. The majoritarian conception defines democracy only procedurally. The partnership conception ties democracy to the substantive constraints of legitimacy. Because legitimacy is a matter of degree, so, on this conception, is democracy. It is an ideal toward which some political communities strive, some more successfully than others. But the partnership conception makes self-government at least an intelligible ideal. The majoritarian conception—or so I shall argue—does not, because it describes nothing that could count as self-government by members of a political minority. Or, for that matter, by individual members of a majority.

This profound contrast between the two conceptions is strikingly illustrated in the debate (principally in the United States but increasingly elsewhere) about the compatibility of democracy and judicial review. The majoritarian conception does not automatically rule out a political arrangement that gives judges the power to enforce a constitution by declaring legislation null and void. Some skilled lawyers and philosophers have argued that judicial review, properly designed and limited, can serve the majoritarian conception by making it more likely that legislation will reflect the settled view of most people. John Hart Ely argued, for instance, that judges must protect the people's power by safeguarding freedom of speech and the press from politicians anxious to hide their corruption or stupidity, and Janos Kis has argued, in the same vein, that judges can protect the people from incumbents who become less enthusiastic about majority will when this is a threat to their continued power.[5]

Still, the majoritarian conception is wary of judicial review, and its acolytes reject judicial power to strike down laws that a steady and informed majority plainly favors: the death penalty, for instance, or prayer in public schools, or, in some American states, restrictions on early abortion. They understand that it is controversial whether a political majority should have the power to adopt such legislation. But they insist that because that question *is* controversial, the majority must be permitted to decide the question for itself. Allowing a small group of lawyers who cannot be dismissed in any general election to decide that fundamental question of governance is contrary to the whole point of majoritarian democracy. On that view, judicial review denies the positive liberty necessary to the dignity of ordinary citizens.[6]

On the partnership conception, however, that familiar argument is starkly circular. It assumes that a political majority has moral authority to decide controversial issues for everyone, but on the partnership conception a majority has no moral authority to decide anything unless the institutions through which it governs are sufficiently legitimate. Judicial review is one possible (though I emphasize, only one possible) strategy for improving a government's legitimacy—by protecting a minority's ethical independence, for instance—and in that way securing a majority's moral title to impose its will on other matters.

Which Model Is Best?

Fairness?

How shall we choose between these two conceptions of democracy? Political scientists list many instrumental benefits of democracy. It is widely assumed that democratic institutions, backed by a free and vigorous press, protect a community against deep and extended corruption, tyranny, and other evils; they make it less likely that officials will govern only in their own interests or those of a narrow class, as military juntas and other dictators commonly do. Democracy has other, more positive advantages. In reasonably prosperous political communities, particularly those with an educated electorate and democratic traditions, democracy improves political stability; indeed, it may be essential to stability in such communities. It allows each of the important interest groups within the community to secure, through alliances and logrolling, what is most important to it. The political freedoms required by democracy also protect economic freedom and the rule of law essential to economic development. It is not obvious, alas, that these practical advantages can be realized in all circumstances. In some—in countries with very weak economies and no experience of democracy—introducing democracy may actually threaten stability or economic development. Or so some political theorists have argued. We need not pursue these issues here, however, because we cannot choose between the two models by asking which would produce more stability or prosperity. There is no general answer to that question—it entirely depends on circumstance—and the fundamental issue is anyway one of principle, not consequence.

We assume that people's dignity requires that they participate in their own government. How does the majoritarian conception of democracy purport to achieve this? The answer may seem obvious: that majority rule is the only *fair* method of governing a coercive political community. Jeremy Waldron, among contemporary political theorists, has set out that case for the majoritarian conception, which he calls "MD," with greatest clarity. "The fairness/equality defense of the majority-decision rule is well known," he declared. "Better than any other rule, MD is neutral as between the contested outcomes, treats participants equally, and gives each expressed opinion the greatest weight possible compatible with giving equal weight to all opinions. When we disagree about the desired outcome, when we do not want to bias the matter up-front one way or another, and when each of the relevant participants has a moral claim to be treated as an equal in the process, then MD—or something like it—is the principle to use."[7]

This is a very general claim, not just about political decisions but about all collective decisions. It offers a general principle of procedural fairness. For people who accept that general principle, the majoritarian conception of democracy is only its application to the political case. I find the popularity of this argument surprising, however, because the majoritarian, counting-heads principle is rather plainly not a fundamental principle of fairness. There is first the problem I earlier discussed: a majority is in any case of no moral significance unless the community of which that group is a majority is the right community. A majority of Japanese and Norwegians has no moral power over Norwegian oil. But even when the community is the right one, majority decision is not always fair. I earlier gave this example: when a lifeboat is over-crowded and one passenger must be thrown over else all will die, it would not be fair to hold a vote so that the least popular among them would be drowned. It would be much fairer to draw lots.

Waldron has said, in response, that if the passengers disagreed about whether it would be fairer to draw lots or vote, then the only fair way to settle *that* dispute would be to vote on which procedure was fairer.[8] That recursive suggestion seems equally wrong: we cannot sensibly treat numbers as deci-sive over the question whether numbers should be decisive. It would not be any fairer for a majority of lifeboat passengers first to vote to hold an election and then to vote to throw the cabin boy out than for them to vote to throw him out directly. When questions of fair procedure are controversial, they are controversial all the way down: there is no default decision procedure to de-cide on decision procedures. (Waldron has recently given a fresh response to this claim.[9])

The evident reasons why a majority vote would be unfair in the lifeboat case apply also to at least some political decisions. Just as the biases and per-sonal dislikes of a majority should not count in deciding which passenger should be thrown overboard, so they are not relevant when a political com-munity decides on the rights of an identified and disliked minority.[10] In the lifeboat case there is an obvious remedy: chance. But chance would not be an appropriate decision procedure in politics. When decisions have vast conse-quences for the lives people lead, leaving those decisions to chance or some other form of oracle is a bad idea; it may have worked, for a time, for the Athenians, but it would not work for us. A majority's opinion about whether to go to war may be no better than some minority's opinion, but it is likely to be better than a decision made by dice.

There are also decisive reasons for rejecting an autocratic or investment-related procedure: citizens should not be treated like orchestra members or shareholders. Some of these reasons are practical: as I said, at least in many circumstances democracy provides stability and protects against corruption. Other reasons rest on assumptions about the outcome of democratic processes: they may be more likely than autocratic procedures to promote the general welfare, defined in some appropriate way, even if they do not do so inevitably. In any case, as we have seen, citizen's dignity requires that they have an im-portant role in their own governance. But none of these reasons for insisting on popular democracy rather than chance or aristocracy in politics favors the majoritarian over the partnership conception of what democracy means. Indeed, because the latter gives more constitutional protection to minorities, it might be expected to provide more stability and to more accurately identify and secure the general welfare.

Political Equality?

Must we say that the majoritarian conception offers something that the partnership conception does not—political equality? That depends on how that further interpretive concept is best understood. We can elaborate political equality as an abstract ideal in three very different ways. We might take political equality to mean, first, that political power is distributed in such a way that all adult citizens have equal influence over political decisions. Each of them has as great a chance as any other adult citizen that the opinions he brings to the political process will in the end become law or state policy. Or we might take political equality to mean, second, that adult citizens have equal impact in that process: that the opinion each finally forms in the process will be given full and equal weight in the community's final decision. Influence and impact are different. A person's influence includes his power to persuade or induce others to his side; his impact is limited to what he can achieve through his own opinion without regard to what others believe.

Third, we might take political equality to mean something quite different: that no adult citizen's political impact is less than that of any other citizen for reasons that compromise his dignity—reasons that treat his life as of less concern or his opinions as less worthy of respect. The first two of these readings take equality to be a mathematical ideal: they presuppose some metric of political power and demand, at least as an ideal, that the power of all citizens be equal on that metric. The third takes political equality to be a matter of attitude, not mathematics. It demands that the community divide political power, not necessarily equally, but in a way that treats people as equals.

When we contrast the first two readings—equal influence and equal impact—it is difficult to think the latter a better interpretation. It makes no sense for me to think that my political power is equal to that of a billionaire or a pop star or a charismatic preacher or a revered political hero when many millions will follow his lead and I am unknown and unpersuasive. So, for that reason, we should prefer the first reading to the second. But the first reading is not only unrealistic but unattractive as well: it could be realized only in a totalitarian society. Some people are always much more influential than others in persuading their fellow citizens how to vote. In his day Martin Luther King had much greater influence over people's opinions than almost any other private citizen, and today Oprah Winfrey, Tom Cruise, a variety of sports heroes, the CEO of Microsoft, the publisher of the *New York Times,* the editors of Fox News, and hundreds of other Americans have special power. We regret some people's special influence because it is grounded in wealth, which we think should make no difference in politics. But we do not regret other people's special influence—Reverend King's, for instance—nor think this a defect in our democracy. On the contrary, we are proud of the power he had.

So if we want a mathematical reading of political equality, we must settle for the second reading after all. This ignores political influence and demands only equal impact: that each person have the same power to control the laws of his community just in virtue of the preferences he holds himself. This kind of equality can easily be achieved in a town meeting, simply by giving each person attending the meeting one vote. It requires considerably more strategy in a huge and complex political community with representative government, electoral districting, and a separation of official powers. Still, even in a continental nation with a government of relatively few people, each with huge power, citizens can each be provided one vote in all elections and electoral districts can be arranged so that each vote counts as much as any other. That goes a considerable distance toward equal impact for all.

Presidents, prime ministers, parliamentarians, and judges then still each have exponentially more immediate impact on law and policy than ordinary citizens do, and once elected they can set off on projects of their own with no concern for public opinion, particularly if they do not worry about reelection. These politicians might be idealists, adopting Edmund Burke's declaration of independence from his electors,[11] or crooks like Richard Nixon's vice president, Spiro T. Agnew, lining their own pockets. But relatively frequent elections and vigilant and free media could make this less likely; in any case it is the best we can do in that direction. If we are drawn to the second reading of political equality, we will think that majoritarian democracy fits that ideal like a glove.

But the second reading remains unpersuasive. It seems irrational to care about equality of impact for its own sake, even when we recognize that equality of influence is unattainable and undesirable. An equal impact, on its own, is of no practical use to people one by one in a community of any size. Suppose you live in a community the size, say, of France. It elects its officials in frequent elections with full adult suffrage, enjoys a constitutional structure that gives every vote the same impact in those elections, provides the most unrestricted version of free speech, and enjoys vigorous, competitive, and politically diverse media. The measure of positive political control these facts provide for you is so small that it can sensibly be rounded off only to zero. Your decision to vote one way or another would not improve to any statistically significant degree the odds of your preference succeeding. People in a large community whose political impact is actually or close to equal have no more power over their own governance, just as individuals, than they would if priests took political decisions by reading entrails. If the political impact of an ordinary citizen with an equal vote is infinitesimal, why should it matter whether the infinitesimal impact each has is equally infinitesimal?

My argument may now appear to have gone too far. It seems to end in the idea that political equality is of no importance at all. Why not then settle for enlightened autocracy? Democracy is said to have the instrumental advantages I mentioned, but these might after all be achieved through a totalitarian government as well. Indeed, many political scientists think these advantages could be more easily achieved by totalitarian government in underdeveloped economies. A dictator might take the necessary soundings to learn what most people want and give it to them without the distraction and expense of elections; he might, for example, enact a fair system of taxation and redistribution modeled on the hypothetical insurance scheme I described in Chapter 16. Do we prefer democracy only because we worry that actual dictators would rule very differently? Is there no case for democracy other than what Judith Shklar called the liberalism of fear?[12]

There is, but we must turn to the third reading of our ideal to find it. Political equality is a matter not of political power but of political standing. Democracy confirms in the most dramatic way the equal concern and respect that the community together, as the custodian of coercive power, has for each of its members. Democracy is the only form of government, short of rule by lottery, that confirms that equal concern and respect in its most fundamental constitution. If any citizen is assigned less electoral impact than others, either because he is denied a vote or they are given extra votes, or because electoral arrangements place him in a district with more people but no more representatives, or for any other reason, then the difference signals a lesser political standing for him unless it can be justified in some way that negates that signal. If the law permitted only aristocrats, or priests, or men, or Christian or white citizens, or property-owning citizens, or citizens with diplomas, to vote, then that implication of lesser concern or respect would be undeniable. It would be no answer, to a woman's demand for the vote, that one person's vote on its own would be of no value at all to her. She might reply that giving all women the vote would be likely to produce legislation that would improve her situation: by changing the rules of marriage and contract, for instance. But she would demand the vote even if she did not favor such change. She would want the dignity, not just the power, of equal participation.

It is crucial now to notice, however, that some electoral arrangements that leave political impact unequal carry no signal of disrespect, no denial of dignity, at all. Given America's unfortunate past racial injustice and the contemporary legacy of that injustice, taking special steps to increase the number of black representatives might well have important advantages for the whole community. It might help to break stereotypes that sustain racial tension and undermine black ambition.[13] It would of course be unacceptable to disenfranchise some white citizens: the vote is so emblematic a badge of equal citizenship that stripping it from any group of citizens would be an irredeemable insult to them. But suppose the goal can be achieved by redistricting that makes the election of black representatives more likely. And that the most efficient form of redistricting to that end would leave the number of voters in different districts somewhat unequal, so that it took somewhat fewer in one district than in another to elect a single representative. It might be either dominantly white or dominantly black voters whose political impact was in that way infinitesimally lowered. Or dominantly neither. In any case, there could be no implication of second-class or diminished citizenship for anyone. It would be silly, in those circumstances, to insist on the greatest possible equality of impact just for its own sake.[14]

To recapitulate. Political equality requires that political power be distributed so as to confirm the political community's equal concern and respect for all its members. Reserving power to any person or group through birth or the spoils of conquest or some aristocracy of talent, or denying the emblems of citizenship to any adult (except perhaps in consequence of a crime or other act against the community), is unacceptable. But arithmetic equality of influence is neither possible nor desirable, and arithmetic equality of impact is essential only so far as deviation means insult. The arithmetic equality of the majoritarian conception therefore has, in itself, no value at all. Majority rule is not an intrinsically fair decision procedure, and there is nothing about politics that makes it intrinsically fair there. It does not necessarily have more instrumental value than other political arrangements. If the legitimacy of a political arrangement can be improved by constitutional arrangements that create some inequality of impact but carry no taint or danger of indignity, then it would be perverse to rule these measures out. That is the fatal weakness of the majoritarian conception. It rightly emphasizes the value of equal impact, but it misunderstands the nature and hence the limits of that value; it compromises the true value at stake, which is positive liberty, by turning equality of impact into a dangerous fetish.

We choose the partnership conception of democracy. I repeat that this is not just a verbal stipulation about how we intend to use a popular honorific. By choosing the partnership and rejecting the majoritarian conception, we declare that there is no automatic or necessary compromise of any genuine political value when constitutional structures are adopted that are somewhat less likely to produce political decisions that match the majority's preferences. However, that declaration leaves open the difficult questions we have only begun to raise. The partnership conception does not automatically demand equal political impact for each citizen's vote. But it does demand this sometimes. When and why?

Representative Government

I suggest a burden of argument. Legitimacy requires a distribution of political power that reflects the equal concern and respect that the community must have for each citizen. That requirement sets a default: any significant difference in the political impact of different citizen's votes is undemocratic and wrong unless it meets two conditions, one negative and the other positive. First, it must not signal or presuppose that some people are born to rule others. There must be no aristocracy of birth, which includes an aristocracy of gender, caste, race, or ethnicity, and there must be no aristocracy of wealth or talent. Second, it must be plausible to suppose that the constitutional arrangement that creates the difference in impact improves the legitimacy of the community.

The first condition rules out the formal electoral discriminations that now belong, we hope, mainly to history, at least in the mature democracies. Adult suffrage is now in principle universal among citizens there for both genders and for all races and religions. In the United States and elsewhere, however, fossil evidence of discrimination persists. American states have in the past created barriers to registration and voting that were only thinly disguised attempts to disenfranchise some despised and feared race or the poor—these often came to the same thing. Some states still do: recently Illinois adopted a rule requiring voters to produce a driver's license or other picture ID. It is disproportionately poor people who lack that identification, and though the Supreme Court allowed the regulation to stand, its decision was mistaken.[15] We cannot take the first condition for granted anywhere.

That condition is automatically satisfied, however, by any constitutional arrangement that lowers the political impact of all citizens across the board; there can be no suspicion of indignity to any person or group when an important decision is left to an elected parliament rather than offered to the people at large in a referendum. If that decision counts as a partial disenfranchisement, it disenfranchises all unelected groups and persons equally. It is then the second condition that is in play, and we should now consider, in that light, the institution of representative government as a whole.

The majoritarian conception treats representative government as a necessary evil. It is obviously necessary: government by enormous town meeting, even on the Internet, is impossible. But representative government is potentially a serious threat to the goal of equal impact because it gives many officials each incalculably greater impact than any ordinary citizen has. The majoritarian conception hopes to reduce that possibility, as I said, by designing procedures of inducement and threat—a free press and the hurdle of frequent elections for incumbents—that make it likely that presidents and parliaments will decide as they think the majority wishes. If that strategy works, then equality of impact is effectively restored: officials become only conduits through which the majority works its will into legislation and policy. In fact, however, the strategy does not—and cannot—work very well, for both good and bad reasons. We do not discourage our officials from following their own conscience and belief in Burke's spirit rather than mimicking what they think their constituents think. We embrace term limits, for example, in the knowledge that these will make lame-duck incumbents more independent. Alas, officials have other, less creditable, reasons for disregarding what the public wants: they need to please large contributors to their reelection campaigns, and what those contributors want is often very different from what the public needs.

The majoritarian conception's defense of representative government is therefore quite weak. It is certainly not strong enough to resist the argument that major issues of principle should be submitted to large-scale referenda rather than to the ordinary political process. The nations of the European Union will continue to confront the question whether their citizens should be allowed to vote directly on new constitutional provisions for the Union, or whether the several parliaments are competent to effect those changes by treaty. The majoritarian conception must favor referenda. Such dramatic issues are not everyday occasions, and the efficiency of government will not be damaged by allowing the public as a whole to decide them.

The partnership conception offers a very different—and more successful—justification of representative government. Because it is citizens in general, not any particular group of them, whose political impact is diminished by assigning enormous power to elected officials, the institution is not an automatic deficit in democracy. On the plausible assumption that elected officials, rather than popular assemblies, are better able to protect individual rights from dangerous swings in public opinion, there can be no general democratic requirement that fundamental issues be put to referenda. So both conditions that our conception of political equality lays down for unequal political impact are met, at least in principle. It is then necessary to look to the details of electoral schedules, districts, and mechanics, and of the division of power among officials, to judge whether these are reasonably calculated to protect the democratic legitimacy they supposedly serve. There can be no algorithm for that test; hence the continuing debates about term limits, proportional representation, and the propriety of referenda. Reasonable people and politicians will disagree about which such structures improve the chance that the community will show equal respect and concern for all and each. But that is the test the partnership conception offers, not the cruder mathematics of majority rule.

Using that test reveals embarrassments. The constitutional system of every mature nation is a cragged riverbed of historical compromises, ideals, and prejudices: these may serve no purpose now, but equally they signal no disrespect for anyone. The United States provides ample illustration. The election of the president by an electoral college rather than by popular vote, and the composition of the Senate, in which sparse and populous states are each alike represented by two senators, ensure that some citizens have greater political impact than others. These inequalities are best explained as political compromises necessary long ago to create the nation. They also once had at least a colorable justification: they were thought helpful in protecting the interests of various minorities from the overweening power of richer parts of the new country. The inequalities cannot be justified in that way now—they are in fact deleterious to politics in various ways—but their preservation reflects entrenchment and inertia rather than any sense of entitlement or disrespect for anyone. Does the partnership conception nevertheless require that these inequalities be eliminated, so far as this is possible?

Elimination would not be possible without a new constitutional settlement in which either states would disappear or the small states that now enjoy an enormous advantage agree to give it up.[16] Even the bare possibility nevertheless poses an important question of principle to which the partnership conception answers: yes, we need a new settlement. The issue is not academic. I emphasized that it makes little practical difference to each citizen whether his own impact is slightly larger or smaller than anyone else's. That fact makes the arithmetical rigidity of the majoritarian conception a fetish. But institutional structures like the composition of the Senate or the mechanics of presidential elections do make a considerable practical difference overall.

Electing the president through a college rather than by direct vote distorts presidential elections: candidates concentrate their attention, and design their policies, to appeal to key "swing" states and largely neglect the others. The structure of the Senate works to the disadvantage of urban centers: legislation more favorable to their interests would be more likely if senators, like congressmen, were apportioned to states by population. If the electoral college or the present inequality of Senate representation served some purpose in promoting equal concern for all, as each was once thought to do, then the disadvantage would be merely an incidental side effect of a justified arrangement and would be acceptable for that reason. But because the inequality serves no such purpose, the disadvantage is arbitrary, and a failure to correct it, if any institution had the capacity to do so, would show an illegitimate insensitivity to the interests or opinions of those so disadvantaged.

Judicial Review

We return, finally, to the great question—old and tired now in the United States but of increasing importance elsewhere—whether judicial review is undemocratic. Should unelected judges have the power to deny the majority what it genuinely wants and its duly elected representatives have enacted? We have in mind substantive judicial review: the power of judges not simply to ensure that citizens have the information they need to properly assess their own convictions, preferences, and policies, or to protect citizens from an incumbent government anxious unfairly to perpetuate its mandate, but actually to strike down legislation whose majoritarian pedigree is undeniable. The majoritarian conception declares: no. The partnership conception replies: not necessarily.

Substantive judicial review certainly creates a limited, but within its limits vast, disparity of political impact. In America it takes only five Supreme Court justices to undo what representatives of millions of ordinary citizens—or those ordinary citizens themselves in a referendum—have done. But the first condition the partnership conception sets out is nevertheless met. That difference in political impact holds between judges and everyone else: there is no discrimination of birth or wealth in place. The second condition is therefore crucial. Is it plausible that judicial review improves democratic legitimacy overall?

Constitutional judges are typically appointed rather than elected, and their terms extend beyond—in some cases very far beyond—the terms of presidents and parliaments who appointed them. The American people can fire a senator who voted to confirm a Supreme Court justice when the senator is next up for reelection, but they cannot fire the justice he voted to appoint. These facts figure prominently in the perennial argument whether judicial review is undemocratic: the fact that judges are not elected seems cardinal among the reasons for thinking that they pose a greater threat to democracy than presidents, prime ministers, governors, or parliamentarians do. This is, however, a crude simplification; in fact a red herring.

In modern times the appointment of a American Supreme Court justice is a heavily publicized event with very great political consequences for both the president who nominates and the senators who must vote on his nomination. The excitement created by a vacancy, or even an impending one, begins long before any actual nomination. The Senate hearings are televised, media comment is intense, and senators receive daily cascades of advice and threats from constituents and interest groups. The American public as a whole has vastly more influence over who becomes a justice than it has over which senator is elected from a small state and then becomes chairman of a crucial congressional committee or investigation or which unelected official becomes secretary of defense or chairman of the Federal Reserve Bank, each of whom has very great power for good or evil.

True, the public loses control over what a justice does once appointed. But it loses control over elected officials as well, and though it can refuse to reelect them, some of them have much greater power, until the day of new judgment arrives, than single justices have over their lifetimes. A president can cry havoc and let slip the dogs of war. He may be right or wrong to do so, but the power is in any case incomparable. George W. Bush was one of the most unpopular presidents in history, but he remained adamant in pursuit of the policies that made him unpopular. The majoritarian conception of democracy might suppose, as I said it did, that politicians will always be anxious to do what the majority wants. But history teaches otherwise.

Now compare the power that judges on constitutional courts have to defy the will of the people. Unlike presidents, prime ministers, and governors, constitutional judges have no power to act independently. They sit in panels of several members, and the decisions of a panel can usually be reviewed by the full court, which may consist of a great many judges. In the American Supreme Court all the justices sit on each decision (unless some must be excused for disability or reasons of conflict). So the power of any individual judge is limited by the need to attract a majority of other judges to his view.

A phalanx of like-minded justices can indeed strike down popular laws, impair popular policies, and critically alter our electoral institutions and processes. They can make very serious mistakes in exercising that power. The Supreme Court did great damage in ruling large parts of President Franklin Roosevelt's New Deal legislation unconstitutional in the 1930s and, in the early years of Chief Justice Roberts's tenure, in striking down programs to relieve racial tension and discrimination.[17] The Court damaged democracy itself both in the way it resolved the 2000 presidential election and in its recent 5–4 ruling that corporations cannot be prevented from spending what they wish on negative television advertising to defeat legislators who oppose their interests.[18] Still, presidents, prime ministers, and senior legislators who head important committees can do more damage on their own than judges can do collectively. President Herbert Hoover had greater responsibility for economic tragedy than the Supreme Court that opposed Roosevelt's remedies did, and even the Supreme Court's worst decisions of recent years do not match in consequence those a president made. Alan Greenspan, the longtime chairman of the Federal Reserve Bank, is thought by several critics to be in some significant part responsible, through his failures of oversight, for the great 2008 crisis in world credit markets. If so, he ruined more lives over a few years than any single justice has done, on his own, even during decades of tenure. An independence index that noticed that constitutional judges are not elected, but also took into account all the other relevant factors and dimensions of power and accountability, could not confidently rank judicial review as overall more damaging to political equality, on any measure, than several other features of complex representative government.

That is not, however, the main question now. This is rather the second of our two conditions. Does the institution of judicial review contribute overall to the legitimacy of a government? Representative government is indeed necessary: some temporary concentration of power in a few hands is indispensable if a large political community is to survive and prosper. That is not true of judicial review; large nations have survived and prospered without it, and some still do. Any defense of judicial review as democratic must take some other form: it must argue that judicial review improves overall legitimacy by making it more likely that the community will settle on and enforce some appropriate conception of negative liberty and of a fair distribution of resources and opportunities, as well as of the positive liberty that is the subject of this chapter.

Whether that argument can succeed for any political community obviously depends on a host of factors that vary from place to place. These include the strength of the rule of law, the independence of the judiciary, and the character of the constitution judges are asked to enforce. Judicial review may well be less necessary in nations where stable majorities have a strong record of protecting the legitimacy of their government by correctly identifying and respecting the rights of individuals and minorities. Unfortunately history discloses few such nations, even among the mature democracies. The recent reactions of both the United States and the United Kingdom to terrorist threats illustrates a failure of nerve and honor in both these somewhat different political cultures, for instance.

Nothing guarantees in advance that judicial review either will or will not make a majoritarian community more legitimate and democratic. Other strategies for supervising and correcting majoritarian politics can be imagined that might prove superior. Perhaps, for example, the upper house of the British Parliament will be reformed by electing members (without comic titles or dress) for a single longish term and making former members of the

House of Commons ineligible. Such a body would enjoy much more popular support than the present institution but would remain sufficiently insulated from party politics so that it might be entrusted with barring legislation that it deemed contrary to Britain's Human Rights Act. Much less radical changes could be imagined that might improve the performance of existing constitutional bodies and courts: I have elsewhere recommended, for example, that justices of the American Supreme Court be subject to long term limits.[19]

History is not decisive of the large question whether judicial review can be expected to improve legitimacy in the future. But history counts. I am denying what many lawyers and political scientists claim: that judicial review is inevitably and automatically a defect in democracy. But it does not follow that any democracy has actually benefited from the institution. Whether the American Supreme Court has in fact improved democracy in the United States depends on a judgment you and I might make differently. For years I was accused of defending judicial review because I approved of the decisions the Supreme Court actually made. I am no longer open to that charge. If I had to judge the American Supreme Court only on its record during the last few years, I would judge it a failure.[20] But I believe that the overall balance of its historical impact remains positive. Everything now turns on the character of future Supreme Court nominations. We must keep our fingers crossed.

19

Law

Law and Morals

The Classical View

I have written more about law than other parts of political morality. My aim in this chapter is not to summarize my jurisprudential views in any detail but rather to show how they take their place within the integrated scheme of value this book attempts.[1] I can therefore be—at least relatively—brief. I concentrate on what is no doubt the hottest of the chestnuts burning lawyers' fingers for centuries: What is the relation between law and morals? I begin by describing how that problem has traditionally been conceived by almost all legal philosophers, including once myself, and then argue for a sharp revision in how we understand the issues in play.

Here is the orthodox picture. "Law" and "morals" describe different collections of norms. The differences are deep and important. Law belongs to a particular community. Morality does not: it consists of a set of standards or norms that have imperative force for everyone. Law is, at least for the most part, made by human beings through contingent decisions and practices of different sorts. It is a contingent fact that the law in Rhode Island requires people to compensate others whom they injure negligently. Morality is not made by anyone (except, on some views, a god), and it is not contingent on any human decision or practice. It is a necessary, not contingent, fact that people who injure others negligently have a moral obligation to compensate them if they can.

I am describing morality as most people understand it: what I called in Chapter 2 the "ordinary" view. Some philosophers reject this description: they are conventionalists or relativists or skeptics of some other form. They think that morality is more like law in all the ways I distinguished: that it belongs to communities, that it is made by people, that it is contingent. I suggested in Part One why I believe this view indefensible: for now I only mean to describe morality as you and I understand it. But the orthodox picture explains just as well how relativists and conventionalists see the relation between law and morals. They agree that these are different systems of norms and that problems arise about the connections between them, even though they think that both law and morality are man-made.

The classical jurisprudential question asks: How are these two different collections of norms related or connected? One kind of connection is obvious. When a community decides what legal norms to create, it should be guided and restrained by morality. It should not, except in very exceptional emergency circumstances, make laws it believes unjust. The classical question asks about a different kind of connection. How does the content of each system affect the content of the other as things actually stand? Questions arise in both directions. How far do our moral obligations and responsibilities depend on what the law in fact provides? Do we have a moral obligation to obey the law whatever it is? How far do our legal rights and obligations depend, as things stand, on what morality requires? Can an immoral rule really be part of the law?

We reviewed the first set of these questions in Chapter 14. We concentrate now on the second set. How far is morality relevant in fixing what the law requires on any particular issue? Lawyers have defended a great variety of theories. But I will consider only two of these: what is called "legal positivism" and what we may call "interpretivism." These labels are not important, because nothing in the argument I'll make—that the traditional way of understanding these theories is misleading—depends on my labels' historical accuracy.

Here is a very general account of the two theories. Positivism declares the complete independence of the two systems. What the law is depends only on historical matters of fact: it depends finally on what the community in question, as a matter of custom and practice, accepts as law.[2] If an unjust law

meets the community's accepted test for law—if it was adopted by a legislature and the judges all agree that the legislature is the supreme lawmaker—
then the unjust law really is law. Interpretivism, on the other hand, denies
that law and morals are wholly independent systems. It argues that law includes not only the specific rules enacted in accordance with the community's
accepted practices but also the principles that provide the best moral justification for those enacted rules. The law then also includes the rules that follow
from those justifying principles, even though those further rules were never
enacted. Interpretivism, in other words, treats legal reasoning as I have argued in this book we must treat all interpretive reasoning. It treats the concept of law as an interpretive concept.

Actually there are several concepts of law, and it is necessary now briefly
to distinguish among these.[3] We use "law" in a sociological sense, as when
we say that law began in primitive societies; an aspirational sense, as when we
celebrate the rule of law; and a doctrinal sense we use to report what the law is
on some subject, as when we say that under the law of Connecticut fraud is a
tort. Positivism and interpretivism are both theories about the correct use of
the doctrinal concept. Positivism has traditionally treated that concept as criterial: it has aimed to identify the tests of pedigree that lawyers or at least legal
officials share for identifying true propositions of doctrinal law. Interpretivism
treats the doctrinal concept as interpretive: it treats lawyers' claims about what
the law holds or requires on some matter as conclusions of an interpretive argument, even though most of the interpretive work is almost always hidden.

Forgive a paragraph of autobiography. When more than forty years ago I
first tried to defend interpretivism, I defended it within this orthodox two-
systems picture.[4] I assumed that law and morals are different systems of
norms and that the crucial question is how they interact. So I said what I
have just said: that the law includes not just enacted rules, or rules with pedigree, but justifying principles as well. I soon came to think, however, that the
two-systems picture of the problem was itself flawed, and I began to approach the issue through a very different picture.[5] I did not fully appreciate
the nature of that picture, however, or how different it is from the orthodox
model, until later when I began to consider the larger issues of this book.

The Fatal Flaw

There is a flaw in the two-systems picture. Once we take law and morality to
compose separate systems of norms, there is no neutral standpoint from which

LAW   403

the connections between these supposedly separate systems can be adjudi-
cated. Where shall we turn for an answer to the question whether positivism
or interpretivism is a more accurate or otherwise better account of how the
two systems relate? Is this a moral question or a legal question? Either choice
yields a circular argument with much too short a radius.

Suppose we treat the question as legal. We look to legal material—
constitutions, statutes, judicial decisions, customary practices, and the rest—
and we ask: What does the correct reading of all that material declare the relation between law and morality to be? We cannot answer that question without
a theory in hand about how to read legal material, and we can't have such a
theory until we have already decided what role morality plays in fixing the
content of the law. When we ask whether the legal material demonstrates or
denies a connection between law and morality, do we suppose that the material includes not only rules with a pedigree in conventional practice but also
the principles necessary to justify those rules? If not, then we have built positivism in from the start and must not feign surprise when positivism emerges
at the end. But if we do include justifying principles, then we have built in
interpretivism.

If we turn to morality for our answer, on the other hand, we beg the question in the opposite direction. We can say: Would it be good for justice if
morality played the part in legal analysis that interpretivism claims it does?
Or is it actually better for the moral tone of a community if law and morals
are kept separate as the positivists insist? These questions certainly make
sense; they are indeed key jurisprudential questions. But according to the
two-systems picture they can produce only circular arguments. If law and
morals are two separate systems, it begs the question to suppose that the best
theory of what law is depends on such moral issues. That assumes we have
already decided against positivism.

Analytic Jurisprudence?

The two-systems picture therefore faces an apparently insoluble problem: it
poses a question that cannot be answered other than by assuming an answer
from the start. That logical difficulty explains what would otherwise be a remarkable fact: the turn in Anglo-American jurisprudence, by positivists beginning in the nineteenth century, to the surprising idea that the puzzle
about law and morals is neither a legal nor a moral problem but instead a
conceptual one: that it can be settled through an analysis of the very concept

of law. (To be more precise: that it can be settled through an analysis of what I called the "doctrinal" concept of law.)[6] We can excavate the nature or essence of that concept without making any prior legal or moral assumptions, the positivists claimed, and then we see plainly that the actual content of law is one thing and what the law should be quite another, so that law and morals are conceptually distinct. Something even more curious happened. Other lawyers, who rejected positivism, nevertheless accepted this account of their problem's character. They tried to show that philosophical analysis of the doctrinal concept of law reveals, contrary to positivism, that morality does have a role in legal reasoning.

We have already noticed, in Chapter 8, the fallacy in these shared assumptions. We cannot solve the circularity problem of the two-systems picture through an analysis of the concept of law unless that concept can sensibly be treated as a criterial (or perhaps as a natural-kind) concept. But it cannot be. There is no agreement among lawyers and judges in complex and mature political communities about how to decide which propositions of law are true. No wonder positivists have had such difficulty in explaining the kind or mode of conceptual analysis they have in mind. John Austin, a nineteenth-century positivist, said that this was just a matter of the correct use of language, which is plainly wrong. H. L. A. Hart, though he called his most influential book *The Concept of Law,* never offered much by way of explanation of what he took conceptual analysis to be.[7] When he wrote that book, in Oxford, the dominant account of analysis among Oxford philosophers supposed that analysis consists in making evident the hidden convergent speech practices of ordinary users of the language. But there are no convergent practices to expose. The doctrinal concept of law can only be understood as an interpretive concept with the character and structure we reviewed in Chapter 8. So defending an analysis of that interpretive concept can only mean defending a controversial theory of political morality. An analysis of the concept must assume from the start an intimate connection between law and morality. The supposed escape from the circularity problem is no escape at all.

There is guidance as well as correction in this explanation. Because the doctrinal concept of law is an interpretive concept, we must begin any analysis of that concept by identifying the political, commercial, and social practices in which the concept figures. These practices assume that people have, among other political rights, rights with a special feature: these are legal rights because they are enforceable on demand in an adjudicative political institution such as a court. We construct a conception of law—an account of the grounds needed to support a claim of right enforceable on demand in that way—by finding a justification of those practices in a larger integrated network of political value. We construct a theory of law, that is, in the same way that we construct a theory of other political values—of equality, liberty, and democracy. Any theory of law, understood in that interpretive way, will inevitably be controversial, just as those latter theories are.

Law as Morality

A Tree Structure

We have now scrapped the old picture that counts law and morality as two separate systems and then seeks or denies, fruitlessly, interconnections between them. We have replaced this with a one-system picture: we now treat law as a part of political morality. That will sound absurd to some readers and paradoxical to others. It seems to suggest, idiotically, that a community's law is always exactly what it should be. Many readers will think that I have finally pressed my ambition to unify value too far: I have indeed become Procrustes sacrificing sense to a philosophical theory. In fact I have in mind something much less revolutionary and much less counterintuitive.

The latter parts of this book have seen a tree structure growing. We saw how personal morality might be thought to flow from ethics and then how political morality might be seen to flow from personal morality. Our aim has been to integrate what are often taken to be separate departments of evaluation. We can easily place the doctrinal concept of law in that tree structure: law is a branch, a subdivision, of political morality. The more difficult question is how that concept should be distinguished from the rest of political morality—how these two interpretive concepts should be distinguished to show one as a distinct part of the other. Any plausible answer will center on the phenomenon of institutionalization.

Political rights can be distinguished from personal moral rights only in a community that has developed some version of what Hart called secondary rules: rules establishing legislative, executive, and adjudicative authority and jurisdiction.[8] Legal rights can sensibly be distinguished from other political rights only if that community has at least an embryonic version of the separation of powers Montesquieu described.[9] It is then necessary to distinguish two classes of political rights and duties. Legislative rights are rights that the community's lawmaking powers be exercised in a certain way: to create and administer a system of public education, for instance, and not to censor political speech. Legal rights are those that people are entitled to enforce on demand, without further legislative intervention, in adjudicative institutions that direct the executive power of sheriff or police. The law of contract gives me a right, on demand, to force you to repay my loan. The political obligation we discussed in Chapter 14—to obey whatever laws lawmaking institutions adopt—is a legal obligation because it can be enforced on official demand in and through such institutions. Of course, both kinds of rights may be controversial: it may be controversial that I do have a right that a particular educational scheme be adopted or that I do have a right enforceable on demand that you repay what I claim to be a loan. The difference is not one of certainty but of opportunity. Legislative rights must wait their turn: in a democracy the vagaries of politics will determine which legislative rights will be redeemed and when. Legal rights are subject to different vagaries, but in principle they entitle individual members of the community to secure what they ask through processes directly available. Legislative rights, even when acknowledged, are of no immediate force; legal rights, once acknowledged, are immediately enforceable, on demand, through adjudicative rather than legislative institutions.

The distinction has no necessary sociological consequence. Claims about legislative rights play an important role in politics even when there is little chance that they will be recognized in parliamentary action; legal rights play their most important role in social and commercial life when there is no prospect of or even interest in adjudicative enforcement. But the distinction is nevertheless philosophically illuminating: it teaches how we should understand political theories and theories of law. General political philosophy treats, among many other issues, legislative rights. A theory of law treats legal rights, but it is nevertheless a political theory because it seeks a normative answer to a normative political question: Under what conditions do people acquire genuine rights and duties that are enforceable on demand in the way described?

That question may be put at different levels of abstraction: it may be asked about a particular political community, like Belgium or the European Union, or, most abstractly, about everywhere or nowhere. I emphasize that it is a question of political morality but—as this distinction among levels of abstraction assumes—ordinary political facts are very likely to figure in the answer. It must be part of any responsible answer, at any level of abstraction, that historical facts about legislation and, perhaps, social convention do play a role. How great or exclusive a role these play is a matter of contest. Legal positivism argues that such historical acts or conduct is exclusively decisive in deciding what legal rights people have. Interpretivism offers a different answer, in which principles of political morality also have a part to play. Once we see these positions as rival normative political theories, not as rival claims about unpacking criterial concepts, we are able to correct a historical mistake. Too much jurisprudence has traveled from some declaration about the essence or very concept of law to theories about rights and duties of people and officials. Our journey must be in the opposite direction: vocabulary should follow political argument, not the other way around. As we shall soon see, ancient jurisprudential puzzles, such as the puzzles of evil law, take very different shape when we take that order of argument to heart.

We have now placed legal rights in our evolving tree structure and so filled out the one-system picture of law and politics. Legal rights are political rights, but a special branch because they are properly enforceable on demand through adjudicative and coercive institutions without need for further legislation or other lawmaking activity. There is nothing mysterious or metaphysical in this way of accommodating law in our structure: it supposes no emergent forces. Nor—this is crucial—does it deny the distinctness of questions about what the law is and what it ought to be.

Is and Ought: Family Morality

I emphasize that last claim—that the integrated, one-system picture does not deny the obviously essential distinction between what law is and what it should be. Here is a banal domestic story: the development of a special moral code or practice for a single family. You have two children: a teenage girl, G, and her younger brother, B. G has promised to take B to a sold-out and much-heralded pop concert for which she has been lucky enough to acquire two tickets. But someone she has been anxious to date calls, and she offers the place to him instead. B protests and comes to you; he wants you to make G keep her word. An army of questions arises. Do you have legitimate associational authority, as a parent, to tell G what to do or to tell B what to accept? Do they have distinct associational obligations to do or to accept what you say, just as your children? If you think that you do have that authority, and that they do have that obligation, then are coercive measures appropriate—threats that will induce G to keep her promise even though she does not wish to do so or does not think that she should? Are there conditions on your use of coercive authority beyond your conviction that she should keep her promise?

If so, what are those further conditions? How far are they supplied or shaped by your family's history? Does it matter—and if so, in what way—how you have exercised your authority on similar occasions in the past? Or, if you have a partner, how that partner exercised a similar authority? What makes a past occasion similar? What if you have revised your opinion about the importance of promising? You used to think promises should almost never be broken; now you are attracted to a more flexible view. How far should you regard yourself as required by your past decisions to treat new claims in the old way? Do you have to announce your changed views in advance of the events that give rise to new arguments? Or can you immediately decide new controversies as you now think right? Need you try to anticipate, as you reflect on these issues, the other controversies that will inevitably arise? How far must you adjust or simplify your arguments now so that your rulings provide adequate guidance to allow the family to anticipate what you will decide in the future?

The family story nicely illustrates how a distinction between what law is and what it ought to be can arise as a complexity within morality itself. As you decide the domestic questions, you construct a distinct institutional morality: a special morality governing the use of coercive authority within your family. This is a dynamic morality; as pronouncements are made and enforced on concrete occasions, that special family morality shifts. At some point a difference clearly emerges between two questions. What conditions hold, now, on the use of coercive authority within the family, given its distinct history? What conditions would a better family history, reflecting better answers to questions like those I listed, have produced? It is crucial to see that these two different questions are *both* moral questions and that they must undoubtedly attract different answers. It would be wrong to think that the special family history has created a distinct nonmoral code, like traditions of dress, that have some form of authority within the family that is not a moral authority.

That would be a mistake because the reasons that you and other members of the family have for deferring to this history are themselves moral reasons. They draw on principles of fairness that condition coercion—principles about fair play, fair notice, and a fair distribution of authority, for instance, that make your family's distinct history morally pertinent. We may call these structuring principles because they create your distinct family morality. If you made a decision now that did not respect those structuring principles— for example, by imposing a standard on G that you refused to enforce in her favor on some earlier occasion—your decision would be not simply surprising, like wearing a tie to a picnic, but unfair. Unfair, that is, unless some new and better interpretation of those principles shows why it is not unfair. And, of course, any new interpretation of these principles, like any interpretation of social history, is itself a moral exercise: it calls on moral conviction. These facts certainly do not erase the distinction between what the family morality is and what it should have been. The best interpretation of the structuring principles may well require that some decision now regretted nevertheless be followed as a precedent. Fresh interpretation of these principles might well mitigate the difference between family and more general morality. But it cannot erase the difference. You may well feel obliged to command what you wish you did not have to command.[10]

What Difference Does It Make?

Theory

If lawyers and laymen take up the integrated, one-system theory of law in place of the dead-end two-systems model, legal philosophy and practice will shift. The substance of the old confrontation between positivism and interpretivism would remain, but, as I said, in a political rather than conceptual form. A political global positivist would need arguments why justice should never count in deciding how the constitutional or substantive law of a political community should be interpreted, and it is hard to imagine where he might find such arguments. But a narrower, more selective kind of positivism defended on political grounds might well seem persuasive to some. A positivist might argue, for example, that ambiguous or vague statutes should be read in whatever way the legislature that adopted them would most likely have decided if confronted with the choice. He might say that making interpretation turn on a historical test in that way would improve predictability; that though that test might not eliminate uncertainty and controversy, it would substantially reduce them.[11] Or he might say that allowing even long-dead elected legislators to decide political issues, even counterfactually, is more democratic than entrusting those issues to the moral sensibilities of unelected contemporary judges. In any case, jurisprudence would become both more challenging and more important. Treating legal theory as a branch of political philosophy, to be pursued in philosophy and politics departments as well as law schools, would deepen both disciplines.

Evil Law

Certain other changes in substantive legal theory might follow as well. If we treat law as a branch of political morality, we need to distinguish between legal and other political rights. I have suggested one way: that we classify legal rights as those that are enforceable on demand in the way I described. Much academic writing rejects that suggestion, however. Legal philosophers argue, for instance, about an ancient jurisprudential puzzle of almost no practical importance that has nevertheless had a prominent place in seminars on legal theory: the puzzle of evil law. The Fugitive Slave Act, passed by the American Congress before the Civil War, declared that slaves who escaped to free states remained slaves and required officials of those states to return them into slavery. Judges asked to enforce the Act faced, as some of them described it, a moral dilemma. They believed that though the Act was wicked, it was nevertheless valid law.[12] They therefore thought they had to choose among three unpleasant alternatives: enforcing what they knew to be grave injustice; resigning, which would only mean that other officials would enforce that injustice; or lying about what they thought the law was.

This description of their dilemma seems to presuppose the two-systems account of law and morality. It seems to require a firm distinction between the questions of what the law is and whether judges should enforce that law. But the integrated account all but erases the difference between these two questions. It distinguishes law from the rest of political morality, in effect, by defining a legal right as a right to a judicial decision. It seems to force us to say either that the Fugitive Slave Act was not valid law after all, which seems contrary to near-universal opinion, or that judges did have a duty to enforce that wicked law.

We should remember, as we begin our response to this objection, the decisive objections to the two-systems picture we noticed earlier. It is not an option; we must find some way of explaining the evil law puzzle within the integrated conception. Set the question of nomenclature—should we call the

Fugitive Slave Act law—aside for a moment. Concentrate first on the underlying moral issue. Did judges have a political obligation, given their role and circumstances, to rule in favor of slaveholders claiming their escaped "property"? This is a more complex question than might first appear. The United States Congress (let us assume) was sufficiently legitimate so that its enactments generally created political obligations. The structuring fairness principles that make law a distinct part of political morality—principles about political authority, precedent, and reliance—gave the slaveholders' claims more moral force than they would otherwise have had. But their moral claims were nevertheless and undoubtedly undermined by a stronger moral argument of human rights. So the law should not have been enforced. That is the right answer, let us assume, to the basic moral question.

Now return to nomenclature. We seem to have a choice. We might say that the slaveholders had, in principle, a political right to regain their slaves on demand but that this right was trumped, in the language I used in Chapter 14, by an emergency—in this case a moral emergency. We express that thought best by saying what most lawyers would say: that the Act was valid law but too unjust to enforce. Or we might say that the slaveholders did not have a right to what they asked even in principle. We express that conclusion by saying what some other lawyers would say: that the Act was too unjust to count as valid law.

The first account, and therefore the first way of putting the point, seems preferable in these circumstances. It expresses nuances that the second smothers. It explains why the judges confronted with the Act faced, as they said, a moral dilemma and not simply a prudential one. The second option would seem more accurate, however, in another, very different, case that is also often cited in academic seminars. The hideous Nazi edicts did not create even prima facie or arguable rights and duties. The purported Nazi government was fully illegitimate, and no other structuring principles of fairness argued for enforcement of those edicts. It is morally more accurate to deny that these edicts were law. The German judges asked to enforced them faced only prudential dilemmas, not moral ones.

The integrated account of law allows this discrimination. The dead-end two-systems picture does not. However, the important question posed by these familiar academic examples is the moral one we first considered. It would be misleading, in my opinion, to say flatly either that the Fugitive Slave Act was not valid law, or that the Nazi edicts were valid law. Misleading in both cases because these descriptions obscure morally important aspects of each case and differences between them. But the infelicity of expression would not amount to conceptual error. The ancient jurisprudential problem of evil law is sadly close to a verbal dispute.

Partial Enforcement

Other judges and writers depend on the two-systems picture in other ways. Some argue, for instance, that the United States Constitution creates legal rights that are not properly enforced by courts: this seems, once again, to assume a distinction between theories of law and theories of adjudication. When the United States D.C. Circuit Court overruled a lower court decision that ordered the government to admit Uighur detainees wrongly held in Guantánamo Bay, it explained, "Not every violation of a right yields a remedy, even when the right is constitutional."[13]

Lawrence Sager, a prominent defender of that thesis, offers examples like this one.[14] A constitution declares that people have a right to state-financed health care. A constitutional court believes that it is not well placed to adjudicate all the delicate questions of budget allocation and medical science that it would face if it tried to decide exactly which health plan citizens were entitled to have. So it declines to enforce that constitutional right directly. It concedes that a government that put in place no plan at all would be in violation of its citizens' legal rights. But it refuses to require any such plan. However, if government does establish a health care system, the court would rule on citizens' claims that the rules of that system discriminate illegitimately or refuse care arbitrarily. In these circumstances, Sager and others wish to say that citizens do have a legal right to health care, granted by the constitution, but that courts enforce only part of what they are legally entitled to have. Citizens must look to legislation for the most important part: to have some health care rather than none.

This is indeed an available way to describe the situation: no one would misunderstand. The different vocabulary I suggest seems at least equally natural, however. We might say that not all the rights a constitution declares are legal rights. Some, like those touching foreign policy, or those much more efficiently enforced by other branches of government, are best treated as political but not legal—that is, as rights not enforceable by private citizens on demand. Others, like a right to the equal protection of any health care scheme that a government does adopt, are indeed legal rights. Which of these rather different ways of describing the situation is theoretically sounder?

The first description—that some legal rights are not enforceable on demand—might be tempting if we could sensilbly adopt the two-systems view and a positivist theory of how we should decide what the law is. We might then say that though certain constitutional rights meet the tests for valid law and are hence legal rights, there are independent reasons why courts should not try to enforce them. But once we reject the two-systems view as self-defeating, there seems no sound theoretical basis for that position. It would make little sense to say what we said about the Fugitive Slave Act: that citizens have a prima facie constitutional right to medical care on demand that is however trumped by some emergency that prevents judges from actually enforcing it. In the Slave Act case, the structuring principles of fairness that distinguish legal from other political rights do argue for enforcement: they support the claims of the slaveholders. In the medical case, it is these very principles, which include principles about the best allocation of political power in a coercive state, that supply the argument against enforcement.

The Morality of Procedure

The two-systems picture created an important distinction between process and substance: between the procedures through which law is created and the content of the law that is created. The long debate about law and morals concentrated on substance. Is an immoral law really law? Does justice help decide whether people swindled by Bernie Madoff can sue the Securities and Exchange Commission for negligence? The debate left process largely alone: it seemed plain to most academic lawyers that the methods through which law is created are a matter of local convention whose properties are fixed entirely by that convention.[15] Indeed, that assumption seems essential to the two-systems picture. It would be hard to defend positivism, even on that picture, if judges disagreed about important issues of constitutional procedure. But once we reject the two-systems model, and count law a distinct part of political morality, we must treat the special structuring principles that separate law from the rest of political morality as themselves political principles that need a moral reading.

When I was a law student in Britain, more than half a century ago, I was told that in that country, unlike America, the legislature—Parliament—is supreme. That was held to be a cardinal example of what was just true as a matter of unchallengeable law: it went without saying. But it hardly went without saying in an earlier century: Lord Coke disagreed in the seventeenth century, for instance.[16] Nor does it go without saying now. Many lawyers, and at least some judges, now believe that Parliament's power is indeed limited. When the government recently floated the idea of a bill that would oust the courts of jurisdiction over detainees suspected of terrorism, these lawyers claimed that such an act would be null and void.[17] What changed, and then changed again?

The answer seems clear enough. Once, in Coke's time, the idea that individuals have rights as trumps over the collective good—natural rights—was very widely accepted. In the nineteenth century a different political morality was dominant. Jeremy Bentham declared natural rights nonsense on stilts, and lawyers of that opinion created the idea of absolute parliamentary sovereignty. Now the wheel is turning again: utilitarianism is giving way once again to a recognition of individual rights, now called human rights, and parliamentary sovereignty is no longer evidently just. The status of Parliament as lawgiver, among the most fundamental of legal issues, has once again become a deep question of political morality. Law is effectively integrated with morality: lawyers and judges are working political philosophers of a democratic state.

American constitutional lawyers have debated whether the very abstract substantive constitutional clauses—those, for example, that guarantee rights to free speech and religion, to freedom from cruel and unusual punishment, to equal protection of the laws, and to due process of law—should be read as moral principles.[18] But interpretation of the more concrete clauses of the document has usually been thought to depend on history, not morality. Two recent Supreme Court cases illustrate that assumption. The first of these turned on the Second Amendment's guarantee of some constitutional right to firearms. The Court offered an extended discussion of English law in the eighteenth and earlier centuries to support its ruling that this amendment grants individual citizens rights against a flat prohibition on handguns. The dissenting arguments appealed to the same period of history to contradict that conclusion.[19] The second case arose under a constitutional clause that allows Congress to suspend the right of habeas corpus only in special circumstances but does not specify who is otherwise entitled to the writ. A 5–4 majority of the Court held that aliens detained at Guantánamo Bay were entitled to habeas corpus.[20] The strongly worded dissenting opinion insisted that only classes of people who were entitled to the writ in the eighteenth century were entitled to it now.[21] The majority opinion did not object to that claim, but ruled that the history was inconclusive and held that the alien detainees could therefore bring actions under the writ.

The Court's debates in these cases would make some sense if we adopted the two-systems model of law and political morality. History might then seem decisive in deciding how the Constitution's more technical clauses should be read. But history seems much less relevant once we accept that constitutional interpretation aims at making best sense of the Constitution's words as provision for just government. The circumstances of the eighteenth century were entirely different from those that confront any nation now, and practice then was governed in good part by moral and political standards we long ago rejected. We must therefore do our best, within the constraints of interpretation, to make our country's fundamental law what our sense of justice would approve, not because we must sometimes compromise law with morality, but because that is exactly what the law, properly understood, itself requires.

Epilogue: Dignity Indivisible

Once More: Truth

The big bang of the Galilean revolution made the world of value safe for science. But the new republic of ideas became itself an empire. The modern philosophers inflated the methods of physics into a totalitarian metaphysics. They invaded and occupied all the honorifics—reality, truth, fact, ground, meaning, knowledge, and being—and dictated the terms on which other bodies of thought might aspire to them. The question has now become whether and how the world of science can be made safe for value.

The great variety of isms we studied in Chapter 3 tried to meet that challenge. Philosophers become existentialists, emotivists, anti-realists, expressivists, constructivists, and anything else they could imagine. But each of these oases dried up, so each generation of philosophers imagined and wandered to a new one. That parade will not stop anytime soon. But the isms are all unsatisfactory, because the idea they share—that value judgments can't *really* be true—loses any sense when the pointless italics are removed. They are all grounded, whatever their mechanics or decorations, in a supposedly external skepticism that in one way or another swallows itself.

Some philosophers—"realists"—protested against the imperial assumption, which they called "scientism." But as we saw, mainly in Chapter 4, their break with establishment metaphysics was for the most part not a clean one: they worried still about how judgments of value might satisfy at least some minimal test the metaphysics of science had set, some test of convergence or ground or the power to explain facts of conviction or behavior. Once we take seriously enough the profound independence of morality, ethics, and other forms of value, however, we find that none of these accommodations is necessary or works. We need a cleaner break, a new revolution. Of course, we need to distinguish responsible from irresponsible opinion. We particularly need that distinction in politics, when justice is at stake, and we cannot have the distinction without taking on ideas of truth and falsity as well. But we must find our conceptions of truth and falsity, responsibility and irresponsibility, facts and realism, within the realms of value itself—on as clean a sheet as possible. We must abandon colonial metaphysics.

We have touched on a postcolonial conception of truth many times in this book: in explaining why politics needs truth, unmasking external skepticism, defining moral responsibility, locating truth in interpretation, distinguishing interpretive concepts, and finally, in taking truth to be itself an interpretive concept. Our journey has been steadily one of liberation. Ethics and morality are independent of physics and its partners: value is in that way freestanding. We cannot certify the truth of our value judgments through physical or biological or metaphysical discoveries; no more can we impeach them that way. We must make a case, not supply evidence, for our convictions, and that distinction demands a kind of integrity in value that in turn sponsors a different account of responsibility.

Does the disappointment remain? It is hard for us, in our time, fully to escape the gravity of scientism and therefore fully to grasp the independence of value. But remember the most important lesson of Part One: there must be a right answer about the best thing to do, even if that answer is only that nothing is. That is not a trick: it is a way of reminding yourself that skepticism is not a default. Any conviction that nothing matters must be as much the target of your suspicion and doubt—and misplaced hope for external validation—as any more positive conviction. If you do think that nothing matters, remember that that is also a conclusion that other people, who think as hard and long as you, do not accept. There is no escape from the isolation of believing what others do not. Skepticism or nihilism is certainly no escape.

Remember also that there is a great deal that you *do* believe about how to live. If you pursue the responsibility project of Chapter 6, you will probably achieve at least some limited integrated set of opinions that carries visceral authenticity for you. If you do, what kind of hesitation or doubt would then make sense? Why shouldn't you simply believe what you then believe? Really *believe* it? It cannot matter that psychodynamics or cultural history or genetic dissection, rather than truth itself, explains why you believe what you do. No causal explanation of any kind could validate any conviction, including a skeptical one. True, you might have believed something else. But this is, in fact, what you do believe. You might come not to believe it later, of course. Further responsible reflection might produce that change. But if you have been responsible, you have no reason, pending further reflection, not to believe—fully believe—what you believe. This is not quietism: there is nothing it asks us to be quiet about. It is only telling it like it is.

What if you have not managed confidence in any even rough opinion about how best to live, not even that there is no best way to live? You are uncertain. But uncertainty too, as we saw, assumes that there is truth to be had. You may well find, as you live, that you are following some opinion. Perhaps, as Sartre supposed, you are building a style though you never pause to notice it. Or you may confront your problem more self-consciously: climb a mountain, find a guru, or join a mystic movement. Or you might not: you might lead your life as just one damn thing after another, not defiant in your skepticism but only aimless because you lack even that. You are then, at least in my opinion, not living well. But there is nothing to be done except to wait. Perhaps only for Godot.

Good Lives and Living Well

We wanted not simply to identify the independence of value but to find at least a rough template for the unity of value. We wanted to vindicate a hedgehog's search for justice in a much more inclusive theory of ethics and morality. I end by returning to the core ethical issue in our structure.

Someone lives well when he senses and pursues a good life for himself and does so with dignity: with respect for the importance of other people's lives and for their ethical responsibility as well as his own. The two ethical ideals—living well and having a good life—are different. We can live well without having a good life: we may suffer bad luck or great poverty or serious injustice or a terrible disease and a premature death. The value of our striving is adverbial; it does not lie in the goodness or impact of the life realized. That is why people who live and die in great poverty can nevertheless live well. Even so we must each do what we can to make our own life as good as it could have been. You live badly if you do not try hard enough to make your life good.

The most arresting focus for life is death. We study a life best retrospectively, as it appears near its end. Then we cannot escape the question whether the joys and tears, the glitter and prizes and treats, have come to anything that can quiet the dread or do more than mock the silliness of having cared. Our two principles of dignity seem most stark from that perspective. The second commands us to take personal responsibility for the choices that we have made. We concentrated in Part Five on the political dimension of that responsibility: though we are never free of the vocabularies and pressures of our culture, we must nevertheless insist on freedom from domination. The positive requirements are equally important. A constantly examined life is narcissistic; a poor life. But living well must include some awareness, from time to time, of the values the life exhibits or denies; living must be more than finding oneself pulled by unexamined habit through worn grooves of expectation and reward. The wholly unexamined life, as the ancient philosophers warned us, is also a bad one. Some effective ethical conviction, at least sometimes engaged, is essential to responsibility in living.

There are dimensions to authenticity. Doing it your way is creative even if the "it" that you do is familiar. Style counts; in my view it counts very much. But style is not enough: appraisal is also important. You do not live as well as you might if you have never had occasion to reflect on what living well means for you in your situation. Skepticism might be the cost of that examination: you may come to think that nothing matters in how you live. But living with that thought, right or wrong, gives you more dignity than never even to have considered the possibility. For many people a good life is one observant in a particular religion. They may be right or wrong in the cosmology this assumes, but in either case their lives lack full dignity if they have never even pondered that cosmology.

Our first principle has a different, more substantive, force. Good lives are not trivial, and someone's life does not achieve the needed importance just because he thinks it does. Someone who spends his life in the trivial hobby I mentioned—collecting matchbook covers—does not create a good life, even if his collection is of unmatched completeness and even if he acts always with great dignity, always treating others with proper respect for the importance of their lives. His life may be good for some other reason; otherwise it is wasted.

It is difficult to say what gives weight as well as dignity to a life: what else it needs to make it good. Some people's lives are made good by great and durable achievement, but as we noticed this can be true for only very few people.[1] Most good lives are good for much more transitory effects: for skill in some challenging craft or raising a family or making the lives of other people better. There are a thousand ways in which a life can be good; but many more ways, other than triviality, in which it can be bad, or at least less good than it might have been.

It can be bad through poverty, but the economics of good and bad lives are complex. I summarize now a distinction and a point I made earlier and elsewhere.[2] When I come to consider what life would be good for me, I must distinguish between two aspects of my situation: the parameters that affect the answer—my culture, background, talents, tastes, and allegiances—and the limitations that make it difficult or impossible for me to lead the life—or any of the lives—that those parameters pick out as good. Disease and physical handicaps count as limitations, not parameters; they do not help to define what lives would be good for me but may rather doom me to a bad one.

My material resources and economic, social, and political opportunities may, however, be either parameters or limitations. I must count those that are due entirely to the stage of economic development that my community has reached as parameters: I cannot suppose that my life is bad just because my historical period or geographical platform has not achieved the prosperity that other generations or more prosperous continents will know or have known. If, on the other hand, my resource or opportunity is less because I or my community have been treated unjustly, then that injustice is a limitation, not a parameter. Whether relative poverty defines or blights a life depends, that is, on whether the poverty is unjust. Even if people who are cheated by modern society have substantially more resources than their ancestors had in some distant and just past, those ancestors may have been better placed to lead good lives.

Plato and other moralists argued that an unjust distribution of wealth has ethical disadvantages not only for those who have too little but also for those who have too much. Someone unjustly rich must devote more of his life to politics if he is to retain his self-respect than he would otherwise wish or think fulfilling. He owes duties of political association to other members of his political community, and these include doing what he can to secure justice for them. In an age of participatory politics this must be more than just voting for justice. So long as politics is financed through private funds, he must give resources to politicians that he would rather use for his own life, and he must do whatever else would significantly help. His time is no longer his own.

Grave injustice—a nation split between affluence and desperate poverty—has further and even more dramatic consequences for the relatively affluent: it makes it difficult for most of them to lead as good a life as they could in less unjust circumstances. Some of them, who have remarkable talent in some direction, can use their greater wealth more effectively to pursue lives of genuine achievement. The ethical question, for them, is whether they can do so with dignity. For the rest—the untalented rich—the impact of injustice on their lives is pervasive, because it counts against the value of a life that it is led with other people's money, and nothing they can do with their additional wealth can make up that value shortfall.[3] Rich suffer as well as poor, though the poor are usually more aware of their misfortune.

Cultures have tried to teach a malign and apparently persuasive lie: that the most important metric of a good life is wealth and the luxury and power it brings. The rich think they live better when they are even richer. In America and many other places they use their wealth politically, to persuade the public to elect or accept leaders who will do that for them. They say that the justice we have imagined is socialism that threatens our freedom. Not everyone is gullible: many people lead contented lives without wealth. But many others are persuaded; they vote for low taxes to keep the jackpot full in case they too can win it, even though that is a lottery they are almost bound to lose. Nothing better illustrates the tragedy of an unexamined life: there are no winners in this macabre dance of greed and delusion. No respectable or even intelligible theory of value supposes that making and spending money has any value or importance in itself and almost everything people buy with that money lacks any importance as well. The ridiculous dream of a princely life is kept alive by ethical sleepwalkers. And they in turn keep injustice alive because their self-contempt breeds a politics of contempt for others. Dignity is indivisible.

But remember, finally, the truth as well as its corruption. The justice we have imagined begins in what seems an unchallengeable proposition: that government must treat those under its dominion with equal concern and respect. That justice does not threaten—it expands—our liberty. It does not trade freedom for equality or the other way around. It does not cripple enterprise for the sake of cheats. It favors neither big nor small government but only just government. It is drawn from dignity and aims at dignity. It makes it easier and more likely for each of us to live a good life well. Remember, too, that the stakes are more than mortal. Without dignity our lives are only blinks of duration. But if we manage to lead a good life well, we create something more. We write a subscript to our mortality. We make our lives tiny diamonds in the cosmic sands.

Notes

1. Baedeker

1. Isaiah Berlin, *The Hedgehog and the Fox: An Essay on Tolstoy's View of History* (London: Weidenfeld and Nicolson, 1953), 3.

2. Much of the fox's ammunition relies on substantive moral pluralism: the thesis that sound moral principles and ideals inevitably conflict with one another. See Berlin, *The Crooked Timber of Humanity: Chapters in the History of Ideas,* ed. Henry Hardy (London: John Murray, 1991); Thomas Nagel, "The Fragmentation of Value," in *Mortal Questions* (Cambridge: Cambridge University Press, 1979).

3. See John Rawls, *Political Liberalism* (New York: Columbia University Press, 1996).

4. I first described and defended this thesis long ago. See "Objectivity and Truth: You'd Better Believe It," *Philosophy & Public Affairs* 25 (Spring 1996): 87–139. I have been lecturing about that and other issues in this book off and on since then, and am boundlessly grateful to many commentators and critics over those years.

5. See Crispin Wright, *Truth and Objectivity* (Cambridge, Mass.: Harvard University Press, 1992); and Kit Fine, "The Question of Realism," *Philosopher's Imprint* 1, no. 2 (June 2001), www.philosophersimprint.org/001001/.

6. In book 3 of his *Treatise* Hume said, "In every system of morality . . . the author proceeds for some time in the ordinary way of reasoning, and establishes the being of a God, or makes observations concerning human affairs; when of a sudden I am surpriz'd to find, that instead of the usual copulations of propositions, *is* and *is*

not, I meet with no proposition that is not connected with an *ought,* or *ought not . . .* [no reason is given] for what seems altogether inconceivable, how this new relation can be a deduction from others, which are entirely different from it" (L. A. Selby-Bigge edition, 469). The interpretation set out in the text has been accepted by many philosophers, including Richard Hare (*The Language of Morals* [Oxford: Clarendon Press, 1952], 29, 44), who encapsulated it in what he called "Hume's Law." But it has also been challenged; for example, by Alistair MacIntyre, who argued that, in ruling out a "deduction" from fact to norm, Hume did not rule out other modes of inference (MacIntyre, "Hume on Is and Ought," *Philosophical Review* 68 [1959]) and who noted that Hume himself seemed often to pass from psychological reports to moral claims. It makes no difference to my argument whether my description and use of Hume's principle is a misinterpretation of his argument or whether he violated that principle himself. But, as we shall see in Chapter 3, Hume's principle, at least as I have formulated it, is far from uncontroversial.

2. Truth in Morals

1. In this terminology I follow Bernard Williams, *Ethics and the Limits of Philosophy* (Cambridge, Mass.: Harvard University Press, 1985), 174–96.

2. Just for a start, contemporary texts on moral philosophy discuss intuitionism, realism, emotivism, expressivism, projectivism, reductive naturalism, nonreductive naturalism, quasi-realism, minimalism, Kantian constructivism, and Humean constructivism. I have something to say about each of these theories in Part One, but not always by name.

3. Much of this decline is described in Paul Boghossian, *Fear of Knowledge: Against Relativism and Constructivism* (Oxford: Oxford University Press, 2006).

4. A. J. Ayer, *Language, Truth, and Logic* (London: Gollancz, 1936).

5. Richard Hare, *The Language of Morals* (Oxford: Clarendon Press, 1952); Hare, *Freedom and Reason* (Oxford: Clarendon Press, 1963).

6. Gibbard, *Thinking How to Live* (Cambridge, Mass.: Harvard University Press, 2003), 181.

7. Thomas Nagel quotes Conrad's wonderful description of this form of internal skepticism. "It was one of those dewy, clear, starry nights, oppressing our spirit, crushing our pride, by the brilliant evidence of the awful loneliness, of the hopeless obscure insignificance of our globe lost in the splendid revelation of a glittering, soulless universe. I hate such skies." See Joseph Conrad, *Chance,* Oxford World Classics edition (Oxford: Oxford University Press, 2002), 41; Nagel, *Secular Philosophy and the Religious Temperament* (Oxford: Oxford University Press, 2010), 9.

8. I emphasize the independence of the projects of moral philosophy and social science because some philosophers describe the former projects in a way that does not make the difference as clear as it might be. Peter Railton, for instance, offers a

distinction between "normative theories" of morality, which he takes to consist in first-order, substantive moral judgments systematically arranged, and external, second-order "funding" theories, which he describes as offering "a fairly general, coherent account of what sort of thing morality is, what it presupposes or entails, how it stands in relation to the rest of human activity and inquiry, and what it would need to be in good order." See Railton, "Made in the Shade: Moral Compatibilism and the Aims of Moral Theory," in Jocelyne Couture and Kai Nielsen, eds., *On the Relevance of Metaethics* (Calgary: University of Calgary Press, 1995), 82. Railton's list of questions might be understood as inviting a social-scientific inquiry to determine the different ways in which people use and respond to moral judgments in particular communities, the different grounds they cite for morality's authority, and whether there is sufficient structure and enough agreement in people's moral opinions in some community so that the institution of morality helps to provide stability and efficiency there. No social-scientific theory of that kind could carry—or rebut—any skepticism about the status of value judgments as candidates for objective truth. But this does not seem to be what Railton intends. He does not believe that a "funding theory" would be only an exercise in social science; he says that, in addition to science, "funding theories usually draw heavily upon the philosophy of language and mind, the theory of action, metaphysics and epistemology." The metaphysics and epistemology he has in mind are concerned with such nonempirical issues as whether there is anything in the world that can make moral judgments true and whether people can be said to have good grounds for their moral convictions. He imagines a "funding" theory that argues that, according to the metaphysical or epistemological criteria it deploys, morality is not in good order because it cannot deliver the objective truth at which it aims. That funding theory would be an external error-skeptical theory like Mackie's. He imagines another that argues that morality is in good order because, properly understood, it aims not at objective truth but only at the useful projection of emotion or attitude. That would be an external status-skeptical theory. We must take care to distinguish genuine scientific inquiries about morality, which cannot support any form of external skepticism, from philosophical theories like these.

9. Richard Rorty, *Contingency, Irony, and Solidarity* (Cambridge: Cambridge University Press, 1989).

3. External Skepticism

1. See Aaron Garrett, "A Historian's Comment on the Metaethics Panel at Justice for Hedgehogs: A Conference on Ronald Dworkin's Forthcoming Book," in *Symposium: Justice for Hedgehogs: A Conference on Ronald Dworkin's Forthcoming Book* (special issue), *Boston University Law Review* 90, no. 2 (April 2010) (hereafter BU): 521.

2. Russ Shafer-Landau, "The Possibility of Metaethics," BU: 479.

3. See, e.g., Penelope Maddy, *Realism in Mathematics* (Oxford: Clarendon Press, 1990).

4. Michael Smith and Daniel Star suggest this mistake. Smith, "Dworkin on External Skepticism," BU: 479; Star, "Moral Skepticism for Foxes," BU: 497.

5. See Shafer-Landau, "The Possibility of Metaethics," and Star, "Moral Skepticism for Foxes." Star assumes, in the course of his discussion of the point, that the thesis that ought implies can is not a moral principle. But it certainly seems to be. It contradicts some plainly moral positions, including a view some commentators attribute to Nietzsche—that it is a tragedy that though every human being ought to live greatly, only very few can manage it. Star says, however, that it does not follow from the fact that people may reject that principle on moral grounds in some circumstances that it is "always" a moral principle. But since it has the same meaning when denied as it has when asserted, how can this not follow? In any case, what else could "ought implies can" be *but* a moral principle? It is not a factual generalization. Or a natural law. It is not a logical or semantic principle. Does it belong to some as yet unnamed class of non-normative ideas?

6. (1) One set of challenges relies on the idea of performative obligations I discuss in Chapter 14. Social practices are matters of fact, and certain social practices are taken to generate obligations. The institution of promising, for instance, declares that if someone promises, he has an obligation to keep his promise. Some institutions do not require even an act as voluntary as promising. Children have duties to their parents just in virtue of their biological or legal relationship. Should we say that in cases like these the social facts of convention generate moral responsibilities on their own? Some philosophers have argued that they do, and have cited this fact as a counterexample to Hume's principle. (See Searle, "How to Derive 'Ought' from 'Is,'" *Philosophical Review* 73 [1964]). For powerful criticism of this view, see James Thomson and Judith Thomson, "How Not to Derive 'Ought' from 'Is,'" *Philosophical Review* 73 (1964). My own view is set out in Chapter 14. Such institutions do not create obligations from scratch: they assume more basic moral principles that give institutions moral forces.

(2) Some contemporary philosophers—"moral naturalists"—hold that moral properties are identical with natural properties and challenge Hume's principle for that reason. They offer this analogy. We have discovered, through scientific inquiry, that the property of being water and the property of having the chemical structure H_2O are the same property: anything that has that chemical structure is water. We might discover a parallel kind of identity in the case of moral concepts: we might discover, for instance, that the property of being condemned in the King James Version of the Bible is the same as the property of being morally wrong, or that the property of conducing to the general welfare is the same property as being morally right. If so, then demonstrating that an ordinary fact exists—that a practice is condemned in the King James Version or that an act will favor the general welfare—is enough, on its own, to demonstrate the truth of a moral claim.

This argument does not yet challenge Hume's principle, however, because, though the proposition that water and H_2O are identical is a scientific discovery, the claim that biblical condemnation is identical with being wrong, or that favoring welfare is identical with being right, is naturally understood as itself a moral claim. (See Railton, "Facts and Values," in *Facts, Values, and Norms: Essays toward a Morality of Consequence* [Cambridge: Cambridge University Press, 2003], 43–68.) If so, then any argument that cites biblical condemnation or welfare consequences to support a moral position is an argument that includes a moral premise or assumption, as Hume's principle says any such argument must. However, some moral naturalists argue that these identity claims are *not* moral claims but rather describe a special kind of ordinary fact: facts about concepts. (See Richard Boyd, "How to Be a Moral Realist," in Geoffrey Sayre-McCord, ed., *Essays on Moral Realism* [Ithaca, N.Y.: Cornell University Press, 1988].) They adopt the "causal" theory of meaning, developed in the arguments of Saul Kripke and Hilary Putnam (Kripke, "Naming and Necessity," in Donald Davidson and Gilbert Harman, eds., *Semantics of Natural Language* [Dordrecht: Reidel, 1972]; and Putnam, "The Meaning of 'Meaning,'" *Minnesota Studies in the Philosophy of Science* 7 [1975]).

On this theory, what a concept of a certain kind designates is fixed by historical facts about which natural kinds have attracted the concept's designation. So "water" refers to the stuff, whatever it is, that has caused people to call it water. If we discover, through scientific study, that water necessarily has a certain molecular structure, then a substance on another planet that has all the surface properties of water is nevertheless not water if it does not have that molecular structure. Having that structure, or not, settles the question of whether a stuff is water. Moral naturalists hope to apply this theory of reference to moral concepts. Suppose we discover that a particular natural property of an action—the property, say, of favoring the general welfare—is the property that regulates what people call good or morally required, in much the same way as a molecular composition regulates what people call water. We can then say that the natural property of favoring the general welfare is identical to the moral property of being good or morally required, not because we accept a moral principle connecting welfare and rightness, but in virtue of a matter of ordinary linguistic fact. If this argument is successful, then Hume's principle is indeed false. (See Railton, "Facts and Values.")

But the argument seems mistaken in several ways. It makes assumptions about technical issues in semantics that seem unsustainable. (See Terence Horgan and Mark Timmons, "Troubles for New Wave Moral Semantics: The Open Question Argument Revived," *Philosophical Papers* 21 [1992].) A different mistake is more important. The moral naturalist's argument assumes that moral concepts belong to the family of concepts—these are often called "natural-kind" concepts—whose reference can sensibly be identified causally. In Chapter 8 I explain why this assumption is wrong. There is no one descriptive property, even a complex one, that has regulated the use of "wrong" as water has regulated the use of "water." I argue in Chapter 8 that moral concepts belong to a different family of concepts—I call these interpretive concepts—whose meaning cannot be stated except through judgments of value. If this is correct, then no theory of the kind the moral naturalists offer, about the meaning of moral concepts, can challenge Hume's principle, because any such theory embeds moral claims. That explains an inevitable reaction to the naturalist's argument. It seems inconceivable that whether it is right to torture terrorist suspects or unjust not to provide universal health care depends on how people have used "wrong" or "unjust" in the past. When we understand that moral concepts are interpretive, not natural-kind concepts, we see why.

(3) Two other issues discussed later in this book can also be seen to put Hume's principle at risk. (a) In Chapter 4 we consider the causal impact hypothesis, which states that people can interact causally with moral truth through some form of perception, and the causal dependence hypothesis that, if the causal impact hypothesis is false, it follows that no one can have any reason to hold any moral position. The latter principle is itself a moral principle—a piece of moral epistemology. The former is factual and, if it were true, would threaten Hume's principle. I argue in Chapter 4 that both these hypotheses are false. (b) Later in this chapter, as part of a general survey of status skepticism, we take up a different philosophical claim: that because moral convictions are intrinsically motivating, they cannot be construed as beliefs that can be true or false. If that claim holds, and if it is just a matter of psychological fact whether moral convictions are intrinsically motivating, then this philosophical claim also challenges Hume's principle. I reject the claim later in this chapter, however.

(4) Finally, the fact/value distinction is said itself to be illusory because factual claims are themselves impregnated with value (see, e.g., Hilary Putnam, *The Collapse of the Fact/Value Dichotomy and Other Essays* [Cambridge, Mass.: Harvard University Press, 2002]). I believe that the claim of a "collapse" of fact into value is overstated. Very important distinctions between the two domains survive even once we recognize the important truth that assumptions of epistemic value—simplicity, coherence, intellectual elegance, and beauty—sometimes help to fix what we take to be scientific truth and cannot themselves be tested scientifically without question begging. See Chapter 4. I describe what I take to be the most important of these surviving and deep distinctions in Chapter 7. But even if we accepted the claim of collapse in its most extravagant form, and concluded that every statement of fact is a value judgment, Hume's principle would not be threatened. On the contrary, it would become trivially true.

7. John Mackie, *Ethics: Inventing Right and Wrong* (New York: Penguin Books, 1977), 36–38.

8. Ibid., 38–42, 40.

9. See, e.g., Bernard Williams, "Internal and External Reasons," in his collection *Moral Luck* (Cambridge: Cambridge University Press, 1981), 101–13: Richard Joyce, *The Myth of Morality* (Cambridge: Cambridge University Press, 2001).

10. Williams, "Internal and External Reasons," 101–13.

11. Richard Joyce apparently has a contrary view. He treats the concept as what I call in Chapter 8 a criterial concept (see Joyce, *The Myth of Morality*, 102). That mistake, as I take it to be, has an important impact on his argument.

12. I should say, out of caution, that these nonmetaphysical, down-market translations of my further claims are not meant to endorse the "deflationary" theory of truth or, indeed, any other theory of truth. I consider such theories in Chapter 8.

13. See the online *Stanford Encyclopedia of Philosophy* (plato.stanford.edu/) articles "Cognitivism and Non-Cognitivism," "Judgment Internalism," and "Moral Motivation" for some sense of the variety of theories on this subject in the field. See also Mark Van Roojen, "Moral Cognitivism vs. Non-Cognitivism," *Stanford Encyclopedia of Philosophy,* June 7, 2009, plato.stanford.edu/entries/moral-cognitivism/; and Connie Rosati, "Moral Motivation," *Stanford Encyclopedia of Philosophy*, October 19, 2006, plato.stanford.edu/entries/moral-motivation/.

14. Shakespeare, *Richard III,* act 1, scene 1.

15. See G. E. M. Anscombe, *Intention,* 2nd ed. (Oxford: Basil Blackwell, 1963), section 32.

16. Milton, *Paradise Lost,* book 4.

17. The simplest form of the view would be first-personal: torture is wrong if it disgusts me. That plainly entails a substantive judgment: torture would be acceptable if it didn't disgust me. The most usual form of the view, I believe, is this: what makes an act morally wrong is that contemplating that act produces a particular kind of reaction in most people, or in most members of a particular community. It follows from that formulation that if one day people in general, or in the stipulated community, ceased to react in that way, torture would cease to be wicked, just as rotten eggs would cease to be disgusting if they no longer disgusted anyone. The thesis that torture would cease to be wicked if it were no longer so regarded is of course a highly controversial first-order moral position. However, the dispositional account might take different forms. It might hold, for example, that what makes torture wrong is the reaction, not of whichever kind of people happen to exist from time to time, but of *us,* that is, of people with the physiological structure, basic interests, and general mental dispositions that people actually have now. (See Crispin Wright, *Truth and Objectivity* [Cambridge, Mass.: Harvard University Press, 1992], 114.) In that case it would no longer follow that torture would cease being wicked if human beings developed very different general interests or neural wiring. But some plainly substantive and controversial claims would still follow: for instance, that torture would not have been wicked if economic or other circumstances had been different as human reactions evolved, so that creatures with our general interests and attitudes had not been revolted by it. The dispositional account might take other forms than these two; it might attempt to fix the extension of moral properties in other ways. But just as any philosophically illuminating account of the disgustingness of rotten eggs

yields counterfactual claims about the circumstances in which rotten eggs would not be or have been disgusting, so any illuminating account of moral properties as secondary entails counterfactuals that state substantive moral positions.

18. Lady Macbeth: "I have given suck, and know/How tender 'tis to love the babe that milks me" (I, vii, ll.54–55). Macbeth had no children.

19. Richard Rorty, "Does Academic Freedom Have Philosophical Presuppositions?" in Louis Menand, ed., *The Future of Academic Freedom* (Chicago: University of Chicago Press, 1996), 29–30.

20. Smith, "Dworkin on External Skepticism," agrees that the speech-act version of status skepticism has "basically" been abandoned. He calls attention, however, to a version of the two-games strategy that he believes my arguments do not touch. "What distinguishes beliefs about moral matters of fact from beliefs about nonmoral matters of fact, external status skeptics now say, is that beliefs about moral matters of fact are entirely constituted by desires about non-moral matters of fact, while beliefs about non-moral matters of fact are not" (p. 518).

By way of background, consider the following argument. When we accept that some proposition is true, it remains a distinct and important philosophical issue what in the world makes it true—in what its truth consists or, as Kit Fine puts it, what "grounds" its truth (Kit Fine, "The Question of Realism," *Philosopher's Imprint* 1, no. 2 [June 2001], www.philosophersimprint.org/001001/). So though an external status skeptic might accept that "Cheating is wrong" is true, he might deny that its truth consists in the moral state of affairs of cheating being wrong. He might insist instead that its truth consists in some psychological state of affairs—of particular people having particular attitudes or desires. However, that would not help him out of the predicament I describe. He wants to be able to agree with anything substantive that a nonskeptic can say; he wants to be able to say, for instance, that the wrongness of cheating is a basic moral fact whose truth in no way depends on people's attitudes. If he denied that very popular judgment, he would plainly be taking up a substantive moral position. His skepticism would be internal. So he wants to be able to deny that the wrongness of cheating consists in a psychological state when he is playing the game of substantive morality, but assert it, saying that true moral beliefs are indeed constituted by attitudes, when he plays a distinct, philosophical, second-level game. But, as I argue in the text, he cannot do that unless he can restate the propositions in one of the two games or the other so as to make them consistent. He cannot do that, so he must choose between the two propositions. He must finally decide whether the truth of cheating being wrong is constituted just by attitudes, in which case his skepticism is internal, or whether it is constituted by the wrongness of cheating, in which case he is not a skeptic at all.

Smith agrees that this argument fails, for this reason, to support an external skepticism. But he suggests that the argument for that position improves when we ask what a moral belief, rather than a moral fact, consists in. He cites a recent article to illustrate this strategy. James Drier considers the phenomenon described by the proposition "Julia believes that knowledge is intrinsically good." He suggests that the difference between non-naturalism and naturalism "must, it seems to me, amount to the idea that the property of goodness enters into explanations of [such] phenomena that expressivists would explain by other means" (Drier, "Meta-Ethics and the Problem of Creeping Minimalism," *Philosophical Perspectives* 18 (Ethics) [2004]: 41. I am not sure what kind of "explanation" Drier has in mind or how Smith thinks Drier's suggestion bears on my argument. A "realist" need have no different opinion from an "expressivist" about Julia's phenomenology or her brain states. Nor about the causal history of her belief. As I argue in Chapter 4, a "realist" can consistently adopt any personal-history causal explanation of anyone's moral convictions that any kind of skeptic might offer. What kind of explanation does Drier then have in mind?

Perhaps he means to ask whether it is Julia's desires or the moral facts she asserts that play the more basic or fundamental role in any metaphysical account of the situation. But however we understand this question (if we do), the crucial issue remains the same as when we focused, in the last paragraph, not on belief but on moral facts themselves. Does the "explanation" Drier has in mind include, at any stage or at any level or mode of metaphysical depth, a claim or assumption that knowledge is not intrinsically good? or not really or not intrinsically good? or something of the sort? If so, then once again the "expressivist" in question is not an external but an internal skeptic. Taking his whole account together, he advances a substantive view of the matter. His view may be metaphysical, but it also expresses a negative substantive conviction about goodness. But if not—if no opinion of that sort figures in or is entailed by his account of Julia's belief—then he is not a skeptic at all. If this is "what external status skeptics now say," they have not improved their position. (I do not suggest any doubt that there are important metaphysical issues that bear on the question whether the philosophical theories of realism and anti-realism about any domain can be distinguished and, if so, how. See, e.g., Fine, "The Question of Realism." But only that these issue are orthogonal to the question I take up, which is the possibility of a genuine external skepticism.)

21. Gibbard suggests this in his recent book, *Thinking How to Live* (Cambridge, Mass.: Harvard University Press, 2003), 183–88. Blackburn in conversation and correspondence.

22. Gibbard has consistently described his moral theory as "expressivist." (He once called himself a "noncognitivist" as well, but he has now withdrawn that latter description [Allan Gibbard, *Thinking How to Live*, [183]). He explains his philosophical project this way: he means to "ask what states of mind ethical statements express" (183). He uses "ethical" to include "moral" and uses "express" in a sense closer to "means," as in "boo" expresses disapproval, than to "signal," as in "boo" expresses an inarticulate mind. His conclusion: moral judgments express acceptance of a plan for living. That sounds skeptical of the ordinary view, at least initially, because people

who hold that view think that their moral judgments express beliefs that acts are right or wrong rather than the acceptance of plans. But Gibbard argues that an expressivist in his sense can sensibly say everything that ordinary people say about the truth and objectivity of moral judgment. He can explain the truth-claiming features of morality by describing them as internal to the plans accepted by people who make moral judgments. "Normative claims can be true or false, independent of our accepting them. To accept this is, roughly, to restrict your plans to ones that are not contingent on which plans, in the contingencies you plan for, you would accept if that contingency obtained" (6). That sounds like the two-game strategy I described: the expressivist offers a kind of explanation, at the level of explanation, that allows him to say everything a realist might say at the level of moral engagement. And, indeed, Gibbard distinguishes two games in much the way the strategy I describe requires: he distinguishes questions of the "internal adequacy" of his account, by which he means its success in mimicking the ordinary view, from questions about its "external adequacy," by which he means its success as an explanation of the internal phenomena (184–88).

He is therefore right to confront my suggestion (published in an earlier article, "Objectivity and Truth: You'd Better Believe It," *Philosophy & Public Affairs* 25 [Spring 1996]: 87–139, and repeated in the text) that if an expressivist fully succeeds in that mimicking project, he erases any difference between himself and those he takes to be his "realist" opponents. Gibbard calls this "a strange worry" (184). He insists that even if he and I fully agree about what makes sense at the internal, engaged level, we disagree at the philosophical level because his theory offers a better explanation of what happens at the engaged level. It better explains what state of mind moral judgments express. The ordinary view I defend cannot, he says, answer the question he takes as central to moral theory: Why does what we ought to do matter for what to do? (184). He presents his supposedly more successful answer in this dictum: "I say that the concept of ought just *is* the concept of what to do" (184, italics his). To have an opinion about what is right or wrong just is to have a plan, or part of a plan, about how to live.

However, I suggested that a two-games strategy collapses not because it proposes a different explanation for the same phenomena—that is what most theories do—but because it converts its supposed second-order explanation into part of the first-order phenomenon being explained. His dictum seems a good example. The question he says it answers—Why do what we ought to do?—is a first-order substantive ethical question that philosophers have been trying to answer since the beginning. (This book attempts an answer in its later parts.) We can understand Gibbard's dictum, as an answer to that ancient question, in one of three ways. (1) We can take the dictum as a description of people's state of mind when they express moral convictions. It then encounters two problems. First, it seems false. Some people very carefully plan to do what they think morally wrong, not out of weakness of will but out of straightforward and self-conscious perversity, just because it is wrong. I offered examples: Gloucester and Satan. Second, Gibbard's dictum, understood as just description, does not respond to the question he says it answers. Any such description, even if accurate, would leave entirely open the substantive question: Why be moral? (2) We might treat the dictum as declaring a philosophical position: that there is a conceptual connection between thinking we ought to do something and planning to do it, so we cannot sensibly doubt that the thing to do is what one ought to do. Then it holds that Gloucester and Satan were talking nonsense—committing themselves to plans and rejecting those plans in the same breath. This is implausible. (3) Or we can understand the dictum as staking out a substantive position in the ancient debate. On this understanding, Gibbard makes the strong claim that "the thing to do" is never other than what morality allows. That states a first-order ethical conviction, not a second-order explanation.

Simon Blackburn's views have apparently shifted over the years, but he seems at least once to have held a theory that exemplifies the two-games strategy described in the text. He insisted that moral judgments are best understood as projections of attitudes and emotions. (See, e.g., Simon Blackburn, "Reply: Rule-Following and Moral Realism," in Andrew Fisher and Simon Kirchin, eds., *Arguing about Metaethics* [New York: Routledge, 2006], 471.) He called himself a "projectivist" and a "quasi-realist," and he explained these self-descriptions in status-skeptical terms. He said he was improving on Ayer's emotivism, for example. (See his autobiographical remarks at www.philosophynow.org/issue35/35blackburn.htm.) He said, "I take an emotivist's starting point: we see the meaning of moral utterances as essentially exhausted by their role in expressing the speaker's attitude" (*Essays in Quasi-Realism* [Oxford: Oxford University Press, 1993], 19). He said he "holds that our nature as moralists is well explained by regarding us as reacting to a reality which contains nothing in the way of values, duties, right and so forth" (*Arguing about Metaethics*, 471.) But he was also at great pains, in many articles and books, to show that a projectivist like himself could "adopt the intellectual practices supposedly definitive of [moral] realism." He insisted, for example, that a projectivist who agrees with Hume that values are a "new creation" produced by human response to a morally inert world can nevertheless say that the wrongness of cruelty does not depend on any human response to a morally inert world. He seemed to invoke the idea of two games or "businesses" to explain this apparent puzzle. "There is only one proper way to take the question 'On what does the wrongness of wanton cruelty depend?': as a moral question with an answer in which no mention of our actual responses properly figures . . . As soon as one uses a sentence whose simple assertion expresses an attitude, one is in the business of discussing or voicing ethical opinion." But: "If one attempts to discuss external questions one must use a different approach—in my case, a naturalism that places the activities of ethics in the realm of adjusting, improving, weighing, and rejecting different sentiments or attitudes." And: "The projectivist . . . has a perfect right to confine external questions of dependency to domains where real states of affairs, with their causal relations, are in question. The only things in this world are the attitudes of people . . . moral properties are not in this world at all, and it is only because of this that naturalism remains true" ("How to Be an Ethical Anti-Realist," in Blackburn's *Essays in Quasi-Realism* [Oxford: Oxford University Press, 1993], 173–74).

I am assuming that Blackburn imagined a philosophical "business" distinct from moral "business," so that a philosopher might be skeptical about the ordinary view in the former game but not in the latter. There is an alternate interpretation: that when he speaks of the "external" world of "naturalism" and of "real states of affairs," he has in mind not a distinct philosophical world where he can deny the objective truth of moral judgment but rather the world of social scientists, sociologists, and psychologists whose business is to offer causal personal-history explanations of how people come to hold their moral convictions. On this second interpretation, his remarks about the absence of moral properties "in this world" mean only what is obviously true: that questions about the truth of moral convictions do not arise when we try to explain why someone holds the convictions he does.

I believe that the first of these two interpretations of the "external" world fits the body of Blackburn's work better than the second does, however. Otherwise he wouldn't say that "in my case" the business of explanation would mean naturalism: under the second interpretation, that would of course be true for everyone. Moreover the project of creating a projectivist "mimicking" of the ordinary view itself assumes skepticism about the ordinary view as it stands. Consider, for example, his argument why a projectivist can insist that it would still be wrong to kick dogs even if no one thought it wrong. A projectivist can say this, Blackburn says, because a projectivist "approves of a moral disposition" that, given the belief that no one minds kicking dogs, "yields the reaction of disapproval as an output; he does not approve of one which needs belief about our attitudes as an input in order to yield the same output, and this is all that gets expression in the counterfactual" (Blackburn, "Rule-Following and Moral Realism," in S. Holtzmann and C. Leich, eds., *Wittgenstein: To Follow a Rule* [London: Routledge, 1981], 179).

That is the language of status skepticism. Ordinary people who hold the ordinary view think, on the contrary, that what gets "expression" in the counterfactual is the belief that it would be wrong to kick dogs even if everyone thought otherwise.

23. Ronald Dworkin, *Taking Rights Seriously* (Cambridge, Mass.: Harvard University Press, 1977), chapter 6.

24. See Rawls, "Justice as Fairness: Political not Metaphysical," in *Collected Papers*, ed. Samuel Freeman (Cambridge, Mass.: Harvard University Press, 1999), 386, 400n19.

25. Rawls, "Kantian Constructivism in Moral Theory," in *Collected Papers*, 303, 346.

26. Ibid., 350.

27. See Onora O'Neill, "Constructivism in Rawls and Kant," in *The Cambridge Companion to Rawls,* ed. Samuel Freeman (Cambridge: Cambridge University Press, 2002), 347.

28. I defend and try to begin that kind of project in *Is Democracy Possible Here?* (Princeton: Princeton University Press, 2006).

29. Christine Korsgaard believes that Rawls was given an "axiom" defining liberalism so that he had only to find a suitable procedure for satisfying that axiom (Korsgaard, "Realism and Constructivism in Twentieth Century Moral Philosophy," in *Philosophy in America at the Turn of the Century* [Charlottesville, Va.: Philosophy Documentation Center, 2003], 99, 112). "Since liberalism claims that political policies are justified only when they are acceptable in the eyes of the citizens," she says, "we must be able to offer reasons in support of these coercive policies that are acceptable to all the citizens." If "acceptable" means "could be accepted," the constraint is too weak: conversion is always possible. If it means "will be accepted," it is too strong: there are no policies that will be accepted by everyone we count as reasonable in any state. Korsgaard says that her own version of constructivism begins in the idea that moral judgment has a practical function to play. Of course moral judgment, like any other activity, plays many functions. She means, I take it, that moral judgments are in some way exhausted by their practical problem-solving role. If they were, however, they would perform that role very badly. We do not first identify a practical problem we have, like needing to live together in peace, then find a practical solution to that problem, and then decorate our solution with moral confetti. We need moral concepts even to identify the problems we need to solve. We want to live with others not just in peace, which might be achieved by a variety of tyrannies, but in a just society whose institutions treat every citizen fairly by respecting their equal status. We want a society that is really just, not that we declare just because it is the upshot of a selection device we stipulate. So we cannot solve that problem without first deciding what justice requires. What "works" for us depends on the right understanding of moral concepts, not the other way around; we need some independent, nonconstructivist, way to decide what the right understanding is.

30. Nadeem Hussain and Nishi Shah, "Misunderstanding Metaethics," in *Oxford Studies in Meta-ethics,* vol. 1, ed. Russ Shafer-Landau (New York: Oxford University Press, 2006), 268.

4. Morals and Causes

1. You shouldn't think this. See my *Sovereign Virtue* (Cambridge, Mass.: Harvard University Press, 2000), 409–26.

2. See G. E. Moore, *Principia Ethica* (Cambridge: Cambridge University Press, 1903); Richard Price, *Review of the Principal Questions in Morals* (1757).

3. Moral naturalism, discussed in Chapter 3, supports the causal impact hypothesis. If moral properties are identical to natural properties, and these natural properties interact with human minds, then moral properties do that as well. Nicholas Sturgeon's argument along those lines is framed as a response to an influential book by Gilbert Harman. See Sturgeon, "Moral Explanations," in David Copp and David Zimmerman, eds., *Morality, Reason and Truth* (Totowa, N.J.: Rowman and Allanheld, 1985), 49–79, reprinted in *Arguing about Metaethics,* ed. Andrew Fisher and Simon Kirchin (New York: Routledge, 2006), 117. Harman argued that moral facts, if there were any, could not explain our moral convictions, and concluded that there are no moral facts. See Harman, *The Nature of Morality: An Introduction to Ethics* (New York: Oxford University Press, 1977). Sturgeon challenges Harman's premise. He thinks the fact that Hitler was a monster explains what Hitler did, and what Hitler did explains why we think him a monster, so this is an instance of a moral truth explaining a moral conviction. Harman said that we must test this sort of causal claim by asking a counterfactual question: Would we still have believed Hitler a monster even if he wasn't? If the answer to that question is no, then we can conclude that Hitler's being a monster caused us to think him one. But, Harman says, we have no reason to think the answer is no. Sturgeon points out correctly that we can understand the counterfactual two ways. We may take it to ask whether, if Hitler's behavior had been different in ways that made him not a monster, we would have believed him one. The answer to that question probably is, at least for most of us: no. Or we can take it to ask whether, if Hitler was what he was and did what he did, but that didn't make him a monster, we would have believed him one. Sturgeon rightly says that the premise of the question so understood is unintelligible because it asks us to imagine a different world exactly like ours, with Hitler behaving exactly as he did, but different only in the single fact that in that world Hitler wasn't a monster. If there were morons—moral particles whose configuration made moral judgments true or false—this might make sense. The other world could be just like ours except that the morons were differently arranged. But because moral judgments are true in virtue of reasons, not morons, the premise of this counterfactual is indeed unimaginable.

Sturgeon draws two conclusions and twice runs these together. First, he concludes that because the only intelligible way of framing Harman's counterfactual yields, at least for most people, a negative answer, Hitler's monstrosity must explain why most people think him a monster. But that is a mistake, because on that understanding the counterfactual doesn't bear on the question of causation at all. The ghost of Joseph Goebbels knows all the historical facts that made Hitler a monster, but these facts haven't caused that ghost to hold my opinion. It does seem natural to say that Hitler's being a monster explains why he acted as he did, and why I think him a monster. But that is best understood as a compressed statement of the following fuller version. Hitler's personality caused him to act as he did and, because I think people who act as he did are monsters, his personality in that way caused me to think him a monster. Nothing in that fuller description attributes causal power to the truth that Hitler was a monster, and the fuller description leaves nothing out that is causally relevant. (See Crispin Wright, *Truth and Objectivity* [Cambridge, Mass.: Harvard University Press, 1992], 195.) Sturgeon draws a second conclusion: that Harman is wrong in thinking his argument licenses the skeptical conclusion that there are no moral facts. I agree. Harman is wrong to draw that conclusion even though he is right that moral facts don't cause moral convictions, because the causal dependence thesis I discuss in the next section is false.

4. Mark Johnston argues persuasively, against expressivist and dispositional accounts of aesthetic and moral qualities, that beauty is not in the eye of the beholder ("The Authority of Affect," *Philosophy and Phenomenological Research* 63, no. 1 [2001]: 181). Your lover really is beautiful, although you might have to take the right interest in her to see it. You do not reason or infer her beauty. You see it the way a chessmaster sees a stalemate in three moves. But this cannot be, in either of those cases, a causal kind of perception. You see that the boys burning a cat are depraved, but the sense in which you see that provides no further evidence or argument for their depravity as an eyewitness's seeing does provide further evidence of a stabbing. If someone disagreed with your judgment, and you were able to provide some argument in its favor, that argument wouldn't turn on your truthfulness or your ability to detect depravity or whether you were in the right position to detect it. It would turn on the reasons you offered to show that what the boys were doing was depraved. Your immediate moral and aesthetic reactions reflect experience and deep assumptions, the way the chessmaster's reaction does; any argument about beauty or depravity that follows your claim would be a justification, not a more detailed report of what you saw.

5. Plato, *Phaedrus* 247e–249d; *Phaedo Ph.* 65e–66a; G. E. Moore, *Principia Ethica* (Cambridge: Cambridge University Press, 1903). See also the moral sense theorists: e.g., Shaftesbury, *An Inquiry Concerning Virtue, or Merit* (1699); Reid, *An Inquiry into the Human Mind on the Principles of Common Sense*, ed. Derek R. Brookes (Edinburgh: Edinburgh University Press, 1997); Hutcheson, *An Essay on the Nature and Conduct of the Passions and Affections. With Illustrations on the Moral Sense* (Dublin: J. Smith and W. Bruce, 1728).

6. I describe three such theories here.

Nagel. Morality, on Thomas Nagel's view, is a matter not of occult particles but of reasons. People have a faculty of reason, and this faculty allows them, in the right circumstances, to reach credible conclusions about what they have most reason to do. They exercise this faculty by a process of progressive objectification, that is, by struggling to prescind from their own particular desires, interests, and ambitions to consider what reasons people in general, or no one in particular, has for action. Through this process people are able to leave behind their personal perspective, which their own interests dominate, to struggle toward an impersonal perspective from which moral judgment is possible. (Nagel, *The View from Nowhere* [Oxford: Oxford University Press, 1986], chapters 8 and 9.)

I discuss Nagel's contrast between these two perspectives at several points in this book. Its pertinence now lies in the connection it draws between two issues: the best explanation of how moral opinion is formed and whether moral opinion can be objectively true. He takes the key question in the contest over the latter issue to be whether the process of objectification he describes is possible for human beings or whether they are inevitably trapped in a personal perspective, limited by their own interests and inclinations.

> The subjectivist would have to show that all purportedly rational judgments about what people have reason to do are really expressions of rationally unmotivated desires or dispositions of the person making the judgment—desires or dispositions to which normative assessment has no application. The motivational assumption would have to have the effect of *displacing* the normative one—showing it to be superficial and deceptive . . . Subjectivism involves a positive claim of empirical psychology. (*The Last Word* [Oxford: Oxford University Press, 1997], 110–11.)

"Express" in this context is a causal, not a semantic, idea. The subjectivist argues that people's moral convictions are best explained as the upshot of personal desires or dispositions rather than judgments they make from some impersonal standpoint that allows those desires and dispositions no causal role. Nagel believes that the subjectivist cannot show that this "displacement" occurs in every case. But that is, as he says, a question of empirical psychology, and we might therefore test Nagel's description of the crux of the contest by imagining that the subjectivist succeeds. The subjectivist is able to show that personal inclinations and other aspects of personal history always figure indispensably in any full explanation of why someone holds the moral opinions he does. Why would any form of skepticism follow from that empirical demonstration?

Hume's principle stands in the way. The empirical fact that no one holds a moral opinion that is not best explained by his hidden desires cannot by itself make any moral opinion false or not true. You feel passionately that affirmative action is deeply insulting and unfair. You believe that your opinion states an objective truth; it would still be true, that is, even if everyone came to think the opposite. Your psychotherapist convinces you, however, that some long-forgotten but traumatic childhood experience, when you were denied a treat in order that someone less fortunate might have it, provides the best explanation of why you hold that conviction so passionately; in fact, he convinces you that but for that long-forgotten trauma you would not think affirmative action unfair. It would hardly follow that affirmative action is not, after all, unfair. That depends on the moral arguments that can be made in favor of that moral conclusion, not whether your appreciation of those arguments was the sole cause of your forming the conviction. So the empirical triumph of the subjectivist would be of no use in establishing his philosophical position. Later in this chapter I imagine that everyone who has had a certain brain scan thinks affirmative action fair. I argue that those who changed their minds after a brain scan have no reason, just in that fact, to revert to their former opinion. The empirical demonstration Nagel imagines is only a more easily conceivable example than that one.

How someone has reached his convictions does bear on moral responsibility but not on whether his convictions are objectively true. I distinguish responsibility from truth in Chapter 6, and I argue that no one is morally responsible unless he draws his opinions from a reasonably well-integrated and authentic system of conviction. But even moral responsibility would not be undermined by the subjectivist's success in his empirical claims. Responsibility requires the integration I just described, but it is not destroyed by any deeper explanation of why an agent has come to hold the convictions that he has successfully integrated. So neither the soundness nor the responsibility of our convictions can be challenged by the subjectivist's empirical psychology.

Wiggins. David Wiggins has been energetic in the project to salvage something from the causal impact hypothesis. He calls it a "mark" of truth that a proposition p, in any domain, can be true only if there are circumstances in which someone can believe that p "precisely because p." He thinks that this condition is fulfilled when "there is nothing else to think" but p, so that the question whether moral judgments can be true is the question whether there can be circumstances in which that condition holds. I state his interesting argument at length.

> My suggestion is that someone believes that p precisely because p . . . if there is a good explanation of their coming to believe that p which leaves the explainer himself no room to deny that p . . . The first example may as well be perceptual: "Look, the cat is on the mat. So, given John's perceptual capacities and his presence near the cat, no wonder he believes the cat is on the mat. There is nothing else for him to think about the cat and the mat." This explanation, which leaves no room to deny that the cat is on the mat, answers the question, "Why does John believe the cat is on the mat?" Next, and in the second place, consider the analogous but utterly different question, "Why does Peter believe 7 + 5 = 12?" and an explanation that runs on the following pattern: "Look, 7 + 5 = 12; no calculating rule that makes it possible to use numbers to count things leaves room for any other answer. [Explainer proves this.] So no wonder Peter, who understands the calculating rule which leaves no room for any other answer, believes that 7 + 5 = 12." Let us call such explanations for the existence of a belief vindicatory explanations of the belief . . . By the same token, ethical objectivism will be committed (simply by virtue of its commitment to the possibility of truth in ethics) to saying that an ethical

subject matter, no less than perceptual and arithmetical subject matters, will admit vindicatory explanations of (at least some) moral beliefs. An example might run as follows: "Look, slavery is wrong, it's wrong because . . . [here are given many, many considerations, fully spelled out, appealing to what some-one already knows and understands if they know what slavery is and what 'wrong' means, all these considerations working together to leave no alterna-tive, for one who is so informed, but to think that slavery is wrong]; so no wonder twentieth-century Europeans, who would accept that . . . and whose beliefs are so many of them downwind of such considerations as . . . believe that slavery is wrong. They believe that it is wrong for just the kind of reasons why there is nothing else to think but that it is wrong." (Wiggins, *Ethics: Twelve Lectures on the Philosophy of Morality* [Cambridge, Mass.: Harvard University Press, 2006], 366–67.)

Wiggins apparently accepts something like the causal dependence hypothesis I discuss later in the text (notice the reference to "the possibility of truth in ethics") and tries to satisfy its condition without supposing any mechanism of causal interac-tion between moral truth and human minds. He thinks it important to proceed as he does here, by considering a perceptual and a mathematical example of there being "nothing else to think" before moving to the moral case. But I believe the quoted phrase has such different import in each of these three contexts that it is more help-ful to turn to the moral case, which is our concern, directly. The statement that there is nothing for a modern European to think but that slavery is wrong can naturally be read in two quite different ways. It might be taken to state a psychological or cultural or even biological fact: that for one reason or another a modern European has only one thought on the matter available to him. His education and culture simply do not permit him to doubt that slavery is wicked. Or it might be taken to state a moral truth: that it is so plainly true that slavery is wrong that no other opinion about the matter is even remotely plausible. This latter interpretation must be what the "ex-plainer" means to say if his statement "leaves [him] himself no room to deny" that slavery is wrong. In fact, to serve Wiggins's purpose, this statement that there is nothing else to think must be read as a combination of the two claims I just distin-guished: that a contemporary European cannot possibly think other than that slav-ery is unjust, and that slavery is plainly unjust. But the combination can achieve nothing more by way of vindication than either claim can on its own. The cultural claim provides an explanation but no vindication; the moral claim presupposes vindi-cation, so it cannot supply any. The slavery example is not after all a case of someone's "believing that *p* precisely because *p*." (See Crispin Wright's comments in *Truth and Objectivity*, 194ff, on Wiggins's suggestion.)

As I said, Wiggins thinks that the perceptual and mathematical cases help to ex-plain the moral case. But the sense of "there is nothing else to think" is different in these cases, and it may be useful to notice the differences. The cat's being on the mat probably does cause the thinker to think that the cat is on the mat. We have theories of optics and biology that explain this, or so we think; they explain how the presence of the cat on the mat causes people with normal perceptual, cognitive, and linguistic abilities to think that the cat is on the mat. And that explanation, if successful, does vindicate the perceptual claim. It does leave the explainer unable to deny that the cat is on the mat. In the mathematical case there really is nothing else to think, at least after pertinent training, but that five and seven make twelve (in spite of Descartes's claim that God could have made it otherwise). But though the position of the cat causes beliefs about its position, seven and five do not cause people to think that together they make twelve. A Darwinian explanation of why it is nevertheless true that there is nothing else to think is popular, however. This supposes that the evolution of human beings could not have proceeded to the point it did long ago if successful techniques of counting and primitive numerical manipulation had not been—as amateurs of evolution often put it—hardwired into their brains, and of course no such techniques could be evolutionarily successful unless they dictated that seven and five make twelve. This explanation does, in that way, implicate truths of mathematics in its account of why people believe true mathematical propositions. But it still falls short of a mathematical version of CI, that is, of supposing that the truths of mathematics themselves exercise any causal influence on human brains. The full neo-Darwinian story, if some version of it actually is plausible, can be told without supposing any such influence: it is not that mathematical truth interacts with human brains, but rather that ancestors of human beings whose brains were not shaped to count properly did not survive. Once again, the difference between that story and common-garden perception of physical facts is striking and important. "I see that it is raining," said by someone looking out the window, offers a justification for his belief that it is raining. "I see that Fermat's last theorem can be proved," said even by a famous mathematician, does not offer even the beginning of a justification for his belief. It only promises a justification that remains to be offered.

Some scientists and philosophers believe that a parallel neo-Darwinian story can be told about the development of some of our moral convictions. They suggest that it helped human beings to evolve that they were members of communities that inculcated the wrongness of the most dramatic forms of antisocial behavior. It is much less clear than it seems in the mathematical case that the survival value of the convictions so inculcated depended on their truth. It may be, for instance, that convictions of savage tribal loyalty were indispensable to the evolution of our species into its present form, but it hardly follows that these convictions, which unfortunately survive, are morally correct. In any case, however, even if we think the convictions that were allegedly essential to survival are all true, it does not follow, any more than it does in the mathematical case, that moral truth, rather than the morally neutral processes of evolution, is causally responsible for their genesis and survival.

McDowell. John McDowell firmly rejects "intuitionism." (See McDowell, "Projection and Truth in Ethics," in his *Mind, Value, and Reality* [Cambridge, Mass.: Harvard University Press, 1998], 157.) He denies that people can perceive value, rightness, or wrongness in objects or events the way they can perceive shape and other purely physical properties. But he also rejects "projectivism," a form of skepticism that holds that values are not properties of anything in the external world at all, that value judgments must be understood as expressions or projections of attitude onto a normatively blank universe (151). He hopes to develop a third position through an extended, though limited, analogy to the perception of colors and other secondary properties that depend for their sense and truth both on properties of objects and on the phenomenological reactions of human beings to those properties.

He says: "An object's being red is understood as something that obtains in virtue of the object's being such as (in certain circumstances) to look, precisely, red" (McDowell, "Values and Secondary Qualities," in *Reason, Value, and Reality,* 133). This explanation of color properties does not follow either an intuitionist or a projectivist model: rather it combines observations about the properties of a tomato with those about the reactions people normally have looking at tomatoes. A tomato does not have the property of redness intrinsically; it would not be red if it did not look red in appropriate circumstances. But it would nevertheless be a mistake to deny that a tomato has in itself a property in virtue of which it is red. It has the property of being disposed to produce a certain kind of reaction—a redness reaction—in those circumstances. We can restate that property as a property of surface texture but only when we have determined that it is that texture that accounts for that disposition.

In McDowell's view, a perceptual model of color therefore has a different structure from either an intuitionist or a projectivist explanation of value. Intuitionism gives an explanatory priority to some property of value inherent in an object or event: it supposes, as McDowell puts it, that the inherent value is the parent of the admiring reaction it produces in people with a suitable sensibility. A projectivist model, in contrast, makes the reaction parent to the property. It supposes that value is only what our reactions paint over the world. But in color perception neither the object nor the reaction is the parent of the other; McDowell calls them siblings (ibid., 166). The characteristic response of people to a red object is indispensable to the phenomenon. But so are the objective features that give the tomato the disposition to evoke that response. McDowell suggests an analogous "sibling" explanation of value: the property of some object in meriting admiration and the admiration it elicits are both essential parts of the explanation of value.

He is careful to notice that the analogy between value judgment and color perception is imperfect, in two ways. The texture of the tomato causes a reasonably well-understood chain of physical events that ends in the redness sensation, but there is no analogous physical series initiated by positive or negative value. Color attribution is rarely contentious—we think we can explain to someone's satisfaction that a tomato is red even though it does not appear red to him. But value attribution is very often controversial. McDowell thinks these differences do not spoil the usefulness of the comparison. It allows us to recognize the crucial fact that we are not forced to choose between intuitionist and projectivist accounts of value judgment. We can explain the origin of such judgments through an account in which both object and respondent are indispensable, an account that allows us to say that there is indeed value in the world though it arises only in combination with convictions of value in people.

I believe, however, that the differences do destroy the usefulness of the comparison. Causation is central to the sibling story. We cannot suppose that objects themselves contain a color-related property without identifying that property causally: it is the property that accounts for the object's disposition to cause color reactions. If the causal impact hypothesis I describe in the text is wrong, as McDowell assumes it is in rejecting intuitionism, then we cannot identify a value property in a parallel way. The sibling story therefore has no application to value judgment. It might seem plausible, or at least attractive, to infer from the near-uniform reaction to athletic grace that there must be some property in a graceful performance in virtue of which it is disposed to generate admiration. But we would have no such temptations in the case of controversial moral judgment: capital punishment cannot be thought to house some disposition that makes it either admired or detested.

McDowell seems in other ways to borrow the trappings of causation without its mechanics. He says that it makes sense for people to say, "If the reasons for condemning capital punishment weren't good reasons, I wouldn't condemn it." But, as I said in the text, if those reasons really are good ones, there is no way even to imagine a world otherwise like ours in which they are not, which means no one has any basis for supposing that he would not condemn capital punishment in such a world. McDowell takes from David Wiggins another shadow-of-causation idea: that an explanation of why someone holds the opinions he does can be "vindicatory" because it leaves the explainer no room to deny the opinion so explained. Earlier in this note I discussed Wiggins's suggestion that we can sometimes explain someone's conviction by pointing out that "there is nothing else to think." McDowell suggests that a sibling explanation would also be vindicatory. But it would not be because, again as explained in the text, anyone offering such an explanation would have to have already vindicated, in some other way, the opinion he so explains.

Summary. Philosophers want to find some connection between the way in which we form our moral convictions and the truth of those convictions. Nagel finds the connection in a faculty of reason operating from an impersonal perspective, Wiggins in a Cartesian nothing-else-to-think, and McDowell in a tenuous analogy with sense perception. They hope for some such connection because the alternative I believe correct—the radical independence of the truth of conviction from the manner of its production—strikes them as unsatisfactory. They find it hard to sustain their faith that the world of conviction is a world of truth and yet also accept that we have no better reason for our convictions than the rest of our convictions. However, Mc-Dowell elsewhere seems content with the radical independence of moral truth. He accepts the familiar challenge that we must "earn the right" to speak of truth in the moral context and believes that philosophers who appeal to intuitions fail to meet it. But he is clear that the challenge can be met only from within the substance of morality ("Projection and Truth in Ethics"). I would put the point somewhat differently. We do not need to "earn" the raw proposition that moral opinions can be true, because the claims of global skeptics about morality are themselves moral opinions. But we must earn the right to particular moral opinions, including skeptical opinions, if we think those true. In any case, I agree with McDowell that we earn the right he speaks of only in one way: through substantive moral argument that is vindicated by nothing but more moral argument.

7. Our strange discoveries would, of course, pose other puzzles. If we thought the beliefs the peculiar force caused were invariably true, we would have to account for the correlation. What correlation we thought we had to explain would depend on our independent moral convictions. We might have to show, for instance, a correlation between the force and suffering.

8. Harman, *The Nature of Morality*; Sturgeon, "Moral Explanations."

9. Sharon Street presses this objection (Street, "Objectivity and Truth: You'd Better Rethink It," homepages.nyu.edu/~jrs477/Sharon%20Street%20-%20Objectivity%20and%20Truth.pdf). She accepts the main theoretical claims of Part One of this book, but dissents from what she calls my "realism," by which she means my opinion that moral convictions can be true independently of people's attitudes. "My strategy," she says, ". . . is to adopt wholesale almost all of the major points that Dworkin argues for—but with one major exception . . . Dworkin's endorsement of realism—understood exactly as he himself wishes to understand it, namely as an 'internal' normative claim." She prefers a version of internal "antirealism" according to which people only have reasons that are given to them by their own evaluative attitudes. Caligula has reason to torture prisoners for the pleasure he takes in their screams, and no competing moral reason not to do that. She argues that, because the causal impact hypothesis is false, our moral convictions would be extremely unlikely to be true if we took them to be other than mind-dependent in that way. She suggests the following distinction between morality and at least part of our science. Our beliefs about what she calls "manifest surroundings," like trees and boulders in our neighborhood, are very likely be true because we have an explanation of how we came to those beliefs—a Darwinian explanation—that suggests that they are true. She concedes the sense in which that explanation is circular: Darwinian theory is part of our science and thus part of what we use that theory to explain. But that theory nevertheless provides what she calls "non-trivially question-begging reasons" for believing what we believe.

We have nontrivially question-begging reasons for our moral convictions as well, however. Later in this book I defend a general theory of legitimacy in government and I rely on that general theory to support a variety of opinions about the redistribution of a nation's wealth. That general theory is part of my overall set of convictions, just as Darwinian theory is part of Street's overall science, and if I am allowed to take the truth of that general theory of equality into account, as she does for Darwinian explanations, then the probability of my observations about redistribution also being true are not tiny but impressive—larger, in my ignorant layman's view, than the probability that string theory will stand up to later discovery and imagination. In Chapter 6 I describe a theory of moral responsibility: a theory about the responsible way to test our moral and ethical convictions. I believe that the probability of a moral conviction that survives those tests being true is much greater than the probability of convictions that have not been tested in that way or that fail the test. Appealing to a theory of moral responsibility to gauge the plausibility of a conviction about redistribution does not seem any more trivially circular than Street's appeal to Darwin. "What then is the difference," she asks, "between the manifest surroundings case and the normative case?"

> The answer lies in the distinction between answers to the skeptical challenge that provide *internal reason* to think that the causes might have led us to the hypothesized independent truth versus answers that provide *no reason whatsoever* to think that the causes might have led us to the hypothesized independent truth. The general question we are asking in both the manifest surroundings case and the normative case is "Why think that the causes described by our best scientific explanations would have led us to the truth in this domain?" In answer to this question, it is unsatisfactory to reply, "My judgments in this domain are true, and they're also the ones that the causes described by our best scientific explanations led me to." Such a reply offers no *reason* for thinking that the causes led us to the truth; it merely reasserts that they did. (Street, "Objectivity and Truth," 26)

This paragraph reveals a hidden premise in Street's argument: the causal dependence hypothesis. It supposes that if there is no internal causal reason to think our convictions true, it follows that there is no good internal reason at all. That does not follow: the causal dependence hypothesis is false for the reasons I give in this chapter. Moreover, Street elsewhere says that it is false. She says she is not insisting on what she calls a "causal epistemology" for morality. She says she accepts Hume's principle in the way I understand it; if Hume's principle is true, then the causal dependence thesis *must* be false. She only asks, she says, for *some* epistemology for the normative domains of morality and ethics. But that is exactly what a theory of moral responsibility is meant to provide: it aims to provide a suitable account of the kinds of reasons we ought to have to suppose a conviction true. Any such theory may of course be wrong. But it must be shown wrong by a rival normative theory. Is this trivially circular because a theory of good moral argument is part of the overall moral theory it hopes to defend? We are back to the same point: scientific reasoning is in exactly the same position. So the causal dependence thesis is alive in Street's arguments, denied but still potent.

10. Because your personal identity is defined by your genetic composition, many of the imagined stories in which "you" have radically different beliefs are actually stories in which you do not exist. I had to imagine that I was adopted by a fundamentalist family instead of having been born of fundamentalist parents; if I had been born to such parents, I would have been someone else. Many of the most important influences of genes and culture on your beliefs are not accidental but constitutive of your identity. But even if everyone in all ages and places held the same opinions about all matters of moral conviction, even if this consensus was inevitable for deep biological reasons, even if it was therefore false that your opinions might well have been different, none of these facts would provide the slightest evidence that the convictions everyone shares are true. Whether they are true is a matter for moral argument, not personal or species history. We must in any case decide what is better to do, or think or admire, without any historical or cosmic certificate that we are right.

11. Chapter 8 qualifies this statement in ways I cannot anticipate in any detail here. It may be possible to construct some very abstract, near-platitudinous statement of requirements on knowledge that hold across all intellectual domains. But this abstract statement would by hypothesis be permissive, not restrictive, of different and less abstract accounts of knowledge in different domains.

12. For exposition, see Michael Behe, *Darwin's Black Box: The Biochemical Challenge to Evolution* (New York: Free Press, 1996); William Dembski, *Intelligent Design: The Bridge between Science and Theology* (Downers Grove, Ill.: InterVarsity Press, 1999); Dembski, *The Design Inference* (New York: Cambridge University Press, 1998).

13. See, e.g., Elliot Sober, "What Is Wrong with Intelligent Design?" *Quarterly Review of Biology* 82, no. 1 (March 2007): 3–8.

14. *Tammy Kitzmiller, et al. v. Dover Area School District, et al.* (400 F. Supp. 2d 707 Docket no. 4cv2688).

15. See, e.g., Alvin Plantinga, *Warranted Christian Belief* (New York: Oxford University Press, 2000).

16. See Plantinga's "Aquinas/Calvin" model, in ibid., 167ff.

17. Wright, *Truth and Objectivity*, 200.

18. See Peter Railton, "Moral Realism," *Philosophical Review* 95, no. 2 (April 1986): 163–207.

5. Internal Skepticism

1. I mainly do not distinguish between indeterminacy and incommensurability. I treat the former as including the latter.

2. This helpful term was proposed by Ruth Chang. See her introduction to the collection of essays *Incommensurability, Incomparability, and Practical Reason*, ed. Ruth Chang (Cambridge, Mass.: Harvard University Press, 1997).

3. *District of Columbia, et al. v. Dick Anthony Heller*, 128 S. Ct. 2783 (2008).

4. See the discussion of moral conflict in Thomas Nagel, "War and Massacre," *Philosophy & Public Affairs* 1, no. 2 (1972): 123–44.

5. Leo Katz, for example, believes, as I do, that most claims of indeterminacy are really examples of ignorance. But he includes in that judgment, as I do not, all claims that two artists in different genres are "on a par" with one another. See Katz, "Incommensurable Choices and the Problem of Moral Ignorance," *University of Pennsylvania Law Review* 146, no. 5 (June 1998): 1465–85.

6. Joseph Raz, "Incommensurability," in *The Morality of Freedom* (New York: Oxford University Press, 1986), 321–66.

7. See Martha Minow and Joseph William Singer, "In Favor of Foxes: Pluralism as Fact and Aid to the Pursuit of Justice," in *Symposium: Justice for Hedgehogs: A Conference on Ronald Dworkin's Forthcoming Book* (special issue), *Boston University Law Review* 90, no. 2 (April 2010): 903; Ronald Dworkin, *Law's Empire* (Cambridge, Mass.: Harvard University Press, 1986), 10.

8. For a fuller exposition of the argument of this paragraph, see "No Right Answer?" in my book *A Matter of Principle* (Cambridge, Mass.: Harvard University Press, 1985).

6. Moral Responsibility

1. Jean Piaget, *The Moral Judgment of the Child* (London: Kegan Paul, Trench, Trubner, and Co., 1932); Lawrence Kohlberg, *Essays on Moral Development*, vol. 1: *The Philosophy of Moral Development* (San Francisco: Harper and Row, 1981); James Rest, *Development in Judging Moral Issues* (Minneapolis: University of Minnesota Press, 1979); Carol Gilligan, "In a Different Voice: Women's Conceptions of Self and Morality," *Harvard Educational Review* 47, no. 4 (1977): 481–517.

2. Not all moral philosophers agree. See Jonathan Dancy, "Ethical Particularism and Morally Relevant Properties," *Mind* 92 (1983): 530–47.

3. John Rawls, *Lectures on the History of Moral Philosophy* (Cambridge, Mass.: Harvard University Press, 2000), 148.

4. See Richard H. Fallon Jr., "Is Moral Reasoning Conceptual Interpretation?" in *Symposium: Justice for Hedgehogs: A Conference on Ronald Dworkin's Forthcoming Book* (special issue), *Boston University Law Review* 90, no. 2 (April 2010) (hereafter BU): 535; Amartya Sen, "Dworkin on Ethics and Freewill: Comments and Questions," BU: 657.

5. See, e.g., Martha Minow and Joseph Singer, "In Favor of Foxes: Pluralism as Fact and Aid to the Pursuit of Justice," BU: 903. "It may actually be true that our values conflict" (906).

6. Feynman, *QED: The Strange Theory of Light and Matter* (Princeton, N.J.: Princeton University Press, 1985), 10, 12.

7. See T. M. Scanlon, *What We Owe to Each Other* (Cambridge, Mass.: Belknap Press of Harvard University Press, 2000).

8. See Nagel, *Secular Philosophy and the Religious Temperament* (Oxford: Oxford University Press, 2010). See the discussion of Nagel's views in Chapter 7.

9. Fallon, "Is Moral Reasoning Conceptual Interpretation?"

7. Interpretation in General

1. Ludwig Wittgenstein, *Philosophical Investigations* (Oxford: Blackwell, 1953).

2. For example, I do not argue that my account of interpretation in this chapter fits what is often called the interpretation of data by scientists. But perhaps it does. We might treat scientific interpretation as what I later call explanatory interpretation.

3. See *San Antonio Independent Sch. Dist. v. Rodriguez,* 411 U.S. 1. (1973).

4. F. R. Leavis, *Valuation in Criticism and Other Essays,* ed. G. Singh (Cambridge: Cambridge University Press, 1986).

5. Cleanth Brooks, "The Formalist Critics," in Julie Rivkin and Michael Ryan, eds., *Literary Theory: An Anthology,* 2nd ed. (Oxford: Blackwell, 2004), 24.

6. The opinion is not confined to academic lawyers: some judges off duty are fond of the same expressions. See Stephen Guest's account of a radio discussion in which the eminent judge Lord Bingham participated (Guest, "Objectivity and Value: Legal Arguments and the Fallibility of Judges," in Michael Freeman and Ross Harrison, eds., *Law and Philosophy* [Oxford: Oxford University Press, 2007], 76–103).

7. Ronald Dworkin, *Law's Empire* (Cambridge, Mass.: Harvard University Press, 1986), 313–27; but see Antonin Scalia, *A Matter of Interpretation: Federal Courts and the Law* (Princeton: Princeton University Press, 1998), 16–18.

8. William Wimsatt and Monroe Beardsley, "The Intentional Fallacy," in Wimsatt, *The Verbal Icon: Studies in the Meaning of Poetry* (Lexington: University of Kentucky Press, 1954), 3–18.

9. "Does the author appear otherwise than as first reader? The distancing of the text from its author is already a phenomenon of the first reading that, in one move, poses the whole series of problems that we are now going to confront concerning the relations between explanation and interpretation. These relations arise at the time of reading" (Paul Ricoeur, "What Is a Text? Explanation and Understanding," in *Hermeneutics and the Human Sciences: Essays on Language, Action and Interpretation,* trans. John Thompson [Cambridge: Cambridge University Press, 1981], 149).

10. See Dworkin, *Law's Empire*, particularly chapter 9.

11. Julian Bell, "The Pleasure of Watteau," *New York Review*, February 12, 2009, reviewing Jed Perl, *Antoine's Alphabet: Watteau and His World* (New York: Knopf, 2008).

12. *New York Review of Books*, February 12, 2009, 13.

13. See John Updike's *Claudius and Gertrude* (New York: Knopf, 1993).

14. *The Norton Anthology of Theory and Criticism*, ed. Vincent Leitch, William Cain, Laurie Finke, Barbara Johnson, John McGowan, and Jeffrey Williams (New York: W. W. Norton, 2001), 6–7.

15. Jean-Paul Sartre, "Why Write?" in *Twentieth Century Literary Criticism*, ed. David Lodge (London: Longman, 1972), 371, 375. He added that to make literature "come into view a concrete act called reading is necessary, and it lasts only as long as this act can last. Beyond that, there are only black marks on paper" (371).

16. F. R. Leavis, *The Great Tradition* (Harmondsworth: Penguin, 1972), 176, 173.

17. Leavis, *Valuation in Criticism*, 100.

18. Cleanth Brooks, *The Hidden God: Studies in Hemingway, Faulkner, Yeats, Eliot, and Warren* (New Haven: Yale University Press, 1963), chapter 4, 57; Brooks, *The Well Wrought Urn: Studies in the Structure of Poetry* (New York: Harcourt, Brace, 1947), chapter 10.

19. Roy Foster, *W. B. Yeats: A Life*, vol. 2: *The Arch-Poet 1915–1939* (New York: Oxford University Press, 2003), 322–24.

20. Brooks, *The Well Wrought Urn*, 185.

21. *Norton Anthology of Theory and Criticism*, 1450.

22. Foster, *W. B. Yeats*, 328; Northrop Frye, "The Archetypes of Literature," in *Norton Anthology of Theory and Criticism*, 1445–57.

23. Of course not all history is sensibly treated as interpretive. Much is just retrieval of information from the past: who won what battles and what weapons were at their disposal, for example. However, the radical opinion that history is interpretive even at that level has been defended (Hayden White, *Metahistory: The Historical Imagination in Nineteenth-Century Europe* [Baltimore: Johns Hopkins University Press, 1973]).

24. Butterfield had particularly in mind Thomas Macaulay, who was the most celebrated and influential of the Whig historians. Macaulay saw the history of Britain as a smooth progression to a more perfect society. "The history of our country," he wrote in the first paragraph of his most famous work, "during the last hundred and sixty years is eminently the history of physical, of moral, and of intellectual improvement" (*The History of England from the Accession of James I* [London: Penguin Classics, 1979]). Butterfield was contemptuous of such optimism and moral judgment, but he at least flirted with "general ideas" himself, including the important claim that political necessity rather than moral inspiration produced the greater liberty in Britain that Macaulay celebrated.

25. Herbert Butterfield, *The Whig Interpretation of History* (New York: Norton, 1965), 13.

26. Ibid., 71.

27. Jung, "On the Relation of Analytical Psychology to Poetry," in *The Spirit in Man, Art and Literature,* 4th ed. (Princeton: Princeton University Press, 1978).

28. John Dover Wilson, "The Political Background of Shakespeare's Richard II and Henry IV," *Shakespeare-Jahrbuch* (1939): 47.

29. Greenblatt, *The Power of Forms in the English Renaissance* (Norman, Okla.: Pilgrim Books, 1982), 6.

30. E. D. Hirsch, *Validity in Interpretation* (New Haven: Yale University Press, 1967), 6–10.

31. T. S. Eliot, "Tradition and the Individual Talent," in *The Sacred Wood: Essays on Poetry and Criticism* (London: Methuen, 1920).

32. Frederic Jameson, *The Political Unconscious: Narrative as a Socially Symbolic Act* (London: Methuen, 1981), 73, 85.

33. Terry Eagleton, *The Function of Criticism: From the Spectator to Post-Structuralism.* London: Verso.

34. See Lyn Mikel Brown, *Girlfighting: Rejection and Betrayal among Girls* (New York: New York University Press, 2003).

35. See Dworkin, *Law's Empire,* 266–75.

36. Stanley Fish, *Is There a Text in This Class?* (Cambridge, Mass.: Harvard University Press, 1980), 147.

37. Ibid., 167, 180, 174.

38. Leavis, *Valuation in Criticism,* 93.

39. I summarize in these paragraphs a complex and extensively debated issue in the philosophy of language. See W. V. O. Quine, *Word and Object* (Cambridge, Mass.: MIT Press, 1960); and D. Davidson, "A Coherence Theory of Truth and Knowledge," in D. Henrich, ed., *Kant oder Hegel?* (Stuttgart: Klett-Cotta, 1983).

40. Quine, *Ontological Relativity: And Other Essays* (New York: Columbia University Press, 1969), 27.

41. Donald Davidson, "Radical Interpretation," *Dialectica* 27 (1973): 314–28.

42. See, e.g., John Wallace, "Translation Theories and the Decipherment of Linear B," in E. Lepore, ed., *Truth and Interpretation: Perspectives on the Philosophy of Donald Davidson* (Oxford: Basil Blackwell, 1986), 211.

43. "Three Varieties of Knowledge," in Donald Davidson, *Subjective, Intersubjective, Objective* (New York: Oxford University Press, 2001), 214.

44. Coleridge, "Biographia Literaria," in *Norton Anthology of Theory and Criticism,* 681.

45. Annette Barnes reports this description in Stoppard's lecture at Johns Hopkins University. See her *On Interpretation* (Oxford: Blackwell, 1988), 166.

46. Edwin Baker suggested that people prefer "most reasonable" to "true" because the former allows comparative judgments while the latter does not. (Baker, "In

Hedgehog Solidarity," in *Symposium: Justice for Hedgehogs: A Conference on Ronald Dworkin's Forthcoming Book* [special issue], *Boston University Law Review* 90, no. 2 [April 2010]: 759. But "true" allows comparatives as well: we are comfortable saying that one view is closer to the truth than another, and we can say this even when we cannot claim full truth for any view. In her interesting book *On Interpretation,* Annette Barnes distinguishes "true" from "acceptable." She limits truth in interpretation to correct judgments of "artistic intent." "While only one of the two incompatible interpretations can be true," she says, "the other can make the most sense of the work, or make the work a more significant or successful work" (78–79). In that case, she says, the latter interpretation "could compete with the demand that the interpretation be true" (60). The value theory of interpretation I defend in the text denies the competition: these are only two ways of describing the overall best interpretation.

47. See Georg Henrik von Wright, *Explanation and Understanding* (Ithaca, N.Y.: Cornell University Press, 1971), 5.

48. Philosophers of science call attention to the importance of what Hilary Putnam and others have called "epistemic" values. See Hilary Putnam, *The Collapse of the Fact/Value Dichotomy and Other Essays* (Cambridge, Mass.: Harvard University Press, 2002). Scientists prefer simple to more complex theories, and elegant to inelegant theories (Judith Wechsler, ed., *On Aesthetics in Science* [Cambridge, Mass.: MIT Press, 1981]; Brian Greene, *The Elegant Universe: Superstrings, Hidden Dimensions, and the Quest for the Ultimate Theory* [New York: Vintage, 2000]; Greene, "The Elegant Universe," *NOVA,* PBS TV miniseries, WGBH Educational Foundation, 2003 [interviews with string theorists about the role of elegance and related considerations in string theory]). We must take care to distinguish these epistemic values from justifying goals. Simplicity and elegance count in deciding which of different theories or hypotheses to prefer. They are hypotheses about truth that cannot be tested directly because any test would employ them. They are not, however, assumptions about the purposes of scientific study or theory. We prefer an elegant to an inelegant theory of the universe, but we do not study the universe to find examples of elegance. We might, after all, find an elegant explanation of the number of rocks in Africa.

49. Willard V. O. Quine, "Two Dogmas of Empiricism," in *From a Logical Point of View: Nine Logico-Philosophical Essays,* 2nd ed. (Cambridge, Mass.: Harvard University Press, 2006), 37–46.

50. David Whitehouse, "Black Holes Turned 'Inside Out,'" *BBC News,* July 22, 2004, news.bbc.co.uk/1/hi/sci/tech/3913145.stm.

8. Conceptual Interpretation

1. For an argument that we should not so agree, see Timothy Williamson, *Vagueness* (New York: Routledge, 1994).

2. Saul Kripke, *Naming and Necessity* (Oxford: Blackwell, 1972); Hilary Putnam, "The Meaning of 'Meaning,'" *Minnesota Studies in the Philosophy of Science* 7 (1975): 131–93.

3. See my *Justice in Robes* (Cambridge, Mass.: Belknap Press of Harvard University Press, 2006), 218–19, 223–27.

4. I mean not to exclude other types of concepts: perhaps we should recognize mathematical kinds, for instance. I discuss, as interpretive concepts, those amenable to interpretation on the value theory defended in Chapter 7.

5. I understand Crispin Wright to suppose that a discourse is not assertoric at all without shared paradigms. See Wright, *Truth and Objectivity* (Cambridge, Mass.: Harvard University Press, 1992), 48.

6. Some readers may think it better to treat all concepts, including those I designate as criterial or natural-kind concepts, as interpretive. I do not agree, but my arguments do not depend on rejecting that view. They depend only on accepting that the ethical, moral, and political concepts I later discuss are interpretive.

7. This is not simply a matter of something important turning on the issue. If you and I bet a huge sum on whether the next person through the theater door would be bald, we would have to call off the bet, not engage in some complex interpretation, if the next person was a very close case.

8. Thomas Nagel, "The Psychophysical Nexus," in Paul Boghossian and Christopher Peacocke, eds., *New Essays on the A Priori* (New York: Oxford University Press, 2000).

9. See "Pluto Not a Planet, Astronomers Rule," August 2006, news.nationalgeo graphic.com/news/2006/08/060824-pluto-planet.html. But see "Pluto IS a Planet!" www.plutoisaplanet.org: "Welcome to the main web page for the Society for the Preservation of Pluto as a Planet! We here at SP3 believe strongly that Pluto's status as a planet should not be in question . . . Please join us on our mission to keep Pluto a planet and find out what you can do to support our noble cause."

10. John Rawls, *A Theory of Justice* (Cambridge, Mass.: Harvard University Press, 1971), 5.

11. This is not a further difficulty for the status skeptics I discussed in Chapter 3 who insist that we must treat claims about the good or what ought to be done as disguised commands or recommendations or projections of an attitude or emotion. If we accepted their advice we could say, not that general moral concepts are criterial, but that moral disagreement is genuine because it reflects difference in recommendation or attitude or emotion. But we cannot take this suggestion seriously as an interpretation of actual moral experience. We all know the difference between commanding someone to shut the door and declaring that he has a moral duty to shut the door. Treating moral claims as commands or recommendations or projections is not an interpretive conclusion. It is a heroic attempt to rescue moral experience from external skepticism by reinventing it as something else. In Part One we found external skepticism impossible even coherently to formulate; we have no need of rescue.

12. There are difficulties in this account: perhaps some other large mammal looks sufficiently like a lion that many people have called it a lion. But the idea of a natural-kind concept supposes that once people are made aware that there are fundamental biological differences between the animal to which the word has been attached and the different animal they have also been calling a lion, they correct their mistake. If that were not true—if they insisted that the different animal was also a lion—a different hypothesis would be called for. We might then decide that the concept of a lion in actual use is not a natural-kind concept after all but a criterial one: it describes what has a certain kind of appearance. Or that there are two concepts rather than one in play and that these are often confused, producing cases of spurious agreement or disagreement.

13. Donald Davidson, "The Structure and Content of Truth" (The Dewey Lectures, 1989), *Journal of Philosophy* 87 (1990): 279–328; Davidson, *Truth and Predication* (Cambridge, Mass.: Belknap Press of Harvard University Press, 2005).

14. Wright, *Truth and Objectivity*.

15. It has also been called by other names, and the name as well as the theory is controversial. There is an excellent discussion of different versions of the theory and objections to it under the title "The Deflationary Theory of Truth" in the *Stanford Encyclopedia of Philosophy*, plato.stanford.edu.

16. Bernard Williams, *Truth and Truthfulness: An Essay in Genealogy* (Princeton: Princeton University Press, 2004).

17. It might be useful to point out, in view of Benjamin Zipursky's reading, that though I relied on the platitude of repetition in my discussion of external status skepticism in Part One, I did not commit myself to the deflationary theory, which holds that the repetition exhausts truth, or to any other philosophical theory of truth. See Benjamin C. Zipursky, "Two Takes on Truth in Normative Discourse," in *Symposium: Justice for Hedgehogs: A Conference on Ronald Dworkin's Forthcoming Book* (special issue), *Boston University Law Review* 90, no. 2 (April 2010): 525. I argued that skeptical claims cannot be construed as other than moral claims themselves. Nor do I intend to accept, as he fears I do, a correspondence theory of truth for science. I mention it as a candidate for that role, as I say, only to have an example to contrast with interpretation.

18. This suggestion is in certain respects like those of Crispin Wright (see his *Truth and Objectivity*). He describes a "minimalist" concept of truth defined by what he calls "platitudes" that can be deployed in a variety of domains. Some of these domains, he says, provide more "realism" than others. For instance, a domain is more "realist" if its propositions have "wide cosmological role," that is, if they can figure in the explanation of a wide variety of propositions in other domains. He sets out what he calls "the makings of a prima facie case" that morality fails that test and then adds that if so that is "bad" though not "catastrophic" news for moral realism (198). He offers a further "cognitive command" standard: a domain is more realist in which it is a priori that a failure of convergence in opinion reflects an independent cognitive

failure of some kind. Morality fails that test as well: we may well disagree about the justice of a foreign policy with people who rely on the same information we have and are subject to no more distorting influences than we are. The abstract concept I contemplate in the text, on the contrary, is not platitudinous or minimalist: it requires a substantive conception of inquiry that allows us to understand claims of truth in different domains as claims of unique success. Nor, in my view, are some of the domains that allow unique success more "realist" than others: they are all real. It is not "bad news" that morality fails the wide cosmological and cognitive control tests. The injustice of a foreign policy is not less real because the injustice explains no physical or mental phenomena or because those who disagree suffer from no independent cognitive defect. Many philosophers believe that we could have no warrant for claiming exclusive truth in such circumstances and that any account of truth that did not deny our warrant would be vacuous or too lenient. But—though by now I risk irritation in the repetition—that is itself a moral opinion that must be supported not by Archimedean epistemology but by some argument that shows the moral importance of cognitive command.

19. I am grateful to David Wiggins for pointing this out to me. For Wiggins's illuminating study of Peirce's theories, see his "Reflections on Inquiry and Truth," in Cheryl Misak, ed., *The Cambridge Companion to Peirce* (Cambridge: Cambridge University Press, 2004).

20. Peirce, "The Fixation of Belief" (1877), in *Collected Papers of Charles Sanders Peirce*, vol. 5, ed. Charles Hartshorne, Paul Weiss, and Arthur Burks (Cambridge, Mass.: Harvard University Press, 1931–1958), 375.

21. That may not be an irresistible conclusion. We might consider a more complex interpretive account that took only risible examples as paradigms but yet claimed some analysis of these paradigms that permitted events unlikely to provoke laughter nevertheless to be funny. It seems dubious, however, that any such interpretation would be persuasive.

22. Kit Fine pointed out to me the connection between interpretive concepts and the paradox of analysis.

23. R. M. Hare, *The Language of Morals* (Oxford: Oxford University Press, 1952), 121; Hare, *Freedom and Reason* (Oxford: Oxford University Press, 1963), 21–29.

24. See John McDowell's discussion of this subject, "Reason, Value and Reality," in *Mind, Value, and Reality* (Cambridge, Mass.: Harvard University Press, 1998).

25. Bernard Williams, *Ethics and the Limits of Philosophy* (London: Fontana, 1985).

26. T. M. Scanlon, "Wrongness and Reasons: A Reexamination," in *Oxford Studies in Metaethics*, vol. 2, ed. Russ Shafer-Landau (Oxford: Oxford University Press, 2007).

27. I do not suggest that either Plato or Aristotle accepted the distinction between moral and ethical values I have used in this book.

28. Terence Irwin, *Plato's Ethics* (Oxford: Oxford University Press, 1995).

29. Plato, *Laches,* in *Plato: Laches. Protagoras. Meno. Euthydemus,* trans. W. R. M. Lamb (Cambridge, Mass.: Harvard University Press, 1924).

30. *Plato: Statesman. Philebus. Ion,* trans. Harold North Fowler and W. R. M. Lamb (Cambridge, Mass.: Harvard University Press, 1925).

31. Irwin, *Plato's Ethics,* 75.

32. Aristotle, *Nicomachean Ethics,* trans. Roger Crisp (Cambridge: Cambridge University Press, 2000), VII.11–14 and X.1–5.

33. The *Stanford Encyclopedia of Philosophy,* in the entry for Aristotle's *Ethics,* notes, "A common complaint about Aristotle's attempt to defend his conception of happiness is that his argument is too general to show that it is in one's interest to possess any of the particular virtues as they are traditionally conceived. Suppose we grant, at least for the sake of argument, that doing anything well, including living well, consists in exercising certain skills; and let us call these skills, whatever they turn out to be, virtues. Even so, that point does not by itself allow us to infer that such qualities as temperance, justice, courage, as they are normally understood, are virtues. They should be counted as virtues only if it can be shown that actualizing precisely these skills is what happiness consists in. What Aristotle owes us, then, is an account of these traditional qualities that explains why they must play a central role in any well-lived life." The author of the essay suggests, in response, that Aristotle meant to address only those already educated to a love of the virtues. I believe that treating Aristotle's account as interpretive, weaving together conceptions of particular virtues with an overall conception of happiness, provides a more satisfying answer.

9. Dignity

1. See Michael Smith, "The Humean Theory of Motivation," and Philip Pettit, "Humeans, Anti-Humeans, and Motivation," both in Andrew Fisher and Simon Kirchin, eds., *Arguing about Metaethics* (London: Routledge, 2006), 575, 602.

2. See, e.g, John Stuart Mill, *Utilitarianism,* ed. J. M. Robson (1861; Toronto: University of Toronto Press, 1963); Henry Sidgwick, *The Methods of Ethics* (London: Macmillan, 1874); Thomas Nagel, *Equality and Partiality* (New York: Oxford University Press, 1991), chapter 7.

3. See my *Sovereign Virtue: The Theory and Practice of Equality* (Cambridge, Mass.: Harvard University Press, 2000), 242–54; and my "Foundations of Liberal Equality," in Stephen Darwall, ed., *Equal Freedom: Selected Tanner Lectures on Human Values* (Ann Arbor: University of Michigan Press, 1995), 190, 229–34.

4. See, for example, Philip Roth's imagined debate between Leo Tolstoy and Nathan Zuckerman on the issue (Roth, *American Pastoral* [New York: Vintage, 1998]).

5. Though I was once tempted. See Dworkin, *Sovereign Virtue,* 263–67; and Dworkin, "Foundations of Liberal Equality," 190, 195, 258–62.

6. Christine Jolls has very usefully compared this distinction to one made by so-cial scientists studying people's contentment with their lives (Jolls, "Dworkin's Living Well and the Well-Being Revolution," in *Symposium: Justice for Hedgehogs: A Confer-ence on Ronald Dworkin's Forthcoming Book* [special issue], *Boston University Law Re-view* 90, no. 2 [April 2010]: 641). Performance value, she suggests, may be compared to people's ranking of their experiences one by one, while product value is comparable to their ranking of their life as a whole. She points out, however, correctly, that my re-marks about the importance of the narrative quality of a life as a whole qualify these associations. I take the research she describes to suggest that people evaluate experi-ences differently when placed in the context of a whole life. Commuting ranks very low as an isolated event, but the tedium disappears in any evaluation of the life engaged in an occupation that commuting permits. The oncologist cannot enjoy his conversation with lung cancer victims, but he takes satisfaction in his career nevertheless. It is the isolation of the discrete lived events evaluated in the Princeton study she describes that, to my mind, renders the study, undoubtedly important in a variety of ways, less signifi-cant for ethics than the narrative evaluations that Jolls compares them with.

7. See Thomas Nagel, *Mortal Questions* (Cambridge: Cambridge University Press, 1991); and Bernard Williams, "Moral Luck," in *Moral Luck* (Cambridge: Cam-bridge University Press, 1981), 20–40.

8. See Dworkin, *Life's Dominion* (New York: Knopf, 1993), chapter 7.

9. John Rawls, *A Theory of Justice* (Cambridge, Mass.: Harvard University Press, 1971), 214–21.

10. See the section "Science and Interpretation" in Chapter 7.

11. Dworkin, *Sovereign Virtue;* Dworkin, *Is Democracy Possible Here? Principles for a New Political Debate* (Princeton: Princeton University Press, 2006).

12. Leon Kass, *Life, Liberty and the Defense of Dignity: The Challenge for Bioethics* (San Francisco: Encounter Books, 2004).

13. T. M. Scanlon, *What We Owe to Each Other* (Cambridge, Mass.: Belknap Press of Harvard University Press, 2000); Scanlon, *Moral Dimensions: Permissibility, Mean-ing, Blame* (Cambridge, Mass.: Belknap Press of Harvard University Press, 2008).

14. Stephen L. Darwall, "Two Kinds of Respect," *Ethics* 88, no. 1 (October 1977): 36–49.

15. See James Griffin, *Well Being: Its Meaning, Measure, and Moral Importance* (New York: Oxford University Press, 1986), chapter 1.

16. There are pure cases of pain, not just the pain of injury or disease but even, I imagine, of extreme hunger. But even these are limited: much pain is also, like most pleasure, parasitic on judgment. Envy, disappointment, and shame can be intensely, even viscerally, painful but are parasitic on judgment.

17. See, e.g,, Robert Nozick, *Anarchy, State, and Utopia* (New York: Basic Books, 1974), 42–45. For a literary illustration of this point, see Ray Bradbury, *Dandelion Wine* (New York: Doubleday, 1957), chapter 13.

18. Lionel Trilling, *Sincerity and Authenticity* (Cambridge, Mass.: Harvard University Press, 2006).

19. Friedrich Nietzsche, *The Gay Science,* trans. Walter Kaufman (New York: Vintage Books, 1974), §290: "One thing is needful—to 'give style' to one's character—a great and rare art! It is practiced by those who survey all the strengths and weaknesses of their nature and then fit them into an artistic plan until every one of them appears as art and reason and even weaknesses delight the eye."

20. Jean-Paul Sartre, *Existential Psychoanalysis* (Chicago: Regnery, 1962).

21. See Thomas Scanlon, "Preference and Urgency," in *The Difficulty of Tolerance: Essays in Political Philosophy* (Cambridge: Cambridge University Press, 2003), 70, 74.

22. Friedrich Nietzsche, *Ecce Homo: How One Becomes What One Is* (Oxford: Oxford University Press, 2007).

23. See Nagel, "Secular Philosophy and the Religious Temperament," in his book of the same name (Oxford: Oxford University Press, 2010), chapter 1.

10. Free Will and Responsibility

1. I believe this is much the same understanding of decision as Thomas Nagel offers of action, though I'm not sure that spiders make decisions. See Nagel, *The View from Nowhere* (New York: Oxford University Press, 1986), 111.

2. Certain now-famous experiments conceived by Benjamin Libet, an experimental psychologist, at least illustrate this hypothesis, though they hardly demonstrate that it is true. An experimental subject is asked spontaneously to raise whichever of his hands he wishes: scans indicate that the brain activity that ends in his raising one hand begins a small fraction of a second before the different brain activity begins that constitutes awareness of which hand he will raise. Libet concludes that the subject's decision to raise his right hand is not the cause of his raising his right hand, but only another effect of whatever did make him raise his right hand. He is careful to point out that his results do not preclude the possibility that the subject may interrupt any behavior begun in advance of a decision by a fresh decision: I may initiate an act of shoplifting unaware but cancel it once I become aware that I am about to steal. That possibility, Libet believes, is enough to protect moral responsibility: I am responsible if I do not intervene to cancel some decisions I should have cancelled. Epiphenomenalists suppose, however, that *all* decisions, including decisions to cancel a process begun unconsciously, are side effects rather than causes. (Patrick Haggard, "Conscious Intention and Motor Control," *Trends in Cognitive Neuroscience* 9, no. 6 [June 2005]: 290–96; Alfred Mele, *Free Will and Luck* [Oxford: Oxford University Press, 2006], chapter 2.)

3. For a sample, see Gary Watson, ed., *Free Will* (Oxford: Oxford University Press, 2003); Robert Kane, ed., *The Oxford Handbook of Free Will* (Oxford: Oxford University Press, 2005).

4. Thomas Nagel has insisted throughout his career on a distinction between two sources of truth about ourselves and our place in the world: a subjective, personal perspective and an objective, impersonal one from which we try to understand ourselves as part of the natural world. He believes that the free will problem arises, and is insoluble, because we cannot help finding inconsistent ideas true when we turn from one perspective to the other. We cannot escape a conviction of freedom in the personal perspective that disappears in the objective one.

> The objective view seems to wipe out such autonomy because it admits only one kind of explanation of why something happened—causal explanation—and equates its absence with the absence of any explanation at all . . . [T]he basic idea which it finds congenial is that the explanation of an occurrence must show how that occurrence, or a range of possibilities within which it falls, was necessitated by prior conditions and events. (*The View from Nowhere*, 115)

For reasons set out in this chapter, I think that the impersonal perspective Nagel has in mind is not appropriate to considering ethical and moral questions about responsibility (as distinct from scientific or metaphysical questions about freedom) unless that perspective is made pertinent by some independent moral or ethical principle such as the "causal control" principle I consider and reject later in this chapter. I agree, of course, that that perspective is mandatory to some issues: when we consider the nature of the external world as it is apart from the way any particular creature perceives it. However, Nagel offers a general reason for thinking the impersonal perspective always pertinent to any question about ourselves, including the question of responsibility. Taking up that perspective, he says, "reflect[s] our own disposition to view ourselves, and our need to *accept* ourselves, from outside. Without such acceptance we will be in a significant way alienated from our lives" (*The View from Nowhere*, 198). That seems to me to put the questions in the wrong order. Whether we alienate ourselves from our lives when we suppose that our responsibility for some action does not turn on any causal explanation of that action depends on whether that is a plausible view of the basis of responsibility.

In an equally influential study, Peter Strawson denied that the objective standpoint is right for considering issues of judgmental responsibility (Strawson, "Freedom and Resentment," in *Freedom and Resentment and Other Essays* [London: Methuen, 1974]). Strawson argued that attributions of responsibility are central to a network of human emotions and reactions of blame, resentment, and guilt that we could not abandon without ceasing to be the kinds of creature we are. He declared, in a passage Nagel sets out in his own discussion:

> Inside the general structure or web of human attitudes and feelings of which I have been speaking, there is endless room for modification, redirection, criticism and justification. But questions of justification are internal to it. The exis-

tence of the general framework of attitudes itself is something we are given with the fact of human society. As a whole, it neither calls for, nor permits, an external "rational justification." ("Freedom and Resentment," 23)

Strawson treats the problem of responsibility as arising within a narrative of motives and reactions and holds that we have no reason to test that system by asking whether its assumptions are verified by causal explanations situated in the natural world. Nagel thinks this a mistake

> because there is no way of preventing the slide from *internal* to *external* criticism once we are capable of an external view. The problem of free will . . . arises because there is a continuity between familiar "internal" criticism of the reactive attitudes on the basis of specific facts, and philosophical criticisms on the basis of supposed general facts. (*The View from Nowhere*, 125)

Nagel here states an important, and I believe popular, argument in favor of the causal control principle I later discuss and for taking up the impersonal perspective that principle requires. Our ordinary judgments make exceptions to the general principle that we are responsible for what we do; in Nagel's view these exceptions can be justified only by assuming something like that principle. I think this popular argument wrong, however. In the text I argue that, on the contrary, the causal control principle is inadequate to justify the exceptions Nagel has in mind, and that these exceptions can in fact be justified only through a different principle that does not make responsibility an impersonal causal issue. So in my view Nagel's argument for rejecting Strawson's internal perspective actually tells in Strawson's favor. I should add, however, that I find Strawson's own argument—that we could not possibly abandon our sense of judgmental responsibility—an inadequate basis for declaring our ordinary judgments of responsibility philosophically respectable. We need a defense of our ordinary judgments, not just a confession of our inability to doubt them. We need to show that we have no reason to doubt them. That is one aim of this chapter.

5. Nagel, *The View from Nowhere*, 114–15.

6. See Galen Strawson, "The Impossibility of Mental Responsibility," *Philosophical Studies* 75 (1994): 5–24.

7. True, we commonly separate blameworthiness from wrongness: we think that someone who murders has done something wrong even if he was insane at the time and is therefore not to blame. Incompatibilists assume that that distinction would still hold if determinism were true: though it would then follow that no one was ever blameworthy, it would not follow that nothing was ever the wrong thing to do. But that depends on why we think certain acts wrong. On any plausible theory, concepts of responsibility figure just as pervasively in identifying wrongful acts as in adjudicating blame for those acts. Yes, some philosophers, including some utilitarians, believe that an act is wrong if it has bad consequences, whatever the mental state of the

agent. Someone who gives to charity acts wrongly if, unknown and unknowable to him, he would have improved overall happiness by spending on his own pleasure instead. This is not plausible. Someone does wrong when he harms someone else deliberately or negligently, without justification, but not when his acts cause the same suffering wholly unintentionally and unforeseeably. Then he is not only not to blame but has done nothing wrong. That discrimination is built into the definition of discrete moral rules: we cannot commit murder or steal or embezzle or lie or betray our friends inadvertently. You do not break your promise to help me in need if there is no way you can know that I am in need. These discriminations are justified by assumptions about judgmental responsibility: knowledge or negligence matter for wrongness because they matter for responsibility. It would not be a mistake, therefore, to say that an idiot, who cannot understand that guns kill, does not act wrongly when he fires. We usually put the point differently: we say that he does act wrongly though he has an excuse. That makes it easier to explain why he is dangerous and must be restrained. It also poses no risk to the clarity of society's prohibition of murder. Any attempt to qualify the prohibition with nuanced judgments of responsibility might erode its value. But that different way of describing his situation is available only because he acts in circumstances in which normal people would be responsible for murder. An idiot would not do the wrong thing shooting a stage gun in a play if even a normal person would have no reason to think the gun was loaded. Our identification of right and wrong is therefore parasitic on judgments of responsibility and culpability. If we really came to think that there was no difference between the responsibility of someone who secretly loaded the stage gun and someone who fired it unawares, we would have no reason to think the first of these acts morally wrong and the second not.

What about character? Having a bad character is different from posing a threat; someone with chicken pox poses a threat but need not have a bad character. On views I find plausible the distinction, once again, trades in concepts of responsibility. Someone has a bad character if he is prone to act badly—to do what it is wrong to do. If there is nothing that it is wrong to do, then no one has a bad character. Some people—those who are prone to kill as well as those with chicken pox—are dangerous because they are likely to cause harm. But that is the most we can say. What about liability responsibility? If I am not to blame for an act that caused someone else damage, if I did nothing wrong in acting that way, then why should I bear his cost?

What about prudence? I would think myself imprudent if I was hit by lightning taking my small boat out in an expected storm, but not if I was struck in a wholly unexpected and unpredictable one. But if determinism erases all grounds of self-blame in the former case, because it was predetermined that I would act in that way, then what ground is left for declaring myself imprudent? I can think I have a reason for acting in one way rather than another only when I take that alleged reason to affect how I should behave. If determinism means that there is no way I should behave because nature or fate has already determined how I will behave, then its annihilating power is catholic across reasons. If determinism rules out having reasons of some particular kind—reasons to criticize myself if I act in one way rather than another—then it rules out the very idea of having reasons to act in one way rather than another. Hurricanes are not blameworthy when they kill. Nor do they violate moral norms or display morally bad character. Nor are they imprudent when they swerve into cold air and dissipate. If determinism is true and means that we have no judgmental responsibility, then we are all—hurricanes and people—just large and small disturbances on nature's sea.

Could we at least save judgments about good and bad states of affairs? Can't we say that it is good when people are happier, even if no one ever has judgment responsibility for bringing that state of affairs about? That must depend, again, on your theory of why states of affairs are good or bad. It is good when great cathedrals are built and when people establish lives full of pleasure and achievement in their own or others' eyes. If robots could be made happy, however, I would see no value in their happiness, though much value in the science that made them happy. If people lack judgmental responsibility, there might be no more value in their own happiness than in robotic happiness.

8. The great defense lawyer Clarence Darrow was a pessimistic incompatibilist who therefore thought punishment wrong. He told the judge trying Richard Loeb and Nathan Leopold, students of Nietzsche, for the thrill murder of young Bobby Franks, "Nature is strong and she is pitiless. She works in her own mysterious way, and we are her victims. We have not much to do with it ourselves. Nature takes this job in hand, and we play our parts. In the words of old Omar Khayyam, we are only 'Impotent pieces in the game He plays / Upon this checkerboard of nights and days, / Hither and thither moves, and checks, and slays, / And one by one back in the closet lays.' What had this boy to do with it? He was not his own father; he was not his own mother; he was not his own grandparents. All of this was handed to him. He did not surround himself with governesses and wealth. He did not make himself. And yet he is to be compelled to pay." See Douglas O. Linder, "Who Is Clarence Darrow?" www.law.umkc.edu/faculty/projects/ftrials/DARESY.htm (1997).

9. David Dolinko suggested that example.

10. Robert Kane, who has written about free will for many years and edited several collections of essays on the free will issue, says that he agrees with 90 percent of my views on that subject and that he rejects, as I do, the causal principle (Kane, "Responsibility and Free Will in Dworkin's Justice for Hedgehogs," in *Symposium: Justice for Hedgehogs: A Conference on Ronald Dworkin's Forthcoming Book* [special issue], *Boston University Law Review* 90, no. 2 [April 2010] [hereafter BU]: 611). He thinks I overlook Aristotle's view that even though people are often not in control—when drunk, for instance—they are responsible for what they do then because they

NOTES TO PAGES 230–237

were in control at the earlier time when they decided to drink in excess. But, Kane continues, if determinism is true, then people have never been in control, so that Aristotle's ground for insisting on their responsibility does not hold. That conclusion follows from determinism, however, only if we do accept the causal principle that Kane says he rejects. The contrast shows, I believe, the almost intuitive assumption of many of the best writers on the subject that something like the causal control principle is correct, and that those who reject it, like Hume, have made an elementary mistake.

11. Bernard Williams, *Shame and Necessity* (Berkeley: University of California Press, 1973).

12. See W. F. R. Hardie, "Aristotle and the Freewill Problem," *Philosophy* 43, no. 165 (July 1968): 274–78; Thomas Hobbes, *Leviathan,* ed. R. E. Flatman and D. Johnston (New York: W. W. Norton, 1997), 108; David Hume, *An Enquiry Concerning Human Understanding,* ed. P. H. Nidditch (Oxford: Clarendon Press, 1978), 73; T. M. Scanlon, *Moral Dimensions: Permissibility, Meaning, Blame* (Cambridge, Mass.: Belknap Press of Harvard University Press, 2008).

13. Hume, *Enquiry Concerning Human Understanding,* 73.

14. Roderick Chisholm, "Human Freedom and the Self," in Watson, ed., *Free Will* (Oxford: Oxford University Press, 1982); Peter Van Inwagen, *An Essay on Free Will* (Oxford: Clarendon Press, 1983).

15. "[I] ask the incompatibilist to explain more exactly what kind of freedom he believes that morally significant choice must have, and to explain how choices that were free in this sense could have a special licensing power. I do not myself see how these questions can be given satisfactory answers" (Scanlon, *Moral Dimensions,* 206). See also Scanlon's comments on an earlier draft of this chapter. Scanlon, "Varieties of Responsibility," BU: 603.

16. See, e.g., J. J. C. Smart, "Free Will, Praise and Blame," *Mind* 70, no. 278 (1961): 291–306. See also Nagel, *The View from Nowhere;* Nagel, "Moral Luck" (1979), reprinted in his *Mortal Questions* (Cambridge: Cambridge University Press, 1991).

17. Jean-Paul Sartre, *Existentialism Is a Humanism* (1945 lecture) (New Haven: Yale University Press, 2007).

18. He may not be technically guilty of an attempt in law because, assuming that epiphenomenalism is true, he achieved nothing beyond a mental act. But he is ethically and morally in the same position as the frustrated murderer.

19. See Galen Strawson, "Impossibility of Mental Responsibility," 13.

20. Susan Wolf argues, in effect, that Mother Teresa is free and responsible because she does what is right for the right reasons but Stalin is not free or responsible because he does not (Susan Wolf, "Self-Interest and Interest in Selves," *Ethics* 96 [1986]; Wolf, *Freedom within Reason* [New York: Oxford University Press, 1990]). I find her distinction unpersuasive, but in any case she is not arguing from anything like the causal control principle.

21. Peter Strawson, *Freedom and Resentment*.

22. But suppose the guru, instead of predicting and then reproducing the painting, actually made it. He transmitted radio signals that manipulated the artist's cerebellum so that the artist's arm moved as the guru dictated. We wouldn't give the artist credit then, of course. Now suppose that the radio signals also made the artist think that the thousands of decisions he was making were his own decisions. He thought, as he painted, that he was making his own painting, not someone else's. But he was wrong. Making artistic decisions yourself means bringing to bear your own sense of the various aesthetic values in play and your own skill in exhibiting those values in a concrete work. That is why the capacity control principle makes some level of the second, regulative, capacity essential to responsibility. And that is why someone else's painting through you is different from your painting by yourself, even if your aesthetic values and skills were predestined to take exactly the form they do. Our artist is brainwashed, we are now assuming, into thinking that it is his own artistic genius that is now displayed on the canvas before him. I imagined that a hypnotized patient might be in that position. But when he learns that the canvas actually signals the artistic skills of someone else, and his own only by accident, if at all, he will abandon all pride—or shame—in what he has done. We can turn this screw through more twists of fantasy. We imagine that the guru didn't radio discrete hand movements to the artist's brain but rather implanted the more general tastes—a sense of the artistic possibilities of abstract expressionism, perhaps—to which the artist responded. Or—a more difficult case still—that the guru implanted the more concrete insight that this genre might be exploited brilliantly by swinging leaking paint cans over a prone canvas. We can in this way manufacture hard cases for any judgment about the artist's responsibility. These fantasy cases are hard, however, because we imagine two decision-makers rather than one, and the facts make it unclear whose values and skills a particular decision should be understood as exhibiting. That complication is absent when it is nature, rather than an Arctic guru, that has shaped an artist's skills, taste, and judgment.

23. Of course our lives would change in ways we cannot hope even to imagine if we each discovered techniques like the guru's that allowed us to predict everyone else's behavior with even a tiny fraction of his accuracy. We certainly cannot imagine predicting our own behavior in that way, which means we could not fully predict the behavior of those whose lives we affect. But the difficulty of imagining such a world does not challenge the assumption that judgmental responsibility would survive.

24. Williams, *Shame and Necessity*, 55.

25. Ibid., 72–72.

26. We must distinguish opportunity from capacity in cases in which someone's mistaken view of the world leads to bad results. Someone who is normally good at forming beliefs about the world doesn't realize that the white substance in the sugar bowl is arsenic. He is judgmentally responsible for spooning it into his guest's coffee: it is

appropriate to hold his act up to standards of proper conduct. Whether he is at fault depends on whether his mistake was reasonable in the circumstances, which in turn depends on whether he had a reasonable opportunity to discover the truth and was negligent in not taking that opportunity. The idiot's case is different; it would be wrong to approach the question of his responsibility in that way. Instead we should say that he is not judgmentally responsible for his acts: it is a mistake to treat his behavior as subject to ethical or moral evaluation. I am grateful to a reader for the Harvard University Press for suggesting that I distinguish the ordinary-mistake kind of case.

27. See quotations from Elbert Hubbard and Edna St. Vincent Millay on ThinkExist.com.

28. Anita Allen believes, rightly, that the discussions of mental disease in this chapter and elsewhere are unsophisticated (Allen, "Mental Disorders and the 'System of Judgmental Responsibility,'" BU: 621). She thinks that a competent philosophical account of these pathologies has not been written. I had no intention to provide such an account but only to characterize mental disease sufficiently to rebut the assumption that our attitudes toward the judgmental responsibility of victims of such disease shows that we accept the causal control principle.

29. See Hugo Adam Bedau, "Rough Justice: The Limits of Novel Defenses," *Report* (The Hastings Center) 8, no. 6 (December 1978): 8–11.

30. American Law Institute, "Model Penal Code" (proposed official draft) (Philadelphia: Executive Office, American Law Institute, 1962).

31. Not necessarily. Seana Shiffrin has pointed out, in discussion, that duress can sometimes destroy these capacities through intense fear.

32. Compare my discussion of justice as a parameter of the good life in *Sovereign Virtue: The Theory and Practice of Equality* (Cambridge, Mass.: Harvard University Press, 2000), chapter 6.

11. From Dignity to Morality

1. I defend that view in *Life's Dominion* (New York: Knopf, 1993).

2. Ronald Dworkin, *Sovereign Virtue: The Theory and Practice of Equality* (Cambridge, Mass.: Harvard University Press, 2000), chapter 6. I discuss ethical parameters in Chapter 9.

3. R. M. Hare, *Freedom and Reason* (Oxford: Oxford University Press, 1965), 130.

4. See Tamsin Shaw, *Nietzsche's Political Skepticism* (Princeton: Princeton University Press, 2007), particularly chapter 5. Shaw points out that Nietzsche is often taken to be an "anti-realist" who denies the existence of objective and universal values, and she denies that reading. She argues that Nietzsche is skeptical about the legitimacy of any coercive political state, not because he doubts the objective character of value but because he doubts that those likely to become political leaders have the

ability to discover objective value. See also Simon May, *Nietzsche's Ethics and His War on "Morality"* (New York: Oxford University Press (1999).

5. Nietzsche, *Ecce Homo*, trans. W. Kaufmann (New York: Vintage, 1967), II:9.

6. *Thus Spoke Zarathustra*, in *The Portable Nietzsche*, ed. Walter Kaufmann (New York: Viking, 1954).

7. Ibid., I:15.

8. Nietzsche, *Beyond Good and Evil*, trans. W. Kaufmann (New York: Vintage, 1966), §228.

9. Nietzsche, *The Will to Power*, trans. Walter Kaufman and R. J. Hollingdale (New York: Random House, 1967), 944.

10. *The Antichrist*, in Kaufmann, *The Portable Nietzsche*, 11.

11. See Thomas Hurka, *Perfectionism* (Oxford: Oxford University Press, 1993), 75.

12. May, *Nietzsche's Ethics*, 13, 12.

13. Aristotle, *The Nicomachean Ethics*, 572–73.

14. Bernard Williams illustrates the psychological dilemmas in an admittedly extravagant example: a tourist to a dictatorship is told that ten innocent prisoners will be killed unless he himself kills one of the ten. Williams, "A Critique of Utilitarianism," in J. J. C. Smart and Bernard Williams, eds., *Utilitarianism For and Against* (Cambridge: Cambridge University Press, 1973), 76, 98.

15. See Peter Singer, *The Life You Can Save: Acting Now to End World Poverty* (New York: Random House, 2010). See also Thomas Nagel, "What Peter Singer Wants of You," *New York Review of Books*, March 25, 2010.

16. This distinction marks much of his work. See the discussion in Chapter 10 of his views about free will and judgmental responsibility. I have particularly in mind, in the discussion here, his book *Equality and Partiality* (New York: Oxford University Press, 1991), e.g., 14.

17. Ibid., 31.

18. T. M. Scanlon, *What We Owe to Each Other* (Cambridge, Mass.: Belknap Press of Harvard University Press, 2000).

19. Immanuel Kant, *Groundwork of the Metaphysic of Morals*, trans. H. J. Paton (New York: Harper and Row, 1964), 58.

20. Ibid., 35.

21. For a recent illustration, see Robert N. Johnson, "Value and Autonomy in Kantian Ethics," in *Oxford Studies in Metaethics*, vol. 2, ed. Russ Shafer-Landau (Oxford: Oxford University Press, 2007).

22. See the many discussions of Kant's ambitions in John Rawls, *Lectures on the History of Moral Philosophy* (Cambridge, Mass.: Harvard University Press, 2000).

23. John Rawls, *Collected Papers*, ed. Samuel Freeman (Cambridge, Mass.: Harvard University Press, 1999), 346.

24. Ibid., 315.

25. Ibid., 312.

26. See the discussion of Rawls's constructivism in Chapter 3.

27. Ronald Dworkin, *Justice in Robes* (Cambridge, Mass.: Belknap Press of Harvard University Press, 2006), chapter 9.

28. Scanlon, *What We Owe to Each Other.*

29. Colin McGinn, "Reasons and Unreasons," *New Republic,* May 24, 1999.

12. Aid

1. See Ronald Dworkin, *Sovereign Virtue: The Theory and Practice of Equality* (Cambridge, Mass.: Harvard University Press, 2000), chapter 1.

2. In his recent book *Moral Dimensions: Permissibility, Meaning, Blame* (Cambridge, Mass.: Belknap Press of Harvard University Press, 2008), Thomas Scanlon explores different ways in which an agent's intentions might or might not affect the permissibility of what he does. The argument of this chapter is, I believe, an instance of his suggestion that the "meaning" of an act may make it permissible or impermissible. "If someone acts with no regard whatsoever for the interests of another person, then this has a certain meaning—it indicates something significant about his attitude to that person and about their relationship with each other—whether or not it was his intention to convey." This is not a matter of the significance anyone else finds in the act but the significance he "has reason to assign to it, given the reasons for which it was performed" (53–54).

3. Thomas Scanlon, "Preference and Urgency," *Journal of Philosophy* 72 (1975): 665–69.

4. See the discussion of "expensive tastes" in my *Sovereign Virtue,* chapter 2.

5. Criticism at the Boston University Law Review conference (mentioned in the Preface) helped me correct an impression that my earlier draft had left: that an example I gave of a high threshold for rescue was meant as necessary as well as sufficient for a duty of rescue. See Kenneth W. Simons, "Dworkin's Two Principles of Dignity: An Unsatisfactory Nonconsequentialist Account of Interpersonal Moral Duties," in *Symposium: Justice for Hedgehogs: A Conference on Ronald Dworkin's Forthcoming Book* (special issue), *Boston University Law Review* 90, no. 2 (April 2010) (hereafter BU): 715.

6. Criticism at the Boston University Law Review conference also made me realize the importance of this aspect of the issue. See Kwame Anthony Appiah, "Dignity and Global Duty," BU: 661; and F. M. Kamm, "What Ethical Responsibility Cannot Justify: A Discussion of Ronald Dworkin's *Justice for Hedgehogs,*" BU: 691. Jeremy Waldron and Liam Murphy raised similar issues in discussions of the draft at the NYU Colloquium in Legal, Moral and Political Philosophy.

7. For an argument that equal respect requires that we take account of the confrontation dimension in rescue cases, see Richard W. Miller, "Beneficence, Duty and Distance," *Philosophy & Public Affairs* 32, no. 4 (2004): 357–83.

8. Janos Kis offered this suggestion in a paper at a Holberg Prize symposium held at NYU in 2008.

9. Kenneth Simons cites empirical evidence of the difference confrontation makes. See Simons, "Dworkin's Two Principles."

10. See Dworkin, *Sovereign Virtue,* chapters 8 and 9.

11. See Peter Singer, *The Life You Can Save: Acting Now to End World Poverty* (New York: Random House, 2009).

12. For a lottery in which each person has a 1/3 chance, see John Broome, "Selecting People Randomly," *Ethics* 95 (1984): 38–55. For one in which each group has a 1/2 chance, see John Taurek, "Should the Numbers Count?" *Philosophy & Public Affairs* 6 (1977): 293–316.

13. In what is certainly one of the most quoted philosophical remarks of the last century, Bernard Williams said that if you think about whether you are justified in saving your wife rather than several strangers, you have "one thought too many" (Williams, "Persons, Character, and Morality" [1976], reprinted in his *Moral Luck* [Cambridge: Cambridge University Press, 1981], 1–19).

14. For a discussion of the role of bizarre examples in philosophical argument, see Kamm, "What Ethical Responsibility Cannot Justify." I believes she misunderstands my views on this score. See my "Response," BU: 1073.

13. Harm

1. Indeed, our assignment responsibility requires more than this minimum. You must have substantial control over what your body does—where you can take it and what you can use it to do—as well. That further control responsibility must be limited, however, to protect the control responsibility of others over their lives: you must not have control responsibility that would include damaging me or my property, for instance. So the criminal and tort law of any morally sensitive community will require fine judgments. But the most basic level of control responsibility, over what happens to your body, does not need to be limited and has therefore been treated as a necessary condition of dignity.

2. See Ronald Dworkin et al., "Assisted Suicide: The Philosophers' Brief," *New York Review of Books,* March 27, 1997, 41–47.

3. *Washington v. Glucksberg,* 521 U.S. 702 (1997).

4. *The T.J. Hooper,* 60 F.2d 737 (2d Cir. 1932).

5. An earlier draft of this sentence wrongly suggested that the required standard of due care is relative to the agent's ambitions rather than his opportunities and resources. A standard so relative would have ridiculous consequences. I meant, and have revised the paragraph to make plainer, what I said in *Law's Empire* (Cambridge, Mass.: Harvard University Press, 1986), 301ff. I am grateful to John Goldberg and Kenneth W. Simons for bringing this to my attention. See Goldberg, "Liberal

Responsibility: A Comment on *Justice for Hedgehogs*," 677, and Simons, "Dworkin's Two Principles of Dignity: An Unsatisfactory Nonconsequentialist Account of Interpersonal Moral Duties," 715, both in *Symposium: Justice for Hedgehogs: A Conference on Ronald Dworkin's Forthcoming Book* (special issue), *Boston University Law Review* 90, no. 2 (April 2010).

6. For an illuminating elaboration, see Mark Geistner, "The Field of Torts in *Law's Empire*," Inaugural Lecture of the Sheila Lubetsky Birnbaum Professorship of Civil Litigation, NYU Law News website, www.law.nyu.edu/news/GEISTFELD_BIRNBAUM_LECTURE.

7. This is a simplified presentation of a very complex set of theories. Frances Kamm offers all you might wish of the complexity. See, e.g., Kamm, "The Doctrine of Triple Effect and Why a Rational Agent Need Not Intend the Means to His End," in *Intricate Ethics: Rights, Responsibilities, and Permissible Harm* (Oxford: Oxford University Press, 2006), 91–129.

8. Judith Thompson, "The Trolley Problem," *Yale Law Journal* 94 (1985): 1395–1415; Frances Kamm, "The Trolley Problem," in *Morality, Mortality*, vol. 2: *Rights, Duties, and Status* (New York: Oxford University Press, 2001), 143–72.

9. John Harris, "The Survival Lottery," *Philosophy* 49 (1974): 81–87.

10. See the discussion of that principle, and that consequence, in Chapter 9.

11. Scanlon argues for a distinction between the deliberative question of what an agent should do and the critical question whether the agent reflected in the right way on the deliberative question. See T. M. Scanlon, *Moral Dimensions: Permissibility, Meaning, Blame* (Cambridge, Mass.: Belknap Press of Harvard University Press, 2008), chapter 1, "The Illusory Appeal of Double Effect." Whether a military leader aims to kill enemy noncombatants in a bombing raid or only knows that the raid will kill them is relevant to the critical question, Scanlon believes, but not to the deliberative question of permissibility unless the difference affects the number of noncombatants actually killed. But if the bombing would bring the war to an end sooner, thereby saving many more thousands of civilian lives on both sides, why is it justified only when it also has immediate military advantage? Scanlon sets out a principle to distinguish the cases (28), but this seems only to restate that requirement and not to explain it. I try to provide a justification in the text. This does not rely on motive in the way Scanlon finds objectionable. It does not ask a commanding general to identify what he most hopes to achieve by his raid. It asks whether his decision can be justified without assuming that this is the best use of the lives of the civilians he will kill. In some very different kinds of cases, however, motive does seem relevant to permissibility as well as to criticism. It would be permissible for a landlord to deny an apartment to a black pianist only if and because he objected to his all-night practicing rather than his race.

12. *Rochin v. California*, 342 U.S. 165 (1952).

13. For a discussion of this important ethical issue, see my book *Life's Dominion* (New York: Knopf, 1993).

14. Thompson, "The Trolley Problem."

15. The distinction between bad luck and usurpation is relevant in other contexts as well. See my *Sovereign Virtue: The Theory and Practice of Equality* (Cambridge, Mass.: Harvard University Press, 2000), chapter 13: "Playing God: Genes, Clones and Luck."

14. Obligations

1. The classic discussion is Wesley Hohfeld, *Fundamental Legal Conceptions as Applied in Judicial Reasoning*, ed. W. W. Cooke (New Haven: Yale University Press, 1919).

2. See David Lewis, *Convention* (Cambridge, Mass.: Harvard University Press, 1969).

3. John Rawls suggests that the duty of justice, which requires us to support and comply with just institutions, is a natural duty. (Rawls, *A Theory of Justice* [Cambridge, Mass.: Harvard University Press, 1971], 115, 334.)

4. Ibid. 342–43. Rawls refers to H. L. A. Hart, "Are There Any Natural Rights?" *Philosophical Review* 64 (1955): 185–86.

5. Robert Nozick, *Anarchy, State, and Utopia* (New York: Basic Books, 1974), 93–95.

6. David Hume, *A Treatise of Human Nature*, 3.2.5–14/15–524.

7. G. E. M. Anscombe, "Rules, Rights, and Promises," in her *Ethics, Religion, and Politics: Collected Philosophical Papers* (Minneapolis: University of Minnesota Press, 1981), 97–103.

8. Scanlon suggests that a promise is best understood as a conventional means of acknowledging that the requirements of his Principle F are satisfied in the circumstances. I believe that understates the function and importance of the institution. The various clauses of Principle F can be satisfied to different degrees, and it may therefore be controversial whether its conditions are sufficiently satisfied to engage moral responsibility in any particular case. That is particularly true of the requirement that A "lead" B to form certain beliefs. If you had called me several times urging me to go to the conference I described so that we could talk, the reassurance I would think I have been given would be greater than if you had mentioned the matter more casually, and the difference would then be pertinent not only to whether you had acquired some prima facie moral responsibility toward me but the strength of that responsibility—whether some conflicting and more important invitation you subsequently received would provide an adequate excuse for skipping the conference. A promise serves its function by declaring that the encouragement offered is at the highest level of intensity and is sufficiently intense to put the bar very much lower for the other conditions.

Some of Principle F's clauses need not necessarily be satisfied to any degree in order that an obligation be created, moreover. As I suggest below in this note, A may acquire an obligation even if B does not actually expect A to do as he says. Satisfying other clauses may not be necessary either; it might be debated, for instance, whether A must know that B wants reassurance—it may be enough that A strongly wants to reassure him and that B knows that even if B doesn't particularly want reassurance. We should therefore say that, absent an explicit promise or promise denial, the general situations that Principle F contemplates are morally fluid. Much depends on circumstance, and reasonable people can disagree in many circumstances. For the reasons and in the way described in the text, an explicit promise or promise denial makes the situation markedly less fluid.

Scanlon finds the following difficulty in his own formulation of Principle F. Suppose A promises to help B plow B's fields tomorrow. According to the first step in Principle F, A incurs an obligation only if he succeeds in convincing B that he will help plow B's field. However A cannot convince B of that unless B comes to think that A will have a reason to plow. In some circumstances the only reason B might sensibly suppose A to have (after B has finished helping A plow A's field) is the obligation he supposes that A incurred through his promise. So the argument for an obligation cannot get started: its first step presupposes its conclusion. (This is a version of the circularity problem I mentioned at the outset of the text discussion.) Scanlon hopes to solve this problem by appealing to a further principle that forbids A to promise unless he reasonably believes that he will perform. B is entitled to believe that A respects that principle as well and therefore to think that A will perform without relying on any assumption that A has incurred an obligation. Once B has formed that belief, the conditions of Principle F are satisfied and A does have that obligation (Scanlon, *What We Owe to Each Other* [Cambridge, Mass.: Belknap Press of Harvard University Press, 2000], 308). Critics reasonably comment that B should not conclude from the fact that A has a reasonable belief that he will perform when he makes the promise that he will have a reason to perform at a later time. See, e.g., Niko Kolodny and R. Jay Wallace, "Promises and Practices Revisited," *Philosophy & Public Affairs* 31, no. 2 (2003): 119. The first step in Scanlon's principle F is too strong. It is not necessary that A convince B that he will keep his promise or respect some other form of assurance in order for A to incur an obligation. A has an obligation if he promises and other conditions are met, even if B thinks it possible or even likely that A will renege. B must have had some reason to make the bargain in that case, of course, but, with some effort, we can imagine one. He might have wanted an occasion to display A's bad character to the world, for instance. Or he may have wanted generously to help A plow A's field without acknowledging that he does not trust A's word. Or he might himself doubt that A has an obligation—perhaps B thinks that A is unaware that B's field is much harder to plow. B might think that A has no obligation for that reason but hope that A will think he does. In all these cases A may still have an obligation to plow B's field tomorrow, whether or not B expects A to plow it or thinks that A does have that obligation.

9. Scanlon, *What We Owe to Each Other,* 304.

10. Charles Fried, *Contract as Promise: A Theory of Contractual Obligation* (Cambridge, Mass.: Harvard University Press, 1982), chapter 2, 9.

11. My colleagues Kevin Davis and Liam Murphy have generously pressed me on this issue.

12. Thomas Scanlon reminded me of this practical argument for some role obligations.

13. Ronald Dworkin, *Law's Empire* (Cambridge, Mass.: Harvard University Press, 1986), 68–73.

14. Richard Fallon raises questions about this discussion. See Richard H. Fallon Jr., "Is Moral Reasoning Conceptual Interpretation?" in *Symposium: Justice for Hedgehogs: A Conference on Ronald Dworkin's Forthcoming Book* (special issue), *Boston University Law Review* 90, no. 2 (April 2010) (hereafter BU): 535.

15. Robert Paul Wolff, *In Defense of Anarchism* (New York: Harper and Row, 1970).

16. I am indebted to Susanne Sreedhar and Candice Delmas for persuading me of the importance of the question whether legitimacy is a matter of degree (Sreedhar and Delmas, "State Legitimacy and Political Obligation in *Justice for Hedgehogs*: The Radical Potential of Dworkinian Dignity," BU: 737). Much of this paragraph is a response to them.

15. Political Rights and Concepts

1. James Griffin misunderstands this suggestion. See James Griffin, *On Human Rights* (Oxford: Oxford University Press, 2008), 20, repeated in Griffin, "Human Rights and the Autonomy of International Law," in Samantha Besson and John Tasioulas, eds., *The Philosophy of International Law* (Oxford: Oxford University Press, 2010). Of course, political rights do not hold only against a government that aims to improve the general good. The trump test sets a standard that a claim of right must meet—the interest it protects must be sufficiently important that it would overcome even a generally proper political justification. The test does not suggest that people have no rights against tyrants whose aims are not proper. A right may be regarded as a trump, moreover, even though it might not trump the general good in cases of emergency: when the competing interests are grave and urgent, as they might be when large numbers of lives or the survival of a state is in question. Then, we might say, the trump gets trumped not by an ordinary justification but by a higher trump. See my "Rights as Trumps," in Jeremy Waldron, ed., *Theories of Rights* (Oxford: Oxford University Press, 1985). It is controversial among political philosophers, moreover, whether groups of individuals have political rights—whether we can properly speak of the rights of an ethnic minority within a larger political community, for instance. See, e.g., Will Kymlicka, *Liberalism, Community, and Culture* (Oxford: Oxford University Press, 1989). My own view is that only individuals have political

rights, though these rights include a right not to be discriminated against because they are members of some group and may also include a right to benefits in common with other members of their group—a right, for instance, that legal proceedings be available in their group's language. However, I shall not pursue this question here. My argument holds equally for group political rights if there are any.

2. The metaphor is not universally admired. See Robin West, "Rights, Harms, and Duties: A Response to *Justice for Hedgehogs*," in *Symposium: Justice for Hedgehogs: A Conference on Ronald Dworkin's Forthcoming Book* (special issue), *Boston University Law Review* 90, no. 2 (April 2010) (hereafter BU): 819, and my "Response" in that issue.

3. Charles Beitz, *The Idea of Human Rights* (Oxford: Oxford University Press, 2009), 96ff.

4. See, e.g., John Rawls, *The Law of Peoples,* 2nd ed. (Cambridge, Mass.: Harvard University Press, 1999); Joseph Raz, "Human Rights without Foundations," in Samantha Besson and John Tasioulas, eds., *The Philosophy of International Law* (Oxford: Oxford University Press, 2010), 321ff.; John Skorupski, "Human Rights," in Besson and Tasioulas, *Philosophy of International Law,* 357.

5. In *On Human Rights,* Griffin makes what he calls "personhood" the touchstone of human rights; he says that respect for personhood requires guarantees of welfare, liberty, and autonomy, and that these are therefore human rights (149). He accepts the challenge described in the text: to explain why human rights differ from other political rights. But he believes the challenge can be met by a more refined description of what personhood itself requires. "On the personhood account . . . the cut-off point is when the proximate necessary conditions for normative agency are met . . . there will be hard interpretive work to be done on the idea of 'proximate necessary conditions for normative agency' to make it sharper edged" (183). But, as Joseph Raz has pointed out, this is unhelpful. On the one hand, if the conditions Griffin has in mind are those necessary for a very limited autonomy, they are too easily met. Even slaves make some decisions. On the other hand, if the conditions are taken to be those necessary for a substantial degree of welfare, liberty, and autonomy, then the problem remains of distinguishing between human rights and other political rights. Where is the line to be drawn? See Raz, "Human Rights without Foundations." Griffin's response seems only to confirm Raz's complaint. He suggests that "practicalities" will help us to determine the "threshold" of autonomy that human rights protect, but that "considerable work" is necessary to find the right threshold (347–49).

Charles Beitz believes that human rights should be identified not through some "top down" principle, like respect for personhood, but through interpretation of human rights practice, guided, as it must be, by a sense of the point of that institution (Beitz, *The Idea of Human Rights*). But as we noticed throughout Part Two of this book, interpretation of that kind requires general principles that can fix the best justification of the raw data of that practice, and these must be "top down" principles of the kind Beitz wants to avoid. He recognizes the need to distinguish human rights from other political rights; he says that human rights are narrower than the political rights that define a just society (142). But his suggested standards for the necessary distinction seem unpromising. He says that some requirements of justice are less urgent than others, that some purported rights would be harder than others to enforce internationally, and that some requirements of justice can sensibly be thought to vary among societies with different economic, social, and cultural backgrounds (143). The second of these standards mixes the question whether it would be permissible for the international community to intervene, if it could do so effectively, with the different question whether it can indeed do so effectively. These speak to different conditions for intervention that are best kept distinct and, in any case, are irrelevant to all cases except barbarism, because only these justify intervention. His first standard requires a metric for urgency that, when supplied, may not produce the right results. How should we rank in urgency, for instance, rights to expression of racist opinion, abortion, expensive lifesaving renal dialysis, same-sex marriage, and no imprisonment without a fair trial? The third standard does not discriminate between justice and human rights; the former as well as the latter vary to some degree with national background, and the standard does not tell us why human rights vary more than justice does.

6. Ronald Dworkin, *Is Democracy Possible Here? Principles for a New Political Debate* (Princeton: Princeton University Press, 2006).

7. Robert D. Sloane, "Human Rights for Hedgehogs? Global Value Pluralism, International Law, and Some Reservations of the Fox," BU: 975.

8. The puzzle is as old as Plato's *Euthyphro* (Plato, *The Last Days of Socrates,* trans. Hugh Tredennick and Harold Tarrant (Harmondsworth: Penguin Books, 1993). For more modern treatments, see, e.g., Ralph Cudworth, *A Treatise Concerning Eternal and Immutable Morality* (1731; New York: Cambridge University Press, 1996); Mark Schroeder, "Cudworth and Normative Explanations," *Journal of Ethics and Social Philosophy* 1 (2005): 1–27.

9. Bishop R. C. Mortimer was attracted to this suggestion. "The first foundation is the doctrine of God the Creator. God made us and all the world. Because of that He has an absolute claim on our obedience. We do not exist in our own right, but only as His creatures, who ought therefore to do and be what He desires" (Robert C. Mortimer, *Christian Ethics* [London: Hutchinson's University Library, 1950], 7).

10. Harry Frankfurt assumes this is what equality means. See his "Equality as a Moral Ideal," in William Letwin, ed., *Against Equality: Readings in Economic and Social Policy* (London: Macmillan, 1983), 21. Frankfurt argues against "the doctrine that it is desirable for everyone to have the same amounts of income and wealth (for short, 'money')."

11. John Rawls, *A Theory of Justice* (Cambridge, Mass.: Harvard University Press, 1971).

12. See, e.g., R. George White, "The High Cost of Rawls' Inegalitarianism," www.jstor.org/stable/448214.

13. See Derek Parfit, *Equality or Priority* (Lawrence: University of Kansas, 1995).

14. The term "trickle down" is used mainly as a pejorative. The theory itself, often called Reaganomics, is vigorous though discredited. See "Live Free or Move," editorial, *Wall Street Journal,* May 16, 2006.

15. Isaiah Berlin, "Two Concepts of Liberty" (1958), in *Four Essays on Liberty* (Oxford: Oxford University Press, 1969); Bernard Williams, "From Freedom to Liberty: The Construction of a Political Value," *Philosophy & Public Affairs* 30, no. 1 (2001): 3–26.

16. Equality

1. See Eduardo Porter, "Race and the Social Contract," *New York Times,* March 31, 2008.

2. See my *Sovereign Virtue: The Theory and Practice of Equality* (Cambridge, Mass.: Harvard University Press, 2000), chapter 3.

3. Sen says that his recent book, *The Idea of Justice* (Cambridge, Mass.: Harvard University Press, 2009), marks an important "departure" from standard theories of justice—he cites, among others, John Rawls's and my own work—that are concerned only to describe ideally just institutions and are therefore of no use in guiding the comparative judgments we must make in the real and very imperfect world. But Rawls's two principles of justice are tailor-made for the comparative real-world judgments Sen has in mind. There is, in fact, an astronomically extensive literature of philosophers, political scientists, economists, lawyers, and even politicians applying Rawls's theories to actual concrete political controversies. (A sample can be harvested by typing "Rawls" and the name of any particular controversy into a Google search.) In my own case, Sen may not have taken full account of my discussion "Back to the Real World," in chapter 3 of *Sovereign Virtue,* which describes in some detail how the abstract theory of justice I defend in that book can be used to justify comparative judgments about improvements in justice. Nor of the entire part II—half—of *Sovereign Virtue,* which is devoted, as that book's subtitle promises, to the "practice" rather than the "theory" of equality. I discuss there, again in some detail, the application of the general theory of part I of that book to practical improvement on present policies in the fields of taxation, health care, racial justice, genetic policy, abortion, euthanasia, freedom of speech, and the regulation of elections. I have also tried to explain practical consequences of my views in general journals, particularly the *New York Review of Books.*

Sen's own work in developmental economics has been enormously important and useful. His views on the causes of famine have been particularly influential. He has brought a wealth of Eastern, particularly Indian, history, literature, and philosophy to the attention of Western readers; his latest book is particularly rich in such information. However, *The Idea of Justice* does not support Sen's claim of a departure in normative political philosophy: in fact he offers less help in real-world judgment than do the theories he means to depart from. His comments on particular political issues are either uncontroversial—he condemns slavery—or noncommittal. He appeals to a variety of standards for comparative judgment of existing structures, but at far too abstract a level to be useful in comparative judgment. He endorses the spirit of Adam Smith's "impartial observer" test, which recommends the decisions that an ideal and impartial judge would reach. But that test, unless construed in a utilitarian way, lacks bite: it does not tell us what theory a beneficent spectator would deploy to decide issues now controversial. Sen says that policy should focus (though not exclusively) on promoting equality in what he calls "capabilities" (see the discussion of "capabilities" in note 6 below). But he concedes the wide variations in people's rankings of the importance of these capabilities and does not recommend any way of choosing among these rankings in the face of serious disagreement. He believes that free democratic discussion among ideally public-spirited citizens would be helpful to comparative judgment. He does not say how this thought is helpful in real communities that include a great many followers of, say, Sarah Palin. It is not helpful, in the world of real politics, only to call for due consideration of a large variety of factors that everyone concedes relevant without also offering some overall scheme to suggest how these different factors should be weighted in a practical decision about a controversial issue.

4. Baker's ambitious and impressive article was completed just before his tragic death (C. Edwin Baker, "In Hedgehog Solidarity," in *Symposium: Justice for Hedgehogs: A Conference on Ronald Dworkin's Forthcoming Book* [special issue], *Boston University Law Review* 90, no. 2 [April 2010] [hereafter BU]: 759). He believed, contrary to my own opinion, that citizens need have no more concern for their fellow citizens when they act together in politics than they need have when they act as individuals. Politics, he thought, should be understood as a competitive activity in which each citizen works to advance his own values and goals by winning a collective political decision to create an ethical environment he approves. There are losers as well as winners in this competition. Political majorities must be tolerant of minorities: they must not coerce them to embrace the majority's values or otherwise violate their liberty or other rights. But majorities need not otherwise refrain from using politics to shape the community to their own convictions about good lives. They need not try to be neutral out of concern for those who disagree with them.

Baker also disagreed with me, in a parallel way, about democracy. He agreed on the need for what I call, in Chapter 18, a partnership conception of that ideal. But he thought that I favor an "epistemic" interpretation of partnership in which the community's role is limited to identifying and enforcing a correct theory of distributive and political justice, while he favored a "choice" interpretation in which majorities choose the values that define the community as a whole. "This alternative sees people in the partnership as trying to convince each other about, and as acting as a partnership to pursue, ethical ideals. It treats equality of respect, not equality of concern, as the sovereign virtue." He thought that conceiving of citizens as "reason-giving" partners in "communicative action" as well as in competition with one another allows us to provide a more secure basis for principles of justice than a view like mine is able to provide. He adopted Jürgen Habermas's view that people in conversation commit themselves to certain principles, and that it is these commitments that identify justice for them.

It will be helpful in considering his views to distinguish two questions. First, do the members of a coercive political community have an obligation, when they design an economic structure, to treat the fate of each citizen as equally important? Second, are they obliged not to adopt laws that can be justified only by assuming the truth of ethical ideas controversial within the community? This chapter answers the first question: yes. Though Baker denied the need for equal concern, I am not sure he actually meant to disagree. I think he rather associated equal concern with a "yes" answer to the second question. There is nothing in his picture of a choice democracy that would suggest that a majority should not have equal concern for the fate, as distinct from the values, of all fellow citizens. Turn to the second question. Baker believed that the majority in a choice democracy should have the power to select texts for public education that reflect their values and to establish a particular religion as official. I believe he underestimated the coercive power of that kind of control. (See my *Is Democracy Possible Here? Principles for a New Political Debate* (Princeton: Princeton University Press, 2006). Baker's version of tolerance would not in fact encourage the "reason-giving" he hoped for among citizens. On the contrary: a majority confident of its power to choose public school textbooks would have little reason to try to explain itself to those left out. For a frightening contemporary example, see Russell Shorto, "How Christian Were the Founders?" *New York Times*, February 11, 2010. The conception of liberty I describe in Chapter 17, which allows the ethical environment to be set organically, so far as possible, through individual choices one by one rather than by collective action, provides much more incentive for conversation aimed at persuasion.

5. Richard Arneson, "Equality and Equal Opportunity for Welfare," *Philosophical Studies* 56 (1989): 77–93; and G. A. Cohen, "On the Currency of Egalitarian Justice," *Ethics* 99 (1989): 906–44.

6. See my *Sovereign Virtue*, 301–303. In his *Inequality Reexamined* (Cambridge, Mass.: Harvard University Press, 1992), Amartya Sen describes the "capabilities" that should figure in such a calculation to include capacities to bring about "being happy, having self-respect, taking part in the life of the community, and so on." These seem to be welfarist notions, though I offered in those pages an alternative characterization. In *The Idea of Justice* Sen adds that "happiness does not generate obligations in the way that capability must do" (271), but it is not plain whether this judgment is meant to change his earlier opinion.

7. Sen, *The Idea of Justice*, 265.

8. See "Ronald Dworkin Replies," in Justine Burley, ed., *Dworkin and His Critics* (Malden, Mass.: Blackwell, 2004), 340ff.

9. I describe the story summarized here in much greater detail, and consider its implications for tax and other political policy, in *Sovereign Virtue,* chapter 2.

10. Freeman suggests, in the course of a very instructive essay, that an ambition to charge people the true opportunity costs of their choices in work and consumption cannot help us to fix a theory of justice in distribution because what we take true opportunity costs to be depends on which such theory we have already assumed (Samuel Freeman, "Equality of Resources, Market Luck, and the Justification of Adjusted Market Distributions," BU: 921). If we decide that a utilitarian scheme is most fair, for instance, then we will think that the true opportunity costs of a person's choices are those fixed by the price system that best promotes utility. If we think some other theory of justice superior, we will take true opportunity costs to be those set by prices in an economic system that enforces that other theory. So even if we assume that asking someone to pay the true opportunity costs of his choices respects his responsibility for his own life, we cannot draw any conclusion from that assumption about which theory of justice is best.

However, the conception of equality of resources described in the text uses the idea of opportunity costs at a more basic level. Any defensible interpretation of equal concern supposes that no one in a political community is initially entitled to more resource than anyone else; it asks whether any reason consistent with that assumption justifies an economic system in which some prosper more than others. Utilitarians, Rawlsians, and other theorists offer such reasons: that treating people with equal concern requires maximizing their average welfare, or protecting the situation of the worst-off group, or something of the sort. They then offer models of economic systems that these different assumptions would justify, and, as Freeman says, any such model carries with it its own distinct calculation of the true opportunity costs of one person's choices to others'. Equality of resources, on the other hand, offers the idea of a fair distribution of opportunity costs, not as derivative from other reasons for allowing deviation from flat equality but as itself a reason for deviating and limiting the scope of such deviation. It defines true opportunity costs recursively as those measured by prices in a market in which all have equal resources and in which insurance against risks of different sorts is marketed on equal terms. The yield of that market then structures, through taxation and redistribution, future markets in which prices set true opportunity costs. So the ambition to make people responsible for their choices is at work in that conception of distributive justice right from the start.

11. See the discussion in *Sovereign Virtue,* chapters 8 and 9.

12. I recommend Ripstein's account of my views about distributive justice. See his essay "Liberty and Equality," in Arthur Ripstein, ed., *Ronald Dworkin* (Cambridge: Cambridge University Press, 2007), 82. He cites the mandatory character of the insurance scheme as an objection (103). He also comments that though the insurance scheme is designed to separate tastes from handicaps, it actually assumes

that distinction, because it does not suppose that people can insure against having expensive tastes. I did not intend the scheme to help make that distinction, which I assumed could be made independently through what I described as an identification test. A taste is not a handicap for an agent who does not wish not to have it. See my "Ronald Dworkin Replies," in Burley, *Dworkin and His Critics,* 347ff. See also my "Sovereign Virtue Revisited," *Ethics* 113 (October 2002): 106, 118ff. It is worth noting here, however, that the insurance scheme does operate to enforce the distinction through the phenomenon of moral hazard. Insurers will not insure against a risk whose cultivation is under the control of the insured and cannot be assumed to be undesirable to him. Nor will they insure, except at extravagant premium, against a risk when it would be expensive and particularly difficult to prove that its cultivation was not desired and not under the insured's control. This is not just a convenient side effect of the insurance scheme. It reflects the connection between that scheme and the view of judgmental responsibility defended in Chapter 10. I also recommend another thoughtful discussion of the mandatory-insurance objection in the course of a detailed and careful study of equality of resources: Alexander Brown, *Ronald Dworkin's Theory of Equality: Domestic and Global Perspectives* (Basingstoke: Palgrave Macmillan, 2009). Brown's study has the great virtue of discussing the role of that conception of equality in global justice, which, as he notices, I have so far not taken up.

13. Sen discusses the hypothetical insurance strategy at some length in *The Idea of Justice,* 264–68. I can best respond through the inelegant vehicle of a list. (1) He discusses comments I made in an earlier book about his "capability" approach. See *Sovereign Virtue,* 299–303. He denies that this approach is welfarist. I offered reasons why it could easily be so interpreted: see the discussion of "capabilities" in note 6 above. (2) He says of the alternative interpretation I offered—that the capabilities approach "is only equality of resources in a different vocabulary" (*Sovereign Virtue,* 303)—that even if that were so, the capabilities approach would be superior because it identifies what is finally important rather than focusing on resources, which, as I have conceded, are mere means. But first, though some people might deem capabilities important for their own sake (that is also true of resources: some people value them as sources of freedom even if they do not use them), others will value them only so far as they can use them to lead lives they find desirable. Like resources, most capabilities, for most people, are only instrumental. Second, as I have several times said in a variety of places, it doesn't follow from the fact that sensible people value resources as means to better lives that government should aim to make people equal not in resources but in the goodness of their lives. This chapter argues that any such program would impair personal responsibility. (3) Sen's remaining comments are specifically about the insurance strategy. He says that an insurance market cannot reflect relative disadvantage. That seems incorrect, for reasons Adam Smith made plain. In deciding how much coverage to buy against unemployment or low wage or

disability, people will naturally take into account not only their absolute need but how they would fare relative to others in different situations. (4) Sen next says that the insurance device supposes individuals acting as "atomistic operators" rather than as part of a process of "public reason." But the insurers I imagine can have the benefit of as much public and private discussion as a flourishing community will generate, as well as the benefit of a shared culture that reflects different strands of opinion. They must finally decide for themselves, but that hardly means that they must decide in an isolation chamber. (5) He declares that my focus "in common with other transcendental institutionalist approaches, is on getting to perfectly just institutions (in one step)." That is wrong; see the discussion of Sen's claim in note 3 above. (6) He says that I take for granted the "existence, uniqueness and efficiency of perfectly competitive market equilibria, which he needs for his institutional story to be entirely unproblematic" (267). He doesn't say why I need this unreal assumption, and I have denied that I do. See, e.g., *Sovereign Virtue,* 79; "Sovereign Virtue Revisited"; *Is Democracy Possible Here?* 115; as well as this and the preceding paragraphs of this text. (7) He concludes, reluctantly, that I betray "institutional fundamentalism" and "innocence" in my assumption that fixing just institutions will solve all human problems, and in my pretense, as he sees it, that the hypothetical insurance scheme has "imperial powers" (267–68). But I disavow any such assumption or pretense. The insurance scheme plays a role in the more complex integrated theory of justice described here. It does nothing "one shot." It offers advice about marginal gains in distributive justice in imperfect communities, and it takes into account the wisdom of flexible insurance policies that can be adjusted to reflect changes in circumstances and ambitions, and also the need sometimes to temper justice with compassion. See my "Sovereign Virtue Revisited."

14. *Sovereign Virtue,* part II.

17. Liberty

1. Benjamin Constant, *"The Liberty of the Ancients Compared with That of the Moderns"* (1819), in Biancamaria Fontana, trans., *Political Writings* (Cambridge: Cambridge University Press, 1988), 309–28; Isaiah Berlin, "Two Concepts of Liberty" (1958), reprinted in *Four Essays on Liberty* (Oxford: Oxford University Press, 1969), 118–72.

2. Charles Fried, *Modern Liberty and the Limits of Government* (New York: W. W. Norton, 2006); Stephen Breyer, *Active Liberty: Interpreting Our Democratic Constitution* (New York: Knopf, 2005).

3. Berlin, *Four Essays on Liberty,* xlix.

4. H. L. A. Hart, "Are There Any Natural Rights?" *Philosophical Review* 64 (1955).

5. See Nicholas Clee, "And Another Thing . . . Morality in Book Publishing," *Logos* 10 (1999): 118, 119.

6. See my discussion of Edwin Baker's version of this argument in Chapter 16.

7. James Fleming raises, among other important matters, the question of how far government may attempt to influence citizens' ethical opinions and decisions by means short of coercion. As the text reflects, I try to distinguish between a community's moral and ethical environments. I do not believe government shows the right respect for individual ethical responsibility when it officially endorses one opinion, controversial among citizens, about what counts as a good life. But as I emphasized in *Life's Dominion* (New York: Knopf, 1993), government does not deny respect for ethical responsibility when it acts to improve people's sense of the gravity of that responsibility. Nor does it by designing compulsory public education to emphasize that gravity and to display imaginatively a range of important and profound responses to it. As Fleming points out, these distinctions require difficult boundary judgments distinguishing government programs aimed to heighten ethical responsibility from those either endorsing or coercing particular choices. But if the distinction reflects important principles, as I think it does, then we must make those judgments as best we can. Fleming notes the distinction I make in *Life's Dominion* between arguments inside-out and outside-in. Though the structure of this book may suggest the latter, I tried to show, in the advance summary of Chapter 1, that its underlying structure is inside-out.

8. See "Principle, Policy, Procedure," in my book *A Matter of Principle* (Cambridge, Mass.: Harvard University Press, 1985), chapter 3. This article is discussed by Robert Bone in "Procedure, Participation, Rights," in *Symposium: Justice for Hedgehogs: A Conference on Ronald Dworkin's Forthcoming Book* (special issue), *Boston University Law Review* 90, no. 2 (April 2010): 1011.

9. I have somewhat lengthened this discussion of free speech from an earlier draft to respond to fears Edwin Baker expressed in the article discussed in Chapter 16 that my defense was not full-throated and did not give liberty pride of place. No value has pride of place in an integrated account of them all, since each relies on the others. But I mean this defense to be full-throated.

10. *Brandenburg v. Ohio*, 395 U.S. 444 (1969).

11. See my *Sovereign Virtue*, chapter 3, "The Place of Liberty."

12. *Life's Dominion*. I mean to incorporate the argument of that book here and only summarize its main conclusions.

13. *Roe v. Wade*, 410 U.S. 113 (1973); *Planned Parenthood of Southeastern Pa. v. Casey*, 505 U.S. 833 (1992).

14. I emphasize that this must be treated as an ethical issue rather than one about protecting impersonal values like great paintings or natural treasures. Government may properly tax its citizens to fund museums, but not conscript them to guard works of art themselves at great personal cost. The case for prohibiting abortion must include the distinctly ethical judgment that even an early abortion reflects a mistaken understanding of the character of life's importance.

18. Democracy

1. John Locke, *Two Treatises of Government,* ed. Peter Laslett (Cambridge: Cambridge University Press, 1960). Janos Kis called my attention to the value of Locke's statement.

2. Ronald Dworkin, *Sovereign Virtue: The Theory and Practice of Equality* (Cambridge, Mass.: Harvard University Press, 2000), chapter 10; Dworkin, *Freedom's Law* (Cambridge, Mass.: Harvard University Press, 1996), introduction, 1; Dworkin, *Is Democracy Possible Here? Principles for a New Political Debate* (Princeton: Princeton University Press, 2006).

3. Stephen Macedo suggests that the term "majoritarian" is so hard accurately to define, and so confusing in its uses, that it should be dropped from discussions of democracy (Macedo, "Against Majoritarianism: Democratic Values and Institutional Design," in *Symposium: Justice for Hedgehogs: A Conference on Ronald Dworkin's Forthcoming Book* [special issue], *Boston University Law Review* 90, no. 2 [April 2010] [hereafter BU]: 1029). I have not followed that suggestion here because I have used the term before and fear that it would be misleading or at least clumsy to avoid it. But I agree with the spirit of his suggestion.

4. This is much weaker than what John Rawls requires of a "well-ordered" society (Rawls, *A Theory of Justice* [Cambridge, Mass.: Harvard University Press, 1971], 453–62) because it does not include any requirement, very unlikely to be met, that citizens share the same conception of justice.

5. John Ely, *Democracy and Distrust: A Theory of Judicial Review* (Cambridge, Mass.: Harvard University Press, 1980), chapter 5, "Clearing the Channels of Political Change," 105–34; Janos Kis, "Constitutional Precommitment Revisited," NYU Colloquium Paper, September 3, 2009, www.law.nyu.edu/ecm_dlv2/groups/public/@nyu_law_website__academics__colloquia__legal_political_and_social_philosophy/documents/documents/ecm_pro_062725.pdf.

6. See Jeremy Waldron, "The Core of the Case against Judicial Review," *Yale Law Journal* 115 (2006): 1346.

7. Ibid., 1387.

8. Ibid., 1387n112.

9. Waldron is unsure what claim I mean to make through the lifeboat example (Waldron, "A Majority in the Lifeboat," BU: 1043). I intend only a very limited and highly circumscribed point—only that the majoritarian principle is not, as his statement I quoted claims it to be, a general principle of fairness independent of context—that is, an "intrinsically" fair process. His own fresh discussion in this essay suggests that he agrees. He says that a majority of passengers should be invited to choose from a menu of procedures to select which of them should be thrown overboard, but now adds that majority decision should not be on the menu. But if there are reasons why majority rule should not be on that menu, then these are equally

reasons why a majority should not be authorized to pick from the menu unless it includes no option that would antecedently and in a known way favor some passengers over others. Waldron's own suggestion, choosing death for the oldest or least healthy passengers, would be ruled out by that test. We do want a procedure that does not bias the process from the start. But head-counting would be very unlikely to satisfy that condition. This is most certainly not an argument that majority rule is never a fair method of decision. On the contrary I insist that it is appropriate in politics when conditions of legitimacy are met. Waldron believes he has other arguments against judicial review, beyond the intrinsic fairness of the majority decision principle. I agree that the lifeboat case has no power whatever to impeach any such argument he offers; I certainly do not regard that example, as he fears I do, as a "knockdown" argument against a majoritarian conception of democracy. He refers to the extended case I have made over several years for a different conception, a case summarized and elaborated in this chapter. He declares that the lifeboat example adds nothing whatever to that case. He is absolutely right. That example is directed only at what I take to be a mistaken philosophical assumption that should not figure in the argument. The example is not intended to replace or even bolster the positive case I make here.

A further issue. Waldron says in this essay that he has never received an honorable answer to a question he has been asking for twenty years. Why, if it is not intrinsically fair, is majority rule appropriate on final appellate courts like the Supreme Court, which decides many very important cases by a 5–4 vote? The choice among checks on majoritarian procedures must of course depend on which options are available. Judicial review is an available option for checking legislative and executive decisions. It is also an available option for checking judicial review itself through a hierarchal system of appellate courts, and most systems of judicial review use further judicial review as a check in that way. But of course judicial review is not available to check the decision of the highest appellate court; if it were, the court would not be the highest. It does not follow that if the judges in this series of reviews disagree, the disagreement should be settled by a vote among them. A Supreme Court's 5–4 decision might overrule the unanimous decisions of a great many more judges on lower courts. But the head-counting procedure does hold on the Supreme Court itself, and it makes perfect sense to ask what other alternatives, beyond judicial review, are available. We can easily imagine some. Constitutional courts might give more votes to senior judges on the ground that they have more experience. Or more votes to junior judges because they are likely to better represent popular opinion. The Supreme Court does give each justice an equal vote, but it also gives some justices much more power than others in shaping constitutional law. When the Chief Justice is in the majority, he decides the often crucial question who will write the opinion for the Court; when he is in the minority the senior justice in the majority does. No vote decides that issue. The Court's practice of adopting majority rule for the verdict itself can sensibly be challenged. But because judicial review is logically not an option at that stage, the choice of a majority decision procedure hardly suggests that that procedure is intrinsically fairer than a different process that includes judicial review.

10. In general, political procedures aimed at a collective good should take care to separate so far as possible what I have called the "personal" from the "external" preferences of the population, and count only the former. See Ronald Dworkin, *Taking Rights Seriously* (Cambridge, Mass.: Harvard University Press, 1977), chapter 9. A straightforward majority vote in politics cannot achieve that separation. I am grateful to Waldron for pointing out the relevance of my old distinction. See Waldron, "A Majority in the Lifeboat," 1043.

11. Edmund Burke, "Speech to the Electors of Bristol," in *The Works of the Right Honourable Edmund Burke*, vol. 1 (London: Henry G. Bohn, 1855), 178–80.

12. Judith N. Shklar, "The Liberalism of Fear," in Nancy L. Rosenblum, ed., *Liberalism and the Moral Life* (Cambridge, Mass.: Harvard University Press, 1989), 21–38.

13. Dworkin, *Sovereign Virtue*, chapters 11 and 12.

14. In *Hunt v. Cromartie*, 532 U.S. 234 (2001), the Supreme Court upheld a redistricting creating a dominantly black district because it could not be proved that the gerrymandering was intended to benefit a race rather than a political party. The latter goal, it assumed, was constitutionally permissible but the former not.

15. *Crawford v. Marion County Election Board*, 553 U.S. 181 (2008).

16. It has been proposed that states agree, one by one, to cast their electoral votes in presidential elections for the popular-vote winner. If enough states agreed so that their combined electoral votes would elect a president, no further loser in the popular vote could be elected. However, states could drop out of the system at any time. The more serious problem of the distortion of representation in the Senate could not be solved even by constitutional amendment. At least the Constitution so provides in Article V.

17. *Parents Involved in Community Schools v. Seattle School District No. 1*, 551 U.S. 701 (2007). For criticism, see Ronald Dworkin, *The Supreme Court Phalanx: The Court's New Right-Wing Bloc* (New York: New York Review of Books, 2008).

18. *George W. Bush v. Al Gore*, 531 U.S. 98 (2000); *Citizens United v. Federal Elections Commission*, decided January 21, 2010. See my articles in the *New York Review of Books*: "A Badly Flawed Election," January 11, 2001, and "The Decision That Threatens Democracy," May 13, 2010.

19. Dworkin, *Is Democracy Possible Here?* 158–59.

20. Dworkin, "The Supreme Court Phalanx."

19. Law

1. This chapter is meant to supplement my books *Law's Empire* (Cambridge, Mass.: Harvard University Press, 1986) and *Justice in Robes* (Cambridge, Mass.: Belknap Press of Harvard University Press, 2006), not substitute for them.

2. According to what is called "soft" positivism, morality can figure among the tests of law if some legal document with historical pedigree, like a constitution, so stipulates. See H. L. A. Hart, *The Concept of Law,* 2nd ed. (Oxford: Oxford University Press, 1994), postscript, 250, 265.

3. These distinctions among legal concepts are explained more fully in my *Justice in Robes,* introduction.

4. Ronald Dworkin, *Taking Rights Seriously* (Cambridge, Mass.: Harvard University Press, 1977), chapter 2.

5. Ibid., chapter 3.

6. Stephen Guest and Philip Schofield have pointed out to me, however, that in his *A Fragment of Government* Jeremy Bentham candidly bases his fundamental "arrangement" of legal materials on the moral principle of utility. The text is available at www.efm.bris.ac.uk/het/bentham/government.htm. So Bentham, widely regarded as the most important of the early positivists, once based his analysis of law on moral theory, not conceptual analysis. Bentham was a closet interpretivist.

7. Hart, *The Concept of Law.*

8. Ibid.

9. Charles de Montesquieu, *The Spirit of the Laws* (Cambridge: Cambridge University Press, 1989).

10. I drew a pertinent contrast between the justice and the integrity of a legal system. See my *Law's Empire,* particularly chapter 11.

11. For a political argument in favor of originalism, see Antonin Scalia, *A Matter of Interpretation* (Princeton: Princeton University Press, 1999). See my response to Scalia in that book, pp. 115–27. For a recent discussion arguing against the assumption that historical meaning is objective, see Tara Smith, "Originalism's Misplaced Fidelity: 'Original' Meaning Is not Objective," *Constitutional Commentary* 26, no. 1 (2009): 1. See also my *Law's Empire,* chapter 9.

12. The legal question whether the Fugitive Slave Act was valid law includes the question whether it was constitutionally valid. In my view it was not—see "The Law of the Slave-Catchers," *Times Literary Supplement,* December 5, 1975 (a review of *Justice Accused,* by Robert Cover). But I am prescinding from that issue now.

13. *Jamal Kiyemba v. Barack Obama,* decided February 18, 2009, Opinion of Senior Circuit Court Judge Randolph. The court was speaking arguendo. It did not hold that the detainees had a constitutional right to enter the United States.

14. Sager, "Material Rights, Underenforcement, and the Adjudication Thesis," in *Symposium: Justice for Hedgehogs: A Conference on Ronald Dworkin's Forthcoming Book* (special issue), *Boston University Law Review* 90, no. 2 (April 2010) (hereafter BU): 579.

15. Robert G. Bone is an exception. He offers an illuminating account of the moral dimension of procedural issues (Bone, "Procedure, Participation, Rights," BU: 1011). He discusses, among other topics, my article "Principle, Policy, Proce-

dure," in my book *A Matter of Principle* (Cambridge, Mass.: Harvard University Press, 1985).

16. "Edward Coke's Reports," in *The Selected Writings of Sir Edward Coke,* vol. 1 (Indianapolis: Liberty Fund, 2003), 1–520.

17. See Jeffrey Jowell, "Immigration Wars," *The Guardian,* March 2, 2004. See also comment on the idea by Lord Justice of Appeal Sir Stephen Sedley, "On the Move," *London Review of Books,* October 8, 2009.

18. See Ronald Dworkin, *Freedom's Law: The Moral Reading of the American Constitution* (Cambridge, Mass.: Harvard University Press, 1996).

19. *District of Columbia, et al., v. Dick Anthony Heller,* 554 U.S. ____ (2008).

20. *Rasul v. Bush,* 542 U.S. 466 (2004).

21. Ibid. (Scalia dissenting).

Epilogue

1. For an illuminating account of lives thought good, see Keith Thomas, *The Ends of Life: Roads to Fulfillment in Early Modern England* (Oxford: Oxford University Press, 2009), reviewed by Hilary Mantel, "Dreams and Duels of England," *New York Review of Books,* October 22, 2009.

2. "Foundations of Liberal Equality," *The Tanner Lectures on Human Values,* vol. 11 (Salt Lake City: University of Utah Press, 1990); Ronald Dworkin, *Sovereign Virtue: The Theory and Practice of Equality* (Cambridge, Mass.: Harvard University Press, 2000), chapter 6, "Equality and the Good Life."

3. I explain this difficulty in more detail in *Sovereign Virtue,* chapter 6.

Index

Abortion, 42–43, 53–54, 91, 95, 369, 376–378, 482n14
Absoluteness, of moral truth, 54–55
Abstraction, 38, 176–177, 180–181, 183
Absurdity, 217
Accident, 77, 79–80, 80–82
Action, deciding on: value judgments and, 24, 25; moral positions and, 48–49; moral reasoning and, 49–50; indeterminacy and, 93–94; moral conviction and, 104–113, 121; value of responsibility and, 111–112; value account of interpretation and, 151; thick and thin concepts, 181; political morality and, 188. *See also* Decision procedures
Addiction, 239, 240
Adequacy, of moral arguments, 37–38, 39
Adverbial value, 88, 94
Affirmative action, 70–71, 73, 74, 391
Agape (altruistic love), 260
Aid: morality and, 14–15; Hume's principle and, 44–45; duty and, 194; dignity and,

271–275; metrics of harm and, 274–276; metrics of cost and, 276–277; confrontation scale and, 277–280; number of victims and, 280–283; value of hypothetical cases and, 283–284; personal responsibility and, 300; liberty and, 371, 376; moral reasoning and, 468n2
Allen, Anita, 466n28
Ambivalence, interpretation and, 125–128
American Revolution, aims of, 128, 129
Among School Children (Yeats), 137–138
Amoralists, 57, 58
Analytic jurisprudence, 403–405
Anarchism, 318
Anthropology, external skepticism and, 35
Antigone, 90
"Anti-realist" philosophy, 9–10
Appraisal respect, 205–206
Archimedean epistemology, 25, 82, 86
Aristotle, 186–188, 198, 230, 260, 457n33, 463–464n10

Art, living well and, 196–197, 203

Art criticism, 130, 133–134

Artistic merit, 92–93, 123, 125, 178, 199, 465n22

Assignment responsibility, 103, 288, 469n1

Assisted suicide, 289

Associative obligations, 301, 311–317

Assumptions, 44–45, 132, 148, 317

Astrology, 40–41, 83

Atheism, 40, 41, 215–216, 339

Attempted action, 232

Austere view, of morality, 192–193

Austin, John, 404

Authenticity: morality and, 192–193; dignity and, 209–214, 256, 261; balance and integrity, 262–263; aid and, 277; goal of living well and, 420

Author's intention theory, 130, 150

Autonomy: authenticity and, 212; Kant's principle and, 265–266, 267; Rawls and, 267–268, 269

Ayer, A. J., 32

Badness and moral luck, 200–202

Baker, Edwin, 352, 452–453n46, 477–478n4

Balance and integrity, 260–264

"Barely true" judgments, 114, 116–117, 120, 153–154

Barnes, Annette, 453n46

Beitz, Charles, 333, 474–475n5

Belief: moral motivations and, 56, 57–58, 59; forming scientific opinion and, 69; physical world and, 71; religious conviction and, 83–85; personal history and, 234–235; capacity control and, 244, 245; evidence and, 248; moral truth and, 419. See also Moral conviction

Benevolent dictatorships, 390

Bentham, Jeremy, 17, 18, 414, 486n6

Berlin, Isaiah, 1, 350, 364–368

Blackburn, Simon, 33, 63, 435n22

Blackwell, Basil, 370

Bodies, personal control of, 288–289

Boone, Robert G., 486–487n11

Brooks, Cleanth, 126, 137, 138

Bush, George W., 340, 397

Butterfield, Herbert, 138–139, 451n24

Cairo Declaration of Human Rights, 332, 340

Campaign finance limitations, 374, 397

Capacity control, 228–229, 249, 465n22, 465–466n26

Capitalism, 357–358

Capital punishment, 294–295, 299, 329, 334

Categorical imperative, Kant's, 63, 110

Categorical reasons, 42–44, 49, 51

Causal control, 228–229, 231–241, 249

Causal dependence hypothesis (CD), 70, 76–80, 442n6, 447–448n9

Causal impact hypothesis (CI): causes of moral convictions and, 70–75; moral responsibility and, 113–114; interpretive concepts and, 168; moral truth and, 235; Hume's principle and, 430n6; moral naturalism, 438–439n3; Nagel and, 439–441n6; Wiggins and, 441–443n6; McDowell and, 444–445n6

Causal responsibility, 103

Causation, truth and, 174

Causes, of moral convictions: status skepticism and, 55; moral truth and, 69–70; causal impact hypothesis (CI) and, 70–75; causal dependence hypothesis (CD) and, 76–80; accident and, 80–82; integrated epistemology, 82–86; moral progress and, 86–87; value of responsibility and, 111–112

Censorship, 369, 370, 372–373

Certainty, moral arguments and, 95–96, 99–100

Chance, determinism and, 233–234

Character, 242–243, 462n7

Cheating, 28, 32–33, 48

Children: causal control and, 238; capacity control and, 245–246; associative obligations and, 311, 313, 316, 319; family morality, 407–409

Choices. *See* Decision procedures

Christian philosophers, 16, 17

Circular reasoning, 38, 84–85, 100, 162–163, 188

Civil disobedience, 318, 321, 323

Coercion: authenticity and, 212, 213; judgmental responsibility and, 227; capacity control and, 245; political obligations and, 319–320, 321; liberty and, 365; legal rights and, 407; family morality, 408

Cognitive capacity, 244, 245, 247, 248, 249

Coherence theory of truth, 108–109, 113, 120, 175, 213

Coke, Edward, 414

Coleridge, Samuel Taylor, 150

Collaborative interpretation, 135–138, 143; critical legal studies and, 144; radical translations and, 148; moral reasoning and, 157; interpretive concepts and, 162; psychological state theory of interpretation and, 175

Colonialism, democracy and, 381

Colonial philosophy, 9, 418

Command economy, 356–357

Commands, moral judgments and, 32, 454n11

Commercial speech, 373

Compatibilism, 12–13, 223, 229–230

Compensation: unintended harm and, 290; equality and, 358, 359, 360

Competition harm, 285–289, 295, 297, 299, 347, 358

Competitive interpretation, 139–144

Complementary interpretation, 139–144, 146–147

Concept of Law, The (Hart), 404

Conceptual interpretation, 136; disagreement and, 157–158; types of concepts, 158–160; interpretive concepts and, 160–170; relativism and, 170–171; truth and, 172–180; thick and thin concepts, 180–184; Plato and Aristotle, 184–188; analytic jurisprudence and, 403–405

Conflicts: indeterminacy and, 90; moral responsibility and, 113; in value, 118–120

Confrontation scale, 277–280

Connection, dignity and, 214–215, 217

Consent, political obligations and, 318–319

Consequence, of a life, 198–199. *See also* Living well, goal of

Consequentialism, 18; Nietzsche and, 260; aid and, 273, 281; harm and, 285, 287; double effect principle and, 293–294, 294–295; associative obligations and, 314

Conservatism, 352–353, 363

Constant, Benjamin, 364–365, 365–366

Constitutional interpretation: indeterminacy and, 90; psychological state theory of interpretation and, 128, 129; Kant's principle and, 266; double effect principle and, 295; liberty and, 369; abortion and, 377; partial enforcement and, 412; legal procedure and, 414–415

Constitutions, 64–65, 332

Constructivism, 63–66

Contempt, 309, 336

Contingency, 155–156, 400–401. *See also* Accident

Contradictory convictions, 106, 108

Control: judgmental responsibility and, 227–231; causal control, 228–229, 231–241, 249; harm and, 288; unintended harm and, 290–291

Convention, 26–28, 300–303, 309–310, 314–317

Conventionalism, 401

Convictions, 132, 153–154. *See also* Moral conviction

Correspondence theory of truth, 174–175, 179

Cost, metrics of, 276–277

Courage, 106, 181–182, 185, 187

Crime and punishment: capacity control and, 246–247; capital punishment, 294–295, 299, 329, 334; double effect principle and, 294–295; harm and, 299;

Crime and punishment *(continued)*
human rights and, 336–337; liberty and,
367; due process rights and, 371–372;
incompatibilism and, 463n8
Criminal organizations, 315, 321
Criterial concepts, 158–160; interpretive
concepts and, 163, 164–165, 165–166;
moral concepts and, 167–168; truth and,
173; thick and thin concepts and, 181–182;
equality and, 346; political morality
and, 349, 350; liberty and, 367; law and,
402, 404
Critical judgment, ambivalence and, 125,
126–127
Critical legal studies, 143–144
Cultural relativity, 34, 45–46, 54. *See also*
Relativism; Social context

Darrow, Clarence, 463n8
Darwall, Stephen, 205–206
Davidson, Donald, 148
Death, causing, 285–286
Death, events after, 201, 208, 420
Decision procedures: conceptual interpretation and, 160; interpretive concepts and,
161, 167, 168; truth and, 172–173; free
will and, 220, 221; judgmental responsibility and, 223–224, 225–227, 228; causal
control and, 231, 232, 238–240; determinism and, 233–234; capacity control and,
241–242, 243–246; insanity defenses and,
248–250; balance and integrity, 261–262,
263–264; Scanlon and, 270; aid and,
271–284; promises and, 305, 306; evil law
and, 410, 411
Default judgments, 90–96
Deflationary theory of truth, 173, 455nn15,17
Deliberate harm, 287, 288, 291–292, 297
Democracy: justice and, 4–5; conceptual
interpretation and, 163; political obligations and, 320, 322–323; political morality
and, 344–345, 349–350; political rights and
concepts, 347–348; liberty and, 366, 367;

positive liberty and, 379–385; models of,
385–392; representative government and,
392–395; judicial review and, 395–399
Desiderata, 118
Desire: moral reasoning and, 49, 50; moral
motivations and, 56, 57–58; conflict and,
118; moral responsibility and, 193; judgmental responsibility and, 226; moral conviction and, 235; well-being and, 273
Despair, 88
Determinism: free will and, 220, 222;
judgmental responsibility and, 224, 225,
227–228, 461–462n7; Hume and, 230;
chance and, 233–234; rationality and,
234–236; causal control and, 238; capacity
control and, 247, 248; Kant's principle
and, 267
Difference principle, 346
Dignity: respect and self-respect, 13–14,
14–15, 19, 205–209, 255–260; morality and,
191–195; goal of living well and, 195–199,
419, 420–421, 422; badness and moral
luck, 200–202; ethical principles and,
202–205; authenticity and, 209–214;
religious temperament and, 214–218;
moral philosophers on, 258–260,
264–270; balance and integrity, 260–264;
harm and, 287, 289, 299; double effect
principle and, 295, 296–297; promises
and, 304, 305; associative obligations
and, 312, 315; political obligations and,
320–321, 330; human rights and, 335–336,
337–338; liberty and, 364, 367–368,
375–376; abortion and, 377–378; democracy and, 379–380, 391
Diminished responsibility, 248–250, 250–252
Disagreement: interpretation and, 131–132,
133–134; value account of interpretation
and, 150–151; conceptual interpretation
and, 157–158, 158–160; paradigms and,
160–162; interpretive concepts and,
166–167, 168, 169; about truth, 172–178;
moral concepts and, 180–181

Discrimination, 169, 393

Distributive justice: equality and, 2–4, 346, 351–352, 355–356; political morality and, 349; paternalism and, 361–362; resource equality and, 363; liberty and, 374–375. *See also* Justice

Diversity: of moral claims, 47–48, 55, 59, 113; of religious convictions, 84–85

Double effect principle, 291–299, 470n11

Drier, James, 433n20

Due care, standards of, 291

Due process, right to, 4, 329, 371–372

Duress, 251

Duty. *See* Obligations

Eagleton, Terry, 142

Economic systems: laissez-faire economics, 2–3, 352–354, 362–363; constructivism and, 63–64; human rights and, 332, 334–335; equality and, 346–347, 356–357; political morality and, 349; democracy and, 386; goal of living well and, 421

Egalitarianism, 269, 332. *See also* Equality

Elected officials, 393, 394, 397

Election processes, 382, 389, 390

Electoral college, 394–395, 485n16

Eliot, T. S., 141–142

Ely, John Hart, 384

Emotions, venting, 32, 36, 53, 62, 68, 435n22

Empirical demonstration, 27, 28–29

Encouragement, responsibility and, 304–308

Enforcement, 410–411, 412–413

Enlightenment, 16–17, 230, 349

Envy test, 356–358

Epiphenomenalism, 220, 232–233, 240, 247, 248, 459n2

Epistemic values, 453n48

Epistemology, 16, 82–86

Equality: justice and, 2–4, 351–352; resource equality and, 2–4, 5, 273, 354–356, 356–363, 374–375, 479n10; constructivism and, 64; moral responsibility and, 112–113; dignity and, 260–261; aid and, 273–274;

political morality and, 330–331, 349; political rights and concepts, 346–347; false conceptions of, 353–356; democracy and, 386, 388–392, 477–478n4

Equality of opportunity, 363

Equality of resources, 356–363; distributive justice and, 2–4, 363; democracy and, 5, 479n10; aid and, 273; welfare and, 354–356; liberty and, 374–375

Equal-worth principle, 205

Error, moral conviction and, 122, 155

Error skepticism: moral truth and, 32–33, 35–36; internal skepticism and, 33–34; moral reasoning and, 40, 49–51; moral judgments and, 46–47; external skepticism and, 46–51; diversity of moral claims and, 47–48; moral motivations and, 48–49

Ethical independence, 368–371, 385, 418

Ethical parameters, 215–216, 323

Ethical responsibility, 202–203, 230, 482n7. *See also* Moral responsibility

Ethics: moral philosophy and, 13–14, 15; morality and, 19, 191; moral truth and, 25; moral reasoning and, 50; rationality and, 50, 51; global internal skepticism and, 88; indeterminacy and, 93–94; moral responsibility and, 112–113; Plato and Aristotle, 184; dignity and, 191–218; good life and living well, 201–202; free will and responsibility, 219–252

"Eudemonia" (happiness), 184, 187

European Convention on Human Rights, 332, 334

European Union, 381–382

Evidence, for moral truths, 27, 28–30, 37–39; diversity of moral claims and, 47–48; intelligent design and, 83–84; interpretive concepts and, 101–102; moral responsibility and, 115, 116; belief and, 248

Evil, problem of, 16

Evil law, 410–412

Ex ante equality, 358–360, 363

Exemptions from responsibility, justification of, 243–246

Existentialism, 18, 209, 210, 231

Expectations, creating, 304–308

Experimental evidence, 72–73, 74–75

Explanatory interpretation, 136, 138–139, 143, 144, 157, 162

Ex post equality, 358–360

Expressivism, 33, 63, 433–434n22, 439n4

External skepticism: moral truth and, 26, 31–32; error skepticism and, 32, 46–51; status skepticism and, 32–33, 52–59; as moral position, 40–44; Hume's principle and, 44–46; language games and, 59–63; constructivism and, 63–66; meta-ethical issues of morality and, 67–68; causal impact hypothesis (CI) and, 70, 71–72; global internal skepticism and, 89; ordinary view, of morality and, 100; ambivalence and, 126–127; truth and, 172; self-respect and, 209; Nagel and, 460–461n4

Fairness: causal impact hypothesis (CI) and, 73; obligations and, 302–303; democracy and, 348, 385–388, 392; family morality and, 408–409

Fallon, Richard, 118

Family morality, 407–409

Fault, goal of living well and, 201

Federalism, 381

Feminist criticism, 143

Feynman, Richard, 115

Fiction, 60, 61

Filters of conviction, 107–109, 112, 117

Fine, Kit, 432n20, 456n22

First-order issues, of morality. See Substantive issues, of morality

Fish, Stanley, 145–146

Fleming, James, 482n7

Foreign policy, 33–34, 104–105

Formalism, 137

Foster, Roy, 137–138

Frankfurt, Harry, 475n10

Frankfurter, Felix, 295

Freedom: liberty and, 4, 345, 363–368; Kant and, 19; free will challenge and, 221, 222; Kant's principle and, 265–266

Freeman, Samuel, 356, 479n10

Free-riding principle, 302–303

Free speech rights, 4, 329, 371, 372–374

Free will: responsibility and, 12–13, 219–252; moral responsibility and, 103–104; causal control and, 231–241; capacity control and, 241–248; incompatibilism and, 464n15

Freud, Sigmund, 17

Fried, Charles, 307, 308

Friendship, 180–181, 313, 316, 317, 319

Fry, Northrup, 138

Fugitive Slave Act (1850), 410–411, 413

Funding theory, 426–427n8

Game theory, 19

Gay marriage, 69–70

General welfare: dignity and, 272–275, 354–356; political morality and, 329–330; democracy and, 387–388

Genocide, 336

Geology game, 60, 61

Gibbard, Allan, 33, 63, 433–435n22

Global internal skepticism, 34, 46–47, 88, 127

God: moral truth and, 28; internal skepticism and, 34; external skepticism and, 41, 42; error skepticism and, 46–47; causal impact hypothesis (CI) and, 72; religious conviction and, 83–84; moral progress and, 87; human rights and, 340, 341, 342–343

Goldberg, John, 469–470n5

Good life, having: Plato and Aristotle, 184–187; moral responsibility and, 191, 200–202, 419–423; dignity and, 195–199; goal of living well and, 195–199; Nietzsche and, 259; aid and, 273, 277; associative obligations and, 312; equality and, 355. *See also* Living well, goal of

Goodness, 168–169, 182, 185, 341, 343

Government: constructivism and, 64–65; political obligations and, 317–318; human rights and, 335; liberty and, 345, 346, 365; laissez-faire economics and, 352–354; government regulation, 357, 367–368, 369–370, 373; representative government and, 392–395; ethical responsibility and, 482n7. *See also* Democracy; Political morality

Great Britain, representative government and, 398–399

Greatness, value judgments and, 89, 92–93, 137–138, 178

Greek philosophers, 15–16, 180, 184–188, 198, 421–422

Greenblatt, Stephen, 140–141

Greenspan, Alan, 397–398

Griffin, James, 473n1, 474n5

Group political rights, 473–474n1

Guantánamo Bay detention camp, 106

Guest, Stephen, 486n6

Guilt, 201

Gun rights, 414

Habeas corpus rights, 414–415

Hand, Learned, 291

Haneke, Michael, 146

Happiness, 185–186, 187, 259, 355, 457n33. *See also* Living well, goal of

Hare, Richard, 32–33, 257, 425–426n6

Harm: morality and, 14, 15; relational responsibility and, 103; aid and, 271; metrics of, 274–276; competition and, 285–289; unintended harm, 290–291; double effect principle and, 291–299; personal responsibility and, 300; promises and, 303–304, 305, 310–311; associative obligations and, 313, 314; political obligations and, 320; tribal obligations and, 324; human rights and, 337; liberty and, 345–346, 371, 376

Harman, Gilbert, 438n3

Harris, John, 294

Hart, H. L. A., 367, 404

Hate speech, 372–373

Hawking, Stephen, 154–155

Health care policies, 4, 332, 412

Hedonism, 207

Hirsh, E. D., 141

Historical interpretation: interpretation and, 123, 124, 451n23; explanatory interpretation and, 136, 138–139; political morality and, 350; U.S. Supreme Court and, 399; legal positivism and, 409–410; law and, 414–415, 486n11

Hobbes, Thomas, 17, 18–19, 194, 230

Holism, 154, 155

Holmes, Oliver Wendell, 373

Homo economicus, 17–18

Honesty, 118–119, 120

Humanism, 215, 216

Human rights, 332–344, 414, 474–475n5

Hume, David, 17, 19, 57, 194, 230, 303, 435n22

Hume's principle, 17, 222; external skepticism and, 44–46; causal impact hypothesis (CI) and, 71, 430n6, 440–441n6; causes of moral convictions and, 75; causal dependence hypothesis (CD) and, 77; moral responsibility and, 99; value judgments and, 116; morality and, 193; obligations and, 302; human rights and, 341; moral naturalists and, 428–429n6

Hypothetical cases, value of, 283–284, 297–298

Idealism, 66, 109

Incompatibilism, 223, 227, 229–230, 461n7, 463n8, 464n15

Independence: authenticity and, 211–213; judgmental responsibility and, 229; harm and, 288; ethical independence, 368–371, 385, 418

Independence of value, 9–11; moral philosophy and, 19; moral truth and, 23–40, 418; evidence of moral truth and, 38, 39; external skepticism and, 40–69; meta-ethical issues, of morality and, 67–68; causes of moral convictions and, 69–87; internal skepticism and, 88–96; skepticism and, 99–100

Independent interpretation, 139–144

Indeterminacy: external skepticism and, 44; internal skepticism and, 89–90, 90–96, 449n5; uncertainty and, 91–93; moral conflicts and, 118–119; radical translations and, 148–149; truth and, 178

Injury. *See* Harm

Insanity, judgmental responsibility and, 243–244

Insanity defenses, 246, 248–250

Insincerity, 28, 104, 108, 111

Institutionalization, 405

Insurance, 358, 360–361, 479–480n12, 480–481n13

Integrated epistemology, 82–86, 100, 101

Integration, morality and, 119–120, 192

Integrity, 242–243, 259, 260–264, 283–284

Intelligent design, 83–84

Intentions, of authors and originators, 128–129, 134, 135–136, 149–150, 450n9

Internal skepticism: moral truth and, 26, 30–32, 33–35, 37, 178–179; typology and, 88–90; indeterminacy and default, 90–96; moral conviction and, 99; literary criticism and, 146; interpretation and, 155; self-respect and, 209; Nagel and, 426n7, 460–461n4

International law, 337

Interpretation: truth and, 123–134; types of, 134–144; interpretive skepticism, 144–147; radical translation, 147–149; value account and, 149–152; science and, 152–156; conceptual interpretation, 157–188; promises and, 310–311; associative obligations and, 316–317

Interpretive concepts: political morality and, 6–7, 15, 345–348; moral reasoning and, 12, 38–39, 51; moral philosophy and, 19; justice and, 66, 169–170; moral responsibility and, 99–122; moral truth and, 120–122; conceptual interpretation and, 158–170; paradigms and, 160–163; usage and, 163–164; migration of concepts and, 164–166; moral concepts, 166–170; good life and living well, 195; dignity and, 204; capacity control and, 229; causal control and, 240–241; political rights and concepts, 349–350; liberty, 364–368; democracy and, 379–380, 382–383; law and, 404–405

Interpretive skepticism, 144–147, 147–149

Interpretivism, law and, 401, 402–403, 407

Intuition: causes of moral convictions and, 75, 115; religious conviction and, 85; causal control and, 241; aid and, 283; McDowell and, 444n6, 445n6

Inventory of the universe, 168

Investment luck, 358–359

Iraq war, 27, 116

Irony, 36

Irresponsibility, 104–107. *See also* Moral responsibility; Responsibility

Irwin, Terence, 184–185

Is Democracy Possible Here? (Dworkin), 328

Islam, 340

Ivan Illyitch (Tolstoy character), 208

Jameson, Frederic, 142

Jefferson, Thomas, 339–340

Johnston, Mark, 439n4

Jolls, Christine, 458n6

Joyce, Richard, 431n11

Judgmental responsibility, 103, 104; free will and, 221, 223, 461–462n7; decision procedures and, 223–224; third-person judgments and, 224–225; responsibility system, 225–227; goal of living well and, 230–231; causal control and, 231–241;

capacity control and, 241–248, 465–466n26; insanity defenses and, 248–250; insurance and, 480n12

Judicial review, 348, 380, 384–385, 395–399, 484–485n9

Justice: equality and, 2–4, 352; liberty and, 4; democracy and, 4–5, 383–384; law and, 5–6, 403; political obligations and, 15, 321–322, 322–323; constructivism and, 63–64, 66; interpretive concepts and, 66, 160–161, 162, 166–167; relativism and, 169–170; Plato and, 185; diminished responsibility and, 251–252; Rawls and, 267–268, 268–269; property rights and, 375; goal of living well and, 422, 423

Justification of conviction, 48, 79–80, 86, 116–117, 128, 171

Kamm, Frances, 470n7

Kane, Robert, 463–464n10

Kant, Immanuel: morality and, 14, 19, 193; constructivism and, 63; moral philosophy and, 109, 110; self-respect and, 255; Nietzsche and, 259; dignity and, 264–267; aid and, 272

Kant's principle, 19, 260, 264, 273–274, 287

Katz, Leo, 449n5

Kindness, 118–119, 120

King, Martin Luther, Jr., 389

Kis, Janos, 384–385

Korsgaard, Christine, 437n29

Lady Macbeth (Shakespeare character), 60

Laissez-faire economics, 2–3, 352–354, 362–363

Language. *See* Semantic distinctions

Language games: status skepticism and, 53; external skepticism and, 59–63; projectivism and, 62–63; moral truth and, 68; conceptual interpretation and, 175–176; speech-act skepticism and, 432n20; expressivism and, 434n22

Language, Truth, and Logic (Ayer), 32

Law: justice and, 5–6; obedience to, 302, 317–318, 401; international law, 337; natural law, 339–340, 414; equality and, 353–354; morality and, 400–409; purpose of, 409–415; evil law, 410–412. *See also* Legal judgments

Leavis, F. R., 126, 137, 138, 146

Legal judgments: error skepticism and, 46; indeterminacy and, 90, 91, 94–95; evidence and, 116; interpretation and, 123–124, 131, 133, 142–144; ambivalence and, 125–126; psychological state theory of interpretation and, 129–130; collaborative interpretation and, 136; value account of interpretation and, 149–150; interpretive concepts and, 164–165; relativism and, 170, 171; judgmental responsibility and, 224–225; causal control and, 232; insanity defenses and, 248–250; Kant's principle and, 266; unintended harm and, 291; democracy and, 348

Legal positivism, 94–95, 401–404, 407, 409–410, 413

Legal procedure, 413–415, 486–487n11

Legal rights, 331–332, 406, 410, 412–413

Legislative rights, 406

Legitimacy, of government: political obligations and, 317–318, 321–323; political morality and, 330; moral authority and, 344; democracy and, 384, 385, 392; representative government and, 394; judicial review and, 396, 398, 399; evil law and, 411

"Letting nature take its course," 298–299

Liability responsibility, 103, 211, 290–291

Liberal legalism, 144

Libertarianism, 332

Liberty: justice and, 4; constructivism and, 63–64; moral contradictions and, 106; security and, 118; political morality and, 330–331, 344–345, 477–478n4; political rights and concepts, 345–346, 368–378;

Liberty *(continued)*
  dimensions of freedom and, 363–368;
  equality and, 422–423
Liberty of the Ancients and the Liberty of the
  Moderns, The (Constant), 364–365,
  365–366
Libet, Benjamin, 459n2
Life, judging the value of a, 51. *See also*
  Living well, goal of
Life's Dominion (Dworkin), 328
Literary criticism: interpretation and, 123,
  124, 131, 135, 139–142; ambivalence and,
  126–127, 127–128; psychological state
  theory of interpretation and, 130;
  collaborative interpretation and, 135–136,
  136–138; interpretive skepticism and,
  145–146; value account of interpretation
  and, 150
Living well, goal of: ethical principles and,
  191–192; moral concepts and, 193–194;
  religious conviction and, 194–195; dignity
  and, 195–199; moral responsibility and,
  200–202, 328, 419–423; self-respect and,
  205–209; authenticity and, 209–214;
  religious temperament and, 214–218;
  judgmental responsibility and, 221,
  226–227, 230–231; capacity control and,
  242, 244–245, 247; moral philosophy and,
  258–260, 267, 270; balance and integrity,
  260–264; aid and, 272–273, 275; promises
  and, 308; equality and, 355; liberty and,
  369. *See also* Good life, having
Lottery, choosing by, 281, 283, 294, 298, 348,
  469n12
Luck, 357–358, 358–359, 360
Lying, 192, 305, 306

Macaulay, Thomas, 139, 451n24
Macedo, Stephen, 483n3
MacIntyre, Alistair, 425–426n6
Mackie, John, 47, 48, 49
Majoritarian model of democracy, 383–384,
  385–392; democracy and, 347–348, 380,

386–387, 483–484n9; liberty and, 370;
  representative government and, 393–394;
  judicial review and, 395–396, 398–399,
  484–485n9; elected officials and, 397;
  minority groups and, 477n4
Marxist interpretation, 139, 142
Material implications, capacity control
  and, 247
McDowell, John, 444–445n6, 446n6
Mental deficiency: judgmental responsibility
  and, 226–227; determinism and, 234;
  causal control and, 237, 238–239; capacity
  control and, 244, 245, 246, 466n28;
  insanity defenses and, 250
Mental telepathy, 72–73
Meta-ethical issues, of morality, 10, 11;
  moral truth and, 24, 122; skepticism and,
  31; status skepticism and, 52, 60; external
  skepticism and, 67–68; interpretive concepts and, 166; Star and, 428n5
Metaphysical questions: morality and,
  24–26; error skepticism and, 32; language
  games and, 60–61; moral truth and,
  417–418
Methodology, truth and, 179–180
Migration of concepts, 164–166
Military action, 333, 334
Mill, John Stuart, 18, 345, 349, 367, 373
Minimalism, truth and, 455–456n18
M'Naghten Rule, 250
Moral arguments: moral truth and, 26, 27,
  37, 39; causal dependence hypothesis
  (CD) and, 77, 78; indeterminacy and, 95;
  interpretive concepts and, 164; thick and
  thin concepts and, 184
Moral authority, 342, 343, 344
Moral claims, 53–54, 76–77, 172, 173
Moral compartmentalization, 105–107, 108
Moral concepts: interpretive concepts,
  166–170; thick and thin concepts,
  180–184; Plato and Aristotle, 184, 187;
  Socrates and, 185; goal of living well and,
  193–194

Moral conflicts, 118–120

Moral contradictions. *See* Contradictory convictions

Moral conviction: law and, 5; moral truth and, 47–48, 68, 69–70, 120–121, 235; motivations for action and, 48, 49; status skepticism and, 52, 55; amoralists and, 57; personal behavior and, 58; political morality and, 64–65; causal impact hypothesis (CI) and, 70–75; causal dependence hypothesis (CD) and, 76–80; accident and, 80–82; integration and, 82–86, 192; moral progress and, 86–87; internal skepticism and, 99; responsibility and, 100–101, 111–113; moral irresponsibility and, 104–107; as filter, 107–109; liberty and, 368–369; Gibbard and, 434–435n22; personal history and, 436n22; neo-Darwinism and, 443n6

"Moral facts," 9; moral truth and, 29; status skepticism and, 32, 433n20; speech-act skepticism and, 55; constructivism and, 65; causes of moral convictions and, 70; obligations and, 302; God and, 343

Morality: responsibility and, 11–13; dignity and, 14–15, 191–195, 255–270; moral philosophy and, 15–19; origins of, 16–17; moral truth and, 25; types of, 117; ethics and, 191; aid, 271–284; harm, 285–299; obligations, 300–324; law and, 400–409

Morality games, 62–63

Moral judgments: status skepticism and, 32–33, 59, 431–432n17; external skepticism and, 35–36; moral truth and, 37–38; skepticism as moral position and, 41; Hume's principle and, 46; error skepticism and, 46–47; moral motivations and, 56; belief and, 57–58; meta-ethical issues and, 67; causal dependence hypothesis (CD) and, 76–77; indeterminacy and, 90; truth and, 176; Scanlon and, 269–270; constructivism and, 437n29. *See also* Value judgments

Moral luck, 200–202

Moral motivations, 48–49, 56–58

Moral naturalism, 428–430n6, 438–439n3

Moral objectivity. *See* Truth

Moral particles (morons), 32, 42–43, 76, 117, 120

Moral philosophers, 18, 19; Greek philosophers, 15–16, 184–188; Christian philosophers and, 16; Enlightenment philosophers, 16–17; causal impact hypothesis (CI) and, 72; causal dependence hypothesis (CD) and, 76; value systems and, 109–110, 111; interpretation and, 134–135; moral truth and, 439–446n6

Moral philosophy: truth and, 7–11, 23–26, 172–173; schools of thought and, 15–19; skepticism as moral position and, 40–44; responsibility and, 109–111; conceptual interpretation and, 157; thick and thin concepts and, 181–182; capacity control and, 230; moral truth and, 417–418

Moral pluralism, 425n2

Moral reasoning: interpretive concepts and, 12, 38–39; moral truth and, 27–28, 37–38, 179–180; external skepticism and, 40–44; causal dependence hypothesis (CD) and, 78–79; causes of moral convictions and, 81–82; ordinary view of morality and, 100; interpretation and, 153–154, 156; conceptual interpretation and, 157–158; thick and thin concepts and, 183–184; determinism and, 233–234; Scanlon and, 270

Moral responsibility: interpretive concepts and, 99–104, 162–163; moral actions and, 104–113, 194; moral truth and, 113–122, 441n6; value theory of interpretation and, 177; conceptual interpretation and, 179–180; desire and, 193; goal of living well and, 196, 419–423; capacity control and, 246–247; Kant's principle and, 266, 267; integrity and, 283–284; promises and, 304, 306–307, 308–310; associative obligations and, 315; political obligations

Moral responsibility *(continued)*
  and, 317–318; abortion and, 376–377.
  See also Responsibility
Moral schizophrenia, 105
Moral seriousness, literary criticism and, 137
Moral truth: moral philosophy and, 23–26,
  417–418; ordinary view of, 26–28; evidence and, 28–30, 37–39; internal and external skepticism, 30–35; error and
  status skepticism, 32–33; status skepticism
  and, 35–37, 52, 59–60; Hume's principle
  and, 46; diversity of moral claims and,
  47–48; motivations for action and, 49;
  categorical reasoning and, 51; speech-act
  skepticism and, 54; constructivism and,
  65; moral conviction and, 68, 69–70, 80,
  81, 235; causal dependence hypothesis
  (CD) and, 78; interpretive concepts and,
  101–102, 120–122; personal history and,
  113; moral responsibility and, 113–122;
  ambivalence and, 125–126; moral
  reasoning and, 179–180; Rawls and,
  267–268; aid and, 283; human rights
  and, 338–339; religious conviction and,
  340–341, 342, 343
"Morons." *See* Moral particles (morons)
Mortimer, R. C., 475n9
Mother Teresa, 236, 237, 242
Motivations, for action, 48–49, 56–58, 194
Mountains, language games and, 61
Mrs. Jellyby (Dickens character), 313

Nagel, Thomas: religious temperament and,
  215–216, 217; free will challenge and, 220,
  221, 460–461n4; goal of living well and,
  261, 262; internal skepticism and, 426n7;
  causal impact hypothesis (CI) and,
  439–441n6
National boundaries, democracy and, 380–381
Natural-kind concepts, 159–160, 165,
  168–169, 428–430n6, 455n12
Natural law, 339–340, 414
Nazism, 33, 257, 322, 411, 438–439n3

Negation, moral positions and, 42
Negative liberty, 5, 365, 366, 367
Negative moral judgments, 46, 88–89
Neo-Darwinism, 35, 46, 85, 443n6
New Criticism, 142
New Deal, 397
Nicomachean Ethics (Aristotle), 186
Nietzsche, Friedrich, 18; authenticity and,
  209–210, 213, 214; Nagel and, 216; dignity
  and, 258–260, 459n19; political morality
  and, 466–467n4
Nihilism, 209; authenticity and, 213
Noncognitivism, 33

Objective value: goal of living well and, 196;
  authenticity and, 213–214; dignity and,
  255–258, 259; aid and, 275, 276–277, 281–282
Obligations: moral responsibility and, 15,
  194; thick and thin concepts and, 182;
  convention and, 300–303; promises and,
  303–311; associative obligations, 311–317;
  political obligations, 317–323, 330; tribal
  obligations, 323–324; religious conviction
  and, 342; law and, 401; family morality,
  407–409; Principle F, 471–472n8
"One thought too many," 314, 469n13
Opportunity costs, 356, 357, 362, 375, 479n10
Ordinary speech, 52–53, 54, 61, 62
Ordinary view, of morality, 26–28; internal
  skepticism and, 34; moral reasoning and,
  49, 111; status skepticism and, 56; external
  skepticism and, 100; conceptual interpretation and, 163–164; judgmental responsibility and, 225–226; causal control and, 238;
  harm and, 286; value of hypothetical cases
  and, 297; law and, 400–401; expressivism
  and, 433–434n22
Organ donation, 294
Originalism, law and, 486n11

Pain, 458n16
Paradigms, interpretive concepts and,
  160–163, 176

Paradox of analysis, 180

Parents and children, 312, 313, 314, 316, 407–409

Parliamentary systems, 380, 393, 398–399, 413–414

Partial enforcement, law and, 412–413

Particularization, aid and, 278

Partnership model of democracy, 383, 384, 385–392, 394–395, 477–478n4

Partnerships, associative obligations and, 313

Paternalism, 289, 336, 337, 361–362, 370

Peirce, Charles Saunders, 177–178

People, the, democracy and, 380–382

Performance value, 197–198, 242, 423, 458n6, 465n22

Performative obligations, 301, 428n6

Performing arts, 146–147, 178–179

Personal behavior: moral conviction and, 48–49, 58; moral motivations and, 57; good life and living well, 200–202; self-respect and, 206–207; authenticity and, 212; free will and, 219–220, 222–223; making promises and, 308–310

Personal beliefs, constructivism and, 66

Personal history: causal impact hypothesis (CI) and, 73–74; causal dependence hypothesis (CD) and, 77, 79; moral conviction and, 80–81, 101, 107–108, 112, 436n22, 448n10; moral progress and, 87; moral truth and, 113, 122; free will challenge and, 221; determinism and, 233–234; belief and, 234–235; psychological impossibility and, 236–237; judgmental responsibility and, 251; family morality and, 407–409; goal of living well and, 421

Personal loyalty, 106

Personal relationships, obligations and, 301–303, 311–317

Personal responsibility: distributive justice and, 2, 3; liberty and, 4, 365; ethics and, 13; internal skepticism and, 30–31; moral conviction and, 79; relational responsibility, 102, 103; free will challenge and,

222–223; capacity control and, 246; harm and, 287–288, 289; double effect principle and, 296–297; associative obligations and, 311–317; human rights and, 336–337; equality and, 353, 356, 357–358, 359, 360, 361–362, 363; welfare and, 354–355; insurance and, 360–361; moral truth and, 418–419

Personal standards, moral compartmentalization and, 106–107

Personhood, human rights and, 474–475n5

Pessimistic incompatibilism, 223, 224, 237, 240

Philosophical speech, 52, 53

Philosophy games, 62–63

Physical world: empirical demonstration and, 28–29; causes of belief and, 71; fundamental laws and, 114–115

Pirandello, Luigi, 227–228

Planets, definition of, 165–166

Platitudes, truth and, 172–173, 455–456n18

Plato, 180, 184–188, 198, 421–422

Pleasure, 186, 206–207, 273. See also Living well, goal of

Pluralism. See Social context

Pluto, 165–166

Poetry, 7, 141–142, 147, 150, 152, 214, 357

Political equality, 388–392

Political impact: democracy and, 388–389, 389–390, 391; representative government and, 393, 394–395; judicial review and, 396

Political influence, 388, 389, 391

Political morality: equality and, 2–4, 351–363; liberty and, 4, 364–378; democracy and, 4–5, 379–399; law and, 5–6, 400–415; interpretive concepts and, 6–7, 157; moral truth and, 7–8, 418; ethics and, 13, 14; justice and, 15; constructivism and, 63–65; moral compartmentalization and, 106–107; moral responsibility and, 112–113; thick and thin concepts and, 182; moral philosophers on, 188, 264, 268–269; authenticity and, 212; aid and, 275; associative

Political morality *(continued)*
  obligations and, 312; political rights
  and concepts, 327–350; goal of living
  well and, 421–422; majority rule and,
  477n4
Political obligations, 317–323
Political philosophy, 110–111, 133, 162
Political rights and concepts: rights,
  327–332; human rights, 332–344,
  473–474n1; liberty, 345–346, 368–378;
  equality, 346–347; democracy, 347–348;
  interpretive concepts and, 349–350; law
  and, 405–406
Political stability, 385–386
Political standing, 390–391
Positive liberty, 5, 365, 366, 372, 379–385, 392
Positive moral judgments, 46–51, 90–91, 92,
  94–95
Postmodernism, 30
Poverty: judgmental responsibility and, 251;
  equality and, 346–347, 351–352; democ-
  racy and, 393; goal of living well and,
  419, 420, 421
Pragmatist theory, 175, 177–178
Precedent, legal judgments and, 116
Prejudice, 282, 336, 351
Preventative war, 104–105
Primary and secondary qualities, status
  skepticism and, 58–59
Principle F, 307, 308, 471–472n8
Procedural justice, 5, 413–415
Product value, 197, 198, 216
Projectivism, 33, 62–63, 435–436n22, 444n6
Promises, 15, 303–311
Property rights, 4, 342, 374–375
Proximity, aid and, 278
Prudence, judgmental responsibility and,
  462–463n7
Psychological impossibility, 236–237
Psychological state theory of interpretation,
  128–130, 137, 141, 149–150, 175
Psychology, 70–71, 136
Psychopathology, 239, 247

Quasi-realism, 33, 63, 435n22
Queer entities, 47, 48, 49
Quietism, 25, 67, 419
Quine, Willard, 147–148, 149

Race and ethnicity, 323, 324, 473–474n1
Radical translations, interpretation and,
  147–149
Railton, Peter, 426–427n8
Rationality, 50, 51, 234–236
Rationalization, 104, 108
Rawls, John: constructivism and, 63–64,
  65, 437n29; Kant and, 110; justice and,
  166–167; balance and integrity, 263–264;
  dignity and, 267–269; equality and, 346,
  352; political morality and, 349, 476n3
Raz, Joseph, 474n5
Realism: moral truth and, 9–10, 417–418;
  external skepticism and, 37; constructivism
  and, 65; meta-ethical issues, of morality
  and, 67; causal impact hypothesis (CI) and,
  70, 71; Street and, 446n9
Reality game, 60–61
"Reason," interpretive concept of, 50–51
Recognition respect, 205–206
Redundancy theory, 175
Referenda, 382, 394
Reflective equilibrium, 263–264
Regret, 201, 208
Regulative capacity, 244, 245–246, 248, 249
Relational responsibility, 102, 210–211,
  327–328
Relativism, 145, 146, 170–171, 401
Religion, human rights and, 335
Religious conviction: integrated epistemol-
  ogy and, 83–85; moral responsibility and,
  194–195, 202–203; authenticity and, 213,
  214; judgmental responsibility and, 230;
  dignity and, 256, 257–258; human rights
  and, 339–344; liberty and, 370
Religious freedom, 371, 375–378
Religious temperament, dignity and,
  214–218

Representative government, 392–395. *See also* Democracy

Rescue cases, 274, 278, 279, 280–283, 292–293, 468n5

Resource equality. *See* Equality of resources

Respect for others, 255–260, 266, 420–421. *See also* Self-respect

Responsibility: morality and, 11–13; moral truth and, 38, 113–122, 418–419; skepticism and, 41; moral assumptions and, 45; causes of moral convictions and, 80; interpretive concepts and, 99–104; types of, 102–104; morally responsible action and, 104–113; interpretation and, 131, 142, 144; authenticity and, 210–211; free will and, 219–252; political rights and concepts, 328. *See also* Moral responsibility

Responsibility system, 225–227, 227–231, 237–240, 241

Revolution, political obligations and, 323

Richard of Gloucester (Shakespeare character), 57

Ricoeur, Paul, 130

Rights: liberty and, 4; aid and, 281; obligations and, 301, 302–303; political rights and concepts, 327–332; political morality and, 328–329; human rights, 332–344, 414, 474–475n5; judicial review and, 398; law and, 405–406, 414; partial enforcement and, 412

Ripstein, Arthur, 361, 479–480n12

Risk, 199, 306, 360–361

Risk transfer, 290

Roberts, John, 397

Role obligations. *See* Associative obligations

Rorty, Richard, 36, 59–61, 62–63

Sacrifice, 195, 294, 298

Sager, Lawrence, 412

Sailing to Byzantium (Yeats), 138, 146

Salience, aid and, 278

Same-sex marriage, 369

Sanctions, human rights and, 333–334

Sartre, Jean-Paul, 18, 136, 210, 231

Scalia, Antonin, 486n11

Scalotopic brain scans, 77–79

Scanlon, Thomas: dignity and, 204–205, 269–270; capacity control and, 230; Nagel and, 262; aid and, 275–276, 468n2; double effect principle and, 295, 470n11; Principle F, 307, 308, 471–472n8

Schofield, Philip, 486n6

Science: forming scientific opinion and, 69, 72–73, 82–83, 121–122; scientific principles, 114–115; interpretation and, 123, 151, 152–156, 450n2; interpretive concepts and, 165; truth and, 177, 203, 428–429n6; free will and, 221–222; epistemic values, 453n48

Scientific method, 82–83, 179

Secondary qualities, 58–59

Second-order issues, of morality. *See* Meta-ethical issues, of morality

Security, 106, 118

"Seeing" events, moral truth and, 27, 72, 73–74, 74–75, 116–117

Self-abnegation, morality of, 18, 19, 287

Self-conception, 185, 207–208, 235

Self-determination, 323, 381

Self-government: liberty and, 365, 366; free speech rights and, 372; democracy and, 379–380, 380–382, 384; goal of living well and, 423

Self-interest: moral philosophy and, 17–19; moral reasoning and, 50; moral irresponsibility and, 104, 107; moral responsibility and, 192, 194; aid and, 272; harm and, 285–286; promises and, 309; associative obligations and, 313; free speech rights and, 374

Self-respect: moral responsibility and, 112–113, 194, 246; ethical principles and, 203; dignity and, 205–209, 255–260; Kant and, 255, 265; balance and integrity, 262–263; aid and, 277; political obligations and, 320; abortion and, 378

Semantic distinctions: status skepticism
    and, 52–56; moral conflicts and, 120;
    moral truth and, 121–122; interpretation
    and, 124; radical translations and,
    147–149; conceptual interpretation and,
    158, 163–164; thick and thin concepts
    and, 183; evil law and, 410–412
Semantic expressivism, 56
Semantic independence, 55
Sen, Amartya, 352, 476–477n3, 478n6,
    480–481n13
Senate, U.S., 394–395
Seurat, Georges, 199
Sexuality, 33, 312, 376
Shafer-Landau, Russ, 41–42
Shakespeare, William, 128, 129, 209
Shaw, Tamsin, 466–467n4
Shiffrin, Seana, 466n31
Shklar, Judith, 390
Sidgwick, Henry, 18
Simons, Kenneth W., 469–470n5
Sincerity, 111–112, 126, 209, 305
Six Characters in Search of an Author (Piran-
    dello), 227–228
Skeptical pertinence, 55
Skepticism: moral philosophy and, 17; moral
    truth and, 25, 26, 29–30, 178–179; internal
    skepticism, 30–32, 33–35; external skepti-
    cism, 31–32, 40–68; error skepticism, 32–33;
    status skepticism, 35–37; independence
    of value and, 99–100; interpretation
    and, 131; interpretive skepticism,
    144–147; radical translations and,
    147–149; conceptual interpretation and,
    175–176; goal of living well and,
    208–209
Slavery, 86, 87, 298
Smith, Adam, 477n3, 480–481n13
Smith, Michael, 63, 432–433n20
Social context: moral skepticism and, 31;
    neo-Darwinism and, 35; morality and,
    45–46, 47–48; moral truth and, 54; moral
    conviction and, 70–71, 101; interpretation

and, 130–134; conceptual interpretation
    and, 136, 170–171; value account of
    interpretation and, 150–151; authenticity
    and, 211–212; obligations and, 301–302,
    319–320, 321, 322, 408, 428n6; associative
    obligations and, 311–312, 314–315; human
    rights and, 338–339; law and, 401–402,
    406–407; goal of living well and, 421
Social programs, 361, 363
Social value, of moral philosophy, 110
Socrates, 110, 184–185
Sovereignty, human rights and, 333–334
Sovereign Virtue (Dworkin), 328, 476n3
Spare-parts lottery, 294, 298
Special view, of human value, 255–258
Speech-act skepticism: status skepticism
    and, 52–56; moral motivations and,
    56–57; language games and, 60, 432n20
Stalin, Joseph: moral reasoning and, 49, 50;
    ethics and, 51; psychological impossibility
    and, 236, 237; capacity control and, 242;
    political obligations and, 322
Star, Daniel, 428n5
Status skepticism, 433–436n22; moral truth
    and, 32–33, 35–37; internal skepticism
    and, 34; as moral position, 40; speech-
    act skepticism and, 52–56, 432–433n20;
    external skepticism and, 52–59; moral
    motivations and, 56–58; primary and
    secondary qualities and, 58–59; moral
    judgments and, 431–432n17
Statutory intentions, 129–130, 133
Stoppard, Tom, 150
Strangers, 271–284, 285–299
Strawson, Galen, 224, 235–236
Strawson, Peter, 220, 460–461n4
Street, Sharon, 446–448n9
Sturgeon, Nicholas, 438–439n3
Subjectivism: truth and, 7–8, 9; unity of
    value and, 11; moral truth and, 23–24,
    27–28; internal skepticism and, 34; moral
    conviction and, 121; causal impact hy-
    pothesis (CI) and, 440n6

Subjectivity, 54–55, 255–258, 259

Subordination, associative obligations and, 312, 313

Substantive issues, of morality, 10; moral truth and, 24; skepticism and, 31; external skepticism as, 40–44; status skepticism and, 52, 56, 59–60; indeterminacy and, 89; interpretive skepticism and, 178–179; Gibbard and, 434–435n22

Supreme Court, U.S.: judicial review and, 396–397, 397–398; term limits and, 399; historical interpretation and, 414–415; majority rule and, 484–485n9; minority groups and, 485n14

Sydney Carton (Dickens character), 206, 208

Taxation: distributive justice and, 3–4; progressive taxation, 166; equality and, 353, 363; liberty and, 369; property rights and, 374, 375

Tea Party conventions, 66

Templates, of moral responsibility, 109–110

Temptation, causal control and, 239–240

Term limits, 399

Tests and standards: value judgments and, 92–93, 106–107, 137–138, 145–146; law and, 133, 409–410; metrics of harm and, 275–276; metrics of cost and, 276–277; confrontation scale and, 277–280; defining human rights and, 333–335; human rights and, 338; envy test and, 356–358; liberty and, 368; representative government and, 394–395

Theology, 16, 340–342

Theory of Justice, A (Rawls), 63

Thick and thin concepts, 180–184

Thinking, good or bad. *See* Moral reasoning

Third-person judgments, 224–225

Tolerance, moral responsibility and, 112–113

Torture, 251, 336–337, 431–432n17

Totalitarianism, 366, 390

Town meetings, 389

Translations, 147–149, 170–171

Trials, human rights and, 337

Tribal obligations, 380

Trickle-down economics, 347

Trilling, Lionel, 209

Trolley case, 293–294, 295, 297–298, 298–299

Truth: value judgments and, 7–8; moral philosophy and, 7–11; interpretive concepts and, 123–134; interpretation and, 137, 151–152, 172–180; interpretive skepticism and, 144–145; science and, 152–153, 154–155; capacity control and, 244. *See also* Moral truth

Truth-aptness, 175–176

Two Concepts of Liberty (Berlin), 364–365, 365–366

Typology, internal skepticism and, 88–90

Uncertainty: skepticism and, 34–35, 44; indeterminacy and, 91–93, 95–96; moral conflicts and, 118–119; interpretation and, 156; associative obligations and, 316

Unintended harm, 290–291, 295–296

Unity of value, 1, 7, 11, 119, 419–423

Universal Declaration of Human Rights (1948), 332, 334, 337, 338

Universality, of moral claims, 54, 255–258, 266, 271–272

Universe, conception of, 214–218

Utilitarianism: interpretive concepts and, 66; moral progress and, 87; moral responsibility and, 115, 194; justice and, 162; Nietzsche and, 259; political morality and, 329, 330, 349; human rights and, 332; liberty and, 345; equality and, 354; democracy and, 383; legal procedure and, 414; free will and, 461–462n7

Value account, interpretation and, 135–136, 149–152, 175

Value judgments: truth and, 7–8, 9, 11; moral reasoning and, 12; moral truth and, 24, 25, 26, 417, 418; error skepticism and, 32; Hume's principle and, 44–45, 116;

Value judgments *(continued)*
  indeterminacy and, 89; "barely true"
  judgments and, 114; ambivalence and,
  127–128; collaborative interpretation and,
  136–138; interpretive skepticism and,
  145–146; thick and thin concepts and,
  181–182; McDowell and, 444–445n6
Values: unity of value, 1; interpretive
  concepts and, 7, 160–161; moral independence of, 9; moral truth and, 23–26; moral
  philosophy and, 109–110; of responsibility,
  111–113; conflicts in, 118–120; truth and,
  173–174; goal of living well and, 197;
  dignity and, 204, 217–218, 255–258;
  authenticity and, 213–214; Kant's principle
  and, 265; aid and, 273–274; God and, 343
Value theory of interpretation, 130–134, 141,
  177
Victims, number of, 280–283
Virtue: responsibility as, 102–103, 103–104,
  210; truth and, 176; virtue theorists, 182;
  Plato and Aristotle, 184, 185–188
Voting rights, 392–393

Waldron, Jeremy, 386, 387, 483–484n9
Watteau, Antoine, 133–134

Wealth, 346–347, 421–422
Welfare. *See* General welfare
Well-being, 272–273
Westphalian conception of sovereignty,
  333–334
What We Owe to Each Other (Scanlon),
  269–270
Whig historical interpretation, 138–139,
  451n24
Wiggins, David, 441–443n6, 456n19
Williams, Bernard: moral reasoning and,
  49–50, 51, 467n14, 469n13; truth and, 173,
  174; thick and thin concepts and, 181, 182;
  capacity control and, 243–244; political
  morality and, 350
Wilson, J. Dover, 139
Wittgenstein, Ludwig, 60, 124, 160
Wolf, Susan, 464n20
Worship, religious temperament and, 217
Wright, Crispin, 86, 172–173, 455–456n18
Wrongdoing, dignity and, 271–272

Yeats, William Butler, 137–138, 146

Zarathustra, 259
Zipursky, Benjamin, 455n17